Encyclopedia of Women in the Renaissance

Encyclopedia of Women in the Renaissance

Italy, France, and England

DIANA ROBIN, ANNE R. LARSEN,
AND CAROLE LEVIN, EDITORS

ABC⬥CLIO

Santa Barbara, California   Denver, Colorado   Oxford, England

Library of Congress Cataloging-in-Publication Data
Encyclopedia of women in the Renaissance : Italy, France, and England /
edited by Diana Robin, Anne R. Larsen, Carole Levin.
    p. cm.
  Includes bibliographical references and index.
  ISBN-10: 1-85109-772-4 (hardcover : alk. paper)
  ISBN-10: 1-85109-777-5 (ebook)
  ISBN-13: 978-1-85109-772-2 (hardcover : alk. paper)
  ISBN-13: 978-1-85109-777-7 (ebook)
  1. Women—History—Renaissance, 1450–1600—Encyclopedias I. Robin,
Diana Maury II. Larsen, Anne R. III. Levin, Carole, 1948–

  HQ1148.W67 2007
  305.48'80900902403—dc22

                  2006038854

11 10 09 08 07   1 2 3 4 5 6 7 8 9 10

Production Editor: Kristine Swift
Editorial Assistant: Sara Springer
Production Manager: Don Schmidt
Media Editor: John Withers
Media Resources Coordinator: Ellen Brenna Dougherty
Media Resources Manager: Caroline Price
File Management Coordinator: Paula Gerard

This book is also available on the World Wide Web as an ebook. Visit http://www.abc-clio.com for details.

ABC-CLIO, Inc.
130 Cremona Drive, P.O. Box 1911
Santa Barbara, California 93116–1911

This book is printed on acid-free paper ∞

Manufactured in the United States of America

For Judith Hallett, muse, mentor, and dear friend.
Diana Robin

To Carolyn Charnin, a true friend whose wisdom
and counsel I always value.
Anne Larsen

For my dear friend Jo Carney, for her many years of
courage, generosity, and wisdom.
Carole Levin

Contents

Women in the Renaissance: A Historical Encyclopedia

Contributors

Martha Ahrendt
Green Bay, Wisconsin

Hariette Andreadis
Texas A&M University

Kory Bajus
University of Nebraska–Lincoln

Deborah Lesko Baker
Georgetown University

Debra Barrett-Graves
California State University–East Bay

Cathleen Bauschatz
University of Maine

Marlo M. Belschner
Monmouth College

Pamela J. Benson
Rhode Island College

Lynn Botelho
Indiana University of Pennsylvania

Susan Broomhall
The University of Western Australia

Abigail Brundin
University of Cambridge

Julie D. Campbell
Eastern Illinois University

Jo Carney
The College of New Jersey

Grace E. Coolidge
Grand Valley State University

Jane Couchman
Glendon College, York University

Ann Crabb
James Madison University

Joy M. Currie
University of Nebraska–Lincoln

Nancy Dersofi
Bryn Mawr College

Diane Desrosiers-Bonin
McGill University

Jane Donawerth
University of Maryland–College Park

Bruce Edelstein
New York University in Florence

Tim Elston
Newberry College

Gary Ferguson
University of Delaware

Sheila ffolliott
George Mason University

Catherine Field
University of Maryland–College Park

Hannah Shaw Vickers Fournier
University of Waterloo

Amy Gant
University of Nebraska–Lincoln

Amyrose McCue Gill
University of California at Berkeley

Cynthia Gladen
Portland, Oregon

Teresa Grant
University of Warwick

Melanie Gregg
Wilson College

Julia L. Hairston
University of California, Rome Study Center

Nancy Hayes
St. Ambrose University

Shawndra Holderby
Mansfield University

Brenda M. Hosington
University of Montreal

Vittoria Kirkham
University of Pennsylvania

Carrie F. Klaus
DePauw University

Alexandra M. Korey
University of Chicago

Mary Ellen Lamb
Southern Illinois University

Anne R. Larsen
Hope College

Carole Levin
University of Nebraska–Lincoln

Kathleen M. Llewellyn
Saint Louis University

Kathleen Perry Long
Cornell University

Nadia Margolis
Leverett, Massachusetts

Mary B. McKinley
University of Virginia

Lianne McTavish
University of New Brunswick

Sara Mendelson
McMaster University

Shannon Meyer
University of Nebraska–Lincoln

Gerry Milligan
College of Staten Island

Catherine M. Müller
Neuchatel, Switzerland

Jonathan Nelson
Syracuse University in Florence

Karen Nelson
University of Maryland–College Park

Marie-Thérèse Noiset
University of North Carolina–Charlotte

Tara Nummedal
Brown University

Michele Osherow
University of Maryland–Baltimore County

Carol Pal
Stanford University

Letizia Panizza
Royal Holloway, University of London

Holt Parker
University of Cincinnati

Daria Perocco
Università di Venezia

Graziella Postolache
Washington University in St. Louis

Alisha Rankin
Trinity College, University of Cambridge

Sid Ray
Pace University

Régine Reynolds-Cornell
Agnes Scott College

Anya Riehl
University of Illinois–Chicago

Louis Roper
SUNY–New Paltz

Joann Ross
University of Nebraska–Lincoln

Sarah Gwyneth Ross
Northwestern University

Marian Rothstein
Carthage College

Brigitte Roussel
Wichita State University

Rinaldina Russell
City University of New York, Queens College

Lisa Sampson
University of Reading

Martine Sauret
University of Minnesota

Deanna Shemek
University of California, Santa Cruz

Linda Shenk
Iowa State University

Brandie R. Siegfried
Brigham Young University

Núria Silleras-Fernández
University of California, Santa Cruz

Martha Skeeters
University of Oklahoma, Norman

Janet Smarr
University of California, San Diego

Sara Jayne Steen
Montana State University

Kevin Stevens
University of Nevada, Reno

Jane B. Stevenson
University of Aberdeen

Marguerite Tassi
University of Nebraska–Kearney

Fran Teague
University of Georgia

Emily Thompson
Webster University

James Grantham Turner
University of California, Berkeley

Jane Tylus
New York University

Retha Warnicke
Arizona State University

Elissa Weaver
University of Chicago

Lynn Westwater
The George Washington University

Jane Wickersham
The Newberry Library

Merry Wiesner-Hanks
University of Wisconsin–Milwaukee

Corinne Wilson
Washington University in St. Louis

Kathleen Wilson-Chavelier
The American University of Paris

Colette H. Winn
Washington University in St. Louis

Mary Beth Winn
SUNY–Albany

Diane S. Wood
Texas Tech University

Tara Wood
Arizona State University

Richardine Woodall
York University

Cathy Yandell
Carleton College

Naomi Yavneh
University of South Florida

Irene Zanini-Cordi
Florida State University

Gabriella Bruna Zarri
University of Florence

Carla Zecher
The Newberry Library

Introduction

In a now-classic essay published thirty years ago, the historian Joan Kelly asked the question, "Did Women Have a Renaissance?" Challenging conventional representations of early European history, Kelly answered her own question with a resounding "no." At the time, she was responding to the received historiography of the Renaissance as an age of "great men," the florescence of the arts, and the recovery of the culture of Greco-Roman antiquity. This was a history from which women had effectively been purged. Indeed, until the 1980s, little attention had been paid to early European women. But Kelly's bold essay galvanized interest in women's collective past and prompted scholars to test her argument. In the three decades since the publication of her work, an avalanche of books, articles, and, most influentially, editions and translations of works by early women writers themselves has enabled us to redefine the idea of the Renaissance and to reevaluate the varied roles women assumed during the period between roughly 1350 and 1700.

In his introduction to Scribner's six-volume *Encyclopedia of the Renaissance,* Paul F. Grendler noted that the study of women stands among the three most important developments in recent work on early modern European history, flanked only by research in humanism and social history. The new scholarship has shown that notable women of this period came from a variety of social and economic ranks. In the age of the Reformation and the Renaissance, women played significant roles in the revival of the classical tradition and the rise of national literatures, religious reform, art and music, pol-

itics and statecraft, and science and medicine. Women of the Renaissance were widely experienced in both work and family. The *Encyclopedia of Women in the Renaissance* brings together the newest scholarship in a broad array of issues. The articles are written for students and teachers at all levels, and the reading public in general.

The very term "Renaissance" has been recently contested, with some social historians perceiving the rubric as too oriented toward literary and artistic developments. Some scholars have preferred the descriptor "early modern" as less encumbered by the cultural baggage of the pre-Kellian age. Yet no term can in fact be completely free of historiographical biases, and we have chosen to use "Renaissance" as broadly inclusive in that it reflects a specific period that was neither completely medieval nor entirely modern. Just as we use the term inclusively, so too our chronology is comprehensive. The Renaissance self-consciously began in fourteenth-century Italy with a group of writers, artists, and thinkers who looked back to the ancient world for inspiration. This generated a movement known as humanism, which reflected ethical and epistemological as well as artistic values, and spread throughout Europe, still having a major impact in England, France, and other Euopean countries at the end of the seventeenth century. While this encyclopedia focuses primarily on Italy, France, and England, it takes other regions into account and covers about three hundred and fifty years.

The title of this collection, *Encylopedia of Women in the Renaissance,* is important in that it emphasizes the plural—women, not woman— and the multiplicity of experiences women had. We cannot speak of the "Renaissance woman" or even the Italian, French, or English Renaissance woman. Women's experiences changed not only as they crossed geographic and chronological boundaries, but also in terms of social and economic status, religious belief, and access to education. This encyclopedia has over one hundred and fifty biographical entries on specific women artists, writers, musicians, patrons, religious leaders, and medical practitioners. There are articles on nuns, working-class women, and women of the elite classes. There are essays on topics ranging from amazons and alchemy, marriage and midwifery, prostitution, the book trade, the figure of the hermaphrodite, to Sappho. There are essays on such public roles as women's involvement in religious reform, education, medical care, entertainment at courts, salons, and homes; and the more domestic issues such as marriage, birth control, and child rearing. Above all, there are articles on feminism, the idea and ideology of gender, and the concept of woman and sexuality in the Renaissance.

One of the great values of early modern women's scholarship is its collaborative nature, and we, the editors, have found it a benefit as well as a pleasure to work not only with one another but with our many contributors and our advisory board: Janet Smarr, Deanna Shemek, Julia Hairston, Letizia Panizza, Elissa Weaver, and Paul Gehl. We would like to thank Margaret King and Paul Grendler for their indispensable advice at the beginning of the project. We would also like to express our gratitude to Amy Gant and her assistant Erica Wright at the University of Nebraska for their expertise and their work on the project. Above all, we owe a debt of thanks to our editors at ABC-CLIO, without whose advice, enthusiasm, and technological sophistication this encyclopedia could not have been produced.

Chronology

1307	Dante (1265–1337), *The Divine Comedy.*
1309–1378	Papacy at Avignon.
1337–1453	Hundred Years' War: Series of wars between France and England. In the end, England is expelled from all of France, except Calais.
1341	Francesco Petrarca (1304–1374) is crowned with laurel, Rome.
1347–1361	The Black Death decimates the population of Europe.
1351–1353	Giovanni Boccaccio (1313–1375), *Decameron.*
1363–1404	Philip the Bold (Burgundy).
1364–1380	Charles V (France).
1373–1394	Geoffrey Chaucer (ca. 1343–1400), *Canterbury Tales.*
1377	Papacy reestablished in Rome, Pope Gregory XI.
1377–1399	Richard II (England).
1378–1417	Great Schism.
1381	Peasants' Revolt in England.
1397	The Medici family founds its bank, laying the foundation for one of the greatest ruling families in Italian history.
1399–1413	Henry IV (England).
1405	Christine de Pizan circulates in manuscript her *Le livre de la cité des dames* (The Book of the City of Ladies), the first world historical interpretation of women's lives by a woman.
1415	The English led by King Henry V rout the French at the Battle of Agincourt.
1417–1436	Brunelleschi's Dome of Florence Cathedral.
1419	Alliance between Burgundy and England.
1419–1467	Philip the Good (Burgundy).
1420	English occupy Paris.
1422–1461	Charles VII (France).
1429	Charles VII is crowned king of France.
1431	Joan of Arc is executed.
1434	Cosimo de Medici establishes rule in Florence.
1436	French recapture Paris from English.
1447–1455	Pope Nicholas V establishes Vatican Library.
1450	Mercenary leader Francesco Sforza seizes power in Milan.
1451	Isotta Nogarola publicly debates Ludovico Foscarini in Verona on whether Adam or Eve bears greater responsibilty for the Fall.
1453	Turks capture Constantinople.
1454	Peace of Lodi (end of wars between Milan, Venice, Florence).

1455–1487	Wars of the Roses in England.
1455–1456	Johannes Gutenberg (ca. 1400–1467) invents printing with movable metallic type.
1461–1483	Louis XI rules France.
1462–1463	Platonic Academy is established in Florence under the patronage of Cosimo de' Medici.
1461–1470	Reign of King Edward IV of England.
1469–1492	Lorenzo de Medici ("the Magnificent") rules Florence.
1471–1484	Pontificate of Sixtus IV.
1478	Ferdinand V of Aragon and Isabella of Castile, with authorization of Pope Sixtus IV establish Spanish Inquisition.
1480	Lodovico Sforza seizes power in Milan.
1485	Battle of Bosworth ends the Wars of the Roses and Henry Tudor is crowned King of England (Henry VII); Botticelli paints *The Birth of Venus.*
1485–1499	Laura Cereta's autobiographical Latin letterbook circulates in manuscript in the Veneto.
1492	Christopher Columbus (1451–1506) discovers the New World; Rodrigo de Borja y Borja is elected as Pope Alexander VI; Jews are expelled from Spain.
1493	Maximilian I becomes Austrian Emperor.
1494	Ludovico Sforza becomes Duke of Milan.
1494	Charles VIII of France invades Italy.
1495–1498	Leonardo da Vinci (1452–1519) paints his *Last Supper* in Milan.

1498	Savonarola is burned at the stake in Florence.
1499	Louis XII (1498–1515) of France seizes Milan.
1501–1504	Michelangelo sculpts the statue *David.*
1502–1503	Leonardo da Vinci (1452–1519) paints *Mona Lisa.*
1507	Margaret of Austria is appointed Regent of the Netherlands.
1508	Raphael enters service of Pope Julius II.
1508–1512	Michelangelo paints the ceiling of the Sistine Chapel.
1509	Henry VIII becomes King of England (until 1547).
1513	Leo X is elected pope; Machiavelli's *The Prince* published.
1515	Francois (Francis) I becomes king of France (until 1547).
1516	Ariosto's *Orlando furioso* published.
1519	Charles V of Spain (1500–1556) becomes Holy Roman Emperor.
1517	Martin Luther (1483–1546) posts the 95 Theses (Wittenberg, Saxony); Reformation begins.
1521	Machiavelli's *Art of War* published.
1522	Luther's translation of the Bible.
1525	Francis I of France is captured at Pavia.
1527	Troops of Charles V, Holy Roman Emperor, sack Rome and capture Pope Clement VII.
1529	The Ottoman Turks besiege Vienna.
1532–1534	Henry VIII breaks with Rome, establishes English Church (Anglican).

1535–1541   Michelangelo paints the *Last Judgement* in the Sistine Chapel.

1536   Execution of Anne Boleyn.

1538   Titian paints *Venus of Urbino;* the first edition of Vittoria Colonna's collected poetry inaugurates the print-debuts of a series of important women writers in Italy.

1538–1560   Hélisenne de Crenne's novel *Les angoysses douloureuses qui procedent d'amours* (The Torments of Love) is reprinted in eight editions.

1540–1541   Ignatius Loyola (1491–1556) founds the Jesuit Order.

1541   Calvin establishes reformed church in Geneva.

1542   Paul III opens the Inquisition.

1546–1563   Council of Trent.

1547   Henry II ascends the throne of France.

1547–1553   Edward VI, King of England.

1553–1558   Mary Tudor, Queen of England.

1555   Peace of Augsburg; salonnière and poet Louise Labé publishes her *Oeuvres* (Works) with the prominent Lyon printer Jean de Tournes.

1556   Charles V abdicates the throne of Spain and the Holy Roman Empire. His son Phillip II rules Spain from 1556 to 1598, while his brother Ferdinand I becomes the Holy Roman Emperor (1556–1564).

1558–1570   Four editions of the Italian heretic Olimpia Morata's *Omnia opera* are published in Basel.

1558–1603   Elizabeth I, Queen of England.

1559–1580   Sophonisba Anguissola, court painter to King Philip II of Spain, completes a series of paintings for the royal family in Madrid.

1560   The poet Laura Battiferra publishes the first book of her collected poetry in Florence.

1562–1598   Wars of Religion in France during the reigns of Francis II (1559–1560), Charles IX (1560–1574), Henry III (1574–1589).

1564   Maximilian II becomes Holy Roman Emperor (rules until 1576).

1568–1648   Dutch Wars of Independence.

1569–1570   Rebellion of Catholic nobility in northern England.

1570s   The Dames des Roches, mother and daughter, inaugurate their important literary salon in Poitiers.

1571   Italian and Spanish forces defeat the Ottoman Turks in the Battle of Lepanto.

1572   Massacre of Saint Bartholomew's Day in Paris.

1576   Rudolf II is elected Holy Roman Emperor (until 1612).

1582   Pope Gregory XIII, reform of the calendar.

1587   Mary, Queen of Scots, is executed.

1588   Spanish Armada.

1589   Henri III of France is assassinated. Henri IV renounces Protestantism to become King of France; Venetian dramatist, Isabella Andrieni stars in a performance of her play *La pazzia di Isabella* in Florence.

1592   Shakespeare produces *Comedy of Errors.*

1598   Edict of Nantes grants Huguenots freedom of worship and equal rights.

1599	Globe Theatre established; Shakespeare's *Julius Caesar; As You Like It* produced.
1603	James I (James VI of Scotland) becomes King of England (until 1625).
1609	Louise Bourgeois publishes her handbook on gynecology and obstetrics, *Observations diverses,* in Paris.
1610	After the assassination of Henry IV of France, Louis XIII ascends the throne.
1612	Artemisia Gentileschi executes her famous painting, *Judith Slaying Holofernes,* in Naples.
1618–1648	Thirty Years' War in Germany.
1619	Ferdinand II becomes the Holy Roman Emperor (until 1637).
1620	Pilgrims sail from England in the Mayflower.
1624–1642	Cardinal Armand du Plessis de Richelieu consolidates royal power and enhances France's international standing.
1625	Charles I becomes King of England.
1637	Ferdinand III is elected Holy Roman Emperor (until 1657)
1639	France enters Thirty Years' War.
1641	Marie de Gournay publishes her feminist essay, *L'Egalité des hommes et des femmes* (The Equality of Men and Women) in Paris.

1642–1646	English Civil War.
1643–1661	Cardinal Jules Mazarin directs the French government due to infancy of King Louis XIV.
1647–1659	French-Spanish War.
1648	Peace of Westphalia ends Thirty Years' War.
1648–1653	French civil war.
1649	Charles I of England is executed.
1653	Oliver Cromwell dissolves the English Parliament.
1655	Margaret Cavendish publishes the first utopia authored by a woman, *The Description of a New World Called The Blazing World,* in London.
1657	Leopold becomes the Holy Roman Emperor.
1660	English monarchy is reestablished: Charles II.
1661	Louis XIV is crowned King of France.
1682	Louis XIV establishes French court at Versailles.
1683	Turks besiege Vienna.
1685	James II is crowned King of England; Louis XIV revokes the Edict of Nantes.
1688	James II of England is deposed; Aphra Behn publishes the most popular of her numerous novels, *Oroonoko, or the Royal Slave,* in London.

A

Abortion and Miscarriage

Early modern medical treatises explained how women could avoid miscarriage and abortion, often using both terms to refer to inadvertent pregnancy loss. In her *Observations diverses sur la stérilité, perte de fruict, foecondité, accouchements et maladies des femmes et enfants nouveaux naiz* (Various Observations on Sterility, Miscarriage, Fertility, Childbirth and Diseases of Women and Newborns) of 1609, for example, French midwife Louise Bourgeois urged pregnant women to remain calm, because passions such as anger disrupted the flow of nutritive blood to the unborn child. English midwife Jane Sharp offered similar advice in her *The Midwives Book* of 1671, suggesting a powder women could take to "hinder abortion," which included coriander and wine. The majority of European obstetrical treatises cautioned pregnant women against lifting heavy objects, riding in bumpy carriages, and raising their hands over their heads.

These descriptions could have provided information about what to do if ending a pregnancy was desired. Denis Fournier wrote his *L'accoucheur méthodique* (The Methodical Man-Midwife) of 1677 in French, but used Latin to convey remedies designed to expel a dead child or retained afterbirth from the womb, fearing untrustworthy persons might use the recipes to induce abortion. Yet the deliberate termination of pregnancy was not always considered an immoral act during the early modern period. Interventions at an early stage—before ensoulment, thought to occur at around thirty days for boys and forty-five days for girls—were considered contraceptive rather than abortive techniques. Following ancient tradition, medical practitioners as well as the church distinguished between formed and unformed fetuses in the womb.

Legal and religious sanctions against induced abortion were more severe for later pregnancies but did not necessarily govern women's behavior. According to historian Angus McLaren, early modern abortions would have been mostly self-induced, with women turning to abortionists only if other remedies had failed and they could afford it. Classicist John Riddle has collected herbal remedies with consistent ingredients such as rue, myrtle, myrrh, and pennyroyal, arguing they were used as effective abortifacients. Riddle's research indicates that both medieval and early modern women were interested in contraception and abortion, but various scholars question his approach, which relies on modern scientific tests and assumes herbs have not changed over time. Historian Helen King claims that Riddle furthermore fails to appreciate the historical belief that menstruation was crucial to the health of the female body. Recipes designed to "bring forth the menses" were not always abortifacients, as he suspects. Pregnancy was notoriously difficult to determine during the early modern period, and the absence of menstruation or sensation of movements in the womb could indicate other conditions. A swelling womb might contain wind, water, or a "false conception," such as a fleshly mole lacking life. These early modern understandings of the female body stubbornly resist modern ways of thinking about pregnancy.

Lianne McTavish

See also the subheadings Childbirth and Reproductive Knowledge; Midwives and Licensing Male Midwifery; The Practice of Pharmacology and Laywomen (under Medicine and Women); Contraception and Birth Control.

Bibliography

Dunstan, G. R., ed. *The Human Embryo: Aristotle and the Arabic and European Traditions.* Exeter, UK: University of Exeter Press, 1990.

King, Helen. *Hippocrates' Woman: Reading the Female Body in Ancient Greece.* London: Routledge, 1998.

McClive, Cathy. "The Hidden Truths of the Belly: The Uncertainties of Pregnancy in Early Modern Europe." *Social History of Medicine* 15, no. 2 (2002): 209–227.

McLaren, Angus. *A History of Contraception: From Antiquity to the Present Day.* Oxford: Blackwell, 1990.

Riddle, John M. *Contraception and Abortion from the Ancient World to the Renaissance.* Cambridge, MA: Harvard University Press, 1992.

Riddle, John M. *Eve's Herbs: A History of Contraception and Abortion in the West.* Cambridge, MA: Harvard University Press, 1997.

Rütten, Thomas. "Receptions of the Hippocratic Oath in the Renaissance: The Prohibition of Abortion as a Case Study in Reception." *Journal of the History of Medicine and Allied Sciences* 51, no. 4 (1996): 456–483.

Jeanne d'Albret, queen of Navarre and Protestant leader. Portrait by unknown artist. (Bettmann/Corbis)

Albret, Jeanne d' (1528–1572)

Queen of Navarre, sovereign of Béarn, duchess of Vendôme, Protestant leader, author of Mémoires et poésies *and letters*

Jeanne d'Albret was born at Saint-Germain-en-Laye on 16 November 1528, the only child of Henry d'Albret, king of Navarre, and Marguerite de Navarre, the sister of Francis I, king of France. Both parents rarely spent time with their daughter during her childhood. Eager to have a son, they neglected her; her education, which was supervised by the humanist Nicolas Bourbon, was directed by Aymée de Lafayette, a friend of her mother's, in the Norman countryside. In 1537, Jeanne d'Albret became an instrument both to her father and her uncle's policy. At the request of Francis I, she moved closer to court, to the chateau of Plessis-les-Tours, as her father considered using her to recover the kingdom of Navarre by marrying her to the son of Charles V, the Habsburg emperor of the Holy Roman Empire. However, Francis I arranged a marriage alliance with the duc de Cleves in 1541. Marguerite de Navarre, ambivalent about this alliance, managed to delay it by having the duc de Cleves agree to wait before the consummation of the marriage because Jeanne d'Albret was only twelve years old at the time. Jeanne d'Albret wrote a couple of testimonies with witnesses to protest against the marriage, was whipped on the order of her mother to comply with the king of France's demands, and also defied Francis I before the wedding. Nonetheless, she was carried to the altar on 13 June 1541 to marry the duc de Cleves at Châtellerault. After the latter betrayed Francis I, the marriage was annulled and dissolved by Paul III on 12 October 1545 on grounds that the marriage was never consummated and that Jeanne d'Albret never ceased to protest against the union.

In 1548, as a pawn to the new king of France, Henry II, Jeanne d'Albret was to marry Antoine de Bourbon, duc de Vendôme (First Prince of the Blood) to provide the king with an alliance with the Hapsburgs. Although her parents were also against this second alliance, Jeanne d'Albret was content with it and the marriage was celebrated on 20 October 1548. Their union led to two children, Henry (the future Henry IV), born on 14 December 1553 and Catherine, born in 1559.

The rise of Calvinism in the 1550s was accompanied by a lenient enforcement of legislation against heresy. Thus Antoine de Bourbon joined the movement, mostly out of political interest: his claims to Spanish Navarre having been ignored by both Philip II of Spain and Henry II of France, he hoped that they would in turn be more accommodating to him for fear of the spread of heresy. Despite Jeanne d'Albret's long-standing interest in Calvinism, she did not announce her conversion until Christmas Day 1560. Both Jeanne d'Albret and her husband encouraged the Reformation in their domains of Navarre.

The constant Catholic pressure, soon to be followed by a counteroffensive in February 1562, forced Antoine de Bourbon to convert back to Catholicism in January 1562, leaving Jeanne d'Albret alone at the head of the Calvinist cause, supported by both Calvin and Queen Elizabeth I. During the First Civil War (1562–1563), Jeanne d'Albret chose strategic neutrality, as Antoine de Bourbon threatened to repudiate her. She fled the court, leaving her son in the care of her husband. When Antoine de Bourbon died on 17 November 1562, Jeanne d'Albret resumed control of her son's education, reinstating his Protestant tutors, although Henry was retained at court away from his mother. From 1563 to 1567, Jeanne d'Albret guaranteed the religious autonomy of Béarn, establishing Calvinism. She founded the framework of a unified Calvinist Church by the autumn of 1563. In February 1564, she issued the *simultaneum,* a declaration of liberty of conscience for all her subjects. Catherine de Médicis, hoping to pacify the troubles and unite the leaders to the crown, offered Jeanne d'Albret protection from her enemies provided that she join the court.

Jeanne d'Albret resumed the second phase of her reform in 1566 in a more authoritarian manner by reforming morals and purging "idolatry" from churches in her lands, which led to the Third Civil War (1569–1570). Jeanne d'Albret then abandoned neutrality and went with her children to join the leaders of the Huguenots, the prince of Condé and Admiral Gaspard de Coligny, at La Rochelle, the center of Huguenot activity. She established a Protestant college and held the first Protestant synod in April 1571, where the Confession of La Rochelle, a uniform creed of the French Reformed Church, was written. Jeanne d'Albret believed in her absolute right over her subjects and showed intolerance with her confirmation of the D'Arros edict of January 1570, which closed Catholic churches and required obedience to the Calvinist church.

In the final stage of her life, Jeanne d'Albret struggled with Catherine de Médicis, who wanted the alliance of their children, Henry de Navarre and Marguerite de Valois, to guarantee the peace negotiations and stop a French alliance with England. After a difficult marriage treaty, Jeanne d'Albret accepted the conditions, but died suddenly in Paris on 9 June 1572, before the celebration of the marriage. It was believed that she may have been poisoned. Her letters cover her political and religious activism, while her memoirs seek to justify her actions as a leader of the Huguenot cause.

Corinne Wilson

See also Marguerite de Navarre; Power, Politics, and Women; Religious Reform and Women.

Bibliography

Primary Works

Albret, Jeanne d'. *Lettres d'Antoine de Bourbon et de Jehanne d'Albret.* Edited by de Rochambeau. Paris: Renouard, 1877.

Albret, Jeanne d'. *Mémoires et poésies.* Edited by Alphonse de Ruble. Geneva: Slatkine, 1970. (Originally published in Paris, 1893.)

Secondary Works

Bainton, Roland H. "Jeanne d'Albret." In *Women of the Reformation in France and England.* Pages 43–73. Boston: Beacon Press, 1973.

Bryson, David. *Queen Jeanne and the Promised Land: Dynasty, Homeland, Religion and Violence in Sixteenth-Century France.* Boston: Brill, 1999.

Roelker, Nancy Lyman. "The Appeal of Calvinism to French Noblewomen in the Sixteenth Century." *Journal of Interdisciplinary History* 2 (Spring 1972): 391–418.

Roelker, Nancy Lyman. *Queen of Navarre Jeanne d'Albret 1528–1572.* Cambridge, MA: The Belknap Press of Harvard University Press, 1968.

Alchemy

Stretching back to antiquity, alchemy's long textual tradition is largely male. With only a few exceptions, women appear in the alchemical corpus as symbolic figures, personifications of fundamental alchemical principles, not as authors or practitioners themselves. In the Renaissance, however, alchemical knowledge became accessible to a new range of people, both male and female; as a part of this expansion, a small number of women began to carve out a place as practitioners, patrons, and authors. Initially, women were most likely to participate in practical alchemical operations that verged on medicine or household tasks, such as making cosmetics and dyes. By the mid-seventeenth century, however, female alchemists began to engage in alchemy as a philosophical pursuit, taking their place alongside male natural philosophers in elucidating nature's secrets.

Alchemy has encompassed a wide variety of ideas and practices throughout its long history, including natural philosophical inquiries into the nature of metals; the production of mineral and metallic medicines; spiritual practices linking changes in matter to changes in the alchemist's soul; practical techniques for producing dyes, artificial gemstones, and pearls; and, most famously, the transmutation of metals. In the Renaissance, practical and medicinal alchemy in particular flourished. Practitioners of all sorts took advantage of newly printed and translated alchemical texts, translations, and anthologies, as well as the market for recipes and techniques both to gain access to

Woodcut frontispiece from Marie Meurdrac's Accessible and Easy Chemistry for Women, *published in 1666. (Othmer Library, CHF)*

alchemical knowledge and to sell their expertise in return.

Women participated in alchemy's sixteenth-century expansion as well, though in largely private, informal ways that historians have yet to trace fully. Because there was no formal training in alchemy in universities, guilds, or colleges, women could access alchemical knowledge in the same way that most men did: by cobbling together an alchemical education from a few vernacular texts, by learning techniques from other practitioners, or perhaps by buying a recipe from another peddler of alchemical secrets. Women could also draw on their experience with traditional activities that utilized similar techniques, such as distilling water and cooking. Those who could read or whose social status put them in a scholarly milieu may also have supplemented this kind of household knowledge with a theoretical understanding of alchemical theory and practice. A very small number of women went on to use their alchemical knowledge publicly, authoring texts or pursing employment for wealthy patrons. Most women's alchemical practice before the seventeenth century, however, remains almost invisible, documented not in printed texts, but only in letters, contracts, and other manuscript documents, if at all.

These archival traces suggest that in the sixteenth century women did participate informally in alchemy as students, assistants, or practitioners. In England, for instance, Mary Sidney, countess of Pembroke (1561–1621), was known for her interest in making medicines; although her precise involvement in alchemical projects remains unclear, she might well have joined the alchemical activities of the physicians and scholars associated with her household. In Central Europe, Duchess Sibylla of Württemberg (1564–1612) clearly shared her husband Duke Friedrich's (ca. 1550–1608) interest in patronizing alchemical projects, for she signed a contract with an alchemist named Andreas Reiche, binding him to teach her and her son the theory and practice of alchemy. Women of more humble backgrounds certainly staffed some of the laboratories set up by wealthier patrons, even as servants or managers. In Bohemia, Salome Scheinpflugerin worked in the laboratory of the Bohemian magnate Wilhelm Rosenberg (1535–1592) in the 1570s and 1580s. Her fellow alchemists' comments suggest that they accorded her a certain amount of authority in managing the laboratory. Such tiny glimpses suggest that women did participate in alchemy in Renaissance Europe, although the full extent and nature of their involvement await further historical research.

Two examples from the sixteenth century stand out: Isabella Cortese, whose alchemical secrets first appeared in print in 1561 in Venice under the title *I secreti della signora Isabella Cortese* (The Secrets of Signora Isabella Cortese), and Anna Maria Zieglerin (ca. 1550–1575), who worked at the court of Duke Julius of Braunschweig-Wolfenbüttel (1528–1589) in the 1570s. Little is known about Cortese other than what appears in *I secreti*, where she recounted her alchemical education. She evidently learned more from her travels in central Europe than from traditional alchemical texts, which she dismissed as "only fictions and riddles" (Cortese 1561, 19). The formulaic elements in her autobiography, as well as the uncertain provenance of the book, however, make it a problematic autobiographical source; the text may initially have been a private manuscript intended for family that somehow found its way into a print shop, where it was embellished for the market. However it ended up in print, *I secreti* was hugely successful, appearing in at least fifteen Venetian editions and one German translation in the sixteenth and seventeenth centuries. Cortese's book was one of several "books of secrets" that appeared in Italy in the mid-sixteenth century, revealing practical secrets of nature that appealed to an aristocratic audience, such as how to make perfumes, cosmetics, oils, and distilled waters, as well as how to work with metals.

As the only printed book by a female alchemist in the sixteenth century, Cortese's book was an anomaly. Although she did not publish, Anna Zieglerin did pursue her own alchemical work at the Northern European court of Duke Julius of Braunschweig-Wolfenbüttel. Zieglerin initially arrived at court with her husband, who came to work as an alchemical assistant there, but she quickly set up her own laboratory and hired at least one assistant. She also completed a short treatise, which contained recipes for a golden oil she called "lion's blood" as well as its uses in preparing the philosopher's stone, medicines, artificial gemstones, and fertilizing fruit trees. Zieglerin's alchemy was particularly focused on fertility and childbirth, suggesting that she was reinterpreting male alchemists' efforts to create an artificial human, or homunculus. Zieglerin quickly distinguished herself from the other alchemists at court (including her husband) through her connections to a mysterious adept named Count Carl, who, she claimed, not only had unique alchemical expertise but was also the son of the legendary early sixteenth-century medical practitioner Paracelsus (1493–1541). Despite initial favorable attention from the ducal court, Zieglerin and her fellow alchemists all found themselves unable to deliver on their promises (including Count Carl, who turned out not to exist after all). The male alchemists were ultimately executed for fraud and treason, while Zieglerin was executed for sorcery and adultery. These highly unusual charges against Zieglerin indicate that the Wolfenbüttel authorities found it difficult to comprehend her alchemical practice, forcing it instead into the more familiar categories of magic and witchcraft.

Cortese and Zieglerin both seem to be exceptional in that they sought a kind of publicity for their work that most women who pursed alchemy in the sixteenth century did not. In the seventeenth century, however, a number of learned women included alchemy in their scholarly pursuits. Like their learned male counterparts, Kristina Wasa, queen of Sweden (1626–1689), Marie le Jars de Gournay (1565–1645), and Marie Meurdrac (fl. 1666) all understood alchemy as a path to the knowledge of nature and included it in their studies. Women certainly continued to pursue practical alchemical projects and to assist their husbands and brothers, but by the mid-seventeenth century they could stake a public claim to be alchemical philosophers as well.

Tara Nummedal

See also Gournay, Marie de; the subheading The Practice of Pharmacology and Laywomen (under Medicine and Women).

Bibliography
Primary Works
Cortese, Isabella. *I secreti della signora Isabella Cortese, de'qvali si contengono cose minerale, medicinali, arteficiose, & alchimiche, & molte de l'arte profumatoria . . . Con altri bellissimi secret aggiunti. . . .* Venice: Giovanni Variletto, 1561.
De Gournay, Marie Le Jars de. *Apology for the Woman Writing and Other Works.* Translated and edited by Richard Hillman and Colette Quesnel. Chicago: University of Chicago Press, 2002.
Secondary Works
Åkerman, Susanna. *Queen Christina of Sweden and Her Circle: The Transformation of a Seventeenth-Century Philosophical Libertine.* Leiden and New York: E. J. Brill, 1991.
Eamon, William. "Science and Popular Culture in Sixteenth Century Italy: The 'Professors of Secrets' and Their Books." *Sixteenth Century Journal* 16 (Winter 1985): 471–485.
Eamon, William. *Science and the Secrets of Nature: Books of Secrets in Medieval and Early Modern Culture.* Princeton, NJ: Princeton University Press, 1994.
Hunter, Lynette, and Sarah Hutton, eds. *Women, Science and Medicine 1500–1700: Mothers and Sisters of the Royal Society.* Thrupp, Stroud, Gloucestershire, UK: Sutton, 1997.
Nummedal, Tara. "Alchemical Reproduction and the Career of Anna Maria Zieglerin." *Ambix* 48 (July 2001): 56–68.
Patai, Raphael. "Maria the Jewess—Founding Mother of Alchemy." *Ambix* 29 (November 1982): 177–197.
Tosi, Lucia. "Marie Meudrac: Paracelsian Chemist and Feminist." *Ambix* 48 (July 2001): 69–82.

Amazons

Amazons appear with some frequency in late medieval and early modern literature, from Christine de Pizan's *The Book of the City of Ladies* (1405) to Shakespeare's *A Midsummer Night's Dream* (1595) to Thomas Heywood's *Exemplary Lives . . . of the Nine Most Worthy Women* (1640). Amazons grew in popularity in the sixteenth century not only because of the revival of interest in classical mythology and literature but also because of the stories explorers of the Americas and Africa told of Amazonian encounters in the New World; the topical interest resulted in the depiction of the exotic Amazon queen and her female community in dramatic productions, poems, prose romances, and masques.

The representation of Amazons comprised several common features: Amazons were alleged to live in self-sufficient, all-female societies; they were reputed to be warrior women who removed one breast in order to use weapons more skillfully; they mated with men periodically, primarily for reproductive purposes; they raised their daughters but abandoned their sons, killed them, or forced them to perform domestic duties for the Amazon community. Any of these behaviors would have challenged the paradigm of the ideal woman in early modern England; collectively, they depicted a model of female monstrosity. Some authors were drawn to the exotic otherness of the Amazon women, while others were fascinated by their transgressive attention to military prowess rather than domestic matters. On occasion, British writers evoked the Amazon myth to represent their nation and its female regent as formidable in war, but for the most part even Elizabethan iconography avoided Amazonian connections. In general, the figure of the Amazon was appropriated to represent the violation of the natural order, and as such she was both a fascinating and frightening figure in the early modern imagination.

One exception to the predominant view of Amazons as threatening comes from the French woman writer, Christine de Pizan. In Pizan's *The Book of the City of Ladies* (1405), the Amazonian community is upheld as exemplary for its resourcefulness and cooperation. In her revisionist history of women, Amazon women exist peaceably within the boundaries of their own government but are also capable of negotiating successfully with the threats posed by male forces. For Pizan, what is most striking and ad-mirable about the Amazons is the orderly and reasonable governance of the female community. In contrast to Pizan's positive depiction of a well-structured Amazonian government is the work of Protestant reformer John Knox, whose polemic against women on the throne, *The First Blast of the Trumpet Against the Monstrous Regiment of Women* (1558), cites the Amazons as emblematic of the dangers of female sovereignty. Knox was responding in particular to the many contemporary examples of queenship in England and on the Continent that he found abhorrent: Catherine de Médicis, Mary Stuart (Queen of Scots), and Mary Tudor. Although Knox was opposed to the Catholicism of these female rulers, he also insisted that their positions of power represented a monstrous perversion of the natural order in the tradition of the Amazons.

Edmund Spenser's epic poem, *The Fairie Queene* (1590–1596), illustrates even further the association between Amazons and the exercise of female power. Both the figures of the good, just warrior Britomart and the monstrous Radigund are Amazonlike, suggesting the dichotomous implications of the Amazonian figure who could demonstrate strength and justice but who could also threaten the natural order. In a version of the Hercules-Omphale legend, Spenser describes a roomful of weakened men who are ordered to keep spinning under the direction of Amazonian women, their participation in domestic duties a sign of their emasculation. Ben Jonson's Jacobean *The Masque of Beauty* (1609) presents an interesting variation on the Amazonian motif because the star role of the Amazon queen in the drama was played, according to Jonson, by Queen Anne of Denmark herself; as both performer and patron of the work, Anne was implicitly endorsing the association between her position of power—however secondary it was to that of King James I of England—and the Amazon figure.

In Shakespeare's *A Midsummer Night's Dream* (1595) and again in *The Two Noble Kinsmen* (1613), a play on which he collaborated with John Fletcher, the Amazon represents no such threat to orthodox patriarchy. Hippolyta, the Amazon queen who figures in both plays, was, according to many legends, conquered and courted by Theseus. Shakespeare's Hippolyta does not represent female agency, as in Pizan, nor a political threat, as in Knox; rather, she is depicted as a relatively passive character whose power has been suggested in the play but then erased, as is the female community she represents.

If many of the early modern works exploiting the Amazon legends reveal a cultural anxiety about female rule, other works reflect unease about constructions of sexuality. Sir Walter Raleigh, an enthusiastic advocate of exploration, wrote of the Amazons after his expedition to South America in search of the gold treasures of El Dorado. In the *Discovery of Guiana* (1596), Raleigh is interested in locating Amazons geographically and historically, a theme he treats more fully in *The History of the World* (1614). Both works are preoccupied with the sexual and reproductive practices of the Amazon community that imply control and agency on the part of the women. Sir Philip Sidney's pastoral romance, *The Arcadia* (ca. 1580), also suggests that the Amazonian figure was associated with an unnatural sexuality. In this work, a central male character disguises himself as an Amazon to gain closer access to the woman he wishes to court; cross-dressing as a seduction strategy is not uncommon in the romance genre, but the particular form of transvestism implies a connection between Amazonian representation and emasculation.

During the later seventeenth and eighteenth centuries, Amazons continue to appear in literary texts, but it was the early modern period that found the figure of the Amazon particularly compelling.

Jo Eldridge Carney

See also Androgyne; Hermaphrodite as Image and Idea; Masculinity, Femininity, and Gender; Querelle des Femmes; Transvestism.

Bibliography
Schwartz, Kathryn. *Tough Love: Amazon Encounters in the English Renaissance.* Durham, NC: Duke University Press, 2000.
Shepherd, Simon. *Amazons and Warrior Women: Varieties of Feminism in Seventeenth-Century Drama.* New York: St. Martin's Press, 1981.

Amboise, Catherine d' (ca. 1482–1550)

French author, literary patron

Daughter of Charles I d'Amboise and Catherine de Chauvigny, Catherine d'Amboise belonged to the powerful and wealthy d'Amboise family. She was married three times: first to Christophe de Tournon who left her widowed at age seventeen, then in 1501 to Philibert de Beaujeu (d. 1540), and lastly, at age 65, to Louis de Cleves. Biographical information comes chiefly from her writings: *Book of the Prudent and Imprudent* and *Complaint against Fortune,* both in prose, and *Devout Epistles,* in verse. *Book of the Prudent,* dated 1 July 1509, offers an illustrated catalogue of men and women from history, mythology, and the Bible, noted for their prudence or lack thereof. Prudence is recognized through adversity, and, while Catherine seeks consolation in writing of her own personal tragedies (the loss of her parents, her first husband, and their only child), she underscores the difficulties faced by women authors: limited access to learning, inexperience in writing, and feminine modesty, which curtails discussion of "dishonorable" subjects. These difficulties justify the charitable reception of women's work, just as Catherine's gender, along with her God-given intelligence and reason, leads her to recount the good that has come from women.

Catherine declares that she regularly retires to her study to compose "lamentations and feminine regrets," but her next two works probably date from after 1525. The autobiographical *Complaint against Fortune* relates how the author (*dame pasmee*) faints upon receiving sad news (of her nephew's death in 1525). She is resuscitated by Dame Raison, who advises her not to accuse Fortune but to accept adversity as part of God's order. Raison accompanies Catherine to the Park of Divine Love, where she finds Patience seated at Tree of the Cross.

This allegorical journey may have inspired the penitential verses called *Devout Epistles*. For the first epistle to Christ, Catherine apparently rewrote a text that Jean Bouchet had dedicated to Gabrielle de Bourbon (d. 1516). The second epistle to the Virgin concludes with an unusual *chant royal,* which is followed by a third epistle assuring Christ's grace and pardon, as depicted in the accompanying miniature by a ring brought from heaven to the kneeling author.

Like her illustrious uncle, Cardinal-Archbishop George d'Amboise (d. 1510), Catherine was a patron, notably to her nephew, the poet Michel d'Amboise. Catherine's works are preserved in deluxe, abundantly illustrated manuscripts displaying her name and arms and depicting the author. Probably intended as gifts for family members, especially her niece and heir, Antoinette d'Amboise, they reflect a strong tradition in early Renaissance France of aristocratic women writing, illustrating, and dedicating their works.

Mary Beth Winn

See also the subheading Literary Patronage (under Literary Culture and Women).

Bibliography

Primary Works

Catherine d'Amboise. *La Complainte de la Dame pasmee contre Fortune.* 3 manuscripts: Paris, Bibliothèque Nationale de France, n.a.fr. 19738; SMAF Ms. 97–9, on deposit at the Bibliothèque Nationale de France; and London, in private hands, sold by Sam Fogg. An edition by Ariane Bergeron is forthcoming, based on her thesis (2002) for the Ecole des Chartes, Paris.

Catherine d'Amboise. *Le Livre des Prudens.* Paris: Bibliothèque de l'Arsenal, Ms. 2037.

Catherine d'Amboise. *Les Devotes Epistres.* Paris: Bibliothèque Nationale de France, Ms. fr. 2282.

Catherine d'Amboise. *Les Devotes Epistres.* Edited by J.-J. Bourassé. Tours: Mame, 1861.

Catherine d'Amboise. *Les Devotes Epistres.* Edited by Yves Giraud, with introduction, transcription, and reproduction of original manuscript on facing pages. Friburg: Éditions Universitaires, 2002.

Catherine d'Amboise. *Les Devotes Epistres.* Edited by Catherine M. Müller, with substantial introduction and notes. Montreal: Ceres (Inedita et rara: 16), 2002.

Catherine d'Amboise. *Poésies.* Bibliothèque Nationale de France, fr. 2282.

Secondary Works

Berriot-Salvadore, Evelyne. *Les Femmes dans la société française de la Renaissance.* Geneva: Droz, 1990.

Orth, Myra D. "Dedicating Women: Manuscript Culture in the French Renaissance, and the Cases of Catherine d'Amboise and Anne de Graville." *Journal of the Early Book Society* 1, no. 1 (1997): 17–39.

Souchal, G. "Le Mécénat de la famille d'Amboise." *Bull. Soc. Antiq. de l'Ouest et des Musées de Poitiers* part II, XIII, no. 4 (1976): 567–612.

Andreini, Isabella (1562–1604)

Italian playwright, actor, poet

Isabella Andreini's renown was owed not only to her great talent and erudition but also to her keen ability to manage her public image. She was born in Padua in 1562 into the Venetian Canali family, and at age fourteen she joined the well-known *commedia dell'arte* company, the Gelosi. In 1578 she married a fellow member of the company, Francesco Andreini, with whom she performed and managed the troupe's activities. Her correspondence reveals that she was able to negotiate delicate political situations for procuring patronage, and, because Andreini's creative life is integrally tied to financial concerns, her career required her to participate in what have traditionally been perceived as the early modern male's social spaces.

Andreini is first remembered as a celebrated actor. With the theater troupe the Gelosi, she most frequently performed the role of female love lead. When invited to perform in all-female environments, she would also play male roles such as the character Aminta in Tasso's

Isabella Andreini, Italian playwright, actor, and poet. Engraving by unknown artist. (Maria Bandini Buti, Enciclopedia biografica e bibliografica italiana: poetesse e scrittrici*)*

ing genre of *commedia dell'arte,* her acting eschewed the buffoonery of the so-called "vulgar comics." Her stage roles and literary production combined humanist values such as neo-Platonic meditation on the soul with popular Christian discourses of marriage and family.

Andreini's literary publications demonstrate a familiarity with classical sources, often citing Aristotle, Plato, or the Greek and Roman playwrights directly. Her published works include about five hundred poems, one pastoral play, correspondence, and a collection of scenes for comic plays. Here too, her works often advocate the centrality of marriage and motherhood to the health of society. It is in fact her adherence to the precepts of the "virtuous woman" in her writings and in her personal life that prompted many writers throughout the centuries to praise her as a model to be emulated by young women. It is also this fact that might make some twenty-first-century scholars pause before hailing her work as protofeminist. For example, her pastoral play *Mirtilla,* which in part demonstrates some interesting rewritings of traditionally misogynist scenes, concludes with all of its female characters being cajoled or persuaded into marrying men that they do not seem to desire. Furthermore, her well-known missive, "Letter on the Birth of Women," argues that daughters bring more happiness to fathers than do sons since women are submissive and are content to live in the "sweet prison" of the household. Both her play and her letters at times might suggest a certain critique of the limited roles of women, but they stop short of the direct social criticism found in other contemporary women writers.

We should not forget, however, that it is precisely because Andreini was able to portray herself as a "virtuous woman" that she was able to assert her career *as* a woman actress and writer in the most prominent circles of the time. Through her staged mastery of language utterance alone, Andreini perforce demands that the audience recognize a female body and female voice that controls the *logos,* the long

play by the same name. Although she and her company became closely associated with the Gonzaga court at Mantua, Andreini enjoyed fame in all of the important courts of Italy and beyond the Alps at the French court of Henry IV and Queen Marie de Médicis in 1603–1604. It was on her journey returning home in 1604 that she died in Lyon on 10 June, during the birth of what would have been her eighth child.

Because professional actresses of the period had a social status not different from that of prostitutes, Andreini faced a challenge in crafting her public image as a virtuous woman. Her choices in her stage career and literary production are notably marked by their humanist themes, the stamp of what was considered high culture. Some of Andreini's most famous roles were in a series of plays under her own name, *Lucky Isabella, Jealous Isabella,* and, the best-known, *Isabella's Madness.* Although these works belonged in great part to the entertain-

argued territory of men. This relationship between language and the discourse surrounding women is most interesting if we consider her best-known comic work, *Isabella's Madness,* performed for the wedding of Ferdinand I de' Medici and Christine of Lorraine. The character's madness is caused when she is abducted by a young man, and it is characterized in two phases. In one moment Isabella sings French *chansons* and speaks in foreign languages, while in the other she imitates the dialects of the fellow characters on stage. Madness, which is a common topos in *commedia dell'arte,* is thus marked by linguistic confusion, a confusion that allowed for the demonstration of Andreini's virtuosic linguistic and vocal skills as well as providing a chance for the actress to address the French bride in her own language. When Isabella's character regains her senses by drinking magic waters, she delivers a discourse on the sublime and Platonic nature of love.

If madness opened the space for performative virtuosity, her return to more fashionable themes on humanist thought allowed Andreini to demonstrate her own exceptional learning, bolster the image of performers and women, and finally appeal to the contemporary tastes of Italian courts, thus securing continued support and patronage. It is this image of erudite thinker and virtuous woman that marks Andreini's life. She was praised during her own life and for centuries after in Christian terms as a mother, devout wife, and woman of virtue while she was also regarded as an artist and student of classical thought. In recognition of her achievements, Andreini was invited to become a member of the Academy of the Intenti of Pavia in 1601, and, in that same year, her first book of poetry was published. The portrait that accompanies the frontispiece of her *Rhymes* shows Andreini dressed as a member of the high bourgeoisie with eyes cast sideways, depicting the gaze of a woman aware of the subversive theatricality of her person and her work. For example, we see in the first and most famous poem in her collection, one of the ear-

liest literary examples of a woman artist who expresses the link between illusory stage performance, poetry, and life. In an age slow to slough off the influence of Petrarchism, Andreini begins her collection of poems not with an apology of her amorous verse, but with a warning of the dangers of artifice and art:

> If anyone should ever my neglected verses read,
> let him not believe in these pretended passions,
> For, on stage, I am accustomed to treating
> imagined loves with untrue affects. (1601)

This attention to theatricality and artifice associates Andreini's poetry with the baroque works of contemporary poets such as Marino and Tasso, who were admirers of the poetess. Her verse also contains large numbers of poems written about a female object of desire. Though this has often been called Andreini's unique appropriation of the male voice, we may view these verses within the theatrical context that Andreini herself has declared, one that calls attention to her lifetime on a stage of feigned passions and—to borrow her own word from the same poem—"representations" of human emotion.

Though her poetry and correspondence are rich and quite extensive, it is her pastoral play that stands as Andreini's literary masterpiece. *Mirtilla* is a fully scripted play that tells of the desires of shepherds and nymphs, ending in the conjugal pairings of three couples. Andreini's pastoral is loosely based on Tasso's *Aminta,* yet the seasoned *commedia dell'arte* actress chooses to stage action that Tasso left to narration. Most notably, Andreini stages the attempted rape of the nymph Filli by the Satyr and effectively reverses the female role of sexual object into one of shrewd manipulator of seduction and power. Andreini composes a highly dramatic and comedic scene that engages both male and female bodies in the erotic tensions of the audience's gaze. As the Satyr gets closer to undressing and violating the nymph, she outwits him by suggesting that she wishes to tie him to a tree and kiss and caress his body. The shrewd nymph, a role famously played by Andreini herself, then binds the powerful Satyr and leaves him to lament his emotional and physical helplessness. Andreini's literary production thus oscillates between conventional and radical representations of women and ultimately escapes an easy classification. Finally, it is in the scene in *Mirtilla* where nymphs compete for men's attention in a singing competition that we may find Andreini's truest depiction of her career. Such a competition is a gendered reversal of the chivalric tournaments, where knights battled for the kiss of their ladies, but it may also in some manner mirror the real-life situations faced by Andreini as a diva of the stage in which her company would perform multiple plays with different leading ladies; for we know that when Isabella performed at the wedding of the Medici duke to his French bride, she would have been in direct competition with the other show produced that same week—this one led by Vittoria Piisimi.

Andreini knew through experience that women in the early modern period were judged based on their talents, merits, and reputation. She thus challenges our understanding of women's history in that she provides an example of a woman who demonstrates the necessity of women to be professionally trained, educated, and talented in a competitive and public world. Hers was a tenuous position of performer both on and off stage, where she operated within the social and economic spheres of men by portraying herself as both an erudite humanist and a conventional Christian wife without seeking to reconcile one with the other.

Gerry Milligan

See also Literary Culture and Women; Theater and Women Actors, Playwrights, and Patrons.
Bibliography
Primary Works
Andreini, Isabella. *La Mirtilla: A Pastoral.* Translated by Julie Campbell. Tempe: Arizona Center for Medieval and Renaissance Studies, 2002.

Andreini, Isabella. *Lettere.* Edited by Francesco Andreini. Venice, 1607. (Published many times after 1607.)
Andreini, Isabella. *The Madness of Isabella.* In *Scenarios of the Commedia dell'Arte.* Translated by Henry Salerno. New York: Limelight Editions, 1996.
Andreini, Isabella. *Mirtilla, favola pastorale.* Verona, 1588; Ferrara, 1590; Venice, 1590; Milan, 1605.
Andreini, Isabella. *Rime.* Milan, 1601; Paris, 1603; Milan, 1605.
Stortoni, Laura Anna, and Mary Prentice Lillie. *Women Poets of the Italian Renaissance.* Pages 221–249. New York: Italica Press, 1997.
Secondary Works
Dersofi, Nancy. "Isabella Andreini." In *Italian Women Writers.* Edited by Rinaldina Russell, 18–25. Westport, CT: Greenwood Press, 1994.
Macneil, Anne. *Music and Women of the Commedia dell'Arte in the Late Sixteenth Century.* Oxford: Oxford University Press, 2003.
Tylus, Jane. "Women at the Windows: Commedia dell'arte and Theatrical Practice in Early Modern Italy." *Theatre Journal* no. 49 (1997): 323–342.

Androgyne

The most familiar source of the figure of the androgyne is the myth recounted by the comic poet Aristophanes in Plato's *Symposium* describing a quasi human creature, four-armed, four-legged, with two faces and two sets of genitals (*Symposium,* 189e–192b). These early quadruped-humans existed in three forms: those who were entirely male; those who were entirely female; and those who were half male and half female. Thus, according to Plato's myth, there were originally three sexes: the male, the female, and the hermaphrodite or androgyne. When these four-legged protohumans tried to attack the gods, Zeus ordered them cut in half to reduce their strength, while he moved their genitals from the backs to the fronts of their bodies so that they could procreate in their reduced state. But these creatures, now humans, longed to be reunited with their other halves: the male-female creatures sought union with the opposite sex, while the descendants of the male-male and female-

female quadrupeds yearned to be made one again with members of their own sex.

Poets in the Renaissance expected their audience to be familiar with Plato's androgyne, and they used it as a metaphor of the joining of lover and beloved, bringing two bodies together as they were meant to be according to Aristophanes' myth. These poetic references, all by male poets, are almost all to male-female pairings. In such cases, the androgyne includes the beloved more as a marker of the poet's desire than as a way of depicting the woman who is immediately subsumed in the new "androgyne." The latter is how the androgyne is evoked by a female poet, Louise Labé, in the "Debate of Folly and Love." There, Apollo, defending Love, explains that man requires woman who "Causes him to have two bodies, four arms, and two souls more perfect than the first men in Plato's Symposium."

The term "androgyne" was also applied to a lesbian couple celebrated in French literature: Diane, a noblewoman of the highest order, and Anne, a lady of lower rank. The French Renaissance poets Pierre de Ronsard, Etienne Jodelle, and Pontus de Tyard wrote about their love; in each case the male poet spoke in the voice of Anne, declaring her love for Diane. In Ronsard's elegy, the figure of the androgyne marks the friendship of two women declared to be "pure" (1948, l. 9) and "holy" (1948, l. 10). The poem is equivocal, seemingly depicting their bond as a deep friendship rather than a homoerotic relationship, although the total effect is that it was both. The body is subordinate to the friendship that makes them one. Their "same shared body" might be intended merely as a metaphor of the unity created by their friendship. The apparent erotic associations of a reference to "my mistress" are perhaps blurred by the difference in the social standing of the two women made explicit at the end of the poem (1948, ll. 129–130); the word might apply to a servant/mistress relationship as well as to an erotic one. Their friendship is earlier compared to that of Orestes and Pylades, a type of true

friendship. Building on this comparison, Anne declares herself ready to die for her friend. The androgyne references ("half," "same shared body") are expressions of the intensity of this friendship, preparing its ultimate statement in the evocation of the Platonic notion of the fusion or exchange of lovers' souls, which by the time this poem was published was heavily charged with sexual implications from its frequent other (heterosexual) contemporary literary uses.

The names of Anne and Diane, presumably the same two women, reappear in a sonnet by Etienne Jodelle, whom he also associates with the androgyne. Summarizing Plato's rendering of the meaning of the myth of the androgyne, Jodelle passes from male-male couplings to heterosexual ones and finally to lesbian pairings. Again, the audience is expected to be familiar with these choices and the speaker is one of the women. Jodelle's sonnet is more openly homoerotic than Ronsard's elegy, taking no pains to veil the eroticism in a system of equivocations: we are dealing with the "ardent fires" of a "total love." Both poems refer to the possible anagram of Anne in Diane as a kind of marker of the physical joining of the two.

The androgyne also can be traced to another source, of which the Renaissance was equally aware. The Bible, in Genesis 1:27, declares: "God created man in his own image, in the image of God created he him; male and female created he them." Since this precedes the creation of Eve, there is a tradition predating Christianity and taken up by early Christian fathers, interpreting the hesitation between singular and plural as marking an androgyne, a single human creature containing both genders. The passage, including the shift from singular to plural and the declaration that humankind was created in the image of God is echoed in Genesis 5:1–2: "In the day that God created man, in the likeness of God made he him; Male and female created he them, and blessed them, and called their name Adam in the day when they were created." Gender rather than sex is at issue in this tradition: man here is understood as having been made in the image of God, who is both immaterial and contains all things, including male and female. Genesis 1 is an authorizing text for the spiritual androgyne, as a state of prelapsarian man with greater resemblance to the *image* of God. Once Eve is created, there are two separately *sexed* beings who through marriage are to be "one *flesh*" (Gen. 2:24), a familiar image repeated several times in the New Testament. Genesis 2 is the authorizing text for the Mosaic androgyne as a marriage figure. The marital androgyne serves as a metaphor binding married women to their husbands, and, like the usual poetic use of the Platonic androgyne, it does not have much to tell us about women. In contrast, the spiritual androgyne of Genesis 1 was equally available to Renaissance women and men, creating a possibility, a likeness to the image of God, to which all humans had equal rights of access. Marguerite de Navarre provides perhaps the most moving use of the idea in her poem "The Prisons" (1989, ll. 921–930), where she speaks of the essence of God reflected in the divine androgyne, using it to demonstrate women's (as well as men's) access to the divine.

Marian Rothstein

See also Hermaphrodite as Idea and Image; Marguerite de Navarre; Masculinity, Femininity, and Gender; Querelle des Femmes; Sappho and the Sapphic Tradition.

Bibliography
Primary Works
Jodelle, Etienne. *Œuvres Complètes.* 2 vols. Edited by Enea Balmas, vol. 1.379. Paris: Gallimard, 1965–1968.
Labé, Louise. *The Debate of Folly and Love.* Translated by Anne-Marie Bourbon. New York: Peter Lang, 2000.
Labé, Louise. *Œuvres Complètes.* Edited by François Rigolot. Paris: Flammarion, 1986.
Marguerite de Navarre. *Les Prisons.* Edited by Simone Glasson. Geneva: Droz, 1978.
Marguerite de Navarre. *Prisons.* Translated by Claire Lynch Wade. New York: Peter Lang, 1989.
Plato, *Symposium.*
Ronsard, Pierre de. *Elegies, mascarades et bergerie (1565).* In *Œuvres Complètes.* Edited by Paul Laumonier, 13: 170–176. Paris: Didier, 1948.
Secondary Works
Merrill, Robert Valentine, and Robert J. Clements. *Platonism in French Renaissance Poetry.* New York: New York University Press, 1957.
Rothstein, Marian. "The Mutations of the Androgyne: Its Functions in Early Modern France." *Sixteenth Century Journal* 34, no. 2 (2003): 409–437.

Anguissola, Sofonisba (b. ca. 1532–1625)

Italian painter born in Cremona

Sofonisba Anguissola is best classified as "the first great woman artist of the Renaissance" (Perlingieri 1992). Like her younger contemporary, the Bolognese painter Lavinia Fontana, Anguissola was praised by contemporary theorists, including Georgio Vasari, for her skill in portraiture. Unlike most women artists of the early modern period, however, Anguissola was recognized not only for her technical competence (*diligenza,* a category of praise commonly awarded to women), but also for her inspired ability to invest her subjects with "life"—a creative capacity that was coded masculine and thus usually reserved for the greatest male practitioners of the visual arts. Yet Vasari considered Anguissola's portraits as "truly alive" (*vive*), "lacking nothing except speech," and "executed so well that they appear to be breathing and absolutely alive" (Jacobs 1997, 51).

Like many women artists and writers of her time, Anguissola enjoyed the strong support of her father. Amilcare Anguissola, a nobleman and connoisseur of art, saw to the education of his six daughters, Sofonisba, Elena, Lucia, Europa, Minerva, and Anna Maria, in addition to their brother, Asdrubale. Lucia, Europa, and Anna Maria Anguissola were also known to contemporaries for their abilities as painters, but to a lesser degree than their elder sister. Most artists of the Renaissance era, male and

Sofonisba Anguissola, Italian painter. Self-portrait. (Palazzo Spada/Library of Congress)

female, were the children of artists. Anguissola presents a different paradigm: she was a noblewoman who did not use her painting as a pastime or "accomplishment," but instead conducted herself as a professional. Although the Anguissola family of Cremona was noble, their finances were in a perilous state by the time Amilcare Anguissola began to think of his son's patrimony and his daughters' dowries. The education of all his daughters may have enhanced their marriage prospects, supplementing their less than optimal financial dowries with cultural cachet. Several scholars have suggested in particular that part of Amilcare's motivation for encouraging Sofonisba to make a professional career out of her evident talent was the hope that she would be able to help restore the family resources. In the event, Sofonisba did use part of her salary from the Spanish court to support her family back in Cremona. After her father's death in 1573, Anguissola assisted her younger brother Asdrubale, returning him to

solvency when he found himself in especially dire straits (1578) and later (1589–1590) gave him an annual stipend of 800 lire (Garrard 1994, 618, n. 107). In 1606, she requested that her lifetime pension from the Spanish crown be transferred to Asdrubale (Perlingieri 1992, 193). Amilcare arranged for Sofonisba and her sister Elena to study with Bernardino Campi from about 1545 to 1549; thereafter Sofonisba studied with Bernardino Gatti (*il Sojaro*). Under Campi's guidance, she developed her facility with the mannerist style, which characterizes much of her oeuvre. Anguissola's studies with Gatti sharpened her taste for genre scenes, inventive approaches to portraiture, and an anecdotal mode of visual storytelling— aesthetic choices that set her work apart from the sometimes stifling formality attendant to Mannerism (*DBI* 1961, 322).

Anguissola's father also corresponded with Michelangelo concerning her artistic education. Several of Amilcare's letters attest that the illustrious artist served informally as her instructor and also that he came to admire her work. In 1557, Amilcare wrote to Michelangelo requesting that he send one of his drawings to Sofonisba "so that she may color it in oil, with the obligation to return it to you faithfully finished by her own hand" (Garrard 1994, 614, n. 100). One of her own drawings, *Asdrubale Bitten by a Crab,* was a study piece that Michelangelo suggested (Hochman 1993, 72). In 1558, Amilcare wrote again to Michelangelo expressing his gratitude that, "such an excellent gentleman, the most virtuous above all others, deigns to praise and judge the paintings done by my daughter Sofonisba" (Garrard 1994, 614–615, n. 100).

In addition, Amilcare took pains early in his daughter's career to publicize her talent. In 1556, he sent two of her self-portraits to the duke of Ferrara. In 1558, he invited the writer Annibal Caro to visit his home and loaned him one of her self-portraits. Anguissola received numerous commissions during the course of her career. Her most notable patron was King Philip II of Spain, who hired her as a court portraitist in 1559. She moved to Madrid about 1560 and remained at her post as portraitist and lady-in-waiting until around 1580, enjoying not only the king's sponsorship in the abstract, but considerable financial remuneration. Her annual pension was 100 ducats (Garrard 1994, 618, n. 107). In addition, Philip arranged Anguissola's marriage (1572) to Fabrizio Moncada, a native of Palermo and the brother of Francesco II, viceroy of Sicily. The queen, Elizabeth of Valois, provided Anguissola with a dowry of three thousand ducats (Murphy 2003, 38).

Widowed around 1580, Anguissola intended to return to her native Cremona. On her journey homeward, however, she met the Genovese nobleman Orazio Lomellini, whom she soon married. Established in Genoa by 1584, Anguissola became an important salonnière in that city, hosting at the Lomellini palazzo both artists and famous literary figures (*DBI* 1961, 323 and Garrard 1994, 618). She spent the final years of her long life in Palermo where, in 1623, the portraitist Anthony Van Dyck met her. He has left an affecting description of this remarkable career woman, whom he greatly admired, which reveals that even as a nonagenarian and nearly blind, Anguissola retained her memory and sharp wit (Garrard 1994, 577, n. 43).

Works

Anguissola's family portraits and self-portraits constitute a significant portion of her oeuvre. Paintings featuring her family members include *Portrait of a Nun* (1551; her sister Elena; London, Yarborough Collection), *Portrait of Asdrubale* (ca. 1556; Cremona: Museo Civico ala Ponzone), *Portrait of a Lady* (ca. 1556; probably her mother, Bianca Ponzone Anguissola; Cremona: Museo Civico ala Ponzone), and *The Family Group* (ca. 1558; Minerva, Amilcare, and Asdrubale Anguissola; Niva, Nivaagaards Malerisamling). Anguissola's most famous painting, *The Chess Game* or *Anguissola Sisters Play-*

ing Chess (1555; Poznan, Museum Narodowe), is both a family portrait and genre scene. This work has elicited much scholarly interest, in part because it represents a striking typological departure: rather than depicting her three noble sisters and their nurse with traditional "feminine" props such as needlework, prayer-books, or pets, she shows them engaged in an *intellectual* game. In the same vein, her *Old Woman Studying the Alphabet Instructed by a Girl* (1550s; Florence, Uffizi Gallery) portrays women edifying themselves.

Anguissola's self-portraits similarly emphasize her own diverse talents. She depicts herself holding the painter's tools (1552; Florence: Uffizi Gallery); playing the clavichord (ca. 1555–1556; Naples: Museo Nazionale di Capodimonte; and 1561; Althorp: Collection Earl Spencer); reading (1550s; drawing in black chalk; Florence: Uffizi); and holding medallions (ca. 1555; Boston: Museum of Fine Arts) or books with Latin inscriptions. Her earliest securely dated self-portrait (1554; Vienna: Kunsthistoriches Museum) depicts the artist holding a book open to a page that reads, in Latin, *Sophonisba Anguissola virgo seipsam fecit* (Sophonisba Anguissola, a maiden, painted this image of herself). Through these devices, Anguissola underscored her participation in artistic, musical, and literary culture. She also contravened gender assumptions concerning female sensuality and irrationality by emphasizing her sobriety and self-mastery in her self-portraits: she usually appears with tightly bound, unornamented hair and wearing high-collared black dresses in the conservative Spanish style (Garrard 1994, 583–586, 594–595). As Mary Garrard has shown, moreover, the double portrait called *Bernardino Campi Painting Sofonisba Anguissola* (1550s; Siena: Pinacoteca Nazionale) can be seen to mimic tropes of female inferiority by destabilizing the subject-object relationship (Garrard 1994, 556–564). Anguissola continued to paint her own image well into her nineties. Her *Self-Portrait* (ca. 1610; Bern: Gottfried Keller Collection) emphasizes once again her status as a woman of letters and client of the Spanish crown. Commissioned by Philip III, who continued to pay her the lifetime pension that his father had granted to her, this portrait shows Anguissola holding in one hand a letter addressed "to His Catholic Majesty" and in the other a book, which she keeps open with one finger to mark her place (Perlingieri 1992, 193–194). Her final *Self-Portrait* (ca. 1620; Niva: Nivaagards Art Museum) constitutes a subtle meditation on her age and increasing frailty.

In the course of her long career, Anguissola worked steadily as a professional portraitist. She painted intellectual men (*Portrait of a Dominican Astronomer,* 1555; whereabouts unknown), artists (*Portrait of Giorgio Giulio Clovio,* 1578; Mentana: Zeri Collection), and clerics (*Portrait of a Dominican Monk,* 1556; Brescia: Pinacoteca Tosio Martinengo; *Portrait of a Monk,* ca. 1556; England: Private Collection). She was also a popular portraitist among men and women of the nobility. Her works in this genre, most of which belong to her Spanish period, include *Portrait of Massimiliano Stampa* (1557; Baltimore: Walters Art Gallery); *Portrait of Don Sebastian of Portugal* (1572; Madrid: Fundaciòn Casa de Alba); several portraits of *Queen Isabel de Valois* (ca. 1561; Milan: Pinacoteca de Brera; 1561, Vienna: Kunsthistoriches Museum; 1563–1565; Madrid: Prado Museum); *Portrait of Don Carlos* (ca. 1560; Madrid: Prado Museum); *Portrait of Queen Anne of Austria* (ca. 1570; Glasgow: The Stirling Maxwell Collection, Pollok House, Glasgow Museums and Art Galleries); *Portrait of the Infantas Isabella Clara Eugenia and Catalina Micaela* (ca. 1569–1570; London: Buckingham Palace, Royal Collection); *Portrait of Margarita Gonzaga* (1571; Derbyshire: Captain Patrick Drury-Lowe Collection); *Portrait of Doña María Minrique de Lara y Pernstein and One of Her Daughters* (ca. 1574; Prague: Central Gallery of Bohemia); *Portrait of the Infanta Isabella Clara Eugenia* (ca. 1578; Madrid: Prado Museum); and *Portrait of Philip II* (Madrid ca. 1551: Prado Museum).

Anguissola also made several contributions in the field of religious painting. These works include her *Holy Family* (1559; Bergamo: Accademia Carrara); *Madonna Nursing Her Child* (1588: Budapest: Museum of Fine Arts); *Holy Family with Saints Anne and John* (1592; Florida: Lowe Art Museum, University of Miami); and *Pietà* (1550s; Milan: Pinacoteca di Brera).

The successful career of Sofonisba Anguissola attests the degree to which ambitious early modern women were able to make their mark on contemporary culture. One of Anguissola's distinctive achievements, as Mary Garrard has argued, was to present herself in such a way that she avoided both the dismissive category "only a woman" and the equally problematic category of the "exceptional" woman. In Garrard's words, Anguissola fashioned herself with "not so much virility as to offend, but enough to stake her serious claim on culture" (Garrard 1994, 588). She also set an example for painting as a socially acceptable profession for women, an example that encouraged other women artists of her era (Pagden 1995, 10; Perlingieri 1992, 210). No less important, Anguissola pioneered "psychological intimacy in portraiture" (Perlingieri 1992, 210).

Anguissola enjoyed widespread recognition from artists, art critics, and humanists. In addition to encomia from writers like Vasari and Caro, her appearance alongside other famous women in the encyclopedias of female biography that poured out of the Italian presses in the sixteenth and seventeenth centuries reified her legacy. One male biographer noted that Sofonisba "not only created the most wonderful and beautiful things with her brush, but also desired to write with her pen (since she was very learned) certain things, which have been much praised and appreciated by *virtuosi*" (Chiesa 1620, sig. U7r). Another biographer classified her in his collection of 845 famous women as "a musician, writer and above all an exceptionally fine painter" (*musica, letterata, e soprattuto rarissima pittrice*); he devoted four pages to her transcategorical excellence (Ribera 1609, sig.

Rr2r et seq.). Testimony of this kind reinforced the image that Anguissola fashioned for herself: she was not "only a woman" and indeed not only a painter, but also a Renaissance woman in the fullest sense of the term.

Sarah Gwyneth Ross

See also Art and Women; Fetti, Lucrina; Fontana, Lavinia; Gentileschi, Artemisia; Nelli, Plautilla.

Bibliography
Primary Works
Chiesa, Franceso Agostino della. *Theatro delle donne letterate, con un breve discorso della preminenza, e perfettione del sesso donnesco.* Mondovi, Italy: Giovanni Gislandi e Gio, Tomaso Rossi, 1620.
Ribera, Pietro Paolo de. *Le glorie immortali de'trionfi, et heroiche imprese d'ottocento quarantacinque Donne Illustri antiche, e moderne.* Venice: Evangelista Deuchino, 1609.
Secondary Works
Dizionario biografico delgi Italiani. Rome: Istituto dell'Enciclopedia Italiana, 1961.
Garrard, Mary D. "Here's Looking at Me: Sofonisba Anguissola and the Problem of the Woman Artist." *Renaissance Quarterly* 47, no. 3 (Autumn 1994): 556–622.
Hochman, Michel. "Les dessins et les peintures de Fulvio Orsini et la collection Farnèse." *Mélanges de l'ècole françqise de Rome* (CV 1993): 49–83.
Jacobs, Fredrika. *Defining the Renaissance Virtuosa: Women Artists and the Language of Art History and Criticism.* Cambridge: Cambridge University Press, 1997.
Jacobs, Fredrika. "Woman's Capacity to Create: The Unusual Case of Sofonisba Anguissola." *Renaissance Quarterly* 47, no. 1 (1994): 74–101.
Murphy, Caroline P. *Lavinia Fontana: A Painter and Her Patrons in Sixteenth-Century Bologna.* New Haven, CT: Yale University Press, 2003.
Pagden, Sylvia Ferino. *Sofonisba Anguissola: A Renaissance Woman.* Exhibition catalog. Washington, DC: National Museum of Women in the Arts, 1995.
Perlingieri, Ilya Sandra. *Sofonisba Anguissola: The First Great Woman Artist of the Renaissance.* New York: Rizzoli, 1992.
Pinessi, Orietta. *Sofonisba Anguissola: un "pittore" alla corte di Filippo II.* Milan: Selene, 1998.

Anna of Denmark (1574–1619)

Wife and queen consort of King James VI of Scotland (James I of England)

Anna of Denmark was born 12 December 1574, the second of seven children of Frederick II, king of Denmark-Norway, and his queen consort, Sophia. She is particularly known as a patron of the arts, especially the court masque and her involvement in court politics. Married to the Scottish monarch, James VI, by proxy in May 1589, her new spouse collected her for her coronation on 17 May 1590. The couple had seven children themselves, only three of whom—Henry, prince of Wales, the future Charles I, and Elizabeth, the "Winter Queen" of Bohemia—saw their sixth birthday.

Customarily regarded as "frivolous," Anna's reputation has received new scholarly luster, thanks, in large part, to the development of a better appreciation of her behavior prior to her arrival in London. Students of Jacobean England have long known of her role as a patron of arts, especially of her fondness for masquing, but have tended to regard her employment of dramatists and her own appearances in their theatrical creations as squibs fired by a largely impotent political personality who supposedly lacked the seriousness and intellectual ability to make any substantial contribution to the character of reality during the reign of her husband, the archetypical patriarch.

Anna certainly played the *litterateur,* but she also, as befit the well-educated daughter of a capable mother, continually involved herself in "high politics" in both Scotland and England. Shortly after she arrived in her home, she befriended Henrietta, countess of Huntly and daughter of her new husband's favorite and cousin, Esmé Stewart, and aligned herself with Huntly's brother, Lodovick Stewart, duke of Lennox, and John Erskine, earl of Mar, against their enemy, James's chancellor, Sir John Maitland, to the extent that Maitland had to petition for her favor after a two-year battle. She then allied herself with the chancellor against Mar.

Anna's safe delivery of a son in 1594 cemented this realignment as she opposed the Stewart tradition, continued for Prince Henry

Anna of Denmark, wife and queen consort of King James VI of Scotland. Engraving by G. Barrie and Son. (Library of Congress)

by her husband, of handing over their heirs to the governance of the Erskine family. For the next ten years, she tussled with James over the Erskines' control of her child—for all of the king's notorious fondness for young men, their passionate marriage involved alternate periods of loggerheads and reconciliation as Anna bore children routinely. Although implicated in the Gowrie plot in 1600—two of her closest attendants were sisters of the treacherous earl—the queen finally won the war when she collected Henry from Stirling Castle on her way to join her husband in England following his accession to that throne in 1603 as James I.

Like James, Anna found that the relative wealth of the English realm permitted flights of previously unimaginable fancy, which she indulged, especially and notoriously, in the production of court masques. The larger English stage also, though, offered new opportunities for political maneuvering; indeed, her involvement in English politics predated her physical arrival in the kingdom when a group of noblewomen, including Lucy, countess of Bedford, Penelope, Lady Rich, and Mary, countess of Pembroke, made their way north to meet the new queen at Newcastle. These ladies comprised part of a substantial faction, a relict of the failed rebellion of the earl of Essex in 1601, opposed to Spain and its English supporters. Although the nature of her own religion remains uncertain, Anna found an affinity with this group, and she associated herself with them for the rest of her life.

Prior to Robert Cecil's death in 1612, the maneuvers of the anti-Spanish faction remained small in scale, and the death of the prince of Wales in November of the same year was a severe personal, as well as political, blow. But afterward, their activities became more noisome, especially after the death of Henry Howard, earl of Northampton, in 1614. Most famously, Anna and friends—George Abbott, archbishop of Canterbury, Henry Wriothesley, earl of Southampton, and William Herbert, earl of Pembroke—maneuvered a new favorite, George Villiers, into the king's affections at the expense of the pro-Howard Robert Carr.

The queen and her associates, though, had interests in policy as well as politics. Her councilors, including Sir Edwin Sandys, and their circle played vital roles in the Virginia Company; a number of significant works espousing British "improvement" were dedicated to Anna, including Captain John Smith's procolonization *The Generall Historie of Virginia, New-England and the Summer Isles.* The queen took charge of the English government while James returned to Scotland during 1617.

Despite Prince Henry's death, as the mother of the "spare" Prince Charles, Anna might have continued to exercise considerable significance in British affairs. Unhappily, even as Villiers began his political ascent, she developed pleurisy and became seriously ill by the end of 1617. She died 2 March 1619.

Louis H. Roper

See also Literary Culture and Women; Power, Politics, and Women; Sidney, Mary Herbert; Theater and Women Actors, Playwrights, and Patrons.

Bibliography

Alsop, J. D. "William Welwood, Anne of Denmark and the Sovereignty of the Sea." *Scottish Historical Review* 59 (1980): 155–159.

Barroll, Leeds. *Anna of Denmark, Queen of England: A Cultural History.* Philadelphia: University of Pennsylvania Press, 2000.

Lewalski, Barbara K. "Enacting Opposition: Queen Anne and the Subversion of Masquing." In *Writing Women in Jacobean England,* 15–43. Cambridge, MA: Harvard University Press, 1993.

Roper, Louis H. "Unmasquing the Connections between Jacobean Politics and Policy: The Circle of Anna of Denmark and the Beginning of the English Empire, 1614–18." In *High and Mighty Queens of Early Modern England.* Edited by Debra Barrett-Graves, Jo Eldridge Carney, and Carole Levin, 45–59. New York: Palgrave Macmillan, 2003.

Anne of Brittany (Anne de Bretagne; 1477–1514)

Duchess of Brittany, twice queen of France

Anne de Bretagne, born in Nantes, was the daughter of Duke Francois II de Bretagne and Marguerite de Foix. Anne's mother died when she was a small child; her father lived only until Anne was eleven years old. Upon the death of her father, the child became duchess of Brittany. At the age of thirteen, Anne was married by procuration to Maximilian I, archduke of Austria. The procuration was later declared defective and the marriage not binding. In 1491 Anne married the French king Charles VIII, son and successor of Louis XI, to stabilize relations between France and Brittany. The following year Anne was crowned queen of France. Charles and Anne's firstborn, Charles-Orlando, lived only until the age of three. Their other three children were stillborn or died in infancy. Charles died in 1498 without leaving an heir to the throne. Upon her husband's death, Anne reacquired the title of duchess of Brittany, a title she had been forbidden to use since her marriage.

The man who would be Anne's second husband, Louis d' Orleans, was declared king of France on 8 April 1498, becoming Louis XII. He married Anne in January 1499, a few weeks after his marriage to Jeanne de France was annulled. Late that year a daughter, Claude, was born to the king and queen. At the age of six, Claude was promised to Francois d'Angoulême, later Francois I, over the strong objections of her mother. In 1510 their second daughter was born, Renée de France, subsequently duchess of Ferrara.

Anne was a pious woman, eminently respectable. Her court came to be known as a school of good conduct for young noble girls. Although she possessed a tumultuous temper and a revengeful streak, Anne, known as the Good Duchess, was deeply generous to friends, allies, and the poor. She died of natural causes on 9 January 1514.

Kathleen M. Llewellyn

See also Power, Politics and Women; Renata di Francia.

Bibliography

Matarasso, Pauline. *Queen's Mate: Three Women of Power in France on the Eve of the Renaissance.* Aldershot, UK; Burlington, VT; Singapore; Sydney: Ashgate, 2001.

Minois, Georges. *Anne de Bretagne.* Paris: Fayard, 1999.

Ryley, M. Beresford. *Queens of the Renaissance.* Williamstown, MA: Corner House Publishers, 1982.

Anne of Cleves (1515–1557)

Fourth wife of King Henry VIII of England

Born 22 September 1515 in Düsseldorf, Anne of Cleves is distinguished from the English monarch's other wives by the brevity of her marriage, which lasted a mere six months. Soon after their wedding on 6 January 1540, Henry sought an annulment and thereafter treated Anne as an honorary sister. Their marriage was officially annulled by an act of parliament on 12 July 1540. Anne received a considerable divorce settlement of £4,000 per

Anne of Cleves (1515–1557), the fourth wife of King Henry VIII of England. Portrait by anonymous artist. (Library of Congress)

annum, as well as significant properties, such as Bletchingley Manor, Richmond Palace, and Hever Castle, on condition that she remain in England. During her seventeen years as a foreigner in England, Anne of Cleves enjoyed a privileged position at court as the first lady of England, after the queen and Henry's daughters. When Henry died in 1547, the Privy Council confiscated Bletchingley Manor and Richmond Palace. As compensation, Anne was granted two Kentish estates, Penshurst Place and Dartford Priory. After a lingering illness, she died on 16 July 1557 at Chelsea Manor at the age of forty-one.

Daughter of John III of Cleves and Maria of Jülich-Berg-Ravensberg, Anne was born into a politically powerful Protestant family, which ruled territories known as the Duchy of Jülich-Cleves. Anne had two sisters, Sybilla and Amelia, and a brother, William, who became

duke of Cleves in 1539. Sybilla married the zealous Lutheran Johann Frederick, elector of Saxony, who became the head of the Schmalkaldic League of Protestant princes and cities. Anne's lineage can be traced back to Edward I of England and John II of France. In 1527, when Ann was twelve, her father arranged a precontract for her marriage to Francis of Lorraine. After her father died, the precontract apparently became void. Anne spent most of her early years at the ducal court in Düsseldorf and left her homeland for England at the age of twenty-four.

Anne of Cleves' marriage to Henry VIII was the result of a calculated diplomatic effort. Henry's Privy Councillor Thomas Cromwell orchestrated the courtship, intending to secure England's alliance with Cleves and by extension a host of Protestant states. The political spur to the marriage was the peace alliance signed in 1539 by two Catholic powers, Francis I of Spain and Charles V of France. Cromwell sought to protect English interests by urging Henry VIII to ally himself with a Protestant enemy of France. Ironically, soon after Henry and Anne's marriage took place, relations between Francis I and Charles V became hostile, and Henry forged an amicable agreement with Spain.

A remarkable aspect of Henry VIII's courtship negotiations involved a portrait of Anne of Cleves. Wishing to gauge the appearance and character of his prospective bride, Henry VIII sent his court painter, Hans Holbein, abroad to capture Anne's image. Two betrothal portraits of Anne of Cleves are extant: one is an exquisite miniature, now in the Victoria and Albert Museum, and the other is a full-size picture, now in the Louvre. Both offer realistic depictions of her as a solemn young woman in Flemish dress, attractive with fair skin and a modest demeanor. The miniature was set in an ivory case carved in the form of a Tudor rose. Two portraits of Anne from the workshop of Barthel Bruyn the Elder in Cologne reveal a more angular face and sober character. Although no record of Henry's reaction to Holbein's pictures exists, we can assume he found them pleasing since he did not halt the marriage negotiations. Nicholas Wotton, a member of Henry's privy chamber, offered a believable counterpart to Holbein's portrait, which he verified as lifelike, when he described Anne as a virtuous daughter attached to her mother, strictly brought up, and skilled with the needle. According to Wotton's report, Anne could read and write in High Dutch but was not literate in other languages. She could not sing or play an instrument, because these activities were considered too "light" for a woman of her class. She was intelligent and temperate, especially regarding overindulgence in food and drink.

The marriage treaty was concluded on 4 October 1539; Anne arrived in England in late December of that year. On New Year's Day, Henry VIII staged his first meeting with his future wife, which proved mortifying and predictive of the failed relationship to come. Disguised as messengers, he and his gentlemen of the privy chamber surprised Anne in Rochester. They entered her room, disturbing her while she was watching bear baiting from a window. She could not communicate in English and would not have known the identity of the king. Her reaction, therefore, left much to be desired. Henry left the room in disappointment and then returned as the king of England; Anne humbled herself in his presence, but their interview did not go well. The king conveyed to Cromwell how little he liked her from their first meeting. Their marriage was apparently never consummated. Anne revealed ignorance about sexual matters when questioned, and Henry claimed to have been too repulsed by Anne to carry through with his marital obligation. The grounds for divorce were threefold: Anne's prior marriage contract with Francis of Lorraine, Henry's unwillingness to enter into the marriage, and its nonconsummation. Having no better option, Anne agreed to a divorce. In political terms, Henry recognized that he must keep peace with the duke of Cleves; he therefore offered Anne financial independence. He required her to stay in England, however, so that he could ensure that her correspondence to her family did not compromise the delicate political alliance between states.

Anne resided primarily at Hever Castle in Kent. She never remarried, essentially enjoying the authority and freedom of a widow. She established good relations with Mary Tudor, with whom she shared Catholic affinities, and took an interest in Elizabeth Tudor, both future queens of England. Her wedding ring motto, "God send me wel to kepe," ironically describes her circumstances in England; she was well kept indeed, but at the price of her rightful social position as queen, her family's honor, and an heir to the English throne. Anne of Cleves is buried in Westminster Abbey.

Marguerite Tassi

See also Boleyn, Anne; Catherine of Aragon; Howard, Catherine; Howard, Frances; Parr, Katherine; Power, Politics and Women; Religious Reform and Women.

Bibliography
Fraser, Antonia. *The Wives of Henry VIII.* New York: Vintage Books, 1994.

Lindsey, Karen. *Divorced, Beheaded, Survived: A Feminist Reinterpretation of the Wives of Henry VIII.* Reading, MA: Addison-Wesley, 1995.

Plowden, Alison. *Tudor Women: Queens and Commoners.* New York: Atheneum, 1979.

Saaler, Mary. *Anne of Cleves: Fourth Wife of Henry VIII.* London: Rubicon Press, 1995.

Warnicke, Retha M. *The Marrying of Anne of Cleves: Royal Protocol in Early Modern England.* Cambridge: Cambridge University Press, 2000.

Weir, Alison. *The Six Wives of Henry VIII.* New York: Grove Weidenfeld, 1992.

Aragona, Eleonora d'. *See* Eleonora d'Aragona.

Aragona, Giovanna d' (1502–1577)

Duchess of Tagliacozzo; patron of artists, poets, editors, and the printing industry; active in the religious reform movement in Naples

Giovanna d'Aragona, daughter of Duke Ferdinando di Montalto and Castellana Cardona and the granddaughter of King Ferrante of Naples, was born in 1502 in the castello on the island of Ischia, where her parents and the other members of the Aragonese court took refuge when Naples fell to the king of France and his army. There on Ischia, where Giovanna grew up, the forty-year-old widow Costanza d'Avalos gathered a circle of literary men and women around her, the poet Vittoria Colonna, the wife of d'Avalos's nephew Ferrante Francesco d'Avalos, among them. D'Avalos herself had taken up arms and had driven the French off the island when they attempted to lay siege to the castello.

In 1521 Giovanna d'Aragona married Vittoria Colonna's brother, Ascanio Colonna, in the Castel Novo in Naples. By then the French had left Naples, ceding the kingdom to the king of Spain. On their marriage, the couple inherited the titles duke and duchess of Tagliacozzo, a Colonna fiefdom in Abruzzo. Giovanna and Ascanio's marriage brought together the interests of the powerful Colonna clan and the Aragonese royals in Naples. After the birth of her sixth and last child in 1535, Giovanna d'Aragona left her husband and withdrew with her children to the d'Avalos castello on Ischia, where she took part in the literary salon around Costanza d'Avalos and Vittoria Colonna. Despite attempts of many to reconcile the couple, Giovanna and Ascanio continued to live in separate domiciles for the rest of their lives.

Giovanna Aragona's withdrawal to Ischia signaled a period of increasing closeness between Vittoria Colonna and her sister-in-law. Naples was already the epicenter of the religious revival in Italy at this time, even before the early months of 1536 when the Spanish theologian Juan de Valdés came to Naples and the *spirituali* movement he led was born. D'Aragona, her sister Maria, and the Colonna women, Vittoria Colonna and her cousin by marriage Giulia Gonzaga Colonna, were among the first to join the religious circle around Valdés. These women and their mentor Costanza d'Avalos remained inseparable, and together they constituted the core of Valdés's followers in Naples. Giovanna d'Aragona's long and close relationship with Vittoria Colonna took on a new dimension as they listened together to the sermons of Ochino and Valdés.

Colonna was unable to persuade d'Aragona to give the marriage another try, though at her urging, Paul III (pope 1534–1549) sent his own envoy to Ischia to influence Giovanna to return to Ascanio, but after two years the pope's ambassador returned to Rome, his mission a failure. In 1539, Ascanio Colonna and other lords in the region extending from Abruzzo to Campagna refused to pay the new salt tax the new pope had levied. For two years both Vittoria Colonna and Giovanna d'Aragona worked behind the scenes, writing letters and meeting face to face with the pope's envoys and the representatives of Emperor Charles V in their efforts to head off war between Paul and his vassals. But in March 1541, the Salt War began in earnest. The pope's ten thousand men marched on Paliano. Early that summer they razed Ascanio Colonna's fortifications at Marino, Rocca di Papa, and finally in January 1543 they destroyed Paliano. Ascanio remained banished from his lands until 1549, only to be arrested and imprisoned five years later in Naples by an envoy of his former patron, Charles V, on charges of treason.

At the end of 1555, Giovanna d'Aragona found herself facing imminent danger from two fronts: the office of the Inquisition in Rome and the newly inaugurated pope, Paul IV (Gian Pietro Carafa), who was virulently anti-Reform and anti-Spanish—and no friend of the Colonna. By late summer that year Giovanna's son, Marcantonio Colonna, and the viceroy of Naples had signed treaties of alliance with Spain and Milan, while Paul awaited massive shipments of men and materiel from France. A decade and a half after the Salt War of 1541, the pope and the Colonna were gearing up for a second war. Virtually hostages of the pope, d'Aragona and her entourage sat in the Colonna palace, a stone's throw from the Vatican. On 31 December at around midnight, Giovanna walked through the city gates unrecognized in the coarse shawl and boots of a peasant, and from there she fled to Naples with her children, secretaries, and servants. D'Aragona's flight from Rome and her treatment at the hands of Pope Paul triggered protests from the men of the presses in Venice, thousands of whose books the Inquisition had confiscated or destroyed. An attack on Giovanna d'Aragona—the patron of the presses, literary academies, and poets—was an assault on their own lives and work. Two major works paying tribute to Giovanna d'Aragona Colonna were published in Venice: the first, a 524-page anthology published in 1555 by Girolamo Ruscelli, containing commemorative works by virtually every living poet in Italy; the second, a dialogue by Giuseppe Betussi that came out in 1556.

By 1560, Paul IV and Ascanio Colonna were both long dead, the latter having died in prison in Naples where he languished for four years after his arrest. That year d'Aragona returned in triumph to her home in the Colonna palace in Rome. Though d'Aragona retained her Spanish-leaning politics and her ties with the Jesuits, she remained a prominent cultural figure in both Rome and Naples until her death in 1575.

Diana Robin

See also Aragona, Maria d'; Colonna, Vittoria; the subheading Literary Patronage (under Literary Culture and Women); Power, Politics and Women; Religious Reform and Women.

Bibliography

Primary Works

Betussi, Giuseppe. *Le Imagini del tempio della signora donna Giovanna Aragona. Dialogo di M. Giuseppe Betussi . . . .* Florence: Torrentino, 1556.

Colonna, Vittoria. *Carteggio.* 2nd ed. Edited by Ermanno Ferrero and G. Mueller, with a supplement by Domenico Tordi. Turin: Loescher, 1892.

Reumont, Alfredo. "Di Vittoria Colonna: a proposito dell'operetta Vittoria Colonna, par J. Lefevre Deumier." *Archivio storico italiano,* n.s. 5 (1857): 143–145.

Ruscelli, Girolamo, ed. *Del Tempio alla divina signora donna Giovanna d'Aragona, fabricato da tutti i più gentili Spiriti, & in tutte le lingue principali del mondo.* Venice: Plinio Pietrasanta, 1555.

Secondary Works

Alberigo, Giuseppe. "Aragona, Giovanna d'." *Dizionario biografico degli italiani [DBI],* 3: 694–696. Rome: Istituto dell' Enciclopedia Italiana, 1961.

Alberigo, Giuseppe. "Aragona, Maria d'." *Dizionario biografico degli italiani [DBI],* 3: 701–702. Rome: Istituto dell' Enciclopedia Italiana, 1961.

Brundin, Abigail. *Vittoria Colonna.* Aldershot, UK: Ashgate, forthcoming.

Caro, Gaspare de. "Avalos, Alfonso." *Dizionario biografico degli italiani [DBI],* 4: 612–616. Rome: Istituto dell' Enciclopedia Italiana, 1962.

Patrizi, G. "Colonna, Vittoria." *Dizionario biografico degli italiani [DBI],* 27: 448–457. Rome: Istituto dell' Enciclopedia Italiana, 1982.

Petrucci, Franca. "Colonna, Ascanio." *Dizionario biografico degli italiani [DBI],* 27: 271–275. Rome: Istituto dell' Enciclopedia Italiana, 1982.

Robin, Diana. *Publishing Women. Salons, the Presses, and Religious Reform in Renaissance Italy.* Chicago: University of Chicago Press, 2007.

Vassalli, Donata Chiomenti. *Giovanna d'Aragona, fra baroni, principi e sovrani del Rinascimento.* Milan: Mursia, 1987.

Aragona, Maria d' (1502–1568)

Marchesa del Vasto; patron of artists, poets, literary academies, and the printing industry; active in the reform movement in Naples and Milan

Daughter of Duke Ferdinando di Montalto and Castellana Cardona and the granddaughter of King Ferrante of Naples, Maria d'Aragona was born in 1503 in the d'Avalos castello on Ischia, one year after its chatelaine Costanza d'Avalos took up arms herself and drove off the French who were bombarding the island *fortezza*. Growing up in the d'Avalos castle, d'Aragona absorbed the rich cultural milieu Costanza d'Avalos cultivated. The poet Vittoria Colonna, who married d'Avalos's nephew, Ferrante Francesco d'Avalos, also lived at the castello and was an active participant in Costanza's literary circle. On Ischia Maria met for the first time the poets Sannazaro, Giovio, Tansillo, and Bernardo Tasso, among other literary men she would later entertain in her own salons in Naples, Milan, and Pavia.

In 1523, Maria d'Aragona married Costanza's grandnephew, Marchese Alfonso d'Avalos del Vasto. Del Vasto, like the husbands of Colonna and her sister Giovanna, was a military man in the emperor Charles V's service. During the mid-1530s Maria, Giovanna d'Aragona, Costanza d'Avalos, Vittoria Colonna, and Colonna's cousin by marriage, Giulia Gonzaga, became disciples of the widely influential Spanish theologian Juan de Valdés, attending the lectures and discussions of Scripture he held at his house in Chiaia. Valdés and the d'Avalos-Colonna women also attended the sermons of the radical reform preacher Bernardino Ochino, and they met regularly at the lodgings of Giulia Gonzaga in the convent of San Francesco delle Monache in Naples.

In 1538, Charles V named Maria's husband governor of Milan. Del Vasto and Maria d'Aragona abandoned their homes in Naples and Ischia, settling into the ducal palace in Milan. While del Vasto, who had already served under Charles at Pavia, Tunis, and Naples, was constantly in the field with his army, d'Aragona assumed the responsibility of organizing the court, promoting a cultural program in Milan similar to the one she had instituted in Naples. Once in Milan, she remained loyal to Valdés's disciple Pietro Carnesecchi, and she continued to correspond with Cardinal Seripando, though he had already come under the Inquisitors' attack in Rome. Del Vasto and Maria also sought to bring Ochino to Milan in 1540, though the friar fled Italy for Protestant Geneva in 1541, without having visited the Lombard capital. Bernardo Cappello, a distinguished member of Maria's circle of poets, portrayed her as the queen of a dazzling court. The habitués of her salon included Paolo Giovio, Girolamo Muzio, Pietro Arentino, Giulio Camillo, and Bernardo Spina, all of whom had taken part in Costanza's circle on

Ischia. Maria's well-connected secretary Luca Contile chronicled the lives and times of the marchesa, her husband, and her sister Giovanna in his collected *Lettere,* which were subsequently published in Venice.

In 1544, in one of the worst massacres of the century, del Vasto lost twelve thousand of his men in the battle he fought against the French at Ceresole. A disgraced man, del Vasto never recovered from the wounds he sustained at Ceresole; he died in 1546. D'Aragona moved her entourage out of the ducal palace in Milan and resettled with her seven children and her sister Giovanna in Pavia, where she reestablished her salon and inaugurated the literary academy Chiave d'Oro with Contile, Aretino, and many others from her Milan circle. In February 1547, d'Aragona boarded a ship at Cumae with her whole household and sailed to Ischia. Later that month she and her sister, reinaugurated their salon at the Castel dell'Ovo in Naples.

But on May 13 a popular rebellion erupted in the city. The viceroy of Naples, Pedro di Toledo, turned his cannons on the people, and he closed the city's literary academies, imprisoning their leaders, the poets Ferrante Carafa and Angelo di Costanzo. Driven out of their own venue, d'Aragona collaborated with writers well connected to Venetian editors and printers, such as Aretino, Doni, Giovio, Cappello, and Molza, who had been the mainstays of the academies she patronized in Milan and Pavia. Through d'Aragona's efforts, a number of Venetian presses published works honoring her and her sister since they had continued to stand behind the Naples literary establishment in the face of threats from the Inquisition and the book burnings that had spread throughout the cities of the peninsula. In 1551, the literary academy of the Dubbiosi in Venice launched plans for a work to be titled *Il Tempio alla divina signora donna Giovanna d'Aragona* (Temple for the Divine Lady Giovanna d'Aragona); and, in 1552, the prominent Venetian editor Girolamo Ruscelli published a tribute to

Maria d'Aragona under the title *Lettura . . . sopra un sonnetto . . . alla divina signora Marchesa del Vasto* (A Lecture . . . on a Sonnet in Honor of the Divine Lady, the Marchesa del Vasto). With Ruscelli's commemorative volumes for the d'Aragona sisters in the works, the stage was set for the Venetian print debut of the Naples salon. In 1551/1552, the Venetian editor Lodovico Dolce announced the publication of the first of four anthologies featuring the Neapolitan writers who had frequented Maria d'Aragona's circle. Poems by Maria's deceased husband led off both the second and third editions of the *Rime di diversi napoletani,* and Maria's patronage remains palpable in the choice of poets included.

Maria d'Aragona d'Avalos del Vasto lived out the last decade and a half of her life in Naples. When she died in her native city in 1568, many writers and editors active in the Venetian literary scene—among whom were Contile, Betussi, Muzio, and Tansillo—wrote eulogies praising her brilliance and beauty. Both d'Aragona sisters were remembered as champions of the press, patrons of literature and the arts, and leaders in the struggle for religious reform in Italy.

Diana Robin

See also Aragona, Giovanna d'; Colonna, Vittoria; Power, Politics and Women; Religious Reform and Women; *see also* the subheading Literary Patronage (under Literary Culture and Women).

Bibliography

Primary Works

Betussi, Giuseppe. *Le Imagini del tempio della signora donna Giovanna Aragona. Dialogo di M. Giuseppe Betussi. . . .* Florence: Torrentino, 1556.

Colonna, Vittoria. *Carteggio.* 2nd ed. Edited by Ermanno Ferrero and G. Mueller, with a supplement by Domenico Tordi. Turin: Loescher, 1892.

Dolce, Lodovico, ed. *Rime di diversi signor napoletani . . . .* Venice: Gabriel Giolito, 1552, 1555.

Ruscelli, Girolamo, ed. *Del Tempio alla divina signora donna Giovanna d'Aragona, fabricato da tutti i più gentili Spiriti, & in tutte le lingue principali del mondo.* Venice: Plinio Pietrasanta, 1555.

Ruscelli, Girolamo, ed. *Lettura di Girolamo Ruscelli, sopra un sonnetto dell' illustriss. signor Mar-chese della Terza alla divina signora Marchesa del Vasto.* Venice: Giovan Griffio, 1552.

Secondary Works

Alberigo, Giuseppe. "Aragona, Giovanna d'." *Dizionario biografico degli italiani [DBI],* 3: 694–696. Rome: Istituto dell' Enciclopedia Italiana, 1961.

Alberigo, Giuseppe. "Aragona, Maria d'." *Dizionario biografico degli italiani [DBI],* 3: 701–702. Rome: Istituto dell' Enciclopedia Italiana, 1961.

Caro, Gaspare de. "Avalos, Alfonso." *Dizionario biografico degli italiani [DBI],* 4: 612–616. Rome: Istituto dell' Enciclopedia Italiana, 1962.

Patrizi, G. "Colonna, Vittoria." *Dizionario biografico degli italiani [DBI],* 27: 448–457. Rome: Istituto dell' Enciclopedia Italiana, 1982.

Petrucci, Franca. "Colonna, Ascanio." *Dizionario biografico degli italiani [DBI],* 27: 271–275. Rome: Istituto dell' Enciclopedia Italiana, 1982.

Robin, Diana. *Publishing Women. Salons, the Presses, and the Counter-Reformation in Renaissance Italy.* Chicago: University of Chicago Press, 2007.

Vassalli, Donata Chiomenti. *Giovanna d'Aragona, fra baroni, principi e sovrani del Rinascimento.* Milan, 1987.

Aragona, Tullia d' (1505/1510–1556)

Italian writer and courtesan who published a neo-Platonic dialogue, Petarchan sonnets, and a choral anthology

By the time she had reached her thirties, Tullia d'Aragona had established herself as one of the most versatile and original women of letters of her time. Luminaries such as Bernardo Tasso, Benedetto Varchi, Sperone Speroni, and Girolamo Muzio represented her in their works, and Jacopo Nardi even claimed in his 1536 translation of Cicero that she was the "one and only heir of Tullian eloquence," punning on Cicero's middle name. Yet alongside a Nardi, Muzio, or Varchi, authors such as Pietro Aretino, Agnolo Firenzuola, and Giambattista Giraldi Cinzio ferociously attacked d'Aragona for putting on airs, starving her poor husband, or selling herself to a particularly repulsive German client, in vituperation of her other occupation as courtesan, or rather perhaps because she chose to fashion herself as an intellectual and as a woman of letters rather than as a courtesan.

D'Aragona was born sometime between 1505 and 1510 in Rome to Giulia Campana, a courtesan from Adria, a small town in northern Italy, halfway between Ferrara and Venice. The identity of d'Aragona's father has been much debated, yet he seems to have been Cardinal Luigi d'Aragona, illegitimate grandson of Ferdinando d'Aragona, king of Naples. D'Aragona's wedding certificate in the State Archives of Siena identifies her father as Costanzo Palmieri d'Aragona, but given that many of d'Aragona's contemporaries—excluding her detractors—accepted her claim of noble paternity, this second figure has been interpreted as a member of the d'Aragona family recruited to marry Giulia Campana as a cover-up for the cardinal's illicit activities. D'Aragona spent the first part of her childhood in Rome and, upon Luigi d'Aragona's sudden death in 1519, she supposedly left the city to spend a number of years in Siena. By June 1526, she was back in Rome in the company of Filippo Strozzi, as attested by one of his letters to Francesco Vettori. D'Aragona's relationship with Strozzi was rather long-lived, for we find her in his company five years later, in 1531. Yet she was not based solely in Rome. In the years from 1528 to 1543, d'Aragona's presence is noted in Venice, Bologna, Ferrara, and Siena.

In Venice, d'Aragona purportedly frequented the circles of Pietro Aretino and Sperone Speroni, who used her as a character in his *Dialogo d'amore,* published in 1534, although composed before 1528. In a letter to Speroni, Aretino deplored the flattering treatment d'Aragona received in his *Dialogo.* D'Aragona was apparently present in Bologna in 1530 during the negotiations between Pope Clement VII and Emperor Charles V, subsequent to the Sack of Rome, as attested to by a pasquinade lamenting her departure from Rome. In 1535, d'Aragona and Campana left Rome for her mother's hometown of Adria, where Penelope d'Aragona was

born, according to Muzio. Scholars have long disagreed whether Penelope is d'Aragona's sister or daughter, given that twenty to twenty-five years separate the siblings. Although this is not an entirely implausible age difference, one might question the need to leave Rome for the birth, if the mother were in truth Giulia Campana rather than d'Aragona.

We next find d'Aragona in Ferrara, where—in June 1537—she had only recently arrived and attended sermons by the reformist priest Bernardo Ochino. In a sonnet in which she addresses him by his first name, d'Aragona responds to Ochino's admonitions against dancing and music making; she reminds him of the importance of free will, as the greatest gift that God has given us. It is interesting to note that Vittoria Colonna was also in Ferrara at the same time as d'Aragona and apparently also listened to Ochino preach, although we can safely assume that the two women of letters never met.

On 8 January 1543, in Siena, d'Aragona married a certain Silvestro Guicciardi of Ferrara, although nothing more is heard of this relationship or of this man, except for a quip later offered by Agnolo Firenzuola that d'Aragona let her husband die of hunger. From d'Aragona's will, redacted in 1556 and preserved in the Capitoline Archives in Rome, we learn that she eventually had a son, named Celio, yet given that he was in the care of Pietro Chiocca and a minor, although of an indeterminate age, we do not know whether Guicciardi was his father. D'Aragona remained in Siena for several years until she was forced to flee in either late 1545 or early 1546 because of political unrest there. She had sided with the Noveschi, who had temporarily fallen into disfavor. Along with other Sienese nobles, she sought refuge in Florence, in the court of Cosimo I and from this venue continued her literary activities. By August 1546, she was living in a villa just outside Florence, near the Mensola River, where she received numerous visitors, many of them poets who later exchange verse with her in her choral anthology. In 1547, she was attacked for disobeying sumptuary legislation, as she had been earlier in Siena. D'Aragona appealed directly to Eleonora di Toledo, duchess of Florence, and to Duke Cosimo I, who exempted d'Aragona because of her rare knowledge of poetry and philosophy. Perhaps due to this episode, in 1547 d'Aragona published both her *canzoniere* (or sonnet sequence) and her dialogue on love with the Venetian publisher Gabriele Giolito.

In October 1548, d'Aragona announced in a letter to Varchi that she would be leaving Florence for Rome in a few days. The following year she is mentioned in a document used to tax prostitutes working in Rome to help defray the costs of rebuilding the Santa Maria Bridge across the Tiber (now known as the Ponte Rotto); at the time, she was living near Palazzo Carpi, just around the corner from Monsignor Giovanni Della Casa, who later authored the *Galateo.* Recent research indicates conclusively that d'Aragona continued to write and cultivate patrons connected with the Venetian presses after her return to Rome. In 1553, two new poems by d'Aragona not contained in the 1547 edition of her *Rime* were published in a volume titled *Il sesto libro delle rime di diversi eccellenti autori,* which was the sixth book in a best-selling poetry anthology series inaugurated by the Venetian printer Giolito in the 1550s. In addition, I have discovered two previously unknown and unpublished autograph sonnets by d'Aragona that bear the date 1552; these are dedicated to Duchess Giovanna d'Aragona Colonna and her son Marcantonio Colonna. Tullia d'Aragona's final work, the epic poem *Il Guerrino, altramente detto il Meschino,* was published posthumously by Sessa in 1560. Her last will and testament, dated 1556, the year of her death, reveals that she had moved to a much less prestigious area of town (Trastevere) and was boarding in a house.

D'Aragona's *Rime della signora Tullia di Aragona; et di diversi a lei* represents one of the earliest sonnet sequences published by a woman

poet (her 1547 text is second only to Vittoria Colonna's in 1538). Moreover, the *Rime* ranks as the first published exemplar of the choral anthology (that is, a single volume of verse attributed to a sole author, even though a number of different authors may have contributed to it). Although the choral anthology is characterized by its existence as a single volume, its origins are to be found in the tradition of correspondence poetry. Known in the English lyric tradition as answer poetry, correspondence poetry consists of an initial poet's *proposta,* almost exclusively in the form of a sonnet, which stimulates a response (or *risposta*) from his or her poetic interlocutor. This form of cultural capital was widespread in the courts, academies, and salons of early modern Italy and Europe, as reflected in both the manuscript and print traditions that detail those activities. Indeed one of the implicit assumptions about correspondence poetry is that its practitioners are figures of significance in their time; the poetic exchange virtually always takes place between well-known figures. In d'Aragona's case, her interlocutors may be divided into three different categories: recipients, correspondents, and dedicators. Recipients are those to whom she addressed a poem or poems; correspondents are those who exchanged sonnets with her; and dedicators are those who wrote poems to her or about her to which she did not respond. Besides the previously mentioned Muzio, Varchi, and Ochino, some of these figures include Cosimo I, Eleonora di Toledo, Pietro Bembo, Giulio Camillo, Simone Porzio, Cardinal Ippolito de Medici, Rodolfo Baglioni, and Anton Francesco Grazzini. D'Aragona made use of her cultural and intellectual intercourse with prominent political, military, and literary figures to fashion an image of herself as an equally prominent and proud woman of letters and frequently reiterates throughout her *canzoniere* that she seeks to acquire literary fame.

Also published in 1547 was her neo-Platonic dialogue *Della infinità di amore.* The dialogue is situated in d'Aragona's home, which functioned as a literary salon, presumably in Florence. The participants are Tullia, Benedetto Varchi, and Lattanzio Benucci, although other unnamed gentlemen are present. In Muzio's prefatory letter, he claims responsibility for having published the dialogue without d'Aragona's consent and that in the original manuscript the female speaker was named Sabina, which he changed to Tullia for reasons of historical verisimilitude. Of course, it is entirely possible that d'Aragona orchestrated the entire affair herself, just as she did to have Muzio change her pastoral name from Tirrhenia to Talia, as he himself recounts in a letter to Antonio Mezzabarba. The dialogue consists of a lively debate between Tullia and Varchi (these are the names attributed to the characters in the text) on the nature of love. The Tullia speaker in particular presents an interesting contrast to the poetess of the *Rime*. Her style of argument oscillates between playing dumb and then artfully leading her prey into an intellectual trap. She seems at times spunky, at times submissive, haughty and humble, arrogant and ancillary. A recent article by Lisa Curtis-Wendlandt, however, has also emphasized the philosophical importance of d'Aragona's dialogue as she deviates from and counters traditional neo-Platonic doctrine as it had been developed in other dialogues on love of the period.

Several nineteenth-century Italian literary historians have questioned d'Aragona's authorship of her final work, *Il Meschino, altramente detto il Guerrino*. Their reasons range from a lack of similarities between her *Rime* and *Il Meschino,* to the poem's posthumous publication, to contradictions between the preface and the poem itself, or to the ability of a woman with limited literary capabilities who lived a life roaming from city to city and died relatively young to compose a thirty-six canto epic poem. Only in the nineteenth century was d'Aragona's authorship questioned. Textual and historical evidence have led modern scholars to believe that d'Aragona wrote *Il Meschino* upon her reentry to Rome in 1548 and completed it before her death in 1556. The poem recounts the adventures of Guerrino, a personage of noble blood who is captured by pirates as an infant and sold into slavery. His adventures in search of his parents take him to various parts of Europe, Turkey, Africa, India, and even Purgatory and the Inferno. To compose her poem, d'Aragona transposed into octaves *Il Meschino di Durazzo,* a popular late fourteenth-century chilvaric prose text written by Andrea da Barberino. *Il Meschino,* published in 1560, although composed at least four years earlier, ranks as the first in a series of epic poems authored by women such as those by Moderata Fonte, Lucrezia Marinella, Margherita Sarrocchi, and Margherita Costa and explores the construction of gender and subjectivity, through the voice of the narrator, for example. The poem also echoes the complexities of an important moment in early modern European history—its encounter with Islam at the same time that the hegemony of the Roman Catholic church was being challenged from within. Although the events in the poem take place during the ninth century, the text's representation of foreign culture in general and Muslim culture in particular reveals an intensity characteristic of the Counter-Reformation, the period during which the poem was composed, but with a difference. *Il Meschino* provides a refreshingly nondogmatic and at times tolerant representation of Islam. Just as gender identity may be tried on, so may religious identity. And although *Il Meschino* wholeheartedly endorses Christianity, the fortuity of one's religious membership and the potential for varying historical truths regarding religion are made explicit. The poem thus contributes to twentieth-century debates on the relativity of identity of any sort—religious, sexual, and even personal—as the hero's allegiances vary while he learns new aspects regarding his past.

Julia L. Hairston

See also Courtesans and Prostitution, Italy; the subheadings Salons, Salonnières, and Women Writers; Virtual Salons: Women in Renaissance Dialogues; Sonnet-Writing (under Literary Culture and Women); Toledo, Eleonora di.

Bibliography

Primary Works

D'Aragona, Tullia. "Dialogo della infinità di amore." *Trattati d'amore del Cinquecento.* Edited by Giuseppe Zonta, 185–248. Bari: Laterza, 1912.

D'Aragona, Tullia. *Dialogo della signora Tullia d'Aragona della Infinità di Amore.* Venice: Gabriel Giolito de' Ferrari, 1547.

D'Aragona, Tullia. *Dialogue on the Infinity of Love.* Translated by Rinaldina Russell and Bruce Merry. Chicago: University of Chicago Press, 1997.

D'Aragona, Tullia. *Il Meschino, altramente detto il Guerrino. Fatto in ottava rima dalla signora Tullia d'Aragona. Opera nella quale si veggono e intendono le parti principali di tutto il mondo, e molte altre dilettevolissime cose, da essere sommamente care ad ogni sorte di persona di bello ingegno.* Venice: G. B. and M. Sessa, 1560.

D'Aragona, Tullia. *Il Meschino detto il Guerrino.* 12 vols. Parnaso Italiano. Edited by Francesco Zanotto, vol. 5. Venice: Giuseppe Antonelli, 1839.

D'Aragona, Tullia. *Le rime di Tullia d'Aragona cortigiana del secolo XVI.* Edited by Enrico Celani. Bologna: Commissione per i testi di lingua, 1968. (Originally published in 1891.)

D'Aragona, Tullia. *Rime della Signora Tullia di Aragona; et di diversi a lei.* Venice: Gabriele Giolito, 1547.

Secondary Works

Allaire, Gloria. "Tullia d'Aragona's *Il Meschino* as Key to a Reappraisal of Her Work." *Quaderni d'Italianistica* 16, no. 1 (1995): 33–50.

Bausi, Francesco. " 'Con agra zampogna'. Tullia d'Aragona a Firenze (1545–48)." *Schede umanistiche* 2 n.s. (1993): 61–91.

Bongi, Salvatore. "Rime della Signora Tullia di Aragona; et di diversi a lei." In *Annali di Gabriel Giolito de' Ferrari.* Vol. 1, 150–199. Rome: Principali Librai, 1890.

Curtis-Wendlandt, Lisa. "Conversing on Love: Text and Subtext in Tullia d'Aragona's *Dialogo della infinità d'amore.*" *Hypatia* 19, no. 4 (2004): 75–96.

Hairston, Julia L. "Out of the Archive: Four Newly-Identified Figures in Tullia d'Aragona's *Rime della Signora Tullia di Aragona et di diversi a lei* (1547)." *MLN* 118 (2003): 257–263.

Jones, Ann Rosalind. *The Currency of Eros: Women's Love Lyric in Europe, 1540–1620.* Bloomington: Indiana University Press, 1990.

Smarr, Janet L. "A Dialogue of Dialogues: Tullia d'Aragona and Sperone Speroni." *MLN* 113 (1998): 204–212.

Art and Women (ca. 1400–1650)

This essay considers European women as makers and consumers of art as well as how women figured in visual representation. Expectations for behavior based on gender—prescribing different paths for men and women—informed every aspect of women's relationships to art in the early modern era. "Artist" was a male-gendered concept, expectations for art patronage differed, and art theory and artworks themselves participated in reproducing gender norms. Six subheadings follow: Artists; Theory; Patronage; Representation of Women; the Nude; Public Squares.

Artists

The lack of reliable biographical data and works that can be confidently attributed to specific women artists greatly complicates the problem of assessing the full impact of artwork by women in European history. With names gleaned from Pliny, Boccaccio and other writers repeated the names of some ancient women artists in their catalogues of famous women, but these remain just names. Pervasive institutional structures inhibited girls from becoming professionals and producing the kind of works considered art today. Artistic training required a residential apprenticeship with an established master and thus was not possible for women, most of whom were closely guarded to protect family honor. Guild rules inhibited the possibilities for some working class women.

Almost all of the few women with professional careers in the Renaissance had artist fathers or brothers. Some began work in the family workshop, a pattern common in trades, and then moved on: Barbara Longhi of Ravenna (1552–1638) trained with her father, then developed an independent career painting religious works; Susanna Horenbout of Ghent (active ca. 1520–1550) worked as an illuminator for her father and went on to an independent career in England; the father of Fede Galizia of Milan (ca. 1578–ca. 1630s) was a miniaturist, but she became an easel painter. Printmaker Diana Mantuana (ca. 1547–1612) received training from her father and brother but obtained the right to make and sell her own prints in Rome. Elisabetta Sirani of Bologna (1638–1665) learned from her father, eventually assuming responsibility for his workshop, where her sisters also worked. The Bolognese Lavinia Fontana (1552–1614) and the Roman Artemisia Gentileschi (1593–1652) had father-teachers who painted large-scale works; both went on to independent careers. Jacopo Tintoretto in Venice, however, kept his daughter, Marietta Robusti (ca. 1552–1590), in his workshop, even though the Habsburgs expressed interest in her working abroad as a portraitist.

Art Theory

Renaissance art theory also marginalized women's contrbutions. Giorgio Vasari devoted one biography to a woman artist, Bolognese sculptor Properzia de' Rossi (fl. 1514–1529), in his *Lives* (1550, 1568), the first systematic history of art, but folded in mention of many others into this exceptional life. Rather than situating her with other artists irrespective of gender, he equates her with women accomplished in a variety of fields from poetry to soldiering. Leon Battista Alberti (incidentally, the author of an influential treatise on the family that spelled out specific gender roles) also wrote on art and architecture. In his treatise *On Painting* (1435), he declared *istoria* (narrative) to be the most important genre in the visual arts because its didactic potential demanded great intelligence from its makers, who in turn be-

came the most esteemed practitioners. Practical matters contributed to the exclusion of women from making such religious, mythological, or historical subjects because they typically decorated ecclesiastical, civic, or domestic interiors and, especially in Italy, were executed in *fresco,* a medium that called for work on location. These works, moreover, required human figures in action, often in perspective settings, and most women's training neither included drawing from the male nude nor mastering the mathematics-based perspective system. Still life and portraiture were theorized as less mentally challenging than narrative, preceding—it was argued—from direct recording without the need for an intellectual filter. Some women artists did produce commercially successful narratives, among them Lavinia Fontana and Elisabetta Sirani. Artemisia Gentileschi developed a specialty depicting heroic women, biblical (Judith, Susanna) and historical (Lucretia, Cleopatra). Nevertheless, the greater part of objects produced by women remained outside what developed into the top genre in the hierarchy of art history categories.

The Flemish Clara Peters (1594–after 1657) pioneered in still life, and the Italians Fede Galizia and Giovanna Garzoni (1600–1670), the French Louise Moillon (1610–1696), and several Dutch women achieved commercial success in the genre. Portraiture, however, became the most socially acceptable outlet for women, leading to prestigious appointments. Lavinia Fontana portrayed the aristocracy of her native Bologna; she also received commissions for altarpieces, even one from the pope for a major Roman basilica. Some women portraitists obtained prestigious court appointments. Sofonisba Anguissola (ca. 1532–1625), from Cremona, became a court painter in Spain, producing the requisite images of members of the royal family; significantly, her appointment was as lady-in-waiting to the queen, Elizabeth of Valois. Miniature portraitist Susanna Horenbout served as companion to Henry VIII's third wife, Anne of Cleves, for her journey to England. Marriages brought women painters from the Southern Netherlands into court circles: Catharina van Hemessen (1528–after 1587) came with her musician husband to Spain in the household of Mary of Hungary, and Levina Terlinc (ca. 1520–1576), daughter of illuminator Simon Bening, came with her husband to England, where documents record her working for the Tudors but firmly attributed works are lacking. Such appointments permitted these women artists significantly more freedom of movement compared to their nonprofessional peers.

Throughout the Middle Ages, nuns, most of whom remain anonymous, produced devotional objects—especially textiles and books. In the Renaissance, within convents, nuns undertook works in a variety of media. Suor Plautilla Nelli (1523–1588) in Florence executed frescoes; Caterina Vigri (ca. 1413–1463) in Bologna made panel paintings; Lucrina Fetti in Mantua (active 1614–1673) produced portraits for the Gonzaga court and paintings of saints for her convent; Cecelia and Maria Sobrino (seventeenth century) painted for their Carmelite convent in Spain; and the la Hyre sisters (seventeenth century) were similarly active as artists in their French convent. Nun artists' works, however, were considered expressions of their religious vocation, not professional art.

In the seventeenth century, a handful of women gained admission to European artistic academies: Artemisia Gentileschi to the Florentine *Accademia del Disegno;* possibly Caterina Ginnasi (1590–1660), Elisabetta Sirani, and Giovanna Garzoni to the Roman *Accademia di San Luca;* genre painter Judith Leyster (1609–1670) to the Haarlem Guild of St. Luke; and flower painter Cathérine Duchemin (1630–1698) to the French academy. The Florentine academic experience informed Artemisia Gentileschi's work, but in most cases, women's memberships were not fully commensurate with men's.

As Albrecht Dürer said upon seeing the work of Susanna Horenbout, "It is a great marvel that a woman should do so much." Considering all these factors, the women who attained success as masters occupied exceptional positions. Anguissola's father and some women themselves learned to exploit their exceptional status to gain notoriety.

Consumers/Audience

Men and women of all social classes had access to artworks decorating churches and public squares, although women spent less time in public spaces than men. Elite women remained within the family residences. Men and women in religious communities had access to the monumental and smaller artworks in their respective houses, but outsiders' access was limited. Specialized iconographies for conventual women developed. Women across the economic spectrum owned small devotional images and portraits of family members. Those in wealthier families interacted with objects (trays and bowls) associated with birth and decorated accordingly and with painted furniture—bed frames and chests, in particular—some of which bore narrative decorations exemplifying proper female behavior via prototypes like Lucretia or Griselda.

Patronage

Art patronage and collecting the required money were necessary, so only a few women commanded the resources sufficient to be active. There is no pattern of women patrons seeking out women artists. Piety and family solidarity governed the expression of their patronage. Women regularly commissioned art for display in family funerary chapels, although their portraits seldom appeared in them. Wealthy widows with access to their own resources sponsored architecture expressive of the same concerns for piety and family. Women also commissioned personal objects, especially books of hours and portraits. Margaret of Austria (1480–1530), regent of the

Netherlands, and Catherine de Médicis (1519–1579), queen mother and regent in France, surrounded themselves with portraits of family members that demonstrated the extent of their networks. In an age when many women ruled as queens regnant or regents, art patronage provided them the means to establish or undergird their power. Elizabeth I of England (1533–1603) actively regulated how she was portrayed, while French queen regent Marie de Médicis (1575–1642) commissioned Rubens to commemorate her life in monumental allegories for display in her Paris palace. Nuns engaged in collective patronage for their convents, but there were few female equivalents to the influential public corporate bodies of men who actively commissioned works of art and architecture.

Representation of Women

Artworks reaching a broad audience included representations of women, especially biblical and classical heroines and saints. Images of Eve, Mary, and the saints appeared in a variety of media (painting, sculpture, glass, metalwork, and needlework) throughout the entire Christian world prior to the Reformation; afterward they appeared in decorations only in Catholic churches, but religious art continued to be produced for private consumption. As they provided images for devotion, such works also encoded exemplary female behaviors, both good and bad. Female figures also regularly appear in sacred and secular settings, not, however, as agents of narratives, but rather as personifications of abstract qualities. From the fourteenth-century frescoes in the Sala della Pace in Siena's town hall to the seventeenth-century papal tombs in St. Peter's in Rome, female personifications embodied virtues ideally pertaining to the active male subjects portrayed. The most probable encounter a woman would have with an artist would be if she had her portrait painted. Portraits were made in conjunction with marriage and, especially in the case of royalty, for

exchange with prospective spouses. Other portraits commemorated the birth of a child. The self-portraits of Hemessen, Anguissola, Fontana, Peeters, Leyster, Gentileschi, Sirani, and the first English-born woman painter, Mary Beale (1633–1699), present interesting commentary on the representational tradition and their multiple identities. Portraitlike but generic representations of women served in an aesthetic discourse: the depiction of a beautiful woman signaled the painter's skill.

The Nude

Depictions of female nudes, notably Eve, emerged in the fifteenth century but came to prominence in the sixteenth century in both painting and sculpture. In monumental form, the male nude, following ancient traditions, connoted heroism; the female nude, however, carried other meanings. In court contexts internationally, Titian, Cellini, and artists associated with Fontainebleau produced erotically charged female nudes. When allegorized as *Vanitas,* the female nude assumed a moralizing tone. In 1563, the reforming Council of Trent restricted nudity in art in public places, but the depictions of the female nude continued to be made. Artemisia Gentileschi's heroines demonstrate her expertise with the female nude.

Public Squares

Shrines to the Virgin and other saints occur throughout European cities, but monumental sculpted female personifications and heroines appeared in some public spaces, especially in France and Italy. Indicative perhaps of increasing fears about women's public role, Donatello's *Judith and Holofernes,* conceived in the fifteenth century as an expression of republican virtue, became controversial in the early sixteenth, when the Florentine herald recommended its removal from the Piazza della Signoria.

Sheila Folliott

See also Anguissola, Sofonisba; Fetti, Lucrina; Fontana, Lavinia; Gentileschi, Artemisia; Nelli, Plautilla.

Bibliography

Brown, David Alan, ed. *Virtue & Beauty: Leonardo's Ginevra de' Benci and Renaissance Portraits of Women*. Washington, DC: National Gallery of Art, 2001.

Chadwick, Whitney. *Women, Art, and Society*. London: Thames and Hudson, 2002.

Ferino-Pagden, Sylvia, and Maria Kusche. *Sofonisba Anguissola, a Renaissance Woman*. Washington, DC: National Museum of Women in the Arts, 1995.

Garrard, Mary D. *Artemisia Gentileschi: The Image of the Female Hero in Italian Baroque Art*. Princeton, NJ: Princeton University Press, 1991.

Goffen, Rona. *Titian's Women*. New Haven, CT, London: Yale University Press, 1997.

Hamburger, Jeffrey. *Nuns as Artists: The Visual Culture of a Medieval Convent*. Berkeley: University of California Press, 1997.

Jacobs, Fredrika H. *Defining the Renaissance Virtuosa: Women Artists and the Language of Art History and Criticism*. Cambridge: Cambridge University Press, 1997.

Johnson, Geraldine, and Sara F. Matthews-Grieco. *Picturing Women in Renaissance and Baroque Italy*. Cambridge: Cambridge University Press, 1997.

King, Catherine. *Renaissance Women Patrons: Wives and Widows in Italy, c. 1300–c. 1550*. Manchester, UK, New York: Manchester University Press, 1998.

Murphy, Caroline P. *Lavinia Fontana: A Painter and Her Patrons in Sixteenth-Century Bologna*. New Haven, CT, and London: Yale University Press, 2003.

Nelson, Jonathan, ed. *Suor Plautilla Nelli (1523–1588): The First Woman Painter of Florence*. Fiesole, Italy: Cadmo, 2000.

Reiss, Sheryl, and David Wilkins, eds. *Beyond Isabella: Secular Women Patrons of Art in Renaissance Italy*. Kirksville, MO: Truman State University Press, 2001.

Tinagli, Paola. *Women in Italian Renaissance Art: Gender, Representation, Identity*. Manchester, UK, New York: Manchester University Press, 1997.

Wood, Jeryldene M. *Women, Art, and Spirituality: The Poor Clares of Early Modern Italy*. Cambridge: Cambridge University Press, 1996.

Askew, Anne (ca. 1521–1546)

English theologian; Protestant martyr

Anne Askew died in 1546, at the end of Henry VIII's reign. She burned at the stake for refusing to recant her religious views. She left behind two works that were published posthumously. *The First Examination of Anne Askew* (1546) and *The Latter Examination of Anne Askew* (1547) present Anne's own account of her interrogations at the hands of her inquisitors. In addition, they include several letters and statements of her beliefs, as well as a translation of Psalm 54. The works provide riveting first-person drama while shedding light on several religious and political controversies of the early English Reformation.

Askew was born in South Kelsey, Lincolnshire, around 1521, the fifth of six children born to Sir William Askew and Elizabeth Wrottesley Askew. Askew's writings clearly show a woman well educated for the time. Her *Examinations* indicate a strong familiarity with rhetoric and Scripture. Yet Askew's writings also provide an image of a woman at odds with her society's ideal of womanhood. Instead of a modest, silent helpmate to her husband, Askew spoke out in public, took pen to paper to tell her story, and argued vociferously with her inquisitors—going so far as to chastise them for their errors.

The political import of Askew's works becomes clear during her interrogation and torture, as her inquisitors attempt to pressure Askew into naming members of Queen Katherine Parr's circle as reformers and fellow heretics. The attempt to bring down the queen failed when Askew refused to implicate anyone associated with the throne. Her refusal to name names apparently resulted in her being racked by Lord Chancellor Thomas Wriothesley and Sir Richard Rich personally. Askew's voice comes to modern readers only through the filter of those who published her writings. John Bale, a Protestant propagandist and later bishop of Ossory, obtained Askew's writings sometime shortly after her death in 1546. He recognized the propaganda value her writings represented and their potential use to further the cause of Protestantism. As Elaine Beilin points out, Bale dispenses with the difficulty that Askew presents—strong, courageous, and outspoken instead of weak, silent, and modest—by attributing her strength entirely to God. In contrast, Askew presents herself as assured, strong, and educated. She may indeed have believed that God worked through her, but not because she was a woman. Beilin argues that Askew may have decided to write her accounts for self-justification. Askew was certainly aware of her society's constraints on women, and her writings reflect her need to establish herself as an honest, God-fearing woman certain of her own righteousness. Where Askew uses her account of torture and interrogation to portray herself as a defender and teacher of the faith, Bale sees not a strong woman, but God's hand. As Thomas Betteridge argues, John Bale's commentary frames and dominates Askew's writings, diminishing the authority with which Askew asserts her faith. Bale's edition ran into several editions and was wildly popular.

Askew's writings were next published in 1563 by John Foxe in his great compendium of Protestant martyrs, *Acts and Monuments*. Foxe eliminated Bale's commentary, though he did provide his own comments, focusing his attacks on Askew's tormentors. The inclusion of Askew's work in *Acts and Monuments* again co-opts her work to the greater cause of Protestantism, minimizing the individual effect of the work. Indeed, as Thomas Freeman and Sarah Elizabeth Wall argue, Foxe shaped our view of Askew just as surely as did Bale, though more subtly. Foxe's work, however, ensured that Askew's writings would be available for posterity and could provide a role model and also influence generations of Protestant English women and men. Askew's influence on the English Reformation and on English women was recognized in the decades following her death. Bathsua Makin, another Englishwoman and writer, wrote in 1673, "Our very Reformation of Religion, seems to be begun and carried on by Women."

Modern scholars have examined Askew's works from a variety of perspectives. Her writings offer scholars a glimpse into the mind and personality of an educated gentlewoman—though it was not until the late twentieth century that the value of these works for gender history was recognized. The complexity of Askew's rhetoric and its rarity as the writing of a woman make Askew's work a valuable part of early modern English literature.

Tara Wood

See also Parr, Katherine; Religious Reform and Women.

Bibliography

Primary Work

Beilin, Elaine V., ed. *The Examinations of Anne Askewe.* New York and Oxford: Oxford University Press, 1996.

Secondary Works

Beilin, Elaine V. *Redeeming Eve: Women Writers of the English Renaissance.* Princeton, NJ: Princeton University Press, 1987.

Berry, Boyd. "Of the Manner in Which Anne Askew 'Noised It.'" *Journal of English Germanic Philology* 96, no. 2 (April 1997): 182–203.

Betteridge, Thomas. "Anne Askew, John Bale, and Protestant History." *The Journal of Medieval and Early Modern Studies* 27, no. 2 (Spring 1997): 265–284.

Freeman, Thomas S., and Sarah Elizabeth Wall. "Racking the Body, Shaping the Text: The Account of Anne Askew in Foxe's 'Book of Martyrs.'" *Renaissance Quarterly* 54, no. 4.1 (Winter 2001): 1165–1196.

Aubespine, Madeleine de L' (1546–1596)

Dame de Villeroy, French poet, and author of moral discourse

Madeleine de L'Aubespine was the daughter of Secretary of State Claude de L'Aubespine and the wife of Nicolas de Neufville, seigneur de Villeroy, who later became secretary of state under the reign of Charles IX and Henry III. Well-known in the aristocratic circles, she became a "lady-of-honor" to Catherine de Médicis. Worldly minded, bright, and erudite (as her translation of Ovid's *Heroides* attests), Madeleine de L'Aubespine soon began to receive the most famous poets and prominent

figures of her time at her residence in Con-
flans-l'Archevêque, near Paris, and in her hotel
near the Louvre. Among her celebrated guests
were Rémy Belleau, who dedicated one of his
"precious stones" to her; Ronsard, who regarded her as his "spiritual daughter"; and
Philippe Desportes, who celebrated her in numerous love poems under the name of
Rosette, Callianthe, and Cléonice. Madeleine
de L'Aubespine's poems remained handwritten
until 1926–1927, when they were published
for the first time and subsequently raised questions about their authorship.

The talent of Madeleine de L'Aubespine
does not lack originality or imagination. In her
poetry may be found images of a square moon,
fish that fly, and dry water that create a universe
of the absurd that confuses and fascinates,
thereby foreshadowing the poetry of Théophile
de Viau. On the other hand, some poems announce the elegies of Marceline Desbordes-
Valmore, while others reveal a philosophical
approach in her writing, as they are addressed
to a God whose leniency perplexes her.
Nonetheless, the poetry of Madeleine de
L'Aubespine does not resemble the sober discourse assembled in the *Cabinet des saines affections,* which recent studies have attributed to
her. The volume was published five times between 1584 and 1600 in Paris (the first three
editions appeared anonymously from Abel
L'Angelier, a well-known printer specializing
in humanist writings) and was also translated
into both German and Italian in 1623. Themat-
ically related to Montaigne's *Essais,* the *Saines
affections* also draw on classical sources such as
Seneca, Plutarch, Cicero, and Epictitus.

The author of *Saines affections* firmly believes
in the effectiveness of philosophy as the only
way to reach spiritual happiness. Philosophical
thought is molded into a meditation on man's
condition and destiny, leading to a practical
morality, which places at the forefront the exercise of reason and the practice of virtue. As
another way to praise human reason and its im-
mense benefits, Madeleine de L'Aubespine develops a program to control passion, which is
responsible for vanity, ambition, envy, sadness,
and ingratitude. Like Plutarch, she believes that
passions are not necessarily bad, but they must
be restrained, and like Cicero, she proposes the
conciliation of virtue with happiness. Like
Montaigne, she condemns social ethics and
vices and places self-knowledge at the center of
her thinking. However, unlike the author of the
Essais, she never becomes the object of her
own discourse, preferring a generic "we" to a
personal "I." Indicative of the feminine writer
are the variegated style, an affinity for definitions and "recipes for the soul," as well as the
renouncement of self. Madeleine de L'Aubespine applied her talent to both poetry and discourse, the latter a favorite humanist genre that
began to flourish along with moral reflections
between 1580 and 1625.

Graziella Postolache

See also Education, Humanism, and Women; Literary Culture and Women.

Bibliography
Primary Works
L'Aubespine Madeleine de. *Cabinet des saines affections.* Edited by Colette H. Winn. Paris: Champion, 2001.
L'Aubespine Madeleine de. *Cabinet des saines affections. Derniere edition, nentee de XII. Discours et
quelques Stances sur le mesme sujet. Par Madame
de Rivery.* Paris: Antoine du Breuil, 1595.
L'Aubespine Madeleine de. *Des saines affections.*
Paris: Abel L'Angelier, 1584 or 1594.
L'Aubespine Madeleine de. *Les chansons de Callianthe.* Edited by Roger Sorg. Paris: L. Pichon,
1926.

Secondary Works
Balsamo, Jean. "Abel L'Angelier et ses dames: les
Dames des Roches, Madeleine de l'Auspepine,
Marie le Gendre, Marie de Gournay." In *Des
femmes & des livres, France et Espagnes XIV e–
XVII e siècle.* Edited by Dominique de Cour-
celles and Carmen Val Julian, 117–136. Paris:
Ecole des Chartes, 1999.
Louviot, Louis. "Cabinet des Saines affections
(1595)." In *Revue des Livres Anciens,* vol. II. Edited
by Fontemoing et Cie, 274–282. Paris: 1917.
Sorg, Roger. "Une fille de Ronsard, la bergère
Rosette." *Revue des Deux Mondes* 13 (1923):
128–144.

B

Bacon, Anne Cooke
(ca. 1528–1610)

Writer, religious reform thinker, and translator
Motivated by religious piety and a remarkable education, Anne Cooke Bacon was one of the most prominent and prolific women writers in Renaissance England. Scholars have called attention in particular to the transformation her writing underwent after the death of her husband, Sir Nicholas Bacon, in 1579. While he lived, Cooke Bacon translated religious works, modestly keeping the focus on the ideas of others. When she became a widow, she assumed a new voice and tone—assertive and often domineering—in letters of advice not only to her adult sons but to prominent male political figures as well.

Born in 1527 or 1528 to Sir Anthony Cooke and Lady Anne Fitzwilliam, Cooke Bacon received, in her youth, a rigorous education in history, classics, philosophy, and theology that undergirds all her writings. In 1548, her translations of sermons by the Italian Calvinist Bernardino Ochino were first published. Over the next twelve years, they were printed two more times in tandem with another (male) translator's work. In 1564, Cooke Bacon translated from the Latin the official text justifying the Church of England. Her translation, *Apologie of the Church of England,* became the official edition, superseding the existing translation.

Cooke Bacon's learning and religious conviction also remain central in the letters she wrote as a widow. Acting on her Protestant, nonconformist beliefs, she wrote numerous letters to support Puritan preachers. For example, in 1584/1585, she wrote to William Cecil requesting a private conference at court for several Puritan preachers. Such advocacy matches her ongoing support of nonconformist preachers through local appointments and financial assistance. Cooke Bacon's religious zeal took a more private turn in her letters to her two adult sons, Anthony and Francis. Between 1592 and 1596 alone, she wrote them over one hundred letters. She admonishes them to practice godly living, offers political counsel, and dictates the terms on which she will rescue them from repeated debt. Her financial independence gave her power over her sons, and she used this power to assert opinion with unflinching authority. Her sons, however, were not the only recipients of her chastising letters. In 1596, she wrote Robert Devereux, earl of Essex, reprimanding him for sexual misconduct. Strong-willed and learned, Anne Cooke Bacon, who died in 1610, achieved a rare independence and prominence in the patriarchal world of Renaissance England.

Linda Shenk

See also Education, Humanism, and Women; Literary Culture and Women; Religious Reform and Women; Translation and Women Translators.

Bibliography
Primary Work
Bacon, Lady Anne Cooke. *Anne Cooke Bacon.* Edited by Valerie Wayne. Burlington, VT: Ashgate, 2000.
Secondary Works
Hogrefe, Pearl. *Women of Action in Tudor England: Nine Biographical Sketches.* Ames: Iowa State University Press, 1977.
Magnusson, Lynne. "Widowhood and Linguistic Capital: The Rhetoric and Reception of Anne Bacon's Epistolary Advice." *English Literary Renaissance* 31, no. 1 (2001): 3–33.
Stewart, Alan. "The Voices of Anne Cooke, Lady Anne and Lady Bacon." In *"This Double Voice": Gendered Writing in Early Modern England.* Edited by Danielle Clarke and Elizabeth Clarke, 88–102. New York: St. Martin's Press, 2000.

Barton, Elizabeth (ca. 1506–1534)
Roman Catholic nun, mystic, and martyr

In the early 1530s, Henry VIII's decision to divorce Catherine of Aragon and leave the spiritual authority of the pope was unpopular among conservative religious groups and individuals in England, including William Warham, archbishop of Canterbury, Sir Thomas More, John Fisher, bishop of Rochester, and many religious houses such as the Benedictine community of Saint Sepulchre. A member of the convent since 1526, Elizabeth Barton became a participant in the complaints against Henry, when the visions and revelations that she had received since she was sixteen turned political in nature.

Barton served on an estate belonging to Archbishop Warham when she first began receiving visions and communication from the Virgin Mary. Warham, always the careful churchman, established a commission to investigate the truthfulness of Barton's claims, the results of which were favorable according to the chief examiner, Dr. Edward Bocking. After joining the convent, Barton's reputation for holiness and special access to the divine will spread throughout England and soon she began speaking out against the king's policies.

In 1533 with the divorce secured, Henry began a full assault upon Roman Catholicism, and Barton and her followers became a political liability. Barton's own rhetoric against her king had increased in its vehemence, now openly predicting that Henry would lose the throne and that he would die a villain's death. In November 1533, authorities arrested Barton and soon she confessed that her revelations were fraudulent. Barton and some of her more politically important supporters had to endure a public humiliation at St. Paul's Cross on 23 November 1533. Additionally, authorities spread their nets farther and arrested Fisher and More, implicating both as supporters of Barton. Eventually, Barton and five others, including Dr. Bocking, were convicted of treason and executed at Tyburn field 21 April 1534, while More and Fisher faced the axe a year later on additional charges.

The events surrounding Elizabeth Barton point to Henry's fear that Barton and people like her could stir up rebellion. While she spoke out in one of the only mediums available to women at the time, her political prophecies were too threatening to a monarch who thought constantly of securing his dynasty at any cost.

Timothy G. Elston

See also Religious Reform and Women.

Bibliography
Rex, Richard. *Henry VIII and the English Reformation.* New York: St. Martin's Press, 1993.
Scarisbrick, J. J. *Henry VIII.* Berkeley: University of California Press, 1968.
Watt, Diane. *Secretaries of God: Women Prophets in Late Medieval and Early Modern England.* Woodbridge, UK and Rochester, NY: D. S. Brewer, 1997.

Battiferra, Laura (Laura Battiferri Ammannati; 1523–1589)
Italian poet, active in the court of Eleonora di Toledo and Cosimo I de' Medici

A marvel of learning, talent, and virtue among her contemporaries, Laura Battiferra degli Ammannati flourished as a poet in mainstream cultural networks of sixteenth-century Italy. Her life falls into three phases, marked by the cities where she lived, always in courtly circles: Urbino (1523–1549), Rome (1549–1555), Florence (1555–1589). Neither a widow like Vittoria Colonna and Veronica Gàmbara, nor a courtesan like Tullia d'Aragona and Veronica Franco, nor a virtuosa like Gaspara Stampa, she writes within the Petrarchist tradition as a loving, happy wife. In a forty-year creative partnership, ended only by her death, she and the Florentine sculptor and architect Bartolomeo Ammannati practiced their respective art forms and promoted each other's work. Battiferra published two books, which contain her sonnets and her translation of the Penitential Psalms. These and a third overarching collec-

Laura Battiferra degli Ammanati, Italian poet. Portrait by Bronzino, ca. 1561. Palazzo Vecchio, Florence. (Alinari Archives/Corbis)

tion of *Rhymes,* left incomplete in manuscript at her death, document a career that mirrors intellectual, religious, and artistic trends on the Italian peninsula from the late Renaissance into the Catholic Reformation.

A natural daughter of the cleric Giovan'Antonio Battiferri of Urbino and his concubine Maddalena Coccapani of Carpi, Laura was born on St. Andrew's Day (13 November) 1523 in the city of her paternal ancestors. Her father, educated as a humanist, accumulated wealth from plural ecclesiastical benefices, notably his appointment as scriptor of briefs (letters) in the Apostolic Chamber at the Vatican. His daughter's tutor, he can be credited with her early education and beautiful chancery script, preserved in her eighteen surviving letters and others she penned for her husband to high-ranking correspondents (Michelangelo, the grand duke Francesco de Medici).

From the papal brief of her legitimation, signed by Pope Paul III on 9 February 1543,

we know that Laura had a brother named Ascanio and a half brother, Giulio. Although she mourned her father's death in poetry (1561), her sonnets are silent on her mother and siblings. Notarial documents tell of bitter contention between Ascanio and his father, who took the extraordinary step of disinheriting the son in favor of a female, making Laura a wealthy woman. After her legitimation she married Vittorio Sereni of Bologna, an organist in the service of Duke Guidobaldo II Della Rovere of Urbino. Her handsome dowry, set at one thousand *scudi,* was to have been doubled at the duke's suggestion. (Compare Chiara Matraini of Lucca, who sued her son to recover a dowry of three hundred *scudi.*) Giovan'Antonio, however, never paid in full, and after Sereni's early death (1549), his brother as heir blocked the money from passing to Laura and her second husband. Two letters (1558, 1559) and a sonnet Battiferra sent to Duke Guidobaldo attest to this long struggle.

Battiferra's first datable body of verse is a nine-sonnet sequence of grief at her loss of Sereni. Influenced by Colonna and Gàmbara, this poetry of widowhood represents its author as a new laurel descended from the nymph Apollo loved (Ovid, *Metamorphoses* I, 452–467) and Francesco Petrarca's elusive lady. She, a "plant accustomed to plaint," hopes to bloom with flowers and fruit (write good poetry). Perhaps she composed her mournful sonnets in an Urbino convent, where, according to a document of 20 July 1549, Duke Guidobaldo forcibly placed her for her own protection because, while waiting for her father to come from Rome and fetch her, she had been left without any suitable female companion or even food to eat.

On 17 April 1550 the twenty-six-year-old widow married Bartolomeo Ammannati, employed in Rome on commissions from Pope Julius III. With the bride's father officiating, the wedding took place at the Holy House of Mary in Loreto, one of Christendom's most venerated pilgrimage shrines. The couple resided five years in the papal city, to which Battiferra declares a fond attachment in some of her finest sonnets. During this period she developed an important professional friendship with Annibal Caro, secretary to the powerful Cardinal Alessandro Farnese and a poet whom no other Vatican courtier could rival for widely reaching contacts in the world of letters. His name and those of others in the Roman orbit to whom she addresses verse float at the pinnacle of society: Pope Paul III; Livia and Ortensia Colonna; Ersilia Cortese Del Monte, niece of Julius III; Lucrezia Soderini, of the great banking family; Eufemia, a fashionable Neapolitan singer and poet.

The death of Julius III in 1555 precipitated Laura's forced move to Florence, where Bartolomeo had found a new patron in Cosimo I de Medici. Her sonnets of this period bespeak wrenching loneliness, but Benedetto Varchi, literary lion king on the Arno, helped her "laurel" take root. By 1560, she had assembled enough poems—and people—to fill her *Primo libro dell'opere toscane* (First Book of Tuscan Works). Dedicated to the Medici duchess Eleonora di Toledo, this polyvocal anthology celebrates Duke Cosimo's conquest of Siena in a diplomatically ordered "virtual salon" with 187 poems: 146 by the author and 41 by distinguished male correspondents, among them Varchi, Caro, il Lasca (Anton Francesco Grazzini), Agnolo Bronzino, and Benvenuto Cellini. Mostly sonnets, including a sequence for her husband Fidia (Phidias), it achieves pleasing variety by integrating other forms: madrigals, *canzonette* or odes, *sestina,* canzone, *terza rima* in translations of Jeremiah's lament and a hymn attributed to Saint Augustine (actually Peter Damian), and *verso sciolto* (free verse) in an eclogue.

Bronzino's *Portrait of Laura Battiferra* (Florence, Palazzo Vecchio), a profile that implies her likeness to the Trecento poets Dante and Petrarca, probably celebrates the new book. Congratulations flew to her from poets across Italy, prominent men, and the prolific Laura

Terracina of Naples, with whom she exchanges sonnets. The year 1560 saw her induction as the first woman ever into the prestigious Sienese *Accademia degli Intronati* (Academy of the Dazed), where she took the humorous nickname *la Sgraziata* (The Graceless Woman). Her sonnets begin to appear in volumes by others, and her Florentine publisher Giunti sends her a *Rimario* (Rhyming Dictionary) compiled from Giovanni Della Casa's poetry in an edition of 1564.

In that same year she published her second book, *Salmi penitentiali del santissimo profeta Davit . . . con alcuni suoi sonetti spirituali* (Penitential Psalms of the Most Holy Prophet David . . . with Some of Her Spiritual Sonnets), free-verse experiments that announce her knowledge of Latin, the Bible, and its commentaries. Sent to Guidobaldo's duchess, the pious Vittoria Della Rovere, it offers the Psalms individually to cloistered nuns in Florence and Urbino (one of the latter her aunt Cassandra Battiferra). A third collection entitled simply *Le rime* (The Rhymes), transcribed by a Jesuit (1580s?), was intended to contain all she had written, except as preserved in collections by others. Rediscovered in 1995, this forgotten trove reflects her intensifying religious sentiments in years when the Ammannati became Jesuit sponsors. The final entry, which breaks off after seventeen stanzas of *ottava rima,* is an epic based on the biblical Samuel with poignant sympathy for Hannah, infertile as the poet herself apparently was. To the same late period belongs her one known prose work, the "Orison on the Birth of Our Lord," an impassioned meditation on the Nativity inspired by the *Spiritual Exercises* of Ignatius Loyola.

Ammannati buried his wife on 3 November 1589 in San Giovannino, the Florentine Jesuit church they together had helped remodel (today San Giovannino degli Scolopi). For their funeral chapel he commissioned Alessandro Allori's *Christ and the Canaanite Woman* (ca. 1590), a Gospel miracle that still hangs in place and depicts Laura as an older woman, kneeling in witness with a devotional book. Another late portrait by Hans van Aachen is lost. In addition to her own three poetry books, she assisted as editor in preparing a commemorative anthology for Varchi (1566), contributed generously to other major funerary anthologies (for Michelangelo, the Medici duchess, and princes), and composed verse set to music or displayed on floats in processions for great Florentine festivals.

Battiferra's unique literary identity rests first on real talent and remarkable learning, from the Bible to Ignatius Loyola; from Virgil and Ovid to Vittoria Colonna; from the Tuscan classics Dante and Petrarca to Sannazzaro, Bembo, Della Casa, Aragona, Matraini, and Gaspara Stampa. She favors men with Urbino ties like Antonio Gallo, Bernardo Cappello, and Bernardo Tasso, and she follows closely in the footsteps of her mentors, Caro and Varchi, especially the latter. Second, in an artistic persona she herself seems to have constructed, Laura is metaphorically a laurel, at once successor to the Tuscan master sonneteer and namesake of his lady. Fellow poets pick up her cues with punning compliments to this amazing "Dafne." They canonize her as a "new Sappho" and embrace her in *cenacoli,* or coteries, moving between great country villas and patrician city dwellings, sometimes gathering at Battiferra's own fireside. Fame during her lifetime carried her writing well beyond Italy, as far as the imperial courts of Prague and Madrid. Still praised by literary historians in the eighteenth century, as of the nineteenth she disappears except for trickles of memory that recall her *Penitential Psalms* and a handful of autobiographical "pastoral" sonnets. The bulk of her production—a corpus of more than five hundred poems, four hundred that she herself wrote and over a hundred addressed to her by literary correspondents—was all but forgotten. The very qualities that won praise from her contemporaries have distanced Battiferra's writing from our postmodern world— classical learning, a Mannerist style of wit, ver-

satility as an occasional poet, and Catholic Reformation religious values.

Vittoria Kirkham

See also the subheading Sonnet Writing (under Literary Culture and Women); Toledo, Eleonora di.

Bibliography

Primary Works

Battiferra, Laura. *Il primo libro delle opere toscane.* Edited by Enrico Maria Guidi. Urbino: Accademia Raffaello, 2000.

Battiferra, Laura. *Il primo libro dell'opere toscane di M. Laura Battiferra degli Ammannati.* Naples: Bulifon, 1694. (Originally printed in Florence: Giunti, 1560 [based on the holograph, Florence, Biblioteca Nazionale, Ms. Magl. VII, 778].)

Battiferra, Laura. *I sette salmi penitentiali del santissimo profeta Davit. Tradotti in lingua Toscana da Madonna Laura Battiferra Degli Ammannati . . . insieme con alcuni suoi Sonetti spirituali.* Florence: Giunti, 1564. (Reprinted in 1566, 1570.)

Battiferra, Laura. *I sette salmi penitentiali di David con alcuni sonetti spirituali.* Edited by Enrico Maria Guidi. Urbino: Accademia Raffaello, 2005.

Battiferra, Laura. *Lettere di Laura Battiferri Ammannati a Benedetto Varchi.* Edited by Carlo Gargiolli. Bologna: Commissione per i testi di lingua, 1968. (Originally printed in 1879.)

Kirkham, Victoria, ed. and trans. *Laura Battiferra degli Ammannati and Her Literary Circle: An Anthology.* Chicago: University of Chicago Press, 2006.

Secondary Works

Kirkham, Victoria. "Creative Partners: The Marriage of Laura Battiferra and Bartolomeo Ammannati." *Renaissance Quarterly* 55 (2002): 498–558.

Kirkham, Victoria. "Dante's Fantom, Petrarch's Specter: Bronzino's Portrait of the Poet Laura Battiferra." In *"Visibile parlare": Dante and the Art of the Italian Renaissance.* Edited by Deborah Parker, 22–23. *Lectura Dantis* (Special issue) (1998): 63–139.

Kirkham, Victoria. "La poetessa al presepio: Una meditazione inedita di Laura Battiferra degli Ammannati." *Filologia e critica* 27, no. 2 (2002): 258–276.

Kirkham, Victoria. "Laura Battiferra degli Ammannati benefattrice dei Gesuiti fiorentini." In *Committenza artistica femminile.* Edited by Sara F. Matthews, and Grieco and Gabriella Zarri. *Quaderni storici* 104, no. 2 (2000): 331–354.

Kirkham, Victoria. "Laura Battiferra's 'First Book' of Poetry: A Renaissance Holograph Comes

Out of Hiding." *Rinascimento* 35 (1996): 351–391.

Kirkham, Victoria. "Sappho on the Arno: The Brief Fame of Laura Battiferra degli Ammannati." In *Strong Voices, Weak History: Early Women Writers and Canons in England, France and Italy.* Pages 174–196. Ann Arbor: University of Michigan Press, 2005.

Beaufort, Lady Margaret (1443–1509)

Countess of Richmond and Derby, mother of Henry VII of England, the first of the Tudor kings

Lady Margaret Beaufort was the daughter of John Beaufort, duke of Somerset, and granddaughter of Edward III by his third son, John of Gaunt and Gaunt's mistress Katherine Swynford. The family that was given the name Beaufort was made legitimate by an act of the English parliament. Margaret's first marriage to Edmund Tudor resulted in the birth of her only child, Henry. Following the death of Edmund Tudor, Margaret remained active in the lives of the Yorkist kings Edward IV and Richard III and their courts. While her son was safely away from England, Margaret plotted against Richard III, hoping this would lead to the crowning of her son as king of England. In 1485 he defeated Richard at Bosworth Field and started the Tudor dynasty as Henry VII. If the crown had been decided strictly on the right of inheritance, Margaret would have had a claim to the throne following the victory at Bosworth Field. To avert that possibilty, Henry VII claimed the throne by right of conquest as well as inheritance, and Margaret Beaufort assumed her role as the king's mother.

Margaret enjoyed a central role in the monarchy of Henry VII. Her experience from the Wars of the Roses allowed her to advise her son on both internal and international affairs. Especially during her son's reign, Margaret was a scholar and patron of such printers as William Caxton. She also founded the Lady Margaret professorships of divinity at Oxford and Cambridge in 1502. When Henry VII died in 1509, he appointed his mother executrix of his will. Margaret died on 29 June 1509, just two months after her son.

Shawndra Holderby

See also Power, Politics and Women; on her patronage of Caxton, *see also* Printers, the Book Trade, and Women.

Bibliography

Jones, Michael K., and Malcolm G. Underwood. *The King's Mother, Lady Margaret Beaufort, Countess of Richmond and Derby.* Cambridge: Cambridge University Press, 1992.

Routh, E.M.G. *Lady Margaret: A Memoir of Lady Margaret Beaufort, Countess of Richmond and Derby, Mother of Henry VII.* London: Oxford University Press, 1924.

Seward, Desmond. *The Wars of the Roses: Through the Lives of Five Men and Women of the Fifteenth Century.* London: Constable; New York: Viking, 1995.

Simon, Linda. *Of Virtue Rare, Margaret Beaufort, Matriarch of the House of Tudor.* Boston: Houghton Mifflin Company, 1982.

Beaujeu, Anne de (Anne de France; 1461–1522)

Unofficial regent of France and duchess of Bourbon

Anne de Beaujeu provides an example of female political authority in a country where the Salic Law prevented women from assuming the crown. She also illustrates the tension between an increasingly centralized monarchy on the one hand and feudal independence on the other, having supported both causes at different times in her life. Probably born in 1461, Anne de Beaujeu was the oldest of the surviving children of Louis XI, king of France, and the one said to resemble him most intellectually and temperamentally. When this king died in 1483 leaving a thirteen-year-old Charles VIII on the throne, Anne and her husband, Pierre de Beaujeu, as his guardians, assumed control. In so doing they resisted Louis d'Orléans, the next in line to the throne, who wished to be named regent. Louis and his supporters sought help from the estates-general, who met in 1484 but who ultimately supported Anne's cause. Referred to as *Madame la*

Anne de Beaujeu, Duchess of Bourbon and unofficial regent of France. Portrait by anonymous artist. (Library of Congress)

Grande (Grand Madam), Anne was recognized by the court and by foreign emissaries as the person actually ruling France during the early years of Charles's reign.

In 1488 she and Charles VIII squelched a noble uprising, the *Guerre Folle* (the Foolish War), led by Louis d'Orléans and Francis II, duke of Brittany. Charles then married the new duchess of Brittany, Anne, to ensure the duchy's loyalty to France. Meanwhile Pierre de Beaujeu's two older brothers had died, leaving Pierre with the Bourbon inheritance. Anne and her husband were now the richest and most powerful nobles in France. In 1491, after the loss of one infant and fifteen years of childlessness, Anne gave birth to a daughter, Suzanne. As Charles VIII grew increasingly independent of his older sister, Anne redirected

her attention to her own lands and feudal duties, though she remained his advisor while retaining her ties to the court. When Charles died suddenly in 1498 leaving no heirs, Louis d'Orléans became king of France. Neither his previous attacks on the crown nor his well-known personal vices inspired confidence in his subjects, so the support of Anne de Beaujeu and her husband were instrumental in a smooth accession to the throne. Anne agreed to overlook their antagonistic past and did not hinder the annulment Louis immediately requested from her physically disabled sister, Jeanne. In exchange Louis XII waived the royal rights to the Bourbon inheritance in the case that Anne and Pierre did not have a male heir. Once all this had been established, the Bourbon's relationship with Louis XII and his new queen, Charles's widow Anne de Bretagne, became quite cordial. Anne de Beaujeu no longer held any direct influence, however, over the governance of the French state.

In 1504 or 1505, after the death of her husband and before she arranged a marriage for her daughter, Anne wrote Suzanne a book of lessons, *Les Enseignements d'Anne de France, duchesse de Bourbonnois et d'Auvergne, à sa fille Susanne de Bourbon,* modeled on the book that Louis IX had written for his daughter, the one her own father had written for Charles, and the writings of Christine de Pizan. Anne's version contains conventional advice on the appropriate behavior for noblewomen. During her unofficial regency, Anne had overseen the education of many young noblewomen at court, including Louise de Savoie, Marguerite d'Autriche, and Diane de Poitiers. The humble feminine figure that emerges from the *Enseignements,* however, seems at odds with their independent author. More easily recognizable are the anxieties about life as an older widow distant from court. The *Enseignements* ends with a tale about a noblewoman who bravely sacrifices her only child for the honor of her family and the interests of the king. Suzanne was, in fact, married shortly thereafter to a cousin to protect the integrity of the Bourbon inheritance.

In contrast to the moral of her tale, however, the interests of a noble family and those of the crown did not always overlap. Before she died, Anne witnessed the opposition of two adults whom she had raised from chilhood: her son-in-law, the connétable de Bourbon, and Louise de Savoie, mother of Francis I, successor to Louis XII. Louise and her son, suspicious of the wealth and power of the connétable, the Bourbon heir, challenged his inheritance. After losing the domain that Anne had so carefully built up and defended during her lifetime, the connétable, perhaps with Anne's bitter approval, responded by betraying the French king Francis I—the other cause that Anne had defended so staunchly during her brother's reign. Anne died in 1522, before this ultimate betrayal.

Emily Thompson

See also Education, Humanism, and Women; Pizan, Christine de; Power, Politics, and Women.

Bibliography

Primary Works

Anne de France. *Les Enseignements d'Anne de France, duchesse de Bourbonnois et d'Auvergne, à sa fille Susanne de Bourbon.* Edited by A. M. Chazaud. Moulins: Desrosiers, 1878.

Brézé, Jacques de. *La Chasse, Les Dits du Bon Chien Souillard et Les Louanges de Madame Anne de France.* Edited by Gunnar Tilander. Lund. Sweden: Carl Bloms, 1959.

Secondary Works

Matarasso, Pauline. *Queen's Mate: Three Women of Power in France on the Eve of the Renaissance.* Burlington, VT: Ashgate, 2001.

Maulde, M. de. *Anne de France, Duchesse de Bourbonnais, et Louis XII.* Paris: Imprimerie Nationale, 1885.

Pélicier, P. *Essai sur le Gouvernement de la Dame de Beaujeu: 1483–1491.* Chartres: Imprimerie Edouard Garnier, 1882.

Pradel, Pierre. *Anne de France 1461–1522.* Paris: Publisud, 1986.

Viennot, Eliane. "Une Nouvelle d'Anne de France: L'Histoire du Siège de Brest." In *Devis d'amitié. Mélanges offerts à Nicole Cazauran.* Edited by Jean Lecointe, Catherine Magnien, Isabelle Pantin, and Marie-Claire Thomine, 139–150. Paris: Champion, 2002.

Bectoz, Claude Scholastique de (d. 1547)

Learned abbess in the province of Dauphiné, philosopher, poet and correspondent

An abbess at the Monastery Saint Honorat in Tarascon from 15 March 1542 to 17 March 1547, Claude Scholastique de Bectoz is one of the most frequently cited learned woman in early modern French and Italian biographies for her delightful conversation, her great piety, her outstanding management and reform of the convent, her exceptional knowledge of science, and her mastery of Latin prose and French verse. King Francis I frequently visited her with his mother Louise de Savoie and his sister Marguerite de Navarre, accompanied by renowned poets and secretaries of their royal entourage. Because of her talent, Claude was Denys Faucher's preferred pupil. This famous humanist introduced her to learned men who, like Antoine Arlier of Languedoc, engaged in Latin correspondences with her.

The daughter of Jacques de Bectoz and Michelette de Salvaing, from well-known families in the province of Dauphiné, Claude was compared to Greek academicians for her philosophy and civility and to Sappho for her verses. In fact, her extant French *chanson,* written in response to a poem by Bonaventure des Périers, demonstrates such ethical and aesthetic values. To the male poet's tragic view on love as a deceptive and deluding feeling, Claude de Bectoz opposes an optimistic definition, transforming her correspondent's nostalgia for courtly love into a tangible redeeming force inspired by neo-Platonic *amitié* and Christian *agapè.* Claude's wisdom and courtesy, as well as her capacity to resolve arduous intellectual and moral questions, made her into a sought-out courtly interlocutor. As a place of frequent gatherings for both humanists and ecclesiastics, her convent became a philosophical salon unique in cultural history.

Catherine M. Müller

See also Education, Humanism, and Women; the subheading Latin Learning for Women (under Literary Culture and Women); Sappho and the Sapphic Tradition.

Bibliography

Primary Works

Arlier, Antoine. *Correspondance d'Antoine Arlier, humaniste languedocien, 1527–1545.* Edited by E. J. N. Pendergrass. Geneva: Droz, 1990. (A few of Claude de Bectoz's letters appear on pp. 114, 177, 198.)

Coste, Hilarion de. *Les eloges et les vies des reynes, des princesses et des dames illustres en piété, en courage et en doctrine.* Vol. III: 755–761. Paris: S. Cramoisy, 1647.

Della Chiesa, Francesco Agostino. *Theatro delle donne letterate con un breve discorso della preminenza, e perfettione del sesso donnesco.* Pages 283–285. Mondovi: Giovanni Gislandi e Giovanni Tomaso Rossi, 1620.

Des Périers, Bonaventure. *Œuvres françoises.* 2 vols. Edited by L. Lacour. Nendeln, Liechtenstein: Kraus Reprint, 1973. (Originally printed in Paris: P. Jannet, 1856; Claude's *chanson* is on p. 163.)

Des Périers, Bonaventure. *Recueil des œuvres de feu Bonaventure des Periers.* Lyons: Jean de Tournes, 1544. (Idem, p. 185.)

Domenichi, Lodovico. *La nobiltà delle donne.* 272–272ᵛ. Venice: Gabriel Giolito di Ferrarii, 1549.

Secondary Works

Berriot-Salvadore, Evelyne. *Les femmes dans la société française de la Renaissance.* Geneva: Droz, 1990.

Müller, Catherine M. "*En donnant lieu à la main feminine:* lecture de quelques dialogues poétiques des XVᵉ et XVIᵉ siècles." In *De vrai humain entendement: études sur la littérature française à la fin du Moyen Age, hommage à Jacqueline Cerquiglini-Toulet.* Recherches et Rencontres, Vol. 21. Edited by Yasmina Foehr-Janssens and Jean-Yves Tilliette, 65–82. Geneva: Droz, 2004.

Beguines

Developing in the twelfth and thirteenth centuries out of both an upsurge of lay religious activity and the monastic trend toward apostolic poverty, beguines were women who undertook an active religious life in urban areas of medieval and early modern Europe. Particularly strong and numerous in the Low Countries, and also found in Germany, France, and Italy, beguines were a distinctively urban phenomenon, probably because of the prevalence of single female urban migration in this period. Although many early beguines were born to the lower nobility or wealthy tradespeople, as the movement gained in popularity, women from the middle or lower ranks of society became common in beguinages. These women, either single or widows, found marriage neither appealing nor practicable and rejected it in favor of entering into some kind of religious life. The term "beguine" therefore generally refers to women who lived a religiously inspired ascetic or philanthropic life outside of monasteries.

Beguines did not live in nunneries (although, for some women, the beguinage became a halfway point on the way to the monastery). Beguines took simple vows of chastity and poverty, instead of the solemn vows of nuns, and they were not enclosed in monastic institutions. Instead, beguines attempted to combine the contemplative and active roles in their religious lives. They rejected the economic and material gains of commerce and inheritance and, embracing the ideal of apostolic poverty, engaged in labor that was intended to be penitential, charitable, and useful to Christian society, relying solely on that work to support themseves. Liberated from the social responsibilities of property and family, some beguines devoted their lives to the care of the indigent, most often through nursing or teaching. Mary of Oignies, one of the earliest beguines in the Low Countries, left her home in Nivelles to nurse the lepers in Willambroux in 1191. Mary was also married, but convinced her husband to take simple vows of chastity with her and work alongside her in the leper hospital. Other beguines made their living through spinning thread, weaving, or other forms of manual labor.

It was rare for a woman to undertake the beguine life while still married; Mary's life story, however, demonstrates the advantages of the beguine life, in that it was far more flexible than solemn vows or enclosure in nunneries. Living and working arrangements for beguines were extraordinarily diverse. In the twelfth century most beguines lived as independent individuals or in small, informal shared quarters, in groups from two or three to eight or ten women. Beguines nursed the poor and sick and taught young women of all social classes reading, writing, and spiritual devotion, but they also engaged in manual labor, such as spinning or weaving. Although most beguines placed a high spiritual value on their work in the community, they also strongly believed in contemplative prayer. Beguines in the Low Countries were often involved in death vigils or the burial prayers of both family members and strangers. Some beguines did embrace the contemplative ideal and immured themselves as anchoresses in cells next to parish churches. Even immured anchoresses, however, taught younger girls and boys Christian devotion within the confines of their cells.

In the Low Countries, France, and Germany in the thirteenth century onward, the most common living arrangements were the convent and the court. The convent was a house in which an association of beguines lived together or close by and placed themselves under the rule of a "mistress." The beguines promised to follow certain rules and contribute to the house's common fund for the duration of their stay. These convents did not have private chapels; beguines attended the local parish church for their spiritual needs. Courts, most common in the Low Countries, were groups of houses, usually built just outside the city walls, arranged in a circle around a central chapel and ruled by an elected and limited-term *magistra*. (Beguine courts could also require an entrance fee for those wishing to live in them.) They included houses for individual beguines, as well as for beguines living in groups, and provided space for the ill and indigent, including individual beguines who

could no longer work due to illness or age. Courts were large enough that male clergy might live on the premises to administer the sacraments to the beguines.

In general, however, beguines did not employ rigid organizational structures. They also did not submit themselves formally to administration by any male religious order, although many beguines had informal relationships with Dominicans or Franciscans, who acted as confessors and spiritual directors and who administered the sacraments. But the lack of formal affiliation with a male order meant that beguines were not systematically overseen or controlled by male religious. Beguines had both supporters and detractors among the male church hierarchy. To supporters, such as James of Vitry, beguines were "the faithful of Christ serving the Lord under the rule of the Gospel." Others were not so enthusiastic, but acknowledged that beguines were unique role models of charity and devotion within the urban milieu. But for many within the church, the lack of male supervision automatically made beguines suspect of scandalous behavior and susceptible to heresy. In 1274 Guibert of Tournai, a Franciscan master in theology at Paris, accused beguines of interpreting Scripture independently and falsely. The Council of Vienne (1311–1312) condemned beguines, and their male and less numerous counterparts, beghards, for expressing opinions contrary to Catholicism concerning the Trinity. Pope John XXII, in 1318, admonished bishops to watch beguines carefully for signs of heresy but to allow nonheretical beguines to continue with their unique religious lifestyle. The condemnations of Vienne, however, provided the impetus for the suppression of beguines in the German territories. Beguines in France, Italy, and the Low Countries continued to be suspect of heresy, particularly Catharism and the heresies of the Free Spirit.

The beguinages not closed down in the fourteenth and fifteenth centuries operated under increasing restrictions. Members were more restricted in their physical movement outside the convent or court, for example, and when they did move into the public sphere they were instructed to keep their heads veiled and eyes averted. The Protestant Reformation brought even greater religious controversy to beguines, and the Council of Trent's decrees (1545–1563) continued the movement toward the forced enclosure and regulation of female religious. Some beguine courts in the Low Countries, however, survived into the nineteenth and early twentieth centuries, propagating their unique brand of religious devotion and active Christian service.

Jane Wickersham

See also Religious Reform and Women.

Bibliography

Primary Works

De Vitry, Jacques. *The Life of Mary d'Oignies.* Translated by Margot H. King. Toronto: Peregrina Press, 1989.

Eymeric, Nicolau, and Francisco Peña. *Directorium Inquisitorum.* Venice: Apud Marcum Antonium Zalterium, 1595. (Indiana University Microform Collection, Canon 5; originally published in Rome, 1578.)

Secondary Works

Bailey, Michael D. "Religious Poverty, Mendicancy, and Reform in the Late Middle Ages." *Church History* 72, no. 3 (September 2003): 457–483.

Geybels, Hans. *Vulgariter Beghinae: Eight Centuries of Beguine History in the Low Countries.* Turnhout, Belgium: Brepols, 2004.

Lambert, Malcolm D. *Medieval Heresy: Popular Movements from Bogomil to Hus.* London: Edward Arnold, 1977.

Murk-Jansen, Saskia. *Brides in the Desert: The Spirituality of the Beguines.* Maryknoll, NY: Orbis Books, 1998.

Simons, Walter. *Cities of Ladies: Beguine Communities in the Medieval Low Countries, 1200–1565.* Philadelphia: University of Pennsylvania Press, 2001.

Behn, Aphra (ca. 1645–1689)

Novelist, playwright, poet, and Tory activist

Aphra Behn was born near Canterbury, Kent, in the middle to late 1640s, of a Catholic fam-

Aphra Behn, English playwright, novelist, and Tory activist. Portrait by Sir Peter Lely. (Library of Congress)

ily named Johnson. In 1663 the family traveled to Surinam, where according to Behn's account in her autobiographical novel *Oroonoko* (1688), her father had been appointed "Lieutenant-General of Six and thirty Islands, besides the Continent of Surinam" by Lord Francis Willoughby. Her father died on the voyage, and Aphra remained in Surinam for several weeks awaiting a ship home, along with her mother, sister, and brother. Here she befriended the "royal slave" Oroonoko, whose story she recounted twenty-five years later. After her return to England, Aphra married an otherwise unidentified "Mr. Behn," who died some time before 1666. As a young widow, Behn was sent by the courtier Thomas Killigrew on an intelligence mission to Flanders in July 1666 as an agent in Lord Arlington's secret service. Her assignment was to persuade William Scot, son of regicide Thomas Scot and a friend of Behn's from her stay in Surinam, to provide military information against the Dutch. Although Behn later claimed that she had used Scot's intelligence to give advance warning of the Dutch plan to sail up the Thames in 1667, at the time her reports were discounted and she ended up briefly in debtors' prison in 1668 (Cameron 1961).

Behn is best-known as the first English-woman to earn her living as a writer. During the 1660s Behn began to frequent court literary and theatrical circles. She counted among her friends such well-known literary figures as Dryden and the "theatrical" Howards, the earl of Rochester, poets Katherine Philips and Edmund Waller, playwrights Thomas Otway and Nahum Tate, as well as actors like Eleanor Gwyn. She also befriended lawyers from the Inns of Court like John Hoyle, a notorious bisexual and Whig sympathizer. During Behn's lifetime, gossip alleged that Behn and Hoyle were romantically linked; after her death a series of "Love Letters to a Gentleman," supposedly written to Hoyle, were printed at the end of the posthumous *Histories and Novels* (1696). Behn's first published literary ventures were two plays, *The Forc'd Marriage* (1670) and *The Amorous Prince* (1671), and a miscellany of her own and her friends' poetry and short prose pieces associated with the theater, entitled *Covent Garden Drolery* (1672). In twenty years she wrote seventeen plays under her own name, beginning with *The Amorous Prince* (written before 1670 but not published until 1683), and ending with two posthumous comedies, *The Widow Ranter* (1690) and *The Younger Brother* (1696). Several anonymous comedies have been attributed to Behn, including *The Woman Turn'd Bully* (1675), *The Counterfeit Bridegroom* (1677), and *The Debauchee* (1677), the latter two adapted from plays by Brome and Middleton. As a beneficiary of royal patronage and a secret Catholic, Behn became a strong supporter of the Tory cause during the political struggles of the 1680s. Her allegiance is clearly reflected in the plays, satirical verse, and short prose pieces she produced during this period, beginning with her comedy *The Roundheads* (1681). A lengthy political roman á clef, *Love Letters Between a Nobleman and his Sister* (1684), was loosely based on the scandalous elopement of the Whig chief, Forde Grey, Lord Warke, with his sister-in-law Henrietta Berkeley.

Although Behn earned much of her income through her dramatic works, notably her greatest hit, *The Rover* (1677), she also produced poetry, short stories, novels, and various occasional pieces. In addition to her own writings, she edited four miscellanies of verse and prose and translated several popular works from the French, including Bernard de Fontenelle's best-selling popular account of Newtonian science, *Entretiens sur la Pluralite des Mondes* (1686), under the English title *A Discovery of New Worlds* (1688). *Oroonoko, or, the Royal Slave* (1688), Behn's most popular and widely known novel, was adapted posthumously for the stage by Thomas Southerne in 1696. Behn suffered ill health during the late 1680s, living just long enough to witness the triumphant ascendancy of the Whigs during the Glorious Revolution of 1688–1689. She died on 16 April 1689, five days after the coronation of William and Mary, and was buried in Westminster Abbey.

Sara H. Mendelson

See also Literary Culture and Women; Philips, Katherine; Theater and Women Actors, Playwrights, and Patrons.

Bibliography

Primary Work

Behn, Aphra. *The Works of Aphra Behn.* Edited by Janet Todd. Columbus: Ohio State University Press, 1992.

Secondary Works

Cameron, William. *New Light on Aphra Behn.* Auckland: University of Auckland Press, 1961.

Hughes, Derek. *The Theatre of Aphra Behn.* London: Palgrave, 2001.

Mendelson, Sara. *The Mental World of Stuart Women: Three Studies.* Chapter 3. Amherst: University of Massachusetts Press, 1987.

O'Donnell, Mary Ann. *Aphra Behn: An Annotated Bibliography of Primary and Secondary Sources.* 2nd ed. Burlington, VT: Ashgate, 2004.

Todd, Janet. "Aphra Behn." In *Oxford Dictionary of National Biography.* Oxford: Oxford University Press, 2004.

Bess of Hardwick (Elizabeth Talbot; ca. 1527–1608)

Countess of Shrewsbury, member of Queen Elizabeth I's court, and one of the wealthest women in England in the 1590s

Bess of Hardwick, a daughter of a modest landowner, John Hardwick, and Elizabeth Leake, had to start building her fortune almost from scratch. Endowed with down-to-earth practicality, shrewdness, and, most important, the ability to succeed at the game whose rules favored men, Bess became one of the wealthiest women in England. She built mansions at Chatsworth, Oldcotes, Workshop, and Bolsover; the pinnacle of her dynastic ambition was Hardwick Hall in Derbyshire (completed in 1597). Bess even became a grandmother of a potential heir to the English throne when, in 1574, she contrived a marriage between her daughter Elizabeth Cavendish and Charles Stuart, earl of Lennox, a union that produced Arbella Stuart. Although this marriage got Bess in trouble with Elizabeth I, she was soon forgiven by her queen, who enjoyed Bess's vibrant personality.

Bess's rise to wealth was firmly linked to her marital career. At about age fourteen, Bess married Robert Barley only to become a widow at the age of sixteen. She was to survive three more husbands: Sir William Cavendish, whom she married in 1547 and who fathered all of Bess's eight children; Sir William St. Loe, whom she wedded in 1559; and finally George Talbot, sixth earl of Shrewsbury, who became her husband in 1567 and with whom Bess was to share the honor and hardship of caring for Mary Stuart, Queen of Scots, when she was Elizabeth I's prisoner in England. Bess's last marriage disintegrated under pressure of this challenging task—sixteen years (1569–1584) of mounting expenses, discomfort, and stress. Bess spent several years in reluctant separation from her embittered husband, waiting in vain for reconciliation. By the time of Talbot's death, Bess was an expert in dealing with the legal system designed to keep property in the hands of men. As a widow, she retained a portion of her husbands' estates, and she bought land in the name of her sons. Bess left a fortune to her family, and she is still widely remembered for erecting the magnificent Hardwick Hall, a monument to one remarkable woman's success on her journey from poverty to splendor.

Anya Riehl

See also Cavendish, Elizabeth Brackley and Jane Cavendish; Elizabeth I; Power, Politics, and Women; Stuart, Arbella.

Bibliography
Primary Work
Stowe, J. *The Chronicles of England*. 1587.
Secondary Works
Durant, David N. *Bess of Hardwick: Portrait of an Elizabethan Dynast*. London: Peter Owen, 1999. (Originally printed in 1977.)
Hubbard, Kate. *A Material Girl: Bess of Hardwick, 1527–1608*. London: Short Books, 2001.

Boleyn, Anne (1507–1536)

Second wife of King Henry VIII of England, patron of religious reform activists, executed on the king's orders

Anne Boleyn was born in 1507 to Elizabeth Howard, daughter of the second duke of Norfolk, and Sir Thomas Boleyn, future earl of Wiltshire. Probably the eldest of their three children, Anne's sister, Mary, became William Carey's wife and Henry VIII's mistress, and her brother George, future Lord Rochford, joined Henry VIII's privy chamber. In 1513, Anne began studying French at the court of Margaret of Savoy, regent of the Netherlands. In 1514, she removed to France as maiden of honor to Mary Tudor, who wed Louis XII. After his death, Anne attended Claude, Francis I's consort, and his sister Margaret d'Alencon. Anne became fluent in French and learned to sing, to play musical instruments, and to do needlework.

She entered the English court in 1521 but was soon expelled for contracting a secret betrothal with Lord Henry Percy. In 1526, when she returned as Catherine of Aragon's maiden of honor, Henry was planning to end his marriage on the grounds that God was causing the

Anne Boleyn, second wife of King Henry VIII of Engand. Portrait by unknown artist. (Corel)

death of his male infants to punish him for violating a Levitical law when he wed Catherine, his brother Arthur's widow. After petitioning Pope Clement VII for an annulment, Henry wrote love letters to Anne, who was absent from court in 1528, recovering from the sweating sickness and for other reasons. Seventeen of his letters are now at the Vatican. Despite Clement's refusal to nullify his marriage, Henry wed Anne on 25 January 1533.

By authority of the Appeals Statute, Archbishop Thomas Cranmer invalidated Henry's alliance with Catherine and then validated the one with Anne. She was crowned on 1 June and gave birth to Elizabeth on 7 September. As queen, she patronized evangelicals, supervised her royal chapel, and won rewards for her relatives, including the marriage of Mary Howard, daughter of the third duke of Norfolk, to Henry's illegitimate son, Henry Fitzroy, duke of Richmond. Anne failed to accomplish her most important duty, for she was unable to give birth to a healthy son, suffering miscarriages in 1534 and 1536. Citing the dispatches of the Imperial ambassador, Eustace Chapuys, some writers claim that after she was delivered of a male fetus of perhaps three-and-one-half months in January 1536, Thomas Cromwell, the king's principal minister, deserted her evangelical faction for the Catholic faction. He allegedly betrayed her because her support for the French alliance was preventing England's rapprochement with Emperor Charles V, Catherine's nephew. Cromwell subsequently manipulated Henry into executing Anne and marrying Jane Seymour. As no other evidence verifies this conspiracy theory, it is more likely that Cromwell was deceiving Chapuys to prevent his learning that Anne's fetus was deformed, a tragedy that contemporaries interpreted as God's punishment for their parents' sins, especially their sexual misconduct. Blaming Anne's promiscuity for the deformity, Henry ordered her and her five apparent lovers incarcerated in the Tower of London. Just before her arrest on 2 May, Anne's thoughts turned to Elizabeth, and she asked Matthew Parker, future archbishop of Canterbury, to monitor her well-being.

The indictments accused Anne of witchlike, lecherous behavior, of enticing the five men with French kisses to perform sexual acts with her. The accused were her brother, George Boleyn, Lord Rochford, Sir Francis Weston, William Norris, William Brereton, and Mark Smeaton, all of whom were executed. No effort was made to ensure that she was with the men at the time and place stated in the indictments. For instance, they claimed she met Rochford on 5 December 1535 at Westminster when she was with Henry at Windsor. Also arrested but released were Richard Page and Thomas Wyatt, who may have composed sonnets to her. These accusations of witchlike behavior led Nicholas Sander and other Catholic writers to describe her as physically disfigured. She did not, as they claimed, have a sixth finger or a wen on her throat.

At the Tower, she confessed to rejecting Weston's and Norris's attentions. Incredibly, some writers have interpreted these admissions as proof that she was actually the men's courtly lover. For spiritual comfort, she asked her jailors to place the sacrament in a closet near her chamber. At her trial on 15 May, although she swore that she was faithful to her husband, she was convicted of treason. Two days later, Cranmer pronounced her marriage to Henry invalid, perhaps citing as grounds her alleged witchlike powers. At her execution on 19 May, she prayed to God to give the king a long reign and asked witnesses to think the best of her. After the Calais executioner beheaded her with one stroke of a special sword, she was buried at St. Peter ad Vincula at the Tower.

Retha Warnicke

See also Power, Politics, and Women; Religious Reform and Women; Witchcraft, Witches, and Witch-Hunting.

Bibliography

Ives, Eric. *Anne Boleyn*. Oxford: Blackwell, 1986.
Warnicke, Retha M. *The Rise and Fall of Anne Boleyn: Family Politics at the Court of Henry VIII*. Cambridge, UK: Cambridge University Press, 1989.

Book Trade. *See* Printers, the Book Trade, and Women.

Borgia, Lucrezia (1480–1519)

Duchess of Ferrara, patron of poets, musicians, and the Venetian publisher Aldo Manuzio (Aldus Manutius)

Lucrezia Borgia, noblewoman and controversial figure of the Italian Renaissance, was born in Rome, the natural daughter of Cardinal Rodrigo Borgia, the future Pope Alexander VI (1492–1503). She was one of four children the cardinal had from Vannozza Cattanei, the others being Juan, Cesare (ca. 1475–1507), and Joffre. After spending the first years of life in her mother's house, she was moved to the Orsini palace on Monte Giordano to be brought up

Lucrezia Borgia, duchess of Ferrara. Portrait by unknown artist. (Leonard de Selva/Corbis)

under the tutelage of Adriana de Mila, confidant and first cousin to Cardinal Rodrigo. Nothing is known about the education she received. Borgia was conversant in both Italian and Catalan, the latter being the language spoken in her family, and she is supposed to have composed poems in both languages, but she was described by no one as a poet and no verse by her is mentioned anywhere.

Pope Alexander loved Lucrezia Borgia "to a superlative degree," in the expression used by the Ferrarese ambassador in Rome in his dispatch to Duke Ercole d'Este on 4 April 1493. His attachment to her did not prevent him from using her as a pawn in his political strategy and in the advancement of his dynastic aims. In 1491, as he was endeavoring to establish the fortunes of his sons in Spain, Alexander betrothed Borgia to two Spanish noblemen, first to Cherubino Juan de Centelles, brother of the count of Oliva and Valencia, and, almost immediately after, to Gasparo of Procida, son of Count of Aversa, of a Valencian family that had moved to the kingdom of Naples. The contracts of both betrothals, which for a short period overlapped, were annulled when Alexander became an ally of Charles VIII of France and Ludovico Sforza, ruler of Milan (1452–1508). As a consequence, on 12 June 1493, Lucrezia Borgia, then thirteen, was married by proxy to Giovanni Sforza, count of Cotignola and vicar of Pesaro, a vassal of the church belonging to a cadet branch of the house of Sforza. By 1495, however, as Charles retreated to France, the pontiff's political allegiances switched. He now aimed at a match for Cesare with the Neapolitan royal house of Aragon and at an eventual takeover of that kingdom. Marital relations between Borgia and Giovanni Sforza were made increasingly difficult until, on 20 December 1497, their marriage was annulled by the Vatican on grounds of nonconsummation. The following year, Borgia was already married to Don Alfonso, duke of Bisceglie, natural son of Alfonso II of Aragon.

Although the new union was a happy one—a son, named Rodrigo, was born on 14 October 1500—soon Cesare wanted for Borgia a marriage more consonant to his new plans. The Neapolitan scheme having failed, at present he intended to carve a domain of his own out of the papal territory of Romagna and actively sought the financial and military support of Louis XII of France. Alfonso was first attacked in the street by paid assassins, and, having survived the attack, on 18 August 1500 he was strangled in his bed. Even before the murder, the pope let it be known that Lucrezia Borgia was to marry Alfonso d'Este, son of Ercole, duke of Ferrara. The match would establish for Cesare an advantageous alliance with both France and the Este, guarantee his acquisition of Romagna, and increase his chances of taking possession of Bologna and Florence.

Borgia's betrothal to Alfonso was a turning point in her life. From this moment on, the pope's daughter ceased to be a pawn in her family's political machinations, and her deter-

mination to take charge of her life became paramount. During the negotiations for her marriage, Borgia was effective in mediating between the Duke of Ferrara—who had consented to the marriage only under Alexander's threat to deprive him of his domain—and the objections her father kept raising to the duke's demands: that he be paid two hundred thousand ducats, that Ferrara's annual dues to the church be remitted, and that several ecclesiastical benefices be conferred on the house of Este. Ercole came to appreciate the diplomatic skill exercised by his future daughter-in-law in her own interest and in that of the house of Este; furthermore, notwithstanding the rumors about incest and about her participation in murderous plots, the reports that the duke received about Borgia from his agents described her as intelligent, lovely, and exceedingly gracious, a lady of whom it was impossible to suspect anything sinister. The wedding ceremony took place in Rome in December 1501: Alfonso was not present, and the rings were exchanged between the bride and Ferrante d'Este, who stood in lieu of his brother. Then, richly dressed and accompanied by a splendidly attired retinue, Borgia rode at the head of a spectacular procession through papal territories, entering Ferrara in triumph. Soon, her vitality, kindness, and amiability ingratiated her to her family-to-be and to the Ferrarese people. The popularity thus became important to her one year after the wedding, when Pope Alexander died, depriving her of her base of power. Three years later Alfonso became duke of Ferrara and Borgia its duchess.

Ferrara could boast of one of the most cultured courts in Italy, one that will be forever associated with such poets as Matteo Maria Boiardo (1441–1494) and Ludovico Ariosto (1474–1533). The court was also a center for music and theater, and disposed of a well furnished classical and humanistic library. The Este were the sponsors of a university as well as a renowned school of painters and architects. Although not keenly interested in cultural matters, Borgia kept in touch with members of the local literary circle. Devoted to her were Tito Vespasiano Strozzi (1424–1505) and his son Ercole (1473–1508), two humanistic poets who figured prominently in the court bureaucracy: Borgia gave her support to Aldus Manutius (1449–1515) in his attempt to establish an academy to his own specifications. Aldus made her the executor of the will he drew up in 1509, and in 1513, on her recommendation, he published the Latin verse of both Strozzi. With Pietro Bembo (1470–1547), the future pundit of Italian literature, Borgia carried on a romantic affair from the moment of her arrival in Ferrara until 1505. At this time, on what seems to have been sober considerations of decorum and prudence, Bembo left Ferrara. In Venice he published and dedicated his dialogue on love, *Gli Asolani,* to her. Lucrezia Borgia's lifelong, passionate, and fully reciprocated attachment, however, was for Francesco II Gonzaga (1484–1519), Marquis of Mantua, husband of her sister-in-law, Isabella d'Este. Their intense liaison, which was risky but not without practical advantages for the safety of the duchy, was managed by Borgia with circumspection. All the while, her vivacity and love of pleasure, as well as her constant attentiveness to promote the interests of the Ferrarese dynasty, secured the regard of her husband, as they had ingratiated his father before.

Throughout the years, Borgia provided for the living expenses of her entourage—ladies-in-waiting, singers, musicians, and secretaries. She cared for the welfare of Rodrigo, her child by Alfonso of Bisceglie, who lived in the south of Italy under the tutelage of his paternal relatives, as well as for the upbringing of Cesare's natural offsprings, Girolamo and Camilla, who resided near her. An insight into her merciful character is also given by her continued concern for Cesare himself. At the death of their father in 1503, when *il Valentino* was still at Faenza and Forlì, Lucrezia supplied him with money and troops; later, when he was a prisoner at Medina del Campo in Castille, she did

her utmost to bring about his liberation. But Borgia's chief concern was to succeed as a reigning consort to Duke Alfonso.

After Ercole's death in 1505, the new duke had established the bureau of the *Exemine* for the examination of private petitions and had placed his wife in charge of it. In 1506, as he left on a military campaign against Venice, he nominated her governor regent. From 1508 to 1512, Borgia was the de facto ruler of Ferrara, while her husband campaigned against Pope Julius II, who was advancing toward Ferrara at the head of an army with the intention of restoring the Este fiefs to the direct control of the church. As before, she carried out her office with intelligence and justice, giving proof of remarkable administrative abilities and of a sharp understanding of military matters. As late as 1518, when Alfonso was called to Paris by the French king, the duchess was again left in charge of the city. By this time Borgia and Alfonso were a partnership in all respects, in the political and military defense of the duchy, in the exercise of a strong religious piety, in their intimate relations, and in the parental care of their children.

While performing her administrative tasks, Borgia was almost continuously pregnant. After some miscarriages and the death of a newly born child, on 14 April 1509 she gave birth to the future duke of Ferrara. He was named Ercole in honor of his grandfather. In the next ten years, five more children were born: Ippolito, Alessandro, Eleonora, Francesco, and Isabella Maria. The difficult pregnancies, the miscarriages, and the premature births had greatly weakened her fiber. Shortly after Alfonso's return from Paris in 1519, the duchess died giving birth to Isabella Maria. She was thirty-nine years of age.

Rinaldina Russell

See also Este, Isabella d'; the subheading Literary Patronage (under Literary Culture and Women); Power, Politics, and Women; on her patronage of the printer Aldus Manutius, *see* Printers, the Book Trade, and Women.

Bibliography

Primary Works

Contemporary letters bearing on Lucrezia's life are found in manuscript form in the following archives:

Correspondence of Ercole I with Gain Luca Pozzi and Gherardo Saraceni, his ambassadors in Rome: Ambasciatori Esteri, Roma 1501–2, b Correspondance of Gian Luca Pozzi, Ferrarese ambassador in Rome, with Ercole I d'Este. Acton MSS. Add. MSS 4757. Cambridge University Library Archives. Usta 12, in Archivio di Stato di Modena, Archivio Segreto Estense.

Correspondence of Francesco Gonzaga to Lucrezia Borgia, Lucrezia to Ercole I, Ercole I to Lucrezia, Lucrezia to Alfonso I d'Este, Alfonso I to Lucrezia: Carteggio dei Principi Esteri, busta 1181; in busta 141; in Camera Ducale, Minutario, busta 5, Minute Ducali, busta 69; in Casa e Stato, busta 141; Carteggio dei Principi Estensi, busta 75, respectively. All documents are in Archivio di Stato di Modena, Archivio Segreto Estense.

Correspondence of Gian Luca Pozzi, Ferrarese ambassador in Rome, with Ercole I d'Este: Acton MSS. Add. MSS 4757. Cambridge University Library Archives.

Correspondence of Lucrezia Borgia to Francesco Gonzaga: Autografi 84, busta 1–4, serie E. XXX 1.2; busta 1189, in Archivio di Stato di Mantova. (Also in Archivio Gonzaga.)

Letters to Isabella d'Este from Bernardino di Prosperi, her informant in Ferrara, 1502–1519: Serie E XXX 1.3, buste 1238–47. Archivio di Stato di Mantova. Archivio Gonzaga. An extensive listing of documentary sources is found in Sarah Bradford, *Lucrezia Borgia* (in Secondary Works), pp. 368–371.

Alberi, Eugenio. *Le Relazioni degli ambasciatori veneti al Senato.* Firenze: Società Editrice Fiorentina, 1839–1863.

Bembo, Pietro. *La grande fiamma: lettere 1503–1517.* Edited by Giulia Raboni. Milano: R. Archinto, 1989.

Bembo, Pietro. *The Prettiest Love Letters in the World: Letters Between Lucrezia Borgia and Pietro Bembo, 1503–1519.* Translation and preface by Hugh Shankland. Wood engravings by Richard Shirly Smith. Boston: D. R. Godine, 1987.

Burchard, Johannes. *At the Court of the Borgia, Being an Account of the Reign of Pope Alexander VI, Written by His Master of Ceremonies, Johann Burchard.* Edited and translated by Geoffrey Parker. London: The Folio Society, 1963.

Sanuto, Marino (Marin Sanudo). *I diarii di Marino Sanuto (MCCCCXCVI-MDXXXIII) dall' autografo Marciano ital. cl. VII codd. CDXIX-CDLXXVII.* Edited by Rinaldo Fulin, Federico Stefani, Nicolò Barozzi, Guglielmo Berchet, and Marco Allegri. Venezia: F. Visentini, 1879–1903.

Secondary Works

Bellonci, Maria. *The Life and Times of Lucrezia Borgia.* Translated by Bernard and Barbara Wall. New York: Harcourt Brace, 1939.

Bellonci, Maria. *Lucrezia Borgia; la sua vita e i suoi tempi.* Milano: A. Mondadori, 1939.

Bradford, Sarah. *Lucrezia Borgia: Life, Love and Death in Renaissance Italy.* New York: Viking Penguin, 2004.

Catalano, Michele. *Lucrezia Borgia, duchessa di Ferrara; con nuovi documenti, note critiche e un ritratto inedito.* Ferrara: Taddei, 1920.

Farinelli Toselli, Alessandra, ed. *Lucrezia Borgia a Ferrara.* Ferrara: Liberty House, 2002.

Gregorovius, Ferdinand. *Lucretia Borgia: According to Original Documents and Correspondence of Her Day.* Translated from the third German edition by John Leslie Garner. New York: Appleton, 1903.

Gundersheimer, Werner I. *The Style of a Renaissance Despotism.* Princeton, NJ: Princeton University Press, 1973.

Bourbon, Catherine de (1559–1604)

Princess of Bourbon and duchess of Bar-Lorraine, Calvinist who died in exile

Catherine de Bourbon was born in Paris, daughter of Jeanne d'Albret and Antoine de Bourbon and granddaughter of Marguerite de Navarre. Sister to Henry IV, she served as regent on four occasions during the period of her brother's reign in Navarre: first from 1577 to 1578, again in 1582, a third time from 1583 to 1587, and finally in 1588. Descended from a long line of strong-willed and influential women, Bourbon was well equipped to withstand the numerous adversities that plagued her life: the early loss of her parents, the forced abandonment of her beloved, Charles de Bourbon (the Count of Soissons), and her unhappy marriage in 1599 to Henri de Lorraine (the duke of Bar), which was eventually annulled by Clement VIII in 1603, just months before her death, at a time when she mistakenly believed she had at last achieved a much-longed-for pregnancy. A staunch Calvinist in a Catholic kingdom, Catherine de Bourbon was unwilling to renounce her Protestant faith and was ultimately exiled from her brother's court. Despite constant political and sentimental dramas, Catherine de Bourbon refused to submit to the demands of those around her and managed to cultivate a life of lucid piety and intellectual freedom, qualities made evident in what remains of her correspondance (224 letters written between 1570 and 1603) and her poetry (five short devotional compositions written in 1595, addressed to her spiritual mentor Théodore de Bèze). Catherine de Bourbon's later years were marked by heavy financial burdens and ill health. She died in Nancy of tuberculosis at the age of forty-five.

Melanie Gregg

See also Albret, Jeanne d'; the subheading Letter Writing (under Literary Culture and Women); Marguerite de Navarre; Religious Reform and Women.

Bibliography

Primary Work

Bourbon, Catherine de. *Lettres et poésies de Catherine de Bourbon (1570–1603)*. Edited by Raymond Ritter. Paris: Champion, 1927.

Secondary Works

Armaille, Marie Celestine Amélie, Comtesse de. *Catherine de Bourbon: soeur d'Henri IV.* Paris: Didier et Cⁱᵉ, 1865.

Melchior-Bonnet, Sabine. *Catherine de Bourbon, l'insoumise.* Paris: NiL Éditions, 1999.

Ritter, Raymond. *Catherine de Bourbon 1559–1604: La soeur d'Henri IV.* Paris: J. Touzot, 1985.

Tucoo-Chala, Pierre. *Catherine de Bourbon: Une calviniste exemplaire.* Biarritz, France: Atlantica, 1997.

Bourbon, Gabrielle de (ca. 1460–1516)

French princess, author of moral and spiritual treatises, bibliophile, and art patron

The life and works of Gabrielle de Bourbon are of great interest to religious, literary, and art historians. Rarely have there been so many archival documents available for any woman of the early modern period, allowing us to capture her personality, religious aspirations, artistic and literary tastes, and daily activities. As the daughter of Gabrielle de La Tour and Louis de Bourbon and the wife of Louis II de La Trémoille, she was closely related to the royal family and thus at the center of the French political and cultural arena. Raised as a worthy descendant of King Saint Louis, Gabrielle de Bourbon was a devout and well-read princess fully aware of the responsibilities connected with her rank. The portraits decorating her apartments, the precious books filling her impressive library, the fascinating letters she wrote to her husband (almost always away at war) all attest to the crucial role she played. In addition to being the main administrator of her domain and the preceptor of her only son Charles, prince of Talmont and godchild to King Charles VIII (and later that of her grandson Francis), she was a generous patron and an important writer who authored a book of conduct destined for her ladies, *L'Instruction des jeunes filles* (unfortunately lost), as well as several devotional treatises.

Her three extant works, entitled *Petit traicté sur les doulleurs de la Passion du doulx Jesus et de sa benoiste mere* (Short Treatise on the Travails of the Passion of the Meek Jesus and of His Blessed Mother), *Le voyage spirituel entreprins par l'ame devote pour parvenir en la cité de bon repoux* (The Spiritual Journey Undertaken by the Devout Soul to Reach the City of Good Repose), and *Le fort chasteau pour la retraicte de toutes bonnes ames fait par le commandement du glorieux sainct esperit* (The Fortified Castle for the Retreat of All Good Souls Built on the Order of the Glorious Holy Spirit), are strongly inspired by medieval mystery plays, allegorical life pilgrimages, and Marian poetry, and they serve both devotional and didactic purposes, as instruments of personal spiritual growth and edification of laypeople. Nourished by Cistercian mysticism, these texts offer precious insights on laywomen's spirituality in the early Renaissance.

Catherine M. Müller

See also Beguines; the subheading Literary Patronage (under Literary Culture and Women).

Bibliography
Berriot-Salvadore, Evelyne. *Les femmes dans la société française de la Renaissance.* Geneva: Droz, 1990.
Berriot-Salvadore, Evelyne. "Le miroir des princesses, un modèle de dévotion séculière au début du XVIe siècle." In *La Bible et ses raisons. Diffusion et distorsions du discours religieux (XIVᵉ–XVIIᵉ siècle).* Edited by Gérard Gros, 77–96. Saint-Étienne: Publications de l'Université de Saint-Étienne, 1996.
Bourbon, Gabrielle de. *Le fort chasteau pour la retraicte de toutes bonnes ames fait par le commandement du glorieux sainct esperit.* Paris: Bibliothèque Mazarine, ms. 978, f. 31–45ᵛ.
Bourbon, Gabrielle de. *Le voyage spirituel entreprins par l'ame devote pour parvenir en la cité de bon repoux.* Paris: Bibliothèque Mazarine, ms. 978, f. 1–29ᵛ.
Bourbon, Gabrielle de. *Œuvres spirituelles (1510–1516).* Textes de la Renaissance, vol. 26. Edited by Evelyne Berriot-Salvadore. Paris: Champion, 1999.
Bourbon, Gabrielle de. Petit traicté sur les doulleurs de la passion du doulx Jesus et de sa benoiste mere. *Chartrier de Thouars: Archives Nationales, 1 AP 220.*

Bourbon-Montpensier, Charlotte de (1546/1547–1582)

Princess of Orange, wife of William of Orange and de facto secretary of state, Roman Catholic nun and abbess turned Huguenot

Charlotte de Bourbon-Montpensier was the daughter of Louis de Bourbon, duke of Montpensier and Jacqueline de Longwy. When she was professed as a nun of the convent of Jouarre in 1559 at the age of thirteen (later to be elected abbess at eighteen), she made a formal oral and written protest that she was being professed against her will. After she left the convent in 1571 and adopted the Protestant faith, Charlotte cited this documentation to justify to her father her decision to renounce her vows.

On the advice of Jeanne d'Albret, Charlotte sought refuge with Frederick III, elector of the Palatinate, a strong Calvinist. Here she met William of Orange, Stadhouder of the Netherlands; she became his third wife in 1575. William's leadership of the Dutch revolt against Spanish Catholic domination brought poverty and struggle to his family; Charlotte supported his cause and created a home for his children by his first two marriages and for her own six daughters. The letters she exchanged with her husband illustrate how, during his frequent absences, he entrusted her with maintaining his alliances at home, negotiating financial support, and communicating advice and information. In an exchange of letters with her father, her brother Francis, and other relatives, Charlotte skillfully pursued reconciliation with her father, as much for her husband's as for her own sake.

Charlotte died in 1582, exhausted from bearing six children in seven years and from having nursed William back to health after an assassination attempt.

Jane Couchman

See also Albret, Jeanne d'; Power, Politics, and Women; Religious Reform and Women.

Bibliography
Primary Works
Couchman, Jane, trans. "Charlotte de Bourbon, Princess of Orange: Lettres et documents (1565–1582)." In *Writings by Pre-Revolutionary French Women.* Pages 107–121. New York: Garland, 2000.
Delaborde, Jules. *Charlotte de Bourbon, princesse d'Orange.* Paris: Fischbacher, 1888.
Secondary Works
Bainton, Roland. "Charlotte de Bourbon." In *Ladies of the Reformation in France and England.* Pages 89–111. Boston: Beacon Press, 1973.
Couchman, Jane. "Charlotte de Bourbon's Correspondence: Using Words to Implement Emancipation." In *Women Writers in Pre-Revolutionary France.* Edited by Colette H. Winn and Donna Kuizenga, 101–117. New York: Garland, 1990.

Bourgeois, Louise (Louise Boursier; 1563–1636)

Midwife to Queen Marie de Médicis, renowned author of medical textbooks translated into many languages

Born in Paris, Louise Bourgeois in 1584 married the king's surgeon Martin Boursier, with whom she had five children. She led a very happy life. But during the Religious Wars, the Boursier family was forced to leave Paris and find refuge in Tours, where they suffered a life of financial difficulties. Returning to Paris, Louise Boursier became a midwife to provide financial assistance to her family. In spite of opposition from within the profession, she practiced for five years among the poor and became a registered midwife in 1598. This period of her life is recounted at the beginning of her *Recit veritable de la naissance de messeigneurs et dames les enfans de France* (True Account of the Birth of the Sons and Daughters of France).

In 1601, a wonderful opportunity was offered to Louise Boursier: Queen Marie de Médicis was looking for a midwife. Demonstrating a strong sense of authority and loyalty, Louise Boursier was chosen by the queen to deliver her six children between 1601 and 1610 (the year King Henry IV was assassinated). Louise Boursier was well respected and became the most popular midwife at the court. In 1627, however, Marie de Bourbon Montpensier gave birth to her daughter, Anne-Marie-Louise d'Orléans (La Grande Mademoiselle), and died suddenly of a puerperal fever. Her midwife, Louise Boursier, was accused of negligence by the physicians who did the autopsy. Her popularity began to decline, and she spent the rest of her life writing and publishing very successful books about her art until her death in 1636. Her famous works were read all over Europe. First published in 1609, her *Observations diverses, sur la sterilité, perte de fruict, foecondite, accouchements, et maladies des femmes, et enfants nouveaux naiz* (Various Observations on Sterility, Miscarriage, Ability to Conceive, Childbirth, Female Illnesses, and Infants) provides scientific remarks

Louise Bourgeois, midwife to the Queen of France and author of medical textbooks. Portrait from Louise Bourgeois' Observations diverses, sur la sterilité, perte de fruict, foecondité, accouchements, et maladies des femmes, et enfants nouveaux naiz. *(Courtesy of the Edward G. Miner Library)*

on obstetrics and numerous guidelines for the care of the pregnant woman as well as her infant. Becoming the manual of reference, this book was augmented and published again and again (in 1617, 1626, 1634, 1642, and 1652). It was also translated into Latin, German, Dutch, and English, underscoring the importance of her European reputation at that time. Some parts of her works are of particular interest: *Recueil des Secrets, de Louyse Bourgeois dite Boursier* (Book of Secrets of Louise Bourgeois Boursier), published just before she died (1635), is a compilation of recipes for women for the treatment of ailments such as skin eruptions, painful periods, and the like. The most interesting writings of Louise Boursier are the *Recit veritable* (True Account) and the *Instruction à ma fille* (Advice to my Daughter), both published in 1617, where she presents her short autobiography as well as the spiritual testament of an exemplary midwife.

In her own time, the well-educated and highly competent Louise Boursier was something of an anomaly, first among her male coworkers, who came to resent her as she became a self-confident practitioner, and also among other sworn midwives who saw her as a formidable challenger to their own preeminence in the field because of her marriage to a surgeon and her unusual training (Louise had studied Ambroise Paré's book on obstetrics). Furthermore, important changes were taking place in the medical and surgical professions. For centuries, women, having gained their skills from experience, monopolized midwifery. With the upsurge of medical science in the sixteenth century, physicians became more interested in the art of delivery, and, as organized instruction and licensing became prevalent, these requirements extended also to women engaged in midwifery.

In a time of growing suspicion over women's capacities to handle child delivery, Louise Boursier understood the need for formal training and collaboration with male physicians and surgeons. She saw herself as the founder of a new generation of midwives, more knowledgeable and better trained. In her effort to educate those who would follow her, she published *Instruction à ma fille,* the first treatise in French on the art of midwifery. She recorded her theories on maternity care and her experiences in Parisian society in her *Recit veritable.* This important work provides a unique source of information about midwifery practices in the early modern period as well as insights into the challenges women faced as they entered the professional world.

Colette H. Winn

See also the subheadings Childbirth and Reproductive Knowledge; Midwives and Licensing; Male Midwifery (under Medicine and Women).

Bibliography

Primary Works

Bourgeois, Louise (dite Boursier). *Observations de Louyse Bourgeois ditte Boursier, Sage-femme de la Royne. Livre Deuxiesme* (suivi du texte du *Recit veritable,* et de l'*Instruction à ma fille*). Paris: Abraham Saugrain, 1617. (Reedited Rouen: La Veuve T. Dare, 1626.)

Bourgeois, Louise (dite Boursier). *Observations diverses, sur la sterilité, perte de fruict, foecondité, accouchements, et maladies des femmes, et enfants nouveaux naiz / Amplement traittées, et heureusement practiquées par L. Bourgeois dite Boursier sage femme de la Roine / Oeuvre util et nècessaire à toutes personnes / Dedié à la Royne.* Paris: Abraham Saugrain, 1609.

Bourgeois, Louise (dite Boursier). *Observations diverses (. . .) (Livre III) (suivi du Recit veritable de la naissance de Messeigneurs et Dames les enfans de France. Avec les particularitez qui y ont esté, et pouvoient estre remarquées et de l'Instruction à ma Fille).* Paris: Melchior Mondiere, 1626.

Bourgeois, Louise (dite Boursier). *Recit veritable de la naissance de Messeigneurs et Dames les enfans de France.* Paris: Melchior Mondiere, 1625.

Bourgeois, Louise (dite Boursier). *Recit veritable de la naissance de Messeigneurs et Dames les enfans de France. Instruction à ma Fille et autres texts.* Edited by Francois Rouget and Colette H. Winn. Geneva: Droz, 2000.

Bourgeois, Louise (dite Boursier). *Recueil des Secrets, de Louyse Bourgeois dite Boursier, sage-femme de la Royne Mere du Roy, Auquel sont continués ses plus rares experiences pour diverses maladies, principalement des femmes avec leurs embelissemens.* Paris: Melchior Mondiere, 1635.

Secondary Works

Broomhall, Susan. *Women's Medical Work in Early Modern France.* Manchester, UK: Manchester University Press, 2004.

Kalisch, Philip A., Margaret Scobey, and Beatrice J. Kalisch. "Louyse Bourgeois and the Emergence of Modern Midwifery." *Journal of Nurse Midwifery* 26, no. 4 (1981): 3–17.

McTavish, Lianne. *Childbirth and the Display of Authority in Early Modern France.* Aldershot, UK: Ashgate, 2005.

Perkins, Wendy. *Midwifery and Medicine in Early Modern France: Louise Bourgeois.* Exeter, Devon, UK: University of Exeter Press, 1996.

Rouget, Francois. "De la sage-femme à la femme sage: Réflexion et réfléxivité dans les *Observations* de Louise Boursier." *Papers on French Seventeenth-Century Literature* XXV, no. 49 (1998): 483–496.

Winn, Colette H. "De sage (-) femme à sage (-) fille: Louise Boursier, Instruction a ma Fille (1626)." In *L'éducation des filles sous l'Ancien Regime. Numéro spécial en homage à Linda Timmermans.* Edited by Colette H. Winn. *Papers on French Seventeenth-Century Literature,* XXIV, no. 46 (1997): 61–83.

Bradstreet, Anne (1612/1613–1672)

The first woman to be recognized as an accomplished poet in the New World

Still considered one of the most important early American writers by modern scholars, Anne Bradstreet was born in Northampton, England, in 1612 or 1613. She was the daughter of Thomas Dudley and his wife, Dorothy Yorke Dudley, both wellborn members of the gentry. In 1619, Thomas Dudley became steward to the fourth earl of Lincoln and moved his family to the earl's Sempringham estate. Anne's education and intellect were cultivated in this environment, encouraged by the Elizabethan tradition that valued female education. The residence possessed an excellent library, from which Anne read voraciously. At Sempringham, Anne was often in the company of educated individuals who were familiar with contemporary ideas about the nature of man, the universe, and politics. In 1628, Anne married Simon Bradstreet, a Cambridge-educated man and her father's protégé. Only sixteen when they married, Anne loved her husband with great devotion, remaining loyal to him the entire forty-four years of their marriage. Frail and often ill, Anne delivered eight children between 1633 and 1652, all but one of whom survived her. In 1630, the Dudleys and the Bradstreets sailed upon the *Arabella* with Puritan leader John Winthrop and the other founders of the Massachusetts Bay Company. Reaching Salem, Massachusetts on 22 July 1630, Anne's family relocated several times, each time attempting to improve their worldly estates. Leaving Salem, they settled first in Charlestown, then Newton (present-day Cambridge), Ipswich, and finally Andover.

Written by Anne and first published in 1650, *The Tenth Muse Lately Sprung Up in America* was a collection of poems, both larger in volume and more varied in subject than any previously published book of original poetry by a resident of British North America. The poems portray Anne's desire to express herself as an individual

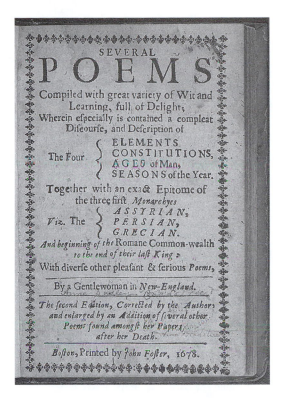

Title page of first American printing of Anne Bradstreet's book of poetry. (Library of Congress)

through her poetry, while carefully living in a society where personal autonomy deferred to the community and poetry was valued only so far as it glorified God. Anne's writing brings to life her daily struggle between the visible and invisible world, the religious and emotional conflicts she experienced as a female writer and as a Puritan. As a Puritan, she struggled to subdue her attachment to the world, but as a woman, she felt strongly connected to her husband, children, and community. While *The Tenth Muse* received general approval and sold well in England, it was not without its critics. Most notably, John Winthrop spoke out against Anne's boldness and willingness to forsake the traditional place of women in Puritan society. That Anne continued to write amid this criticism demonstrates her willingness to act independently, all the while remaining ever conscious of the precarious balance that must be observed lest she be tried and shunned from Puritan Massachusetts as her contemporary Anne Hutchinson had been. Anne Bradstreet died 16 September 1672 in the Bradstreet home in North Andover.

Joann Ross

See also Literary Culture and Women.
Bibliography
Primary Work
Hensley, Jeannine, ed. *The Works of Anne Bradstreet.* Cambridge, MA: Harvard University Press, 1967.
Secondary Works
Martin, Wendy. "Anne Bradstreet." In *Dictionary of Literary Biography,* vol. 24. Edited by Emory Elliott. Detroit, MI: Gale Research Co., 1984.
Stanford, Ann. "Anne Bradstreet: Dogmatist and Rebel." *The New England Quarterly* 39 (1966): 373–389.
Stanford, Ann. *Anne Bradstreet: The Worldly Puritan. An Introduction to Her Poetry.* New York: Burt Franklin and Co., 1974.
White, Elizabeth Wade. "The Tenth Muse—A Tercentenary Appraisal of Anne Bradstreet." *The William and Mary Quarterly* 8 (1951): 355–377.

Bresegna, Isabella (Breseña, Brisegna; 1510–1567)

Neapolitan noblewoman of Spanish birth, religious reform leader in Naples, member of Italian expatriate communities in Germany and Switzerland

The daughter of a Spanish noble, Isabella Bresegna was educated in Naples. In 1527, she married the Spanish captain Garcia Manriquez, with whom she had two sons and two daughters. Frequently absent, the captain let his more business-minded wife administer their wealth. Isabella heard the preaching of Bernardino Ochino at Naples in 1536 and within a few years had joined the circle of followers of Juan de Valdés, along with her close friend Giulia Gonzaga. In 1547 her husband was appointed governor of Piacenza; there,

while helping him govern, she hired or hosted heretics: the Anabaptist Girolamo Busale, Lorenzo Tizzano (who later confessed to the Inquisition discussing Luther's ideas with Giulia and Isabella in Naples), Juan de Villafranca (who supplied Tizzano with Luther's works), and the Lutheran Giovanni Laureto. In 1555, when Piacenza was taken over by the French, her family moved to Milan.

In 1557, as the prosecution of heretics intensified, Isabella fled across the Alps, leaving her family behind. Her brother, sons, and husband (whose brother was grand Inquisitor of Spain) urged her to return, but she replied that she would live only in a place that permitted freedom of conscience. After visiting the reformer Pier Paolo Vergerio in Tübingen, she moved to Zurich, where Ochino was pastor and where her son Pietro joined her. By 1559 she settled in Chiavenna, attending its evangelical church led by Agostino Mainardi. Isabella received visits in Switzerland from fellow expatriates such as Vergerio and Galeazzo Caracciolo. Other reformers dedicated writings to her: Ochino sent her his *Disputo intorno all presenza del Corpo di Gesu Cristo nel sacramento della Cena* (Basel, 1556); Celio Secondo Curione, whose religious ideas had been shaped by Mainardi, dedicated to her his first edition of Olympia Morata's posthumous *Opera omnia* (Basel, 1558).

Janet Smarr

See also Aragona, Giovanna d'; Aragona, Maria d'; Gonzaga, Giulia; Morata, Fulvia Olympia; Religious Reform and Women.
Bibliography
Bainton, Roland H. *Women of the Reformation in Germany and Italy.* Minneapolis: Augsburg Publishing House, 1971.
Casadei, Alfredo. "Donne della Riforma italiana: Isabella Bresegna." *Religio* 13 (1937): 6–63.
Church, Frederic C. *The Italian Reformers, 1534–1564.* New York: Octagon Books, 1974.

C

Cambis, Marguerite de (fl. 1550s)

Baronne d'Aigremont, translator into French of Trissino and Boccaccio

Marguerite de Cambis was born in Alès, near Nîmes, in the province of Languedoc, into a family of rich Florentine bankers, the Cambis, who immigrated for political reasons to Avignon at the beginning of the fifteenth century. Of the six children of Louis de Cambis, governor of Alès, and Marguerite de Pluviers, Marguerite was the youngest. Little is known of her youth, except that in 1550 she became the widow of Pons d'Alairac, Baron d'Aigremont, and that one year later she married Jacques de Rochemore, a doctor of law from Nîmes, best known for his translations of Spanish into French (*Le Favori de court* [The Court Favorite], Anvers, 1557), and of Tuscan into French (*Propos amoureux* [Conversations on Love], Lyons, 1573). Encouraged by her husband and solicited by her father, Marguerite de Cambis used her knowledge of both French and Tuscan to work on translations. In 1554, her first translation of an Italian text, the *Epistre du Seigneur Jean Trissin de la vie que doit tenir une Dame veuve* (Epistle by Lord Jean Trissi on the Conduct That a Widow Should Have), was published by Guillaume Rouillé, a successful erudite printer from Lyons. Unfortunately, this translation (mentioned in 1584 by Antoine DuVerdier in his catalogue of writers and translators of the time) is impossible to find today. Two years later, Marguerite de Cambis again published with Rouillé a translation of Boccaccio, *Epistre consolatoire de messire Jean Boccace, envoyée au Signeur Pino de Rossi* (Consolatory Epistle by Boccaccio to Lord Pino Rossi), dedicated to Loys de Cambis, Baron D'Alez, her father. After 1556, nothing further

is mentioned of her either as a translator or as a writer. Her dedicatory epistle of 1 May 1555 reveals sympathy for the author, Boccaccio, and the addressee, Signor Pino de Rossi (both Tuscans like her ancestors), as well as important information on the circumstances presiding over her translation, her own motivation, and her thought. Far from being a simple remedy for idleness, the translation of Boccaccio's epistle seems to have had a deep and personal resonance for Marguerite de Cambis. In the preface, she gives reasons for her enterprise, aware that she must negotiate her entry into a male-dominated world and maneuver within the social restrictions of her time. (Apart from some religious works, Renaissance texts were translated by men.) Based on her excellent knowledge of French and Tuscan, as Peletier du Mans recommends in his *Art poétique* (1555), her style is accurate, clear, and driven by the principles diffused by the *Pléiade* poets, especially by Du Bellay in his *Deffence et Illustration de la langue françoyse* (Defense and Illustration of the French Language) (1549), and Dolet in *La manière de bien traduire* (On the Best Way to Translate) (1540). Like her contemporaries, she associated translation with imitation, a principle common to scholars during the French Renaissance. Despite the difficulties of the Tuscan language of Trecento, Marguerite de Cambis gave a very satisfactory translation of Boccaccio, which entitles her critics to view it as a starting point in the formation of her literary identity. Her translation is highly indicative of the difficulties that feminine writers encountered when trying to obtain public recognition of their work as good translators, as was the case with Hélisenne de Crenne, Marie de Cotteblanche, Marie de

Romieu, Catherine des Roches, and Gabrielle de Coignard, or as an editor, as in the case of Marie de Gournay. Moreover, translations from the sixteenth century, as important documents for demonstrating the progression of the French language, illustrate the important role that women of the Renaissance played in promoting vernacular languages. In addition, women were also vital in the diffusion in French of works by major Italian writers from the Trecento and Quattrocento, like Dante, Petrarch, Boccaccio, Castiglione, and Ariosto. This enduring interest in Italian literature began during the Italian Wars (1494–1519) and was promoted essentially by women who were queens like Anne de France, Marguerite de Navarre, and Marguerite de Valois, and by erudite printers like Abel l'Angelier, Jean de Tournes, and Guillaume Rouillé.

Graziella Postolache

See also Literary Culture and Women; Translation and Women Translators.

Bibliography

Primary Works

Marguerite de Cambis. *Epistre consolatoire de messire Jean Boccace, envoyée au Signeur Pino de Rossi.* Lyons: Guillaume Rouillé, 1556.

Marguerite de Cambis. *Epistre consolatoire de messire Jean Boccace, envoyée au Signeur Pino de Rossi (1556).* Edited by Colette H. Winn. Paris: Champion, 2003.

Marguerite de Cambis. *Epistre du Seigneur Jean Trissin de la vie que doit tenir une Dame veuve.* Lyons: Guillaume Rouillé, 1554.

Secondary Works

Balsamo, Jean. "Traduire de l'italien: ambitions sociales et contraintes éditoriales à la fin du XVIᵉ siècle." In *Traduire et adapter à la Renaissance.* Edited by Dominique de Courcelles and Carmen Val Julian, 89–98. Paris: Publication de L'Ecole des Chartes, 1999.

Chavy, Paul. *Traducteurs d'autrefois. Moyen Age et Renaissance. Dictionnaire des traducteurs et de la literature traduite en ancien et moyen français (842–1600).* Two volumes. Paris: Champion; Geneva: Slatkine, 1988.

Rickard, Peter. "Le rôle des traducteurs." In *La langue française au seizième siècle. Etude suivie de textes,* 6–14. Cambridge: Cambridge University Press, 1968.

Campiglia, Maddalena (1553–1595)

Vicenzan writer, author of one of the first published pastoral plays by a woman

Relatively little is known about Maddalena Campiglia's life, but it is clear that she was born to parents from the minor civic elite in Vicenza, at that time part of the Venetian republic. She received a good education in letters and music, and was married in 1576 to a local nobleman, Dionisio Colzé. The marriage, contracted perhaps for financial reasons, proved unsuccessful, possibly connected with the fact that the couple remained childless, and by the early 1580s Campiglia was living separately from her spouse. Unusually, she did not choose to observe a religious life as a tertiary in a religious order, as has been posited without conclusive evidence. Instead, as an independent laywoman, she devoted herself to literary and spiritual concerns, as represented in her portrait attributed to Alessandro Maganza. Campiglia's marriage was apparently never formally dissolved, so she remained in this anomalous situation, outside the standard female estates of marriage or widowhood, until her death at the age of forty-two.

Campiglia's writings, all datable from this period of independence, show a remarkable ability to experiment with contemporary literary conventions in order to develop a distinctly feminine voice. Her first known work, published in 1585 (*Discorso sopra l'Annonciatione della Beata Vergine* [Discourse on the Annunciation of the Blessed Virgin]), marks an unusual departure for a woman writer as one of the earliest extended works of devotional prose, following the example of Vittoria Colonna. The edifying spiritual subject matter would have helped to offset any doubts raised by her social position, as would the dedication of the work to a nun from the local nobility (Suor Vittoria Trissina Frattina). Even so, numerous accompanying poetic tributes by male literati—some by members of the prestigious Olympic Academy (Accademia Olimpica) of Vicenza—point to

Campiglia's wider cultural aspirations. These perhaps began to be realized when family connections brought her within the sphere of the Gonzaga dynasty. Her acquaintance in this courtly context with poets like Muzio Manfredi and Bernardino Baldi, as well as patronage by Curzio Gonzaga and Isabella Pallavicino Lupi, Marchioness of Soragna, probably encouraged her composition of fashionable Petrarchan, neo-Platonic, and pastoral verse, as well as her interest in pastoral drama.

Campiglia's *Flori, favola boscareccia* (1588, dedicated to Gonzaga and Pallavicino Lupi) represents, together with Isabella Andreini's *Mirtilla* (1588), the first known female-authored pastoral play in print. This appeared as the form was rapidly gaining popularity in Italy following Tasso's celebrated *Aminta* (printed 1580/1581). Various allusions to the *Aminta* are made in *Flori,* while its emphasis on religious and tragic themes suggests a familiarity also with Guarini's still unpublished masterpiece of the genre, *Il Pastor fido* (printed 1589/1590), and demonstrates the decorous way in which the pastoral mode could be used by a "serious" woman writer. Nonetheless, the introduction of radical changes to the representation of amorous relationships in this Arcadian world provides a more challenging feminine perspective. This is especially true of the main plot which centers around the nymph Flori (a name also used elsewhere to allude to the author). The protagonist is initially mad with love for another (dead) nymph; and even after her "cure" through a societal sacrifice, when she falls in love with a male shepherd, she rejects the standard outcome of marriage in favor of a chaste union more conducive to literary pursuits. The play was widely praised by contemporaries, including Tasso, though the mainly eulogistic verse appearing in an appendix to some editions of the play hints at the unease felt by a few readers regarding its portrayal of female-female desire. It is unclear whether the play was meant for performance; none is recorded.

The following year, Campiglia's pastoral eclogue *Calisa* appeared in an anthology to mark the dynastic wedding of Pallavicino Lupi's son, an occasion that explains its explicit encomiastic allusions. The verse dialogue again presents Flori's love for a nymph, this time Calisa (identifiable as Pallavicino), which invited less polemical parallels with the devotion of the writer for her patron but similarly raised issues concerning female friendship and creativity. This appears to be Campiglia's last substantial work, although she contributed editorial material to a heroic poem by Curzio Gonzaga, as well as verse for various anthologies and as accompaniments to other works. Some unpublished writings were left at her death, and evidence suggests she may have been planning a longer narrative verse composition on the life of Saint Barbara. Campiglia's surviving poetry is mainly in a neo-Platonic or spiritual vein, though surprisingly it includes some rustic verse following a local tradition. Thus, Campiglia may be regarded as having negotiated imaginatively the delicate balance required in preserving her social reputation while venturing more ambitiously into the "public" world of print.

Lisa Sampson

See also Andreini, Isabella; Literary Culture and Women; Theater and Women Actors, Playwrights, and Patrons.

Bibliography

Primary Works

Campiglia, Maddalena. *Calisa, ecloga.* Vicenza: 1589.

Campiglia, Maddalena. *Discorso sopra l'Annonciatione della Beata Vergine, e la Incarnatione del S[ignor] N[ostro] Giesu Christo.* Vicenza: 1585.

Campiglia, Maddalena. *Flori, favola boscareccia.* Vicenza: 1588. (Some editions include an appendix with celebratory verse.)

Secondary Works

Cox, Virginia, trans. *Flori, a pastoral drama.* With introduction and notes by Virginia Cox and Lisa Sampson. Chicago: University of Chicago Press, 2004. (Bilingual edition.)

De Marco, Giuseppe. *Maddalena Campiglia: La figura e l'opera.* Vicenza: 1988. (Includes some verse.)

Mantese, Giovanni. "Per un profilo storico della poetessa vicentina Maddalena Campiglia: Aggiunte e rettifiche." *Archivio veneto* 81 (1967): 89–123.

Milani, Marisa. "Quattro donne fra i pavani." *Museum Patavinum* 1 (1983): 387–412.

Morsolin, Bernardo. *Maddalena Campiglia, poetessa vicentina del secolo XVI: Episodio biografico.* Vicenza: 1882.

Mutini, Claudio. "Campiglia, Maddalena." In *Dizionario biografico degli italiani,* 17: 541–542. Rome: Istituto dell'Enciclopedia Italiana, 1974.

Perrone, Carlachiara. *"So che donna ama donna":* La Calisa *di Maddalena Campiglia.* Galatina: Congedo, 1996. (Includes an edition of *Calisa.*)

Sartori, Diana. "Maddalena Campiglia." In *Le stanze ritrovate: Antologia di scrittrici venete dal Quattrocento al Novecento.* Edited by Antonia Arslan, Adriana Chemello, and Gilberto Pizzamiglio, 57–68. Mirano, Venice: 1991.

Ultsch, Lori J. "Epithalamium Interruptum: Maddalena Campiglia's New Arcadia," *MLN* 120, no. 1 (2005).

Ultsch, Lori J. "Maddalena Campiglia, 'dimessa nel mondano cospetto'?: Secular Celibacy, Devotional Communities, and Social Identity in Early Modern Vicenza." *Forum Italicum* no. 2 (Fall 2005): 350–377.

Cary, Elizabeth Tanfield (ca. 1585–1639)

Lady Falkland, author known for the broad range of her writings including a work for the theater

Elizabeth Tanfield Cary was the first Englishwoman to write and subsequently publish a tragedy, *The Tragedy of Mariam* (1602–1604, published 1613). Cary is also acknowledged for her authorship of *The History of the Life, Reign, and Death of Edward II* (ca. 1627–1628). Further literary works—some extant, some lost—include verse hymns and poems, classical and biblical translations, and advice manuals written for her children.

Many details of Elizabeth Cary's life come from a biography, which one (or more) of her daughters probably wrote. From *Lady Falkland: Her Life* (ca. 1655), scholars frequently cite Cary's deference to her superiors, such as kneeling in her mother's presence and struggling to please her husband. Cary's early affection for learning and her amazing facility with languages are also mentioned. Born into a wealthy English family, Elizabeth Tanfield was contracted to marry Henry Cary in 1602. The arrangement socially elevated Cary and her family through marriage into an aristocratic family while simultaneously providing Henry Cary with a rich dowry. Elizabeth Cary eventually defied her husband when, against his wishes, she embraced the Catholic faith, a decision that confirmed her independent spirit while also placing her in an unfortunate situation in which she endured extreme financial hardships.

Cary's experimentation with the genres favored by authors like Samuel Daniel and Ben Jonson, such as the great house entertainment and the antimasque, affords additional insight into the ways Cary draws connections between domestic and political tyranny in *The Tragedy of Mariam.* As Cary's recent editors have observed, when interpreting her best-known play, any material from *Her Life* also needs to be "considered alongside the play's dramatic inheritance and *Mariam's* position in the history of Renaissance tragedy" (Cerasano and Wynne-Davies 1996, 46).

Debra Barrett-Graves

See also Religious Reform and Women; Theater and Women Actors, Playwrights, and Patrons.

Bibliography

Primary Works

Cary, Elizabeth. *The Lady Falkland: Her Life.* Edited by Barry Weller and Margaret Ferguson. Berkeley: University of California Press, 1994.

Cary, Elizabeth. *The Tragedy of Mariam: The Fair Queen of Jewry.* London: 1613.

Cary, Elizabeth. *The Tragedy of Mariam. Renaissance Drama by Women: Texts and Contexts.* Edited by S. P. Cerasano and Marion Wynne-Davies, 43–75. London: Routledge, 1996.

Secondary Works

Findlay, Alison, Stephanie Hodgson-Wright, and Gweno Williams. *Women and Dramatic Produc-*

tion: 1550–1700. Harlow, UK: Longman, 2000.

Levin, Carole, Debra Barrett-Graves, Jo Eldridge Carney, W. M. Spellman, Gwynne Kennedy, and Stephanie Witham. "Elizabeth Cary." In *Extraordinary Women of the Medieval and Renaissance World: A Biographical Dictionary.* Westport, CT: Greenwood Press, 2000.

Catherine de Médicis (Catherine de' Medici; 1519–1589)

Queen consort and queen mother

Mother of ten children and the last three Valois kings of France, dauphiness, queen, regent, poet, and patron, Catherine de Médicis was born in Florence, Italy, the daughter of Lorenzo de' Medici (II), duke of Urbino, and Madeleine de la Tour d'Auvergne, who was related by her mother Catherine de Bourbon to the royal house of France. She was married at the age of thirteen to Henry II, duc d'Orléans, second son of Francis I who arranged the ceremony to ensure better relationships with Pope Clement VII and prevent the expansion of the empire of Charles V. Unfortunately, the death of the pope ruined the royal hopes. Consequently, Catherine was relegated to a minor role where she remained even when she became dauphiness at the death of her husband's elder brother. Unable to bear any children for the first ten years, she was in the shadow of her husband's mistress, Diane de Poitiers, and the mistress of Francis I, the Duchesse d'Etampes. When Henry II acceded to the throne on 31 March 31 1557, she became queen of France but remained inconspicuous except for a brief period when she acted as regent during Henry's short campaign in Lorraine.

Her political career really began at the death of Henry II in July 1559. She ruled as regent for her second son, Charles IX, until he reached his majority in 1563, and she continued to dominate him for the duration of his reign. During these years, Catherine devoted

Catherine de Médicis, queen of France and mother of three French kings. Portrait by anonymous French painter. Palazzo Pitti, Florence. (Library of Congress)

her energy to maintaining a balance between the Protestant group known as the Huguenots, led by the military leader Gaspard de Coligny, and the Roman Catholics, led by the powerful house of Guise. To establish the dominion of the royal family, she maneuvered between those two groups. During the religious civil wars that began in 1562, Catherine, a Roman Catholic, usually supported the Catholics, though sometimes she was close to the Huguenots. Thus she strove to ensure the independence and political self-government of French royalty.

Her political manipulations also affected the personal affairs of her family. In 1560 she arranged for her daughter, Elisabeth of Valois, to become the third wife of the powerful Roman

Catholic king of Spain, Philip II. She married another daughter, Marguerite de Valois, to the Protestant Henry of Navarre, who later became Henry IV, king of France. Later in 1572, frightened by the growing Huguenot influence over her son, King Charles IX, she hatched a plot to murder the Protestant leader Coligny that led to his death and the deaths of an estimated 50,000 other Huguenots in the St. Bartholomew's Day Massacre (1572). When another of her sons, Henry III, came to power, she started to lose her political influence. For twelve years, France was under the control of the Guises, and the relentless warfare against the Huguenots helped to fortify their power. Constantly intriguing, she used all means possible to prolong the rule of the Valois, even saving her son's honor during the Day of the Barricades (12 May 1588) in the latter's negotiations with Henri de Guise, whose murder, however, was soon ordered by Henry III. Placing her family and the interests of her children first, she died wondering how the last Valois king would remain in power.

Praising her in his *Discours des misères de ce temps* (Discourse on the Miseries of the Times), Ronsard described her as capable of preserving national unity. She attempted to do so when, with the Peace of St. Germain in 1570, she formally declared that the Protestants should gain their own legitimate and independent churches.

Besides her political role, Catherine was also a great patron of the arts. She wrote poetry in Italian and influenced the art and literature of the court through her patronage, particularly of the Pléiade poets. She initiated the construction of a new wing of the Louvre palace, had the Tuileries palace built, enriched the Bibliothèque Royale with many rare manuscripts, and built the château of Monceau and the Hotel de Soissons. She organized the renovation of the castle of Chenonceau. A disciple of Machiavelli, she was a woman of the Renaissance whose main political objective as queen mother was to save her royal children at any cost.

Martine Sauret

See also Art and Women; the subheading Literary Patronage (under Literary Culture and Women); Marguerite de Valois; Poitiers, Diane de; Power, Politics, and Women; Religious Reform and Women.

Bibliography

Primary Work

de la Ferrière, Hector, and Gustave Basguenault de Puchesse, eds. *Lettres de Catherine de Médicis.* 10 vols. Paris: Imprimerie Nationale, 1880–1909.

Secondary Works

Cloulas, Yvan. *Catherine de Médicis.* Paris: Fayard, 1981.

Folliott, Sheila. "Catherine de'Medici as Artemisia: Figuring the Powerful Widow." In *Rewriting the Renaissance: The Discourse of Sexual Difference in Early Modern Europe.* Edited by Margaret W. Ferguson, Maureen Quilligan, and Nancy J. Vickers, 227–241. Chicago: University of Chicago Press, 1986.

Garrisson, Janine. *Catherine de Médicis. L'impossible harmonie.* Paris: Payot, 2002.

Vray, Nicole. *La guerre des religions dans la France de l'Ouest. Poitou, Aunis, Saintonge 1534-1610.* LaCrèche: Geste Editions, 1997.

Catherine of Aragon (1485–1536)

Queen and consort of King Henry VIII

Born to the most Catholic monarchs Ferdinand II of Aragon and Isabella of Castile on 16 December 1485, Catherine of Aragon began her life during one of the most tumultuous eras of Spanish history. Throughout the first six years of her life, Catherine experienced the Spanish Reconquista first hand, and when Isabella exposed her youngest daughter to the rigors of military campaigning, Catherine and her sisters also experienced the training necessary to serve as the next generation of queens throughout Western Europe. Isabella hired the best humanist educators of the late medieval period, mixing nontraditional instruction in the humanities with the traditional training in the domestic arts. Catherine learned Latin and read biblical literature and works of devotion, Ambrose, Augustine, Jerome, Christian and

Catherine of Aragon, queen and wife of King Henry VIII of England. Portrait by unknown artist. National Portrait Gallery, London. (Corel)

pagan classics, and some civil and canon law. She also learned dancing, sewing, spinning, and baking. Her classical education was such that Erasmus later remarked that Catherine was a miracle of feminine learning.

From the age of three, Ferdinand and Isabella had pursued a match for Catherine with Arthur, prince of Wales, the eldest son of Henry VII, king of England. After many years of negotiation and delay, Catherine finally set sail for England and arrived at Plymouth on 2 October 1501, with her marriage at St. Paul's Cathedral taking place a little more than a month later. The English crowds greeted Catherine warmly, and every indication suggested she would have a long, healthy, and successful life first as princess of Wales, and eventually as queen.

The reality of life for Catherine between the fall of 1501 and the spring of 1509 was entirely different. Arthur died just five months

into the marriage, never having consummated their relationship. To make matters worse for Catherine, dowry payments from Spain were late, and Henry VII blamed Catherine's father and chose to mistreat Catherine. For almost eight years, Catherine's position in England was tenuous at best. Though Henry VII had agreed to another marriage arrangement in 1503, this time between Catherine and his remaining son, Henry, Duke of York, the English, king took every opportunity to neglect his daughter-in-law, often failing to provide for her and her dwindling household beyond the barest of necessities. During these dark times Catherine also believed her father and his ambassadors had abandoned her since they failed to provide sufficient finances for her. Upon Henry VII's death in April 1509, Catherine's position once again changed for the better, but not before circumstances had taught her that she was her own best counsel and support.

Henry VIII, claiming it was his father's wish, married Catherine in May 1509. Through 1515, Catherine's place as chief confidant and advisor to Henry had no rival, and she filled her duties as consort and wife, making great use of her education in all fields. Catherine's chief accomplishments during this period included the continued preservation of the Anglo-Spanish alliance and the defeat of James IV, king of Scotland, at Flodden Field. Though Catherine did not actually partake in the battle, the responsibility of maintaining a secure realm was hers alone, since Henry had made her governor of the realm and captain-general of all forces left in England while he went off to war in France. Her loyalty to Henry was unequivocal.

Catherine's chief fault, however, was her inability to produce a healthy male heir. While she had given birth to Princess Mary in 1516 and had had several stillbirths and miscarriages, Henry and many of his nobility were unwilling to lay the destiny of the country in the hands of a woman. Thus by the early 1520s, Henry believed himself in a desperate situation dynastically and sought a way out of the marriage. Through Cardinal Wolsey, in 1529 Henry pushed for an annulment of his twenty-year marriage based upon the belief that he had sinned in marrying his brother's wife. Further complicating the picture and Henry's motive was a young woman with whom he had fallen in love, Anne Boleyn.

From 1527 to 1533, Henry's chief aim was to separate himself from Catherine, regardless of the cost. For Catherine's part, she fought Henry at every turn, wanting to protect her daughter's rights to the throne and her own reputation as queen. Yet, Henry was far too powerful and fearsome a king, who made use of a weakened papacy and a strengthening English parliament to break away from the Catholic church, annul his marriage to Catherine, and marry his then pregnant mistress.

Now the dowager princess of Wales, Catherine spent her remaining years in England believing herself a martyr for the Catholic faith and for her daughter. Henry had Catherine shipped from palace to palace, each succeeding house in worse condition than the one before. Nevertheless, Catherine showed remarkable fortitude during the years 1533–1536, refusing to bend to Henry's demands and always believing she was his legitimate wife. Her death in January 1536, probably of a rare form of cancer, saw her striving to the end in a failed bid to bring Henry back to his senses and to her arms.

Timothy G. Elston

See also Boleyn, Anne; Education, Humanism, and Women; Power, Politics, and Women.

Bibliography

Claremont, Francesca. *Catherine of Aragon.* London: Robert Hale Limited, 1939.

Fraser, Antonia. *The Six Wives of Henry VIII.* London: Weidenfeld and Nicolson, 1992.

Loades, David. *Henry VIII and His Queens.* Gloucestershire, UK: Sutton, 1994. (Reprinted in 1997.)

Mattingly, Garrett. *Catherine of Aragon.* Boston: Little, Brown and Company, 1941.

Starkey, David. *Six Wives: The Queens of Henry VIII.* New York: Harper Collins, 2003.

Catherine of Siena (1347–1380)

Ambassador, mystic, prophet, writer, reformer, martyr, nurse, and virginal "Mamma" to dozens of loyal followers

This is only a partial list of some of the titles wielded by Catherine of Siena in her brief lifetime. Yet it reflects seemingly contradictory aspects of Catherine's career that have caused many scholars to contrast her contemplative life with her active life—the latter exceptional for a woman from a lower-class family, the twenty-fourth of twenty-five children who had no formal schooling. And yet in Catherine's *Dialogue* with God and her almost four hundred letters to kings, popes, senators, and clerics as well as to humble women like herself, one sees continuity rather than contradiction. As Giovanni Getto has put it, we witness in her life "the exterior projection of an interior phenomenon"—a phenomenon that was not valid unless it was communicated and acted upon in a world that for Catherine had no boundaries. The question is not only why she believed in her authority to act, but why so many others believed in her as well.

Born in 1347 on the threshold of the most devastating plague ever to strike Europe, Catherine was early on entranced by transvestite saints and calls to a desert life of solitude. Refusing marriage, she cut off her hair at age twelve and was forced by her irate family to wait on them as a servant and live in a small cell in the basement. Her eventually successful struggle to become a *mantellata,* or third-order Dominican (Catherine was not a cloistered nun, as many think), is a further indication of her desire to rebel against convention and others' expectations for her. In Siena in the 1360s, only widows were permitted to live as *mantellate* in loosely organized communities and administer to the poor, sick, and needy. The connection with a group of women similar to the Beguines of France and Flanders fostered in Catherine deeply held beliefs about charity and the necessity of loving God through one's neighbor, or *prossimo.* As Catherine puts it suc-

Saint Catherine of Siena, ambassador, mystic, prophet, writer, reformer, and martyr. Painting by Fra Bartolommeo. (Arte and Immagini / Corbis)

cinctly in a letter from 1377 to the Countess Bandecca Salimbeni, "we cannot give any service to God, so God has us do it for our neighbors" (Noffke 2001).

Yet fundamental to Catherine's development as a religious leader was what she called the ability to enter the cell of self-knowledge, a spiritual cell that probably had its basis in the small, subterranean room where she spent her adolescence. While the self that she advocates knowing is "nothing" next to God, it is also a self that has been given the power of free will; and in Catherine's claims for the dignity and freedom of that will, she is closer to humanist conceptions of the self than to the thundering threats and chastisements of medieval preachers. For her, the will, much like charity and like life itself, is spoken of as a *donna,* or woman: "Free woman that she is, neither the devil nor

anyone else can force her to sin any more than she chooses to" (Noffke 2001, Letter T44).

This is a will that Catherine exercises (the Italian word *esercitare*—literally, to put something into movement—is ubiquitous in her writing) at every possible opportunity. This is the case even though she claims simultaneously that she is doing only the will of Christ, a claim buttressed by her mystical marriage with Jesus in imitation of that other Catherine, of Alexandria, and by her receiving (invisible) stigmata in Pisa in 1375. Her letters almost always open with the shrill phrase "*Io voglio*" ("I want"), followed by imposing declarations: "I want to see you live in the light and fire of the Holy Spirit"; "I want to see you grounded in true patience"; "I want" (this to Pope Gregory XI) "to see you become a good shepherd." Her desires and those of Christ took her finally to see Gregory in person in Avignon, where the papacy had been based since the early fourteenth century, but they also brought her twice before inquisitors anxious to determine the orthodoxy of these fervently expressed wishes.

Yet of the three earthly missions that preoccupied Catherine in the last five years of her life—the pope's return to Rome, a new Crusade, and procuring peace among the papacy and the Italian states—only the first was a real success. Even that was marred by the refusal of the French and others to accept Gregory's successor, Urban VI, as pope, thereby ushering in the forty-year schism. The world in which Catherine wrote, preached, and worked was a complex and embattled one, struggling to find stability in the wake of plague, brigands, mercenaries, and constant power struggles between various cities and nations. Like her contemporary Petrarch, Catherine dreamt of a united Italy, and the words that end his famous canzone *L'Italia mia*—"peace, peace, peace"— are often Catherine's as well, as they would have been of many others in an age of infighting among families and cities. (Catherine herself was suspected of betraying her fellow Sienese when she spent several months trying to broker a deal with the exiled Salimbeni family outside the city.) Her hope was that, once the papacy was restored to Rome, the Italian peninsula could become united and focus on the real enemy—the Muslims, infidels across the sea who controlled the holy city of Jerusalem that should have been "rightfully" Christian. Gregory's return, however, only infuriated Roman nobles who had been happily governing without him, as well as other parties fearful of papal aggression into their territories. Moreover, the hoped-for reforms within the Church about which Catherine's God is so outspoken in the *Dialogue* were not forthcoming in Catherine's lifetime, even though she came to Rome in the last eighteen months of her life to turn herself into a daily spectacle of grief and penitence, dragging her starved and enfeebled body from Santo Maria sopra Minerva to the papal residence in the hope of persuading Urban and the Roman people to "exercise" their will and act on behalf of charity and God. She died in April 1380 surrounded by the disciples who had taken down every word she had uttered in her final years, including the moving sermon she spoke on her deathbed. Canonized only in 1461 by her Sienese compatriot Pope Pius II, she was pronounced a doctor of the church in 1970 and Patron Saint of Europe in 1999.

These recent titles are welcome because they restore to Catherine the reputation that for centuries had been obscured: a public figure, intent on uniting her fellow Europeans, albeit under the banner of a questionable crusade, and promulgator of an original and intensely humane version of Christian charity. The intervening period had portrayed her as primarily a solitary mystic transfixed by her love for her spouse Jesus Christ and living a life of meditation. Meditation there no doubt was. The *Dialogue* could not have been generated without it, and even some of her letters are said to have been dictated in a trance. But it is important to insist on Catherine's later life as a peripatetic one, divided among Siena, Pisa, Florence, Avignon, Rome, and the little towns and feudal holdings in the Tuscan countryside. Like her favorite author, Saint Paul, she was a *banditore,* or herald, for Christ; like her fellow *mantellate*—many of whom out of jealousy or fear for their own reputations were suspicious of her highly public persona—she practiced charity in a visible and efficacious way: "[I]n my love and hunger for your salvation," she writes the wife of Bernabo' Visconti of Milan, "I would rather act than just talk." This translation of speech into action and her encouragement of others to do the same—she constantly tells popes and city officials to bear fruit—parallels her own inspired translation of the Latin Vulgate into a vernacular that has made her writings—the first in Italian by a woman—supple and remarkably vibrant documents that seek to persuade, harangue, energize, and force others to *esercitare* their own versions of charity.

Why others apparently capitulated to these harangues is one final and not easily answerable question. When one takes into account that Catherine was the contemporary of another forceful and influential woman, Bridget of Sweden, and that she predates by only forty years La Pucelle d'Orléans (Joan of Arc), who for a time had her own loyal followers as she fought to save France, one recognizes the particularity of an era that found leadership in strong and imposing women. On the one hand, there was undoubtedly the mystique surrounding an unlettered woman who was said to have spoken more wisely than learned men when she was called to the court of Urban. Surely, once her orthodoxy was assured, she could only be speaking so knowledgeably because God was working through her. The unsettledness of the times and the open corruptness of the papal curate in Avignon and later in Rome encouraged contemporaries to look for other sources of enlightenment, and Catherine clearly obliged them. On the other hand, Catherine was nothing if not shrewd in both her understanding of human psychology—she is adroit in shaming men into acting like men and fellow religious for having believed false rumors about her—and her manipulation of her public appearances: She could be humble and diplomatic when she needed to be and willingly recognized others' authority over her even as she claimed to have a uniquely intimate relationship with God: "Don't make it necessary for me to complain about you to Christ," she bitingly tells Gregory XI at the end of a letter persuading him to act "like a man" and come back to Rome. In this forceful personality exemplified in hundreds of letters and in a *Dialogue* in which Catherine dares to speak with the voice of *Provvidenza,* or God, we see a commanding and subtle presence that deserves to be placed alongside Dante as the founding mother of Italian literature.

Jane Tylus

See also Beguines; the subheading Letter Writing (under Literary Culture and Women).

Bibliography
Primary Works
Cavallini, Giuliana, ed. *Il Dialogo della divina provvidenza.* Rome: Edizioni cateriniani, 1968.
di Antonio da Siena, Tommaso. *Santa Caterina da Siena: Legenda minore.* Translated by Bruno Ancilli. Siena: Cantagalli, 1998.
Laurent, Marie-Hyacinthe, ed. *Il Processo Castellano. Fontes vitae s. Catharinae Senensis historici.* Milan: Bocca, 1942.
Noffke, Suzanne, trans. *The Dialogue of Catherine of Siena.* New York: Paulist Press, 1980.
Noffke, Suzanne, trans. *The Letters of Catherine of Siena.* Tempe: Arizona Center for Medieval and Renaissance Studies, 2001.
Raymond of Capua. *The Life of Saint Catherine of Siena.* Translated by Conleth Kearns. Wilmington, DE: Michael Glazier, Inc., 1980.
S. Caterina da Siena. *Le lettere.* Edited by D. Umberto Meattini. Milan: Edizioni Paoline, 1987.
Secondary Works
Fawtier, Robert. *Sainte Catherine de Sienne: Essaie de citique des sources, I. Sources hagiographiques.* Paris: De Boccard, 1921.
Fawtier, Robert. *Sainte Catherine de Sienne: Essaie de citique des sources, II. Les oeuvres de Sainte Catherine de Sienne.* Paris: De Boccard, 1930.
Getto, Giovanni. *Saggio letterario su S. Caterina da Siena.* Florence: Sansoni, 1939.
Noffke, Suzanne. *Catherine of Siena: Vision Through a Distant Eye.* Collegeville, MN: Liturgical Press/Michael Glazier, 1996.
Scott, Karen. "*Io Catarina:* Ecclesastical Politics and Oral Culture in the Letters of Catherine of Siena." In *Dear Sister: Medieval Women and the Epistolary Genre.* Edited by Karen Cherewatuk and Ulrike Wiethaus, 87–121. Philadelphia: University of Pennsylvania Press, 1993.
Tylus, Jane. "Caterina da Siena and the Legacy of Humanism." In *Perspectives on Early Modern and Modern Intellectual History.* Edited by Joseph Marino and Melinda Schlitt, 116–144. Rochester, NY: University of Rochester Press, 2001.
Zancan, Marina. "Lettere di Caterina da Siena." In *Letteratura italiana. Le Opere: Dalle Origini al Cinquecento.* Edited by A. Asor Rosa, I: 593–633. Turin: Einaudi, 1992.

Cavendish, Elizabeth Brackley (1626–1663) and Jane Cavendish (1621–1669)

Coauthors of a pastoral play, a drama, and poetry; daughters of William Cavendish, duke of Newcastle, and his first wife, Elizabeth Bassett

The Cavendish sisters, Elizabeth Brackley and Jane, were encouraged by their father to engage in literary pursuits, and they did. They are best known for their coauthored drama, *The Concealed Fancies* (ca.1645), and jointly wrote a pastoral masque and poetry. Their stepmother Margaret Cavendish (who was thirty years their father's junior when she married him in 1645) was also a published author, making the literary women of the Cavendish family as prolific as those of the acclaimed Sidneys.

During the English Civil War, Elizabeth (known as Elizabeth Brackley or E.B. in her manuscripts) and Jane were left at the family estate at Welbeck Abbey with their younger sister Frances while their father and brothers served the Royalist forces. Welbeck Abbey was captured by Parliamentary forces in 1644 and surrendered the following year. It is ironic that this period of confinement for the Cavendish sisters should result in the literary freedom marked by their dramatic text. In *The Concealed Fancies* the authors challenge social attitudes toward both class and gender. The play's heroines educate their suitors on a woman's proper role in marriage; the heroines demand their autonomy and contradict the traditional expectations of obedience. While the play is a comedy ending in multiple marriages, the realities of war serve as a backdrop to these events.

The elements of autobiography in the text are not limited to references of war but extend to the script's preoccupation with a woman's role in marriage. At the time *The Concealed Fancies* was written, Elizabeth would have been married to John Egerton, Viscount Brackley. The two wed in 1636, but Elizabeth remained in her father's home due to her young age. After the Cavendish family vacated Welbeck, Elizabeth went to the Egerton family home. By all accounts, her marriage was a happy one. She continued to write poetry and meditations and raised four children. When she died in 1663 as result of premature labor, Egerton distributed her writings to her family. Jane married Charles Cheney in 1654 and also appears to have made a happy match. She died in 1669 after a series of epileptic fits. Her only extant poem was written on the death of her sister Elizabeth.

Michelle Osherow

See also Cavendish, Margaret; Theater and Women Actors, Playwrights, and Patrons.

Bibliography

Cerasano, S. P., and Marion Wynne-Davies, eds. *Renaissance Drama by Women: Texts and Documents.* London and New York: Routledge, 1996.

Wynne-Davies, Marion, ed. *Women Poets of the Renaissance.* New York: Routledge, 1999.

Cavendish, Margaret (1623–1673)

Duchess of Newcastle, writer of the first utopia written by a woman; author of twenty-three published books including poetry, plays, science fiction, philosophical essays, romances, and autobiography

Margaret Cavendish née Lucas was born in Essex, the youngest of eight children, to a wealthy royalist family. When the English Civil War broke out in 1642, the family moved to Oxford, where Margaret served as lady-in-waiting to Queen Henrietta Maria, the wife of King Charles I of England (1600–1649). In 1644 she followed the queen into exile in Paris. There Margaret met and married the Royalist William Cavendish, the duke of Newcastle, who had commanded the king's forces at Marston Moor. After the execution of King Charles I and Newcastle's official banishment from England in 1549, Margaret and William lived as exiles in Antwerp. It was during this time that Margaret began writing. Margaret and her husband were well acquainted with Thomas Hobbes (1588–1679), the English philosopher, and through him they met René Descartes (1595–1650) and other notable intellectuals. Encouraged by her husband to pursue a career in writing, Margaret produced numerous works in verse and prose. Her first volume of poems was entitled *Poems and Fancies* (1653). Because of its status as a volume of poetry published by a woman, the work was received as an oddity in England. Cavendish's contemporary, Dorothy Osborne, after reading the book, quipped in a letter to Sir William Temple "that there [were] many soberer People in Bedlam" (Battigelli 1998, 4). Two years after the publication of *Poems and Fancies,* Cavendish's next major and most daring work, her fictional utopia, *The Description of a New World, Called the Blazing World* (1655), again elicited disparaging comments from her contemporaries. Cavendish's experience in the English Civil Wars (ca. 1642–1648), reflected in all her writings, is perhaps most palpable in her utopian vision of society in *The Blazing World.*

The first utopian novel to be authored by a woman, *The Blazing World* is today acclaimed as a classic. Critics have also been slow to acknowledge the achievements of the two dozen plays that Cavendish authored. While recent

Margaret Cavendish, duchess of Newcastle and author of twenty-three books. Portrait by unkown artist. (Bettmann/Corbis)

scholars such as Gweno Williams have argued for the performability of her plays and their valence as theater, questions about whether the plays were actually performed remain. Others have noted that Cavendish clearly had a public audience in mind whenever she wrote. In her many prefaces, she defends her writing, considers critical theory, and comments on the material aspects of the publication process. In spite of her own statements about her lack of formal training, comments for which her contemporaries and subsequent critics were only too willing to dismiss Cavendish and her work, Cavendish's writings demonstrate her interest in the cultural and intellectual ideas circulating during her lifetime. Although Cavendish and her subsequent critics publicly stated that she never revised her works or cared about them after they had been published, textual evidence now exists documenting both her revisions and handmade corrections.

Margaret Cavendish gained notoriety because of her unusual dress and eccentric behav-

ior, but it is through the legacy of her varied and extensive writings that her unique literary contributions should be assessed. Among those who criticized Cavendish, Samuel Pepys (1633–1703) dismissed her as a "mad, conceited, ridiculous woman" (Bowerbank 1984, 392). In the twentieth century, Virginia Woolf spoke of the "loneliness and riot" of Cavendish's writings, adding that it was "as if some giant cucumber had spread itself over all the roses and carnations in the garden and choked them to death" (Bowerbank 1984, 392). Recent reception of her work has focused not only on Cavendish's engagement with the philosophical ideas and scientific experiments of her era but also on the originality and depth of her thought.

Debra Barrett-Graves

See also Cavendish, Elizabeth Brackley and Jane Cavendish; Literary Culture and Women; Theater and Women Actors, Playwrights, and Patrons.

Bibliography
Primary Works
Cavendish, Margaret, Duchess of Newcastle. *The Convent of Pleasure and Other Plays.* Edited by Anne Shaver. Baltimore: Johns Hopkins University Press, 1999.
Cavendish, Margaret, Duchess of Newcastle. *The Description of a New World, Called the Blazing World and Other Writings.* Edited by Kate Lilley. New York: New York University Press, 1992.
Secondary Works
Battigelli, Anna. *Margaret Cavendish and the Exiles of the Mind.* Lexington: University Press of Kentucky, 1998.
Bowerbank, Sylvia. "The Spider's Delight: Margaret Cavendish and the 'Female' Imagination." *English Literary Renaissance* 14, no. 3 (1984): 392–408.
Findlay, Alison, Stephanie Hodgson-Wright, and Gweno Williams. *Women and Dramatic Production: 1550–1700.* Harlow, UK: Longman, 2000.
Straznicky, Marta. "Reading the Stage: Margaret Cavendish and Commonwealth Closet Drama." *Criticism* 37, no. 3 (1995): 355–390.
Whitaker, Katie. *Mad Madge: The Extraordinary Life of Margaret Cavendish, Duchess of Newcastle, the First Woman to Live by Her Pen.* New York: Basic Books, 2002.

Cecil, Mildred Cooke (1526–1589)

Member of Elizabeth I's court, known for her humanist education and as an expert reader and translator of Greek and Latin texts

Married to William Cecil, Queen Elizabeth's chief advisor, Mildred Cooke Cecil occupied a rare position in Elizabethan England. She traveled in the inmost circles of high politics and occasionally participated directly in political, typically international, situations. Born on 25 August 1526 to Sir Anthony Cooke and Lady Anne Fitzwilliam, Cooke Cecil became one of the most famous learned women in England during and even after her lifetime. Elizabethan educator Roger Ascham lauded Cooke Cecil for being able to read Greek as easily as English. She had proven this skill by translating Greek works by the early church fathers, St. Basil and St. Chrysostom. A few years after she married Cecil (on 25 December 1545), she offered her translation of a sermon by Saint Basil to Anne Stanhope Seymour, duchess of Somerset, wife to the lord protector of England.

In 1558, the Cecils entered a new phase of political prominence when Elizabeth I ascended the throne and appointed Cecil as principal secretary. This new status, coupled with Cooke Cecil's impressive mind, prompted political figures to request her advice and support. In the years surrounding the Treaty of Edinburgh (1560), Cooke Cecil corresponded with Scottish Protestant leaders on issues that required such secrecy that trusted messengers conveyed the details. In 1567, Queen Elizabeth acknowledged Cooke Cecil's familiarity with Scottish politics (and her experience as a mother) by choosing her to talk with Lady Lennox when her son, Henry Stuart, Lord Darnley, was murdered. In October 1573, Cooke Cecil used her political prowess in a Latin letter to her cousin, Sir William Fitzwilliam, when he was the target of slander as lord deputy of Ireland.

Following Saint Basil's advice against pride, Cooke Cecil avoided public notice. She never published her translations. She engaged ac-

tively in philanthropy, giving to the universities and the local poor, but often so quietly that even her husband did not know of her generosity until after her death on 4 April 1589. Such modesty has shrouded Mildred Cooke Cecil in relative silence.

Linda Shenk

See also Elizabeth I; the subheadings Greek Learning and Women; Latin Learning and Women (under Education, Humanism, and Women); the subheading Letter Writing (under Literary Culture); Translation and Women Translators.

Bibliography

Hogrefe, Pearl. *Women of Action in Tudor England: Nine Biographical Sketches.* Ames: Iowa State University Press, 1977.

Lamb, Mary Ellen. "The Cooke Sisters: Attitudes Toward Learned Women in the Renaissance." In *Silent But for the Word: Tudor Women as Patrons, Translators, and Writers of Religious Works.* Edited by Margaret Patterson Hannay, 107–125. Kent, OH: Kent State University Press, 1985.

Cereta, Laura (Cereto; 1469–1499)

Humanist and feminist, author of a Latin autobiographical letterbook and a comic dialogue

Laura Cereta was born into an urban, upper-middle-class family in Brescia in 1469. She was the daughter of Silvestro Cereto, an attorney and magistrate in Brescia, and Veronica di Leno, whose brother's noble pretensions Cereta mocked. But almost everything we know about Cereta comes from the colorful image she crafted for herself in her own autobiographical letters. She learned Latin grammar and "to draw pictures with a needle" from the nuns at a convent, where she lived from ages seven to nine, wandering its secret passages "under lock and key." She was not educated by her father or by a male tutor but by women. The eldest of six children, Cereta was soon saddled with her siblings' care. But every night, when the labors of the day were done and her sisters and brothers were put to bed, Cereta continued her studies, savoring the

Roman poets, orators, philosophers, and the Bible, and writing until the early hours of the morning. At age fifteen, she saw her chance to get away. She married Pietro Serina, a Venetian merchant with a shop on the Rialto, and she left her childhood home. She had been living with her young husband no more than a year and a half when plague broke out in the Veneto, and first Serina's brother Nicolai and then Serina himself succumbed. For the next thirteen years of her life, the widowed Cereta immersed herself in her grief over Pietro, her studies, and her writing. At the time of her own premature death in 1499, the thirty-year-old humanist had completed a book containing eighty-two Latin letters and a rather bizarre comic dialogue, which was placed first in her book.

Like her Latin-writing predecessor, Isotta Nogarola, Cereta inserted a dialogue into her letterbook. This work so annoyed the eighteenth-century bibliographer Jacopo Morelli that he noted in the Catalog of the Marcian Library in Venice that Cereta's little "farce" had no business in a serious book of humanist letters. Unlike Nogarola's philosophical dialogue, *On the Equal or Unequal Sin of Adam and Eve,* Cereta's work took as her model not Cicero but Lucian, the first-century satirist who fathered a burlesque, fantasy-driven tradition of dialogue writing that gained currency in fifteenth-century Italy. Her comic theater piece for three speakers, *Dialogue on the Death of an Ass,* resembles the short Lucianic dialogues of her humanist forerunners Guarino, Alberti, and Poggio. Based on one of the most popular books in the Renaissance, Apuleius's late Latin novel, *The Golden Ass,* Cereta's dialogue is a murder mystery. We are given clues but not told whether the ass's death was an "assinicide" or an accident. The main speakers include the author herself ("Laura") who delivers the funeral oration and acts as moderator; Soldus, the bereaved miller who owned the ass; and Philonacus, the miller's slave who seems to know more than he should about the alleged murder.

Cereta is believed to have lectured publicly in Brescia in the period 1486–1499 after her husband's death. Certainly the dialogue, *On the Death of an Ass,* was well suited for public performance. Although we have no evidence that she performed specific pieces, some of her letters look like modern newspaper columns and would have been ideal for public readings. One such piece begins: "A nervous, noisy, and incessantly babbling woman, a stranger to everyone, appeared today just as the sun was setting and the evening was coming on; half-naked and holding a snake tightly in her left hand, she danced at the crossroads without embarrassment. An angry commotion broke out somewhere towards the back of the stunned crowd . . . ." In another piece, Cereta reports the suffering the Venetians and their mercenary troops had inflicted on her city, her family, and her neighbors: "The wound brought to Brescian territory bleeds and drips. Almost the whole of Italy and even populous Calabria have come to despoil the single food supply that is here. The army has grown together into one great people, and having crossed the bridge over the Aglio, it replenishes the plains at night."

Two epistolary essays in Cereta's book, one on marriage and a second on women and education, stand among the earliest known polemics that put forward the case for women's rights as a class action. Both letters belong to the inaugural period of the *querelle des femmes,* the debate about gender and woman's nature that continued into the eighteenth century. In both works, Cereta borrows extensively from Boccaccio's catalogue of illustrious women's lives, *De claris mulieribus,* repudiating his misogynistic history of women much as Christine de Pizan did in her *Le Livre de la Cite des Dames* (Book of the City of Ladies, 1405). In her letter on marriage dedicated to Pietro Zecchi, Cereta's cameo treatments of famous ancient women focus on the figure of the maternal, and in particular the female breast, as an emblem of the fecundity, loyalty, and strength of women. Lucretia, Dido, Veturia, Agrippina, and other morally ambiguous examples of mature womanhood in Latin literature are treated in Cereta's essay with homage. "The powers of maternal authority are great," she writes. Iconic of that authority is the nurturing breast of the mother, whose milk saves an old woman and a baby from death by starvation, and the bleeding breast of Lucretia, which brings an end to monarchy in Rome. At the close of this essay, however, Cereta paints a picture of women's lives, both within and outside marriage, that is grim and hard. Women rear their children "amid wailing and all night vigils," they abase themselves to their husbands to avoid being beaten, they are expected to settle family feuds, and they end their lives in a lonely widow's bed.

In her other great feminist essay, addressed to Bibolo Semproni, Cereta argues that access to education equal to that of males should be every woman's birthright. She portrays the history of generations of women poets, scholars, and prophets as a proud lineage (*generositas*) shared by all women. Cereta rejects the humanist model of the brilliant woman as exceptional. Rather, the long history of outstanding women in all walks of life constitutes a virtual "republic of women" (*respublica mulierum*) and testifies to the worth of women as a species.

Among the most moving of Cereta's letters are those she wrote to her husband before he died. Here she reveals the complexity of her roles as his partner, friend, advisor, and lover. The expressiveness of these letters runs the gamut—from flirtatiousness to anger, from tenderness to frank sexual innuendo, from hope to impatience. The marriage was strained by Pietro's many absences from home. Sometimes he disappeared for months at a time. Yet Cereta rises to the occasion when his shop on the Rialto burns to the ground, consoling him and giving wise counsel.

In the nine letters in which Cereta mourns her husband's sudden death, we would expect a ritual excess of grief. And yet her letters to her friends about the death are so rasping, dry, and laconic that they command our attention and cannot be brushed away as mere formulas. "Lamentation alone is left for me to cultivate. Thus my pen, cut down in the bloom of its eloquence, has dried up . . . ," she writes to her old friend, Alberto degli Alberti. Elsewhere she returns to her theme of the welling tears that, in an inversion of consolation, wash away words:

> Rain steals over the eyes and fills them—a rain that not only washes over a widow's face and her anxious heart, but that also purges her memory and her whole mind of the joy of speech. And so, may the gods of literature fight against the other gods for my poor sake.

Though Cereta's work and thought were well known in Brescia during her lifetime, her humanist letterbook and her comic dialogue were not published until long after her death. In 1640, the first printed edition of her collected letters came out in Padua, but the first translation of her book from the Latin was not published until 1997.

Diana Robin

See also Education, Humanism, and Women; Fedele, Cassandra; the subheading Letter Writing (under Literary Culture and Women); Nogarola, Isotta.

Bibliography

Primary Works

Cereta, Laura. *Collected Letters of a Renaissance Feminist*. Edited and translated by Diana Robin. Chicago: University of Chicago Press, 1997.

Cereta, Laura. *Laura Ceretae Brixiensis Feminae Clarissimae Epistolae iam primum e MS in lucem productae*. Edited by Jacopo Filippo Tomasini. Padua: Sebastiano Sardi, 1640.

King, Margaret L., and Albert Rabil, Jr., eds. *Her Immaculate Hand: Selected Works by and About the Women Humanists of Quattrocento Italy*. 2nd rev. ed. Binghamton, NY: Medieval and Renaissance Texts and Studies, 1991.

Secondary Works

Caccia, Ettore. "Cultura e letteratura nei secoli XV e XVI." In *Storia di Brescia, II. La dominazione Veneta (1426–1575)*. Pages 477–527.

Edited by Giovanni Trecanni degli Alfieri. Brescia: Morcelliana, 1961.

Cremona, Virginio. "L'umanesimo Bresciano." In *Storia di Brescia, II. La dominazione Veneta (1426–1575)*. Pages 542–566. Edited by Giovanni Trecanni degli Alfieri. Brescia: Morcelliana, 1961.

Jordan, Constance. *Renaissance Feminism. Literary Texts and Political Models.* Ithaca, NY: Cornell University Press, 1990.

Marsh, David. *Lucian and the Latins: Humor and Humanism in the Early Renaissance.* Ann Arbor: University of Michigan Press, 1998.

Rabil, Albert, Jr. *Laura Cereta: Quattrocento Humanist.* Binghamton, NY: Medieval and Renaissance Texts and Studies, 1981.

Robin, Diana. "Humanism and Feminism in Laura Cereta's Public Letters." In *Women in Italian Renaissance Culture and Society.* Edited by Letizia Panizza, 368–384. Oxford: Legenda, University of Oxford, 2000.

Robin, Diana. "Space, Woman, and Renaissance Discourse." In *Sex and Gender in Medieval and Renaissance Texts: The Latin Tradition.* Edited by Barbara K. Gold and Allen Miller, 165–187. Albany, NY: Charles Platter, 1996.

Childbirth and Reproductive Knowledge. *See* Medicine and Women.

Childhood

Perhaps the best-known fact regarding Renaissance children is that many of them died. Although poor women, who nursed their own children, tended to deliver every twenty-four to thirty months, and wealthier women, able to afford wet nurses, gave birth as often as once a year, 20 to 50 percent of these babies did not survive childhood. Not just plague or childhood ailments, such as measles or scarlet fever, killed children, but also dehydration brought on by diarrhea. Accidents were frequent as well: In an age of open fireplaces and no indoor plumbing, children might be burned, drowned in wells or streams, or mortally injured while engaged in daily chores. Babies, swaddled and brought into bed with mothers or nurses, might be inadvertently smothered in a tragic circumstance known as "overlying," although different scholars question whether such deaths were in fact a form of infanticide or actually SIDS (sudden infant death syndrome, or "crib death"). Even though mortality rates were high for all children, wealthier ones were less likely to perish. In all socioeconomic classes, boys fared better than girls, because girls were nursed for shorter periods of time and often farther from home than were their brothers and who were more likely to be abandoned to foundling hospitals.

This extremely high mortality rate has caused some scholars to question whether Renaissance parents loved their children. Philippe Aries, for example, was highly influential in establishing the argument that early modern mothers and fathers deliberately sought to avoid affective ties, distancing themselves from their offspring both physically (by, for example, placing newborns in the home of a wet nurse and later in the care of a nanny) or psychologically, for example, through the use of nonspecific descriptors such as "it" or "creature." Some historians even posited that childhood was not a recognized developmental period until the modern era.

More recent scholarship, however, looking at a broader range of sources (record books and diaries, for example, as well as popular works such as saints' lives or advice manuals), frames its consideration of family ties within an examination of early modern gender and social constructions. This research makes clear that, while the death of a child might not have been uncommon, it was nevertheless an often devastating blow, greeted with violent grief, prolonged mourning, and, when possible, lasting monuments such as tombs, epitaphs, poems, or paintings.

Evidence of affection is not limited to grief for the dead. Indeed, the turn to naturalism in Italian Renaissance art is epitomized in the depiction of the beautiful young Madonna with an increasingly cherubic baby Jesus, their affective intimacy serving in part to help the viewer identify with the incarnate God's humanity. Moreover, the very existence of a plethora of early modern books and popular advice manuals on upbringing and education suggests that a consuming interest in parenting is far from exclusive to our own modern time period.

Children were a precious commodity and their arrival, especially in upper-class families, was usually celebrated as a "blessed event"; the mother (assuming she survived the ordeal) was presented with gifts, such as fine cloth or clothing, silver forks, spoons, or cups, or, in Italy, a birth salver—a decorative birth tray featuring images of robust baby boys or perhaps the birth of the Virgin or of John the Baptist. Although virtually all child-rearing manuals of the period recommend maternal breast-feeding, the use of wet nurses—whether within or outside the home—was ubiquitous, with girls more likely to be sent out than boys.

Such gendered variations in practice, which (as noted) are often reflected in lower infant mortality rates for males, suggest that, although early modern manuals offered generic recommendations for little boys and girls (who were dressed alike—in dresses, fed the same foods, and offered the same toys), there were probably cultural norms that distinguished sex-specific treatment even of infants and toddlers. Certainly, the birth of a boy, who would carry the family name and patrimony and whose marriage would potentially bring in a dowry, was a greater cause for celebration than that of a daughter, who would require a dowry of her own. Early education, generally supervised by the mother, focused on religion and morality (topics of central importance for both girls and boys) and no doubt included early inculcation of gender roles. By age four or five, playthings reflected and directed children toward their future roles, with girls taught such tasks as spinning, sewing, and cooking rather than woodworking or reading. By seven or eight, a boy began his formal education, preparing for training for a trade or following his father to help in the field. Although there were exceptions, a girl usually remained home to receive domestic training from her mother; in Catholic families of certain classes, she might have been sent to a convent for education and safekeeping either until she was married around the age of fourteen or until she took permanent vows. Taking vows was a step sometimes freely elected, but frequently it was forced on girls by their families, whether to avoid exorbitant dowry costs or to handle an unmarriageable daughter, who might be disabled in some way, illegitimate, or herself carrying an illegitimate child.

While the argument that childhood was unrecognized or children in general devalued has been greatly revised, not every child was wanted. There are widely ranging views regarding infanticide rates, with some scholars positing the ubiquity of the practice and others, notably John Boswell, arguing that it was virtually replaced by the paradoxically loving *abandonment* of children, society's most valued resource following the demographic catastrophe of the Black Death. Whether abandonment was in fact a sign of love, foundling hospitals, where unwanted children could be left anonymously, were an established feature of the early modern city.

Naomi Yavneh

See also Abortion and Miscarriage; Contraception and Birth Control; the subheadings Midwives and Licensing; Male Midwifery; Hospital Administration and Nursing as Careers for Women (under Medicine and Women).

Bibliography

Alexandre-Bidon, Danièle, and Didier Lett. *Children in the Middle Ages, 5th–15th Centuries.* Translated by Jody Gladding. Notre Dame, IN: University of Notre Dame Press, 1999.

Bell, Rudolph. *How to Do It: Guides to Good Living for Renaissance Italians.* Chicago and London: University of Chicago Press, 1999.

Boswell, John. *The Kindness of Strangers: The Abandonment of Children in Western Europe from Antiquity to the Renaissance.* New York: Pantheon, 1988.

Eisenbichler, Konrad, ed. *The Premodern Teenager: Youth in Society, 1150–1650.* Toronto: Centre for Reformation and Renaissance Studies, 2002.

Haas, Louis. *The Renaissance Man and His Children: Childbirth and Early Childhood in Florence, 1300–1600.* New York: St. Martin's Press, 1998.

Hanawalt, Barbara. "Medievalists and the Study of Childhood." *Speculum* 77, no. 2 (2002): 440–460.

King, Margaret L. *The Death of the Child Valerio Marcello.* Chicago: University of Chicago Press, 1994.

Klapisch-Zuber, Christiane. *Women, Family and Ritual in Renaissance Italy.* Translated by Lydia Cochrane. Chicago: University of Chicago Press, 1985.

Cibo, Caterina (Cybo; 1501–1557)

Reform thinker and duchess of Camerino

Caterina Cibo was born at Ponzano near Florence, the granddaughter of the learned patron of the Florentine neo-Platonists, Lorenzo (the Magnificent) de' Medici. As befit her ancestry, she read Latin, Greek, and Hebrew with ease and was well versed in ancient oratory, philosophy, poetry, and patristics. Three years after she married Giovanni Maria da Varano, the duke of Camerino in 1520, she gave birth to a daughter, Giulia. When her husband died of the plague in 1527, Cibo obtained a papal decree granting her sole rights to the duchy should Giulia predecease her. Between 1422 and 1534, she repeatedly fought off the armed attacks on Camerino by neighboring lords, one of whom attempted to rape and kidnap Giulia. In 1535, Cibo engineered a marriage between Giulia and the future duke of Urbino (Guidubaldo Della Rovere). But Pope Paul III, fearing the Duke's growing power in the region, confiscated the duchy, took Camerino for himself, and excommunicated Cibo, Giulia, and Della Rovere. Cibo took refuge with her brother in the Pazzi Palace in Florence. It was only after Cibo's return from Marseilles, where she took part in Catherine de Médicis' wedding to the future King of France, Henri II, that Cibo's clashes with papal authority began to gather steam. In 1533, she joined the poet and reform thinker Vittoria Colonna in rescuing the Capuchins, a primitive monastic order whose independence caused the Pope to oust them from the church. At Cibo's urging, Pope Clement VII took the Capuchins back into his fold and named as their general Bernardino Ochino, a disciple of Juan de Valdés, the leading reform theologian in Italy. Cibo is featured as Ochino's chief interlocutor in his *Seven Dialogues* (1542), a work that dramatizes his conversations with the duchess about the relation between faith and works, the question of predestination versus free will, and other doctrinal issues. After Ochino's flight to Zurich, Cibo turned for intellectual companionship to the Padua-educated Aristotelian, Marcantonio Flaminio. Though no writings of hers survive, Cibo's theology is believed to have evolved from her conversations with Flaminio, Cardinal Reginald Pole, and Pietro Carnesecchi, with whom she met frequently at Carnesecchi's house in Florence in 1541 on the eve of the Inquisition. Cibo was denounced as a "heretic, a follower of heretics, and a teacher of heretics" by a witness at the Holy Office's trial of Cardinal Giovanni Morone in 1557. Nonetheless, she escaped the fate of Carnesecchi, who would be burned in Rome in 1567. Cibo died of natural causes in the Pazzi Palace in Florence, to which she had inherited the usufruct.

Diana Robin

See also Colonna, Vittoria; Education, Humanism, and Women; Religious Reform and Women.

Bibliography

Primary Work

Ochino, Bernardino. *I "dialogi sette" e altri scritti del tempo della fuga.* Ed. U. Rozzo, 147–152. Turin: Claudiana 1985.

Secondary Works

Bainton, Roland H. *Women of the Reformation in Germany and Italy.* Minneapolis, MN: Academic Renewal Press, 1971.

Caponetto, Salvatore. *The Protestant Reformation in Sixteenth-Century Italy.* Translated by Anne C.

Tedeschi and John Tedeschi. Kirksville, MO: Thomas Jefferson University Press, 1999.

Petrucci, F. "Cibo, Caterina." In *Dizionario biografico degli Italiani*. Vol. 25. Rome: Istituto dell Enciclopedia Italiana, 1960.

Claude de France (1499–1524)

Queen of France, duchess of Brittany, countess of Blois, first consort of King Francis I

The "good queen" Claude—today overshadowed by her husband King Francis I—was born in 1499 to Queen Anne de Bretagne and her second husband Louis XII. Bonfires signaled rejoicing throughout the realm for, with the help of Saint Claude, a viable child had been born. The princess, although not the desired son, was fashioned in her mother's pious image to become both sovereign duchess of Brittany and empress (she was engaged to the future Charles V at age two) or queen (of France, as her father, before her first birthday, had secretly declared). A decade later, her sole sibling, Renée de France, the remarkable future Protestant duchess of Ferrara, would again owe her name to another saintly protector of women in search of a child. Thus if Queen Claude inherited Queen Anne's limp, her ability to bear relatively healthy offspring was entirely her own. Her engagement in 1506 and her marriage in 1514 consolidated the first prince of the blood's claim to the throne, but after seven debilitating pregnancies in ten years (Louise, Charlotte, François, Henri, Madeleine, Charles, Marguerite), the tired body of this honored "daughter, wife and mother" of kings collapsed at the tender age of 24.

The canonization of Francis of Paola (1519), promoted by Claude and her mother-in-law Louise de Savoie in gratitude for protection from illness and the births of namesake male heirs, betrays the inextricable intertwining of the two sides of the royal family, programmed from 1498. Claude's parents willfully empowered their female progeny; thus when King Francis I descended into Italy the first year of their respective reign, the pageantry in Lyons depicted him entering Milan to "defend the rights of the two daughters of France." Although a princess raised to be queen, Claude learned to share her husband with other women, and her power and its public expressions with strong female kin, especially Louise de Savoie, named regent in her stead, and her sister-in-law Marguerite de Navarre. Legend and neglect have imposed the image of an ever-with-child, sweet, and submissive queen. Yet this eloquent and cultivated bearer of legitimacy commanded respect and carved out a space of her own in the cities of the realm (the townspeople cast her as Justice and Wise Counsel), in her duchy of Brittany, and in her Loire Valley territories, especially at the castle of Blois. Shortly after his accession, her husband flaunted his monogram "F" and his emblem, the salamander, on the spectacular new façades of the castle of Blois's "wing of Francis I"; but on the cornice and ceremonial staircase and over the fireplaces, these cohabited with his consort's at what was in fact her regal home. Here and elsewhere, her emblems—the ermine, occasionally on a leash with the motto *À ma vie* (To my life), her knotted rope, her swan pierced by an arrow, and her full moon with the device *Candida candidis* (Candid for the candid)—called attention to the queen.

A primer made for this daughter of privilege stages her with her sister Renée, as children tutored by Saint Anne and under the protection of Saint Claude, while learning to read and write; and learning came to be a feature at the heart of the queen's persona. Following her accession in 1515, Claude became mistress of the castle of Blois with its royal library, her mother's manuscripts probably among its precious volumes, to which the king, in an incident of 1516, did not have a key. Her *Book of Prayers,* by the "Master of Queen Claude," returns to the then commonly depicted theme of Saint Anne as educator, but its pages are uncommonly packed with illuminations in which books form an insistent leitmotiv. Saint Genevieve appears twice on the same page, in the lower right margin holding a book along with her standard candle and in the center praying before a second book, its pages open. On another page, a monk reads to Saint Jerome as he expires, and a second open book is placed by the side of the dying man. Saint Luke, instead, is shown both writing and painting, in accordance with tradition, conjuring up Claude's sensitivity to the other arts. In 1518, Pope Leo X presented the queen with Raphael's *Holy Family;* and Andrea del Sarto portrayed the dauphin and honored his mother Claude as *Charity*—in glorification of her fecundity and, after the birth of two girls, her ability to provide a male heir. In the intimacy of her chamber, however, Claude prayed to Sebastiano del Piombo's *Visitation,* her gaze resting upon the pregnant Elizabeth and the pregnant Mary, thoroughly aware of the dangers of her state. Tapestries depicting scenes from Christine de Pizan's *City of Ladies,* these too inherited from her mother, hung in the rooms of the castles of Amboise and/or Blois, frequented by her twelve ladies-in-waiting (including Anne Boleyn and Diane de Poitiers). The writer Anne de Graville commissioned a picture of herself offering her mistress Claude one of the works she dedicated to her, thereby providing us with a rare inside vision of the city of ladies surrounding Claude.

In a final act of independence, the queen bequeathed Brittany not to her husband but to her son, the dauphin. Rather than willfulness, though, sensitivity to the plight of her subjects had colored numerous episodes of her life. During her entry into Nantes in 1518, when the town offered her a costly heart of gold flanked with ermine, she promptly gave it back. Shortly before her death she endowed the building of a cemetery in a suburb of Blois for those who had succumbed to the plague. Such symbolic gestures, combining strength and humility, help us to comprehend why the memory of the short-lived Claude lingered on. Miracles were said to occur around her body, laid to rest in her parents' chapel of Saint

Calais in 1524. Subsequently, her second son, King Henri II (of the seven siblings, only he and his sister Marguerite, future duchesse de Savoie, outlived their father) immortalized her on a monumental tomb at Saint Denis. And in her *Book of Hours,* Catherine de Médicis inserted Claude's portrait near that of Eleonora of Austria, Francis I's second wife, forging an unexpected double embodiment of a powerful queenly ideal.

Kathleen Wilson-Chevalier

See also Anne of Brittany; Boleyn, Anne; Renata di Francia.
Bibliography
Primary Works
Book of Prayers of Claude de France. New York: private collection.
L'Orme, Philibert de, and Pierre Bontemps. *Tomb of François Ier and Claude de France.* Vendée, France: Basilica of Saint Denis.
Primer of Claude de France. Cambridge, UK: Fitzwilliam Museum.
Secondary Works
Avril, François, and Nicole Reynaud. *Les manuscrits à peintures en France 1440–1520,* 319 and nos. 176, 177, 178. Paris: Bibliothèque nationale de France, 1993.
Gringore, Pierre. *Les Entrées royales à Paris de Marie d'Angleterre (1514) et Claude de France (1517).* Edited by Cynthia J. Brown. Geneva: Droz, 2005.
Lecoq, Anne-Marie. *François Ier imaginaire. Symbolique et politique à l'aube de la Renaissance française.* Paris: Macula, 1987.
Néret, Jean-Alexis. *Claude de France femme de François Ier—1499–1524.* Paris: Les Éditions de France, 1942.
Sterling, Charles. *The Master of Claude, Queen of France: A Newly Defined Miniaturist.* New York: H. P. Kraus, 1975.

Clermont, Claude-Catherine de (1543–1603)

Duchess of Retz, key figure in French courtly and literary circles during the reigns of Charles IX, Henri III, and Henri IV

Claude-Catherine de Clermont, the only child of Claude de Clermont-Tonnerre, baron of Dampierre, and Jeanne de Vivonne, a lady-in-waiting to Catherine de Médicis, was born in Paris. Groomed to hold a privileged place in courtly society, Clermont studied Greek, Latin, and other languages, as well as history, philosophy, and mathematics. At an early age she was placed at court, where she became a lady-in-waiting to Marguerite de Valois.

In her late teens, Clermont married Jean d'Annebaut, baron of Retz, who was killed in the Battle of Dreux in 1562. According to contemporary accounts, the marriage was not a happy one. On 4 September 1565, she married again, this time to Albert de Gondi (1522–1602), who took the title of Retz. Gondi's service to the French kings was rewarded in 1573, when he was made a *Maréchal de France,* and again in 1581, when the land of Retz was raised to a duchy. The couple had four sons and six daughters.

Clermont and Gondi entertained lavishly at their country house at Noisy and their Parisian home, the Hôtel de Dampierre, in the Faubourg St. Honoré. In the process, they cultivated one of the most famous literary salons of the period. Sometimes called the *salon vert* of Dyctinne in reference to a description in "*Le Sejour de Dyctinne et des Muses,*" a poem from the Retz album (Bibliothèque Nationale de France: fonds français 25,455, folios 62–65vº), their salon was a haven for lovers of pastoral poetry. "Dyctinne" was Clermont's pseudonym. Among the poets associated with the salon were Étienne Jodelle, Philippe Desportes, Jean-Antoine de Baïf, Pierre de Ronsard, Pontus de Tyard, Remy Belleau, and Amadis Jamyn. Female participants included Marguerite de Valois, Henriette de Clèves, Hélène de Surgères, Gilonne de Goyon, Charlotte de Beaune, Gabrielle de Rochechouart, and Anne de Thou. These and numerous other luminaries of the French court frequented the Retz salon.

An avid scholar, Clermont circulated her work mainly in manuscript, with the possible exception of *Les diverses assiettes d'amour, traduit d'Espagnol en François* (Various Remarks on Love, Translated from Spanish into French), a

translation mentioned in Pierre de l'Estoile's *Memoires* (1515–1611). The unfortunate result is that little of her writing is extant. The influence of Clermont and her circle, however, should not be underestimated. Étienne Pasquier's correspondence with Clermont reveals that her wit and encouragement were strong stimuli for those who frequented her salon. Tyard dedicated the second edition of *Solitaire premier* (The Solitary One, First Book, 1573) to her, and she is believed to be the new Pasithée of his *Nouvelles œuvres poétiques* (1573). Similarly, Jamyn's numerous poems in praise of Artémis include references to Clermont.

In addition to her literary interests, Clermont was noted for her skills in music, oratory, and dance. She studied lute with Adrian Le Roy, who dedicated his *Livre d'Airs de Cour miz sur le Luth* (Book on Court Tunes for the Luth, 1571) to her, and her collection of musical instruments was legendary. In 1573, when Polish ambassadors requested the duc d'Anjou for their king, Clermont gave an impressive Latin oration on behalf of the queen mother. She also participated in the Palace Academy, as is documented by Théodore Agrippa d'Aubigné, who praises her eloquence in debate. (One of her academic emblems was the rose.) Regarding court entertainments, Clermont orchestrated spectacles for banquets given by Henri III at Plessis-les-Tours on 15 May 1577 and Catherine de Medici at Chenonceaux on 18 May 1577, as well as danced in the renowned *Ballet comique de la reine* (The Queen's Comic Ballet) on 15 October 1581 for the wedding of the duke of Joyeuse and Marguerite de Vaudemont.

Intimately involved in French politics, Clermont was associated with various political machinations. For example, her husband was accused of involvement with the St. Bartholomew's Day massacre in 1572, while Clermont was believed to harbor some Protestant sympathies. Moreover, Clermont herself was rumored to have been party to the foiled plot against Charles IX, orchestrated by the count de la Mole and the count de Coconnas in 1574. In spite of entanglements with political intrigue, Clermont was admired throughout her life for her wit, learning, and eloquence. She died on 18 February 1603.

Julie D. Campbell

See also Catherine de Médicis; the subheading The Humanist Curriculum (under Education, Humanism, and Women); Music and Women; Rhetoric, Public Speaking, and Women; the subheading Salons, Salonnières, and Women Writers (under Literary Culture and Women); Translation and Women Translators.

Bibliography

Primary Works

Clermont, Catherine de, Maréchale de Retz. *Album de poesies (Manuscrit français 24255 de la BNF)*. Edited by Colette Winn and François Rouget. Paris: Champion, 2004.

d'Aubigné, Théodore Agrippa. "À mes filles touchant les femmes doctes de nostre siècle." *Œuvres*. Edited by Henri Weber et al., 852–853. Paris: Gallimard, 1969.

L'Estoile, Pierre de. *Memoires pour servir à l'histoire de France (1515–1611)*. Vol. 1. Cologne: 1719.

Pasquier, Étienne. "A Madame la duchesse de Retz." *Lettres Familières*. Edited by D. Thickett. Geneva: E. Droz, 1974.

Secondary Works

Keating, L. Clark. *Studies on the Literary Salon in France, 1550–1615*. Cambridge, MA: Harvard University Press, 1941.

Pommerol, Marie-Henriette. Geneva: E. Droz, 1953.

St-John, Christie Ellen. "The *Salon Vert* of the Maréchale de Retz: A Study of a Literary Salon in Sixteenth-Century France." Ph.D. dissertation, Vanderbilt University, 1999.

Clifford, Anne (1590–1676)

Diarist, genealogist, and philanthropist

Lady Anne Clifford was the only surviving child of George Clifford, earl of Cumberland, and Margaret Russell Clifford, countess of Cumberland. Her entitlements ensuing from that role consumed much of her life. Anne Clifford was born on 30 January 1590. She had a noble upbringing, frequented court, and had as a private tutor the scholar and author Samuel Daniel. Though her parents separated when she was young, they reconciled shortly before the earl's death in 1605. Anne was her father's only heir (her brothers having died in infancy) and was positioned to inherit numerous lands and titles. However, George Clifford designated his brother Francis his inheritor, bequeathing Anne fifteen thousand pounds from the income of the Clifford estates. Arduous legal battles ensued.

In 1609 Anne Clifford married Richard Sackville, both aged nineteen. They became the earl and countess of Dorset and saw the births of three sons and two daughters, with only Margaret (1613) and Isabella (1622) surviving to adulthood. Sackville pressed his wife to resolve her legal disputes and take the cash settlement from her uncle, but Lady Anne remained firm. Her bold show went beyond the home to court. James I directed Anne to accept her uncle's terms, and she refused.

As a means of legitimizing her claims to the Clifford inheritance, Lady Anne began writing. She kept extensive diaries (her Books of Record) and wrote detailed genealogies of both the Clifford and Russell lines. Her own history took an unexpected turn with the early death of Sackville in 1624. In 1630 Anne Clifford Sackville married Philip Herbert, fourth earl of Pembroke and Montgomery, son of Henry, second earl of Pembroke and Mary Sidney. With Herbert, Anne had two sons who died in infancy. The couple spent most of their married life apart.

In 1643 Anne came into her inheritance when both her uncle and his son died, leaving no male heir. She took possession of her properties in 1649 (due to delays caused by the civil war). Herbert died in 1650, and the dowager Anne found herself both independent and financially secure. She made improvements to her family's estates at Applyby, Brough, Broughman, Pendragon, and Skipton. Her generosity was extreme; she restored churches, built almshouses, and founded St. Anne's Hospital, Applyby. She was widely regarded as a woman of intelligence and virtue. She died at Broughham Castle on 22 March 1676.

Michele Osherow

See also Literary Culture and Women.
Bibliography
Lewalski, Barbara Kiefer. *Writing Women in England.* Cambridge, MA, and London: Harvard University Press, 1993.
Spence, Richard T. *LadyAnne Clifford, Countess of Pembroke, Dorset and Montgomery (1590–1676).* Phoenix Mill, Thrupp, Stroud, Gloucestershire, UK: Sutton, 1997.

Clitherow, Margaret (1556?–1586)

Catholic martyr and daughter of a wax chandler

Margaret Clitherow was the first female Catholic martyr of the reign of Elizabeth I. Born in York in 1556, she was the daughter of Thomas Middleton, a wax chandler and sheriff of the City (1564–1565). In 1571 Margaret married John Clitherow, a butcher, and bore him four children. Converted by Dr. and Mrs. Vasavour in 1573–1574, she was imprisoned several times for recusancy. In a 1585/1586 house raid, a child taking lessons in her house revealed "books and church stuff" to the authorities. On 14 March 1585/1586, Margaret was indicted on the charges both of having heard mass and of harboring Jesuit and seminary priests. As a way to protect her friends through not testifying, Margaret refused to plead to her indictment. This resulted in her being condemned to a "sharp death for want of trial" (Mush, 414). She refused to accept that Catholic priests were traitors to the queen's majesty and her laws and felt slandered that it was claimed she harbored priests for harlotry rather than religion. She exculpated her conformist husband by expressing her disappointment that, while he did not share her religious views, she nonetheless "loved him next unto God" (Mush 1877, 426).

She was crushed to death under a weighted door on 25 March 1586, a sharp stone under her back and her hands bound. She begged that she might die in her smock, but the sentence stipulated that she be naked (except for a linen habit). Even some Puritan ministers argued that she should not be executed on a child's evidence, and the sheriff wept as she died.

She had taught herself to read while in prison in order to peruse such works as the Rheims *New Testament* (1582) and William Peryn's *Spirituall Exercyses* (1557).

Teresa Grant

See also Religious Reform and Women.
Bibliography
Primary Work
Mush, John. "Life of Margaret Clitherow" [1586]. In *The Troubles of Our Catholic Forefathers.* Edited by John Morris, SJ, 331–440. London: Burns and Oates, 1877.
Secondary Works
Claridge, Mary (aka Katharine Longley). *Margaret Clitherow.* London: Burns and Oates, 1966.
Longley, Katharine. *Saint Margaret Clitherow.* Wheathampstead: Anthony Clarke, 1986.

Coignard, Gabrielle de (ca. 1550–ca. 1586)

Devotional poet

Although biographical information about Gabrielle de Coignard is limited, some assumptions can be made about her education and social status based on what we know about her family and by what she reveals about her life in her poetry. Her father, Jean de Coignard, a prominent figure of his time, was a counselor at the Parlement of Toulouse. He also served as *Maître ès Jeux Floraux* from 1535 to 1555. Through her father's professional associations, Coignard most likely enjoyed frequent opportunities to mingle with the cultivated and literary elite of Toulouse, a major cultural center in France at the time. Based on her writings, she appears to have been well educated and was raised in the Catholic faith. At the age of twenty, Coignard married Pierre de Mansencal, seigneur de Miramont, a distinguished lawyer and statesman who became *président* of the Parlement of Toulouse just two years after they were married, a position he held until his death a year later in 1573. The couple's first daughter, Catherine, was born in 1571. Their second daughter, Jeanne, was born in 1573. Widowed at the age of twenty-three, Coignard was left to raise their two young daughters alone. In 1594, almost a decade after their mother's death, Jeanne and Catherine de Mansencal published the first edition of their mother's *Œuvres chrestiennes* (Christian Works), a two-part collection of devotional compositions she had written after the death of her husband. This first edition was published in Toulouse by Pierre Jagourt and Bernard Carles. Subsequent editions of Coignard's work appeared in Avignon (1595) and in Lyons (1613).

The first part of the *Œuvres chrestiennes* consists of 129 sonnets, *Les sonnets spirituals* (Spiritual Sonnets), in which Coignard records the struggles she faces in the preliminary stages of her spiritual journey. The sonnets treat a variety of devotional subjects and include penitential confessions, meditations on Christ's Passion, and exaltations of God's glory and grace. Scattered among these fervent and pious reflections are poems in which Coignard devotes attention to more earthly concerns, such as parental responsibility, social conventions, vanity, nature, sickness, and death. On the whole, the sonnets encapsulate the worldly despair the poet strives to overcome in her impassioned pursuit of eternal union with her divine creator.

The second part of the collection, entitled *Les vers chrestiens* (Christian Verses), is made up of twenty-one Biblical meditations of varying length and genre, including *noëls, hymnes, complaintes, stances,* and a *discours. Les vers chrestiens* takes Coignard from the somber and self-absorbed study of spiritual struggle that dominated the sonnets to a more open and uninhibited exploration of the divine. In this section, the poet focuses primarily on the life and suffering of Christ. The composition of each poem in the collection, both in *Les sonnets spirituels* and *Les vers chrestiens,* serves as a means for Coignard to examine and renew her faith through poetic prayer and meditation.

Coignard's *Oeuvres chrestiennes* exemplifies the devotional literature that grew to prominence in the last few decades of the sixteenth century in France under the reign Henri III. During this period of religious conflict and spiritual revival, devotional handbooks, such as Ignatius of Loyola's *Exercitia Spirituali* (Spiritual Exercises, 1548) and Louis of Granada's *Libro de la oración y meditatión* (Book on Oration and Meditation, 1566), became popular among Catholics, who sought more structured methods for practicing their faith. The self-evaluation and symbolic self-flagellation promoted as a means of developing a closer relationship with God in the handbooks of these two Spanish mystics influenced a whole generation of devotional poets. The emotive and introspective analysis Coignard undertakes in the *Œuvres chrestiennes* suggests that she was among the many who subscribed to their methods.

Aside from the various biblical, devotional, and liturgical texts that Coignard drew on in her poetic endeavor, she also demonstrates a familiarity with classical literature, primarily through her numerous references to mythological figures. These allusions are striking in light of her repeated and forceful rejection of paganism. Her work reveals a similar paradox in her admiration for the poetic skills of her contemporaries, such as Ronsard and the poets of the Pléiade, skills to which she aspired at the same time condemning what she considered their ungodly inspiration. In fact, Coignard's poetry is rife with contradiction. The inconsistencies of her creative impetus contribute significantly to the appeal of her work. As a Christian poet, she questioned the motivation of her literary activity, fearing that her writing and the pleasure she gained from it might serve some other objective, contrary to the exclusively devotional purpose she proclaims in her opening sonnets.

Malanie E. Gregg

See also the subheading Sonnet Writing (under Literary Culture and Women).

Bibliography

Primary Works

Coignard, Gabrielle de. *Œuvres chrestiennes.* Edited by Colette H. Winn. Geneva: Droz, 1995.

Coignard, Gabrielle de. *Spiritual Sonnets: A Bilingual Edition.* Edited and translated by Melanie E. Gregg. Chicago: University of Chicago Press, 2004.

Secondary Works

Berriot-Salvadore, Evelyne. *Les femmes dans la société de la société française de la Renaissance.* Geneva: Droz, 1990.

Berriot-Salvadore, Evelyne. "Les héritières de Louise Labé." In *Louise Labé: Les voix du lyrisme.* Edited by Guy Démerson, 93–106. Saint-Etienne, FR: Publications de l'Université de Saint-Etienne, Editions du CNRS, 1990.

Cave, Terence. *Devotional Poetry in France, c. 1570–1613.* Cambridge: Cambridge University Press, 1969.

Marczuk-Szwed, Barbara. "Le thème du péché et son expression poétique dans les *Oeuvres chrestiennes* de Gabrielle de Coignard et dans *Le mespris de la vie et consolation contre la mort* de J. B. Chassignet." *Zeszyty Naukowe Uniwersyteru Jagiellónskiego* MLIV (1992): 51–71.

Salies, Pierre. "Gabrielle de Coignard: Poétesse toulousaine du XVIe siècle." *Archistra* 79 (March–April 1987): 33–43.

Sommers, Paula. "Gendered Distaffs: Gabrielle de Coignard's Revision of Classical Tradition." *Classical and Modern Literature* 18, no. 3 (Spring 1998): 203–210.

Coligny, Louise de (1555–1620)

Princess of Orange, French Huguenot, widow of William of Orange, diplomat, letter writer

Louise de Coligny was a respected noblewoman whose letters document her exercise of informal political influence in France and in the Netherlands during the reigns of Henry IV of France and Maurice of Nassau, stadholder of the Netherlands. Born in September 1555, Louise de Coligny was the daughter of Gaspard de Coligny and his first wife Charlotte de Laval, both leaders of the Huguenot cause in France. They saw to it that Louise received a solid education from her Protestant humanist tutors, in spite of the fact that her childhood was disrupted by the French Wars of Religion. Beginning in September 1568, when her family sought refuge in the Huguenot stronghold of La Rochelle, Louise lived within the community of Protestant nobles who would form her network for the rest of her life, including Jeanne d'Albret and her children Henry de Navarre (the future Henry IV) and Catherine de Bourbon. She married Charles de Téligny there in May 1571. In Paris for the wedding of Henry de Navarre to Marguérite de Valois in August 1572, Gaspard de Coligny was the original target for what grew into the St. Bartholemew's Day Massacre of Huguenots, spreading from Paris throughout France. Téligny was also killed. Louise fled to Berne and then to Basel, returning to France only in 1576 when the Edict of Beaulieu allowed for increased religious tolerance. Louise spent the next seven years mainly at Lierville, a property she had inherited from her husband. In the spring of 1583, William ("The Silent") of Orange, stadholder of the Netherlands, sought Louise's hand in marriage. She became his fourth wife and the stepmother of his ten children. Her own son Henry-Frederik was born in January 1584. Louise de Coligny's second marriage also ended tragically when William of Orange was assassinated by a Spanish sympathizer on 11 July 1584.

In the years immediately after William's death, Louise de Coligny, now dowager princess of Orange, was entirely occupied with ensuring the survival and the upbringing of William's youngest children, especially the six daughters of William's third wife, Charlotte de Bourbon-Montpensier, and her infant son. Having poured all his resources into the fight of the Protestant United Provinces of the Netherlands against the domination of Catholic Spain, William had left only debts. Most of Louise de Coligny's letters at this time are addressed to relatives or to the various estates general of the Dutch provinces, requesting financial support. She offered to her stepdaughters the same excellent education she had received, ensuring that they learned reading and writing, several languages, music, and dancing. She eventually arranged advantageous marriages for them with Protestant noblemen (Louise-Julienne married the elector of the Palatine, Elizabeth the duke de Bouillon, and Charlotte-Brabantine the duke de la Tremoille). For her own son, she dreamed of a place at the French court of Henry IV. The new stadholder, Maurice de Nassau, had other plans for his half-brother, who became stadholder himself in 1625. Louise's attempts to establish her son at the French court and her success in arranging marriages for her stepdaughters were also the first steps in her own self-fashioning as a valued negotiator between her stepson, Maurice de Nassau, and her "cousin" and childhood friend, Henry IV. Her influence was also felt within the French court. Her sons-in-law, the dukes de Bouillon and de la Tremoille, were two of the most influential of the Huguenot nobles who were alienated from Henry IV when he abjured Protestantism and returned to the Catholic faith in order to complete his conquest of France and to enter the pro-Catholic city of Paris. Louise intervened with both of them on behalf of Henry IV, convincing each to support the monarch and the Edict of Nantes, which established religious tolerance in France. After 1594, she divided her time between Nordheim palace in The Hague, her property in Lierville, and the French court. She died in November 1620 at Fontainebleau, where she was the guest of Queen Marie de Médicis. She is buried beside William of Orange in the Niewe Kerk in Delft.

One hundred and ninety-three of the "thousands" of letters Louise de Coligny describes herself as writing have survived, most in the collections of the royal family of the Netherlands (Koninklijk Huisarchief) and in the French National Archives. Louise used the epistolary genre with great skill and grace to develop and maintain her networks and to exercise her influence, skillfully choosing the approach most likely to have an impact on her reader.

Jane Couchman

See also d'Albret, Jeanne; the subheading Letter Writing (under Literary Culture and Women); Power, Politics, and Women; Religious Reform and Women.

Bibliography

Primary Works

Coligny, Louise de. *Correspondance de Louise de Coligny, princesse d'Orange.* Edited by Paul Marchegay and Léon Marlet. Geneva: Slatkine, 1970. (Originally published in Paris, 1887.)

Couchman, Jane. "Lettres de Louise de Coligny aux membres de sa famille en France et aux Pays-bas." In *Lettres de femmes XVIe-XVIIe siècle.* Edited by Elizabeth Goldsmith et Colette Winn. Paris: Champion, forthcoming.

Secondary Works

Bainton, Roland H. "Louise de Coligny." In *Women of the Reformation in France and England.* Pages 113–135. Boston: Beacon Press, 1983.

Berriot-Salvadore, Evelyne. "Louise de Coligny." In *Les Femmes dans la société française de la Renaissance.* Pages 134–139. Geneva: Droz, 1990.

Couchman, Jane. "La lecture et le lectorat dans la correspondance de Louise de Coligny." In *Lectrices d'Ancien Régime.* Edited by Isabelle Brouard-Arends, 399–408. Rennes Presses: Universitaires de Rennes, 2003.

Elaborde, Jules. *Louise de Coligny, princesse d'Orange.* Geneva: Slatkine, 1970. (Originally printed in Paris, 1890.)

Colonna, Vittoria (1490/1492–1547)

Marchesa di Pescara, Italian lyric poet, religious reform leader, prolific letter writer, art and literary patron

Greatly esteemed by her literary peers during her lifetime, Vittoria Colonna became famous as a Petrarchan lyric poet of the highest order and the first woman to turn the genre to female ends with marked success. Her *Rime* went through numerous sixteenth-century editions and she enjoyed great fame as a result, but her public profile was at all times married to a carefully marketed literary *persona* embodying all the necessary traits of modesty, chastity, and piety, so that Colonna effectively laid down the first wholly successful formula for literary production by a secular woman in

Vittoria Colonna, Marchesa di Pescara. Lyric poet and religious reform leader. Painting by Girolamo Muziano. Galleria Colonna, Rome, Italy. (Alinari/Art Resource)

Renaissance Italy. Her interest in reform spirituality colored her poetry in her later years, to the extent that her name was associated with a number of individuals who were tried by the Inquisition or left Italy under the cloud of heresy after the first meetings of the Council of Trent.

Colonna was born into the powerful Roman Colonna clan in 1490 or possibly 1492, at Marino close to Rome, the second child of Fabrizio Colonna and Agnese di Montefeltro. She was betrothed at a very young age to Francesco Ferrante D'Avalos, the Marquis of Pescara, in a political maneuver that established an alliance between the Colonna and the Spanish throne of King Ferdinand of Aragon. The marriage was celebrated in 1509 on the island of Ischia off the coast of Naples, and the couple briefly resided together in the Neapolitan countryside before D'Avalos left on the first of the many military campaigns against the French that were to occupy him for the rest of his life. Colonna herself returned to Ischia, to the court presided over by her aunt by marriage, Costanza D'Avalos, where the well-stocked library and lively court environment no doubt helped to encourage her own literary aspirations. A single poetic "Epistle" to her husband, written during his imprisonment by the French in 1512, is all that survives of Colonna's poetry from this early period, but she is cited with enough frequency by contemporary Neapolitan writers to suggest that her literary work was already enjoying significant scribal publication in and around Naples, if not farther afield.

The almost constant absence of D'Avalos from home, as well as his reputation for valor and heroism in battle, appear to have provided Colonna with the necessary contexts of loss and longing required by the Petrarchan format in which she wrote. This was reinforced in 1525, when D'Avalos died from injuries sustained at the Battle of Pavia, and it is no accident that Colonna's activity and fame as a poet grew exponentially from this date. Widowed, independently wealthy, and childless, she retreated into a convent in Rome as a secular guest and resisted all attempts by her family and the pope to arrange a second marriage. The emphasis in her work on spirituality and the contemplative life was reinforced by the chaste and pious persona she promoted publicly, and, aided no doubt by her wealth and aristocratic status, she was able to formulate a literary voice that commanded considerable respect while preserving the necessary gender decorum.

Colonna's poetry is stylistically impeccable, drawing on the Petrarchan linguistic and imitative models recommended by Pietro Bembo and others in the period, but also, particularly in the more mature work, rich, sensuous, and innovative in ways that may surprise the uninitiated reader. Although the earlier, so-called "amorous" poems are more traditionally Petrarchan in their emphasis on mourning for the deceased consort, later "spiritual" sonnets embrace instead a far more positive celebration of divine love for Christ, which is flavored significantly by the poet's personal interest in the ideas and doctrines of reform. In these later poems Colonna's status as a poetic innovator is clearly established, and indeed her work came to be widely imitated in the later century by writers of both sexes. Bembo himself, grand master of the Petrarchan genre in the sixteenth century, extolled Colonna's talents as a lyricist, rating her alongside the finest male poets of her age and noting in particular the gravitas of her work that was surprising and admirable in a woman.

A first edition of Colonna's *Rime* was published in 1538 and was followed by twelve other editions before the poet's death in 1547. A particular feature of this phenomenal publication history is Colonna's personal distance from all editions of her work that appeared during her lifetime, so that she was able to maintain that her writing was in no way related to any desire for personal fame or acclaim (although this claim is perhaps undermined by the large number of manuscript collections of the sonnets that were also in circulation during the period). Particularly notable in this early publication history is the presence of a critical commentary, written by a young scholar from Correggio (Rinaldo Corso) and first published in 1543, the first scholarly exposition of the work of a living poet in this period, let alone a female poet. A further nine editions of the *Rime* were published before the end of the sixteenth century, when interest in the genre and its practitioners waned. Since then, attention to the poetry has been sporadic, and serious critical consideration has often been undermined by the tendency toward overly biographical readings of these highly stylized and complex verses.

Colonna's published work is not limited to poetry. She also composed prose works on religious themes, initially as letters, which were later published in collections of prose meditations and in separate editions. These writings demonstrate clearly her interest in religious reform, as well as a concerted attempt to define a role for the secular literary female that draws on the examples of the female "apostles" who appear in the New Testament and in traditional hagiographies, most significantly the examples of Mary Magdalene, Catherine of Alexandria, and the Virgin Mary.

While her literary work has been consistently neglected by the critical establishment, Colonna has remained known for her friendships with famous men of her era. She conducted a poetic and spiritual relationship with Michelangelo Buonarroti that was famous in their own era, predicated on their shared interest in reform spirituality and in lyric production, although it was not in any way a love affair, as the sillier Victorian biographies have asserted. Colonna, widely lauded for the quality of her poetry as well as commanding a far higher social status than Michelangelo and more deeply entrenched than her friend in the reformist debates of the period, assumed the position of authority regarding questions of faith in the poems that they addressed to one another. She also commissioned various artistic works from Michelangelo that clearly arise from the same context of reform-minded exploration. Her private manuscript gift of sonnets for Michelangelo, compiled around 1540, includes many poems that were not published in any printed collection of the period and affords a privileged glimpse of the spiritual and lyric material that most inspired and concerned them both.

A second formative friendship in Colonna's life was forged with the English Cardinal Reginald Pole, who played a key role in the doctrinal negotiations at the early sessions of the Council of Trent and was famously vilified by Cardinal Carafa, later Pope Paul IV, for his position of compromise with the reformers over the doctrine of *sola fide*. Pole was Colonna's religious mentor during the 1530s and 1540s, and she left Rome to reside near him in Viterbo. Under his influence she explored the potential of various doctrines of reform, doctrines that were later defined as heretical at Trent (*sola fide,* Predestination) but that in this earlier period clearly colored her literary output.

Colonna ended her life after a lengthy illness in Rome, where in February 1547 she died in the Convent of Sant'Anna de' Funari, shortly after her poetic mentor Bembo. She left behind her a cultural legacy of huge significance in her role at the forefront of vernacular literary production by secular women in Italy, and her example informed the work of women writers well into the following century. This is not to say that later women writers in Italy limited themselves to the Petrarchan genre in Colonna's image: Rather, women began to write and publish in a striking range of genres by the end of the sixteenth century. More crucially, Colonna's example clearly illustrated the close marriage between public persona and literary production in the work of women writers and provided such a successful model of careful negotiation that critics have continued to confuse persona with production ever since. It could certainly be asserted that Colonna's example helped to spawn the huge increase in women writers appearing in Italy in the later sixteenth and early seventeenth centuries, when that country far surpassed all others in Europe for the sheer number of women writing and publishing literary works.

Abigail Brundin

See also Art and Women; the subheadings Sonnet Writing and Letter Writing (under Literary Culture and Women); Religious Reform and Women.

Bibliography

Primary Works

Colonna, Vittoria. *Carteggio.* 2nd ed. Edited by Ermanno Ferrero and Giuseppe Müller with a supplement by Domenico Tordi. Turin: Ermanno Loescher, 1892.

Colonna, Vittoria. *Dichiaratione fatta sopra la seconda parte delle Rime della Divina Vittoria Collonna* [sic] *Marchesana di Pescara. Da Rinaldo Corso. . . .* Bologna: Gian battista de Phaelli, 1543.

Colonna, Vittoria. *Litere della Divina Vettoria* [sic] *Colonna Marchesana di Pescara alla Duchessa de Amalfi, sopra la vita contemplativa di santa Catherina, Et sopra della attiva santa Maddalena non più viste in luce.* Venice: Alessandro de Viano, Ad instantia di Antonio detto il Cremaschino, 1544.

Colonna, Vittoria. *Pianto della Marchesa di Pescara sopra la passione di Christo. Oratione della medesima sopra l'Ave Maria . . . etc.* Bologna: Manutio, 1557.

Colonna, Vittoria. *Rime.* Edited by Alan Bullock. Rome: Laterza, 1982.

Colonna, Vittoria. *Sonetti in morte di Francesco Ferrante d'Avalos, marchese di Pescara: edizione del ms. XIII.G.43 della Biblioteca Nazionale di Napoli.* Edited by Tobia R. Toscano. Milan: Mondadori, 1998.

Colonna, Vittoria. *Sonnets for Michelangelo. The Other Voice in Early Modern Europe.* Edited and translated by Abigail Brundin. Chicago: University of Chicago Press, 2005.

Secondary Works

Besami, O., J. Hauser, and G. Sopranzi, eds. *Concordances to Vittoria Colonna e Galeazzo di Tarsia: Le rime. Archivio tematico della lirica italiana.* Vol. IV. Hildesheim, Germany, Zürich, and New York: Georg Olms Verlag, 1997.

Bianco, Monica. "Le due redazioni del commento di Rinaldo Corso alle *Rime* di Vittoria Colonna." *Studi di filologia italiana* 56 (1998): 271–295.

Brundin, Abigail. "Vittoria Colonna and the Poetry of Reform." *Italian Studies* 57 (2002): 61–74.

Brundin, Abigail. "Vittoria Colonna and the Virgin Mary." *Modern Language Review* 96 (2001): 61–81.

Cox, Virginia. "Women Writers and the Canon in Sixteenth-Century Italy: The Case of Vittoria Colonna." In *Strong Voices, Weak History: Early Women Writers and Canons in England, France, and Italy.* Edited by Pamela J. Benson and Victoria Kirkham. Ann Arbor: University of Michigan Press, 2005.

Dionisotti, Carlo. "Appunti sul Bembo e su Vittoria Colonna." In *Miscellanea Augusto Campana.* Edited by Rino Avesani et al., 257–286. Padua: Antenore, 1981.

Ferino-Pagden, Silvia, ed. *Vittoria Colonna: Dichterin und Muse Michelangelos.* Catalogue for the exhibition at the Kunsthistorisches Museum, Vienna, 25 February–25 May 1997. Vienna: Skira, 1997.

Rabitti, Giovanna. "Vittoria Colonna as Role Model for Cinquecento Women Poets." In

Women in Italian Renaissance Culture and Society. Edited by Letizia Panizza, 478–497. Oxford: European Humanities Research Centre, 2000.

Therault, Suzanne. *Un cénacle humaniste de la Renaissance autour de Vittoria Colonna châtelaine d'Ischia.* Paris: Didier; Florence: Sansoni Antiquariato, 1968.

Contraception and Birth Control

Until recently, historians argued that early modern women had little or no control over their fertility. According to E. P. Thompson, women were uninterested in limiting pregnancies because of extremely high infant mortality rates. Lawrence Stone contends that contraception was virtually unthinkable until sexual pleasure was freed from the constraints of religion during the eighteenth century. Demographic analyses have since shown, however, that the early modern family had on average some four to six children. Baptismal records indicate that births did not occur at a constant rate, as might be expected if birth control was never used. In fact, quantitative studies demonstrate that the number of births markedly declined once a woman reached her midthirties. This data implies the deliberate spacing, delaying, and avoidance of births, likely through various means such as prolonged breast-feeding (which was known to hinder fertility), abstinence, coitus interruptus, and late marriage. Other methods of birth control included both magic (wearing amulets, for example) and medical techniques such as inserting vaginal pessaries of rue and ground lily root combined with castoreum, administering douches designed to cool the womb, and using barrier methods. Condoms were primarily designed to shield men from venereal disease, with the first printed description of them appearing in a discussion of syphilis, in Gabriello Fallopio's *De morbo gallico* (1564).

John Riddle, a scholar of classical antiquity, argues that medical recipes for contraceptives were used to control fertility. Though Riddle collects and analyzes printed recipes, he claims medical writers were not the primary means of transmitting contraceptive knowledge. Instead, it was spread orally, through networks of women. Yet scholars such as Patricia Crawford doubt the efficacy of early methods of birth control, given the clearly high incidence of unwanted pregnancies outside of marriage, while Linda Pollock and Laura Gowing draw attention to the ways in which women were divided, and not simply united, by issues surrounding pregnancy and birth. Other scholars strive to expand the definition of birth control, pointing out that literary and other early modern sources regularly refer to the concealment of pregnancy. According to Etienne Van de Walle, when women disguised their pregnant bodies, gave birth secretly, and then abandoned or killed newborns, they participated in efforts to control births. It was precisely these cases that received the most attention in fictional as well as legal sources in Renaissance Italy, France, and England.

Lianne McTavish

See also Abortion and Miscarriage; Medicine and Women.

Bibliography

Crawford, Patricia. "Sexual Knowledge in England, 1500–1750." In *Sexual Knowledge, Sexual Science: The History of Attitudes to Sexuality.* Edited by Roy Porter and Mikuláš Teich, 82–106. Cambridge: Cambridge University Press, 1994.

Gowing, Laura. "Secret Births and Infanticide in Seventeenth-Century England." *Past and Present* 156 (1997): 87–115.

McLaren, Angus. *A History of Contraception: From Antiquity to the Present Day.* Oxford: Blackwell, 1990.

McLaren, Angus. *Reproductive Rituals: The Perception of Fertility in England from the Sixteenth Century to the Nineteenth Century.* London: Metheun, 1984.

Pollock, Linda. "Childbearing and Female Bonding in Early Modern England." *Social History* 22, 3 (1997): 286–306.

Riddle, John M. *Contraception and Abortion from the Ancient World to the Renaissance.* Cambridge, MA: Harvard University Press, 1992.

Riddle, John M. *Eve's Herbs: A History of Contraception and Abortion in the West.* Cambridge, MA: Harvard University Press, 1997.

Stone, Lawrence. *The Family, Sex, and Marriage in England, 1500–1800.* New York: Harper and Row, 1977.

Thompson, E. P. "Eighteenth-Century English Society Class Struggle Without Class." *Social History* 3 (1978): 133–165.

Van de Walle, Etienne. " 'Marvellous Secrets': Birth Control in European Short Fiction, 1150–1650." *Population Studies* 54 (2000): 321–330.

Convents

The story of women and convents was perhaps never so complex as it became in sixteenth- and seventeenth-century Europe. The Protestant Reformation in Northern Europe, England's break with the Catholic church, and the Wars of Religion in France provoked the dissolution of many houses and turmoil in others. The Catholic reform movements promoted the foundation of new orders and the spread of new forms of spirituality and of active religious communities. The reforms of religious orders instituted by the Council of Trent affected convent life everywhere, most strongly through its insistence on the enclosure (*clausura*) of all women religious, which met with strong opposition from convent women and their families. This history can best be told by country, even by city and institution, since it was conditioned by the religious and political history of the place and by local social and economic conditions, inheritance patterns, and traditions.

Convent populations differed greatly in number and in kind. In the urban centers of Italy, convents were filled with the daughters of the nobility and prosperous merchant class who could not dower and marry them properly and still keep their patrimony intact. In England, a very small percentage of convent women came from the elite aristocracy and upper gentry; most women of those classes married. The larger numbers were women of the parish gentry, but still the numbers were not great and male religious far outnumbered the women. The wealth of English families was land and they were able to pay dowries over time with income from their estates. The rising cost of dowries, therefore, did not threaten to impoverish them, as it did Italians who generally had to pay largely in cash (convent dowries cost them far less). Lower-class women did not become choir nuns; such women were admitted only in small numbers and as lay sisters, or servant nuns. In many areas of Europe where the feudal system remained strong, daughters of the nobility were often appointed as abbesses of important abbeys, often large landholding institutions, and governed territory in the name of their families. Mère Angelique Arnauld (1592?–1661), who, at the age of eight, was sent by her powerful family to the monastery of Port-Royal to become abbess, is one of the most famous examples of this practice, common in France.

To be sure, there were also many constants, aspects of convent structure and life that were similar throughout Europe. Foremost were those ordained by the rules of the religious orders: Convents followed similar liturgical calendars; they shared rituals of religious life, the observance of canonical hours, and the articulation of the day of work, prayer, and relaxation. They provided protection for women, as well as an education, albeit limited, and they offered nuns a certain autonomy of action not possible for most women in the secular world. Their sphere of action was not limited to the private world of their community, since convent women lived off income from properties they owned, money they lent, and the sale of produce and handicrafts; they interacted with secular employees, townspeople (including but not limited to relatives and friends), their secular and clerical governors, confessors, and pastoral visitors.

Convent education and freedom from family responsibilities offered nuns the opportunity to study and to write. In many convents a recorder was appointed to keep account books or to document the history of their foundations and the events of their lives. Nuns composed devotional literature too and hagiographical texts for the edification of their sisters; some wrote and staged plays intended to teach and to entertain their novices and other members of the community (often laypersons as well). Nuns also practiced other arts, especially music; they performed in choir and some learned to compose. Many published their works and earned fame in the world. Fewer nuns achieved renown for the figurative arts, yet in their scriptoria they produced and illuminated manuscript books, and they embellished their own physical surroundings with paintings and sculpture. Nuns also commissioned artworks for their convents and churches. Enclosure kept them inside convent walls but it did not stifle their creativity.

Convents had always provided refuge for women of the upper classes who, because of illness, infirmity, or physical appearance, were not considered suitable for the marriage market. They also took in wives who had proven sterile or who had been mistreated by their husbands. Widows retired to convents; however, because of their worldly experience and the likelihood that they would decide to leave, eventually taking their money with them, they were not always welcome. Special convents were founded for reformed prostitutes and for poor girls in danger of turning to such a life. Most large convents were engaged in child care, taking in infant girls and keeping them until their future could be decided by their families; these institutions also educated secular girls. Beginning in the early sixteenth century new orders were founded that were dedicated to educating young women outside convent walls; the Ursulines were the first, founded by Angela Merici (1470/1474–1540) in Brescia in the 1530s. Other institutions were founded to minister to the poor and the sick: The Oblates of Tor de' Specchi began as early as the mid-fifteenth century, but others followed with increasing frequency. They were to meet with difficulties in the early post-Tri-

dentine period when the church sought energetically to enclose them.

Education and other forms of social work, however, were badly needed by growing city populations, and more institutes grew up that were founded to answer these needs. In France Jane Frances de Chantal (1572–1641) founded the Visitandines, an order devoted to nursing. Mary Ward (1585–1645), an English recusant Catholic, set up schools for girls and teachers in London, Rome, Naples, Cologne, Trier, Vienna, Liége, Munich, and elsewhere, following the example of the Jesuits, but her Institute of the Blessed Virgin Mary, known as the English Ladies, met with the strong opposition of the Society and most of the church hierarchy, who feared the creation of a large religious structure within the church that answered to a female administrator. Her many strong enemies persuaded the pope to issue a bull of suppression, closing most of her foundations; Mary Ward was imprisoned, though later released, and, when she died, of her many schools only two (in Rome and Munich) were still operating. The Institute of the Blessed Virgin Mary received canonical status as a congregation only in 1703. By the late seventeenth century most of the newly founded female religious communities in Europe were active orders; one of the most successful was the Daughters of Charity, founded by pious members of the laity in France together with Vincent de Paul.

Movements for religious reform also shaped the lives of convent women during the period we call the Renaissance. Reform movements of the fifteenth century affected convent women throughout Europe, observants were placed in houses of conventuals, but the experiments met with opposition, often violent. Grassroots reform movements met with more immediate and more long-lived success. New, reformed religious orders were instituted that had male and female branches, principally the Capuchins, Theatines, Barnabites, Oratorians, and Discalced Carmelites, the contemplative order founded by Saint Teresa of Avila. Teresa traveled throughout Spain establishing many houses of convent women dedicated to spiritual perfection. She was a brilliant writer whose autobiographical account of her conversion, her mission, and her mystical experiences is a classic of the genre and a prose masterpiece of the Spanish Golden Age. Two of Teresa's closest collaborators were invited to France to found institutions there, and the popularity of the order—and of Teresa's new spirituality—grew rapidly in all of Catholic Europe.

The Protestant Reformations of the sixteenth century and the Catholic Counter-Reformation produced dramatic effects in convent life. In Northern Europe where Lutheranism and Calvinism took hold, in England with its Anglican reform, and in various areas of France that leaned toward Protestantism, convents were closed and the women pensioned or married. Some houses survived by accepting Lutheran women in their midst, whose charge was to convert those who resisted; in other houses the women fought to preserve their religious and community life. English convents were dissolved between 1534 and 1539, but a number of them were later reestablished in Catholic areas of the continent, in Belgium, France, and Portugal; their fate varied briefly during the return of Catholic monarchs.

Even the convents of Southern Europe, which remained Catholic, found themselves constantly embroiled in controversy. Beginning in the fifteenth century, local civic authorities asserted the right to oversight of the convents in their jurisdiction, establishing new magistracies or enlarging the purview of others for that purpose. This created a double structure of control, civic and ecclesiastical, often in conflict. The post-Tridentine church exercised its control most obviously as it sought to impose enclosure with bricks and mortar as well as decrees. Church authorities walled up doors and windows that gave onto city streets; ordered more locks and keys and smaller open spaces in convent grilles; and made laypersons request permission of the bishop or his vicar to visit the nuns. Yet many exceptions were granted and rules frequently flouted. Convent women protested, sometimes violently, hurling stones at officials come to impose their will. The decrees promulgated at Trent also sought to wrench control of convents from the regulars and entrust them to local bishops; this meant close local supervision and less autonomy for the women, and it too was long resisted. Ultimately, the nuns were forced to concede, but they demanded privileges in exchange for compliance, and the church, which had won, relaxed its demands. The Tridentine reforms to prevent forced religious vocations remained mere formalities that were never effectively instituted. Postulants were interviewed by the bishop before taking vows and asked if they did so willingly, but the answer could only be yes for those who had nowhere else to go. This provoked several eloquent written protests from Arcangela Tarabotti, a Venetian nun, a victim of forced vocation, and an early feminist. Tarabotti accused the inheritance system and those who defended it, fathers, church, and the state, of unfairly denying its victims their god-given free will, finding it in their interest to do so and indifferent to the suffering they caused. She accused men of depriving women of an education out of fear of being surpassed by them, and she argued for a role in public life for women in Italy. It was even more extraordinary that she managed to publish and circulate several works, including her letters; her most important treatise was issued pseudonymously in Belgium and shortly after her death was consigned to the Index of Forbidden Books.

Elissa B. Weaver

See also Religious Reform and Women; Tarabotti, Arcangela; Ward, Mary.

Bibliography

Eckenstein, Lina. *Women Under Monasticism: Chapters on Saint-Lore and Convent Life Between A.D. 500 and A.D. 1500.* New York: Russell and Russell, 1963.

Kendrick, Robert. *Celestial Sirens: Nuns and Their Music in Early Modern Milan.* Oxford and New York: Clarendon Press, 1996.

Leonard, Amy. *Nails in the Wall: Catholic Nuns in Reformation Germany.* Chicago and London: University of Chicago Press, 2005.

Matter, E. Ann, and John Coakley, eds. *Creative Women in Medieval and Early Modern Italy: A Religious and Artistic Renaissance.* Philadelphia: University of Pennsylvania Press, 1994.

Medioli, Francesco, Paola Vismara Chiappa, and Gabriella Zarri. "*De Monialibus* (secoli XVI-XVII-XVIII)." *Revista di Storia e Letteratura Religiosa* 33 (1997): 643–715.

Monson, Craig. *Disembodied Voices: Music and Culture in an Early Modern Italian Convent.* Berkeley: University of California Press, 1995.

Power, Eileen. *Medieval English Nunneries, c. 1275–1535.* New York: Biblo and Tannen, 1964.

Ranft, Patricia. *Women and the Religious Life in Premodern Europe.* New York: St. Martin's Press, 1996.

Scaraffia, Lucetta, and Gabriella Zarri, eds. *Women and Faith: Catholic Religious Life in Italy from Late Antiquity to the Present.* Cambridge, MA: Harvard University Press, 1999.

Sperling, Jutta Gisela. *Convents and the Body Politic in Late Renaissance Venice.* Chicago and London: University of Chicago Press, 1999.

Strasser, Ulrike. *State of Virginity: Gender, Politics and Religion in Early Modern Germany.* Ann Arbor: University of Michigan Press, 2003.

Tarabotti, Arcangela. *Paternal Tyranny.* Edited and Translated by Letizia Panizza. Chicago and London: University of Chicago Press, 2004.

Walker, Claire. *Gender and Politics in Early Modern Europe: English Convents in France and the Low Countries.* New York: Palgrave, 2003.

Weaver, Elissa. "Renaissance Culture in Italian Convents, 1450–1650." In *Convent Theatre in Early Modern Italy: Spiritual Fun and Learning for Women,* 9–48. Cambridge: Cambridge University Press, 2002.

Zarri, Gabriella. "Gender, Religious Institutions and Social Discipline: The Reform of the Regulars." In *Gender and Society in Renaissance Italy.* Edited by J. C. Brown and R. C. Davis. London and New York: Longman, 1998.

Zarri, Gabriella. "The Third Status." In *Time, Space, and Women's Lives in Early Modern Europe.* Edited by Anne Jacobson Schutte, Thomas Kuehn, and Silvana Seidel Menchi, 181–199. Kirksville, MO: Truman State University Press, 2001.

Zemon Davis, Natalie "City Women and Religious Change." In *Society and Culture in Early Modern France,* 65–95. Stanford, CA: Stanford University Press, 1977.

Cookbooks and Recipes

The word "recipe," literally meaning "take" from the Latin *recipere* (to receive), denotes a set of prescriptive instructions for the preparation of food or medicine. In early modern Europe, both women and men invented, collected, and exchanged recipes in manuscript, print, and by word of mouth. In England, the recording of "recipe" (or "receipt") was a popular form of everyday writing, and women circulated recipes exclusively in manuscript until the mid-1650s, when their collections first began to go into print.

Many literate women of the middle and upper classes kept receipt books dedicated solely to the topic of recipes, although occasionally they included other miscellaneous writings, such as poems, hymns, sermons, and family records. These receipt books were often handed down and across generations of women. For example, the receipt book of Englishwoman Mary Granville (ca. 1620–1750) belonged to three generations of women since Mary inherited it from her mother and then left it to her daughter, Anne. The cloistered nuns of the Ursuline Order in rue de Capucins in Paris kept a communal *Catalog of Remedies* (1725), a collection of medicinal remedies circulated among the nuns responsible for providing care to the sick and elderly of the convent.

A particular recipe collection could include culinary or medicinal recipes, or it could include a mix of both. Culinary recipes focused on the preparation of ordinary and exotic foodstuffs: meats, pies, puddings, confections, ales, beers, and chocolate. Mary Baumfylde collected both culinary (such as "to preserue Apricoks or any other greene fruite") and medicinal (such as "a bath for an olde soare") receipts in her notebook (ca. 1626). Medicinal recipes included remedies for purges, ointments, salves, simples, waters, and charms. Lady Grace Mildmay

(1552–1620) from Northamptonshire collected over two hundred and fifty folios of medicinal receipts, and she maintained an extensive lay practice for much of her life. In France, the royal midwife to Marie de Médicis, Louise Bourgeois, published a collection of two hundred and eighty medical and cosmetic recipes, the *Recueil de divers secrets pour diverses maladies,* in 1626, and her popular book was republished into the eighteenth century.

Recipes were exchanged as gifts, given in bids for patronage, and circulated among select coteries, and thus they were social and communal texts (similar to commonplace books), as well as individual ones informed by the writing, reading, and practice of the author/compiler. Women's recipe practice was also informed by male-authored household manuals, herbals, and technical "how-to" books, yet, as a genre, recipe writing was particularly accessible to women given their training and expertise in the areas of preserving, cooking, and household medicine. Recipes were collected on loose scraps of paper, exchanged in letters, written on walls in the home, recorded in diaries, or copied into notebooks (called "receipt books") by the owner or by a hired scribe. Alice Thornton noted a medicinal recipe for curing her mother's cough, which required "the use of bags with fried oats, butter and camomile chopped, [and] laid to her sides . . . ," in her autobiographical *Book of Remembrances* (1668). The Venetian writer, Moderata Fonte, in *The Worth of Women* (1600), used recipes to further her argument advocating for the rights of women. While discussing the difficulty of finding an appropriate remedy to "cure men of their defects" and make them more "respect[ful] and lov[ing]" to women, she systematically catalogs medicinal and culinary recipes for other kinds of bodily ailments (such as using rhubarb "against fevers").

The categories of culinary and medicinal were indistinct for much of the early modern period since every ingestible substance was believed to have humoral properties capable of affecting the individual body's fragile "com-plexion," or balance. This fluidity between the medicinal and culinary, along with the collaborative nature of most collections, made the receipt book a flexible genre, one that enabled female self-expression through the writing and exchange of recipes for the well-being of body, home, and community.

Catherine Field

See also Bourgeois, Louise; Fonte, Moderata; the subheading The Practice of Pharmacology and Laywomen (under Medicine and Women).

Bibliography

Primary Work

Fonte, Moderata. *The Worth of Women.* Edited and translated by Virginia Cox. Chicago: University of Chicago Press, 1997.

Secondary Works

Hunter, Lynette. "Women and Domestic Medicine: Lady Experimenters, 1570–1620." In *Women, Science and Medicine, 1500–1700.* Edited by Lynette Hunter and Sarah Hutton, 89–107. Phoenix Mill, UK: Sutton, 1997.

Pollock, Linda. *With Faith and Physic: The Life of a Tudor Gentlewoman, Lady Grace Mildmay, 1552–1620.* New York: St. Martin's Press, 1995.

Copio Sullam, Sara (1592?–1641)

Influential poet, letter writer, polemicist, and salonnière
The prominent Jewish writer Sara Copio Sullam was born around 1592 to a prominent family in the Venetian ghetto. Her father, Simone Copio, owned lands in the Eastern Mediterranean and dealt in insurance, agricultural goods, and loan banking; her mother, Ricca or Richa de' Grassini in Copio, carried out the family's affairs after Simone's 1606 death. The Copio family was among the wealthier in the ghetto. Simone Copio in his will listed assets of twenty-three thousand ducats, invested in his bank, plus "other merchandise, gold, silver, jewels and things of different kinds."

Sara Copio, who had two younger sisters, married the affluent businessman Giacob Sullam after her father's death, probably by 1609. Sara was likely pleased with the match, since her father in his will directed that his daughters "have husbands to their liking, so long as they are decent, honest and honorable." Giacob seems not to have opposed Sara's literary activity. Sara brought to the marriage significant financial resources: her sizable three-thousand-*scudo* dowry and later, after her mother's death, one-third of her father's estate, over which her father had ordered that she have "absolute control" as long as she retained her Jewish faith. Such financial independence was likely instrumental in Copio Sullam's literary career. Sara and Giacob seem not to have had any children who lived beyond infancy, another factor that probably enabled Copio Sullam's intellectual pursuits.

In her midtwenties, Copio Sullam gained fame in intellectual circles in Venice for her erudition, musical talent, and stunning beauty. (Her erudition was perhaps a trick of fate: her father, who lacked sons, invested resources in his daughter's education that might otherwise have gone to a boy.) She established a literary salon frequented mostly by Christian men—including dramatist and priest Baldassare Bonifacio (1586–1659), poet Numidio Paluzzi (1567–1625), whom she hired as her preceptor, and writer Alessandro Berardelli—but also by rabbi Leon Modena (1571–1648), a major intellectual figure in early modern Venice. Several of these figures were associated with the Accademia degli Incogniti, Venice's most important literary body in the era.

Her intellectual community was coalescing when in 1618 Copio Sullam, inspired by an epic poem on the Old Testament heroine Esther, wrote to the author, Genoese writer and monk Ansaldo Cebà, to express her admiration and spiritual love. The two writers engaged in a sporadic four-year-long correspondence. In 1623, Cebà published his side of their exchange, fifty-three letters, along with poems the two exchanged. He suppressed the letters of Copio Sullam, which have never been found. Despite this exclusion, traces of Copio Sullam's voice are still discernable, since Cebà includes four of her sonnets and adds footnotes that sup-

posedly paraphrase some of her statements. Cebà's letters document his unrelenting attempts to convince his correspondent of the "error" of her Judaism and to effect her conversion. They also show, indirectly, Copio Sullam's rebuffs of these attempts and her proud defense of her faith. The correspondence ends when Cebà realizes Copio Sullam will not convert.

Copio Sullam was still corresponding with Cebà when her associate Bonifacio published the 1621 *Immortalità dell'anima*. The work was a frontal attack on Copio Sullam, whom Bonifacio repeatedly accuses of denying the soul's immortality. His charge amounted to one of heresy. Bonifacio also repeatedly urges Copio Sullam to convert to Christianity, at times suggesting a relation between unorthodox beliefs on the soul and Judaism. Bonifacio's treatise occasioned a prompt reply from Copio Sullam, her 1621 *Manifesto,* in which she interlaces spiritual poetry and forceful prose to debunk Bonifacio's charge. The work—the only one Copio Sullam put to press and the most important piece of her surviving writing—was printed at least three times in 1621, a probable sign of the interest it garnered. In the *Manifesto,* Copio Sullam highlights the gendered nature of the conflict with Bonifacio, framing it as an unfair battle between a defenseless woman and an unchivalrous man, and minimizes the religious aspects of the exchange, carefully avoiding criticism of Christianity and creating a vision of Judaism palatable to Catholics. Bonifacio immediately answered Copio Sullam's treatise with a short and harsh retort, published as the *Risposta al Manifesto* (1621); in it he paradoxically attacks Copio Sullam for her *Manifesto* and charges that she did not write it.

Shortly after the *Manifesto* controversy, other members of Copio Sullam's literary circle—Paluzzi and Berardelli—betrayed her by defrauding her of hundreds of ducats. Copio Sullam fired Paluzzi and took Berardelli to court. After Paluzzi's death in 1625, Berardelli issued an edition of Paluzzi's *Rime* (1626), which repeatedly accuses Copio Sullam of plagiarism and theft and gives Paluzzi credit for the writing attributed to her, including the *Manifesto.* More than a dozen minor writers appear to have banded together to produce a work that countered these charges. The longest section of the work, which remained manuscript, is an intricate narrative on the model of Traiano Boccalini's *Ragguagli di Parnaso.* This section describes Paluzzi and Berardelli's fictional trial and punishment in Parnassus because of Paluzzi's *Rime,* in which "the reputation of a virtuous woman is torn apart with the most explicit lies and with disgusting slander." The work also contains five sonnets by Copio Sullam. This manuscript defense may have helped to repair Copio Sullam's reputation, but the episode with Paluzzi and Berardelli nevertheless seems to have ended her public literary career, since it seems she either could not or chose not to pursue further public literary activity. No information has emerged on Copio Sullam from the late 1620s until her death in 1641 *more veneto.*

When Copio Sullam disappeared from the literary stage, she had only published her *Manifesto.* Ten poems had also been published in other works, most importantly in Cebà's letters and the *Avvisi* manuscript. She also influenced many of the works of her associates. Her skillful writing and her intense intellectual exchange with many prominent writers, often marked by a thwarted desire to establish respectful communication across religious lines, make her the most exceptional example of Jewish female learning in early modern Italy. She seems not to have been in contact with the two other Venetian women writers of the era, Lucrezia Marinella (1571–1653) and Arcangela Tarabotti (1604–1652), though these women's literary careers were also marred by the frequent hostility and charges of plagiarism that beset Copio Sullam. These difficulties impelled Copio Sullam, like her female contemporaries, to take up pen in self-defense and to publish, securing lasting fame.

Lynn Westwater

See also Marinella, Lucrezia; Tarabotti, Arcangela.

Bibliography
Primary Works
Bonifacio, Baldassarre. *Dell'immortalità dell'anima.* Venice: Pinelli, 1621.
Cebà, Ansaldo. *Lettere a Sarra Copia.* Genoa: Pavoni, 1623.
Sullam, Sara Copio. *Manifesto.* Venice: Giovanni Alberti, 1621.
Secondary Works
Adelman, Howard. "The Literacy of Jewish Women in Early Modern Italy." In *Women's Education in Early Modern Europe, A History, 1500–1800.* Edited by Barbara J. Whitehead, 133–158. New York: Garland, 1999.
Boccato, Carla. "Sara Copio Sullam, la poetessa del ghetto di Venezia: episodi della sua vita in un manoscritto del secolo XVII." *Italia* 6, no. 1–2 (1987): 104–218.
da Fonseca-Wollheim, Corinna. "Faith and Fame in the Life and Works of the Venetian Jewish Poet Sara Copio Sullam (1592?–1641)." Ph.D. dissertation, University of Cambridge, 2000.
Fortis, Umberto. *La 'bella ebrea': Sara Copio Sullam, poetessa nel ghetto di Venezia del '600.* Turin: Silvio Zamorani editore, 2003.
Westwater, Lynn. "Sara Copio Sullam: Life and Family" and "Sara Copio Sullam: Literary Life and Works." In "The Disquieting Voice: Women's Writing and Antifeminism in Seventeenth-Century Venice." Ph.D. dissertation, University of Chicago, 2003.

Cornaro, Caterina (1454–1510).

Queen of Cyprus, Venetian humanist, patron of poets, artists, and architects

Born in Venice on 25 November 1454, Caterina was one of the eight children of Marco Cornaro (Corner) and Fiorenza Crispo, daughter of Duke Nicolo Crispo. Caterina was given an education befitting boys and girls whose families were members of the patriciate: humanist studies (poetry, philosophy, history, the classical languages) with an emphasis on the perfection of social skills, as well as dancing and singing. When Caterina was ten she entered the Convent of San Benedetto in Padova as a resident student. Four years later, in 1468, she returned to Venice for her engagement to James II de Lusignan, king of Cyprus.

The union had been engineered by Caterina's father and uncle, Andrea Cornaro, who had strong commercial interests in Cyprus and was very close to the sovereign. James II de Lusignan had obtained the throne of Cyprus after much intrigue and thanks to the support of the Egyptian sultan at Alexandria who, up to that moment, was the titular ruler of the island. This marriage ensured James the protection of the Serenissima for his wealthy but contested dominion and would conversely strengthen Venetian influence in the Mediterranean. Caterina's proxy marriage was a solemn event. On 30 July 1468, Caterina was taken from her father's palace along the Grand Canal on the gilded ship of state, the Bucintoro, and brought to the Doge's Palace. Before the ambassador of Cyprus and the Doge Cristoforo Moro, she was officially married and then sent back to the convent in Padova to complete her education.

In 1471 the Venetian senate created for Caterina the title of Daughter of the Republic and gave her a magnificent dowry of one hundred ducats. In the summer of 1472, escorted by four Venetian galleons and accompanied by family and servants, Caterina left for Cyprus. Two months later, in the cathedral of Famagosta, the marriage was celebrated in person, and she was crowned "Queen of Cyprus, Jerusalem and Armenia." Her husband died in 1473 at the age of thirty-three and her infant son, Prince James III de Lusignan, died a few months later. Caterina thus became, at the age of nineteen, the sole ruler of Cyprus. Caterina's uncle, Andrea Cornaro, and her cousin, Marco Bembo, were victims of a conspiracy that aimed at bringing Cyprus under the control of the Reign of Naples. Venice was quick to send a fleet to Famagosta and to reestablish order. The Venetians now had control over the island and the queen was surrounded by Venetian advisors: The Venetian senate had appointed a council of regents, which gained power over the fifteen years that she ruled. Caterina was still young, and the republic was

Caterina Cornaro, queen of Cyprus and patron of poets and artists. Painting by Titian. Uffizi, Florence, Italy. (Alinari/Art Resource, NY)

afraid she would remarry (a possible candidate was Alfonso, son of the King of Naples). Moreover, there was the danger that, aided by the Cypriots, she would rebel against her Venetian advisors and gain effective control of the island. In 1488, through the mediation of her father and her brother Giorgio, the senate managed to persuade the queen to abdicate her crown to the republic. In exchange, she was allowed to retain the title of queen, her dowry, and the income from many villages in Cyprus.

In 1489 Caterina embarked for Venice where, in the Basilica of St. Mark, she publicly "donated" her reign to the doge. Some time after her return to Venice, during an excursion in the Veneto area, Caterina was charmed by the picturesque district of Asolo and requested it of the republic. The senate conceded Asolo with some neighboring lands, an annual pension, and a bodyguard. She settled in the castle of Asolo and ruled for twenty years, turning out to be, in many ways, a progressive monarch. She introduced the silk industry to the region and improved commerce. Caterina was also a generous patron, and her new court became a center of attraction for poets, painters, and artists. Titian, Giorgione, and Gentile Bellini rendered her portrait, and the queen and her court were depicted by Pietro Bembo, a relative and frequent guest, in his work *Degli Asolani*. Her summer villa, Il Barco, designed by Francesco Grazioli in 1491 in the nearby village of Altivole, was an impressive building with an extravaganza of gardens, fountains, and exotic animals.

Caterina left Asolo and took refuge in Venice in 1509 during the invasion of the troops of Emperor Maximilian. Unfortunately, her resort place was destroyed and, because of the League of Cambrai politics, she could never return. On 10 July 1510 she died in Venice.

Irene Zanini-Cordi

See also Art and Women; Education, Humanism, and Women; the subheading Literary Patronage (under Literary Culture and Women); Power, Politics, and Women.

Bibliography

Primary Works

Bembo, Pietro. *Gli Asolani*. Venice: Aldo Manunzio, 1505.

Colbertaldo, Antonio. *Vita di Caterina Cornaro Regina di Cipro*. Venice: Biblioteca del Museo Correr, ms. cod. 1189/XXVI.

Secondary Works

Antinoro-Polizzi, Joseph. *Lady of Asolo: A Pictorial History of the Life and Times of Caterina Cornaro*. Rochester, NY: Ayers Printing Co., 1985.

Berruti, Aldo. *Patriziato veneto—I Cornaro*. Turin: La Nuova Grafica, 1953.

Piovesan, Luciana, *Storia di Asolo: Il Barco della Regina Cornaro ad Altivole*. Asolo: 1980.

Scarpari, Gianfranco. *Le ville venete*. Rome: Newton Compton Editori, 1980.

Cotteblanche, Marie de
(ca. 1520–ca. 1580)

Translator and linguist

Born into a family of *parlementaires* (members of Paris's *Parlement*), Marie de Cotteblanche was the daughter of Guy de Cotteblanche, a lawyer at the Paris Parlement, and Catherine Hesselin, whom he married in 1517. Her older brother Elie accumulated many honors, becoming a gentleman of the Chambre du Roi in 1571 and knight of the Order of Saint Michel in 1578. Marie had a sister Marguerite, as we learn from the cosmographer François de Belleforest's dedication to them of his pastoral poem, *Chasse d'amour* (Love's Hunt, 1560). The bibliographer La Croix du Maine notes that she was a "*Damoiselle Parisienne, très-docte en Philosophie et Mathématiques*" (Damoiselle Parisienne, very learned in philosophy and mathematics).

Marie de Cotteblanche was also adept at languages. Her only extant work, *Trois dialogues de M. Pierre Messie, touchant la nature du Soleil, de la Terre, et de toutes les choses qui se font et apparoissent en l'air* (Three Dialogues by M. Pierre Messie, concerning the nature of the sun, the earth, and all things that happen and appear in the air), a French translation of three Spanish dialogues by the cosmographer Pedro Mexía (or Mejía, Pierre Messie in French, 1497–1551), was published in 1566 and reissued some twenty-nine times between 1566 and 1643, either independently, in Claude Grujet's translation of Messie's *Diverses Leçons*, or in an anonymous translation of the complete dialogues of Pierre Messie.

Cotteblanche bases her translation on both the original Spanish version (either the 1547 or 1548 editions) and an Italian rendition by Alfonso D'Ulloa published in Venice in 1557. In her numerous marginal annotations, Cotteblanche compares the Spanish and Italian versions, opting sometimes for the one or the other or sometimes coming up with her own formulations. In her dedicatory letter to her friend and patron, Marguerite de Saluces, maréchale de Termes, she thanks the latter for having taught her Italian. She states her knowledge of only Italian, a privileged language at court and among a select group of translators who were state secretaries, writers, and lawyers. Marie de Cotteblanche combines her knowledge of languages with her interest in the sciences. Of the six dialogues by Messie, she retains only the three that concern geophysical and cosmological topics (the sun, the earth, and the meteors). Her choice of a scientific subject matter was not an unusual one for a woman of the elite classes. Many learned women of the nobility and upper gentry were well read in the sciences. Catherine de Médicis, for instance, was interested in astronomy and the natural sciences, Marguerite de Valois and Diane de Poitiers in medical treatises, and Catherine de Clermont, maréchale de Retz, in philosophy and mathematics.

Cotteblanche's choice of the dialogue form, a favorite humanist genre, appealed to a wide readership eager to expand its learning. In her preface, she states her great love for books ("*seuls m'ont faict fidelle compaignie*" [they alone have been my faithful companions]), study, and learning. She was also committed to writing. She viewed her translation as a stylistic exercise, a first attempt to produce a work that would eventually lead to another publication reflecting her own creativity. No other work by her has been published.

Anne R. Larsen

See also Poitiers, Diane de.

Bibliography

Primary Works

Cotteblanche, Marie de. *Trois dialogues de M. Pierre Messie, touchant la nature du Soleil, de la Terre, et de toutes les choses qui se font et apparoissent en l'air.* Paris: Federic Morel, 1566.

La Croix du Maine et Du Verdier. *Les bibliothèques françoises* (1584, 1585). 6 vols. Edited by Rigoley de Juvigny, vol. 1, 88. Graz, Austria: Academische Druck, 1969. (Originally printed in 1772–1773.)

Secondary Works

Berriot-Salvadore, Evelyne. "Les femmes et les pratiques de l'écriture de Christine de Pisan à Marie de Gournay." *Réforme, Humanisme, Renaissance* 16 (1983): 52–69.

La Charité, Claude. "Marie de Cotteblanche, traductrice de Pierre Messie, ou l'espagnol en filigrane de l'italien." In *D'une écriture à l'autre: les femmes et la traduction sous l'Ancien Régime.*
Edited by Jean-Philippe Beaulieu, 211–227. Ottowa: Presses de l'Université d'Ottowa ("Regards sur la traduction"), 2004.

Larsen, Anne R. "Marie de Cotteblanche: préfacière et traductrice de trois dialogues de Pierre Messie." In *Écrits de femmes à la Renaissance.* Edited by Anne R. Larsen and Colette H. Winn, 111–119. *Etudes littéraires* 27.2 (1994).

Larsen, Anne R. "Writing in the Margins: Marie de Cotteblanche's Preface to Her Translation of Pierre Messie (1566)." *Allegorica* 19 (1998): 95–103.

Courtesans and Prostitution, Italy (*cortigiana, cortegiane*)

A courtesan was an educated and talented woman who, in the courtly and urban society of early modern Italy, provided sexual services to wealthy and prominent men. Despite her name, the courtesan was not a direct counterpart to the male courtier (*cortigiano*), who was usually a court diplomat or intellectual. She is also not to be confused with the palace lady or princess (*dama, donna di palazzo*) or with the lady-in-waiting (*donzella, damigella*).

Sexual commerce flourished in early modern Europe. In a society based on the inheritance of wealth through marriage, legitimate offspring—and hence the chastity of marriageable women—appeared essential. Women destined for marriage were kept close to home and far from social life; men wedded late but freely associated, traveled, and worked long before marriage. Prostitution was tolerated in this context because it was thought to deflect male sexual advances away from potential brides, conserving them for the marriage market. Some cities also condoned brothels as a deterrent to homosexual relations, which were thought to threaten population growth by luring men away from procreative sex.

Many were the Italian names for women who traded sex for remuneration: *donna pubblica* (public woman), *meretrice* (meretrix), *puttana* (whore), *donna da partito* (woman of means), *prostituta,* and the like. These terms, however, often convey the speakers' contexts and attitudes rather than the economic status of the women they name. Prostitutes of all kinds could euphemistically be called courtesans, while even celebrity courtesans were regularly insulted as whores. The social status of the early modern prostitute thus lay not in what people called her but rather in her income, which derived from the wealth of her clients.

Lowest on the ladder were orphaned girls and destitute women who walked the streets in search of men willing to trade food and shelter for sex. A middle range included women who registered (and paid taxes) within varyingly legalized versions of the sex trade, including work in the municipal brothels operating in European cities throughout the fifteenth century. Most privileged in the profession were women who earned high incomes not only as sexual partners but also as social companions to prosperous men of their society: the clergy, especially at the powerful papal court; ambassadors and diplomats traveling in the service of princes; noblemen; wealthy merchants; and military officers. In these male orbits of war, politics, and commerce, contact with women was at a premium. The sophisticated, often humanist-influenced circles in which such men moved, moreover, demanded female companions who were not merely beautiful and sexually available, but also socially polished and literate. Prostitutes who marketed these high qualifications came to be known as courtesans.

Perhaps the earliest recorded appearance of this term occurs in the Latin diary of the German Johann Burchard, master of ceremonies at the papal court from 1483 to 1506, who notes that courtesans are "decent prostitutes" (*hoc est meretrix honesta*). Indeed, the Renaissance courtesan probably emerged first in Rome. As the political power of the church expanded, large numbers of young, educated men converged on the Holy City. Advancement within the clergy required vows of celibacy, yet the lavish parties and feasts of the papal court demanded

female guests. By the second half of the fifteenth century, certain women occupying houses owned by St. Peter's Basilica were registered without surnames, by place of origin only (for example, Beatrice di Piemonte, Margherita Fiorentina). This type of self-identification was typical of prostitutes, who often left their cities of birth but adopted professional names reflecting their homelands. The women of St. Peter's were designated in property records as *curialis* (belonging to the curia or court), a term easily translated into the Italian *cortigiana*. The adjective *honesta* (decent, licit), which referred only to the most prestigious of these women, acknowledged not their character but their operation within elite society.

Access to high society distinguished the "decent courtesan" from the staggering number of common prostitutes in major Italian cities. Papal Rome and the naval and trading power of Venice were especially famous for their sex worker populations. Contemporary estimates vary and are probably exaggerated, but one chronicler claimed on the basis of the 1490 census that Rome's fifty thousand inhabitants included more than sixty-eight hundred prostitutes: over 13 percent. Diarist Marin Sanudo (1466–1536) estimated that prostitutes constituted over one-tenth of the Venetian population. These numbers diminished sharply in the later sixteenth century, when Counter-Reformation morality compelled governments to press (unsuccessfully) for the expulsion of all sex workers from within city walls.

A rise to the rank of *cortigiana onesta* required both preparation and luck. Candidates were often trained within their families, since many people could live off the income of one successful courtesan. Literature, music, and dance as well as social skills, proper grooming, and sophisticated style were fundamental to the courtesan's education. Access to lucrative clients required further financial outlays for clothing, cosmetics, and an apartment. Though the investment was considerable, potential profits were also high: the most successful courtesans enjoyed wealth, prestige, fame, and autonomy until about the age of forty, at which time some of them married, some trained younger courtesans, and some retreated into monastic communities. Courtesans in Rome who died with property to bequeath were required by law to leave one-fifth of their wealth to support houses for repentant prostitutes. Whether for legal reasons or due to fears of the afterlife, charitable giving was not uncommon among mature courtesans.

Due to their exceptional visibility, courtesans are among the most historically documented women of early modernity. Contemporary writings in many veins record details about how courtesans lived and died, socialized, spent their money, and interacted with the law. Painters and other artists captured their likenesses. Though they may be portrayed for the viewer as Cleopatra, Venus, Beauty, or simply "a woman," virtually the only models who could dare pose nude or semiclothed for the erotic and allegorical art of the European Renaissance were courtesans. Numerous paintings, engravings, and medallions, in addition, explicitly depict courtesans as such, whether named or anonymous. In these images, courtesans gaze at themselves in the mirror, bathe, solicit clients, play musical instruments, and indeed engage in sexual intercourse. Toward the end of the sixteenth century, Cesare Vecellio included courtesan dress in his book documenting contemporary fashion. Finally, at least two Italian courtesans claim a place in literary history. Tullia d'Aragona (ca. 1510–1556) and Veronica Franco (1546–1591) were attacked as well as praised by their contemporaries for daring to write, but they stand today among the most important poets of the sixteenth century.

Courtesans often projected an idealized view of their lives, but literature and archival evidence (trial records, account books, wills, contracts, and other papers) document the many perils and indignities they faced.

Two Courtesans *(?). Painting by Vittore Carpaccio, ca. 1510–1515. Museo Civico Correr, Venice. (Alinari Archives/Corbis)*

Syphilis, which ran rampant in early modern Europe, was a natural hazard of their trade. Many cities required courtesans to wear yellow veils or bells in public, in an effort to distinguish them from the noblewomen whose fashion and manners they so successfully imitated. Desired and despised, celebrated and shunned, ever occupying a border zone between legality and illegality, courtesans were as subject to coercion, theft, and violence as they were to adulation. Since beauty was their most important professional asset, a popular form of personal revenge against them was disfiguration (usually a cut to the face). Another was gang rape, known in Italy as *il trentuno* ("the thirty-one") in indication of the requisite number of male perpetrators. The public (no quote marks) nature of sex work even moved legal and moral authorities to incorporate prostitutes of all ranks into spectacles devised to entertain or instruct the community at large. These ranged from allegories, in which seminude courtesans paraded as goddesses or virtues, to exemplary shaming rituals and even executions.

In the ambivalent contemporary imagination, courtesans personified beauty, sumptuousness, and erotic liberty, but also vice, treachery, and fraud. No wonder, then, that they frequently appear not only in the copious visual imagery of the period but also in plays, novellas, and songs or that a few courtesans became legends in their time. In one of his best-known novellas (III.42), Matteo Bandello (1485–1561) describes the luxurious Roman apartment of celebrity courtesan Imperia. Her house, he says, appeared to be the dwelling of a princess, furnished as it was in velvets and gold brocade, exquisite carpets, elaborate draperies, and precious ornaments. Bandello recounts Imperia's elegance, but he also narrates the bawdy humor and shameless trickery of another famous courtesan, Isabella de Luna, whose misdemeanors led to her public whipping (II.51; IV.16). The Spanish Francisco Delicado's picaresque dialogue, *La Lozana andaluza* (1528), describes the raucous underworld life of a successful courtesan in Rome; Pietro Aretino satirically depicts the courtesan's cunning survival instincts in his *Dialogues* (1534; 1536); French commentator Pierre Brantôme recalls Italian courtesans with fascination in his *Vies des dames galantes* (1566); and courtesans captivated the English travel writer Thomas Coryat, who marveled over them in his *Coryat's Crudities* (1611). The courtesan appears in popular broadside and pamphlet literature too: In the "Lament of the Ferrarese Courtesan" (ca. 1519–1530) speaks a woman who reached the top of her profession only to be brought low by syphilis, which turns her into a beggar and a pariah.

Luxury prostitution was not an invention of early modernity. On the contrary, some courtesans and their clients compared themselves to ancient Greek and Roman counterparts, casting their activities as a Renaissance revival of those earlier cultures. The legacy of the luxury sex trade, both ancient and modern, remains complex. While it may help sustain glamorized myths about prostitution, it also enriches the long historical record of feminine inventiveness, agency, and resistance.

Deanna Shemek

See also Aragona, Tullia d'; Franco, Veronica.

Bibliography

Cohen, Elizabeth S. "Courtesans and Whores: Words and Behavior in Roman Streets." *Women's Studies* 19 (1991): 201–208.

Larivaille, Paul. *La Vie quotidienne des courtisanes en Italie au temps de la Renaissance.* Paris: Hachette, 1975.

Lawner, Lynne. *Lives of the Courtesans.* Milan: Rizzoli, 1987.

Masson, Georgina. *Courtesans of the Italian Renaissance.* London: Secker and Warburg, 1975.

Otis, Leah. *Prostitution in Medieval Society: The History of an Urban Institution in Languedoc.* Chicago: University of Chicago Press, 1985.

Pecchiai, Pio. *Donne del Rinascimento in Roma. Imperia. Lucrezia figlia d'Imperia. La misteriosa Fiammetta.* Padua: CEDAM, 1958.

Pecchiai, Pio. *Roma nel Cinquecento.* Bologna: Licinio, 1948.

Rosenthal, Margaret F. *The Honest Courtesan: Veronica Franco, Citizen and Writer in Sixteenth-Century Venice.* Chicago: University of Chicago Press, 1992.

Rossiaud, Jacques. *Medieval Prostitution.* Translated by Lydia Cochrane. London: Blackwell, 1988.

Shemek, Deanna. *Ladies Errant: Wayward Women and Social Order in Early Modern Italy.* Durham, NC, and London: Duke University Press, 1998.

Shemek, Deanna. "'Mi mostrano a dito tutti quanti': Disease, Deixis, and Disfiguration in the *Lamento di una cortigiana ferrarese.*" In *Italiana 11: Essays on Gender, Literature, and Aesthetics in the Italian Renaissance. In Honor of Robert J. Rodini.* Edited by Paul A. Ferrara, Eugenio Giusti, and Jane Tylus, 49–64. Boca Raton, FL: 2004.

Trexler, Richard C. *The Women of Renaissance Florence: Power and Dependence in Renaissance Florence.* Binghamton, NY: Medieval and Renaissance Texts and Studies, 1993.

Crenne, Hélisenne de (Marguerite Briet; ca. 1500–ca. 1552)

Novelist, humanist, and feminist

Hélisenne de Crenne is the pseudonym of Marguerite Briet, a noblewoman from Abbeville in Picardy who wrote in Paris during the 1530s and 1540s. Extant notary documents provide a few scanty details about her life. She was married to Philippe Fournel, lord of Crenne, whose holdings provided her pen name. The marriage appears to have been an unhappy one leading to a financial separation. Hélisenne's will lists considerable personal property, including a house on the present Rue Lhomond of the Latin Quarter, and notes that she was living in Saint-Germain-des-Prés, then outside the walls of Paris. She was well educated, possibly in a convent, and knew enough Latin to translate Virgil. Paris of that era was a major center for the printed book. Her influential bookseller and publisher, Denis Janot, produced high-quality books illustrated by a large number of woodcuts. He sold his books in a stall in the Palace of Justice and from his shop in the Rue Neuve Notre Dame, a street now partially visible in Notre Dame's Crypt. Three of Hélisenne's volumes were small books intended to be held in the hands of women readers. Her fourth publication was an expensive folio edition, a sister volume to the extremely popular *Amadis de Gaule,* which was in Janot's press at the same time. Her books were carefully illustrated commercial ventures, especially her 1538 novel *Les Angoysses douloureuses qui procedent d'amours* (The Torments of Love), which was printed eight times by 1560, qualifying it as a best-seller.

Hélisenne de Crenne's *Les angoysses douloureuses qui procedent d'amours* is the first sentimental novel written in French. It tells the story of a woman who is married at age eleven and subsequently falls in love with a handsome stranger. The novel has three parts and an epilogue. The brutal treatment of the first person narrator Hélisenne by her husband in Part One dramatically showcases an unhappy marriage. Hélisenne's jealous husband knocks her down and breaks several teeth while attempting to force her to act less flirtatiously. She remains chaste even though she suffers from the temptation of adulterous love. When her husband fails to bring her back to reasonableness, she is imprisoned in a tower where she records the tale of her disastrous love. The poignancy and psychological realism of this unfortunate situation are responsible for the renewed interest in Hélisenne de Crenne's writing in the second half of the twentieth century when the novel was reissued in four partial and complete editions as well as a reprint. Part One of the *Angoysses* is the most widely read and studied of Hélisenne's writings, and modern readers have identified it as the beginning of the French psychological novel whose successors include Madame de Lafayette's *The Princess of Cleves* and Gustave Flaubert's *Madame Bovary.* They also have appreciated Part One as a so-called "authentic" portrait of a sixteenth-century marriage. Actually, this first portion of Hélisenne's landmark novel was influenced by Giovanni Boccaccio's *Fiametta,* an Italian Renaissance letter elegy.

In Parts Two and Three of the *Angoysses,* Hélisenne de Crenne creates a second first-person narrator, Hélisenne's beloved Guenelic, who, like the hero of Caviceo's *Peregrino,* searches the known world for her, although anagrams reveal the route actually to be between Picardy and Paris. This shift in narrators has long intrigued scholars as a radical experiment in narration. Guenelic, like his beloved Hélisenne, suffers from love and, after much wandering, is reunited with his long lost love. They die shortly afterward, thereby ennobling their chaste passion. The city-states visited have diverse forms of government, a humanist concern shared by Hélisenne, and include a successful woman ruler, the *Princesse Monarque* (Princess Monarch). The *Ample Narration* (Epilogue) is narrated by the faithful knight Quezinstra, who has accompanied Guenelic on his quest. Like Aeneas he travels to the pagan Elysian Fields where the main characters join a panoply of legendary lovers and he is exhorted by the gods to publish the novel in Paris.

Capitalizing upon the success of her novel, in 1539 Hélisenne published *Les epistres familieres et inuectiues de ma dame Hélisenne* (Hélisenne's Personal and Invective Letters), a set of letters loosely in the Ciceronian mode to friends and family and followed by several harsh invectives. Anticipating the epistolary novel, Hélisenne conveys a sense of connectedness in her letter series as she offers consolation and advice to her extended network of correspondents (Letters 1–9). Letters 10–13 change in tone as she describes the illicit passion to which she has succumbed. The coded Letter 13 alludes to her rescue, as seen in the *Angoysses.* Her letter sequences have recently been edited twice and were the first of her works to be translated into English. The five invective letters have elicited the most critical attention. The first three letters present an exchange between Hélisenne and her fictional, misogynist husband. The fourth invective vehemently responds to disparagement of the female intellect with an enumeration of exemplary women akin to Christine de Pizan's *Cité des dames* (City of Women) and includes lavish praise of Marguerite de Navarre, King Francis I's sister. Hélisenne's examples, drawn from antiquity and the Bible, situate the author in the center of the *querelle des femmes.* The last letter of the series defends Hélisenne's own chivalric characters against attack by a contemporary critic named Elenot, a disparager whose identity has been lost.

In its treatment of love, Hélisenne's third major work *Le songe de madame Hélisenne* (The Dream of Madame Hélisenne, 1540) follows in the lineage of the *Roman de la rose* (Romance of the Rose), which sparked Christine de Pizan to launch the *querelle des femmes.* Hélisenne draws on Jean Lemaire's *Illustration de Gaule et singularitez de Troie* to frame the descriptions of the dream. The dreamer sees a man and a woman, mythological figures (Venus and Pallas) and then finally allegorical figures (Sensuality and Reason), which present the discussion of love. As in her novel, chastity and virtue prevail. The three works were intended to be read together and were printed in a single volume several times.

Hélisenne de Crenne's last publication *Les quatre premiers liuvres des eneydes* (The First Four Books of the *Aeneid,* 1541) translates into French prose Virgil's *Aeneid I–IV* for the first time. She relates the story of the fall of Troy and the tragic love of Dido for Aeneas as her final example of love's destructive potential. In other works, Hélisenne's foregrounding of Dido's courageous widowhood and building of Carthage (her *œuvres viriles*) figures the Carthaginian queen as a model of female conduct. In the *Eneydes,* however, her depiction of Dido's self-destructive passion renders her a negative exemplar for women. Beginning as an author of sentimental fiction, Hélisenne de Crenne gradually evolved to become a letter writer, defender of women's intellect, master of the allegorical genre, and finally a Renaissance humanist and disseminator of the classics. Hélisenne de Crenne's reputation has grown steadily, as attested by studies devoted to her writings. Critical editions of the *Angoysses* and *Epistres* will soon be complemented by a new edition of the *Songe.* English translations of these works are already available. While *Angoysses* Part One and the *Epistres invectives* were the first of her writings to be closely studied, scholars are closely examining the rest of her literary production. A recent volume of essays devoted to Hélisenne approach her writing from a number of critical perspectives discovering new sources, finding thematic connections, and studying the architecture of her works. Several essays look closely at the *Angoysses* Part Two as well as the *Songe,* works that have received less critical attention. This volume, as well as the critical editions, offers an extensive bibliography that will doubtless grow as Hélisenne de Crenne assumes her rightful place in the literary canon.

Diane S. Wood

See also the subheading Letter Writing (under Literary Culture and Women); Querelle des Femmes.

Bibliography

Primary Works

Crenne, Hélisenne de. *Les angoysses douloureuses qui procedent d'amours.* Paris: Denis Janot, 1538.

Crenne, Hélisenne de. *Les epistres familieres et inuectiues de ma dame Hélisenne.* Paris: Denis Janot, 1539.

Crenne, Hélisenne de. *Le songe de madame Hélisenne.* Paris: Denis Janot, 1540.

Crenne, Hélisenne de. *Les quatre premiers liures des eneydes.* Paris: Denis Janot, 1541.

Modern Editions and Translations

Crenne, Hélisenne de. *Les angoysses douloureuses qui procèdent d'amours.* Edited by Christine de Buzon. Textes de la Renaissance 13. Paris: Champion, 1997.

Crenne, Hélisenne de. *Les Epistres familieres et invectives.* Edited by Jerry C. Nash. Textes de la Renaissance 8. Paris: Champion, 1996.

Crenne, Hélisenne de. *Les Epistres familieres et invectives de ma dame Hélisenne.* Edited by Jean-Philippe Beaulieu and Hannah Fournier. Montreal: Presses de l'Université de Montréal, 1995.

Crenne, Hélisenne de. *Le Songe.* Edited by Jean-Philippe Beaulieu. Paris: Indigo and Côté-femmes, 1995.

Crenne, Hélisenne de. *Le Songe.* Edited by Jean-Philippe Beaulieu, Diane Desrosiers-Bonin, and Christine de Buzon. *Textes de la Renaissance.* Paris: Champion, forthcoming.

Crenne, Hélisenne de. "Le Songe de Madame Hélisenne." Translated by Lisa Neal. In *Writings by Pre-Revolutionary French Women: From Marie de France to Elizabeth Vigée-Le Brun.* Edited by Anne R. Larsen and Colette H. Winn, 63–105. New York: Garland, 2000.

Crenne, Hélisenne de. *A Renaissance Woman. Hélisenne's Personal and Invective Letters.* Translated and edited by Marianna M. Mustacchi and Paul J. Archambault. Syracuse, NY: Syracuse University Press, 1986.

Crenne, Hélisenne de. *The Torments of Love.* Translated by Lisa Neal and Steven Rendall. Minneapolis: University of Minnesota Press, 1996.

Secondary Works

Beaulieu, Jean-Philippe, and Diane Desrosiers-Bonin, eds. *Hélisenne de Crenne. L'Ecriture et ses doubles.* Etudes et Essais sur la Renaissance 54. Paris: Champion, 2004.

Wood, Diane S. *Hélisenne de Crenne. At the Crossroads of Renaissance Humanism and Feminism.* Madison: Fairleigh Dickinson University Press, 2000.

D

Dames des Roches (Madeleine Neveu, 1520–1587; Catherine Fradonnet, 1542–1587)

Authors, salonnières, feminists

The Dames des Roches, mother and daughter, lived their entire lives in the southwestern city of Poitiers where they belonged to the urban bourgeoisie and nobility of the robe. Madeleine was born into a bourgeois family of notaries in about 1520. She and her daughter Catherine would later adopt the quasi noble name des Roches from a family property owned by Madeleine. The latter was married twice, the first time in 1539 to André Fradonnet, a procurer who was the father of Catherine and who died in 1547, and the second time in 1550 to François Eboissard, seigneur de la Villée, an appeals court lawyer who died an untimely death during the summer of 1578 of an upper respiratory disease.

We know little about Madeleine's education. She reveals in her first ode, published and collected with her other poems in *Les Œuvres* (Works) of 1578, that, when she married, she had little time left for her studies: "In the happy moments of my yesteryear, / I bore my wings close by my side: / But, in losing my youthful freedom, / My feathered pen was clipped before I could fly." She probably continued learning in her spare time by making use of local libraries, for in her poems she displays an astonishing knowledge of Greco-Roman mythology, history, and philosophy, as well as the church fathers, the Bible, and humanist literature. She may have benefited from Poitiers's first period of literary renewal from 1545 to 1555, when humanists and poets such as Joachim Du Bellay, Jacques Pelletier, Jacques Tahureau, Jean-Antoine de Baïf, and many others brought fame to Poitiers's already solid reputation as a humanist center. Madeleine des Roches took charge of Catherine's education, which was unique for her time and her milieu. It was customary for daughters of the upper bourgeoisie to be sent to convent schools or, more rarely, to be tutored at home by male instructors. Catherine, while likely tutored by some of the leading humanists of Poitiers, was guided and inspired primarily by her mother to the awe of their contemporaries. The poet lawyer Scévole de Sainte-Marthe, a cousin of the Dames des Roches, describes his admiration upon hearing "the mother instruct her daughter and speak to her on all the sciences with as much authority as ease," while the daughter would respond by "reciting the beautiful verses of her mother, and hers as well; which she did with such grace that she would win over all the hearts of those who listened." While Madeleine des Roches subscribed to humanist views on the centrality of the mother's role in the education of the young, she deliberately disregarded their strictly utilitarian goals. She never enjoined her daughter to aspire to the traditional feminine virtues of humility, silence, and obedience to a husband. To the contrary, she encouraged her to think of fame and poetic immortality gained through her virtue.

In the 1560s, the Wars of Religion exacerbated the legal difficulties that the Dames des Roches experienced until their death. Poitiers was ransacked by Protestant troops in May 1562 and Admiral Gaspard de Coligny laid siege to the city in 1569, destroying two of Madeleine's townhouses, a loss great enough for her to request an indemnity from the royal treasury. Madeleine also refers to a thirteen-year lawsuit and other legal wrangling. These were the years, however, when they founded a salon and became financially independent upon the death of Éboissard. The first evidence of their literary activities appeared in 1571 with the publication of Caye-Jules de Guersens's play *Panthée,* which he gallantly claimed was Catherine's work and to which Madeleine wrote a liminary poem. As her suitor, he may have wished to persuade her to marry him. Another suitor, Claude Pellejay, dedicated love sonnets to her. Catherine responded with her two-voiced sonnet sequence, "Sonnets from Sincero to Charite" and "Charite to Sincero," in which she assumes the role of the virtuous chaste woman who teaches and refines her lover.

The fame of the Des Roches' salon benefited from two occurrences in the late 1570s. First, in 1577, the ambulatory royal court resided at Poitiers for three months, bringing with it the learned gathering of the Palace Academy. The Dames des Roches were probably invited to court entertainments and likely composed at that time several poems in honor of King Henri III, Queen Louise of Lorraine, and Queen Mother Catherine de Médicis. Catherine could have also composed then her feminist "Masquerade of the Amazons" and "Song of the Amazons," which celebrate the defiance of mythical warrior women who refuse to submit to love and male control of their lives. These poems are among the one hundred and nine pieces included in the 1578 edition of their collected works published by Abel L'Angelier in Paris. The volume contains a wide variety of poetic genres—odes, sonnets, quatrains, octets, epistles, narrative poems, songs, epitaphs, and six dialogues. Among the poems figure Catherine's famous "To my Distaff," in which she attempts to resolve the ideological conflict between the distaff, an emblem of devalued housewifery, and the pen, the tool of the poet, seeker after immortality; "The Strong Woman Described by Solomon," a paraphrase of the Song of the Valiant Woman in Proverbs 31, in which she exploits the figure of the Good Wife to legitimate her scholarly aspirations; and

"Agnodice," an adaptation of a tale by Hyginus, in which she pleads for greater freedom for all women to gain access to books and learning. This first volume was soon followed in 1579 by a second edition containing additional sonnets, Madeleine's request for an indemnity from the king for her two destroyed townhouses, and Catherine's "One Act of the Tragicomedy of Tobias," in which she rewrites the Biblical apocryphal story by turning Sarah, Tobias's bride, and her mother into major characters critiquing male patriarchal structures.

Second, the Dames des Roches's informal coterie acquired even greater prestige when, soon after the publication of the second edition of their collected works in 1579, the *grands jours,* or assizes, brought to Poitiers for three months influential legists accompanied by their wives and children. Henri III commissioned these lawyers of the Paris Parlement to relieve the congestion of the local courts on account of the property damages caused by the civil wars. Upon their arrival in Poitiers, two of the lawyers, Etienne Pasquier and Antoine Loisel, headed for the home of the Des Roches, whose reputation had reached educated circles in Paris. Their ensuing conversation with the two ladies produced one of the best known episodes in sixteenth-century social literary history. Pasquier, seeing a flea on Catherine's breast, suggested that each immortalize the insect in a poetic exchange. No sooner had they complied than a number of the Parisian lawyers and the local habitués of the salon began to produce innumerable *blasons,* punning on the *puce* (flea) exploring the body of the *pucelle* (maiden). These poems were later collected and published by Abel L'Angelier in the ninety-three-folio collection, *La Puce de Madame des Roches* in 1572 and again in 1573. Catherine des Roches's nine poems, or "responses," included in this collaborative volume reappear, along with another seven of her responses on the flea, in 1583 in the *Secondes œuvres de Mesdames des Roches de Poictiers, Mere et Fille* (Second Works of Mesdames des Roches of

Poitiers, Mother and Daughter), which as a whole focuses mainly on Poitiers, its siege in 1569, its *grands jours* and the flea contest, as well as other local events pertaining to the Des Roches coterie. Catherine also included in her portion of the volume two feminist pedagogical dialogues on the education of girls. In the first, "Dialogue of Placide and Severe," two fathers discuss the merits of educating their daughters Iris and Pasithée. Iris, Severe's progeny, is ignorant, flighty, and crazy about men; Pasithée is wise, learned, and skeptical of men. In these dialogues, Catherine synthesizes three opposing views: the age-old traditionalism of the misogynist (Severe), the well-intentioned paternalism of the humanist (Placide), and the independence of the feminist (Pasithée). Whereas in the first of the two dialogues, Catherine's cautious move is to win over her most reticent readers with arguments from Vives and Erasmus, in the women's dialogue, she advances the more radical agenda that the women of the urban upper gentry be allowed to combine *civilité mondaine* (worldly civility), in the form of music, dance, and salon entertainment, with a solid humanist education, a combination more fitting at the time for women of the aristocracy.

In 1586, the Dames des Roches had their last work, *Les Missives de Mes-dames des Roches de Poictiers, Mere et Fille* (The Letters of the Dames des Roches of Poitiers, Mother and Daughter), published in Paris by Abel L'Angelier. They were the first women in France to publish their private letters. The des Roches's last volume contains ninety-six letters, Catherine's 590-lined verse translation of Claudian's *De raptu Proserpinae* (On the Rape of Proserpina), and several "responses," epitaphs, and "imitations" by both mother and daughter.

In the summer of 1587, the plague reached Poitiers. Upon becoming ill, the Dames des Roches dictated their last testament on 8 October, and both died before the end of November. Posthumous *elogia* all claim that they died together on the same day. Scévole de Sainte-Marthe, a close relative of the Dames des Roches, concludes in his *Eloges des hommes illustres* (In Praise of Illustrious Men, 1644) that just as life had united the mother and her daughter, so they were united in death: "[D]eath itself, deaf and inexorable, could not refuse the ardent and noble desire of these two generous Ladies who sought so passionately to live and die together."

Anne R. Larsen

See also Amazons; Education, Humanism, and Women; the subheadings Salons, Salonnières, and Women Writers; Letter Writing (under Literary Culture and Women); Religious Reform and Women.

Bibliography

Primary Works

Des Roches, Madeleine and Catherine. *From Mother and Daughter: Poems, Dialogues, and Letters by Les Dames des Roches. A Bilingual Edition.* Other Voice Series. Edited with critical introductions and translations by Anne R. Larsen. Chicago: University of Chicago Press, 2006.

Des Roches, Madeleine and Catherine. *Histoire et Amours pastoralles de Daphnis et de Chloe escrite premierement en grec par Longus et maintenant mise en françois. Ensemble un debat judiciel de Folie et d'Amour, fait par dame L. L. L. (Loyse Labé Lyonnoise). Plus quelques vers françois, lesquels ne sont pas moins plaisans que recreatifs, par M.D.R., Poictevine (Madame des Roches).* Paris: Jean Parent, 1578.

Des Roches, Madeleine and Catherine. *La Puce de Madame des Roches. Qui est un recueil de divers poemes Grecs, Latins et François, composez par plusieurs doctes personnages aux Grands Jours tenus à Poitiers l'an M.D.LXXIX.* Paris: Abel l'Angelier, 1582, 1583.

Des Roches, Madeleine and Catherine. *Les Missives.* Edited by Anne R. Larsen. Geneva: Droz, 1999.

Des Roches, Madeleine and Catherine. *Les Œuvres.* Edited by Anne R. Larsen. Geneva: Droz, 1993.

Des Roches, Madeleine and Catherine. *Les Secondes Œuvres.* Edited by Anne R. Larsen. Geneva: Droz, 1998.

Secondary Works

Berriot-Salvadore, Evelyne. *Les femmes dans la société française de la Renaissance.* Geneva: Droz, 1990.

Broomhall, Susan. *Women and the Book Trade in Sixteenth-Century France.* Aldershot, UK, and Burlington, VT: Ashgate, 2002.

Diller, George E. *Les Dames des Roches. Étude sur la vie littéraire à Poitiers dans la deuxième moitié du XVIᵉ siècle.* Paris: Droz, 1936.

Jones, Ann Rosalind. *The Currency of Eros: Women's Love Lyric in Europe, 1540–1620.* Bloomington: Indiana University Press, 1990.

Larsen, Anne R. "The French Humanist Scholars: Les Dames des Roches." In *Women Writers of the Renaissance and Reformation.* Edited by Katharina Wilson, 232–259. Athens: University of Georgia Press, 1987.

Olson, Todd. "'La Femme à la Puce et la Puce à l'Oreille': Catherine des Roches and the Poetics of Sexual Resistance in Sixteenth-Century French Poetry." *Journal of Medieval and Early Modern Studies* 32, no. 2 (2002): 327–342.

Sankovitch, Tilde. *French Women Writers and the Book: Myths of Access and Desire.* Syracuse, NY: Syracuse University Press, 1988.

Yandell, Cathy. *Carpe Corpus: Time and Gender in Early Modern France.* Newark, DE: University of Delaware Press; London: Associated University Presses, 2000.

Datini, Margherita Bandini (1357–1423)

Italian writer of letters

Margherita Bandini Datini is known from her extensive surviving correspondence with her husband Francesco Datini (1335–1410). Margherita, of a dispossessed but elite Florentine family, married the self-made, extremely rich "merchant of Prato" in Avignon when she was sixteen and he forty-one. Once the couple returned to Italy, their relationship deteriorated, and they often moved separately between Prato and nearby Florence, writing daily about household, family, business, and politics. Their letters and many others providing information about Margherita are preserved in the Archivio di stato di Prato.

Margherita and Francesco's core problem was a failure to have children. Margherita was considered at fault, since Francesco had illegitimate children, including two during the marriage (which did not help the relationship). Margherita compensated for her infertility through religious devotion and by striving to be the model of an intelligent and competent woman. She had charge of a large household, including apprentices, servants, and visitors, and in Prato she also dealt with Francesco's ambitious building projects, farming, and business.

Margherita's duties included writing letters to Francesco, and her relationship to letter writing is noteworthy for the continuum it demonstrates between illiteracy and literacy. Although evidence indicates that Margherita knew how to read and probably to write at an elementary level from the start of the correspondence, she dictated letters to scribes during most of her marriage. She used a Tuscan dialect untouched by literary concerns, but nonetheless, even in her earliest dictated letters, she prided herself on her talent for oral composition. Then, in the 1390s, when she was in her midthirties, she began to work on improving both her reading and letter writing, probably through intensive practice rather than formal lessons, and in 1399 she produced a spate of twenty-one surviving autograph letters. Her handwriting and placement of text on the page improved noticeably during this period, although her word usage and the way she organized the content changed little. After 1399, she returned to using scribes. She had achieved what she had set out to do, her health was poor, and she no longer cared about impressing Francesco.

Ann Crabb

See also the subheading Letter Writing (under Literary Culture and Women).

Bibliography

Primary Work

Datini, Margherita. *Per la tua Margherita: Lettere di una donna del '300 al marito mercante.* Prato: Archivio di stato, 2002. CD-ROM, with handwriting images.

Secondary Work

Origo, Iris. *Merchant of Prato.* Boston: David R. Godine, 1986. (Originally published in New York: Alfred A. Knopf, 1957.)

D'Ennetières, Marie (Dentières; 1495–1561)

Reform writer and preacher

The D'Ennetières family was of increasing political importance in Tournai during the fifteenth and sixteenth centuries. Born after two older brothers, who married into wealthy noble families, Marie d'Ennetières, the oldest daughter, was sent to the Augustinian convent at Prés-Porchin. It is likely that she attended school there, taking her vows sometime after the death of her mother in 1508. Jeanne de Jussie called her a defrocked abbess (1996, 238), but from the lists that exist, it is clear that Marie never occupied such a position. She showed considerable interest in the new religious ideals that had spread to Tournai by 1520 or the early 1520s at the latest.

By 1527, Marie had left her convent for Strasbourg and had married Simon Robert, a defrocked Augustinian from the Tournai area, who preached there to the community of French-speaking exiles. After the victory of the Reformed party at the Disputation of Bern in January 1528, Simon and Marie accepted Guillaume Farel's invitation to move to the Quatre Mandements, under Bernese rule, located at the eastern end of Lake Léman. By May, the couple had arrived in Bex, a few miles east of Aigle. The couple had at least two children, Marie and Jeanne. As the complete text of Marie's dedicatory letter to Marguerite de Navarre states, the latter was Jeanne Robert's godmother (a3v∞). After serving loyally in Bex and in Aigle for several years, Simon Robert died in the early part of 1533. Marie married the pastor Antoine Froment, Farel's companion in arms, and came to live with him in Geneva in 1535.

After the Genevan council voted to follow the reformed religion in August 1535, Marie was invited to accompany members of the council to the Clarisses's convent in the Old Town (Head 1987). A version of the confrontation between the former nun and the Genevan sisters was written down by Jeanne

de Jussie (*Petite Chronique*). Jeanne portrays her as "*une moinne abbesse, faulce, ridée et de lengue diabolique*" (a monk abbess, false, wrinkled and with a diabolical tongue) (Wengler 1999). A few years later, in her *Defense pour les femmes* (Defence for Women) (a5r∞), Marie would write that women have the duty and obligation to preach, at least among themselves. This she probably did informally during her early years in the city, along with Claudine Levet and a few others (Skenazi 1997).

By the fall of 1535, the reformed canton of Geneva was under heavy siege by the Savoyards, faithful to the Catholic prince-bishop of Geneva, Pierre de La Baume. The siege was finally broken in early 1536 when the Bernese sent an army to attack the Savoyards from the rear. The campaign was so successful that it liberated all of Geneva as well as the lands south of the lake, known as the Chablais, including such towns as Evian and Thonon. By the middle of the year, an account of the transition of the city of Geneva from Catholic to Reformed had been printed under the title *La Guerre et deslivrance de la Ville de Genefve* (The War and Deliverance of the City of Geneva). In 1881, Rilliet attributed this work to Marie d'Ennetières mainly on the basis of the epigraph "*Lisez et puis jugez*" (Read and then judge), which is common to this imprint and to the *Epistre tresutile* (Very useful epistle). This argument seems insufficient, as has been recently shown (Kemp 2004). In addition, work by Isabelle C. Denommé (2004) indicates that, in terms of vocabulary and style, the pamphlet bears many traces of Froment's historical writing. During 1536 and 1537, Froment was an itinerant minister, preaching in Geneva but also in the Chablais. It was finally decided that he should serve instead as a deacon in the church at Thonon.

Reluctantly, Marie, Antoine, and the children left their house in Geneva in the fall of 1537 and moved to Thonon. Around this time, or shortly thereafter, Marie had a girl by Froment, whom they named Judith. Starting in 1537, there was increasing dissension with the authorities in Geneva over religious matters, especially over the rules pertaining to the rite of communion. At Easter 1538, things came to a head, and Guillaume Farel, Élie Coraud, and Jean Calvin were dismissed from the church in Geneva and sent for questioning to Bern. No satisfactory solution was found, so Farel withdrew to Neuchâtel and Calvin went to Basel and then Strasbourg. In addition, over the next few years, things seem to have gone somewhat awry for Antoine and Marie. Coming from a merchant family, D'Ennetières must have seen no conflict between commerce and religion. So Antoine sold various products in the street or at market, including wine. They were cited for behavior unbecoming to a minister by the class of ministers from Thonon at the end of the 1530s.

It was precisely at this time, with Farel and Calvin in exile, Froment eager for a change, and their affairs under examination, that Marie finished writing and had printed in Geneva, with the help of Antoine, her *Epistre tresutile [. . .] envoyee à la Royne de Navarre* (Backus 1991). Under a false address in Antwerp, the pamphlet came out in March 1539. However, almost all of the fifteen hundred copies were immediately seized by the Council, which decreed that henceforth all books must be presented to the magistrate for approval before publication. Froment was called before the Council and his replies were duly recorded. The *Epistre tresutile* was an aggressive work, very much in the vein of the polemical Neuchâtel imprints that Pierre de Vingle had printed during the years 1533–1535 (Denommé 2004). It was clearly an attack on the current leadership in Geneva.

Finally, in 1539, despite wishing to go to Morges, Froment was assigned to lead the church in the small town of Massongy, several miles East of Thonon. This was a singular demotion and rebuff. After moving, the couple continued working in the church and also selling goods with the obvious aim of improving their financial condition. At the same time, they tried to give a good Christian education to their girls, including courses in Hebrew. In the summer of 1546, while Marie was in Geneva, she met Calvin and berated him for wearing a long black gown, which she associated with the garments of the false prophets announced in the Bible. Calvin criticized her in no uncertain terms (McKinley 1999). In 1548, Froment pronounced a series of sermons critical of the reigning political powers in Bern. As a result, he was expelled from his position in Massongy. He would never preach again.

By the end of 1549, the couple were back in Geneva, where they began a new life. Antoine found employment for over a year as an assistant to François Bonivard, recently named official historian of the republic. Politically, Marie and Antoine seem to have moved into the Calvinist camp at this time. It is probably within this context that we must understand the last work by Marie d'Ennetières, the preface to the 1561 edition of Calvin's *Sermon de la modestie des femmes en leurs habillemens* (Sermon on the Modesty of Women in their Clothing). This appears to be Marie's contribution to the pro-Calvinist propaganda campaign leading up to the Poissy Colloquium. She died sometime before 29 November 1561.

William Kemp and Diane Desrosiers-Bonin

See also Religious Reform and Women.
Bibliography
Primary Works
D'Ennetières, Marie. *Œuvres.* Critical edition by Diane Desrosiers-Bonin, William Kemp, Isabelle Crevier-Denommé, et al. Forthcoming.

Dentières, Marie. *Epistle to Marguerite de Navarre and Preface to a Sermon by John Calvin.* Edited and translated by Mary B. McKinley. Chicago: University of Chicago Press, 2004.

Dentières, Marie. *Epistre tresutile faicte et composee par une femme Chrestienne de Tornay, Envoyée à la Royne de Navarre seur du Roy de France [. . .].* Antwerp: M. Lempereur; Geneva: J. Girard, 1539, 32 ff.

Dentières, Marie. *Un Sermon de la modestie des Femmes en leurs habillemens.* 1561.

Froment, Antoine. "Restitution de l'écrit intitulé: *La Guerre et deslivrance de la Ville de Genefve.*"

Edited by Albert Rilliet. *Mémoires et documents publiés par la Société d'histoire et d'archéologie de Genève.* Vol. 20: 309–384. Geneva: Societe d'histoire et d'archeologie, 1879–1888 (1881).

de Jussie, Jeanne. *Petite chronique.* Edited by Helmut Feld. Mayence: Von Zabern, 1996.

Secondary Works

Backus, Irena. "Marie Dentière: un cas de féminisme théologique à l'époque de la Réforme?" *Bulletin de la Société d'Histoire du Protestantisme Français,* 137 (1991): 177–195.

Crevier-Denommé, Isabelle. "La vision théologique de Marie d'Ennetières et le 'Groupe de Neuchâtel.' " In *Le Livre évangélique en français avant Calvin.* Edited by Jean-François Gilmont and William Kemp, 179–197. Turnhout, Netherlands: Brepols, 2004.

Head, Thomas. "A Propagandist for the Reform: Marie Dentière." In *Women Writers of the Renaissance and the Reformation.* Edited by Katharina M. Wilson, 260–283. Athens: University of Georgia Press, 1987.

Kemp, William. "L'épigraphe 'Lisez et puis jugez' et le principe de l'examen dans la Réforme française avant 1540." In *Le Livre évangélique en français avant Calvin.* Edited by Jean-François Gilmont and William Kemp, 241–274. Turnhout, Netherlands: Brepols, 2004.

Kemp, William, and Diane Desrosiers-Bonin. "Marie d'Ennetières et la petite grammaire hébraïque de sa fille d'après la dédicace de l'*Epistre* à Marguerite de Navarre (1539)." *Bibliothèque d'Humanisme et Renaissance* 51 (1998): 117–134.

McKinley, Mary B. "Les fortunes précaires de Marie Dentière au XVIe et au XIXe siècle." In *Royaume de fémynie. Pouvoirs, contraintes, espaces de liberté des femmes, de la Renaissance à la Fronde.* Edited by Kathleen Wilson-Chevalier and Éliane Viennot, 27–39. Paris: Champion, 1999.

Skenazi, Cynthia. "Marie Dentière et la prédication des femmes." *Renaissance et Réforme* 21, no. 1 (1997): 5–18.

Wengler, Elizabeth M. "Women, Religion, and Reform in Sixteenth-Century Geneva." Ph.D. dissertation, Department of History, Boston College, 1999.

Dialogues and Women. *See* the subheading Virtual Salons: Women in Renaissance Dialogues (under Literary Culture and Women).

Dowriche, Anne (fl. 1589–1596)

Epic poet

Born sometime before 1560, Anne Dowriche was the daughter of Sir Richard Edgcumbe and Elizabeth Tregian Edgcumbe of Mount Edgcumbe, Cornwall. A prominent family in Cornwall and Devon, the Edgcumbe men were active in political affairs. Sir Richard and his sons were members of Parliament. In 1580, Anne married Hugh Dowriche, a Puritan minister from Devon, with whom she bore no fewer than three children. Baptismal records exist for Mary (born 1587), Anne (born 1589), and Hugh (born 1594). An older son, Elkana, is mentioned in the will of his paternal grandfather, Thomas Dowriche, in 1590. A further source lists the Dowriche children as Elkana, Mary, Elizabeth, and Walter, indicating the possibility of other births.

Flourishing between 1589 and 1596, Dowriche is best known for *The French History,* a long historical poem that describes the Protestant massacre in and around Paris on St. Bartholomew's Eve, 24 August 1572. Reflecting widely held English sentiment, *The French History* recounts the French civil wars, speaks out against tyranny, and justifies the reformation of the church. Dowriche found inspiration for this poem in Thomas Timme's translation of Jean de Serres's history, known in English as *The Three Parts of Commentaries Containing the Whole and Perfect Discourse of the Civil Wars of France.* Published in 1589, *The French History* was written in alternating heptameters and hexameters.

Dowriche is also known for her poem *Verses Written by a Gentlewoman, upon the Jailor's Conversion,* a religious work on which she may have collaborated with her husband. George Boase also credits Dowriche with *A Frenchman's Songe, made upon the death of ye French King, who was murdered in his own Court, by a traiterouse Fryer of St. Jacobs order, 1st Aug. 1589.* Unfortunately, no copy of this later work is known to have survived.

Joann Ross

See also the subheading The Reform Movement in France (under Religious Reform and Women).

Bibliography
Primary Works
Stevenson, Jane, and Peter Davidson, eds. *Early Modern Women Poets, 1520–1700: An Anthology.* Oxford and New York: Oxford University Press, 2001.
Travitsky, Betty S., and Anne Lake Prescott, eds. *Female & Male Voices in Early Modern England: An Anthology of Renaissance Writing.* New York: Columbia University Press, 2000.

Secondary Works
Beilin, Elaine V. "Anne Dowriche" in *Dictionary of Literary Biography.* Vol. 172. Edited by James K. Bracken and Joel Silver. Detroit, MI: Gale Research Co., 1996.
Martin, Randall, ed. *Women Writers in Renaissance England.* London: Longman, 1997.

Dowry. *See* Marriage.

E

Education, Humanism, and Women
Overview

A revolution in education took place in the period roughly between 1350 and 1600 with the rediscovery of the literary and cultural legacy of ancient Greece and Rome. The new educational movement born from the revival of the poetry, rhetoric, history, philosophy, and art of the ancient world was known as humanism. Four subentries follow in this general survey: Education for Women; The Humanist Curriculum; Latin Learning and Women; Greek Learning and Women.

Education for Women

Two early works must be considered founding texts for the promotion of women's education in the Renaissance: Giovanni Boccaccio's *De mulieribus claris* (On Famous Women, 1362) and Christine de Pizan's *Le Livre de la Cité des dames* (The Book of the City of Ladies, 1404*)*. One of the most commercially successful books published in early modern Europe, Boccaccio's anthology of one hundred and six women's lives from antiquity to the Middle Ages sold out in Italian, French, English, German, and Spanish translations of the work as well as in the original Latin edition. Showcasing the literary accomplishments of such ancient learned women as the poet Sappho, the orator Hortensia, the scholar and epic poet Proba, and the linguist Queen Zenobia of Palmyra (fluent in Latin, Greek, Syriac, and Egyptian), Boccaccio's anthology constituted a history of famous female figures and offered models for modern women to emulate. But while the *De mulieribus* praised learned women as exceptions to their sex, Christine de Pizan's *Cité des dames,* though based on Boccaccio's history, rejected that work's low estimate of the female sex. Pizan's *Cité des dames* called for education for all girls, equal to that of their brothers. While Pizan's *Cité* circulated almost solely in manuscript in the Renaissance, J. Hall McCash notes that the work prompted an "outpouring of female patronage for her writing [in early modern Europe] unprecedented in literary history" (Broomhall 2002, 35). Continuing to spur women's ambitions, numerous catalogues of eminent women's lives followed those of Boccaccio and Pizan in the fifteenth and sixteenth centuries.

The Humanist Curriculum

Despite the legacy of a misogyny deeply embedded in classical and medieval literature, fifteenth-century humanism provided a gateway for women into the literary and cultural mainstream (Robin 1997, 153). The new humanist curriculum introduced a roster of studies that appealed to both women and men. In humanist schools, the study of poetry, languages, rhetoric, moral philosophy, biography, and history supplemented and in some cases supplanted the standard medieval core curriculum of theology, logic, natural philosophy, metaphysics, medicine, mathematics, and astronomy. The new humanist curriculum produced women who published works in every literary genre, served unofficially as their husbands' foreign ministers, acted as regents and coregents of their states, directed their children's educations, practiced medicine, wrote treatises on every branch of knowledge, and became abbesses and nuns who taught in convent schools.

Tim Elston and Diana Robin

See also Convents; Literary Culture and Women; Medicine and Women; Pizan, Christine de; Power, Politics, and Women.

Bibliography

Primary Works

Boccaccio, Giovanni. *Famous Women*. Edited and translated by Virginia Brown. Cambridge, MA: I Tatti Renaissance Library, Harvard University Press, 2001.

Willard, Charity Cannon, ed. *The Writings of Christine de Pizan*. New York: Persea Books, 1994.

Secondary Works

Allen, Sister Prudence, R.S.M. *The Concept of Woman. Volume II. The Early Humanist Reformation, 1250–1500*. Grand Rapids, MI, and Cambridge, UK: William B. Eerdmans, 2002.

Broomhall, Susan. *Women and the Book Trade in Sixteenth-Century France*. Aldershot, UK: Ashgate, 2002.

Grendler, Paul F. *Schooling in Renaissance Italy. Literacy and Learning, 1300–1600*. Baltimore, MD: Johns Hopkins University Press, 1989.

Labalme, Patricia, ed. A. *Beyond Their Sex. Learned Women of the European Past*. New York: New York University Press, 1980.

King, Margaret L. *Women of the Renaissance*. Foreword by Catherine R. Stimson. Chicago: University of Chicago Press, 1991.

Robin, Diana. "Humanism." In *The Feminist Encyclopedia of Italian Literature*. Edited by Rinaldina Russell, 153–157. Westport, CT: Greenwood Press, 1997.

Latin Learning and Women

The Renaissance, beginning in Italy in the fourteenth century, then spreading to Germany, Central Europe, France, Spain, and England in the course of the fifteenth and sixteenth centuries, was among other things, a revival of Classical Latin learning, and this affected women as well as men. One of the first women to benefit is the famous Christine de Pizan (1364–1430), the daughter of an erudite Italian doctor who became physician and court astrologer to the French king Charles V. Though she wrote in Middle French, she received a humanist education. She read extensively in Latin and translated part of Thomas Aquinas's *Commentary on Aristotle's Metaphysics*. Other women connected with scholars active in the Italian universities and medical schools began to study Latin in the fourteenth century. Novella d'Andria, daughter

of a professor of canon law at Bologna, according to Christine de Pizan's *Book of the City of Ladies* (I.36), sometimes substituted for her father as a lecturer.

By the middle of the fifteenth century in Italy, the fashion for giving women a humanist education had extended beyond the universities to some of Italy's ruling families. It was not possible in fifteenth-century Italy for a woman to have a professional career as a humanist (though there is some evidence for women as teachers of other women and of their own children), but for those who were born, or married, into ruling families, a humanist education served as a preparation for rule and the exercise of authority. Since a number of rulers were *condottiere*—essentially, mercenary captains—they came to value educated wives, because such women could govern responsibly and effectively during the months or even years when the head of state was absent on campaign. Battista Sforza (duchess of Urbino, 1445–1472), the noted humanist writer Costanza Varano who was Battista's mother, and their kinswomen exemplify one family's commitment to humanist education for women extending over five or six generations: Battista Sforza's great-grandmother was Battista da Montefeltro (1384–1458), renowned for her poetry and public speaking. Sforza's granddaughter was the even more famous poet Vittoria Colonna (1490–1547). All the generations of women in between were Latin-literate.

Some fifteenth-century Italian women became famous as writers in Latin. The world of the humanists was a small one, and, because it was held together by correspondence, the letter was an important genre. Some women's letters circulated widely: Niccolosa Sanuti, herself a competent Latinist who addressed a long speech in that language to Cardinal Bessarion in 1453, noted in it that "there are many letters and speeches and most elegant verses from Costanza [Varano], wife of Alessandro Sforza, and others, which are in people's hands now" (ed. Frati, 256). In Florence in 1493, the great Greek scholar Angelo Poliziano took the letters the Venetian humanist Cassandra Fedele (1465–1558) had written to his student, Alessandra Scala (1475–1506), in Florence and had Scala recite them before the assembled members of the Florentine academy, a circle that included some of the most celebrated names in Renaissance scholarship, among them the Platonist Marsilio Ficino and Pico della Mirandola. But as Isotta Nogarola of Verona (ca. 1416–1466) discovered, a humanist education could cause problems for a woman. When she wrote a formal letter in Ciceronian Latin to introduce herself to the great educator Guarino da Verona in 1436 and he did not immediately reply, she wrote to him again to say that everyone was laughing at her for putting herself forward, which suggests that her letters were circulated without her permission. Another important Italian woman scholar, Laura Cereta (1469–1499), took control of her letters and edited them herself for (scribal) publication: she refers to "this grand volume of epistles, for which the final draft is now being copied out" in a letter of 1486 (Cereta 1997, 34). Manuscript copies of the resultant book circulated among prominent scholars in Brescia, Verona, and Venice.

Women humanists in Italy also put their learning on display when they delivered public speeches in Latin. Cassandra Fedele presented a Latin oration at a baccalaureate ceremony held at the University of Padua in 1487, and she addressed the doge and the Venetian senate at a state reception for Queen Bona of Poland in 1556. Isotta Nogarola officially welcomed the new bishop Ermolao Barbaro to her city with a Latin oration in 1451 on behalf of the Veronese citizens; and Ippolita Sforza, daughter of Duke Francesco Sforza of Milan, gave a formal speech in Latin at the Congress of Mantua in 1459. Women continued to deliver public orations through the sixteenth and seventeenth centuries, speaking even on occasion at the academies (learned societies), which tended to be all-male clubs. A select few women writers and scholars were inducted into academies. In the sixteenth and seventeenth centuries, women in other parts of Europe also followed the Italian example and made public speeches in Latin.

The advance in women's education in Italy did not go unnoticed in Northern Europe. By the end of the fifteenth century, some German humanists were actively seeking to emulate the Italian example. For example, Margareta Welser (1481–1552) was the product of a family of humanist merchants and corresponded with the greatest of all northern humanists, Desiderius Erasmus. She married Konrad Peutinger, the civic secretary of Augsburg in 1498, by which time she had a considerable knowledge of Latin, and through the years of her marriage she was able to pursue her scholarly interests, despite bearing ten children and giving them, in their turn, a humanist education. Their daughter, Juliane, made a Latin speech to the emperor Maximilian on his visit to Augsburg when she was a little less than four years old, matching the achievement of Battista Sforza, who gave her first public Latin speech at the same age.

In France, the royal court was the center of humanist activity. From the late fifteenth century through the sixteenth, French princesses attained a high level of fluency in their Latin and Greek studies. They were followed in this pursuit by some members of the aristocracy, such as Camille de Morel (1547–after 1611), who became widely known for her Latin eloquence. In Spain, Queen Isabella of Castile (1451–1504), who wrote elegant Latin letters herself, gave her daughters (among them, the future queen of England, Catherine of Aragon (1485–1536) a humanist education, and she promoted Latin literacy in Castilian convents. Just as in France, some Spanish and Portuguese women aristocrats and female members of learned families cultivated Latin, such as Ana Cervatón (early sixteenth century), Catalina Paz (mid-sixteenth century), and, above all, the formidably learned Luisa Sigea (1522–1560).

In England, the Renaissance arrived relatively late and, as in France, via the royal household. Although Margaret Beaufort (1441–1509), mother of Henry VII, was considered one of the most learned women in England in her day, her education was primarily in English and French literature. Humanism arrived at the British court via Beaufort's grandson Henry VIII. Mary, sister of Henry VIII, having been briefly the wife of a French king and thus exposed to the new style of education for women, chose to begin learning Latin as an adult in the 1520s (Watson 1922, 172–173).

Outside the royal family, the Lord Chancellor, Sir Thomas More (1478–1535), who was a close friend of the Dutch humanist Erasmus, was the first known Englishman to give his daughters a humanist education. His daughter Margaret (1505–1544) studied Latin and Greek, married an educated man, and gave a similar education to her own daughter, Mary Bassett, who translated from both Latin and Greek. There were Latin-literate women in the More family down into the seventeenth century: Dame Bridget More (1609–1692), great-great-grandchild of Sir Thomas, was a scholarly Benedictine nun who has left a letter in Latin (Città del Vaticano, Barberini Lat. 8624, no. 35).

Other families who moved in court circles did the same. The three Seymour sisters, Anne, Margaret, and Jane, youngest daughters of the duke of Somerset, were the first Englishwomen to publish a book of their own verse, a collection of Latin distichs on the death of the French king's sister (Margaret de Navarre, or Margaret d'Angoulême, 1492–1549), printed in 1550. Among the most important of their contemporaries were the four highly educated daughters of Sir Anthony Cooke, Mildred (1526–1589), Anne (1528?–1610), Elizabeth (1540–1609), and Katherine (1542?–1583), who were courtiers, writers, patrons, translators, educators, and also wives and mothers of eminent men: Mildred Cooke married the statesman William Cecil (Lord Burghley), and Anne Cooke was the mother of the scientist Sir Francis Bacon

The most significant English woman writer in Latin of the sixteenth century was Elizabeth Jane Weston (1582–1612), born in England but raised at the court of Emperor Rudolf II in Prague. The death of her stepfather, Sir Edward Kelley, left her mother and herself with financial problems, so she set about gaining the sympathy and patronage of a number of important men at court by writing Latin verse. Much of her work was published as a collection with the title *Poems* (1602), then reissued, revised, and extended as *A Maiden's Work* (1608). Her premature death at the age of thirty followed the birth of her seventh child.

In sixteenth-century Italy, women continued to build on the achievement of their predecessors. Noblewomen such as Caterina Cibo (1501–1557), duchess of Camerino, and Veronica Gàmbara (1485–1550), poet and duchess of Correggio, were given a humanist education. Among the most remarkable Latin scholars and writers were Tarquinia Molza of Modena (1542–1617), poet, professional singer, and student of Plato; Olympia Morata (1526–1551), tutor of the duke of Ferrara's daughter Anna d'Este; and Laurentia Strozzi (1514–1591), a Dominican nun from a family of Florentine humanists, who published an ambitious collection of Latin hymns. The fact that Molza and Morata were both gainfully employed at the d'Este court (Molza was a member of an elite group of female musicians known as the *concerto delle donne*) suggests that new professional opportunities were beginning to open up for educated Italian women.

By the mid-seventeenth century, women writing in Latin were to be found all over Europe, including Scandinavia and Poland, and also in South America, where the Mexican nun Sor Juana Inès de la Cruz (1648–1690) wrote with ease in Latin as well as Spanish and Nahuatl. French literary culture generally turned away from Latin (as did Spanish) by the end of the sixteenth century, though a few French-women became known as scholars and translators, most notably Anne Dacier (1651–1720). Many German courts, particularly those of the various branches of the Wittelsbachs, had employed humanist tutors for their princesses by the seventeenth century, and some German professors' daughters were known for their Latin learning, whether as translators, scholars, or writers, but the most spectacular female scholar in Northern Europe was the Dutch Anna Maria van Schurman (1607–1678), who corresponded with leading scholars everywhere on the continent. Her works include an argument for the education of women, translated from the original Latin into many languages, including English (*The Learned Maid, or, Whether a Maid may be a Scholar,* published in England in 1659).

No seventeenth-century Englishwomen achieved this kind of international recognition, but Englishwomen did continue to write in and translate from Latin, notably Lucy Hutchinson (1620–1681), who translated Lucretius, and Rachel Jevon (ca.1627–after 1662), who published a Latin ode on the restoration of Charles II in 1661. Seventeenth-century women Latinists were far less likely to be aristocrats or courtiers than the women Latinists of previous centuries: many of them, from van Schurman, Jevon, and Hutchinson to Mme. de Roquemontrousse of Carpentras in France (fl. 1680s) and Anna Memorata (b. 1615) in Leszno, Poland, were the daughters of educated minor gentry.

Seventeenth-century Italy matched van Schurman with an equally impressive figure, the Venetian noblewoman Elena Lucretia Cornaro Piscopia (1646–1684), who read and wrote seven languages and was the first woman to receive the degree of doctor of philosophy from the University of Padua in 1678, a feat that was reported in many journals throughout Europe. Elsewhere in Italy, women continued to write in Latin, such as the Roman Martha Marchina (1600–1642), whose verse and letters

were collected and published after her death in 1662, and the Sicilian noblewoman Anna Maria Ardoini (1672–1700), who published a collection of Latin verse, *The Rose of Parnassus* in 1682.

While only a small minority of women were ever taught Latin, most European countries show a modest but consistent rise in Latin learning over time, from the fifteenth through the eighteenth centuries. Girls' schools very seldom taught Latin before the late nineteenth century, but in families with a tradition of humanist education throughout this period, girls were encouraged to share their fathers' and brothers' interests and were taught at home, sometimes to considerable effect.

Jane Stevenson

See also entries on the women mentioned.
Bibliography
Primary Works
Beilin, Elaine V., ed. *Protestant Translators: Anne Lock Prowse and Elizabeth Russell.* The Early Modern Englishwoman: The Printed Writings. Aldershot, UK: Ashgate, 1998.

Cereta, Laura. *Collected Letters of a Renaissance Feminist.* Edited and translated by Diana Robin. Chicago: University of Chicago Press, 1997.

Churchill, Laurie J., Phyllis R. Brown, and Jane E. Jeffrey, eds. *Women Writing Latin from Roman Antiquity to Early Modern Europe.* 3 vols. New York and London: Routledge, 2002.

Khanna, Lee Cullen, ed. *Early Tudor Translators: Margaret Beaufort, Margaret More Roper and Mary Basset.* The Early Modern Englishwoman: The Printed Writings. Aldershot, UK: Ashgate, 1998.

King, Margaret L., and Albert Rabil, Jr., trans. *Her Immaculate Hand: Selected Works By and About the Women Humanists of Quattrocento Italy.* Asheville, NC: Pegasus Press, 1997. (Originally published in Binghamton, NY: Medieval and Renaissance Text Society, 1992.)

Morata, Olympia. *The Complete Writings of an Italian Heretic.* Edited and translated by Holt N. Parker. Chicago: University of Chicago Press, 2003.

Nogarola, Isotta. *Complete Writings: Letterbook, Dialogue on Adam and Eve, Orations.* Edited and translated by Margaret L. King and Diana Robin. Chicago: University of Chicago Press, 2004.

Stevenson, Jane, and Davidson, Peter, eds. *Early Modern Women Poets.* Oxford: Oxford University Press, 2001.

Van Schurman, Anna Maria. *Whether a Christian Woman Should Be Educated and Other Writings from Her Intellectual Circle.* Edited and translated by Joyce L. Irwin. Chicago: University of Chicago Press, 1998.

Secondary Works

Clough, Cecil H. "Daughters and Wives of the Montefeltro: Outstanding Bluestockings of the Quattrocento." *Renaissance Studies* 10, no. 1 (1996): 31–55.

King, Margaret L. *Women of the Renaissance.* Foreword by Catherine R. Stimson. Chicago: University of Chicago Press, 1991.

Lamb, Mary E. "The Cooke Sisters: Attitudes Towards Learned Women in the Renaissance." In *Silent But for the Word: Tudor Women as Patrons, Translators and Writers of Religious Works.* Edited by Margaret P. Hannay, 107–125. Kent, OH: Kent State University Press, 1985.

Stevenson, Jane. *Women Latin Poets: Language, Gender and Authority from Antiquity to the Eighteenth Century.* Oxford: Oxford University Press, 2005.

Waquet, Françoise. *Latin, or the Empire of a Sign.* Translated by John Howe. London and New York: Verso, 2000.

Watson, Foster. *Luis Vives: El Gran Valenciano.* Oxford: Oxford University Press, 1922.

Greek Learning and Women

The story of Renaissance women's contribution to the revival of Greek learning comprises two phases. The first relates to their participation in the revival of ancient Greek studies, which was an important aspect of Renaissance culture, though Latin remained the language central to humanist discourse. Beginning at the turn of the fourteenth century, Italians pioneered the rediscovery of classical Greek literature through a greatly accelerated scholarly commerce with the Byzantine world in the fifty years before the fall of Constantinople to the Turkish empire in 1453. The second phase of Greek scholarship, dating from the sixteenth century and more associated with Northern Europe, focused on New Testament studies and the Greek church fathers. The Northern

European interest in Greek was strongly connected with the Reformation and the desire of religious reform scholars to reread and reinterpret what the Scriptures actually said, in the original languages. Women were involved in both enterprises.

Renaissance women's study of classical Greek literature may have been fueled by the recovery of the poetry of Sappho and other ancient Greek women poets. In 1494, Janus Lascaris printed the first edition of the *Greek Anthology:* a large collection of ancient epigrams and short poems in which a number of poems by and about women were preserved. The Parisian scholar-printer Henri Estienne printed Sappho's *Hymn to Aphrodite* twice: first in his Greek edition of the rhetorician Dionysius of Halicarnassus (1546) and two years later in his edition of *Anacreon* (1554). In 1566, Estienne printed a second edition of the *Anthology.* That same year, another almost complete surviving poem of Sappho's, the *phainetai moi kēnos isos theoisin* (That man seems equal to the gods to me), was published in Basel in Francesco Robortello's edition of *Longinus on the Sublime.* This humanist access to Greek women poets was further extended by Fulvius Ursinus's edition of *The Poems of Nine Illustrious Women,* a collection of the works of nine classical Greek women poets, published at Antwerp in 1568. As a result, classical Greek women writers were frequently evoked as foremothers, both by women and by men sympathetic to women's aspirations.

One of the best-known women students of Greek in Renaissance Italy was Alessandra Scala (1475–1506), daughter of Bartolomeo Scala, Chancellor of the Florentine Republic, which had shown itelf particularly hospitable to Byzantine émigrés and their learning. Her Greek teachers were Janus Lascaris, Demetrius Chalcondyles, and the Italian humanist Angelo Poliziano, who wrote six Greek epigrams in her praise in 1493. Alessandra, who played the title role in a salon performance of Sophocles' *Antigone* that year, replied with a recondite epigram of her own (Parker 1997, 268–269). Teodora Chrysoloras (d. 1441), daughter of John Chrysoloras, a lecturer in Constantinople and wife of her father's student Francesco Filelfo, is said to have taught Greek at the University of Bologna, along with another woman, Bettina Sangiorgi (Allen 2002, 935).

In the sixteenth century, the most significant Italian woman writer in Greek was Olympia Morata (1526–1551), whose teacher was a German scholar, Kilian Senf (Sinapius), a resident of Ferrara. Greek was her preferred language for verse composition: the most significant of her Greek poems to survive are imitations of the Psalms in classical Greek. She also wrote dialogues in Greek, now lost, in imitation of Plato. In Modena, Tarquinia Molza (1542–1617) was celebrated as a Platonist. Though she wrote little in Greek (other than some verses), she translated two of Plato's dialogues, the *Crito* and the *Charmides,* and was recognized as a serious student by her teacher Francesco Patrizi, who presents her as such in his *Philosophy of Love.* Molza also demonstrated her knowledge of Plato and neo-Platonist texts in a treatise she wrote for Alfonso d'Este, the *Discourse of love made by Tarquinia Molza to the Grand Duke,* which survives in its original presentation manuscript (Modena, Biblioteca Estense MS g. H. 7. 2, a).

A number of Renaissance Frenchwomen were interested in Greek. The most significant is Edmonda Tusana, widow of the king's printer of Greek, Conrad Neobar, who went on publishing through 1540–1541 after her husband's death before marrying another printer, Jacques Bogard: the work of an academic printer in the sixteenth century involved close supervision of the text, so she was probably Greek-literate. She is likely to have been a relative of Jacobus Tusanus, a professor of Greek, of whom Bogard subsequently published several posthumous editions (Armstrong 1954, 124). Queen Catherine de Médicis also read Greek and owned many Greek books: in 1544, the Florentine envoy, Bernadino

de'Medici, wrote that her knowledge of that language was astonishing (Knecht 1998, 21). The learned Camille de Morel (1547–after 1611) translated from Greek, though she has left nothing written in the language (Utenhove 1568, 67).

After 1500, Northern European women's involvement with Biblical and Christian Greek is also noteworthy. Margareta Welser (1481–1552), the learned wife of Conrad Peutinger of Augsburg, corresponded with Erasmus on his revision of Matthew 20:23, which took into account words recovered from Greek manuscripts. Welser sent him her letter only after she and her husband had checked the Latin Vulgate version and what the Greek writers Origen and John Chrysostom had to say on the subject. Mary Bassett (ca.1522–1572), granddaughter of Sir Thomas More, translated Eusebius's *Ecclesiastical History* from the Greek: she rendered the first book of the *History* into Latin, and then she translated the first five books into English (Eusebius, 1860), offering the manuscript as a gift to Queen Mary Tudor.

More unusually, Lady Jane Fitzalan (1536–1576), daughter of Henry Fitzalan, twelfth earl of Arundel, who worked on classical Greek rather than on patristic texts, "published" in manuscript form a translation of the philosopher Isocrates from Greek to Latin. She also made a complete translation of Euripides' tragedy *Iphigeneia in Aulis* into English, saying of the latter project, "I have always taken an incredible pleasure in this work" (Purkiss 1998). Isocrates seems in particular to have interested women; the French Protestant Catherine de Parthenay, dame de Rohan-Soubise (1554–1631), also ventured a translation of him.

Mildred Cecil, Lady Burghley (1526–1589), was considered one of the most distinguished Greek scholars of her generation in England, "who besides her knowledge in the Latin letters (wherein of a Subject she excelled), such were her studies Exercises and continual meditation in the Greek doctors of the church (especially

Basil, Cyril, Chrysostom and Nazianzen) that she equaled, if not over-matched, any" (Strype 1725, III.ii, 578). This quotation, suggesting that her attention was mostly directed toward Christian writing, is confirmed by her translation of a homily by Basil of Caesarea (extant in London, British Library MS Royal 17 B xviii). She is also one of the few Englishwomen to have written verse in Greek, and a surviving short poem makes it clear that she also read Hesiod (Stevenson and Davidson 2001, 19–21). When the Flemish humanist Karel Utenhove lectured on Thucydides in London, it was Mildred who was his guest of honor and patron (Stevenson 2004, 58). Her sister Elizabeth Hoby Russell (1540–1609) also wrote Greek verse.

Another area of interest that led women to study Greek is medicine: a variety of early modern women were students in particular of the second-century A.D. Greek physician and medical writer, Galen. Dr. Aylmer, who taught Greek to the ill-fated Lady Jane Grey (1537–1554), briefly queen of England, also taught it to his own daughter Judith, who studied Galen and practiced as a physician (Stevenson 2005, 270). Catherine Tishem, or Thysmans (late sixteenth century), mother of the noted Dutch scholar Jan Gruter, taught Latin and Greek to her son and also studied Galen (Forster 1967, 36). Louise Sarrasin of Lyon (d. 1622) similarly used her knowledge of Greek to study medical texts (Pernetti 1757, I: 235–236).

Jane Stevenson

See also entries on the women mentioned.
Bibliography
Primary Works

Eusebius. *Ecclesiastical History.* Translated by Mary Bassett. London: British Library MS Harley, 1860.

Levati, Ambrogio. *Dizionario biografico cronologico, divido per classe, degli uomini illustri V: donne illustre.* 3 vols. Milan: Nicolò Bettoni, 1821–1822.

Morata, Olympia. *The Complete Writings of an Italian Heretic.* Edited and translated by Holt N. Parker. Chicago: University of Chicago Press, 2003.

Patrizi, Francesco. *The Philosophy of Love.* Translated by Daniela Pastina and John L. Crayton. Philadelphia: Xlibris, 2003

Purkiss, Diane, ed. *Three Tragedies by Renaissance Women.* Harmondsworth, UK: Penguin, 1998.

Stevenson, Jane, and Peter Davidson, eds. *Early Modern Women Poets.* Oxford: Oxford University Press, 2001.

Strype, John. *Annals of the Reformation and Establishment of Religion and Other Various Occurrences in the Church of England.* 2nd ed. 4 vols. London: Thomas Edlin, 1725.

Utenhove, Karel. *Caroli Utenhovii F. patricii Gandavensis XENIA seu ad illustrium aliquot Europae hominum nomina, Allusionum (intertextis alicubi Ioach. Bellaii eiusdem argumenti versibus), liber primus.* Basel: T. Guarinus Nervius, 1568.

Secondary Works

Allen, Prudence. *The Concept of Woman II: The Early Humanist Reformation, 1250–1500.* Grand Rapids, MI, and Cambridge: William B. Eerdman, 2002.

Armstrong, Elizabeth. *Robert Estienne, Royal Printer.* Cambridge: Cambridge University Press, 1954.

Forster, Leonard. *Janus Gruter's English Years.* Leiden: Leiden University Press, 1967.

Knecht, R. J. *Catherine de' Medici.* London: Longman, 1998.

O'Donnell, Anne M. "Contemporary Women in the Letters of Erasmus." *Erasmus of Rotterdam Society Yearbook* 9 (1989): 34–72.

Parker, Holt. "Latin and Greek Poetry by Five Renaissance Italian Women Humanists." In *Sex and Gender in Medieval and Renaissance Texts: The Latin Tradition.* Edited by Barbara K. Gold, Paul Allen Miller, and Charles Platter, 247–286. Albany: State University of New York Press, 1997.

Pernetti, Jacques. *Recherches pour servir à l'histoire de Lyon ou Les Lyonnois dignes de mémoire.* 2 vols. Lyon: Chez les frères Duplain, libraires, 1757.

Stevenson, Jane. "Mildred Cecil, Lady Burleigh: Poetry, Politics and Protestantism." In *Early Modern Women's Manuscript Writing: Selected Papers of the Trinity/Trent Colloquium.* The Early Modern Englishwoman: The Printed Writings. Edited by Victoria Burke and Jonathan Gibson, 51–73. Aldershot, UK: Ashgate Publishing, 2004.

Stevenson, Jane. *Women Latin Poets: Language, Gender and Authority from Antiquity to the Eighteenth Century.* Oxford: Oxford University Press, 2005.

Eleonora d'Aragona (1450–1493)

Duchess of Ferrara, chief administrator of ducal building projects and castle fortification in Ferrara, renowned patron of literature and the arts

At the age of twenty-three, Eleonora d'Aragona, daughter of King Ferrante of Naples and Isabella di Chiaromonte, married Ercole d'Este I, duke of Ferrara. Her wedding procession was conducted from Naples through Rome, Siena, and Florence and included approximately fourteen hundred attendants, including the Italian poet Matteo Maria Boiardo and the Italian playwright Niccolò da Correggio. Upon her arrival in Ferrara, Eleonora was received by Ercole I's mother, Rizzarda da Saluzzo. The marriage alliance was advantageous for the Ferrarese because Eleonora's royal lineage outranked her husband's family title. The marriage conveyed great prestige, honor, and income to the court and renewed the ties between Ferrara and Naples that previously had been established with the marriage of Maria d'Aragona (Eleonora's aunt) and Leonello d'Este. Eleonora's marriage to Ercole also brought renewed hope for the continuity of the Este dynasty, because Ercole's predecessor, Borso d'Este, had never had a wife or children.

The duchess quickly fulfilled her wifely duty, bearing seven children with Ercole: Isabella (b. 1474); Beatrice (b. 1475); Alfonso I (b. 1476), who became the Duke of Ferrara, Reggio, and Modena; Ferrante (born 1477); Ippolito (b. 1479), who became a cardinal in 1493; Sigismondo (b. 1480); and Alberto (1481–1482). Eleonora paid great attention to their rearing and education, particularly influencing her daughters' patronage of artists, musicians, scholars, and poets.

Eleonora often controlled the Ferrarese court administration while her husband was at war or on diplomatic visits. In September 1476, while Eleonora remained at home with three children, Ercole's nephew, Niccolò, invaded Ferrara in an attempted coup. Eleonora escaped from the palace apartments with her children to the more fortified castle (Castel Vecchio), not only saving herself but protecting the lives of her children—most important, the male heir to the court. As a consequence, the duke and duchess began major building projects in the castle for increased security in February 1477, including a suite of rooms and loggia for Eleonora. In another notable incident during the War of Venice in 1482, Eleonora maintained economic and social stability when Ercole became ill. She quelled rumors of the duke's impending death, encouraged citizens to remain faithful to Ercole, and raised the Ferrarese spirits by allowing the people to view the recovering duke in his bed (Rosenberg 1997, 125–126). In addition, Eleonora effectively managed household affairs and assisted her husband in daily administration, including his architectural projects and diplomatic and political affairs.

The duchess was a patron and collector. She is known to have commissioned works by Cosmè Tura and Ercole de' Roberti, as well an extensive number of devotional works, some by leading artists of the day, including Andrea Mantegna and Giovanni Bellini. Besides paintings, the duchess donated funds and maintained interest in architectural projects, including the rebuilding of the Clarissian monastery of Corpus Domini (Tuohy 1996, 373) and the convent of S. Gabriele (Tuohy 1996, 377). In addition to her own patronage, other works of art and literature were produced for her or dedicated to her, including illuminated manuscripts, frescoes, panel paintings, and works of literature. The duchess was highly regarded for her piety. Her own religious devotion is cited as an influence on her husband's religious fervor. She maintained her own oratory and cell at the monastery of Corpus Domini and often visited there for retreats. Although the majority of titles in her library were devotional works, it appears that Eleonora was interested in illustrious women in both art and literature. Bartolommeo Goggio wrote *De laudibus mulierum* for Eleonora in the 1480s, focusing on the exploits of famous women from antiquity. This work was known for its protofeminist attitude (Manca 2003, 88). Antonio Cornazzano dedicated *Del modo di regere e di regnare* (On How to Rule and to Reign) to Eleonora, likely around a time she was acting as regent between September 1478 and October 1479, while her husband was away from Ferrara. While providing much of the typical advice about the conduct of a ruler and the qualities needed for governing, such as wisdom and strength, this tome was unusual for its genre in that it specifically related to female leadership. Now lost frescoes at Belfiore, as described by Giovanni Sabadino degli Arienti in 1497, also portrayed atypical subject matter for the time period, that of a contemporary female ruler. These frescoes depicted Eleonora during her triumphal entry into Ferrara and her wedding festivities.

Before her death, she requested to be buried barefoot, wearing penitential robes, in a simple grave, without fanfare. Eleonora died on 11 October 1493 at the age of forty-three and was buried in the monastery of Corpus Domini.

Martha Ahrendt

See also Art and Women; Education, Humanism, and Women; the subheading Literary Patronage (under Literary Culture and Women); Music and Women.

Bibliography

Chiappini, Luciano. *Eleonora d'Aragona, prima duchessa di Ferrara.* Rovigo: S.T.E.R., 1956.

Chiappini, Luciano. *Gli Estensi.* Milan: Dall'Oglio, 1967.

Gardner, Edmund. *Dukes and Poets in Ferrara.* New York: Haskell House Publishers, 1968.

Gundersheimer, Werner. "Women, Learning, and Power: Eleonora of Aragon and the Court of Ferrara." In *Beyond Their Sex: Learned Women of the European Past.* Edited by Patricia H. LaBalme, 43–65. New York: New York University Press, 1980.

Manca, Joseph. "Constantia et forteza: Eleonora d'Aragon's Famous Matrons." *Source: Notes in the History of Art* 19, no. 2 (Winter 2000): 13–20.

Manca, Joseph. "Isabella's Mother: Aspects of the Patronage of Eleonora d'Aragona." *Aurora: The Journal of the History of Art* 4 (2003): 79–94.

Rosenberg, Charles. *The Este Monuments and Urban Development in Renaissance Ferrara.* Cambridge: Cambridge University Press, 1997.

Tuohy, Thomas. *Herculean Ferrara: Ercole d'Este 1471–1505, and the Invention of the Ducal Capital.* Cambridge: Cambridge University Press, 1996.

Elizabeth I (1533–1603)
Queen of England

Elizabeth, born in 1533 the second daughter of Henry VIII by his second wife, Anne Boleyn, ruled England for almost forty-five years and presided over a broadly based religious settlement, a cultural Renaissance, and an England that was developing itself in terms of discovery and trade. She is particularly known for her speech to encourage the troops at Tilbury at the time of the Spanish Armada in 1588.

Elizabeth's Childhood and Youth

Henry had pulled down the Catholic church in England to divorce his first wife, Catherine, mother of only a daughter. Anne Boleyn also had only a girl child, Elizabeth, and was executed in 1536, charged with adultery and treason. Henry's third wife, Jane Seymour, finally gave Henry the son, Edward, he craved. Though he married three more times, there were no more children. Henry died in 1547. His will, which had the force of parliament, gave the throne to Edward and, if Edward died without direct heirs, to Henry's eldest daughter, Mary, and, if she had no direct heirs, to Elizabeth.

Elizabeth had from her earliest memories known the difficulties and dangers for women when their lives were caught in the spotlight of sexuality and power. Not only must she have early learned her mother's fate, she also saw the progression of stepmothers at her father's court. At fifteen she had to listen to rumors that she had become pregnant by Thomas Seymour, widower of her last stepmother Katherine Parr, as he awaited his execution in the Tower. Only her quick wits and

Elizabeth I, queen of England. Portrait by Léopold Massard. (Library of Congress)

self-possession saved her own reputation and allowed her to protect her servants Katherine Ashley and Thomas Parry. Elizabeth spent the rest of Edward's reign living quietly and gaining a thorough humanist education in the classics and foreign languages, enjoying it so much that throughout her reign she did translations for relaxation.

Edward VI's death at age fifteen in 1553 led to a dynastic crisis. Edward had disinherited both his sisters in favor of his Protestant cousin, Lady Jane Grey, recently married to the youngest son of the most powerful man of the realm, John Dudley, duke of Northumberland. But Catholic Mary had such support she succeeded to the throne without a battle. Mary's popularity started to wane when she decided to marry her cousin, Philip of Spain. After the

unsuccessful Wyatt Rebellion in 1554, Mary and her council sent Elizabeth to the Tower, where she was kept for two months. Elizabeth was afraid she would be executed, as her cousin Lady Jane Grey had been. Nothing could be proved against Elizabeth, however, and her life was spared. When Mary died, Elizabeth succeeded her. Few would have believed in November 1558 that her reign would last until 1603.

Elizabeth's Accession

Elizabeth was far more successful than Mary and the other women rulers of her time. During her reign England was not engulfed in civil war, as happened to neighboring Scotland or France. She decided to be a queen for all the English, and she was proud to be pure English, not half-Spanish like her older sister Mary. Elizabeth began her reign emphasizing the theme of national unity. One of Elizabeth's first acts was to appoint William Cecil as her principal secretary. Eventually, he achieved the titles Lord Burghley and Treasurer. It was to be a long and fruitful partnership. Her other loyal servants included Sir Francis Walsingham, Sir Christopher Hatton, and Sir Robert Dudley, earl of Leicester, for many years her favorite.

Religious Settlement and Succession

After the religious upheavals of the previous decades, Elizabeth chose to preside over a broadly based religious settlement. In 1559 parliament defined England's official religion. Services were again to be in English, and mass was abolished. But the wording of the settlement was such that communion could be understood any way people wished. While the theology was Protestant, the services retained some Catholic elements, such as candles, choral music, bell ringing, and vestments for ministers. Elizabeth became supreme governor over the Church of England. Elizabeth was satisfied with the Religious Settlement and wanted no more changes. She desired only outward religious conformity from her subjects and did not want to persecute people for their beliefs. During her reign, however, religion and politics became increasingly intertwined, and Elizabeth found herself pressured by both Roman Catholics and radical Protestants. As her reign progressed, she was unwilling to compromise with the growing Puritan movement, which had support in parliament and among some of her church hierarchy. Edmund Grindal, Archbishop of Canterbury, was suspended from his duties, though not actually deprived of office, over the issue of "prophesying," that is, allowing congregations to hold discussions on Scriptural texts. Elizabeth perceived these meetings as forums for dissatisfactions with the established church, but Grindal refused to suppress them. Elizabeth hoped that Catholicism would just die out naturally; no one was executed for being a Catholic until 1574, but by then Catholics were involved in attempts to assassinate Elizabeth to restore the old religion to England.

In addition to the question of religion, Elizabeth had to deal with another significant issue: the succession. From the beginning of her reign, Elizabeth's council and parliament, fearing the potential chaos if she died without a designated heir, begged her to marry and, they hoped, have a son and heir. In the meantime Elizabeth was under great pressure to name a successor. Elizabeth, however, while she played with courtship and perceived its use as a useful political tool, refused to marry; she also would not name an heir. The example of Henry and his succession of wives would hardly have convinced Elizabeth that marriage was an enviable estate or that, even if she married, she would necessarily have a surviving son or survive the rigors of childbirth herself. Nor did she want someone else to be a rising sun to her setting sun. Elizabeth had a variety of suitors: her former brother-in-law, Mary's husband, Philip II; the Habsburg Archduke Charles; Eric XIV of Sweden; and the sons of Catherine de Médicis, both Henry Duke of

Anjou (later Henry III) and Francis, duke of Alençon, later duke of Anjou. Robert Dudley, to whom Elizabeth eventually gave the title earl of Leicester, was also a forceful suitor for her hand. For years, rumors swept around Elizabeth and Dudley, particularly after the mysterious death of his wife, Amy Robsart, in 1560.

Foreign Relations and Mary Stuart

During the first part of her reign, Elizabeth worked to keep England out of expensive and dangerous foreign entanglements, but by the 1580s conflicts with Spain escalated. When Philip of Spain sent the Armada in 1588, Elizabeth gave a rousing speech to her troops that is said to include the famous words, "I may have the body of a weak and feeble woman, but I have the heart and stomach of a king."

Yet Elizabeth's reign had its share of troubles. Elizabeth had serious problems with her Catholic cousin, Mary Stuart, the Scottish queen. Mary claimed Elizabeth's throne while queen regent in France and then after her return to Scotland. After the murder of Mary's second husband and her remarriage shortly therafter to James Hepburn, earl of Bothwell, the Scottish people rebelled and forced her to abdicate in favor of her infant son James. In 1568 Mary escaped to England and was Elizabeth's "enforced guest" for nineteen years—conspiring to have Elizabeth assassinated—until Mary's execution in 1587.

The Last Years of the Reign

The last years of Elizabeth's reign also had economic difficulties. Inflation and poor harvests caused misery for many of the English, and there was deep fear that the Spanish might attempt another invasion. There were great fears as well that Spain might use Ireland as a base, and the Irish lords were in rebellion over English control. In 1599 Elizabeth's final favorite Robert Devereux, earl of Essex, spectacularly failed at resolving the situation in Ireland and lost favor. Two years later, in 1601, he led a rebellion against her, which, though it failed and he was executed, caused both Elizabeth and England anguish.

It was also, however, a time of great cultural development. In the last decade and a half of her reign William Shakespeare, Christopher Marlowe, and others wrote great plays for the theater, while poets like Edmund Spenser published their work. In 1601 Elizabeth had her final parliament, where she spoke of her love for her people. Though her physicians could not name a specific complaint, by the beginning of 1603 her health began to fail; she died on 24 March 1603. Elizabeth had always refused to name her successor, stating God would take care of England. Her cousin, James VI of Scotland, the son of Mary Stuart, peacefully ascended the throne of England at her death. England under Elizabeth had survived as an independent nation and was not decimated by religious civil wars, as were a number of her continental neighbors. Though there were certainly problems throughout the reign, Elizabeth is one of the best known of all English monarchs, and many describe her as one of the most successful.

Carole Levin

See also Boleyn, Anne; Mary Stuart; Religious Reform and Women.

Bibliography

Primary Works

Marcus, Leah, Janel Mueller, and Mary Beth Rose, eds. *Elizabeth I: Collected Works.* Chicago: University of Chicago Press, 2000.

May, Steven, ed. *Queen Elizabeth I: Selected Works.* New York: Washington Square Press, 2004.

Pryor, Felix. *Elizabeth I: Her Life in Letters.* Berkeley: University of California Press, 2003.

Secondary Works

Doran, Susan. *Elizabeth I and Foreign Policy, 1558–1603.* London and New York: Routledge, 2000.

Levin, Carole. *The Heart and Stomach of a King: Elizabeth I and the Politics of Sex and Power.* Philadelphia: University of Pennsylvania Press, 1994.

Levin, Carole. *The Reign of Elizabeth I.* New York: Palgrave, 2002.

MacCaffrey, Wallace T. *Elizabeth I.* New York: Arnold, 1993.

Elizabeth Stuart (1596–1662)

Queen of Bohemia, grandmother of George I, king of England

Elizabeth Stuart was born 19 August 1596 to King James VI of Scotland and Anne of Denmark. Her father James ascended to the throne of England in 1603 and ruled England and Scotland until his death in 1625. She had two brothers: Henry (1594–1612) and Charles (born 1600, ruled England and Scotland 1625–1649, beheaded 1649).

Elizabeth married Frederick V, elector Palatine and head of the Union of Protestant Princes, on 14 February 1613, and lived in Heidelberg as electress Palatine 1613–1619. In 1619, Protestant Bohemians selected Frederick to rule in place of Ferdinand of Styria, the king chosen for Bohemia by the Habsburgs and supported by the Catholic Alliance. Frederick's coronation in October 1619 resulted in war. Catholic forces stripped Frederick and Elizabeth of Heidelberg in August 1620 and of Prague in November 1620. Frederick and Elizabeth fled Prague and found refuge in The Hague. Elizabeth maintained a household in The Hague from 1621 until 1660 with financial support from various quarters, including England's parliament and the Dutch estates.

Between 1614 and 1632, Elizabeth bore thirteen children. Two died in infancy; one drowned at age fifteen. Her second son, Charles Louis, ruled the Lower Palatinate after it was restored to the family as part of the Peace of Westphalia in 1648. Two other sons, Rupert and Maurice, fought for Cavalier forces during the English Civil War. Sophia, her twelfth child, married Ernst Augustus, duke of Brunswick-Lüneberg; her son George, born 1660, ascended the English throne as George I in 1714.

Elizabeth Stuart died 13 February 1662 in London.

Karen Nelson

See also Power, Politics, and Women; Religious Reform and Women.
Bibliography
Primary Work
Baker, L. M., ed. *The Letters of Elizabeth, Queen of Bohemia.* London: The Bodley Head, 1953.
Secondary Work
Ross, Josephine. *The Winter Queen: The Story of Elizabeth Stuart.* New York: St. Martin's Press, 1979.

Epistolary Culture. *See* the subheading Letter Writing (under Literary Culture and Women).

Este, Isabella d' (1474–1539)
Marchesa di Mantua, patron of artists and poets, prolific letter writer, instrumental musician and singer

Isabella d'Este was the first of six children born to Duke Ercole I d'Este, second duke of Ferrara (1431–1505), and to the daughter of King Ferrante of Naples, Eleonora d'Aragona (d. 1493). Her brother Alfonso I (1476–1524) succeeded Ercole as duke of Ferrara, marrying first Anna Sforza (d. 1497) and then Lucrezia Borgia (1480–1519). Her sister Beatrice (1475–1497) married Ludovico ("il Moro") Sforza (1451–1508) and became duchess of Milan. Their younger brother Ippolito (1479–1520) rose to the ecclesiastical rank of cardinal.

Isabella has been portrayed by many as a female counterpart to the multifaceted Renaissance men who made her century famous. Schooling by humanists and sustained contacts with artists, intellectuals, and diplomats during her childhood prepared her for regency as consort to Francesco II Gonzaga (1466–1519), fourth marchese of Mantua, to whom she was betrothed in 1480. Contemporary accounts describe the child Isabella as verbally and socially precocious, possessing a prodigious memory, an eager learner who enjoyed danc-

Isabella d'Este, Marchesa di Mantua and patron of artists and poets. Painting by Titian, ca. 1536. Kunsthistorisches Museum, Vienna. (Francis G. Mayer/Corbis)

ing, horseback riding, and card games as well as Latin and the reading of chivalric romances.

On 11 February 1490, Isabella married Francesco Gonzaga in the ducal chapel of Ferrara. On 15 February, she made her triumphal entry into Mantua as his bride. From that day until her death, she played a powerful role in the culture and politics of the region, first as marchesa of Mantua and then, after Francesco's death, as an auxiliary figure in the government of their son and heir, Federico II Gonzaga (1500–1540). Isabella and Francesco produced six surviving children. Eleonora (1493–1550) became duchess of Urbino when she married Francesco Maria della Rovere. Federico II was named first duke of Mantua by Habsburg Emperor Charles V in 1530 and married Margherita Paleologo. Daughters Ippolita (1502–1570) and Paola (1508–1569) chose to enter monastic life, thwarting marriage plans on their behalf. The second son, Ercole (also known as Alvise, 1505–1563), pursued a career in the papal court, where he obtained the rank of cardinal; and the third son, Ferrante (1507–1557), became an officer in the imperial forces, marrying Isabella di Capua.

Isabella d'Este is best known as a patron and a collector, a reputation she earned in large part by realizing a single, compact, and spectacular project in Mantua's Ducal Palace. Shortly after her marriage, she began to engage artists to decorate a special suite in her private apartments, designated for the display of paintings, antiquities, and other signs of her culture and her values. Its centerpiece consisted of a small *studiolo* (or study), which communicated via a short staircase with a smaller chamber below it, known as the *grotta* (grotto). Together these two rooms (known as her *camerini*) constituted one of the most impressive expressions of personal culture to be elaborated in the Italian Renaissance. Inspired by the *studioli* of contemporary humanist princes, by medieval and ancient treasury chambers, and perhaps by her mother's apartments in Ferrara, this signature space developed as both an intimate retreat for private meditation and a showcase for select visitors to the Gonzaga court. The *studiolo* featured seven large narrative paintings by Andrea Mantegna, Lorenzo Costa, Pietro Perugino, and (after relocation of her apartments in 1519) Correggio. Increasing the *grotta's* symbolic density were a number of highly wrought intarsia panels as well as Isabella's collections of books, ancient and *all'antica* sculptures, cameos, medallions, and other precious finds. Frescoes, sculpted doorways, gilded ceilings, and tiles bearing enigmatic emblems and mottoes further ornamented these quarters, contributing to an intricate network of significations designed to project an image of the Marchesa as a woman of sov-

ereign taste, substantial learning, and impeccable virtue.

Her art collection included works by Giovanni Bellini, Giancristoforo Romano, Michelangelo, Francesco Francia, Leonardo da Vinci, Titian, and others. (Her portrait was executed by the last three.) Isabella's self-described "insatiable desire for things ancient" and her "appetite" for beautiful things, however, contributed to the Gonzaga household debt; her jewels were pawned repeatedly and for extended periods.

Isabella also devoted enormous attention to the applied arts, insisting on peerless quality in her personal and household acquisitions. Fabrics, gloves, jewelry, crystal, flowers, and buttons were all inspected meticulously by Isabella herself. Many were returned to their purveyors when found inferior to her standards. Her correspondence detailing these purchases documents Isabella's status as a pioneer of fashion, cosmetic, and domestic design. She collaborated in the production of perfumes and cosmetics, exchanged recipes for use in the court kitchen, and worked with advisors on inventions for her clothing and jewelry. The round hat she wears in her portrait by Titian was a signature piece of her wardrobe. Motifs from the emblems decorating the *studiolo* were worked into her jewelry and her gowns.

At the time of her death Isabella's library contained one hundred and thirty-three volumes, including works of Greek philosophy, a wide range of Latin classics (Cicero, Ovid, Pliny, Plutarch, Seneca, Juvenal, and Horace among them), books of music, chivalric romances, theatrical comedies, religious sermons, saints' lives, biographies, and prophecies. Also present were vernacular writings by Dante, Petrarch, Jacopo Sannazzaro, Lorenzo de' Medici, and Pietro Bembo, as well as many minor contemporaries. Her literary friends included Matteo Maria Boiardo, Niccolò da Correggio, Giovanni Sabadino degli Arienti, Mario Equicola, Baldesar Castiglione, Bernardo da Bibbiena, Gian Giorgio Trissino, Bernardo Accolti, Ludovico

Ariosto, and Matteo Bandello, several of whom wrote works in her honor.

Isabella was musically literate, a trained vocalist who studied the clavichord, the lute, the viola da gamba, the *vihuela da mano,* and the *lira da braccio.* Her regular correspondence with the master instrument maker, Lorenzo da Pavia (d. 1517), records her purchase of several fine keyboard and string instruments; she also bought and borrowed instruments from others for her amateur musical activities. She sang alone and in private court companies, both accepting as gifts and commissioning texts to be set to music, especially by the composers Marchetto Cara (d. after 1525) and Bartolomeo Tromboncino (ca. 1470–after 1535).

Privileged, prominent, and proficient as she was, Isabella was nonetheless constrained as a woman to limit her public activities to tasks performed in the name of her husband or that fell traditionally to women at court. While Francesco was away on frequent duty as a *condottiere* (hired officer) in the service of Europe's most powerful princes, Isabella excelled in diplomacy and administrative astuteness, but she was careful to defer officially to her husband's higher authority and to present her decisions as the results of his instructions. Her activism, pragmatism, and discerning judgment are evident in arenas ranging from the pursuit of justice, to the protection of the rights of Mantuan subjects, to the arrangement of marriages for court functionaries, to the defense of women's safety and property. When Francesco was captured and imprisoned by the Venetians (August 1509–July 1510), Isabella acted as Mantua's sole regent, successfully fending off foreign contenders for Gonzaga territories. Subsequent to these events, relations between Isabella and Francesco cooled, partly as a result of suspicions planted by his Venetian captors that Francesco's wife had betrayed him politically. Another factor, however, may have been the marchese's increasingly evident affliction with syphilis, which estranged Isabella from their marriage bed.

Isabella's duties included presiding over the Mantuan court in her husband's absence, but when Francesco was in residence, she herself relished travel on the Italian peninsula. Sometimes her trips were justified by religious pledges to visit holy shrines, as with her 1502 and 1523 travels to Venice; on other occasions her motivations were political, as was true of her 1525 journey to Rome in hopes of securing a cardinalship for her son, Ercole. In many cases she performed combined ambassadorial and social functions, as in her visits to Milan (1491, 1513) or her 1510 travel to Rome and Naples. At still other times, she journeyed merely for pleasure and recreation, as in the case of her regular summer expeditions to Lake Garda. In these contexts Isabella proved a passionate traveler, eager to see the world; an able diplomat with an innate sense of occasion and opportunity; and an excellent travel correspondent. Her descriptions of ceremonies, festivities, and theatrical productions are among the most detailed records to survive from the period. Among her closest friends and occasional travel companions were her sister-in-law, the duchess of Urbino, Elisabetta Gonzaga da Montefeltro (1471–1526), and Emilia Pia da Carpi (d. 1528), both of whom are immortalized in Castiglione's 1528 *Book of the Courtier.*

Soon after Francesco's death from syphilis in 1519, Isabella transferred her apartments to a less central location of the palace. In the next twenty years, she continued to travel, making several trips to Venice and witnessing the sack of Rome in 1527. In 1525, upon the death of her brother-in-law, Cardinal Sigismondo Gonzaga (b. 1469), she purchased Solarolo, a small fief near Imola. There, for the first time in her life, she acted as sole regent and governed according to her own principles and procedures. She died on 13 February 1539 in Ferrara.

Though the Gonzaga-Nevers line ruled until 1707, the Gonzaga court at Mantua essentially vanished with the extinction in 1627 of Vincenzo II, the last heir of the original line. Vincenzo had sold the choicest works from the court's art collection to Charles I of England (1600–1649), and any remaining treasures were carried off in subsequent years under Mantua's domination by Austria and France. Paintings and other objects from Isabella's magnificent *camerini* now reside in museums in Vienna, Paris, London, and New York as well as in Mantua and other Italian cities.

Among the many remnants of Isabella's court still remaining in Mantua, however, are secretarial copies of over twelve thousand of her letters, together with a rich array of Gonzaga correspondence with persons in courts throughout the Italian peninsula and beyond. These documents tell remarkable tales, often in great detail, of the daily life and the extraordinary experience of Isabella d'Este and her generation.

Deanna Shemek

See also Art and Women; Borgia, Lucrezia; Eleonora d'Aragona; the subheadings Letter Writing and Literary Patronage (under Literary Culture and Women).

Bibliography

Bellonci, Maria. *Private Renaissance.* Translated by William Weaver. New York: Morrow, 1989.

Brown, Clifford M. *Per dare qualche splendore a la gloriosa cita di Mantua.* Documents for the Antiquarian Collection of Isabella d'Este. Rome: Bulzoni, 2002.

Brown, Clifford M., and Anna Maria Lorenzoni. *Isabella d'Este and Lorenzo da Pavia.* Documents for the History of Art and Culture in Renaissance Mantua. Geneva: Droz, 1982.

Campbell, Stephen. *The Studiolo of Isabella D'este: Reading, Collecting and the Invention of Mythological Painting.* New Haven and London: Yale University Press, forthcoming.

Cartwright, Julia. *Isabella d'Este Marchioness of Mantua, 1474–1539: A Study in the Renaissance.* London: John Murray, 1907.

Ferino-Pagden, Silvia, ed. *"La prima donna del mondo": Isabella d'Este, Fürstin und Mäzenatin der Renaissance.* Vienna: Ausstellungskatalog des Kunsthistorisches Museum, 1994.

Luzio, Alessandro. *I precettori di Isabella d'Este. Appunti e documenti per le nozze Renier-Campostrini.* Ancona, Italy: A. Gustavo Morelli, 1887.

Luzio, Alessandro, and Rodolfo Renier. *Mantova e Urbino: Isabella d'Este ed Elisabetta Gonzaga nelle relazioni familiari e nelle vicende politiche.* Turin: Roux and Co., 1893.

Prizer, William F. "Una 'Virtù Molto Conveniente a Madonne': Isabella d'Este as a Musician." *The Journal of Musicology* 17, no. 1 (1999): 10–49.

San Juan, Rose Marie. "The Court Lady's Dilemma: Isabella d'Este and Art Collecting in the Renaissance." *Oxford Art Journal* 14, no. 1 (1991): 67–78.

Shemek, Deanna. "In Continuous Expectation: Isabella d'Este's Epistolary Desire." In *Phaethon's Children: The Este Court and Its Culture in Early Modern Italy.* Edited by Dennis Looney and Deanna Shemek. Tempe, AZ: Medieval and Renaissance Texts and Studies, 2005.

Shemek, Deanna. "Isabella d'Este and the Properties of Persuasion." In *Form and Persuasion in Early Modern Women's Letters Across Europe.* Edited by Ann Crabb and Jane Couchman, 108–134. Brookfield, VT: Ashgate, 2005.

Estienne, Nicole (Madame Liébaut or Liébault, "Olympe Liébaut"; ca. 1542–after ca. 1588)

Poet

Born into one of the most influential printing families in sixteenth-century Europe, Nicole Estienne was steeped from her earliest childhood in the liberal arts, ancient languages, and science. The daughter of Charles Estienne, the third son of printing genius Henri (I) Estienne, and Geneviève de Berly, Nicole was first engaged to the poet Jacques Grévin, who celebrates her in his collection *L'Olimpe* (Grévin, 1560). Ironically, posterity has often given to this champion of women's independence the pseudonym created for her by Grévin, to the point of substituting it for her own first name (cf. the Opale Plus catalog of the Bibliothèque nationale de France). The engagement was broken for unknown reasons, perhaps because of the financial disasters of Nicole's father; alternatively, Jacques's conversion to Protestantism may have dissuaded Nicole. In 1561, Nicole married the physician Jean Liébaut, Regent of the Faculty of Medicine of Paris and author of several scientific works.

Nicole Estienne wrote two lost works, *Le mépris d'amour* (Contempt of Love) and *l'Apologie ou Défense pour les femmes contre ceux qui les méprisent* (Defense of Women Against Those Who Spurn Them). In response to the misogynist *Stances du Mariage* by Philippe Desportes (1573), Nicole produced her own *Stanzes,* which remain in manuscript form in the Bibliothèque Nationale de France. While both Desportes' and Estienne's works indubitably originate in the spirit of debate and artful argumentation promoted by the classical rhetorical training of the Renaissance, in the *Stanzes* Nicole Estienne nonetheless defends her sex with aplomb.

Les Misères de la femme mariée, où se peuvent voir les peines et tourmens qu'elle reçoit durant sa vie (Adversities of the Married Woman, in Which the Suffering and Torment She Endures in Her Life Are Exposed, after 1587), Estienne's best known work, at first seems to contradict her *Stanzes* in favor of marriage. But in both works, the author defends the idea of marriage as a sacred alliance potentially full of pleasure, grace, and sweetness, while at the same time criticizing certain practices associated with the institution in sixteenth-century France. In the *Misères* she condemns the age difference between spouses, the intolerance of uneducated husbands who refuse to acknowledge the intelligence of their wives, and domestic violence. The *Misères,* consisting of thirty-five sextets in alexandrine verse, address the leitmotifs of enclosure, domination, repetition, time, and—more obliquely—the importance of writing

The extent to which Nicole Estienne's work is autobiographical remains unknown. Since the author's grievances are registered not against an individual but rather against a group of tyrannical husbands, her avowed mission extends beyond the personal and into the social and political arenas. Nicole's active participation in a number of literary circles is corroborated by the publication of a number of her poems as introductory pieces in collections of other poets (see "Primary Works"). She often

signed her works with the anagrammatic motto *j'estonne le ciel* (I astonish heaven). The anonymous author of a manuscript preserved in the Bibliothèque Nationale de France recounts the following anecdote in an attempt to explain the enigmatic motto: a malicious observer has proposed that Madame Liébaut astonishes not heaven but the canopy of her bed (a pun on *le ciel*) (ms. Fonds Dupuy 844, fol.361r). The poet herself explains the motto as follows: she surprises others by her patience and her strength—like a rock, she resists the waves and never breaks (1587, 43).

The exact year of the author's death remains uncertain. Insofar as she offered an introductory poem to the collection of Baptiste Badere, one can surmise that she was still living in 1588, but she had died by the time of her husband's death in 1596.

Celebrated in her era as a learned woman of considerable wit, accomplishment, and intelligence, Nicole Estienne fell into relative oblivion until the early twentieth century, when a Renaissance scholar placed her among the most gifted women poets of the period (Lavaud 1931, 350). Recently, contemporary critics have analyzed her important role in the debate on marriage, acknowledging both her personal courage and her literary virtuosity. Poet, learned woman, rhetorician, and champion of her sex, Nicole Estienne remains one of the least known among the significant women writers of the period.

Cathy Yandell

See also Literary Culture and Women; Printers, the Book Trade, and Women; Querelle des Femmes.

Bibliography

Primary Works

Estienne, Nicole. *Les Misères de la femme mariée: où se peuvent voir les peines et tourmens qu'elle reçoit durant sa vie. Mis en forme de Stances, par Madame Liebaut.* Paris: Pierre Menier, 1587(?).

Estienne, Nicole. *Les Misères de la femme mariée: où se peuvent voir les peines et tourmens qu'elle reçoit durant sa vie. Mis en forme de Stances, par Madame Liebaut.* In Ilana Zinguer, *Misères et grandeur des femmes au XVIe siècle,* 32–40. Geneva: Slatkine, 1982.

Estienne, Nicole. "A liminary quatrain." In François Béroalde de Verville, *Les Apprehensions Spirituelles, Poemes et autres Oeuvres Philosophiques, avec Les Recherches de la pierre philosophale.* Paris: Timothee Joüan, 1584.

Estienne, Nicole. "A liminary sonnet." In Baptiste Badere, *Devotes meditations chrestiennes, sur la Mort et Passion de nostre Seigneur Jésus Christ.* Paris: Guyon Giffard, 1588. (With "N.E." and signature anagram.)

Grévin, Jacques. *L'Olimpe.* Paris: Robert Estienne, 1560.

Secondary Works

Berriot-Salvadore, Evelyne. "Evocation et représentation du mariage dans la poésie féminine." In *Le Mariage au temps de la Renaissance.* Edited by M. T. Jones-Davies, 215–216. Paris: Klincksieck, 1993.

Larsen, Anne R. "Nicole Estienne." In *Encyclopedia of Continental Women Writers.* Edited by Katharina M. Wilson. New York and London: Garland, 1991.

Lavaud, Jacques. "Quelques poésies oubliées de N. Estienne." *Revue du seizième siècle* 18 (1931): 341–351.

Renouard, Antoine-Augustin. *Annales de l'imprimerie des Estienne ou Histoire de la famille des Estienne et de ses éditions.* Geneva: Slatkine, 1971. (Originally published in Paris: J. Renouard, 1843.)

Reynolds-Cornell, Régine. "*Les Misères de la femme mariée:* Another Look at Nicole Liébault and a Few Questions About the Woes of the Married Woman." *BHR* 64 (2002): 37–54.

Yandell, Cathy. *Carpe Corpus: Time and Gender in Early Modern France.* Newark, NJ: University of Delaware Press; London: Associated University Presses, 2000.

Eve

Chawwah *(related to the Hebrew for "life"), in Jewish mythology the first or second female companion of the primal man Adam ("earth")*

There are as many Renaissance Eves as there are poets, theologians, and artists. In some versions the first female, Lilith, refuses to take a subordinate position and becomes a dangerous, seductive spirit. Incorporation into the Bible transformed this folkloric figure into a

Adam and Eve in Paradise. *Engraving by Albrecht Dürer. Albrecht-Dürer-Almanach. (Library of Congress)*

definitive prototype of Woman, created and immediately punished by God. The brevity and inconsistency of Genesis opened a space into which multiple interpretations were projected. Genesis seems to imagine Eve as a higher-order creature. The male, defective while alone, is first "molded" from mud, the woman later "built" from living flesh, consummating the sequence of creation. Jehovah's questions after the fall presume her more developed moral intelligence, and her punishment (pain in childbirth, subordination to her husband) is meaningless unless beforehand she was an equal or a matriarch.

Ideological pressures forced many Renaissance interpreters to obscure this narrative. Eve must be proved inferior from the start; her "help" in completing humanity makes her a subordinate, an accessory, even an afterthought. The serpent seduces her alone because she is weaker (though the Bible says the man was "with her"), and she then uses her sexual wiles to destroy Adam. How to reconcile these readings of Eve—divinely ordained perfection and a source of sin and death? For the most part theologians emphasize Eve's fallibility, philosophers allegorize her as Sense, and artists make her an ideal nude and/or seductress. Poets compose elaborate love songs for her, blazon her beauty, then abruptly denounce her complicity with Satan. The Virgin Mary (and other charismatic women) become the New Eve, redeeming the faults of the first, who becomes a second Lilith. Only Milton, more Baroque than Renaissance, expresses the entire range of possibilities, creating irresolvable contradictions in his epic *Paradise Lost*.

Though few, some interpreters challenged the notion of Eve's primal subordination. The arguments for the higher ontological status of Eve (and her exemption from blame) of Cornelius Agrippa's *Female Pre-Eminence* (1529) provided a resource for feminists. Luther, Calvin, and the more radical Protestants occasionally imagine Eve as an "equal." Arcangela Tarabotti links the misinterpretation of Eve to "paternal tyranny." Isotta Nogarola (1451) and Aemilia Lanyer (1612) choose a problematic way to prove Eve's greater innocence, emphasizing her emotional tenderness and weakness, as Tarabotti later did, but Lanyer still concludes, forcefully, that men can no longer claim "Sovereignty" on the basis of Eve's guilt: "Then let us have our Liberty again."

James Grantham Turner

See also Lanyer, Aemilia Bassano; Nogarola, Isotta; Querelle des Femmes; Speght, Rachel.

Bibliography

Primary Works

Heale, William. *An Apologie for Women.* Oxford: 1609.

Lanyer, Aemilia. *Poems/Salve Deus rex Judeorum.* Edited by Susanne Woods. New York and Oxford: Oxford University Press, 1993.

Nogarola, Isotta. *Complete Writings: Letters, Dialogue on Adam and Eve, Orations.* Translated and edited by Margaret L. King and Diana Robin. Chicago: University of Chicago Press, 2004.

Speght, Rachel. *A Mouzell for Melastomus.* London: 1617.

Secondary Works

Almond, Philip C. *Adam and Eve in Seventeenth-Century Thought.* Cambridge: Cambridge University Press, 1999.

McColley, Diane Kelsey. *Milton's Eve.* Urbana: University of Illinois Press, 1983.

Norris, Pamela. *Eve: A Biography.* New York: New York University Press, 1999.

Russell, H. Diane, with Bernadine Barnes. *Eva/Ave: Woman in Renaissance and Baroque Prints.* Washington, DC: National Gallery of Art, 1990.

Trible, Phyllis. *God and the Rhetoric of Sexuality.* London: SCM Press, 1992. (Originally published in 1978.)

Turner, James Grantham. *One Flesh: Paradisal Marriage and Sexual Relations in the Age of Milton.* Oxford: Clarendon Press, 1987, 1993, 2004.

F

Fedele, Cassandra (1465–1558)

Venetian humanist, writer, and scholar

Cassandra Fedele was born to citizen-class parents, Angelo Fedele and Barbara Leoni, in Venice. Schooled in Greek and Latin grammar by her father, she studied philosophy, the sciences, and dialectics with the noted scholar of classical literature and Servite friar, Gasparino Borro. When she was sixteen she joined an active circle of scholars at the University of Padua, among whom were Niccolo Tomei, then the leading Aristotelian at the university; the Rimini-born scholar Giovanni Aurelio Augurello; the Brescian theologian Bonifacio Bembo; Panfilo Sasso from Modena; Gianfrancesco Superchio of Pesaro, who was known as Filomuso; and the Paduan painter, sculptor, and philosopher, Girolamo Campagnola. Primed by her regular discussions with such academics as these, Fedele delivered her first public oration at her cousin Bertucio Lamberti's baccalaureate ceremony at the University of Padua in 1487. This speech was immediately published in three printed editions, each titled *Oratio pro Bertucio Lamberto* (Modena 1487; Nuremberg 1488; Venice 1489). Soon afterward, at the invitation of the philosopher Giorgio Valla, she presented a second public lecture before the doge, Agostino Barbarigo, and the Venetian senate, in which she praised the study of literature and addressed the practical question of higher education for women. Her major work, *Epistolae et orationes,* which contained not only all her public lectures but her one hundred and twenty-one Latin letters, circulated widely in manuscript in Italy, though it failed to find a readership north of the Alps until 1636, when it was published posthumously by the Paduan printer Bolzetta.

Cassandra Fedele, Venetian humanist, writer, and scholar. Anonymous engraving from Epistolae & Orationes Posthumae. *(Maria Bandini Buti,* Enciclopedia biografica e bibliografica italiana: poetesse e scrittrici*)*

With the publication of the *Oratio pro Lamberto,* Fedele's reputation as humanist scholar and writer spread beyond the Veneto to Florence, Ferrara, Milan, Germany, and Hungary. Through the Florentine Hellenist Angelo Poliziano, who met her in Venice around 1490, Fedele entered into correspondence with members of Lorenzo de' Medici's circle, exchanging letters not only with Poliziano but also with Pico della Mirandola, the chancellor of Florence Bartolomeo Scala, and Scala's daughter Alessandra, who was also a scholar of Greek. Her correspondence with the members of both her Paduan and her Florentine circles exemplifies the humanist themes typical of her

era: the elevation of reason (*ratio*) to quasi divine status; the supremacy of eloquence
among human pursuits; the civilizing role of
the study of the liberal arts (*studia humanitatis*);
the role of the writer as a cultural critic and
prophet of sorts (*vates*); and lastly the idealiza-
tion of the patronage relationship as a sublime
bond between intellectual and moral peers
(*amicitia*). Though Fedele wrote in the cultivated Latin of Cicero, Seneca, and Pliny the
Younger, her rhetorical style is self-consciously
framed and embellished as female. She defines
herself in terms of her sexual innocence and
her "natural" feminine weaknesses, in both intellectual and physical terms (Robin 2000,
8–9; Robin 1995).

Fedele's letters to and from Italian and European royalty and other nobles showcase her
expertise in the Ciceronian language of patronage. These letters reflect her repeated attempts to win a court appointment with an
annual stipend and to offer her literary services
to such prospective patrons as these. She exchanged letters with Duchess Beatrice d'Este
of Milan, Queen Beatrice d'Aragona of Hungary, Duchess Eleonora d'Aragona of Ferrara,
Marchese Francesco Gonzaga of Mantua, King
Louis XII of France, Duke Lodovico Sforza of
Milan, and Christopher Columbus's patron,
Queen Isabella of Castile,who tried unsuccessfully for the better part of a decade to persuade
Fedele to join her court in Spain (1487–1485).

By the end of the 1490s, Fedele was the
best-known female humanist in Europe. Her
storied literary career, recounted in every early
modern Italian catalogue of famous women,
overshadowed that of her fellow humanists
Isotta Nogarola and Laura Cereta. But what
was recorded both about Fedele's writings and
her personal life was largely a fiction. The biographical tradition praised the beauty of her
Latin poetry and attested to her having written a book entitled *Ordo scientiarum* (The
Order of the Sciences). But no trace of her alleged book or poems has surfaced. Well into
the seventeenth century the early biographical

catalogues characterized Fedele as a lifelong
virgin. But, in fact, Fedele married Gian-Maria
Mappelli, a physician from Vicenza, in 1499,
and she lived with him until his death in 1521.
Little is known about their marriage, though
two tantalizing letters survive in which Fedele
addresses an unnamed physician in unusually
intimate terms (Robin 2000, 40–41). In the
summer of 1515 Fedele and Mappelli set sail
for Retima, Crete, where he practiced medicine for five years. The couple resettled in
Venice in 1520 after nearly losing their lives in
the storm that sank their ship on their return
voyage to the mainland. They survived, but
with nothing but the clothes on their backs.
Widowed the same year that the couple returned to Venice, Fedele spent the 1520s and
1530s desperately looking for employment as a
writer or teacher, but with no luck. As an elderly, single, female scholar, she no longer received the invitations to lecture that she had
enjoyed in her twenties. In 1547, Fedele at last
obtained an appointment from Pope Paul III as
prioress of the orphanage of San Domenico di
Castello in Venice.

Two years before her death, she was invited
to give a public oration before the Venetian
senate and Doge Francesco Venier in 1556, to
commemorate the arrival of Queen Bona
Sforza of Poland in Venice. When Fedele died
in 1558 at the age of ninety-three, the Venetian senate honored her with a public funeral.
She lay in state at the church of San
Domenico; her body was placed on a marble
bier, her white hair bound with laurel.

Diana Robin

See also Cereta, Laura; Education, Humanism,
    and Women; Literary Culture and Women,
    particularly the subheading Letter Writing;
    Nogarola, Isotta; Querelles des Femmes.
Bibliography
Primary Works
For the early modern catalogues with vitae of
    Fedele, see Battista Fregosa (aka Cam-
    pofregosa, 1483), Jacopo Filippo da Bergamo
    (1497), Jean Tixier de Ravisius (1521),
    Giuseppe Betussi (1545), Giovanni Battista

Egnazio (1554), Giacomo Alberici (1605), and Jacopo Filippo Tommasini (1644).

No manuscript collections of Fedele's letters are known; five letters not included in the Tommasini edition are published in Capelli, Cavazzana, Pesenti, and Petrettini (cited in Secondary Works).

Fedele, Cassandra. *Clarissimae Feminae Cassandrae Fidelis Venetae Epistolae et Orationes.* Edited by Giacomo Filippo Tommasini. Padua: Franciscus Bolzetta, 1636.

Fedele, Cassandra. *Letters and Orations.* Edited and translated by Diana Robin. Chicago and London: University of Chicago Press, 2000.

Fedele, Cassandra. *Oratio pro Bertucio Lamberto.* Modena: 1487;Venice: 1488; Nuremberg: 1489.

King, Margaret L., and Albert Rabil, Jr., eds. *Her Immaculate Hand: Selected Works by and About the Women Humanists of Quattrocento Italy.* Binghamton, NY: Medieval and Renaissance Texts and Studies, 1983. (Second revised paperback edition in 1991.)

Secondary Works

Capelli, Adriano. "Cassandra Fedele in relazione con Lodovico Il Moro." *Archivio Storico Lombardo* 3, no. 4 (1895): 387–391.

Cavazzana, Cesira. "Cassandra Fedele erudita veneziana del Rinascimento." *Ateneo Veneto* 29, no. 2 (1906): 73–79, 249–275, 361–397.

Pesenti, G. "Lettere inedite del Poliziano." *Athenaeum* 3 (1915): 299–301.

Petrettini, Maria. *Vita di Cassandra Fedele.* Venice: 1814. (Reprinted in 1842.)

Robin, Diana. "Cassandra Fedele (1465–1499)." In *Italian Women Writers: A Bio-Bibliographical Sourcebook.* Edited by Rinaldina Russell, 119–127. Westport, CT: Greenwood Press, 1994.

Robin, Diana. "Cassandra Fedele's Epistolae (1488–1521): Biography as Effacement." In *The Rhetorics of Life-Writing in Early Modern Europe: Forms of Biography from Cassandra Fedele to Louise XIV.* Edited by Thomas Mayer and Daniel Woolf, 187–203. Ann Arbor: University of Michigan Press, 1995.

Feminism in the Renaissance
Overview

Modern feminism did not spring forth fully formed in the twentieth century when women in the West at last succeeded in their long struggle to gain full legal rights as citizens. Predicated on the absolute equality of women and men, contemporary feminism has deep roots in late medieval and early modern social and political thought.

Renaissance feminism has been defined variously as the product of the late medieval *querelles des femmes* (the debate on women), as the emergence of a new voice of protest in Europe, and as the rise of a new female consciousness, articulated for the first time in the writings of early modern women. Renaissance feminist works praised women's contributions to civilization throughout history in the spheres of government, science, literature, theater, art, music, and war, while they protested the barring of women from access to higher education, the universities, lawmaking, state politics, property ownership, and the workplace. Among the early modern feminists were both men and women. They wrote in a wide range of genres, including treatises, dialogues, letters, dramas, poetry, biographies, histories, and romances. Four subentries follow in this general survey: the Renaissance Inauguration of the Debate on Women, Feminism in Italy, Feminism in France, Feminism in England.

The Renaissance Inauguration of the Debate on Women

Christine de Pizan's *Le Livre de la cité des dames* (The Book of the City of Ladies, ca. 1404–1405) marks the emergence of the feminist voice in Europe. A world history of distinguished women, Pizan's *City of Ladies* was the first important French text in the *querelles des femmes.* Representing a revision of Giovanni Boccaccio's history of women, the *De claris mulieribus* (Famous Women, 1374), Pizan's *City* demonstrates women's equality with men through examples from classical antiquity as well as the Bible and argues that the cause of women's low status is their lack of access to education rather than any inborn deficiency. While Boccaccio's *Famous Women* with its one hundred and six female biographies represents accomplished women as exceptions to the rule of women's assumed inferiority, Pizan's work argues the universality of female virtue (King 1991, 223–224). Women who are portrayed as exotic or even monstrous beings, such as Zenobia of Palmyra and Semiramis of Assyria in Boccaccio's *Famous Women,* are refigured as scholars and builders of town and state in Pizan's *City of Ladies.*

Feminism in Italy

By the end of the fifteenth century in Italy, the rediscovery of the literature of Greece and Rome, humanist educational theory, and the new universal histories of women by Boccaccio and Pizan awakened interest among intellectuals in the nature of woman, women's education, and gender inequity. A succession of defenses of women were commissioned by prominent noblewomen who welcomed rebuttals to such misogynistic works as Guillaume de Lorris's popular *Roman de la Rose* (1265) with its equally woman-baiting complementary text by Jean de Meun. At the request of Bianca Maria Sforza, duchess of Milan, Antonio Cornazzano composed his encomium of women, the *De mulieribus admirandis* (1467). Vespasiano da Bisticci wrote his defense of the female sex, the *Il libro delle lode e commendazione delle donne* (ca. 1480), for the Florentine noblewoman Francesca Acciaiuoli; Giovanni Sabadino degli Arienti dedicated his eulogy, *Gynevera de le clare donne* (1483), to Gynevera Sforza di Bentivogli; Bartolomeo Goggio, his *De laudibus mulierum* (1487) to Eleonora of Aragon, duchess of Ferrara; and Agostino Strozzi, his *Defensio mulierum* (ca. 1501) to Marguerita Cantelma, a friend of Isabella d'Este, then the most influential female patron in Italy.

During the same years that male writers were circulating their defenses of women in the northern courts, a group of Italian women made public the volumes of humanist, Ciceronian-style Latin letters they had authored, again challenging the assumption of women's intellectual inferiority. Among the first large-scale works by women to circulate in manuscript, the letterbooks of Isotta Nogarola (her *Opera omnia,* ca. 1434–1461), Cassandra Fedele (her *Epistolae et orationes,* ca. 1487–1497), and Laura Cereta (her *Epistolae,* ca. 1485–1488) heralded the emergence of female self-fashioning in European literary culture and with it a new feminist consciousness. These fifteenth-century letterbooks (*epistolae familiares*) publicized their female authors' education in the classics and their literary style, while it depicted their ideas, experiences, relationships, and intellectual and emotional responses to the people and events that marked their lives. Fedele's elegant Latin letters made it clear that women should have equal access to higher education; moreover, she argued that issue in an oration she delivered before the Venetian senate. Nogarola publicly questioned the conventional wisdom of Eve's responsibility for the Fall in a debate with the governor of Verona. Of the three women humanists, only Cereta can be characterized as a modern feminist since many of her eighty-three letters directly confront such women's issues as schooling, marriage, child care, widowhood, the problem of gossip, and the fashion industry and its effect on women.

Despite the explosion of women's publishing with the rise of the commercial press in sixteenth-century Italy, it was not until the seventeenth century that women writers launched a frontal attack on the institutions that oppressed women. Works by a group of Venetian feminists—Moderata Fonte's dialogue for seven women *Il merito delle donne* (The Worth of Women, 1600), Lucrezia Marinella's treatise *La nobiltà et l'eccellenza delle donne e mancamenti de gli huomini* (The Nobility and Excellence of Women and the Defects and Vices of Men, 1601), and Arcangela Tarabotti's polemic *La tirannia paterna* (Paternal Tyranny; also published as *La semplicità ingannata,* Innocence Deceived, 1654)—actively urged women to challenge the patriarchal institutions of their city, which these writers saw as based not on innate gender differences but on a simple seizure of power by men. As one of the speakers in Fonte's dialogue argues, "if women are men's inferiors in status but not in worth, [male governance] is an abuse . . . that men have . . . translated into law and custom and it has become so entrenched that they claim . . . that the status they have gained through their bullying is theirs by right" (Cox 1997, 7). The principal speaker Corinna vows not to marry. Refusing to subordinate herself to any man, she also warns her friends against marriage.

Similarly discoursing on Greek philosophy and Roman natural history in her treatise, *La nobiltà et l'eccellenza delle donne,* Lucrezia Marinella attacks the misogynistic arguments of her countrymen. She presents a point-by-point refutation of Giuseppe Passi's vicious *I donneshi difetti* (The Defects of Women, 1599) and exposes the underlying misogyny of her countrymen Giovanni Boccaccio, Ercole and Torquato Tasso, and Sperone Speroni. Forced by her father to take holy orders, the nun Arcangela Tarabotti published a polemic against the dowry system in her *Paternal Tyranny,* which has been described both as a feminist critique of the major texts of contemporary misogyny and "the first manifesto about women's inalienable rights to liberty, equality, and universal education" (Panizza 1999, 1).

Feminism in France

In France from 1540 to 1640, outspoken advocates of female autonomy brought feminism and the *querelles des femmes* to the salons of Paris and Poitiers. Such feminist writers as Hélisenne de Crenne, Madeleine Neveu des Roches and her daughter Catherine Fradonnet des Roches, and Marie le Jars de Gournay (1565–1645) insisted on the importance of independence for women and represented marriage as an institution deeply perilous to that autonomy. Among Hélisenne's major works, her *Les epistres et inuectiues de ma dame* (Familiar and Invective Letters, 1539) portrays the author engaged in a

powerful defense of the female intellect with her fictional, misogynist husband, while her best-selling novel, *Angoysses douloureuses qui procedent d'amours* (The Torments of Love, 1538), tells the story of a woman trapped in a disastrous marriage.

During the chaos and violence of the civil wars of religion in France (1562–1563; 1579–1584), Madeleine and Catherine des Roches established and sustained a salon that became the center of literary activity in Poitiers. The three volumes the Des Roches wrote and published together during these years—*Les Œuvres de Mes-dames des Roches de Poictiers, Mere et Fille* (The Works of the Dames des Roches, Mother and Daughter, 1579), *Les Secondes œuvres . . .* (1583), and *Les Missives de Mes-dames des Roches de Poictiers, Mere et Fille* (The Letters . . . , 1586)—address such issues as education for women, the problem of marriage for women, violence against women, the status of women intellectuals, and female friendship and its connection to female learning.

In 1641, Marie le Jars de Gournay, the prolific polemicist whom Michel de Montaigne would name his "fille d'alliance" (chosen daughter) published the last revisions of her two most influential feminist treatises, *Le Grief des dames* (Women's Grievance) and *L'Egalité des hommes et des femmes* (The Equality of Men and Women, first published in 1622). Like her Italian contemporary, Arcangela Tarabotti, Gournay saw the abuses of patriarchal authority and power in the family and the state as analogues for one another and as mutually reinforcing. Gournay's autobiography, *Apology for the Woman Writing* (revised 1641), exemplifies the trend among early modern women writers of fashioning a print portrait of themselves for public consumption.

Feminism in England

In sixteenth-century England, defenses of women were primarily the preserve of male writers. Among the most influential of these early defenses were Sir Thomas Elyot's *Defence of*

Good Women (1540) and Heinrich Cornelius Agrippa's *Declamation on the Nobility and Preeminence of the Female Sex* (1529; translated from the Latin into English by David Clapam, 1542). Both Elyot and Agrippa opposed Juan Luis Vives' misogynistic *On the Education of the Christian Woman* (1523; translated from the Latin by Richard Hyrde, 1540), which proposed a separate educational program for women suited to their purported inferiority and their one goal in life—chastity (Beauchamp 2002, xlix). Rejecting Vives's and Aristotle's opinions on women, Elyot defended women as men's physical and intellectual equals. Citing Christine de Pizan's Zenobia of Palmyra as his exemplar of the ideal female ruler, Elyot supported a wife's right to disobey her husband to pursue a higher imperative, that of morality (Jordan 1990, 121).

One of the most radical defenses published in the sixteenth century, Agrippa's *Declamation* argued that women and men differed only in "the location of the parts of the body for which procreation required diversity" (Rabil 1996, 43). The *Declamation* espoused complete economic and political freedom for women and characterized both marriage and the convent as forms of state-sanctioned internment, for "when [a woman] has reached the age of puberty, she is delivered over to the jealous power of a husband, or she is enclosed forever in a workhouse for religious" (Rabil 1996, 95; Jordan 1990, 122–125).

The most famous of all English arguments in favor of women's capacity to rule, Edmund Spenser's *Faerie Queen* (1590), was also a defense of Queen Elizabeth's monarchy (reigned 1558–1608). While clearly indebted to Lodovico Ariosto's *Orlando furioso* (1516–1532) and Ariosto's portrayal of his heroine Bradamante, Spenser's *Faerie Queen* departs from its Italian model in ways resonant of the English approach to the *querelle*. As Pamela Benson notes, the essential premise of Ariosto's epic poem is the physical, moral, and intellectual equality of women and men. Spenser's queen, however, is distinguished by her chastity, her femininity,

and her difference from males (Benson 1992, 148–149).

Writers connecting the discourse on women's rights to economic issues enter the debate for the first time in force in the seventeenth century. Ester Sowernam's pamphlet, *Ester Hath Hang'd Haman; or An answer to a lewd pamphlet entituled The Arraignment of Women* (1617), blames men and the patriarchal system for keeping their wives honorable but poor while paying their prostitutes generously yet depriving them of status (Jordan 1990, 300–301). Rachel Speght's *Mousel for Melastomus* (1617) portrays marriage as slavery (Jordan 1990, 298), while Constantia Munda's *Worming of a Mad Dogge* (1617) links the increase in men's abuse of women to the number of misogynistic treatises produced by the presses. An earlier defense of women, *Her Protection for Women* (1589), published under the byline *Jane Anger*, is an advice manual for women in their relationships with men, not a work of protest on behalf of women as a class. The authorship of all four works has been contested, with some scholars attributing them to male writers (Wynne-Davies 1999, 360; Benson 1992, 223–224; Woodbridge 1984, 63–66).

Beyond the defenses of women, a palpably new female consciousness and a novel crafting of the feminine self emerge in seventeenth-century England and can be seen even at the close of the prior century. Modern scholars have credited a number of writings women published (or circulated in manuscript) between the time of Elizabeth I's regency and that of Charles II with having "inverted gender identities and expectations to produce a radically new female-centered commentary [on] . . . love in the early modern period" (Wynne-Davies 1999, 363). Exemplary of such new writings are, among other titles, Isabella Whitney's *A Sweet Nosegay* (1573), Aemila Lanyer's feminist poem, *Salve Deus Rex Judaeorum* (1611), Mary Wroth's prose romance, *The Countess of Montgomery's Urania* (1621), and sonnet sequence, *Pamphilia to Am-*

philanthus (ca. 1620), and Katherine Philips's erotically charged poems to "Rosania" and "Lucasia" (ca. 1650–1660).

Diana Robin

See also Education, Humanism, and Women; entries for the women writers mentioned; Querelles des Femmes.

Bibliography

Primary Works

Agrippa, Henricus Cornelius. *Declamation on the Nobility and Preeminence of the Female Sex.* Translated and edited by Albert Rabil, Jr. Chicago: University of Chicago Press: 1996.

Boccaccio, Giovanni. *Famous Women.* Edited and translated by Virginia Brown. I Tatti Renaissance Library. Cambridge, MA, and London, UK: Harvard University Press, 2001.

Cereta, Laura. *Collected Letters of a Renaissance Feminist.* Edited and translated by Diana Robin. Chicago: University of Chicago Press, 1997.

Des Roches, Madeleine and Catherine. *From Mother and Daughter.* Edited by Anne R. Larsen. Chicago: University of Chicago Press, 2006.

Fedele, Cassandra. *Letters and Orations.* Edited and translated by Diana Robin. Chicago: University of Chicago Press, 2000.

Fonte, Moderata (Modesta Pozzo). *The Worth of Women. Wherein Clearly Revealed Their Nobility and Superiority to Men.* Edited and translated by Virginia Cox. Chicago: University of Chicago Press, 1997.

Gournay, Marie Le Jars de'. In *Apology for the Woman Writing and Other Works.* Edited by Richard Hillman and Colette Quesnel. Chicago: University of Chicago Press, 2002.

Marinella, Lucrezia. *The Nobility and Excellence of Women and the Defects and Vices of Men.* Edited and translated by Anne Dunhill, with an introduction by Letizia Panizza. Chicago: University of Chicago Press, 1999.

Nogarola, Isotta. *Complete Writings: Letterbook, Dialogue on Adam and Eve, Orations.* Edited and translated by Margaret L. King and Diana Robin. Chicago: University of Chicago Press, 2004.

Tarabotti, Arcangela. *Paternal Tyranny.* Edited and translated by Letizia Panizza. Chicago: University of Chicago Press, 2004.

Vives, Juan Luis. *The Instruction of a Christen Woman.* Edited by Virginia Walcott Beauchamp, Elizabeth H. Hageman, and Margaret Mikesell. Urbana and Chicago: University of Illinois Press, 2002.

Secondary Works

Benson, Pamela Joseph. *The Invention of Renaissance Woman: The Challenge of Female Independence in the Literature and Thought of Italy and England.* University Park: Pennsylvania State University Press, 1992.

Jordan, Constance. *Renaissance Feminism: Literary Texts and Political Models.* Ithaca, NY: Cornell University Press, 1990.

King, Margaret L. *Women of the Renaissance.* Chicago: University of Chicago Press, 1991.

Rabil, Albert. "Feminism." In *Encyclopedia of the Renaissance.* Edited by Paul F. Grendler, 336–338. New York: Charles Scribner's Sons, 1999.

Robin, Diana. "Humanism." In *The Feminist Encyclopedia of Italian Literature.* Edited by Rinaldina Russell, 153–157. Westport, CT: Greenwood Press, 1997.

Woodbridge, Linda. *Women and the English Renaissance. Literature and the Nature of Womankind, 1540–1620.* Urbana: University of Illinois Press, 1984.

Wynne-Davies, Marion, ed. *Women Poets of the Renaissance.* New York: Routledge, 1999.

Fetti, Lucrina (d. 1673)

Nun, unofficial painter of the convent of St. Ursula in Mantua

In 1614 Duke Ferdinando Gonzaga invited the Roman painter Domenico Fetti and his family, including his sister Giustina who likewise painted, to live and work in the northern Italian duchy of Mantua. Domenico accepted the appointment, and on 3 December Ferdinando ordered one hundred and fifty *scudi* paid to Giustina Fetti to provide her spiritual dowry for entrance into the prestigious convent of St. Ursula founded by the duke's sister, Margherita. Upon taking the veil in late 1614, Giustina, who took the name Lucrina, became not only a Clarissan nun but also the convent's unofficial painter for the next half century.

Not documented as a painter before her arrival in Mantua, Lucrina's early career was closely tied to that of her brother who remained at the Gonzaga court until 1622. Based on a visual comparison of their paintings and given that the most common way for students of either gender to receive artistic training at the time was through study with a male family member who was already a trained painter, Lucrina almost certainly learned to paint from Domenico. Famed as a painter of both religious subjects and portraiture, Lucrina's renown is attested by contemporary court observers who offer firsthand accounts of her reputation in Mantua. Other chroniclers, many writing in the eighteenth century, demonstrate that her fame extended beyond the local level and beyond her own era.

Sources identify eleven religious paintings of near certain attribution to her. Among her earliest pictures were three works placed in St. Ursula's public church: *St. Mary Magdalen* and *St. Barbara* (dated 1619) on either side of the high altar, and *St. Margaret* in honor of the convent's founder. In *St. Barbara* in particular the dramatic emphasis on curvaceous form and richly patterned robes is clearly indebted to Domenico's baroque style, and the picture exemplifies why observers have posited such a close artistic relationship between the two painters. *St. Barbara* is also a testament to Lucrina's evolving talent, and the detailed fabrics and bold forms it contains foreshadow a more mature style found in her portrait paintings. In 1629 Lucrina also painted a series of pictures on the life and passion of Christ that were located throughout the convent buildings. The internal St. Ursula church contained at least three of them: *Deposition, Adoration of the Shepherds,* and *Oration in the Garden.* Two more paintings from the series decorated the convent's main staircase: one of the angel *Gabriel* and the other an *Annunciation.*

There are seven known portraits by Lucrina, all of Gonzaga women who resided at St. Ursula during Lucrina's lifetime: two portraits of the founder Margherita, two of Eleanora II, one of Eleanora I, one of Catherine de Médicis, and one of Maria Gonzaga. Five of the paintings (one of Margherita de-

Annunciation. *Detail of Virgin Mary from the work by painter Lucrina Fetti. (Arte and Immagini/Corbis)*

picted as a courtly nun, the two presumed wedding portraits of the Eleanoras, and the portraits of Catherine and Maria) constitute a uniform set of formal state portraits. Each portrait shows the subject in three-quarter view wearing richly draped and jeweled gowns. The subjects are characterized by a restrained dignity befitting members of the Gonzaga court and patrons or residents of St. Ursula. Only the portrait of Eleanora I is signed and dated (1622), though the picture of Catherine was also likely painted in the early 1620s and the wedding portrait of Eleanora II was probably painted in 1651, the year of her marriage to Emperor Ferdinand III.

Lucrina's activities as a painter at St. Ursula were complemented by her role in supporting the convent chiefly through inheritance claims connected to Domenico. Financial strains at the convent began within a decade of Margherita Gonzaga's death in 1618. During the

1630s and 1640s, Lucrina exhibited considerable economic and political savvy by making several successful appeals on behalf of the St. Ursula nuns to the ducal court for the collective ownership of Fetti family properties.

Lucrina Fetti likely died in 1673, having resided for nearly six decades at the convent of St. Ursula in Mantua as nun, painter, and financial advocate.

Cynthia Gladen

See also Art and Women; Convents.
Bibliography
Primary Works

Archivio di Stato, Mantua. Archivio Gonzaga, busta 3315. Documenti e suppliche relativi al monastero di Sant'Orsola (1599–1786).

Archivio di Stato, Mantua. Archivio notarile, notaio Angelo Pescatori, busta 7110. "Inventario generale de' Mobili, Arredi, e Suppellettili sagre del monastero di Sant'Orsola" (1786).

Archivio di Stato, Mantua. Demaniali ed Uniti, busta 60, fascicolo 54, no. 21. "Nota de' Quadri trasportati dal Monastero di S. Orsola in questo R. D. Ginnasio di Mantova."

Archivio di Stato, Mantua. Magistrato Camerale Antico, P. V. Donazioni (1600–1619). Mandato ducale del 3 dicembre 1614.

Archivio di Stato, Mantua. Ospedale Civico, libro 84, f.22, Atto di cessione in affitto di uno stabile (1675).

Secondary Sources

Askew, P. "Lucrina Fetti." In *Women Artists: 1550–1950.* Edited by A. Sutherland Harris and L. Nochlin, 124–130. New York: Knopf, 1977.

Baglione, G. *Le vite de' pittori, scultori, architetti, ed intagliatori, dal ponitificato di Gregorio XIII del 1572, in fino a' tempi di Papa Urbano VIII nel 1642.* Rome: 1935. (Originally published in Rome, 1642.)

Baldinucci, F. *Notizie dei professori del disegno, da Cimabue in qua.* Vol. IX. Florence: 1846.

Bazzotti, U. "Margherita Gonzaga e il convento di Sant'Orsola." In *Domenico Fetti, 1588/89–1623.* Edited by E. A. Šafařík, 45–50. Milan: Electa, 1996.

Cadioli, G. *Descrizione delle pitture, sculture ed architetture che si osservano nella città di Mantova, e ne' suoi contorni.* Mantua: 1763; Bologna: 1974.

Chambers, D., and J. Martineau, eds. *Splendours of the Gonzaga* (exhibition catalogue). London: Victoria and Albert Museum, 1981.

Ferrari, D. "Domenico Fetti: note archivistiche." In *Domenico Fetti, 1588/89–1623.* Edited by E. A. Safarik, 63–67. Milan: Electa, 1996.

Gladen, C. A. "A Painter, a Duchess, and the *Monastero di Sant'Orsola:* Case Studies of Women's Monastic Lives in Mantua, 1599–1651." Ph.D. dissertation, University of Minnesota, 2003.

Gladen, C. A. "Suor Lucrina Fetti: pittrice in una corte monastica seicentesca." In *I monasteri femminili come centri di cultura fra Rinascimento e Barocco.* Edited by G. Pomata and G. Zarri. Rome: forthcoming.

Ghirardi, A. "Dipingere in lode del Cielo: Suor Orsola Maddalena Caccia e la vocazione artistica delle orsoline di Moncalvo." In *Vita artistica nel monastero femminile.* Edited by V. Fortunati Pietrantonio, 115–129. Bologna: Editrice Compositori 2002.

Gregori, M., ed. *Pittura a Mantova dal Romanico al Settecento* (exhibition catalogue). Milan: 1989.

Luzio, A. *La Galleria dei Gonzaga venduta all'Inghilterra nel 1627–28.* Rome: 1974.

Zerbi Fanna, M. "Lucrina Fetti pittrice." *Civiltà mantovana* 23–24 (1989): 35–53.

Flore, Jeanne (publication dates 1540–1574)

Pseudonym for a French group of authors who published popular collections of tales (comptes)

Jeanne Flore is known as the author of *Les Comptes Amoureux par Madame Jeanne Flore, touchant la punition que faict Venus de ceulx qui contemnent & mesprisent le vray Amour,* a volume showing the influence of both the *Decameron* and *The Book of the Courtier* and whose *editio princeps* was published in Lyon by Denys de Harsy between 1540 and 1542 or 1543. The author's clear intention was to publish ten tales narrated in ten days and to allow the nine well-educated and refined guests of a generous and congenial host to converse and share ideas in an elegant pastoral setting. The first point of departure from tradition is that the ten protagonists are young women and that they enjoy the freedom of speech and of action usually reserved to men. In this temporary Utopia, the tables have been turned, they make the rules, and men join them only when invited to do so.

The tales they have chosen to share with their companions are the source of lively conversations and debates that reveal bold opinions expressed without fear of reprisals, much laughter, but also very distinct personalities as well as several incidents of unexpected tension.

In spite of claims that the ladies have already gathered for nine days before the final tale is told, the volume offers but seven tales in a somewhat erratic chronology, and the ten names listed in Jeanne Flore's dedicatory epistle to Madame Minerve are not necessarily those of the narrators. One can only surmise that part of the manuscript was lost or that the careless compiler had neither the time nor the means to wait for the three missing tales and the debates they would have invited. Another volume published in Lyon by François Juste in 1540, *La Pugnition de l'Amour contempte, extraict de L'amour fatal de madame Jane Flore,* contains only four of the seven tales.

While Madame Jeanne Flore cannot be robbed of her authorship, it has been ascertained that she is but a pseudonym chosen by a group of talented anonymous authors—one or two of whom may be women—or by the compiler of the tales, all residing in Lyon at the time. Apart from Etienne Dolet and Clément Marot, their identity remains in doubt. Most of their sources were Italian, some already in print, others unknown in France, others yet part of the French medieval and early Renaissance lore, and one is culled from Ovid's *Metamorphoses.* Some tales are peopled by giants, dragons, monsters, fairies, and benevolent creatures; others hint at sorcery, and one tells of vulnerable human beings who are affected not by magic but by their emotions. Mythology is used profusely and sometimes erratically. Far from the Christian world, the most powerful gods are Venus and the god Amour, devoutly worshipped by those who want to know love and to be loved. Most of the heroes suffer from unrequited love and jealousy, old and repulsive husbands are soon dispatched to the relief of their beautiful adolescent brides, and all sincere worshippers of Venus at last enjoy mutual love and sexual gratification.

Madame Flore reappears on the last page of this volume and warns her readers that this amoral world, where the gods remove all obstacles and unloved spouses to help the would-be lovers find happiness, is but a dream. Her sole intention was to denounce the unfairness if not the cruelty of arranged marriages in which both spouses are unhappy because either their ages, their condition, or their own personal feelings make them incompatible. It is doubtful that a single reader believed any of the events narrated in the tales but certain that many enjoyed the audacity and the humor of the debates between the ladies.

A new printing of *La Pugnition*—spelled *punition*—was published in Paris in 1541, but the *Comptes Amoureux* so pleased the public that they were reprinted by various publishers in Paris in 1543 and in 1555 and in Lyon in 1574. No other works or poems were subsequently published under the name of Madame Jeanne Flore, and the Contes Amoureux inspired but a limited number of scholars until 1980, when Gabriel-André Pérouse and his team—CNRS, Université de Lyon—published a thorough and much needed critical edition of the work. A plethora of articles soon resulted from the newly found and still growing popularity of the *Contes Amoureux.* However, *Actualité de Jeanne Flore,* published in 2004 and edited by Desrosiers-Bonin and Viennot, with no less than seventeen articles, provides the broadest and most recent focus on the Contes. A new paperback edition, *Collection Textes et Contre-Textes des Presses de l'Université de Saint-Etienne,* was published in April 2005.

Régine Reynolds-Cornell

See also Literary Culture and Women.
Bibliography
Primary Works
Flore, Madame Jeanne. *Comptes amoureux par Madame Jeanne Flore, touchant la punition que faict Venus de ceulx qui condemnent & mesprisent le vray Amour.* Lyon: Denis de Harsy, 1542?; Paris: Arnoul L'Angelier, 1543; Paris: Poncet le

Preux, 1543; Lyon: Benoist Rigaud, 1574; Turin: Gay and Sons, 1870 (reprint of the 1574 edition); Geneva: Slatkine, 1971 (reprint of the 1870 edition); Saint-Etienne: Publications de l'Université de Saint-Etienne, Spring 2005.

Flore, Madame Jeanne. *Histoire de la belle Rose-monde et du preux chevalier Andro, par Jeanne Flore.* Edited by Albert de Rochas d'Aiglun. Paris: Marchand, 1888.

Flore, Madame Jeanne. *La Pugnition de l'Amour contempné, extraict de l'Amour fatal de Madame Jeanne Flore.* Lyon: François Juste, 1540; Paris: Denys Janot, 1541.

Secondary Works

Bauschatz, Cathleen. "Cebille/Sebille: Jeanne Flore Reader of Christine de Pisan?" *Women in French Studies* (2000): 86–96.

Campanini Catani, Magda. *L'immagine riflessa. La riscrittura delle fonti nei Contes amoureux di Jeanne Flore.* Venice: Supernova, 2000.

Capello, Sergio. "Le Corps dans les Comptes amoureux: Pyralius le jaloux." Udine, *Forum* (2001): 23–42.

Desrosiers-Bonin, Diane, and Eliane Viennot. *Actualité de Jeanne Flore. Dix-sept études réunies par Diane Desrosiers-Bonin et Eliane Vienno avec la collaboration de Régine Reynolds-Cornell.* Paris: Champion, 2004.

Gray, Floyd. "Jeanne Flore and Erotic Desire: Feminism or Male Fantasy?" In *Gender, Rhetoric, and Print Culture in French Renaissance Writing.* Pages 30–46. Cambridge: Cambridge University Press, 2000.

Lavinia Fontana, Bolognese painter. Self-portrait. Uffizi, Florence, Italy. (Scala/Art Resource)

Fontana, Lavinia (1552–1614)

Bolognese painter, member of elite intellectual and ecclesiastical circles in Florence, Rome, and Bologna

Lavinia Fontana was one of the first women painters in European history to have enjoyed professional success. Among the many Bolognese artists of the sixteenth and early seventeenth centuries, she garnered the greater share of praise and some of the most lucrative commissions. Although generally regarded as a portraitist with particular gifts in rendering textiles and jewelry, recent scholarship on Lavinia's æuvre has demonstrated that the affective intensity, use of color, and compositional strategies of her religious works (ranging from large-scale altarpieces to smaller devotional paintings) placed her at the vanguard of Counter-Reformation artistic developments. The lengthy roster of Lavinia's patrons included members of the social, intellectual, and ecclesiastical elite not only in Bologna, but also in Florence and Rome. Much of her prolific career transpired in her native city, but she did move to Rome for the latter part of her life (1604–1614), where she enjoyed papal patronage as the established portraitist at the Vatican Palace, received the rare privilege of membership in the prestigious *Accademia di San Luca,* and may have been the first female artist officially to train apprentices.

Daughter and (eventually) apprentice of the painter Prospero Fontana (ca. 1508–1596), Lavinia's early training in drawing and painting does not seem to have been geared toward a professional career. As art historian Caroline Murphy has demonstrated, Prospero resented the humble status of the painter in Bologna—a city that, unlike Florence, still included painters in the same artisanal guild with saddlers and sword makers. An important component of Prospero's ambitious social strategy was raising his daughter as if she were a noblewoman. Until Lavinia reached her midteens, she learned drawing and painting as "accomplishments," with more emphasis being placed on music and composing elegant letters. Once Prospero's illness and dwindling resources presented obstacles to his work that he could no longer surmount alone, however, he began to train his only child seriously in the painter's craft and to promote her artistic career. In 1577, prior to securing Lavinia's first serious commissions, however, he also assured his daughter's acceptability to elite Bolognese patrons by arranging her marriage to Gian Paolo Zappi, an impecunious minor nobleman from Imola.

The Fontana-Zappi marriage negotiations evince the degree to which a potential husband and his negotiators might consider both a woman's earning power and her intellectual competence to be significant assets. The painter Orazio Sammachini, serving as intermediary between the Fontanas and Zappis, urged Gian Paolo's father to bring the union swiftly to conclusion, as above and beyond Lavinia's piety, virtue, and physical attractiveness, he believed that her art would likely prove lucrative. Sammachini also testified that he had himself witnessed Lavinia write "with her own hand . . . words . . . which are more those of a judicious man and not a woman." Appended to Sammachini's letter was Lavinia's own elegant greeting to her prospective new family. She also provided a self-portrait of herself at the keyboard. To judge by the prompt settlement of the marriage, the Zappis were of Sammachini's own mind.

As a wife, Lavinia's artistic productivity was accompanied by the responsibilities and physical challenges of almost perpetual pregnancy in her fertile years. She gave birth eleven times. Sadly, if all too commonly for the era, only four of her children lived to adolescence, and only three of these, her sons Flaminio, Orazio, and Prospero, survived her.

Despite the challenges that attended being a wife and mother as well as an artist, Lavinia's case demonstrates that gender was by no means an insurmountable obstacle. Like many women artists, intellectuals, and musicians of her era, Lavinia had a powerful weapon against misogyny in her arsenal: a father who both trained and promoted her. Scholars have observed, moreover, that her experience of motherhood and loss may well have given her paintings on the "Holy Family" and "Virgin and Child" themes their particular resonance and poignancy. From another perspective, gender proved useful in garnering publicity insofar as the so-termed "age of the marvelous" viewed a woman's art as doubly miraculous: it was both a triumph of skill and the creation of an "exceptionally" talented woman.

Since women were unable to conclude legal agreements on their own behalf, Lavinia's father and husband negotiated her commissions. Yet she herself exhibited a keen business sense in maintaining these connections. Among her most important patrons and supporters were Cardinal Gabriele Paleotti; the professor and naturalist Ulisse Aldrovandi, whose "cabinet of miracles" Lavinia visited during her youth in her father's company; the historian Carlo Sigonio; the scientist and medical theorist Girolamo Mercuriale; Pope Gregory XIII (the Bolognese Ugo Buoncampagni); and Pope Paul V (Camillo Borghese). Lavinia also cultivated a powerful circle of Bolognese noblewomen. Attuning her skills to her patroness' specifications and desired modes of "self-fashioning," Lavinia became their preferred portraitist. Laudomia Gozzadini, one of Lavinia's noble patrons, describes in her will the Gozzadini family portrait that Lavinia had painted, characterizing it as "a great and beautiful picture [made] by the hand of Lavinia Fontana, the famous painter, honorable in everything."

Praise from male contemporaries highlights Lavinia's successful competition with men in Renaissance artistic culture. "While it is true that in previous centuries women have been seen to compete with men in letters," the painter Francesco Panigarola remarked, "in our century it is Lavinia who does that in the most noble art of painting." The popular Bolognese poet Giulio Cesare Croce, in his *Gloria delle Donne* (Glory of Women, 1590), observed that Lavinia was "unique in all the world, like a phoenix" and painted as well as Michaelangelo, Corregio, Titian, and Raphael. "A new Apelles has arrived," effused Fra Filippo Barbieri, "in the form of a genteel and in this art most skilled creature of a gracious young woman called Fontana [whose portrait subjects were] portrayed so naturally that they only lacked the spirit itself."

Like many artists of the sixteenth century, Lavinia styled herself as an intellectual. Her first important commissions were portraits of the leading male figures in the arts and sciences. Throughout her career, moreover, Lavinia often employed a Latin signatory inscription. Most important, her self-portraits emphasize her accomplishments beyond artistic skill. She depicts herself writing in her study surrounded by antiquities or else at the keyboard. The latter mode was one commonly employed by women artists in the early modern period, both because it evoked Saint Cecilia (whose iconography included the "virginals," suggesting self-mastery with regard to the body and, by association, the virtue of chastity) and because musical skill connoted mental acuity.

Lavinia never received the highest praise for *invenzione* (creativity, making art "breathe with life") that Renaissance art theorists such as Georgio Vasari attributed to the best male painters. With the notable exception of Lavinia's contemporary, Sofonisba Anguissola, theorists summarized a woman's artistic capabilities in the term *diligenza*—that is, attention to detail and accurate if uninventive pictorial rendering. This rule does seem to have applied to Lavinia, but nonetheless her creative output would have done credit to any of her male contemporaries.

In 1611, three years before Lavinia died, the architect and sculptor Felice Antonio Casoni produced an honorary portrait medal. On the face is a portrait bust of Lavinia, encircled by the inscription "Lavinia Fontana Zappi, Painter"; on the obverse is an allegory of *Pittura* (Painting), shown as a woman with hair unbound, hard at work at her easel, and surrounded by the painter's tools. This medal helped to ensure that Lavinia would be remembered as a painter, certainly, but further ennobled her contributions to art history by equating her with the very image of art itself.

Major Works

Lavinia's more ambitious religious compositions include *Christ and the Canaanite Woman* (1566–1577; Venice: private collection), her first "show piece," usually considered to be the work of Lavinia with Prospero's assistance; *Holy Family with Saints* (1578; on loan to Wellesley College, Massachusetts); the altarpiece *Virgin and Child with Saints Catherine, Cosmas, Damian and Donor, Scipione Calcina* (1589; Bologna: San Giacomo Maggiore); *Birth of the Virgin* (ca. 1590; Bologna: Santa Trinità); and *Consecration to the Virgin* (1599; Marseilles: Musée des Beaux-Arts).

On a classical theme, her *Venus and Cupid* (1585; Venice: private collection), *Isabella Ruini as Venus* (1592; Rouen: Musée des Beaux-Arts), and last-known painting, *Minerva Dressing* (1613; location unknown) are outstanding examples. The *Visit of the Queen of Sheba to Solomon* (ca. 1600; Dublin: National Gallery of Ireland) offers a paradigmatic instance of Fontana's treatment of courtly narrative. For biblical narrative, her *Judith with the Head of Holofernes* (1600; Bologna: Museo Davia Bargellini) has received much comment.

Fontana's work in portraiture includes the *Self-Portrait at the Keyboard with a Maidservant* (1577; Rome: Accademia di San Luca) and *Self-Portrait in the Studiolo* (1579; Florence: Uffizi), discussed above. Other portraits that have received substantive analysis are *Carlo Sigonio* (1579; Modena: Museo Civico), *Boy*

Studying with his Father (early 1580s; Cremona: Pinacoteca Civica), *Girolamo Mercuriale* (late 1580s; Baltimore: Walters Museum of Art), *The Gozzadini Family* (1584; Bologna: Pinacoteca Nazionale), and *Costanza Isolani with Courtyard in the Background* (ca. 1586; Sotheby's: New York).

Sarah Gwyneth Ross

See also Anguissola, Sofonisba; Art and Women; Gentileschi, Artemisia.

Bibliography

Primary Work

Croce, Giulio Cesare. *La Gloria delle Donne di Giulio Cesare Croce.* Bologna: 1590.

Secondary Works

Cheney, Liana. "Lavinia Fontana, Boston *Holy Family.*" *Woman's Art Journal* 5, no. 1 (1984): 12–15.

Garrard, Mary D. "Here's Looking at Me: Sofonisba Anguissola and the Problem of the Woman Artist." *Renaissance Quarterly* 47, no. 3 (1994): 556–622.

Jacobs, Fredrika. *Defining the Renaissance Virtuosa: Women Artists and the Language of Art History and Criticism.* Cambridge: Cambridge University Press, 1997.

Jacobs, Fredrika. "Woman's Capacity to Create: The Unusual Case of Sofonisba Anguissola." *Renaissance Quarterly* 47, no. 1 (1994): 74–101.

Murphy, Caroline P. *Lavinia Fontana: A Painter and Her Patrons in Sixteenth-Century Bologna.* New Haven, CT: Yale University Press, 2003.

Schaefer, Jean Owens. "A Note on the Iconography of a Medal of Lavinia Fontana." *Journal of the Warburg and Courtauld Institutes* 47 (1984): 232–234.

Wiesner, Merry E. "Women and the Creation of Culture." In her *Women and Gender in Early Modern Europe.* 2nd ed. Pages 177–185. Cambridge: Cambridge University Press, 2000.

Fonte, Moderata (Modesta da Pozzo, 1555–1592)

Venetian feminist and author of a chivalric poem, a dialogue for women speakers only, a play, and religious poetry

Born to a wealthy family of urban Venice, Moderata Fonte received acclaim throughout the late Renaissance era for her erudite vernacular compositions. Although she wrote in Italian, her works nonetheless attest to a thorough knowledge of classical literature. Fonte is best known today for her dialogue in praise of the female sex, *Il Merito delle donne* (The Worth of Women, published posthumously in 1600), but in her own era she was celebrated more as a poet than as a contributor to the debate on women. A master of the difficult *ottava rima* meter, Fonte most often directed her talent toward arcadian and religious poetry. And, much as her fellow Venetian author and feminist Lucrezia Marinella (1571–1653), had balanced household responsibilities as a wife and mother with a successful career as an author, Fonte also succeeded as a "working mother." In 1583, two years after her debut in print, Fonte married the tax lawyer, Filippo di Zorzi, with whom she had four children. She died in 1592, probably from complications in the birth of her fourth child.

Fonte and her brother Leonardo, orphaned in their early childhood, were adopted by their maternal grandmother and her husband, Prospero Saraceni. A connoisseur of literature, Saraceni was well connected to members of the literary elite, one of whom was a prominent Venetian intellectual and author, Niccolò Doglioni. When Fonte was sixteen years old, her adoptive sister, Saracena, married Doglioni, and Fonte accompanied the young bride into Doglioni's household. Fonte's second adoptive family proved to be a crucial source of support for her career. Doglioni took an active role as Fonte's patron and promoter, and the short biography that he wrote as a preface to his publication of her *Worth of Women* underscores the range and depth of his protégée's learning.

Doglioni attests that Fonte received some of her early education at the convent of Santa Marta in Venice. Recognizing her talent, however, Fonte's grandfather augmented this convent education by providing her with Latin primers and a constant supply of reading material. Doglioni also notes that Fonte actively supplemented her studies by making her brother recite for her what he had learned at the public grammar school each day. He also emphasizes Fonte's competence in Latin as well as her mastery of vernacular literature, mathematics, music, art, and the quintessentially "feminine" accomplishment of fine needlework.

Fonte's first published work was her *Tredici Canti del Floridoro* (The Thirteen Songs of Floridoro, Venice, 1581). Following in the tradition of the chivalric romance, this arcadian poem is also rich in classical allusions. The *Floridoro* does not announce itself as a defense of women. Yet Fonte uses one of her central characters, the warrior heroine Risamante, to make the case that male and female capabilities are equal and that differences between men's and women's social roles are therefore not "natural," but rather the result of education.

The link between women's education and their social roles moves from the periphery to the center of her dialogue for seven female speakers: *The Worth of Women*. This work owes a debt to the dialogues of Baldassare Castiglione (*The Courtier*) and Pietro Bembo (*The Asolani*). Fonte revolutionized the dialogic genre, however, by making all of her speakers women (Cox 1997, 18). Her characters, who represent each stage in a woman's life cycle from adolescence to widowhood, engage in a sustained critique of the patriarchal order and offer an innovative vision of a secular female community.

Fonte's other publications include an occasional poem written for the Venetian doge, *Le feste: rappresentatione avanti il Serenissimo Prencipe di Venetia* (The Celebrations: Performed in the Presence of the Most Serene Doge of Venice, Venice, 1582) and two lengthy religious poems: *La Passione di Christo* (The Passion of Christ, Venice, 1582) and *La Resurrentione di Giesu Christo* (The Resurrection of Jesus Christ, Venice, 1592).

Scholars have long recognized Fonte's written contributions to Renaissance feminism. No less important than her literary work, however, Fonte herself provoked widespread admiration among contemporary biographers

and defenders of women, who touted her as an example of excellence in both "masculine" (literary) and "feminine" (domestic) terms. One encomiast characterized her as "glorious and famous in our era for her writings, which equaled anything written by women of the classical past," while at the same time praising her conduct as a wife and mother (Ribera, sig. Pp3r–v). Fonte demonstrated that the accomplished woman was not ipso facto a transgressor "beyond her sex" but might be culturally normal despite her exceptional intellect. Fonte and her admirers helped to create a more tenable representative category for learned women in literary society—a category that women writers of subsequent eras would increasingly occupy.

Sarah Ross

See also Education, Humanism, and Women; Marinella, Lucrezia.

Bibliography
Primary Works
Fonte, Moderata. *Il Merito delle donne, ove chiaramente si scuopre quanto siano elle degne e più perfette de gli uomini.* Edited by Adriana Chemello. Mirano: Eidos, 1988.
Fonte, Moderata. *Tredici Canti del Floridoro.* Venice: 1581.
Secondary Works
Cox, Virginia. *Introduction to The Worth of Women.* Chicago: University of Chicago Press, 1997.
Cox, Virginia. "The Single Self: Feminist Thought and the Marriage Market in Early Modern Venice." *Renaissance Quarterly* 48 (1995): 513–581.
Labalme, Patricia. "Venetian Women on Women: Three Early-Modern Feminists." *Archivio Veneto* 5th Series, 117 (1981): 81–109.
Ribera, Pietro Paolo di. *Le glorie immortali de'trionfi, et heroiche imprese d'ottocento quarantacinque Donne Illustri antiche, e moderne.* Venice: Evangelista Deuchino, 1609.

Forteguerri, Laudomia (1515–1556?)
Sienese poet and civic leader
Born to parents whose families belonged to the Sienese elite, Laudomia Forteguerri came

of age at a time when women were dominant actors in the cultural affairs of Siena. Forteguerri emerged as a prominent public figure, first in her twenties as a published poet and twenty years later as the leader of a women's regiment during the siege of Siena. She was married twice: in 1535 to Giulio di Alessandro Colombini who died in 1542; and subsequently to Petruccio Petrucci.

A widow at twenty-seven and the mother of three small children, Forteguerri was active in both the Sienese literary salons and the city's religious reform movement. Marc'Antonio Piccolomini's dialogue (ca. 1537), which represents Forteguerri vigorously arguing against the Catholic doctrine of Purgatory with two other female intellectuals, Girolama Carli di Piccolomini and Frasia Marzi, cannot be read as a documentary. Nonetheless it suggests that on the eve of the Inquisition in Rome, elite women in Siena such as Forteguerri, Carli di Piccolomini, and Marzi were actively involved in freewheeling, even heretical readings and discusssion.

Forteguerri's celebrity soon spread beyond Siena when the noted writer and cleric Alessandro Piccolomini delivered a lecture on one of her poems at a meeting of the prestigious Accademia degli Infiammati in Padua. Published with Piccolomini's lecture in Bologna in 1541, Forteguerri's poem was picked up by the Giolito press in Venice and reprinted in the first volume of what would eventually comprise a best-selling series of poetry anthologies. Forteguerri's poem appeared in the Giolito anthology alongside the works of four female lyricists of the 1540s who were already widely acclaimed: Vittoria Colonna, Veronica Gàmbara, Laura Terracina, and the courtesan Francesca Baffa.

Forteguerri dedicated her anthologized poem (entitled *Hora te 'n va superbo*) to Margaret of Austria, Emperor Charles V's daughter, who was visiting Siena en route to Rome where her marriage to the pope's grandson, Ottavio Farnese, was to be celebrated. The poem was part of a suite of five sonnets Forteguerri sent Margaret after her departure. The mis-en-scène in Forteguerri's poetic suite is suggestive of the long Italian tradition of love lyric, from the Roman elegiac poets to Petrarch. Yet Forteguerri's own poetic language is tempered. Her sonnets lack the Petrarchan images of erotic inflammation, icy chills, bodily pain, and psychological suffering that characterize the poems that such sixteenth-century women writers as Isabella di Morra, Gaspara Stampa, and Chiara Matraini addressed to their male lovers—images also found, though more rarely, in the published amatory poems that some women sent to one another in sixteenth-century Italy (Robin 2007; cf. Eisenbichler 2001). Forteguerri's five poems to Margaret portray the drama of an emotional obsession, which begins with the poet's request for a love token and ends with Margaret's silence, the poet's venting of her anger on the goddess Fortuna, and a prayer for divine intervention to bring about Margaret's return.

In 1552, fourteen years after Forteguerri's final meeting with Margaret, her father, Charles V, joined forces with Duke Cosimo I de' Medici of Florence, and for three years they lay siege to Siena, bombarding the city with heavy artillery and laying waste to the surrounding countryside. Between 1552 and 1553, Forteguerri commanded a squadron of a thousand women who were constructing a fortress for the city's defense. Blaise de Monluc, who led the French troops allied with the Sienese Republic against Charles V and Cosimo I, vividly described Forteguerri's all-female regiment as dressed in short velvet outfits that revealed the women's buskins as they labored with picks and shovels and carried baskets of earth on their heads (Monluc 1617, 105–106; Sozzini 1842, 279).

On 17 April 1555, the starving citizens of Siena, many of whom were ill and near death, surrendered their city to Florence and Charles's imperial army. Though Forteguerri's death date is not known, Cerreta believes she either died during the siege of Siena or soon after the surrender of the city (1960, 31), but Zarrilli (1997, 154) argues that Giuseppe Betussi's eyewitness account of her bravery in his *Le Imagini del tempio* (1557, 32r–32v) indicates that she was still alive when he was in Siena in 1556 after the war was over.

Diana Robin

See also the subheading Sonnet Writing (under Literary Culture and Women); Margaret of Parma; Morra, Isabella di; Stampa, Gaspara.

Bibliography

Primary Works

Betussi, Giuseppe. *Le imagini del tempio della signora Giovanna Aragona. Dialogo diM. Giuseppe Betussi.* Venice: Giovanni de' Rossi, 1557.

Monluc, Blaise de Lasseran-Massencome. *Commentaires de Messire Blaise de Monluc. Mareschal de France 1521–1576.* Paris: Martom Gobert, 1617.

Piccolominio, Alessandro. *Lettura del S. Alessandro Piccolomini Infiammato fatta nell'Accademia degli Infiammati.* Bologna: Bartolomeo Bonardo e Marc'Antonio da Carpi, 1541.

Sozzini, Alessandro. *Diario delle cose avvenute in Siena dai 20 Luglio 1550 ai 28 Giugno 1555, scritto da Alessandro Sozzini con altre narrazioni e documenti relativi alla caduta di quella reppublica.* Florence: Piero Viesseux Editore, 1842.

Secondary Works

Belladonna, Rita. "Gli Intronati, Le Donne, Aonio Palerio e Agostino Museo in un Dialogo Inedito di Marcantonio Piccolomini. Il sodo Intronato (1538)." *Bullettino senese di storia patria* 99 (1994): 48–90.

Cerreta, Florindo. *Alessandro Piccolomini. Letterato e Filosofo Senese del Cinquecento.* Siena: Accademia Senese degli Intronati, 1960.

Eisenbichler, Konrad. "Laudomia Forteguerri Loves Margaret of Austria." In *Same Sex Love and Desire Among Women in the Middle Ages.* Edited by Francesco Canadé Sautman and Pamela Sheingoran, 277–280. New York: Palgrave, 2001.

Robin, Diana. *Publishing Women. Salons, the Presses, and Religious Reform in Renaissance Italy.* Chicago: University of Chicago Press, 2007.

Zarrilli, Carla. "Forteguerri, Laudomia." Vol. 49: 153–155. Rome: Instituto dell'Enciclopedia Italiana, 1997.

France, Claude de. *See* Claude de France.

Franco, Veronica (1546–1591)

Venetian poet and courtesan

More famous as a courtesan than as a poet until the beginning of the last century, Veronica Franco is one of the most original female voices of her time. Born to Francesco Franco and Paola Fracassa in 1546 in Venice, she came from a good family in the citizen (*cittadino*) class. Both Veronica and her mother appear in the *Catalogue of All the Principal and Most Honorable Courtesans of Venice* (extant only in manuscript under the title, *Catalogo di tutte le principal et più honorate Cortigiane di Venetia*), both charging the same fee (two *scudi*); Paola is listed as the procuress for both herself and her daughter. If Franco's extremely low published fee is correct, it might be explained by her age: she was perhaps thirteen or fourteen years old when the catalogue was first issued (ca. 1558–1560). She married Paolo Panizza, a physician, but she was soon separated from him. When she drew up her first will at the age of eighteen, she was pregnant with a son, whose father was probably Giacomo de Baballi di Ragusa. Franco herself suggested the child's paternity but never actually affirmed it: "Whether he is the father or not, only the lord God knows," she wrote. In this same will, she instructed her mother to demand the restoration of her dowry from her husband Panizza and to dispose of it at her pleasure, seeing that it originally had come to him from her. She soon understood that if she wanted freedom to act and to consort with whomever as she wished, she would have to make use of the power that her beauty, her sensuality, and, above all, her intelligence gave her.

In her *Rime* (sonnets), Franco never attempted to hide her profession: She flaunted her expertise, unlike Tullia d'Aragona and other poet courtesans, who suppressed the reality of their lives in their published works. The terms "courtesan" and "prostitute" were synonyms in the sixteenth century, but the term *cortigiana* is already found in Venetian diarists and chroniclers from the late fifteenth century on. The term was soon used to designate the various classes within prostitution: courtesan whore, courtesan by lamplight or candlelight, honest courtesan (*cortigiana puttana, cortigiana da lume o da candela, cortegiana onesta*), so that those who were called "honest prostitutes" could be compared with prostitutes of the lowest caste. By the end of the eighteenth century, the two terms had become so distinct from one another that Tassini, Franco's first biographer, found it necessary to change the word *meretrice* (prostitute) to *cortigiana* (courtesan) on the title page of the second edition of his work. Certainly, the distinction was based on the professionalism and lifestyle of the courtesan as well as on her acquired mastery of erotic poetics.

Franco belonged to the highest caste among courtesans. Her fame reached its apex in the summer of 1574, when the Republic of Venice scheduled a night with a courtesan among its festivities for the twenty-three-year-old Henri III of Valois, soon to be crowned king of France. Franco's name was proposed by the patrician Andrea Tron, one of the forty gentlemen in the king's Venetian escort and a mainstay among Franco's clientele. How the king reciprocated is not known; but Franco sent him a portrait of herself with a letter and two encomiastic sonnets, in which she compared Henri to the god Jupiter since he had appeared to her in a benevolent guise: not arrayed in his regal splendor but in human clothing, "to avoid burning mortal eyes," she wrote, alluding to the tragic myth of Semele. Also among her clientele and patrons were Venetians of the highest level, some of whom the Republic would eventually indict on various criminal charges, such as Lodovico Ramberti, Guido Antonio Pizzamano, Giacomo Baballi, Andrea Tron, and Marco, Lorenzo, and Maffio Venier (who would later lampoon Franco).

Franco received a good education, which included the study of Italian literature, though not Latin. She probably knew the great classical authors through the numerous translations into Italian that had been published in Venice in the preceding decades, and these were the sources for her frequent references to classical mythology. She also had training in music and singing, which she made use of in entertaining her clients since musical and poetic skills were obligatory for courtesans of her class, as Aretino makes clear in his *Ragionamenti* (1534). Among Franco's circle we find the name of important artists, writers, and intellectuals with whom she transformed her own house into a salon and whose gatherings she attended. At the salon of Domenico Venier, a skillful poet himself, she met Bartolomeo Zacco, Estore and Francesco Martinengo, G. Gradenigo, G. Molin, Jacopo Zane, Celio Magno, and other members of the Venier family, Lorenzo, Marco, and Maffio. In their salons, Franco's extraordinary poetic gifts thrived, and in 1575/1576, she published a volume of her *terze rime* containing eighteen of her own *capitoli* and seven *capitoli* by her interlocutors. The *capitoli* in response to her *rime* are indicated as the works of anonymous authors (labeled *incerto autore*); in some copies, however, the author of the first *capitolo* is noted as Marco Venier. It has been hypothesized, both on stylistic grounds and because all the poems would have been corrected by a member of the Venier circle (probably Domenico), that Franco herself authored all the *capitoli*.

The great novelty of Franco's writings lies in its content: critics agree that she is a skillful prosodist, but her amatory poetry best exemplifies the originality and brilliance of her voice; as Marco Venier wrote of her work, she is more a follower of Venus than Apollo. She appropriates in her poetry the Bembist Petrarchanism still dominant in the last quarter of the sixteenth century. In her choice of vocabulary and style, she is also influenced by Ariosto's *Rime* and *Satire,* which in part explains her use of the *terzina*.

In 1580, her book *Lettere familiari a diversi* was published, containing a collection of fifty-one letters, including a dedicatory letter to Cardinal Luigi d'Este. With this publication, Franco joins the long line of male authors of letterbooks (*libri di lettere*) in the sixteenth century, a popular genre since its inauguration by Aretino in 1538. The names of the addressees, except those of Henri III and Tintoretto, have been deleted; otherwise the collection follows the standard form given the genre by Francesco Sansovino. The paucity of women's letter collections previous to Franco's in the sixteenth century provides further testimony of her originality and literary genius. There are only five, among which are the *Litere della divina Colonna Marchesana di Pescara alla Duchessa de Amalfi,* whose epistles are devotional in character; the fictional *Lettere di molte valorose donne* (1552) and the *Lettere della molto illustre . . . Lucretia Gonzaga* are both works authored not by women but by Ortensio Lando. Two other editions of collected letters by women precede Franco's: the *Lettere amorose di Madonna Celia, gentildonna romana* (1562) and the *Lettere spirituali della devota religiosa Angelica Paola Antonia De Negri milanese* (1576).

When Montaigne passed through Venice, he noted in his *Journal de voyage en Italie en 1580 et 1581* that Franco had paid homage to him by sending him a copy of her *Lettere familiari et diversi.* Franco's letter collection demonstrates an assumption fundamental to women's epistolary writing in the sixteenth century: that there are three distinct genres of letters – amatory, familiar, and spiritual. Though Franco diligently follows the norms imposed on the genre, nonetheless, she was also capable of expressing the intensity of her feelings in her letters, including, for example, her great pleasure in the conversations she had with learned men. With Bartolomeo Zacco, a noble and cultivated Paduan, she had one of those literary exchanges typical of the time: he first initiated the correspondence by inviting her to write a funeral elegy in honor of his youngest daughter who had recently died.

Courtesans were the frequent targets of literary invective in the sixteenth century. Around 1580, Franco became an object of ridicule herself when Domenico Venier's nephew, whose father Lorenzo Venier had written a satire on the gang rape of another courtesan (*Il trentuno della Zaffetta*), composed a series of poetic attacks on her, one of which was his celebrated satire entitled *Veronica, ver unica puttana* (Veronica, a Truly Unique Whore). In this vicious satire, punning on Franco's name, he alludes to a letter from Machiavelli to Luigi Guicciardini (8 December 1508) about a certain Veronese *puttana,* while parodying a Petrarchan sonnet by Pietro Bembo dedicated to the Brescian noblewoman and poet Veronica Gàmbara—whom Bembo addresses as *Vergine veramente unica e sola* (Virgin, truly unique and extraordinary). While Bembo's sonnet eulogizes Veronica Gàmbara's intellectual beauty, Maffio Venier's satire (which Franco at first thought was composed by Marco Venier) performs a total physical degradation of Franco. Franco responded defiantly with her own declaration of war, saying that she was all the more disposed to enter into poetic combat with him since she was surer of her superiority on the literary battlefield than the amatory one.

Even more consuming of Franco's attention than Venier's poetic venom were the trials that the Holy Office of Venice initiated against her in 1580. On 3 October 1580, charges of heresy against Franco were filed by her sons' teacher, Ridolfo Vannitelli. The teacher's denunciation of Franco seems to have been spurred by Franco's own demand, forwarded to the Patriarch on 20 May 1580, for the excommunication of whoever had stolen certain precious objects from her house, among which were some gold earrings in a silver case. Vannitelli accused Franco of the following violations of ecclesiastical and civil law: practicing witchcraft and magic, playing forbidden games, ignoring the sacraments, consuming prohibited foods on fast days, making pacts with the devil to cause certain German merchants to fall in love with her, pretending to be a married woman in order to adorn herself with jewelry prohibited to prostitutes (and this latter charge asserted that there had never been a record of her marriage to Paolo Panizza). All these accusations could have ruined even a respectable woman if she lacked powerful protectors, as the denunciation itself stated. Beyond addressing these fundamental charges, Franco succeeded in demonstrating that the accusations were the result of a plot to destroy her. Her trial was staged in two sessions, 8 and 13 October 1580: she was interrogated but no witnesses were called, though her second will (1 November 1570) indicates that she had influential enough patrons, who had previously served her as witnesses. On the second day of her trial, she was acquitted of all charges, with no sentence or warning pronounced. During the deposition Franco testified to having given birth six times (there remained living only two sons, Achille and Enea).

Franco herself would later turn accuser, denouncing one Bartolo to the Venetian Holy Office; she accused him of casting spells to harm her servant's son, Andrea, whom Franco named in her will as her "soul-son" (*figlio di anima*). This late act of denunciation on the part of Franco bears no resemblance to a subsequent document, in which she makes an offer to the Venetian republic of a bequest for a home for impoverished women (*Casa del Soccorso*) in return for a guaranteed annuity for herself. Despite the fact that the late eighteenth-century and early nineteenth-century critics of Franco (Cicogna, Tassini, Salza) wanted to see a testimony of her repentance and a change in lifestyle in her last years, no literary or archival evidence has surfaced to support such a view.

That Tintoretto's painting of Franco and the portrait she speaks of in her *Lettere* are one and the same is indicated by a sixteenth-century hand on the reverse side of the portrait, identifying its subject as Veronica Franco. The con-

temporary art historian Paola Rossi has attributed this painting to Domenico Tintoretto, however, and not to Franco's friend Jacopo Tintoretto. Two other publications of the period document Franco's wide circle of literary friends and her exchanges of sonnets with them: Giovanni Fratta's *Panegirico,* an anthology of verses in honor of the doctorate of Giuseppe Spinelli (Padua, 1575), includes a sonnet of Franco's; and Musio Manfredi's *Lettere brevissime* (Venice, 1596) contains a letter he wrote to Franco praising one of her sonnets.

The report of Franco's death on 22 July 1591 notes only that she died at the age of forty-five after twenty days of a fever, whose cause we will never know.

Daria Perocco

See also Aragona, Tullia d'; Courtesans and Prostitution, Italy; the subheadings Sonnet Writing; Letter Writing (under Literary Culture and Women).

Bibliography

Primary Works

Franco, Veronica. *Lettere dall'unica edizione del MDLXXX.* Edited by B. Croce. Naples: Ricciardi, 1949.

Franco, Veronica. *Lettere familiari a diversi della s. Veronica Franca all'illustriss. et reverendiss. monsig. Luigi d'Este Cardinale.* Venice: 1580.

Franco, Veronica. *Poems and Selected Letters.* Edited by A. R. Jones and M. F. Rosenthal. Chicago: University of Chicago Press, 1998.

Franco, Veronica. *Rime.* Edited by S. Bianchi. Milan: Mursia, 1995.

Franco, Veronica. *Terze rime di Veronica Franca al serenissimo signor Duca di Mantova et di Monferrato.* Venice: 1575.

Secondary Works

Adler, Sara Maria. "Veronica Franco's Petrarchan Terze Rime: Subverting the Master's Plan." *Italica* 65 (1988): 213–233.

Barzaghi, Antonio. *Donne o Cortigiane? La prostituzione a Venezia. Documenti di costume dal XVI al XVII secolo.* Verona: Bertani, 1980.

Bassanese, Fiora A. "Private Lives and Public Lies: Texts by Courtesans of the Italian Renaissance." *Texas Studies in Language and Literature* 30, no. 3 (1988): 295–319.

Doglio, Maria Luisa. "Scrittura e 'offizio di parole' nelle *Lettere familiari* di Veronica Franco." In

Lettera e donna. Scrittura epistolare al femminile tra Quattro e Cinquecento. Pages 33–48. Rome: Bulzoni, 1993.

Favretti, Elena. "Rime e lettere di Veronica Franco." *Giornale storico della letteratura italiana* 163, no. 523 (1986): 355–382.

Jones, Ann Rosalind. *The Currency of Eros: Women's Love Lyric in Europe, 1540–1620.* Bloomington: Indiana University Press, 1990.

Lawner, Lynn. *Lives of the Courtesans: Portraits of the Renaissance.* New York: Rizzoli, 1987.

Milani, Marisa. "Da accusati a delatori: Veronica Franco e Francesco Barozzi." *Quaderni veneti* 26 (1996): 12–34.

Rosenthal, Margaret F. *The Honest Courtesan: Veronica Franco, Citizen and Writer in Sixteenth Century Venice.* Chicago: University of Chicago Press, 1992.

Scarabello, G. "Per una storia della prostituzione a Venezia tra il XIII e il XVIII sec." *Studi veneziani* 47 (2004): 15–101, especially 57–61.

Schiavon, Antonia. "Per la biografia di Veronica Franco. Nuovi docuemnti." *Atti dell'Istituto veneto di Scienze, lettere ed Arti* 137 (1978–1979): 243–256.

Zorzi, Alvise. *Cortigiana veneziana: Veronica Franco e i suoi poeti 1546–1591.* Milan: Camunia, 1986.

G

Gaillarde, Jeanne (dates unknown)

One among many talented female poets in the city of Lyons during the 1520s

Seven extant compositions have been attributed to Jeanne Gaillarde. She may have been known as a poet even in Paris because of the subtle response she made to the dithyrambic *rondeau* addressed to her by Clément Marot. As *valet de chambre* of King Francis I, this famous writer must have met her in Lyons between 1522 and 1526, when he accompanied the royal family on a mission. It is probable that Jeanne Gaillarde also became acquainted with Louise de Savoie and Marguerite de Navarre.

Since several persons bearing the same name are to be found in Lyonnaise genealogies, it is impossible to identify with certainty the author of these seven poems or learn more about her life. Nevertheless, we know from ex libris that she owned books, and her fame as a fine poet is confirmed by Renaissance biographers as well as by writers who dedicated works to her and entertained a correspondence with her. Verdun Saulnier has convincingly demonstrated that, in addition to Clément Marot, the brothers Jacques and Germain Colin wrote to and were answered by Jeanne Gaillarde, possibly in the mid-1520s. Although a portion of this poetic exchange has been published in fragmentary fashion already in the sixteenth century (in the works of the male correspondents) and was reproduced by Saulnier, it has not fostered many studies by Renaissance specialists. Yet Jeanne Gaillarde's poetry is worthy of notice for several reasons. First, as vehicles of the renewed ideal of courtly love and behavior so central to the ethos of the French court in this first quarter of the sixteenth century, her love poems propose a definition of perfect love as *bonne amytié* (good friendship) or *amytié non*

commune (noble friendship) full of *honesteté* (virtue) identical to that expressed by Marguerite de Navarre. Secondly, her two political *rondeaux* underscore the importance of Christian virtues and moral conduct at court, commenting on a treason perpetrated against the king (maybe that of Constable Charles de Bourbon in 1527). But there is more. Jeanne Gaillarde is also a daring poet, willing to measure her talents to that of her contemporary male writers. Her best-known *rondeau,* written in response to Marot's praise of her eloquence and *plume dorée* (golden pen/feather) surpassing even Christine de Pizan's talent, is of particular interest for its wit and subtle rhetoric. While adopting preterition to stress her modesty and the impossibility to respond, Jeanne does respond, thereby suggesting that her strategic *captatio benevolentiae* is in fact a gesture of *imitatio* in the same way that her admirer's own poetic style is based on an Erasmian pose of humility. Thus, her explicit refusal to be praised becomes a strategy to implicitly agree with her panegyrist and prove her poetic mastery.

Pernette du Guillet will remember this stylistic *tour de force* in one of her responses to Maurice Scève (*Epigramme VI*). Like her, many Lyonnaise women must have exchanged poems with male authors and gathered in the same poetic circles in the first half of the century (for instance, that of literary patron Jean Du Peyrat, lieutenant of the king in Lyons). Among these female writers we find Jacqueline de Stuard, who entertained a verse correspondence with Bonaventure des Perriers (ca. 1500–1544), and Philiberte de Feurs, who wrote a five-hundred-verse composition entitled *Souspirs de Viduité* (Sighs on Widowhood, ca. 1540), of which only sixty-two lines have been found so far. It is our wish that all of Jeanne's, Jacqueline's, and

Philiberte's poems may be discovered in the near future, in order to delineate a more precise landscape of women's literary presence in the city of Lyons before Louise Labé's publication of her complete works in 1555.

Catherine M. Müller

See also Guillet, Pernette du; Labé, Louise; the subheadings Salons, Salonnières, and Women Writers; Sonnet Writing (under Literary Culture and Women).

Bibliography

Primary Works

Bréghot Du Lut, Claude. *Mélanges biographiques et littéraires pour servir l'histoire de Lyon.* Geneva: Slatkine, 1971. (Originally printed in Lyons: J.-M. Barret, 1828.)

Des Périers, Bonaventure. *Recueil des oeuvres de feu Bonaventure des Periers.* Lyons: Jean de Tournes, 1544. (The extant poem by Jacqueline de Stuard is found on p. 184.)

Du Guillet, Pernette. *Rymes.* Edited by Victor E. Graham. Geneva: Droz; Paris: Minard, 1968.

Feurs, Philiberte de. *Soupirs de vidité.* Partially published in *Bibliothèque,* Antoine du Verdier. Paris: Barthelemy Honorat, 1585.

Gaillarde, Jeanne (?). *Faintises du monde.* Paris: Bibliothèque Nationale de France fr. 14979 (f. 32v and 33r indicate that this manuscript was owned by Jeanne Gaillarde).

Marot, Clément. *Œuvres poétiques complètes.* 2 vols. Edited by Gérard Defaux. Paris: Classiques Garnier, 1990. (The exchange between the poet and Jeanne Gaillarde is reproduced in vol. I, 143–144.)

Saulnier, Verdun. "Documents nouveaux sur Jeanne Gaillarde et ses amis: Clément Marot, Jacques Colin, Germain Colin." *Bulletin de la Société Historique de Lyon* 18 (1952): 79–100.

Secondary Work

Müller, Catherine M. "En donnant lieu à la main feminine: lecture de quelques dialogues poétiques des XVᵉ et XVIᵉ siècles." In *De vrai humain entendement: études sur la littérature française à la fin du Moyen Age, hommage à Jacqueline Cerquiglini-Toulet.* Recherches et Rencontres. Edited by Yasmina Foehr-Janssens and Jean-Yves Tilliette, 65–82. Geneva: Droz, 2004.

Gàmbara, Veronica (1485–1550)

Ruler of Correggio for thirty-two years, poet, and patron of literature and the arts

By the middle of the sixteenth century Veronica Gàmbara was the most frequently published woman poet in Europe, with the exception of Vittoria Colonna. Her poems appeared in no less than eighty poetry anthologies between 1505 and 1754. The frequent citation of Gàmbara and her poetry by the most renowned writers of the later Italian Renaissance represents another measure of her celebrity. Ariosto praised her as "the darling of Phoebus and the choir of Muses" (*Orlando Furioso,* canto 46.3). Bernardo Tasso invoked the power of her art in his *Amadigi.* The prolific Neapolitan poet Laura Terracina dedicated her *Il discorso sopra il principio do tutti i canti di Orlando Furioso* (1549) to Gàmbara, and Lucia Bertana and Vittoria Colonna also eulogized her in their sonnets. A widow for most of her adult life, she worked at building alliances with the most powerful princes in Europe to safeguard her small state, once defending her kingdom alone against the armed attack of a powerful neighboring lord. As ruler of Correggio after her husband's death, Gàmbara transformed her court from the cultural backwater it had been to a magnet for writers, artists, and musicians. Eminent men and women came from all over Italy to pay her court. At the same time, her correspondence and friendships with prominent intellectuals of the period suggests an interest in, if not engagement with, the reformist ideas of the radical theologians Juan de Valdés and Bernardino Ochino, who would later be condemned as heretics. On a par with Gaspara Stampa and Vittoria Colonna, Gàmbara continues to draw praise from modern critics as one of the three greatest women lyric poets of her era.

Born in Prataboino near Brescia a generation after the noted Brescian humanist Laura Cereta, Veronica Gàmbara came from a powerful literary lineage. Daughter of Count Gianfrancesco da Gàmbara and Alda Pia, she saw a role model in her father's aunt, the famous humanist scholar and writer Isotta Nogarola. On her mother's side, she was the niece of Emilia Pia, the principal female interlocutor in Castiglione's *Il Cortegiano* (The Book of the Courtier, published in Venice in 1528). She received the kind of humanist education that most men and some women of her class were given to equip them for their roles as the future governors of their states: her studies included Greek and Latin literature, history, philosophy, scripture, and theology. In 1502 she began to correspond with the most influential proponent of Petrarchanism of the early sixteenth century, the poet Pietro Bembo, whom she looked to not only as the chief architect of her poetic style but as her mentor in forming her literary circle.

In 1509, Gàmbara married the soldier and nobleman Giberto X, lord of Correggio, and from the marriage she had two children: Ippolito, who followed a military career like his father, and Girolamo, who took orders in the church. The unexpected death of her husband in 1518 marked the turning point in Gàmbara's life. While Giberto ruled, the state of Correggio had remained loyal to King Francis I of France, even after 1512 when the forces of the French king had brutally attacked Brescia, Gàmbara's hometown, sacking the city, desecrating its churches, and raping its townswomen. But in 1520, Gàmbara broke with France and pledged her fealty to Charles V and to Spain. In 1529, when Pope Clement VII sent her brother Umberto Gàmbara to Bologna as his ambassador, she traveled to that city herself, where in 1530 the pope crowned Charles V, officially endowing him with the title Emperor of the Holy Roman Empire. Ingratiating herself with both the pope and the emperor in Bologna, in whose retinue Gàmbara's older brother, Brunoro, was already serving, she cultivated new friends from Venice, Rome, Mantua, and Florence, many of whom she would later receive at her court in Correggio. Charles V came to Correggio on 23 March 1530 on his return from Germany. In return for the lavish reception with which Gàmbara welcomed Charles, the emperor promised to safeguard her state from foreign invasion, forbidding his generals to travel through Correg-

gio without his permission. In January 1533 Gàmbara again entertained Charles at her court when he returned to Italy for a new round of talks with the pope. The following year she negotiated the marriage contract of her son Ippolito with Chiara di Correggio, daughter of her cousin Gianfrancesco, to ensure that upon her death Ippolito would succeed to the lordship of Correggio unchallenged.

When Galeotto Pico della Mirandola invaded Correggio in 1538, Gàmbara herself marshaled an army to expel him from her city, and when plague and famine struck her city and the neighboring towns of the Po valley the same year, she mounted a successful campaign to bring relief to her citizens. Meanwhile she continued to craft a good relationship for herself, her signory, and her sons with Clement's successor Pope Paul III (Alessandro Farnese) and his powerful nephews, Pierluigi and Ottavio Farnese, who was the duke of Parma and Piacenza and the husband of the emperor's daughter, Margaret of Austria. Among Gàmbara's other staunch friends and allies during this period were Marchese Alfonso d'Avalos del Vasto and his wife Marchesa Maria d'Aragona of Milan and Naples, and Marchesa Isabella d'Este of Mantua, after whose death she traveled to Mantua accompanied by her daughter-in-law for the wedding of Francesco III Gonzaga and Caterina of Habsburg in 1549. The painter Titian and the poets Bernardo Tasso, Bembo, and Ariosto visited her flourishing court, where the artist Antonio Allegri (known as Correggio) came under her protection and painted a portrait of her that would be celebrated in future centuries. The highly influential publisher's agent and senior editor of the Giolito press in Venice, Lodovico Dolce, never traveled to Gàmbara's court in Correggio, but her collected correspondence reveals an exchange of letters with him in April 1537, notable because Giolito and his associates in Venice published Gàmbara's poetry repeatedly in the popular anthologies they marketed and sold between 1545 and

1560. Gàmbara was one of the few women poets to be inducted into one of the exclusive literary clubs that virtually defined urban culture in sixteenth-century Italy: the Academy of the Sonnacchiosi of Bologna (Fahy 2000, 444).

Gàmbara's poetry represents a synthesis of the Petrarchan style filtered through Pietro Bembo and the Augustan poets Virgil and Tibullus. She favored the sonnet form, but she also wrote a madrigal, a ballad, and stanzas in ottava rima. Among the Petrarchan love poems she addressed to her husband, she wrote a sequence of two sonnets and a madrigal on the beauty of his eyes. Virgilian pastoral verses on the beauty of her native city, typically Augustan themes on the vanity of human wishes, the brevity of life, and the enduring happiness to be found in the pleasures of country living also mark her work. She wrote political sonnets to Charles V, urging him to pursue a policy of peace, and to the pope, exhorting him to oust the Turks from Europe. Her poems warning Pope Paul III that the church of Rome was like a flock without a shepherd and a ship without a pilot indicate that she too espoused certain reformist sentiments common among Italian intellectuals at midcentury, though her religious poetry also includes conventional devotional works as well. In addition, Gàmbara dedicated numerous poems to women, among whom were Vittoria Colonna, Marguerite de Navarre, Maria d'Aragona, and Isabella d'Este.

Gàmbara's published letters, including her long correspondence with the notorious poet and sometime pornographer Pietro Aretino, provide a rich document of her life and culture. One of the most cantankerous figures of the period, Aretino ultimately lambasted Gàmbara in print, dismissing her as nothing more than a "*meretrice laureata*" (erudite whore; Russell 1994, p. 149; Luzio and Renier 1900, 347). Among other events, her letters comment on the wedding of Catherine de Médicis and Henry II in France, Ochino's flight from Italy, and the dashing young Cardinal Ippolito de Medici's death

by poison (a widely held allegation that was never substantiated).

Gàmbara died in Correggio in 1550, leaving an æuvre of sixty-seven poems and one hundred and fifty letters, most of which were not published during her lifetime. Although Gàmbara's poems were printed and reprinted in sixty-eight anthologies in the sixteenth century (Bullock 1989, 100–101), no solo edition of her works appeared in print until Rizzardi's edition of her *Rime* in 1759. A modern critical edition of her complete poetic works is now available by Alan Bullock (1995).

Diana Robin

See also Art and Women; Colonna, Vittoria; Music and Women; the subheadings Salons, Salonnières, and Women Writers; Sonnet Writing (under Literary Culture and Women).

Bibliography

Primary Works

Gàmbara, Veronica. *Rime*. Edited by Alan Bullock. Florence: Perth, 1995.

Gàmbara, Veronica. *Rime e lettere*. With a *Vita* by B. C. Zamboni. Edited by Francesco Rizzardi. Brescia: Rizzardi, 1759.

Stortoni, Laura Anna, ed. *Women Poets of the Italian Renaissance: Courtly Ladies and Courtesans*. Translated by Laura Anna Stortoni and Mary Prentice Lillie, 23–27. New York: Italica Press, 1997.

Secondary Works

Bozzetti, C., P. Gibellini, and E. Sandal, eds. *Veronica Gàmbara e la poesia del suo tempo nell'Italia settentrionale. Atti del convegno Brescia-Correggio, 17–19 ottobre 1985*. Florence: Olschki, 1989.

Diana, Robin. *Publishing Women: Salons, the Presses, and the Counter-Reformation in Sixteenth-Centuy Italy*. Chicago: University of Chicago Press, 2007.

Fahy, Conor. "Women and Italian Cinquecento Literary Academies." In *Women in Italian Renaissance Culture and Society*. Edited by Letizia Panizza, 438–452. Oxford: Legenda, University of Oxford, 2000.

Luzio, Alessandro, and Rodolfo Renier. "La cultura e le relazioni letterarie d'Isabella d'Este Gonzaga. 3. Gruppo lombardo." *Giornale storico delle letteratura italiana* 36 (1900): 325–349.

Pignatti, Franco. "Gambara, Veronica." In *Dizionario Biografico degli Italiani*. Vol. 52. Pages

68–71. Rome: Istituto dell'Enciclopedia Italiana, 1996.

Poss, Richard. "Veronica Gambara: A Renaissance Gentildonna." In *Women Writers of the Renaissance and Reformation*. Edited by Katharina M. Wilson, 47–65. Athens: University of Georgia Press, 1987.

Rabitti, Giovanna. "Lyric Poetry, 1500–1650." In *A History of Women's Writing in Italy*. Translated by Abigail Brundin. Edited by Letizia Panizza and Sharon Wood, 37–42. Cambridge: Cambridge University Press, 2000.

Russell, Rinaldina. "Veronica Gambara (1485–1550)." In *A Bio-Bibliographical Sourcebook*. Edited by Rinaldina Russell, 145–153. Westport, CT: Greenwood Press, 1994.

Gender. *See* Masculinity, Femininity, and Gender.

Gentileschi, Artemisia (1593–1652/1653)

Celebrated Italian painter who worked in Florence, Naples, Rome, and London

Artemisia Gentileschi's career as a painter spanned four decades, during which she demonstrated flexibility in adapting her style from the intense Caravaggism of her early Roman years to the greater classicism of her late life in Naples. Although she traveled both within Italy and to England, worked for important patrons, and was lauded by contemporaries, her artistic education and production were limited by her gender. The expectations of what a female artist should produce influenced her contemporaries to praise her portraits and still lifes. On the other hand, the surviving works show that Artemisia, for reasons of patronage or personal preference, specialized in depicting heroic, often nude, females. Recent studies have revealed Artemisia's role as an important Baroque artist with a relatively well-documented biography.

Born in Rome on 8 July 1593 to the artist Orazio Gentileschi and his wife Prudentia

Judith Beheading Holofernes. *Painting by Artemisia Gentileschi, ca. 1618. Uffizi Gallery, Florence. (Summerfield Press/Corbis)*

Montoni, Artemisia had three brothers but was the only sibling who demonstrated artistic talent. Artemisia learned to paint from her father and developed a similar technique and style. Her first signed and dated work, the Pommersfelden *Susanna and the Elders* of 1610, indicates a precocious understanding of gesture, composition, and lighting. The detailed and unidealistic rendering of the female body points to a feminine sensibility not present in the nudes by her father. Despite this, the sophistication of the work has caused some scholars to suggest that Gentileschi senior contributed to its design or execution.

To supplement paternal instruction, Orazio hired his friend, Agostino Tassi, to tutor Artemisia in perspective. Tassi raped Artemisia in May 1611, a fact attested to by trial records (1612). This rape has been read as a defining factor in the young artist's life, though the extent of its influence on her art has been questioned.

Much attention has been given to her frequent creation of violent images involving heroic women. The Naples *Judith Slaying Holofernes,* a work that shows raw violence of a woman against a man, has been dated to the period around the rape and trial. Unlike male artists' treatments of this subject, Artemisia's rendering shows a strong and determined Judith. Emotion is heightened by stylistic elements like chiaroscuro, alternating bright colors, and strong diagonals leading toward the central action.

Immediately after Tassi's conviction, Artemisia was married to the Florentine artist Pietro Antonio di Vincenzo Stiattesi, and the couple moved to Florence, where Artemisia's artist-uncle, Aurelio Lomi, lived. During her stay in Florence she signed works "Artemisia Lomi" to emphasize this relationship. By 1615 or 1616, Artemisia had secured two important patrons: Michelangelo Buonarroti the Younger, for whom she painted an *Allegory of Inclination* (part of a larger program in the Casa Buonarroti), and Grand Duke Cosimo II, who may have been instrumental in Artemisia's becoming the first woman to be admitted to the prestigious Accademia del Disegno (1616).

During her Florentine period, Artemisia adapted to the patronage and stylistic preferences of the city, but continued to specialize in images of women. Two of the female saints depicted are Medici namesakes: Artemisia painted two Mary Magdalenes (Los Angeles: Sneider Collection; Florence: Pitti) that are believed to have been for the Grand Duchess Maria Maddalena of Austria, and a *Saint Catherine* (Florence: Uffizi) has been seen as homage to Catherine de Médicis. The works from this period take on a more detailed and decorative style in keeping with the courtly atmosphere of Grand Ducal Florence. The prominent "Artemisia gold" dress of the *Penitent Magdalen* (Pitti), in which light luxuriates upon its surface, contrasts with the saint's fervently pious expression. Another gold dress—Artemisia's signature—features in the second *Judith and*

Holofernes (Uffizi), painted for the duke and executed either at the end of the Florentine period or just after the artist's return to Rome. This image is a variation on the painting in Naples of the same subject. In the Uffizi work, Artemisia diminishes the chiaroscuro of the earlier piece to create a visually and emotionally unified triad of figures. More even light also allows her to show greater detail, both in decorative elements like the brocade of Judith's dress and her elaborate cameo bracelet and in unpleasant aspects like the squirting blood that not only runs down the bed but shoots outward in beads. In Florence, Artemisia did paint images of saints and a few Madonnas, but the *Judith and Holofernes* and the roughly contemporary *Jael and Sisera* have received more attention in recent literature because they continue the iconographic trend of heroic females established in her early work.

In 1620 or 1621, Artemisia returned to Rome with her husband and daughter, the only one of four children born in Florence who survived (she may have had another daughter later). Census records show that Stiattesi was absent from their home by 1623 and Artemisia was head of the household. During this decade, Artemisia may have traveled to Genova to help her father who was working there, and she was certainly in Venice in 1627. Few works are securely datable to the period 1620–1628, but some trends can be observed. Artemisia continued to specialize primarily in images of women, but two reclining nudes in the Venetian mode—the Princeton *Venus and Cupid* and a *Cleopatra* (ex-London)—have an erotic charge that appeals to the male gaze. Three portraits also date to this period; two are lost, but the *Portrait of a Condottiere* (Bologna) is signed and dated 1622. Stylistically, the reencounter with Roman Caravaggism led Artemisia to return to this style that had previously influenced both her and her father, while she did not lose the sophistication and decorative manner learned in Florence. Garrard dates the Metropolitan Museum's *Esther Before Aha-*

suerus to Artemisia's Roman period. This painting is consistent with these stylistic observations due to the jaunty, Caravaggesque male figure in conjunction with Esther's ornate dress and jewelry, although the evenly diffused light may point to a later date.

With promises of certain patronage, Artemisia transferred to Spanish-owned Naples. Here, her patrons were the Duque de Alcalá (Spanish viceroy), the Roman collector Cassiano dal Pozzo, and later Don Antonio Ruffo of Sicily. Aside from a trip to England to assist her ailing father with a ceiling decoration for the queen's house at Greenwich (1638–1641), Artemisia spent the rest of her life in Naples. The conservatism of this city and a growing appreciation for the more classicizing Bolognese style forced Artemisia to evolve once again. Her remarkable adaptability is demonstrated in her collaboration, in the 1630s, with Massimo Stanzione and Paolo Finoglio in two religious history cycles, the *Birth and Naming of Saint John the Baptist* for the Hermitage of San Juan at Buen Retiro (now Prado, Madrid) and a series of canvases for the choir at the Duomo of Pozzuoli. In the interest of creating unified cycles, the artists adapted their styles to one another and perhaps intervened on each other's canvases. The style of Artemisia's later works was more influential than her more personal early manner, as can be seen reflected in the art of Cavallino, Guarino, and others. Artemisia died in Naples in 1652 or 1653.

While Artemisia is not mentioned in all the biographies of artists at the time, this could be due to the fact that she produced few publicly accessible frescoes and altarpieces. She is given a section in Baldinucci's *Notizie,* alongside her father and uncle. Her vast patronage network and her admission to the Florentine academy point to an appreciation by contemporaries that, furthermore, was expressed from her Rome period onward in the form of portraits and poems. Two epitaphs dating to 1653 belittle Artemisia's success by making reference to her sexuality.

The twentieth century rediscovered Artemisia. Longhi, in an article of 1916, attempts to distinguish Artemisia's work from her father's and hence opened up a new subject for connoisseurship. Garrard (1989 and 2001) suggests that the general female experience and Artemisia's specific biographical experience produce an emotional indicator that can be used among other factors to distinguish her art. Other methods have also been applied, including psychoanalysis, semiotics, and social history. Bissel (1999) focuses on documents and patronage in the first catalogue raisonée of Artemisia's works; it has been suggested that this traditional art-historical format is unable to incorporate the feminist sensibility necessary to deal with a female artist. Artemisia has recently inspired biographical fictions, some more accurate than others, in the form of novels (Lapierre, 1998; and others), plays, and a controversial film (Merlet, 1998).

Alexandra M. Korey

See also Anguissola, Sofonisba; Art and Women; Fontana, Lavinia; Rape and Violence Against Women.

Bibliography

Primary Works

Baldinucci, Filippo. *Notizie dei professori del disegno da Cimabue in qua.* . . . Edited by F. Ranalli, III, 713–716. Florence: 1845–1847.

Menzio, Eva, ed. *Lettere/Artemisia Gentileschi; precedute da Atti di un processo per stupro.* Milan: Abscondita, 2004.

Secondary Works

Bal, Mieke. *The Artemisia Files: Artemisia Gentileschi for Feminists and Other Thinking People.* Chicago: University of Chicago Press, 2005.

Bissel, R. Ward. *Artemesia Gentileschi and the Authority of Art.* University Park: Pennsylvania State University Press, 1999.

Bissel, R. Ward. "Artemesia Gentileschi: A New Documented Chronology." *Art Bulletin* 50, no. 2 (1968): 153–168.

Christiansen, Keith, and Judith W. Mann, ed. *Orazio e Artemisia Gentileschi.* Milan: Skira, 2001.

Cohen, Elizabeth S. "The Trials of Artemisia Gentileschi: A Rape as History." *Sixteenth Century Journal* 31, no. 1 (2000): 46–75.

Garrard, Mary D. *Artemisia Gentileschi Around 1622: The Shaping and Reshaping of an Artistic Identity.* Berkeley: University of California Press, 2001.

Garrard, Mary D. *Artemesia Gentileschi: The Image of the Female Hero in Italian Baroque Art.* Princeton, NJ: Princeton University Press, 1989.

Harris, Ann Sutherland. "Artemisia Gentileschi: The Literate Illiterate or Learning from Example." *Docere, delectare, movere: affetti, devozione e retorica nel linguaggio artistico del primo barocco romano.* Rome: Edizioni De Luca, 1998.

Lapierre, Alexandra. *Artemisia. Un duel pour l'immortalité.* Paris: Robert Laffont, 1998.

Longhi, Roberto. "Gentileschi, padre e figlia." *L'Arte* xix (1916): 245–314.

Merlet, Agnès. *Artemisia.* Miramax Films, 1998.

Pollock, Griselda. "Review of Mary Garrard's *Artemisia Gentileschi.*" *Art Bulletin* 72, no. 3 (1990): 499–505.

Spear, Richard. "Artemisia Gentileschi: Ten Years of Fact and Fiction." *Art Bulletin* 82 (2000): 568–577.

Gonzaga, Giulia (Giulia Gonzaga Colonna; 1513–1566)

Duchess of Fondi; patron of artists, poets, and Venetian publishers; host of salons at Fondi and Naples; religious reform leader and alleged heretic

Two seemingly conflicting images of Giulia Gonzaga have been handed down in the literature of Renaissance Italy and in documents and historical accounts at our disposal. One description is that of a young chatelaine (from 1527 to 1536) whose beauty and intelligence fired the imaginations of writers and artists. She was painted by the Renaissance masters Angelo Bronzino and Sebastiano del Piombo, and the leading poets of her day, among whom were Ludovico Ariosto, Bernado Tasso, Francesco Berni, Francesco Maria Molza, Luigi Tansillo, Laura Terracina, and Vittoria Colonna, sang her praises. The other image of Gonzaga is that of the inspired animator of Juan de Valdés's spiritual circle in Naples (1536–1541) and leader of the reformist movement within the church of Rome (1542–1566). A coherent view of her

personality emerges if we take notice of the seriousness of character detectable in her behavior since her younger years and connect it to the committed activities of the second part of her life.

Giulia Gonzaga was born to Lodovico Gonzaga, duke of Sabbioneta, and to Francesca Fieschi of Genova, probably in 1513, at Gazzuolo, residence of Gianfrancesco Gonzaga and Antonia del Balzo, her paternal grandparents. She received her primary education at Gazzuolo, which was a small but cultivated court not far from Mantova, and at seven, when the family property was divided among Gianfrancesco's three sons, she was moved with mother and siblings some miles away to the modest castle of Sabbioneta. This was one of the properties that Ludovico, captain of the imperial army, had chosen primarily because of their strategic positions. At Sabbioneta Giulia received a rudimentary education, and in 1526, when she was thirteen, she was married to Vespasiano Colonna, son of the renowned condottiere Prospero Colonna, a widower forty years of age, lame, crippled, and sickly.

After a short residence on the Alban hills, the young bride took up residence in her husband's fief of Fondi, south of Rome, in the midst of a marshy land infested by mosquitoes and roamed over by herds of buffalo. The position of the castle near the Appian Road made it a convenient stop for any company of consequence on its way to the Neapolitan court. The reports sent to their friends by the nobles and literati who were her guests at Fondi created the reputation of Giulia as the most beautiful and beguiling woman of her age and gave her home the sobriquet of "small Athens."

Giulia's fame was greatly enhanced by the flamboyant courtship paid to her by Ippolito de' Medici (1511–1535), the young and handsome scion of the house of Medici, reputed illegitimate son of Giuliano de Medici, duke of Nemours, hence nephew of Pope Clement VII (1523–1534). The fact that the pontiff had made him a cardinal as early as 1531 had not hampered Ippolito's zest for poetry, the arts, the military, the political life, and his enthusiastic pursuit of women. Ippolito himself publicized his infatuation for the celebrated countess by circulating poems in her honor and having himself painted by Titian with a bejeweled blazon of his devotion to her pinned to his cardinal hat. And it is on Giulia's property that he died on 10 August 1535, as he was preparing to leave to join Emperor Charles V in Tunis. His sudden death was most likely due to malaria caught in the marshes surrounding Giulia's castle but was widely attributed to poisoning ordered by Alessandro, duke of Florence, whom Ippolito had alienated by supporting the party of the Florentine republicans. The aura of mysterious allure surrounding the countess of Fondi was elevated to exotic celebrity by a raid carried out in her territories by the much talked-about pirate and Ottoman regent of Algier, Khayr al-Din (d. 1546). After landing on the coast near Gaeta during the night of 8 August 1534, Khayr attacked and sacked the towns of Fondi, Itri, and Borgo di Sperlonga. The inhabitants were slaughtered or taken aboard ship. Warned in time by her servants, Gonzaga managed to escape. Around her flight a legend grew according to which Khayr had planned the abduction of the beautiful countess to make a gift of her to Suleiman II the Magnificent (1520–1566). The news of the raid began to circulate in dozens of fantastic variations, the most tasteful of which remains the eclogue entitled *La ninfa fuggitiva* (The Fleeing Nymph), composed by the elegant court poet Francesco Maria Molza (1489–1544).

As gossipy reports whirled around her name, Giulia found herself burdened by great family responsibilities. Her husband, Vespasiano Colonna, died in 1528. By the power of his will, dated 12 March of that year, Giulia, then fifteen, became sole heir to his property and titles, on the condition that she would not remarry. Vespasiano had also made her guardian of Isabella (1513–1570), his grown-up daughter by his first wife, Beatrice Appiani. In 1531 Isabella married Giulia's brother, Luigi Gonzaga. Luigi, called Rodomonte because of his physical strength and daring, had resided as a youth at the court of Madrid and had become, like his father Ludovico, a captain in the imperial army. Two years later Luigi was killed by a harquebus shot while defending his sister's lands from an incursion led by Napoleone Orsini. Soon after, Giulia's stepdaughter and sister-in-law, Isabella, initiated against her a litigation about the Medici inheritance. The judicial case, which became at times acrimonious, was solved only in 1540 when the ad hoc committee appointed by Emperor Charles V decided in favor of Giulia. About the same time Lodovico Gonzaga died, naming Giulia the guardian of young Vespasiano, Luigi's and Isabella's son. Because of the death of her close male relatives, Gonzaga found it necessary to attend to the administration of her family property and to act as a mother to Vespasiano, who was to inherit the dukes of Sabbioneta's territories and titles. From her correspondence and other documents, it is possible to infer also that Giulia took loving care of many other relatives as well, of her family of servants, and of the people who turned to her for help. Her sense of responsibility and her concern for those in need are confirmed by the careful provisions contained in her last will and testament.

A significant, and seemingly abrupt, change in Giulia's life occurred in 1535, when she was asked by her cousin Ferrante to represent the Sforza clan at the celebrations planned in Naples in honor of the emperor, who was expected to arrive there on his way back from Tunis. During her residence in the city, Giulia met again the theologian and humanist Juan de Valdés (ca. 1490–1541), who in September of the same year had been her guest at Fondi. In his native Spain, Valdés had become a follower of Erasmus and a member of the spiritual group of the *alumbrados*. In 1531, after his tract, *Dialogue of Christian Doctrine,* became suspect to the Spanish Inquisition, he fled his country and found service at the papal court in Rome. In Naples, where he moved in 1535, a circle of aristocrats, prelates, and intellectuals formed around him to study the scriptures and seek in them a direction for their thoughts and conduct. This select group of followers comprised, among others, women like Costanza de Avalos and Isabella Bresegna Manriquez, sister of the Spanish Inquisitor, along with men who, like Bernardino Ochino, Marcanatonio Flaminio, Galeazzo Caracciolo Marquis of Vico, Pietro Martire Vermigli, Pietro Carnesecchi, and Pietro Antonio Di Capua, were to become pivotal figures in the religious events of the next decades. The Christian ideal preached by Valdés was centered on the love for Christ the savior and on perfect trust in the grace of God. His preaching emphasized the inner dimension of religiosity to such an extent as to render irrelevant all ceremonial practices and any structure the church may want to assume. But he never openly objected to the institutions and rituals of the church.

Giulia moved to Naples in 1536 and took up residence, together with a sizable retinue, in the convent annexed to the church of S. Francesco delle Monache of the order of Saint Clare. During Lent she attended the services in the church of San Giovanni Maggiore, and there she heard the sermons delivered by Bernardino Ochino. Perturbed by his predication, Giulia found support and a sense of direction in the discussions she had with the charismatic Valdés. Their conversations were described by him in the dialogue *Alfabeto Christiano,* the first of many works he wrote in Italy. The dialogue has both religious and psychological interest. Valdés clarifies to Giulia the nature of her sense of satiety and restlessness, her dissatisfaction with herself and the world. Serenity and freedom from anxiety and discontent can be achieved, he maintains, if we succeed in nullifying ourselves in our love for God, for humanity, and for the world. The *Alfabeto* came out in Venice in 1545. Giulia's secretary, Marcantonio Magno, who translated the

dialogue from the Spanish into Italian, prefaced his work with a dedication to her, in which he stated that with the first copy of the book he was sending her a portrait of herself, so that she would be able to judge whether he had managed to make her speak in her own language as well as Valdés had been able with his inspired words to lead her to the love of the Holy Spirit.

After Valdés's death in 1541, his followers and several Catholic reformers gathered around the English cardinal, Reginald Pole, at Viterbo—hence their designation as *Ecclesia Viterbiensis.* Giulia who, as Valdés's literary heir, was in the process of circulating and publishing his writings, kept in constant contact with the Viterbo group. From their correspondence and from the depositions underwritten by some of them at the heresy trials in the years to come, we may infer that at this time Giulia did believe in justification by faith alone. According to one of the accused, Apollonio Merenda, she did not know or care about the consequences of such conviction. In 1542 Cardinal Gian Pietro Carafa, the future Pope Paul IV (1555–1559), began a systematic investigation of all presumed heretics. Rather than answering the cardinal's summons to Rome, two eminent members of Valdés's circle, Bernardino Ochino and Pietro Martire Vermigli, took to flight and joined the Protestants beyond the Alps. In the aftermath of these events, the inquisitors sent feelers to Naples to investigate Gonzaga's connections with Ochino. A decade later, Girolamo Morra, Ferrante Gonzaga's agent in that city, in a letter to him dated 11 December 1552, reported that Scipione Rebiba, the archbishop of Naples, was interrogating witnesses on Giulia's activities. This time she was suspected of preaching Valdés's doctrines and of holding secret meetings about them. She became the object of another investigation in 1553. Gonzaga defended herself—the new imputation now was of circulating Valdés's writings—in a letter to her cousin, Cardinal Ercole Gonzaga (1505–1563). This investigative procedure also proved inconclusive and was closed on 9 February 1554. On all occasions, Giulia sustained her reasons with decision and firmness of views, rejecting the accusations with a resolution unsuspected in the perturbed woman of the *Alphabeto* and often reproachfully turning the responsibility for people's behavior on their accusers.

While promoting the message of Valdés—she paid for their publication and made all arrangements with editors and publishers in Venice and abroad—Gonzaga embarked on other dangerous activities. She followed with special attention the events occurring at the final session of the Council of Trent (1561–1563) and tried to push forward in an evangelical direction the plan of internal church reform, favoring the success of those who were ready to compromise with the Protestants. At this time, her informant was Cardinal Girolamo Seripando (1493–1563), delegate to the council and considered by her the spiritual heir of Cardinal Pole, who had died in 1558. Giulia's activities and the principles motivating them can be deduced from the numerous letters she exchanged with Pietro Carnesecchi, a former apostolic protonotary, whom she had introduced to Valdés in 1535. Together they did their utmost to rescue many friends, such as Bartolomeo Spadafora, Apollonio Merenda, Mario Galeota, Bishop Vittore Soranzo, and Cardinal Giovanni Morone, who had become objects of investigation by Cardinal Carafa. Among those Gonzaga helped were also the Marquis Caracciolo of Naples and her best friend, Isabella Bresegna, wife of the governor of Piacenza, don Garcia Manriquez, hence sister-in-law of the Spanish Inquisitor: they escaped to Geneva in 1551 and 1552 respectively. The correspondence between Giulia and Carnesecchi was to form the basis of a final trial for him and led to his execution in 1567.

The Countess of Fondi died in her Neapolitan convent on 16 April 1566, when she was fifty-three years old. The viceroy of Naples seized her correspondence and forwarded it to the newly elected Pope Pius V. After reading the

documentation, the pontiff is said to have exclaimed: "If I had seen it when she still breathing, I would have burned her alive."

Rinaldina Russell

See also Aragona, Giovanna d'; Aragona, Maria d'; Bresegna, Isabella; Colonna, Vittoria; *see also* the subheading Salons, Salonnières, and Women Writers (under Literary Culture and Women); Religious Reform and Women.

Bibliography

Primary Works

Archivio della Congregazione per la Dottrina della fede. Roma: *Sant'Offizio, Decreta, 1548–58,* c.131r.

Archivio di Stato di Mantova. *Archivio Gonzaga* 1922: c.585; 1923: cc.31r, 708r–711r; 6500: cc.45v, 47r–48r; 650: cc. 26, 27v–28r.

Biblioteca Comunale di Guastalla. *Fondo Davolio-Marani* b. 5.

Biblioteca Estense di Modena. *Autografoteca Campori, Giulia Gonzaga.* It contains letters dated February 25, March 25, April 25, May 26, and June 10, 1553.

Carnesecchi, Pietro (1508–1566). *I processi inquisitoriali di Pietro Carnesecchi, 1557–1567.* Edited by Massimo Firpo and Dario Marcatto. Vatican: Archivio segreto vaticano, 1998–2000.

Valdés, Juan de. *Alfabeto christiano.* Translated and edited by Marco Antonio Magno. Venice: Nicolò Bacarini, 1545.

Valdés, Juan de. *Alfabeto Christiano: Which Teaches the True Way to Acquire the Light of the Holy Spirit.* Translated from the Italian of 1546, with a notice of Juan de Valdés and Giulia Gonzaga, by Benjamin B. Wiffen. London: Bosworth and Harrison, 1861.

Valdés, Juan de. "The Christian Alphabet Which Teaches the True Way to Acquire the Light of the Holy Spirit." In *Spiritual and Anabaptist Writers: Documents Illustrative of the Radical Reformation and Evangelical Catholicism as Represented by Juan de Valdés.* Translated by Angel M. Mergal. Philadelphia, PA: Westminster Press, 1957.

Secondary Works

Amante, Bruto. *Giulia Gonzaga, contessa di Fondi e il movimento religioso femminile nel secolo XVI.* Bologna: Zanichelli, 1896. (The appendix contains several letters to Giulia [pp. 407–419] and others by her to friends and relatives, among them Vittoria Colonna, Pietro Carnesecchi, and Cardinal Seripando [pp. 421–482].)

Amante, Bruto. *Memorie storiche e statutarie del Ducato, della Contea e dell'Episcopato di Fondi in*

Campania dalle origini fino ai tempi più recenti.
Fondi, Italy: Emidio Quadrino [s.n.], 1971.
(Originally printed in Rome: Ermanno
Loescher, 1903.)

Benrath, Karl. *Julia Gonzaga. Ein Lebensbild aus der
Geschichte der Reformation in Italien.* Halle, Germany: Verein für Reformationsgeschichte,
1900.

Dall'Olio, Guido. "Giulia Gonzaga." *Dizionario biografico degli italiani* 57. Edited by Mario Caravale and Giuseppe Pignatelli, 783–787.
Rome: Enciclopedia Italiana, 2001.

Firpo, Massimo. *Tra alumbrados e "spirituali": studi
su Juan de Valdés e il valdesianesimo nella crisi religiosa del '500 italiano.* Florence: L. S. Olschki,
1990.

Hare, Christopher (pseudonym of Marian An-
drews). *A Princess of the Italian Reformation:
Giulia Conzaga, 1513–1566, Her Family and
Her Friends.* London, New York: Harper, 1912.

Nieto, José C. *Juan de Valdés and the Origins of the
Spanish and Italian Reformation.* Geneva: Droz,
1970.

Nulli, Siro Attilio. *Giulia Gonzaga.* Milan: Fratelli
Treves, 1938.

Oliva, Mario. *Giulia Gonzaga Colonna: tra rinascimento e controriforma.* Milan: Mursia, 1985.

Tedeschi, John. *The Italian Reformation of the Sixteenth Century and the Diffusion of Renaissance
Culture: A Bibliography of the Secondary Literature, ca. 1750–1997, Compiled by John Tedeschi
in Association with James M. Lattis; with a Historiographical Introduction by Massimo Firpo.* Modena: F. C. Panini; Ferrara: Istituto di studi rinascimentali, 2000.

Gournay, Marie de (1565–1645)

*Professional writer in Paris, moral philosopher,
polemicist for the equality of women, novelist, philologist, and defender of the Jesuits*

Marie de Gournay was born in Paris in 1565,
but she spent a large part of her youth in Picardy, at the castle of Gournay-sur-Aronde.
Her mother and father both belonged to the
aristocracy. Her mother, Jeanne de Hacque-
ville, came from a reputable family of jurists.
Her father, who was Lord of Neufvi and
Gournay, exercised several official charges in
Paris. Marie was the eldest of six children.
After her father's death, when she was only
eleven years old, her mother decided to move
her family from Paris to her country estate in
Picardy. From an early age, Gournay was interested in cultivating her mind, but her mother
did not appreciate the advantages of formal
education for a girl. She felt that her daughters
should only be taught the womanly arts required to attract suitable husbands. Gournay
learned Latin on her own by comparing Latin
texts to their French translations. She acquired
some knowledge of Greek in the same way. In
the *Apologie pour celle qui escrit* (Apology for
She Who Writes), Gournay gives a few details
of her life as a young woman. By the time her
mother died in 1591, the family fortune had
dwindled considerably. Gournay distributed
what was left of it among her brothers and sisters, keeping very little for herself. She then
moved to Paris, determined to live by her pen.
Later, she would receive a small pension from
Richelieu and from Henri IV, but a lack of financial resources plagued her all her life.

In her *Vie de la Demoiselle de Gournay* (Life
of the Demoiselle de Gournay), written when
she was almost sixty years old, Gournay tells of
the impact that Montaigne's *Essais* had on her
life. She had read them by chance when she
was only seventeen or eighteen and had become so enthralled by them that soon her
dearest wish was to meet their author. When
Madame de Gournay took her daughter to
Paris to introduce her to high society in 1588,
Montaigne happened to be in the capital as a
member of the states general called by Henri
III. He was at the same time supervising the
second publication of his *Essais*. Gournay
wasted no time in arranging a meeting with
him. Montaigne was charmed by the intelligence and knowledge of this young woman,
whom he soon named his *fille d'alliance* (chosen
daughter). During his stay in Paris that year, he
made several trips to the castle of Gournay.
Gournay and Montaigne did not see each
other again after his return to Gascony, but
their intellectual friendship endured. She wrote
to him, asking him for advice on her writing.

When he died in 1592, Madame de Montaigne and the philosopher's friends sent Gournay a copy of the *Essais* with Montaigne's latest annotations in the margins, asking her to be their first posthumous editor. Accompanying the *Essais* was a short novel, *Le Proumenoir de M. de Montaigne* (The Promenade of M. de Montaigne), which Gournay had sent to Montaigne in 1588, shortly after his return home.

Gournay dedicated her life to intellectual pursuits. She wrote numerous moral treatises as well as political pieces and philological essays that were published at different periods of her life and later became part of her complete works. She was also a seasoned translator of Virgil. Gournay corresponded with many literary figures and was known in intellectual circles in Paris, yet she was often mocked for her strong views on topics that were considered the domain of men. She never hesitated to take a stand on controversial matters, such as the quarrel of language or the assassination of King Henri IV. Her first published work was *Le Proumenoir de M. de Montaigne* (The Promenade of M. de Montaigne, 1594). It is a short novel adapted from a story by Claude de Taillemont. It has been hailed in the twentieth century as a "feminist" plea for the education of women. *Le Proumenoir* is a very complex work. It introduces many of the themes that would be topics of Gournay's later moral treatises, such as the heavy responsibility of monarchs toward their subjects or the deplorable effects of calumny on people's lives. *Le Proumenoir* had numerous publications during Gournay's lifetime.

In 1595, shortly after the publication of her *Proumenoir,* Gournay produced the first posthumous edition of Montaigne's *Essais,* preceded by a long preface. The preface gives an appraisal of Montaigne's *Essais,* but it also alludes to Gournay's intellectual friendship with Montaigne. The personal tone Gournay used must have displeased her readers because the long preface was replaced by a very short introduction in the 1599 edition of the *Essais.* The evaluation of Montaigne's work included in the long preface did not disappear, however. Gournay modified her text, giving it a dispassionate tone, and appended it to the 1599 edition of her *Proumenoir.* Later, in her 1617 edition of the *Essais,* her lengthy preface would resurface with further modifications and would be totally devoid of sentimentality. If Gournay's appraisal of Montaigne's *Essais* was flattering, as can be expected, the fact that it lists and refutes all the objections made to the *Essais* by Montaigne's contemporaries makes the preface extremely valuable today.

Throughout her life, Gournay wrote a series of moral treatises. Most of them expose the reprehensible conduct of the aristocracy during the reigns of Henri III and Henri IV. Gournay does not hesitate to claim that nobility of heart is more important than the name one bears. She begs the king to recognize the value of his humbler subjects. She condemns some of the most ingrained customs of the aristocrats, such as the duel, which often destroys the king's best warriors. She laments the arrogance of the nobility, their love of gossip, and their casual use of calumny to achieve their ways. She also reproaches the church for its hypocrisy. Two powerful treatises denounce the scorn that patriarcal society directed at intellectual women. *Le Grief des dames* (Women's Grievance) and *L'Egalité des hommes et des Femmes* (The Equality of Men and Women) point out that women are the intellectual equals of men. These treatises attempt to prove that women are the intellectual equals of men and that the ignorance in which they are kept makes them appear inferior. Three of Gournay's longer treatises address the education of the future Louis XIII. These treatises emulate Budé's and Erasmus's earlier works on the education of a crown prince. Gournay insists on the importance of exposing the young prince to models of courage and virtue. She believes that the only way for the prince to acquire the wisdom and knowledge needed to govern is through the examples offered him by the great literary works of antiquity.

Gournay was a staunch admirer not only of Montaigne, but also of Ronsard and the other poets of the Renaissance. When Malherbe's reform of language began to gain popularity at the beginning of the seventeenth century, she took an active part in the quarrel that developed between the defenders of the old generation of writers and the advocates of the new language revolution. She was in no way the only partisan of the old school, but she was its most vocal defender. Gournay's ideas on language and poetry are amply developed in eight treatises that scrutinize the changes advocated by the new school. She pleads to keep the richness that the French language acquired following the publication of the *Deffence et Illustration de la langue françoise* (The Defense and Illustration of the French Language) by Joachim Du Bellay. She opposes the condemnation of numerous words discarded by the growing preciosity. She also rejects the stricter rules of versification imposed by Malherbe, arguing for the importance of inspiration and dismissing Malherbe's technical approach to poetry. Several plays written after Malherbe's victory make fun, after the fact, of Gournay's fiery arguments.

Upon the assassination of King Henri IV, the Jesuits were strongly suspected of having had a hand in his death. Gournay lent her voice to the defense of this religious order. In a seventy-page pamphlet addressed to Marie de Médicis and entitled *Adieu de l'Ame du Roy de France et the Navarre Henry le Grand à la Royne, avec la Defence des Peres Jesuistes* (Farewell of the Soul of the King of France and Navarre, Henry the Great, to the Queen, with the Defense of the Jesuit Fathers, 1610), she strives to prove the innocence of the Catholic order. This political gesture cost her dearly. The Huguenot opposition published an anonymous response to her pamphlet, entitled *Remerciement des Beurrieres de Paris au sieur de Courbazon ou l'Anti Gournay* (Thanks from the Paris Butter Makers to Master Courbazon or the Anti-Gournay), mocking her in the most insulting terms. Gournay's

pamphlet gives a painstaking account of the history of the order, underlining its intellectual excellence, its selflessness, and its good works in France. She also carefully examines the writings of Jesuits who had written on the legitimacy of tyrannicide, a question that was much debated at the time. She clearly shows that the indictment of the Jesuits did not rest on solid ground, a fact that has been corroborated by modern historians.

Gournay reworked her writings all her life. She gave a first edition of her complete works in 1621, under the title *L'ombre de la Damoiselle de Gournay*. (The Shadow of the Damoiselle de Gournay). A second and a third edition appeared in 1634 and 1641 respectively, as *Les Advis ou les presens de la Demoiselle de Gournay* (The Advice or Presents of the Demoiselle de Gournay). The 1641 edition contains all of Gournay's previously published works, except for the preface to the *Essais* and the Defense of the Jesuits, which was never republished after 1610. Gournay died in Paris in 1645.

Marie-Thérèse Noiset

See also Education, Humanism, and Women; Feminism in the Renaissance; Literary Culture and Women.

Bibliography

Primary Works

Gournay, Marie de. *Adieu de l'Ame du Roy de France et de Navarre, Henry le Grand à la Royne, avec la Defence des Peres Jesuistes, par la damoiselle de G.* Paris: Fleury Bourriquant, 1610.

Gournay, Marie de. *Le Proumenoir de M. de Montaigne, par sa fille d'alliance.* Paris: Abel L'Angelier, 1594.

Gournay, Marie de. *Les Advis ou les presens de la Demoiselle de Gournay.* Paris: Toussainct du Bray, 1641.

Gournay, Marie de. *L'Ombre de la Damoiselle de Gournay. Oeuvre composé de meslanges.* Paris: Jean Libert, 1623.

Gournay, Marie de. *Marie le Jars de Gournay, Les Advis ou les presens de la Demoiselle de Gournay.* Vols. I and II. Edited by Jean-Philippe Beaulieu and Hannah Fournier. Amsterdam: Rodopi, 2001 and 2002.

Gournay, Marie de. *Oeuvres complètes.* Edited by Jean-Claude Arnould, Evelyne Berriot, Claude

Blum, Anna Lia Franchetti, Marie-Claire Thomine, and Valerie Worth-Stylianou. Paris: Champion, 2002.

Gournay, Marie de. "Préface à l'édition des *Essais de Montaigne*." Edited by François Rigolot. *Montaigne Studies* I (1989): 7–60. (Originally published in Paris: Abel L'Angelier, 1595.)

Secondary Works

Dezon-Jones, Elyane. *Fragments d'un discours féminin*. Paris: José Corti, 1998.

Hillman, Richard, and Quesnel Colette, eds. and trans. *Apology for the Woman Writing and Other Works*. Chicago: University of Chicago Press, 2002.

Ilsley, Marjorie. *A Daughter of the Renaissance: Marie le Jars de Gournay, Her Life and Works*. The Hague: Mouton, 1963.

Noiset, Marie-Thérèse. *Marie de Gournay et son œuvre*. Namur: Editions Namuroises, Presses Universitaires de Namur, 2004.

Graville, Anne de (ca. 1490–ca. 1540)

Only female writer and translator among the court poets at the court of King Francis I in the first quarter of the sixteenth century

Anne de Graville dedicated her two major works to Queen Claude de France, the first wife of Francis I, thereby becoming a strategic witness on how an early Renaissance woman could have an impact on the highest sphere of society. Her poetic undertakings offer in fact a powerful representation of the court's civic ideals and literary tastes because they reflect the national dream of surpassing Italy and becoming the cultural and political center of the European world.

To serve this idea of *translatio studii et imperii* (transference of letters and dominion), Anne de Graville adapts the works of two major authors of the past, Alain Chartier and Giovanni Boccaccio, into the new linguistic and literary context of the 1520s. She does not translate them literally, but remodels and refashions them to fit the taste of a modern public. In the first of these poems, inspired by *La Belle Dame sans mercy* (The Beautiful Lady Without Mercy, 1424), she rewrites Chartier's octosyllabic

huitains into decasyllabic *rondeaux,* a highly courtly poetic form, and replaces the existing prologue with a praise of her merciful patron. Among many other inserted changes, she eliminates her predecessor's negative views of the merciless lady and her naive suitor, suggesting a new courtly ethos with yet unexplored possibilities of interactions between men and women. Since famous male poets were numerous at the court of Francis I, it may well be the success of this adaptation that prompted the queen to ask Anne de Graville to compose a second poetic work entitled *C'est le beau Romant des deux amans Palamon et Arcita, et de la belle et saige Emilia* (The Beautiful Novel of the Two Lovers Palamon and Arcita and of the Attractive and Wise Emilia). This time the chosen model was Boccaccio's *Teseida* (1339), an epic romance that Anne de Graville transformed into a mirror in which Claude's court could contemplate new heroic and national emblems. Unlike the anonymous fifteenth-century translator of the *Teseida,* who had paraphrased the Italian verse in middle French prose (ca. 1460), the female poet gives new life to the epic grandeur of Boccaccio's *endecasillabo.* Here again, Anne de Graville shows her literary wit and stylistic subtlety as she stresses all the original features of the Cinquecento poem that honors her queen but systematically leaves out misogynistic or old-fashioned traits that would not appeal to a sixteenth-century French readership. In so doing she serves the ethical and aesthetic ideals of her court while assuring her female patron and herself long-lasting fame. These works were never printed but have survived in several *parchemin* and paper manuscripts, including the two richly illustrated copies offered to the queen.

Anne de Graville came from a noble family of Normandy. Her father Louis Mallet de Graville was at the forefront of the political arena as the Admiral of France (1487–1508), a right arm to Louis XI, Anne de Beaujeu, and Charles VIII. The youngest of three daughters, Anne may have been, like her older sisters, a member of Anne de Bretagne's court before becoming Claude de France's lady-in-waiting (probably from 1514 to 1524). As such, she was well acquainted with Marguerite d'Angoulême, Francis I's sister and future queen of Navarre, with whom she shared not only a common taste for literature but also a royal ancestry (their great-grandmothers Bonne Visconti and Valentine de Milan were sisters). The mother of eleven children and an active grandmother, she was also one of the most daring women of the time. Her tenacity and strong will are shown early on when she married her cousin, Pierre de Balsac, against her father's will and eloped with him. When the admiral disinherited her, she filed a suit against him and fought her whole life to get her own rights recognized. After his death in 1516, she was able to win back financially all that had been denied her, including the huge paternal library, which she passed on, together with her own impressive collection, to her daughter, Jeanne, and son-in-law, Claude d'Urfé. Through them, Anne's magnificent manuscripts were inherited by Honoré d'Urfé, whose renowned novel *L'Astrée* bears witness to this seventeenth-century author's familiarity with his great-grandmother's epic romance. Anne's courage is further illustrated by her openness to the Reformation. As a personal friend to Marguerite de Navarre, she offered protection to persecuted writers and reformers (among them Toussain, Œcolampade's pupil) in her mansion at Bois-Maslesherbes.

According to the biographers of her times, Anne de Graville spoke several languages and was also acclaimed for her beautiful singing voice. She was offered several manuscripts (among them a collection of poems composed by members of the *Puy*, a literary circle of Rouen, dedicated to her by their *Prince* [literary judge], Nicolas de Coquinvillier, bishop of Veria) and was cited by Geoffroy Tory in his *Champfleury* as a poet who demonstrated the elegance of the French language. One of the only female writers and translators of the early Renaissance whose major works survived, Anne de Graville is an indispensable link to understanding the history of French literature.

Catherine M. Müller

See also Literary Culture and Women; Marguerite de Navarre; Translation and Women Translators.

Bibliography

Primary Works

Boccaccio, Giovanni. *Teseida delle nozze d'Emilia.* In *Tutte le opere.* General editor, Vittore Branca. Edited by Alberto Limentani, 229–664. Florence: Mondadori, 1964.

Chartier, Alain. *La Belle Dame sans mercy.* Edited by Arthur Piaget. Geneva: Droz, 1949.

Graville, Anne Malet de. *C'est le beau Romant des deux amans Palamon et Arcita, et de la belle et saige Emilia, translaté de vieil langaige et prose en nouveau et rime par madamoiselle Anne de Graville la Malet, dame du Boys Maslesherbes, du commandement de la Royne.* Manuscript. Paris: Arsenal, 5116.

Graville, Anne Malet de. *La Belle Dame sans mercy.* Manuscript. Paris: Bibliothèque Nationale de France, fr. 2253.

Graville, Anne Malet de. *La Belle dame sans mercy. En Fransk dikt författad.* Edited by Carl Wahlund. Uppsala, Sweden: Almqvist & Wiksells Boktryckeri-Aktiebolag ("Skrifter utgifna af K. Humanistika Vetenskapssamfundet"), 1897.

Graville, Anne Malet de. *Le beau Romant des deux amans Palamon & Arcita et de la belle et saige Emilia.* Edited by Yves Le Hir. Paris: Presses Universitaires de France, 1965.

Tory, Geoffroy. *Champfleury. Art et Science de la Vraie Proportion des Lettres.* Foreword by Paul-Marie Grinevald. Tours: Mame ("Bibliothèque de l'Image"), 1998. (Facsimile of Giles Gourmont, ed., Paris: 1529.) (On Anne de Graville, f. Biiii [r–v].)

Secondary Works

Bouchard, Mawy. "Anne de Graville (1492–1544) et la tradition épique au XVIe siècle." In *Littératures* 18 (*L'Écriture des femmes à la Renaissance française,* 1998): 31–63.

Montmorand, Maxime de. *Une femme poète au XVIe siècle. Anne de Graville, sa famille, sa vie, son œuvre, sa postérité.* Paris: A. Picard, 1917.

Müller Catherine M. "Anne de Graville lectrice de 'Maistre Allain:' pour une récriture stratégique de la *Belle Dame sans Mercy.*" In *Lectrices d'Ancien Régime.* Edited by Isabelle Brouard-Arends, 231–241. Rennes: Presses Universitaires de Rennes, 2003.

Müller Catherine M. "Jeanne de la Font et Anne de Graville, translatrices de la *Théséïde* de Boccace au XVIᵉ siècle." In *Les Femmes et traduction du Moyen Âge au XVIIIᵉ siècle.* Edited by Jean-Philippe Beaulieu. Montréal: Presses de l'Université d'Ottawa, 2004.

Orth, Myra D. "Dedicating Women: Manuscript Culture in the French Renaissance, and the Case of Catherine d'Amboise and Anne de Graville." *Journal of Early Book Society for the Study of Manuscript and Printing History* 1, no. 1 (1997): 17–47.

Quentin Bauchart, Ernest. *Les Femmes bibliophiles de France (XVIᵉ, XVIIᵉ, XVIIIᵉ siècles).* 2 vols. II: 380. Geneva: Slatkine Reprints, 1993. (A list of Anne de Graville's own books is on p. 385. Originally printed in Paris: D. Morgand, 1886.)

Greek Learning and Women. *See* Education, Humanism, and Women.

Grey, Jane (1537–1554)

Protestant queen of England and martyr

Lady Jane Grey ruled England as queen for nine days between the reigns of Edward VI and Mary I. Jane, the eldest of three daughters born to Henry Grey, duke of Suffolk and his wife Frances Brandon, was the granddaughter of Henry VIII's younger sister Mary (b. 1496). Though a convinced Protestant and brilliant student, the "nine days' queen" was the pawn in a failed attempt by John Dudley, duke of Northumberland, to control England.

Jane Grey, Protestant queen of England and martyr. Engraving by unknown artist. (Library of Congress)

Educated by some of the leading tutors of the day, Jane proved to be an exceptional student. She acquired proficiency in Latin, Greek, Italian, and French, and she studied Hebrew so that she would be able to read the Old Testament in its original form. She was also an accomplished musician and played the lute and harp, as well as composing her own music. At the age of nine, she was placed in the household of Catherine Parr, Henry VIII's sixth and last queen. Jane remained in this household for two years and under Parr's guidance learned

about life at court and the expectations of her social rank. Jane's parents unsuccessfully promoted her as a possible wife for her cousin, Edward VI. Both Henry VIII and Edward VI believed that the potential for a foreign alliance was too important for England, so Englishwomen were not considered good marriage candidates for Edward.

Lady Jane Grey became an ardent Protestant. She had very little patience for what she saw as the "old religion," Catholicism. She often spoke her mind about what she saw as the childishness of those who continued to follow the ceremonies and practices of the Catholic church.

While Edward VI was still alive and Henry VIII's last will was enforced, Jane was fifth in line to take the English throne, behind Edward's half sisters and Jane's own mother, the duchess of Suffolk. When Edward VI became seriously ill in 1553, his leading advisor, Northumberland (John Dudley), feared the loss of his own power and devised a scheme to keep a Protestant on the throne of England and himself in power. Northumberland married his youngest son, Guildford Dudley, to Lady Jane Grey. He then convinced Edward VI to change the succession. Edward VI's will declared his half sisters illegitimate and removed them from the succession in favor of Jane. Many of Edward VI's councilors had misgivings about the plan; they realized that his will lacked legitimacy. He could only change Henry VIII's order of succession with the permission of parliament, which he did not have.

When Edward VI died, Northumberland had Lady Jane Grey declared queen of England. She reluctantly accepted the crown. Northumberland planned to have his son Guildford declared king, ensuring that he would remain in power, but Jane refused to allow her husband to be crowned king and instead she granted him the duchy of Clarence. For Northumberland's plan to succeed, he needed to capture Mary, the Catholic daughter of Henry VIII and Catherine of Aragon (1516–1558), before she could raise an army. He failed in this, and the country rallied around Mary. While Northumberland was away raising an army against the lawful queen, the council lost its nerve for the coup, declared Northumberland a traitor, and crowned Mary I queen of England. Jane relinquished her claim to the title; she had ruled for nine days. She and her husband, Guilford Dudley, along with others involved in the plot, were tried and found guilty of treason. Most were sentenced to death, but, while Northumberland was executed, Mary I planned clemency for Jane.

This plan changed the following year when Thomas Wyatt rebelled against Queen Mary's proposed marriage to Philip of Spain and Jane's father again attempted to gain support for her rule. Mary believed that she had no choice but to execute Jane and Dudley because, as long as Jane remained alive, she would provide a viable alternative as queen and further plots might center around her. After an unsuccessful attempt to convert Jane back to Catholicism, Mary ordered that her execution be carried out.

Lady Jane Grey was executed on 9 February 1554. Though Jane was only sixteen at the time of her death, she had written a number of letters about her faith that were subsequently published. The tragedy of Jane's brief rule also inspired a number of romances and dramas, especially in the nineteenth century.

Shawndra Holderby

See also Education, Humanism, and Women; Mary I; Power, Politics, and Women; Religious Reform and Women.

Bibliography
Primary Works
Foxe, John. *The Acts and Monuments of John Foxe; with a Life of the Martyrologist, and Vindication of the Work.* Edited by George Townsend. New York, AMS Press, 1965.
Nichols, J. G., ed. *The Chronicle of Queen Jane and Queen Mary.* New York: AMS Press, 1968.
Secondary Works
Chapman, Hester W. *Lady Jane Grey.* Boston: Little Brown and Company, 1962.
Jansen, Sharon L. *The Monstrous Regiment of Women: Female Rulers in Early Modern Europe.* New York: Palgrave Macmillan, 2002.
Plowden, Alison. *Lady Jane Grey: Nine Days Queen.* Phoenix Mill, UK: Sutton, 2003.

Guillet, Pernette du (ca. 1520–1545)

Published poet, member of Louise Labé's circle in Lyon

"*Gentile et vertueuse Dame D. Pernette du Guillet,*" as we read on the title page of her *Rymes,* was born in the upper middle class of Lyons. She died at the age of about twenty-five, most likely of the plague that devastated her native region. We have no authentic portrait of her. Most of the commentaries on her life and personality come either from the poems themselves or from interpretations found in the preface written by her posthumous editor, Antoine du Moulin, or else from poems by Maurice Scève and Jean de Vauzelles that appear at the end of the *Rymes,* as epitaphs, or finally from a few contemporary biographers who did not know her personally but merely speculated from what they heard.

She was well educated. She played the lute and other musical instruments such as the spinet. She knew Italian (Tuscan), Spanish (Castillan), and some Latin, and had started Greek studies. She was an avid reader of French and Italian poets and of Platonic philosophers, and she exhibited a fervent enthusiasm for knowledge. Around 1536 she met Maurice Scève, a prominent poet of the famous *École de Lyon,* who was widely considered to be her mentor. At the beginning of the sixteenth century the society of Lyons had reinvented, for its own purposes, the feminine model of the Italian courtesan. Pernette du Guillet therefore was able to benefit from an exceptional education, like other women of the circles she frequented: elegance, intelligence, culture, charm, and beauty shone through as she undertook artistic and literary activities. She participated in discussions about Italian and French poets, notably in *salons* such as the one held by her friend Louise Labé. Like her, Pernette started writing her own poems that she recited in the Lyons circles. Her *Rymes* reveal a poetic dialogue between her persona and that of Maurice Scève, who also frequented the salon of Louise Labé.

Scève was working on his long Petrarchan work, *Délie. Object de plus Haulte Vertu,* made up of four hundred and ninety-nine *dizains* and published in 1544, when, charmed by the extraordinary intellect of this young poet, he probably thought of her as the perfect initiator to love and knowledge. She became the incarnation of the figure of Délie, a complex muse

adored by the poet. Pernette seems to have made her poetic experience with Scève the greatest endeavor of her short life. He was her elder by about twenty years, so he was able to initiate her to classic and contemporary masterpieces. The admiration she felt and his interest in her aspiring work provoked an intellectual exchange that was not devoid of mutual passion. However, Scève was condemned to celibacy by an ecclesiastical vow, and Pernette's parents had chosen for her Monsieur du Guillet, whom she married in 1538, but without passion. The lovers thus found themselves in the typical courtly situation where the obstacle of forbidden love led them to oscillate between transgression and refusal. Like Louise Labé later on and many brilliant women of her time, Pernette was ill spoken of by prejudiced commentators, but her fame has proven them wrong.

Immediately upon her death, Pernette's husband asked Antoine du Moulin, who worked for the printer Jean de Tournes, to sort out her papers and publish the small stack of poems she had left in a drawer in her room. They appeared under the title *Rymes* in August 1545 in Lyons. Three other editions were published in Lyons and Paris in the sixteenth century, three in Lyons in the nineteenth century, and two in Paris in the twentieth century. Even though Scève is not explicitly named in the *Rymes,* just as Pernette is not named in *Délie,* the Platonic, Petrarchan, and Christian sources provided the two poets with analogous topics, such as the spiritual suffering of the lovers caused by separation, which is typical of the language Petrarch had used in his *Canzoniere.* Thanks to the brilliant circles that nourished the *École de Lyon,* the advent of Petrarchan and Platonic poetry in French enjoyed great success.

The eighty-some poems found and attributed to Pernette du Guillet had to be titled and numbered. They are composed of epigrams (*quatrains, huitains, dizains*), songs, epistles, and elegies. Pernette plays on Scève's name through anagrams and adjectives derived from Latin that echo his name, and she calls him her *Jour* or *Soleil,* or even her *Lumière,* terms that correspond to the figures of the *Lune* and *Ténèbres* found in *Délie.* By theme and style, certain poems of the *Rymes* resemble several *dizains* of Scève to the point that one can read four or five epigrams that differ from *Délie* by only one or two words, which creates an intriguing mirror effect. Yet, through the subtle differences between the epigrams in both works, one can see that the use of the elements of one poem from *Délie* in another from the *Rymes* actually enables each poet to utter a different idea: for instance, Scève's tendency to fall into the somber melancholy of unsatisfied desire and into the infernal cycle of alternating between suffering and hope is consistently uplifted in Pernette du Guillet by a propensity to contentment provided by intellect and creation, because the happiness of the exchange is based on a love defined and felt as divine.

In such a Platonic perspective, even if the separation and renunciation remain difficult, the shared asceticism, while enabling the lovers to reach the *parfaicte amytié* celebrated in France since the publication of Antoine Héroët's *La Parfaicte Amye* in 1542, has the merit of promoting alliances of the heart over arranged marriages. In agreement with neo-Platonic theory, Pernette du Guillet wishes for a union with her beloved, expressed through an enthusiastic ardor that tempers the somewhat austere character of Scève's persona. One may thus consider that the *Jour* and the *Lumière* of Pernette's poetry, while they symbolize the poet who has, by his knowledge and eloquence, enabled both lovers to deepen their understanding of poetic truth, also express the delight that the young woman feels within herself as she creates, thus surpassing the narrow horizon of women's condition.

Therefore, even if the strong poetic personality of Scève put its stamp on the poetic orientation of the young apprentice who was also his inspiration, the two works enrich each other mutually by their multiple points of contact, through experience and poetic invention. Both were also strongly inspired by previous French and Italian poets, and certainly Pernette's poetry derives from imitators of Petrarch and Bembo. Although the young woman did not have the opportunity to further develop or publish her work before she died, it is to be noted that four of her poems, adapted with variations, were set to music during her lifetime.

Brigitte Roussel

See also Education, Humanism, and Women; Labé, Louise; the subheadings Salons, Salonnières, and Women Writers; Sonnet Writing (under Literary Culture and Women); Music and Women.

Bibliography

Primary Works

Charpentier, Françoise. *Louise Labé: Œuvres poétiques, précédées des Rymes de Pernette du Guillet.* Paris: Gallimard, 1983.

Pernette du Guillet. *Poésies de Pernette du Guillet, Lyonnaise.* Lyon: Louis Perrin, 1830.

Pernette du Guillet. *Poètes du XVIe Siècle.* Edited by Albert-Marie Schmidt. Paris: Gallimard/Pléiade, 1953.

Pernette du Guillet. *Rymes.* Critical edition by Victor Graham. Geneva: Droz, 1968.

Pernette du Guillet. *Rymes de Gentile, et Vertueuse Dame D. Pernette du Guillet Lyonnoise.* Lyon: Jean de Tournes, 1545.

Pernette du Guillet. *Rymes de Gentile, et Vertueuse Dame D. Pernette du Guillet Lyonnoize.* De nouveau augmentées. Lyon: Jean de Tournes, 1552.

Secondary Works

Boillet, Danielle, and Marziano Guglielminetti. *Anthologie Bilingue de la poésie italienne.* Paris: Gallimard/Pléiade, 1994.

Hutson, Lorna. *Feminism and Renaissance Studies.* Oxford: Oxford University Press, 1999.

James, Karen Simroth. "On veult responce avoir: Pernette du Guillet's Dialogic Poetics." In *A Dialogue of Voices: Feminist Theory and Bakhtin.* Pages 171–197. Minneapolis: University of Minnesota Press, 1994.

Jondorf, Gillian. "Petrarchan Variations in Pernette du Guillet and Louise Labé." *Modern Language Review* 71, no. 4 (October 1976): 766–778.

Jones, Ann Rosalind. "Assimilation with a Difference: Renaissance Women Poets and Literary Influence." *Yale French Studies* 62 (1981): 135–153.

Lazard, Madeleine. *Images littéraires de la femme à la Renaissance.* Paris: PUF, 1985.

Mulhauser, Ruth. *Maurice Scève.* Boston: Twayne Publishers, 1977.

Rothstein, Marian. "Pernette du Guillet (1520?–1545)." *French Women Writers.* Pages 143–152. Lincoln, NE, and London: University of Nebraska Press, 1994.

Saulnier, Verdun-Louis. "Etude sur Pernette du Guillet et ses *Rymes.*" *Bibliothèque d'Humanisme et de Renaissance* IV (1944): 7–119.

Gynecology and Obstetrics. *See* the subheadings Childbirth and Reproductive Knowledge; Midwives and Licensing; Male Midwifery (under Medicine and Women).

H

Halkett, Anne (1623–1699)

Memoirist at the British royal court, author of devotional writings

Anne Halkett's three love affairs—one involving the married Colonel Bampfield—and her role in the daring 1648 escape of the Stuart heir apparent from St. James's Palace, figure prominently in her *Memoirs* and demonstrate its dual narrative threads of romantic and political intrigue. Written between 1677 and 1678, her largely secular autobiography contains some precursors of the early novel, including naturalistic dialogue and a distinctly self-conscious literary style and structure. It also demonstrates traits of an apology as she contextualizes and explains her actions. Known mainly for her *Memoirs* and from a posthumous biography entitled *The Life of the Lady Halkett* (1701), Anne Halkett neé Murray also wrote twenty-one devotional manuscripts and other pious texts including *Instructions for Youth,* some of which were published posthumously with her 1701 biography.

Anne Halkett's parents, Thomas and Jane Murray, were tutor and governess for the royal family. In her *Memoirs,* Halkett explains that her mother "paid masters for teaching my sister and mee to writte, speake French, play lute and virginalls, and dance, and kept a gentlewoman to teach us all kinds of needleworke."

The tripartite structure of Lady Halkett's autobiography, written about her life from 1623 to 1656, reflects the three significant romantic relationships in her life: Thomas Howard, Colonel Joseph Bampfield, and James Halkett. She narrates her relationship with Thomas Howard, which was forbidden by her mother because of his higher rank as the future Lord Howard of Escrick. In 1648, Colonel Joseph Bampfield enlisted her help in disguising the future James II in women's clothing during the heir apparent's escape from St. James's Palace. United by their Royalist cause, Anne Halkett and Bampfield became romantically involved, although she remained uncertain about his marital status for over six years. Guilt ridden, she severed their relationship when she discovered that he was not a widower as he had claimed.

In her *Memoirs,* Halkett mentions briefly that she treated injured soldiers and the poor, but *The Life of the Lady Halkett* highlights this aspect of her life: "She became very famous and helpful to many, both Poor and Rich (though it was mainly, with respect to the Poor, that She undertook that practice)." Her *Memoirs* conclude in 1656 when, after a four-year courtship, she married Sir John Halkett.

Marlo Belschner

Bibliography
Primary Work
Loftis, John, ed. *The Memoirs of Anne, Lady Halkett and Ann, Lady Fanshawe.* Oxford: Clarendon Press, 1979.
Secondary Work
Walker, Kim. "The Lives of Anne Halkett." In *Women Writing, 1550–1750.* Edited by Jo Wallwork and Paul Salzman, 133–149. Bundorra, Victoria, Australia: Meridian, 2001.

Henrietta Maria (1609–1669)

French-born wife of Charles I of England, mother of Charles II, champion of Roman Catholicism in England, patron of the theater, founder of a convent in France

Henrietta Maria de Bourbon, born 25 November 1609, was the youngest child of Henri IV of France and Marie de Médicis. Her brother was crowned Louis XIII of France upon their father's death in 1610. Henrietta

Henrietta Maria de Bourbon, wife of Charles I of England and mother of Charles II; champion of Roman Catholicism. Painting by Anthony van Dyck. (Alinari Archives/ Corbis)

Maria married Charles I of England in 1625. During Charles's reign, she served as patron for English Roman Catholics, sponsored and performed in masques and ballets at court, and maintained correspondence with politicians and religious officials throughout Europe, including the pope and the royal family of France.

The English Civil War began in 1642; in 1643, Henrietta Maria rallied support for the Royalist cause in northern England. By 1644, civil unrest caused Henrietta Maria to move to France with her unmarried children; she raised money, troops, and arms for her husband's cause from leaders throughout Europe. Charles was beheaded in 1649, and Henrietta Maria

remained in France until the restoration of the English monarchy in 1660. During her lifetime, Henrietta Maria founded the Convent of the Visitation in Chaillot, France; she lived there from 1665 until her death on 10 September 1669.

Henrietta Maria bore ten children, six of whom survived infancy. Her first surviving son, Charles II, born 1630, was crowned king of England in 1660 at the restoration of the English monarchy; her second son, James II, born 1633, ruled from 1685 to 1688.

Karen Nelson

See also Convents; Religious Reform and Women; Theater and Women Actors, Playwrights, and Patrons.
Bibliography
Primary Work
Green, Mary Anne Everett, ed. *Letters of Queen Henrietta Maria, including Her Private Correspondence with Charles the First.* History of Women Microfilm Series. New Haven, CT: Research Publications, 1975. (Originally published in 1857.)
Secondary Work
Plowden, Alison. *Henrietta Maria: Charles I's Indomitable Queen.* Gloucestershire, UK: Sutton, 2001.

Hermaphrodite as Image and Idea

The Renaissance obsession with hermaphrodites, while owing a great deal in its articulation to Aristotle's work on generation (*The Generation of Animals*), to Plato's *Symposium,* and to Ovid's story of Hermaphroditus in the *Metamorphoses,* took some new directions that were crucial to the development of modern (particularly scientific) notions of sex and gender. Already in the Middle Ages, alchemy had developed as an alternative or supplemental system of thought to the official Catholic tradition, both theological and medical. By the mid-sixteenth century, the hermaphrodite had become a central figure in major alchemical treatises such as the *Rosarium philosophorum* (1550). This figure, a two-headed, generally double-sexed human, symbolizes the stage of conjunction, in which disparate elements are fused, only to be destroyed later by fire or corruption. Rather than perfection of the human form being expressed in the male, as in the Aristotelian scheme, perfection in alchemy is achieved through the conjunction of both sexes. It becomes clear in the course of the treatises focusing heavily on sex difference (among them, Clovis Hesteau de Nuysement's *Visions hermétiques,* in addition to the *Rosarium*) that each sex is imperfect in itself and that one is not superior to the other. Both sexes are equally necessary to the successful functioning of the alchemical process, which in philosophical alchemy is the refining of the soul rather than of metals. This effacing of the hierarchy that places the male over the female is significant for early modern societies, based as they are on the assumption of male superiority. This use of the hermaphrodite on a spiritual plane in philosophical alchemy makes it a transcendent figure rather than a monster, and this positive depiction reflects the Platonic tradition of the androgyne. Although comic at its inception, as Aristophanes, in the *Symposium,* describes it as a rounded being cartwheeling about on its arms and legs, the androgyne becomes a serious image of physical and spiritual wholeness and perfection.

Medical treatises of the Renaissance explore the hermaphrodite's status as a monstrous form, falling into the Aristotelian category of excess. But most of these treatises represent the hermaphrodite as human and natural rather than as some subhuman or supernatural monstrosity (as they were considered in ancient Rome). A number of authors—Ambroise Paré, Caspar Bauhin, and Jacques Duval, among others—represent early stirrings of empirical science, calling for direct observation of the ambiguously gendered body and finding a wide range of manifestations of this ambiguity. This is particularly true in the work of Bauhin, a professor of anatomy at the University of Basel, and of Jacques Duval, a surgeon trying to rival the professors of the Sorbonne. These findings call into question the supposedly clear-cut distinc-

tion between male and female, previously elaborated by legal and religious institutions. Still, these treatises are hemmed in by legal strictures concerning hermaphroditism, according to which a hermaphrodite must be designated as male or female. While clinical observations indicated that this distinction was not always clear, social norms dictated that it be made clear, by means of dress, behavior, and carefully established social status (professions and trades permissible for one sex but not the other, participation in the church hierarchy and in religious ceremonies and events, and so on).

While actual instances of hermaphroditism were few, hermaphrodites had a strong hold on the Renaissance imagination, in part because of the alchemical/Platonic hermaphrodite and in part because of the social, even political implications of this figure of ambiguous sex. The hermaphrodite surfaces in court poetry and art, as well as in political pamphlets in Italy, Germany, and France throughout the sixteenth century, appearing much later in similar works in England. A very sophisticated, well-focused campaign of character assassination against Henri III of France uses accusations of homosexuality and bisexuality, linking these accusations to the figure of the hermaphrodite. Eventually, long after Henri's assassination in 1589, a satirical novel written about his court, *L'Isle des hermaphrodites* (The Island of Hermaphrodites), is published (1605), uniting accusations of social disruption, thievery, even murder, with ambiguous sex. Thus, the Renaissance comes full circle to the Aristotelian hermaphrodite as monster of excess. Although Joseph Hall's *Mundus alter et idem* (Another World and Yet the Same, also 1605) presents a dysfunctional Hermaphroditica Island, which in certain points resembles the English court, systematic use of the hermaphrodite for political purposes in England is not adopted until the period preceding the English Revolution. This material follows the same strange trajectory as that directed against Henri III: images of Charles and Henrietta Maria as the perfect spiritual hermaphrodite degenerate into accusations of hermaphroditic bisexuality. By the time of Gabriel de Foigny's *La Terre australe connue* (The Australian Land Revealed, 1676), an account of a utopia inhabited only by hermaphrodites, this figure has lost much of its political force.

The variety of materials published in this period on the subject of hermaphrodites, or prominently featuring them, reveals the dual use of the figure to reinforce social and sexual norms (in many medical treatises and political pamphlets) and to question those norms (in a number of alchemical treatises in particular). Many texts presenting the hermaphrodite suggest that all beings that do not fit into clearly defined ideals of what is masculine and feminine are monstrous, that is, outside the norms of nature. But some texts, particularly discussions of animals believed to be hermaphroditic, portray this ambiguity as natural (Bauhin 1614, Duval 1612). Alchemical texts see transcendence of sexual difference as crucial to the spiritual aspect of the alchemical process. While we now perceive these texts as marginal, hundreds of these treatises were written in this period, and they were extensively published and widely distributed. Their alternative view of the world and of sexual difference was thus far more popular than we are now led to believe. Their suppression by official culture, particularly by the Catholic church, might explain the current obscurity of these texts. The political satires concerning Henri III are revived during the reign of Louis XV; likewise, a resurgence of interest in alchemical texts occurs in the pre-Revolutionary period in France. Most significantly, these texts concerning hermaphrodites embody a debate over the relationship between sexual and gender roles that has been reprised in our own time: what can be seen as "innate" or natural, and what is inculcated by education and social norms?

Kathleen Long

See also Androgyne; Masculinity, Femininity, and Gender; Transvestism.

Bibliography
Primary Works
Aristotle. *On the Generation of Animals.* In *The Complete Works of Aristotle.* Vol. 1. Edited by Jonathan Barnes, 1111–1218. Bollingen Series. Princeton, NJ: Princeton University Press, 1984.

Artus, Thomas. *Description de l'Isle des Hermaphrodites, nouvellemement descouverte.* Edited by Claude Gilbert Dubois. Geneva: Droz, 1996.

Bauhin, Caspar. *De hermaphroditorum monstrosorumque partuum natura ex Theologorum, Jureconsultorumque, Medicorum, Philosophorum, et Rabbinorum sententia libri duo.* Oppenheim: Galleri, De Bry, 1614. (Reprint of the 1600 Frankfurt edition.)

Duval, Jacques. *Des Hermaphrodits, accouchemens de femmes, et traitement qui est requis pour les relever en santé.* Rouen: David Geuffroy, 1612.

Foigny, Gabriel de. *La Terre Australe Connue.* Edited by Pierre Ronzeaud. Paris: Société des textes français modernes, 1990.

Hall, Joseph. *Another World and Yet the Same: Bishop Joseph Hall's "Mundus alter et idem."* Edited and translated by John Millar Wands. New Haven, CT: Yale University Press, 1981.

Maier, Michael. *Atalanta fugiens.* Translated by Joscelyn Godwin. Grand Rapids, MI: Phanes Press, 1989.

Paré, Ambroise. *On Monsters and Marvels.* Translated by Janis L. Pallister. Chicago: University of Chicago Press, 1982.

Rosarium philosophorum. Anonymous English translation from the eighteenth century, made available by Adam McLean in his "Alchemy Virtual Library" at http://www.colloquium.co.uk/alchemy/home.html.

Rosarium philosophorum. Edited by Joachim Telle. Weinheim: VCH, 1992. (Originally printed in Frankfurt, 1550.)

Secondary Works
Cameron, Keith. *Henri III: A Maligned or Malignant King? (Aspects of the Satirical Iconography of Henri de Valois).* Exeter, UK: University of Exeter, 1978.

Daston, Lorraine, and Katharine Park. "The Hermaphrodite and the Orders of Nature: Sexual Ambiguity in Early Modern France." *Gay and Lesbian Quarterly* 1 (1995): 419–438.

Daston, Lorraine, and Katharine Park. "Hermaphrodites in Renaissance France." *Critical Matrix* 1 (1985): 1–19.

Dubois, Claude Gilbert. *L'Utopie hermaphrodite: La Terre Australe Connue de Gabriel de Foigny.* Marseille: Publications de C.M.R., 17, 1981.

Gilbert, Ruth. *Early Modern Hermaphrodites: Sex and Other Stories.* New York: Palgrave, 2002.

Laqueur, Thomas. *Making Sex: The Body and Gender from the Greeks to Freud.* Cambridge, MA: Harvard University Press, 1990.

Poirier, Guy. *L'Homosexualité dans l'imaginaire de la Renaissance.* Paris: Champion, 1996.

Randall, Catharine. "A Surplus of Significance: Hermaphrodites in Early Modern France." *French Forum* 19 (1994): 17–35.

Rothstein, Marian. "Mutations of the Androgyne: Its Functions in Early Modern French Literature." *Sixteenth Century Journal* 34 (2): 409–438.

Yavneh, Naomi. "The Spiritual Eroticism of Leone's Hermaphrodite." In *Playing with Gender: A Renaissance Pursuit.* Edited by Jean Brink, Maryanne C. Horowitz, and Allison Coudert, 85–98. Urbana and Chicago: University of Illinois Press, 1991.

Catherine Howard, fifth wife of King Henry VIII of England. Portrait by unknown artist. (Corel)

Hospital Administration. *See* the subheading Hospital Administration and Nursing as Careers for Women (under Medicine and Women).

Howard, Catherine (ca. 1522–1542)

Fifth wife of King Henry VIII, executed in the Tower of London

After an unsuccessful fourth marriage to Anne of Cleves, Henry turned his attention to the eighteen-year-old Catherine Howard. Catherine was descended from Edward I and was a first cousin of Henry VIII's second wife, Anne Boleyn. Although Catherine was a part of the powerful Howard family, she had grown up far away from the Tudor court. It appears that, although her father had been knighted, he was not ambitious and his career floundered. Catherine's mother died when she was very young, and she was raised in the household of her stepgrandmother, Agnes, duchess of Norfolk, who was an influential figure at court. Catherine could read and write, though she had received little education. Socially, she was naïve. While in the duchess's household,

Catherine had a number of romances, which, though fairly well-known at the time, were kept from Henry VIII. Her most famous relationship was with Thomas Culpepper, a member of Henry VIII's privy chamber. This romance would have repercussions since Catherine and Culpepper would rekindle it during her marriage to Henry VIII.

Catherine had met Henry VIII while she was in the household of his fourth wife, Anne of Cleves. Bitterly dissatisfied with Anne, he divorced her to marry Catherine. By the time of their marriage in 1540, Henry VIII was grossly overweight and his health was deteriorating. His leg was ulcerated, making it difficult for him to walk. Catherine, a young woman in her late teens or early twenties, turned to her former lover, Thomas Culpepper, for comfort. While touring northern England with Henry VIII, Catherine and Thomas carried on a fairly public love affair. When Henry learned of

Catherine's conduct both before and during their marriage, he had her former and current lovers arrested and tortured in the Tower of London. Catherine was found guilty of adultery and treason. She was executed on 13 February 1542.

Shawndra Holderby

See also Anne of Cleves; Boleyn, Anne; Catherine of Aragon; Parr, Katherine.

Bibliography

Fraser, Antonia. *The Wives of Henry VIII.* New York: Alfred A. Knopf, 1992.

Guy, John. *Tudor England.* Oxford: Oxford University Press, 1990.

Jansen, Sharon. *The Monstrous Regiment of Women: Female Rulers in Early Modern Europe.* New York: Palgrave Macmillan, 2002.

Loades, David. *Henry VIII and His Queens.* Gloucester, UK: Sutton, 2000.

Starkey, David. *Six Wives: The Queens of Henry VIII.* New York: Harper Collins, 2003.

Howard, Frances (1590–1632)

Society woman and heiress charged with homicide and political intrigue at the court of King James I

At fifteen, Frances Howard, daughter of Thomas Howard, first earl of Suffolk, wed fourteen-year-old Robert Devereux, third earl of Essex, in a lavish event at Whitehall before King James I of England. In typical fashion for aristocrats, the marriage was a political alliance rather than a joining of lovers. In fact, the newlyweds were judged too young to cohabit, and Essex was sent away to Europe. While her husband was abroad, Frances Howard became active at James's court. On Essex's return in 1609, the two began life as a married couple, but the match was unsuccessful. Howard claimed that Essex was incapable of having sexual relations with her. During this time, she also developed a romantic relationship with Robert Carr, viscount Rochester (later the earl of Somerset) and a favorite of James. The union between Howard and Essex was annulled in September 1613.

Howard, who wanted to marry Robert Carr, became entangled in a plot involving the imprisonment and eventual death of Sir Thomas Overbury, once Carr's close friend and advisor. Overbury disapproved of Carr's forthcoming marriage, perhaps fearing he would lose influence over his friend. Howard and Carr came to view Overbury as the one obstacle to their wedding and also their political ambitions. Through political ill fortune and with Carr's encouragement, Overbury was arrested and taken away to the Tower of London where in a short time he died. Howard and her lover Carr were married in December 1613, just ten days after Overbury's death.

Approximately two years later, when Carr was losing favor with James, an investigation was mounted revealing that Overbury had not died of natural causes but was poisoned. Many at court believed Frances Howard was the instigator of the murder. Carr, Howard, and a number of assumed accomplices were tried and convicted of the murder of Thomas Overbury. Howard pled guilty as charged. Carr claimed to be innocent but was also found guilty. The other alleged accomplices were executed, but the king officially pardoned both Howard and Carr, though they were not allowed to return to court. Howard died in 1632, while her husband survived her.

Because of the sensational nature of the Frances Howard story and its implications as a case study in the partisan and sexual politics of Jacobean England, historians and gender scholars have recently reopened the case. Was Howard in fact guilty of the homicide? Was the traditional view of her as a callous "villainess" a fair assessment? Is it possible that the man who became her husband set her up? Or was she simply a victim of the misogyny of her social class and time?

Amy Gant

Bibliography

Bellany, Alastair. "Carr, Robert, Earl of Somerset (1585/6?–1645)." *Oxford Dictionary of National Biography.* Oxford: Oxford University Press, 2004. Available at: http://0-www.oxforddnb .com.library.unl.edu:80/view/article/4754. Accessed 1 April 2006.

Bellany, Alastair. "Howard, Frances, Countess of Somerset (1590–1632)." *Oxford Dictionary of National Biography.* Oxford: Oxford University Press, 2004. Available at: http://0-www .oxforddnb.com.library.unl.edu:80/view/ article/53028. Accessed 21 Feb 2006.

Lindley, David. *The Trials of Frances Howard: Fact and Fiction at the Court of King James.* New York: Routledge, 1993.

Morrill, John. "Devereux, Robert, Third Earl of Essex (1591–1646)." *Oxford Dictionary of National Biography.* Oxford: Oxford University Press, 2004. Available at: http://0-www .oxforddnb.com.library.unl.edu:80/view/ article/7566. Accessed 21 Feb 2006.

Somerset, Anne. *Unnatural Murder: Poison at the Court of James I.* London: Weidenfeld and Nicolson, 1997.

Humanism. *See* Education, Humanism, and Women.

I

Inglis, Esther (1571—1624)

Calligrapher, miniaturist, and manuscript illuminator
One of the few women in early modern England who can be considered a professional artist, Esther Inglis was a meticulous, gifted calligrapher and miniaturist; during her career she produced over fifty extant manuscripts, which she presented to members of the monarchy and aristocracy in the hope of patronage.

Inglis's parents were French Huguenots who had fled the religious persecution of their homeland around 1570. They moved to Scotland and established a French school in Edinburgh. Though we know little about Inglis's childhood, the fine education and training in calligraphy she received from her parents is evident. In her twenties she married a minister, Bartholomew Kello, who was employed as a scrivener by King James VI of Scotland and who acted as a messenger during the transition between the end of Elizabeth's reign and James's ascension to the English throne. Inglis and her husband moved to England in 1604, and Kello assumed a rectorship in Essex. They had six children, four of whom survived to adulthood; though their marriage was plagued by poverty, there is evidence that it was an otherwise happy relationship.

For the purposes of her work, Esther did not assume her husband's last name; she anglicized her father's name, Langlois, to Inglish, or Inglis. Over her career, she dedicated her works to various powerful patrons, including Queen Elizabeth, King James, Prince Henry, Prince Charles, the Earl of Essex, and members of the Sidney and Herbert families. Most of the texts she illustrated comprise religious verses written or transcribed by Kello; what is most remarkable about these books is their artistic rendering: the books display intricate borders and are bound in leather, silk, or velvet. They are small and delicate, often only a few inches wide. The often microscopic calligraphy is detailed and exquisite. Also notable is the deliberate assertion of self-identity that accompanies these works. In the dedications to several of the books, Inglis employs the modesty topos, apologizing for assuming to present her work to the public since she is only a woman; yet she also takes obvious pride in her work, concluding many manuscripts with a self-portrait and with the motto, *Vive la plume!* Inglis's husband may have used some of her books to gain access to circles of power in his service to the government.

Inglis received recompense for some of her manuscripts, but she was still in debt when she died in 1624. Her portrait, painted in 1595, now hangs in the Scottish National Portrait Gallery.

Jo Eldridge Carney

See also Art and Women; Fetti, Lucrina; Killigrew, Anne; Nelli, Plauilla; Work and Women.

Bibliography

Frye, Susan. "Materializing Authorship in Esther Inglis's Books." *Journal of Medieval and Early Modern Studies* 32, no. 3 (2002): 469–491.

Ziegler, Georgianna. " 'More Than Feminine Boldness': The Gift Books of Esther Inglis." In *Women, Writing, and the Reproduction of Culture.* Pages 19–37. Syracuse, NY: Syracuse University Press, 2000.

J

Joan of Arc (Jeanne d'Arc; ca. 1412–1431)

French national heroine

Joan was born to reasonably well-off peasants (her father held various official posts), in the rural village of Domremy, Lorraine province, France, during the last phase of the Hundred Years War. Educated by her mother in the conventional womanly domestic tasks and prayers, Joan's intelligence and piety were nurtured within an oral, agrarian culture rather than a literate, urban one, although she could sign her name. Very pious and patriotic, even by the standards of simple border province people,

at age twelve or so, she says she first experienced the voices and visions of three popular saints: Michael, Catherine, and Margaret—commanding her to deliver France from English domination and have the Dauphin (Charles VII) crowned as rightful king. Later, having persuaded the Dauphin and his theologians to accept her knightly attire and her mission as divinely—not satanically—inspired, Joan fulfilled her mandate between May (Orléans victory) and July of 1429 (Reims coronation), as celebrated by Christine de Pizan, among others. Additional victories followed but so did defeat, as Charles gradually abandoned

Medieval tapestry depicting the arrival of Joan of Arc at the Chinon Castle. Illustration by unknown artist. (Bettmann/Corbis)

her for political reasons. Pro-English forces captured her at Compiègne in May 1430, then tried and burned her a year later at Rouen. Charles, after completing Joan's work of expelling the English, with papal accord engineered her rehabilitation by 1456, again for his political ends. Although she seems quintessentially medieval, Joan's arguably Renaissance traits include her nationalistic vision of France and skill at self-fashioning through her dress, emblems, letters, and trial testimony: as *La Pucelle* (The Maid—she never called herself Jeanne d'Arc), virginal instrument of France's redemption. She was canonized in 1920.

Nadia Margolis

See also Amazons; Pizan, Christine de.

Bibliography

Primary Works

Fraioli, Deborah A. *Joan of Arc and the Hundred Years War.* Westport, CT, and London: Greenwood Press, 2005.

Hobbins, Daniel, trans. *The Trial of Joan of Arc.* Cambridge, MA: Harvard University Press, 2005.

Taylor, Craig, ed. and trans. *Joan of Arc, La Pucelle: Selected Sources.* Manchester, UK, and New York: Manchester University Press, 2006.

Secondary Works

Beaune, Colette. *Jeanne d'Arc.* Paris: Perrin, 2004.

Margolis, Nadia. *Joan of Arc in History, Literature and Film: A Select, Annotated Bibliography.* New York and London: Garland, 1990.

Jussie, Jeanne de (1503–1561)

Chronicler of the Genevan Reformation

Jeanne de Jussie was born in Jussy-l'Évêque, near Geneva, in 1503. She attended school in Geneva and entered the Convent of St. Clare there in 1521, where she soon became the official *écrivaine* (writer and record keeper). She is best-known for her lively chronicle of the turbulent years leading up to Geneva's adoption of the Protestant Reformation in 1536. In addition to events in her own convent (including a visit by Marie Dentière, author of the *Epistre tresutile* [1539]), Jussie narrates struggles for power between Geneva and Savoy, Geneva's alliance with the Swiss cantons of Bern and Fribourg in 1526 (the *Combourgeoisie*), the expulsion of the bishop in 1533, and the arrival of Reformer Guillaume Farel in 1534. Her story culminates in her convent's departure from Geneva and resettlement in Annecy in 1535. Jussie became abbess in 1548 and died in 1561. Her convent remained in Annecy until its dissolution in 1793. Jussie's chronicle was first published in 1611 by the Frères Du Four in Chambéry as *Le levain du calvinisme,* although John Calvin, who arrived in Geneva in 1536, does not appear in the text. It was published nine times from the sixteenth through nineteenth centuries, including translations into Italian and German. A modern critical edition was published in 1996.

Carrie Klaus

See also Convents; Literary Culture and Women; Religious Reform and Women.

Bibliography

Primary Work

Jussie, Jeanne de. *Petite chronique.* Edited by Helmut Feld. Mainz: von Zabern, 1996.

Secondary Works

Backus, Irena. "Les clarisses de la rue Verdaine / The Poor Clares of the Rue Verdaine." In *Le guide des femmes disparues* (Forgotten Women of Geneva). Edited by Anne-Marie Käppeli, 20–39. Geneva: Metropolis, 1993.

Lazard, Madeleine. "Deux sœurs ennemis, Marie Dentière et Jeanne de Jussie: Nonnes et Réformées à Genève." In *Les Réformes: enracinement socio-culturel.* Edited by Bernard Chevalier and Robert Sauzet, 239–249. Paris: Éditions de la Maisnie, 1985.

Roth, Henri. "Une femme auteur du 16ᵉ siècle: Jeanne de Jussie." *Revue du Vieux Genève* 19 (1989): 5–13.

K

Killigrew, Anne (1660–1685)

Poet and painter of pastoral and antipastoral scenes
Though a member of a family well connected to court circles from early Tudor times until the end of the seventeenth century, few particulars are known about Anne Killigrew. Born in London, daughter of Dr. Henry Killigrew who became chaplain to James II and master of the Savoy (hospital), she became one of Mary of Modena's maids of honor. Mary, the wife of James, brother of Charles II, cultivated a literary culture at court, encouraging her attendants to write, paint, and participate in masques. Killigrew excelled in poetry and painting, the twin talents extolled extravagantly by John Dryden in the ode he wrote to accompany the collection of her poems compiled for publication shortly after her death to smallpox. The detailed descriptions of landscape in her poetry, dotted with classical ruins and gloomy groves, receive literal visualization in her paintings, providing symbolic backdrops for her court portraits. In her poems, including occasional and pastoral verses, as well as three additional works probably from her pen, Killigrew claims a literary and moral kinship with Orinda (Katherine Philips, the royalist poet and translator who became her inspiration), a connection drawn also by Dryden because of the similarity of their deaths.

Although Killigrew did not herself experience the violence of the civil wars and royal execution or turmoil of the interregnum, her poetry registers a keen disapproval of warlike behavior. Like her predecessor Philips, Killigrew's rejection of a turbulent male world of military action and political upheaval leads her into an alternative literary world of a primarily female pastoral community, but unlike Philips, Killigrew's pastoral settings are not idealized moral retreats where platonic friendship provides a soothing antidote to economic and political distress. Death appears to be the only real retreat. Killigrew's pastoral dialogues and complaints are set in infernal and distinctly antipastoral landscapes, although they also appeal to virtue and reason to restore harmony. Her earliest poem in the collection is an epic fragment celebrating Alexander the Great, but her second poem rejects the heroic genre in favor of a lyrical voice singing the praises of heavenly beauty embodied in a strong female figure, the good and gracious queen. Her shift from praising a military male model to a female model of inward virtue becomes a thematic focus for many of her poems. In several pastoral poems, Killigrew alludes to classical myth and scripture in her expressions of concern for female chastity in the face of male inconstancy, in one case voicing Penelope's fear of Ulysses' faithlessness. Having the authorship of some of her poems questioned, Killigrew responded in verse to defend her integrity, voicing the difficulties faced by ambitious women writers.

Nancy Hayes

See also Anguissola, Sofonisba; Art and Women; Inglis, Esther; Literary Culture and Women.

Bibliography

Primary Work

Killigrew, Anne. *Poems.* Introduction by Richard Morton. Gainesville, FL: Scholars' Facsimiles and Reprints, 1967.

Secondary Works

Barash, Carol. *English Women's Poetry, 1649–1714: Politics, Community, and Linguistic Authority.* Oxford: Clarendon Press, 1996.

Williamson, Marilyn. *Raising Their Voices: British Women Writers, 1650–1750.* Detroit, MI: Wayne State University Press, 1990.

L

Labé, Louise (ca. 1520–1566)

A rope maker's daughter, the leading figure in the literary culture of mid-sixteenth-century Lyon, prolific poet, feminist writer

Louise Labé was born sometime between 1520 and 1522 into a well-to-do bourgeois family in Lyon. She lived her entire life in or around this city, which was the cultural center of France during the first half of the sixteenth century, thanks to its commercial dynamism, its role as a center of humanist writing and publishing, and its close ties with neighboring Renaissance Italy. Labé was the daughter of a prominent Lyonnais rope maker, Pierre Charly, and his second wife, Etiennette Roybet. Following Etiennette's premature death in 1523, Pierre promptly remarried, and Labé was therefore raised by her father and her stepmother, Antoinette Taillard. Pierre himself had adopted the name Labé upon his first marriage to Guillemette Humbert, since through this union he assumed ownership of a property named Labé (or L'Abbé) that his wife had inherited from an earlier marriage. Louise Labé maintained this "acquired" family name throughout her life.

Louise Labé, poet and leader in the literary culture of mid-sixteenth-century Lyon. Portrait by Pierre Woeiriot de Bouzey. Bibliotheque Nationale, Paris, France. (Giraudon/ The Bridgeman Art Library)

Although Pierre Labé could not read or write himself, he had his daughter educated not only in "womanly" activities, such as sewing and music, but also, like her brothers, in Classical and modern languages and in military-style sports, such as fencing and horsemanship. It appears that some of Labé's schooling took place at a local convent, where she was able not only to advance her studies with clerical tutors, but also to develop friendships with noblewomen. Indeed, far from the Sorbonne and the Paris court, and energized by the active presence of bourgeois merchants in civic life, Lyonnais society took a flexible stance in respect to certain conventional class and gender rules, namely, that women had to be confined to the domestic sphere.

Paternally arranged marriages, of course, nevertheless remained the norm, and sometime between 1542 and 1544, Labé became the bride of Ennemond Perrin, a bourgeois rope maker in her father's circles who was much older than she. Yet the progressive social strand of Lyon's urban culture made it possible for a gifted woman neither born nor married into the aristocracy to take part in the intellectual community of the city and, more crucially, to write and publish. Labé courageously took advantage of the creative opportunities that Lyon offered her. She hosted and kept company with highly reputed humanists and poets who either resided in or frequented Lyon, among them Maurice Scève and his female collaborator Pernette du Guillet, Clément Marot, Joachim Du Bellay, and Pierre de Ronsard. Her volume of complete works, including a now well-known dedicatory letter, a long mythological prose dialogue, three elegies, and twenty-four celebrated sonnets, in addition to twenty-four more poems written in honor of Labé by her male literary peers, was published in 1555 by Jean De Tournes, one of the premier humanist printers of early modern Europe. The book enjoyed immediate success and was reprinted in three separate editions only one year later. Labé herself, however, appears to have withdrawn from public life around 1557, when she moved to a country estate outside Lyon. Her husband died in the early 1560s, and she survived him by only a few years, passing away in 1566 with little public notice.

Following her death, Labé's legacy became a mixed and conflicted affair. The very independence and intellectual opportunity that she seized from her education and from Lyonnais society, coupled with the social assertiveness and erotic passion of her writings, exposed her not only to admiration, but also to mocking criticism for her supposed penchant for traditionally male activities and to invidious speculation over what may have been her premarital and extramarital love life. This posthumous creation of Louise Labé as *legend* fed her steadily ongoing notoriety, but to a certain extent also drew attention away from her role in Lyon as poet, public intellectual, and social innovator— a phenomenon that critical studies over the past thirty years have finally reversed.

The long-standing duality of Louise Labé's legacy is not surprising when one examines the character and range of her works. In all of them, she situates herself at the heart of the *querelle des femmes,* the long-standing and divisive debate about female nature and the proper roles of women in domestic and social domains. And however progressive her educational and creative milieu may have been, her life and career clearly went counter to the typical Renaissance model of appropriate female behavior and self-expression; her entire body of work sets forth a vision of equality and self-empowerment for women both in society and in interpersonal relationships.

The ninety-line prefatory letter that opens Labé's volume, dedicated to Clémence de Bourges, an aristocratic acquaintance probably made at the convent that both young women attended, has become a fundamental document advancing the issues and aspirations of early modern feminism. Labé first implicitly recognizes the crucial benefits of her own "privileged" schooling by fervently advocating broader availability of education for women, and by urging her female peers, in the most famous sentence of the preface, "to raise their minds a bit above their distaffs and spindles" (*d'eslever un peu leurs esprits par-dessus leurs quenoilles et fuseaus*) so that they can serve in *mutual* partnership with men in private and public life. This plea for equality and reciprocity between women and men is followed by the letter's second fervent entreaty: an appeal to women not only to study but to write, since the act of writing stimulates a process of inward examination and understanding leading finally to a deeper sense of individual selfhood, one that serves as a stronghold in the face of the illusions and disappointments of personal experience.

The feminist assertions of the dedicatory letter provide the polemic context for Labé's other, much longer prose work, a more than two-thousand-line mythological play in prose entitled *The Debate of Folly and Love*. Structured in five "discourses" (loosely corresponding to acts), the *Debate* combines the genres of mythological allegory, Medieval-Renaissance dialogue, and Erasmian satire to restage the letter's key precept of male-female reciprocity by means of an ingenious theatrical enactment: a literal drama pitting against one another the god of Love (*Amour,* or Cupid) and the goddess of Folly (*Folie*) in a dispute over their respective social ranks and roles. Here Labé's controversial critique of conventional male privilege and traditional male-female relations is cleverly communicated through comic argumentative exchanges between the two protagonists, as well as in the witty philosophical speeches given by each character's legal counsel (the gods Apollo and Mercury, respectively) when the couple's quarrel is referred to Jupiter's court of law. By having Jupiter hand down a verdict in which Love and Folly are commanded to coexist peaceably and to recognize their inevitable interdependency, Labé suggests the futility of positing any simplified or inflexible view of gendered relations, whether in public life, or in the arena of romantic or erotic love that forms the inspiration of her own lyric verse.

It is Labé's love poetry—her three hundred-line elegies and twenty-four sonnets (the first of which is written in Italian)—that has gained the greatest acclaim and sealed her ongoing position in the French literary canon. Her verse bears the combined marks of Classical, native French, and Italian influences, among them the famed Latin elegists Propertius, Tibullus, and Ovid; the early French Renaissance court poet, Clément Marot; the fifteenth- and sixteenth-century Florentine neo-Platonists, especially Marsilio Ficino; and, above all, the towering lyric poet of the Italian Renaissance, Francesco Petrarch (1304–1374) and his great French male followers, Maurice Scève, Joachim Du Bellay, and Pierre de Ronsard. When Labé composed and published her verse, the Petrarchan tradition in France was at its height, as poets imitated and responded to how the Italian giant conceptualized the male-female love experience through the perspective of his male speaker in the *Canzoniere.* Stricken by the love of an inaccessible woman (the celebrated Laura), the Petrarchan speaker recounts obsessively the conflicted journey of his spiritual struggles, wrestling to overcome a desire he views as errant and sinful. In this psychic

drama, the female beloved, far from a flesh and blood being, emerges rather as an abstract catalyst fueling the speaker's self-absorption.

When Labé takes up the Petrarchan tradition, her female speaker is clearly no longer the abstract object of male desire, but rather a self-declared subject of desire who reveals her own journey through the trials of love. While recasting in her elegies and sonnets numerous Petrarchan themes and images, she insists on the vital perpetuity of a desire—however painful—which is perceived as so precious, that, in the words of her opening Italian sonnet, she could not live without "the desire so dear to me, / That I cannot live without it, lest I die" (*el desir si caro, / Che mancar non potrà ch'i' non mi muoia*). This desire never provokes in Labé's speaker—as it does in Petrarch's—an obsession with self, since even in her moments of isolation, she reaches out to a broader community of women with an appeal and a promise for *mutual* empathy and support, as in her moving plea in the first elegy: "Women who read these words, / sigh with me for the sorrows you have heard! / Maybe one day I'll do the same for you" (*Dames, qui les lirez, / De mes regrets avec moy soupirez. / Possible, un jour je feray le semblable*).

Labé likewise rejects the privilege given to tortured internal conflict and futile resignation in the Petrarchan male speaker as well as his prayerful anticipation of spiritual union with the beloved after death as the only foreseeable resolution to his crisis. Instead, her speaker fashions scenes—whether longed-for, remembered, or real—in which earthly union, communication, and reciprocity between male and female lovers are realized. Thus, in her most famous sonnet 18, "Kiss Me Again" (*Baise m'encor*), she links the passionately accelerating kisses exchanged with her lover to an interconnected life mutually lived and enjoyed: "and we'll each have two loving lives to tend: / one in our single self, one in our friend" (*Lors double vie à chacun en suivra. / Chacun en soy et son ami vivra*). By envisioning such scenes of union and communion, Labé transforms the Petrarchan notion of desire as a sinful, destabilizing drive into a life-affirming force that, despite the inevitable risks of pain, unattainability, and loss, can produce a mutually fulfilling love relationship with another person as well as a deeper knowledge and understanding of self. Through the itinerary traced in her love poetry, then, Louise Labé proposes an ontological model of an ultimately stable and unified human being who—whatever the vicissitudes of reality—continues to affirm the potential of a fulfilling partnership with another loved human being on this earth.

Deborah Lesko Baker

See also Feminism in the Renaissance; Guillet, Pernette du; the subheadings Salons, Salonnières, and Women Writers; Sonnet Writing (under Literary Culture and Women); Querelles des Femmes.

Bibliography

Primary Works

Lesko Baker, Deborah, and Annie Finch, ed. and trans. *Louise Labé. Collected Poetry and Prose: A Bilingual Edition.* Other Voice Series. Edited with critical introductions and prose translation by Deborah Lesko Baker. Poetry translation by Annie Finch. Chicago: University of Chicago Press, 2006.

Rigolot, François, ed. *Louise Labé: Œuvres complètes.* 2nd ed. Paris: Flammarion, 2004.

Secondary Works

Alonso, Béatrice, and Eliane Viennot, eds. *Louise Labé 2005.* Collection "L'école du genre," special publication no. 1. Saint-Eienne, France: Publications Universitaires de Saint-Etienne, 2004.

Berriot, Karine. *Louise Labé: La Belle Rebelle et le François nouveau, siuvi des Œuvres complètes.* Paris: Seuil, 1985.

Cameron, Keith. *Louise Labé: Feminist and Poet of the Renaissance.* Women's Series. New York: Berg, 1990.

Demerson, Guy, ed. *Louise Labé: Les voix du lyrisme.* Paris: Éditions du CNRS, 1990.

Jones, Ann Rosalind. *The Currency of Eros: Women's Love Lyric in Europe, 1540–1620.* Bloomington: Indiana University Press, 1990.

Lazard, Madeleine. *Louise Labé.* Paris: Fayard, 2004.

Larsen, Anne R., and Colette H. Winn, ed. *Renaissance Women Writers. French Texts/American Contexts.* Detroit, MI: Wayne State University Press, 1994.

Lesko Baker, Deborah. *The Subject of Desire: Petrarchan Poetics and the Female Voice in Louise Labé.* West Lafayette, IN: Purdue University Press, 1996.

Martin, Daniel. *Signes(s) d'Amante: L'agencement des Evvres de Louize Labé Lionnoize.* Paris: Honoré Champion, 1999.

Rigolot, François. *Louise Labé Lyonnaise, ou: La Renaissance au féminin.* Paris: Champion, 1997.

Yandell, Cathy. *Carpe Corpus: Time and Gender in Early Modern France.* Newark, NJ: University of Delaware Press, 2000

La Font, Jeanne de (ca. 1500–1532)

Noted classical scholar, patron, and French poet of Berry

As a writer, a protector of humanists, and a muse, Jeanne de la Font was to Berry what Anne Bégat was to Burgundy and Louise Labé to Lyons. With her French verse adaptation of Boccaccio's *Teseida* (which has mysteriously disappeared), she has been acclaimed by her contemporaries as a poet surpassing Sappho and whose talent has revealed that French women were capable of resurrecting the grandeur of Latin epic poetry. She may have given Queen Claude de France, Francis I's first wife, the idea to ask Anne de Graville to rewrite for her another French version inspired by the same Italian masterpiece.

In 1521, Jeanne, the only child of Jean de la Font (d. 1505) and Françoise Godard of Bourges, married Jacques Thiboust (1492–1555), notary and secretary to Francis I and author of a few administrative, literary, and devotional compositions. When the king of France gave the province of Berry to his sister, Marguerite de Navarre (Marguerite d'Angoulême), she took over his secretary as her own and arranged his marriage with Jeanne de la Font. The city of Bourges had been a religious center for over twenty years, thanks to the patronage of Jeanne de France (d. 1505), the daughter of Louis XI and repudiated wife of Louis XII, who had founded there Sainte-Marie's College and the Monastery of the Annonciade. With the help of the future queen of Navarre, Bourges became, like Paris and Lyons, a cultural center open to political and commercial ties with Italy. Although Marguerite did not reside often in Bourges, she attracted many humanists to the city in the 1520s on account of the renowned professors she appointed at the university. It is in this intellectual climate that Jeanne de la Font and Jacques Thiboust held a cenacle frequented by famous Neolatin and French poets like Jean Second, François Habert, Clément Marot, Charles Fontaine, Nicolas de Bourbon, Jean Milon, and Jean Salomon, who dedicated important literary and scientific works to the royal secretary or to his wife.

At her untimely death, Jeanne de la Font was celebrated in Greek, Latin, and French verse as a woman of great learning who knew all the secrets of French poetry. After Jacques died in 1555, Jacqueline, Jeanne, and Marie Thiboust, the couple's three surviving daughters (out of five children), continued their parents' patronage and literary salon. Jacqueline, born in 1524, had married Pierre Sardé in 1545, a lawyer and counselor who took over his father-in-law's function as secretary of the king. Her sister Jeanne married Jean Du Moulin, another local official. These learned daughters were celebrated by François Habert in his French epistles just as their mother had been by Jean Second in his Latin elegies. Such panegyric works give witness to these women's social and cultural importance in the province of Berry and show the high regard humanists had of their scientific knowledge, their language training, and their poetic performance.

Catherine M. Müller

See also Claude de France; Graville, Anne de; Labé, Louise; Marguerite de Navarre.
Bibliography
Primary Work
Second, Jean. *Ioannis Nicolaii Hagani Opera Omnia, emendatius et cum notis adhuc ineditis Petri Burmanni Secundi, denuo edita cura Petri Bosscha.* 2 vols. Leiden: S. et J. Luchtmans, 1821.
Secondary Works
Boyer, Hippolyte. *Un ménage littéraire en Berry au XVIe siècle. (Jacques Thiboust et Jeanne de La Font).* Bourges: Impr. de la Veuve Jollet-Souchois, 1859.
Müller, Catherine M. "Jeanne de la Font et Anne de Graville, translatrices de la Théséïde de Boccace au XVIe siècle." *Les Femmes et traduction du Moyen Âge au XVIIIe siècle.* Edited by Jean-Philippe Beaulieu. Montréal: Presses de l'Université d'Ottawa, 2004.

Lanyer, Aemilia Bassano (ca. 1569–1645)
English court poet and feminist

Born the daughter of Margaret Johnson and Baptista Bassano, a Venetian-born musician at the court of Elizabeth I, Aemilia Bassano Lanyer grew up in more privileged circumstances than most women of her class because, through her father, she enjoyed access to court circles. Much of what is known about Lanyer's life has been gleaned from the dedicatory poems and epistles in the *Salve Deus,* her major poetic work. Textual evidence suggests that, after her father's death on 11 April 1576, Aemilia benefited from a connection with Susan Montgomery, the countess of Kent, "The noble guide of my ungovern'd dayes" ("To the Ladie Susan" in Lanyer 1993, 18). Through her association with the countess, Aemilia would have had access to humanist works, enabling her to learn about rhetorical traditions as well as to become acquainted with Biblical and Classical texts.

A more private portrait of Aemilia Lanyer emerges from the diary entries of Simon Forman (1552–1611), an astrologer serving at the English court; however, Forman's frustrated sexual advances toward Lanyer may have skewed the information he recorded. A. L. Rowse's claim that the mysterious dark lady of William Shakespeare's *Sonnets* must have been none other than Aemilia Lanyer has been discredited by Woods as a "fantasy [that] has tended to obscure Lanyer as a poet" (Lanyer 1993, xix). What is certain is Lanyer's desire to regain the privileged status she once enjoyed as the mistress of Elizabeth I's Lord Chamberlain

Sir Henry Cary, baron of Hunsdon (1520–1596). Her life after she was hastily married off to a court musician, Alphonso Lanyer, to cover up being pregnant with Lord Hunsdon's child, proved disappointing for her.

Forman records Lanyer's visit to inquire about the possibility of whether the couple would attain higher social standing. Lanyer seemed especially concerned, according to Forman, to learn whether her husband's attempt to gain social favors from his association with Robert Devereux, the second earl of Essex, would succeed. Evidence also suggests that Alphonso presented copies of his wife's works to influential officials. In spite of the couple's efforts to profit from their association with influential patrons, Lanyer's financial and social status fell far short of her expectations. When Alphonso died in 1613, Lanyer struggled to support herself. She tried running a school, but this venture failed after a few years.

Published in 1611, Aemilia Lanyer's book, *Salve Deus Rex Judaeorum* (Hail Lord, King of the Jews) broke new ground in a number of ways. Lanyer redeemed Eve by comparing her transgression to the far greater sin committed by men in their crucifixion of Christ. In her dedication to the work, Lanyer bestowed Saint Peter's keys to the Church not upon a male but a woman: her patron Lady Margaret Russell Clifford, countess of Cumberland. Moreover, she prefaced the *Salve Deus* with eleven dedicatory poems, all of them addressed to women. Finally, Lanyer presented a new Christian biblical history in which women occupied all the central roles (Kennedy 2000, 166). Taken together, Lanyer's protofeminist *Salve Deus* and its companion dedicatory poems, epistles, and concluding "country-house" poem fuse several poetic traditions: the pastoral, the political, and the sacred. Whereas Lanyer's revision of Genesis (in "Eve's Apology"), as Suzanne Woods has noted, "audaciously argues for women's liberty," her finale to the *Salve Deus*—the pastoral poem,"The Description of Cook-ham"—contrasts the beauty and serenity of nature to the corruption and injustice of human society (Lanyer 1993, 381).

Debra Barrett-Graves

See also Eve; Literary Culture and Women.
Bibliography
Primary Work
Lanyer, Aemilia. *Salve Deus Rex Judaeorum*. Edited by Suzanne Woods. New York: Oxford University Press, 1993. (Originally printed in London, 1611.)
Secondary Works
Beilin, Elaine V. "Aemilia Lanyer." *Redeeming Eve: Women Writers of the English Renaissance.* Pages 177–207. Princeton, NJ: Princeton University Press, 1987.
Kennedy, Gwynne. "Aemilia Lanyer." In *Extraordinary Women of the Medieval and Renaissance World: A Biographical Dictionary.* Edited by Carole Levin, Debra Barrett-Graves, Jo Eldrige Carney, W. M. Spellman, Gwynne Kennedy, and Stephanie Witham, 160–167. Westport, CT: Greenwood Press, 2000.
Lewalski, Barbara Kiefer. "Imagining Female Community: Aemilia Lanyer's Poems." *Writing Women in Jacobean England.* Pages 212–241. Cambridge, MA: Harvard University Press, 1993.
Trill, Suzanne. "Feminism Versus Religion: Towards a Re-Reading of Aemilia Lanyer's *Salve Deus Rex Judaeorum.*" *Renaissance and Reformation* 25, no. 4 (2001): 67–80.
White, Micheline. "A Woman with Saint Peter's Keys? Aemilia Lanyer's *Salve Deus Rex Judaeorum* (1611) and the Priestly Gifts of Women." *Criticism* 45, no. 3 (2003): 323–341.

Latin Learning and Women. *See* Education, Humanism, and Women.

Le Gendre, Marie (Dame de Rivery; dates unknown)

Humanist, poet, and author of discourses on moral philosophy

We know little about Marie Le Gendre's life, except that she may have moved from Picardy to Paris and may have possibly been acquainted with aristocratic circles, such as that of the princesse de Conty, to whom she dedicated one of her works, the *Exercice de l'ame vertueuse* (The Practice of the Chaste Soul). Another aristocrat author to whom she addressed a number of sonnets and dedicated a dialogue is her protector, François Le Poulchre, seigneur de La Motte-Messemé. In his diary, *Le Passe-Temps* (The Pastime), Le Poulchre includes her among the erudite ladies of his time, such as Madeleine de L'Aubespine, the Maréchale de Retz, the Countess de Guiche, and the Dames des Roches. Marie Le Gendre addressed a majority of her poems to her husband, a certain Monsieur de Rivery, who probably died in 1595. Her main work, the *Exercice de l'ame vertueuse* (1596–1597), contains twelve moral discourses on friendship, virtue, ambition, passion, and ingratitude, themes that are obviously related to Montaigne's *Essais*. Their content and style reveal affinities with the humanist debates of the Palace Academy: exaltation of virtue and condemnation of vice, as well as classical rhetoric, brevity, and a penchant for definitions. Marie le Gendre may have attended or at least heard about the humanist gatherings of the Palace Academy (founded in the 1560s by Henry III), which brought together the most prominent figures of her day—Baïf, Dorat, Desportes, Du Perron, Jamyn, Pibrac, Ronsard, and Le Poulchre—as well as noble erudite ladies, such as Marguerite de Valois, Madame de Nevers, and the Maréchale de Retz. Marie Le Gendre also composed *Stances,* four short poems that aim at reconciling Christianity with the morality of ancient Stoic philosophy. In another vein, she wrote a lengthy neo-Platonic dialogue, the *Dialogue des chastes Amours d'Eros et de Kalisti* (Dialogue on the Chaste Love of Eros and Kalisti). Inspired by Ficino's *De amore* (On Love) (1484) and by Catherine des Roche's *Dialogue d'Amour, de Beauté et de Physis* (Dialogue of Love, Beauty, and Physis) (1578), Marie Le Gendre's dialogue reflects current Renaissance topics such as love, marriage, and the mother-daughter bond. Finally, she wrote a few Petrarchan sonnets and stances, the *Sonnets à Monsieur de Rivery* (1596–1597), and two poems called *Stances à*

luy-mesme, in which she laments widowhood and idealizes her lost husband. Marie Le Gendre wrote the main part of her work in prose, applying her talent to two favorite humanist genres: discourse and dialogue. Drawing from the same classical sources as did eminent moralists of her age, she wrote on the most popular topics of the Renaissance, echoing Amyot, Bodin, Du Plessis-Mornay, Goulart, Montaigne, Le Caron, and Le Poulchre. The discourse, poems, and dialogue reveal a fundamental unity, based on the author's attempt at reaching self-knowledge and control over passions. They are important documents in the history of humanism that reflect the revival of stoicism in the latter part of the sixteenth century.

Graziella Postolache

See also the subheading Sonnet Writing (under Literary Culture and Women).

Bibliography

Primary Works

Le Gendre, Marie. *L'exercice de l'âme vertueuse.* Edited by Colette H. Winn. Paris: Champion, 2001.

Le Gendre, Marie. *L'exercice de l'âme vertueuse, dedié à tres-haute, tres-illustre, et tres-vertueuse Princesse, Madame de Conty, par Marie Le Gendre, Dame de Rivery: Reveu, corrigé, & augmenté par elle-mesme d'un Dialogue des chastes Amours d'Eros, & Kalisti.* Paris: Jean Le Blanc, 1596.

Secondary Works

Berriot-Salvadore, Evelyne. "Marie Le Gendre et Marie de Gournay à la manière de . . . ." In *Le lecteur, l'auteur et l'écrivain: Montaigne 1492–1592–1992.* Actes du Colloque International de Haïfa, April–May 1992. Edited by Ilana Zinguer, 237–245. Paris: Champion, 1993.

Winn, Colette H. "Les *Discours* de Marie Le Gendre et l'Académie du Palais." In *La Femme lettrée à la Renaissance.* Edited by Michael Bastiaensen, 165–175. Brussels: Université Libre de Bruxelles, Institut Interuniversitaire Renaissance et Humanisme, 1997.

Winn, Colette H. "Marie Le Gendre et l'échec du stoïcisme." In *Women's Writing in the French Renaissance.* Proceedings of the Fifth Cambridge French Renaissance Colloquium, 7–9 July 1997. Edited by Philip Ford and Gillian Jondorf, 207–220. Cambridge: Cambridge French Colloquia, 1999.

Letter Writing. *See* under **Literary Culture and Women.**

Literary Culture and Women
Overview

Women engaged in a wide variety of literary activities in early modern Europe. They organized and hosted evenings for the discussion of new ideas and writings. They wrote and figured as characters in dialogues that simulated salon-style conversation among literary women and men. They circulated their letters and poetry among a wide circle of friends across state and city borders. They authored and acted in plays and pastorals; they published their translations of previously unknown masterworks from Greek and Latin literature; and they were patrons of poets, philosophers, unorthodox thinkers, and editors and publishers. Five subentries follow in this survey: Salons, Salonnières, and Women Writers; Virtual Salons: Women in Renaissance Dialogues; Sonnet Writing; Letter Writing; and Literary Patronage.

Salons, Salonnières, and Women Writers

In literary contexts, the term "salon" is most often associated with the women of the seventeenth and early eighteenth centuries in France, such as Catherine de Vivonne (1588–1665), the marquise de Rambouillet, renowned for her *chambre bleue,* her salon for the intellectuals and courtiers who frequented the Hôtel de Rambouillet, and Madeleine de Scudéry (1607–1701), famous for her *samedis,* or the Saturday meetings of her salon circle. The tradition of women writers hosting and taking part in learned gatherings, however, may be seen much earlier. The foremothers of Vivonne and Scudéry may be found in Renaissance courts and literary circles across the Continent and in England.

Thanks to the pervasive fascination of Renaissance intellectuals with the classical institution of the academy, groups throughout Europe formed to discuss philosophy, literature, music, politics, and science. Although the roots of Renaissance academies and salons may be traced to classical tradition, a contemporary source of inspiration was Baldassare Castiglione's popular work, *The Book of the Courtier* (1528), in which he depicts a group of courtiers and intellectuals at the court of Urbino around 1507. The group's discussions are initiated by Elisabetta Gonzaga, duchess of Urbino, aided by her noble lady-in-waiting, Emilia Pia. Castiglione extols the wit and virtue of these women, and he especially has Gonzaga act as the moral compass to the proceedings, a neo-Platonic touch illustrating the idea that women could fulfill a place in intellectual society, albeit ideally as muses or moral guides. This fictionalized group of brilliant men guided by virtuous women illustrates the "ideal form," as Plato might put it, for Renaissance intellectual society. The reality, however, differed in intriguing ways.

While the majority of participants in academic and salon society during the Renaissance were men, learned women from a variety of social strata, from noblewomen to courtesans, also took part in such groups, although women from such diverse classes were apparently seldom, if ever, in contact with each other. Nonetheless, instead of strictly maintaining positions as "muses" or neo-Platonic guides, women wrote poetry, engaged in philosophical debates, and provided patronage for poets and artists associated with their groups, just as did their male contemporaries. The following selection of women who participated in what we may call Renaissance salon society, the Renaissance academies and salon-style gatherings of literary circles, is by no means exhaustive; it does, however, provide an overview of the types of women involved in such circles in Italy, France, and England and gives a sense of their social *milieux.*

In Italy, Veronica Gàmbara (1485–1550), the niece of Emilia Pia, whom Castiglione immortalized in *The Courtier,* presided over a group of artists, poets, and musicians at her court in Correggio, and Vittoria Colonna (1492–1547), the niece of Guidobaldo Monte-feltro, the duke of Urbino, was active in liter-ary circles in Rome and Naples that were fre-quented by Michelangelo, Pietro Bembo, and Ludovico Ariosto, as well as Jacopo Sannazaro, a leading figure in the humanist academy at the court of Naples. The duchesses Caterina Cibo, Giovanna d'Aragona, and Giulia Gon-zaga inaugurated salons at Fondi and Naples that were driven as much by the concern with poetry and linguistic questions of the period as with religious reform. Laura Battiferri Am-mannati (1523–1589), the illegitimate daugh-ter of Giovanni Antonio Battiferri who was legally recognized by her father and given a humanist education, was a member of the Academy of the Assorditi in Urbino and the Academy of the Intronati in Siena. Other women active in Italian academies and literary circles were those of the courtesan and *virtuose* (musicians and actresses) classes. Gaspara Stampa (ca. 1523–1554), a *virtuosa* renowned for her musical talent as well as her poetry, and Veronica Franco (1546–1591), a courtesan poet, were associated with the Venetian acad-emy of Domenico Venier. Isabella Andreini (1562–1604), an actress, poet, and playwright, was a member of the Academy of the Intenti of Pavia. Finally, the courtesan poet Tullia d'Aragona (ca. 1505–1556) took part in salon gatherings as well as hosting her own. Her par-ticipation in Renaissance salon society is im-mortalized in Sperone Speroni's *Dialogo di amore* (1542), to which Aragona responds in her *Dialogo della infinità di amore* (1547).

The cultural phenomena of academies and literary circles in Italy were reflected at the French court and in the salons that developed in Paris, Lyons, and Poitiers. Marguerite de Navarre (1492–1549), a contemporary of Gàmbara and Colonna, was instrumental in bringing Italian artists to the court of her brother, Francis I, and she presided over her own circle of writers and intellectuals at

Navarre. The sorts of academic and salon soci-ety that flourished in Italy, however, especially blossomed during the reigns of her nephew, Henri II, married to Catherine de Médicis, and his sons.

In Paris, Antoinette de Loynes (1505–1567), Madeleine de L'Aubespine (1546–1596), and Claude-Catherine de Clermont (1543–1603) held literary salons in their homes that were counterparts to the *Académie de poésie et de musique* and the *Académie du palais* at the French court during the sixteenth century. These women were the recipients of numerous poetic addresses by the writers who frequented their salons, including the Pléiade poets, and they and their family members composed poetry, prac-ticed translation, and generally participated in the perpetuation of humanist literary trends. Loynes was married to Jean de Morel, sieur de Grigny, who counted Erasmus among his friends, as well as Jean Dorat, Joachim du Bellay, Ronsard, and Michel de L'Hôpital. Pierre de Nolhac has called the Morel home "*le premier salon littéraire de Paris*" (the first literary salon of Paris) (1921, 541). Clermont was married to Al-bert de Gondi, the *maréchal* and later duc de Retz. She also participated in the court acad-emy during the reign of Henri III. Poets associ-ated with her salon included Étienne Jodelle, Philippe Desportes, Jean-Antoine de Baïf, Pon-tus de Tyard, Remy Belleau, and Amadis Jamyn. Female participants included Marguerite de Val-ois, Henriette de Clèves, Hélène de Surgères, Gilonne de Goyon, Charlotte de Beaune, Gabrielle de Rochechouart, and Anne de Thou. Interestingly, Colette Winn and Francois Rouget point out that Rambouillet was the "*petite cousine*" of Clermont (2004, 17). Many members of the Retz circle were also active in the salon of L'Aubespine, wife of Secretary of State Nicolas de Neufville, sieur de Villeroy. L. Clark Keating writes that these two salons were simultaneously in vogue and that "from the list of their friends it seems that the two households were but alternate gathering places for the poets, humanists, and courtiers who were their contemporaries" (1941, 103). The traditions of these sixteenth-century Parisian salons were carried into the early seventeenth century by Marguerite de Valois (1553–1615), when she returned from exile in Auvergne. French salon society, however, flourished in the provinces as well as in Paris.

Lyons, the major city on the route that linked Paris and northern France to Italy, was an international crossroads for commerce, printing, and the arts. There, in 1544, Maurice Scève published *Délie,* a long sequence of *dizains* based on Petrarchan style, and Clément Marot published a translation of six sonnets by Petrarch (Rigolot 1989, 172). These conditions and developments encouraged the growth of salon society. One of the most famous salons of Lyons was hosted by Marie de Pierrevive, Dame du Perron, the mother-in-law of Clermont and a close friend of Catherine de Médicis. Her husband, Antoine de Gondi, was a Florentine who served as *maître d'hôtel* for Henri II. Lyons was also home to the poets Pernette du Guillet (ca. 1520–1544), the wife of a nobleman, and Louise Labé (ca. 1520–1566), the daughter of a rope maker, both of whom frequented salons popular with the writers who made up the *École lyonnaise.*

Another renowned sixteenth-century French salon was that of the Mesdames des Roches in Poitiers, described by Scévole de Sainte Marthe as "*une Academie d'honneur*" (an Academy of honor) (Keating 1941, 52) where great men gathered. Madeleine des Roches née Neveu (1520–1587) and her daughter Catherine des Roches (1542–1587) hosted numerous literary luminaries, including members of the Pléiade as well as local members of the upper gentry and the nobility of the robe. Their salon especially gained fame when Henri III sent jurists from Paris to Poitiers to aid local courts there in 1579.

The flourishing literary salons and coteries in Paris, Lyons, and Poitiers also spawned the cultivation of such prose narrative genres as the short tale, or *conte* (Jeanne Flore), the novel

(Helisenne de Crenne, Marie de Gournay), the epic romance (Anne de Graville), the moral essay (Madeleine de L'Aubespine, Marie Le Gendre, Marie de Gournay), and the memoir (Charlotte Arbaleste Duplessis Mornay, Jeanne d'Albret, Marguerite de Valois). Experimentation in such prose forms led to the development of the novel in the seventeenth century, a genre increasingly associated with women.

Continental literary trends spread to England, thanks in part to the journeys and literary activities of courtiers and other travelers. While descriptions of salon-like gatherings appear less frequently in contemporary accounts, there were English literary circles that somewhat resembled their European counterparts. One group clearly influenced by Continental literary trends was the Sidney circle. At the group's center were the Sidney siblings, Philip Sidney (1554–1586), Mary Sidney Herbert, countess of Pembroke (1561–1621), and Robert Sidney (1563–1626). Wilton House, the country estate of the countess of Pembroke, was a key gathering place for this group. Poets associated with the Sidney circle included Samuel Daniel, Fulke Greville, and Abraham Fraunce. Especially after the death of her brother Philip, the countess of Pembroke, a young contemporary of Villeroy and Retz, became, like them, a lauded literary circle hostess, poet, translator, and patron, activities also pursued by her younger kinswoman, Lucy Harington Russell, the countess of Bedford (1581–1627). Like Pembroke, Bedford was renowned for her circle, which included John Donne, Samuel Daniel, and George Chapman. Pembroke's niece, Lady Mary Sidney Wroth (ca. 1586–ca. 1652), and daughter-in-law, Susan de Vere Herbert, the countess of Montgomery (1587–ca. 1628), likewise participated in coteries. In "To Sir Robert Wroth," Ben Jonson praises the evening entertainments that Mary Wroth hosts, which suggests that she, like her aunt, provided hospitality for the writers of her circle (Roberts 1983, 16).

Throughout the sixteenth century, women from a variety of backgrounds were participating in the influential groups that constituted Renaissance salon society. If we consider the years spanned by the lives of Bedford, Wroth, and Montgomery, we realize that the "careers" of these women writers, who were participants in the remnants of Renaissance literary society in England, overlapped with those of Rambouillet and Scudéry, women writers of the classical period in France. It seems, then, that Rambouillet and Scudéry ushered in not an entirely new phenomenon with their seventeenth-century salons, but rather a new chapter in women's literary history with their participation in literary society.

Julie D. Campbell

See also entries of the women named in this entry; Religious Reform and Women; Theater and Women Actors, Playwrights, and Patrons; Translation and Women Translators.

Bibliography

Bassanese, Fiora. *Gaspara Stampa*. Twayne's World Authors Series 658. Boston: Twayne, 1982.

Campbell, Julie D. *Literary Circles and Gender in Renaissance Europe: A Cross-Cultural Approach*. Hampshire, UK: Ashgate, forthcoming.

Jones, Ann Rosalind. *The Currency of Eros: Women's Love Lyric in Europe, 1540–1620*. Bloomington: Indiana University Press, 1990.

Keating, L. Clark. *Studies on the Literary Salon in France, 1550–1615*. Cambridge, MA: Harvard University Press, 1941.

Kennedy, William J. *Authorizing Petrarch*. Ithaca, NY: Cornell University Press, 1994.

Larsen, Anne R. *From Mother and Daughter: Poems, Dialogues, and Letters by Les Dames des Roches*. Other Voice Series. Chicago: University of Chicago Press, forthcoming.

Lewalski, Barbara Kiefer. *Writing Women in Jacobean England*. Cambridge, MA: Harvard University Press, 1993.

MacNeil, Anne. *Music and Women of the Commedia dell'Arte in the Late Sixteenth Century*. Oxford: Oxford University Press, 2003.

Nolhac, Pierre de. "Le premier salon littéraire de Paris." *La Revue universelle* 5 (1 June 1921): 537–552.

Rigolot, François. "Clément Marot Imports into French the Petrarchan Sonnet." *A New History of French Literature*. Edited by Denis Hollier, 171–174. Cambridge, MA: Harvard University Press, 1989.

Roberts, Josephine. "Introduction." *The Poems of Lady Mary Wroth*. Pages 3–40. Baton Rouge: Louisiana State University Press, 1983.

Robin, Diana. *Publishing Women: Salons, the Presses, and the Counter-Reformation in Sixteenth-Century Italy*. Chicago: University of Chicago Press, 2007.

Rosenthal, Margaret. *The Honest Courtesan: Veronica Franco, Citizen and Writer in Sixteenth-Century Venice*. Chicago: University of Chicago Press, 1992.

Stortoni, Laura Anna, and Mary Prentice Lillie, eds. *Women Poets of the Italian Renaissance: Courtly Ladies and Courtesans*. New York: Italica, 1997.

Winn, Colette H., and François Rouget. "Introduction." *Album de poesies (Manuscrit francais 25455 de la BNF)*. Paris: Honoré Champion, 2004.

Virtual Salons: Women in Renaissance Dialogues

Dialogue, the written record of a real or fictitious conversation, was one of the most popular genres of the Renaissance. Following the model of Platonic and Ciceronian dialogues, the speakers were usually real historical people, whether or not they actually said what was written. The Lucianic model used fictional characters and classical gods in a dramatic scene. Dialogues could treat any topic, allowing for disagreement and persuasion as well as for a more didactic question-and-answer format.

Although most dialogues are set among men, the inclusion of women in some famous texts created an opening for women writers to legitimize their participation in the genre. Plato's *Symposium* reports a conversation in which Socrates learned from a woman named Diotima. In Bembo *Gli Asolani* (1505) and in Castiglione's *Book of the Courtier* (1528), which expresses a wide range of views on women's roles in society, women, though saying very little, are present at the discussions and interject comments.

On matters of love, sex, beauty, and marriage even men considered that women might have some expertise worth sharing. Male-authored dialogues on love, such as Leone

Ebreo's *Dialoghi d'Amore* (1535) or Sperone Speroni's *Dialogo d'Amore* (1542), made use of female speakers, in one case a neo–Platonic Sophia, in the other a flesh-bound Tullia d'Aragona contrasted with the idealizing Tasso. Bembo's *Asolani* (1505, rev. 1530), Erasmus's *Colloquies* (1518) on marriage and motherhood, Alessandro Piccolomini's *La Raffaella* (1539), Speroni's *Della Dignità delle Donne*, Pontus de Tyard's *Solitaire* (1551), Giuseppe Betussi's *Il Raverta* (1544) and *Leonora* (1552), and Edmund Tilney's *Flower of Friendship* (1568) similarly deemed these topics appropriate for women's speech. Female speakers range from the intellectual Costanza Amaretta of Agnolo Firenzuola's *Ragionamenti* (1525) to the old bawd of Aretino's *Ragionamenti* (1534), who compares a woman's options as wife, nun, or whore.

Dialogues about secular or spiritual education also included and were aimed at women. Lodovico Dolce's *Dialogo della Institutione delle Donne* (1547), in its reading list for women, suggested other dialogues by Plato, Cicero, Castiglione, and Speroni. Spiritual dialogues, such as Juan de Valdés's *Alfabeto cristiano. Dialogo con Giulia Gonzaga* (1536) or Bernard Ochino's *Dialogi sette* (1542), encouraged women to speak about their aims and inner conflicts. Education, both secular and spiritual, was a major topic of women's own dialogue writing.

Conversation, whether with a spiritual mentor or in a domestic or garden setting with friends, was in fact a part of women's lives. Inviting literary models, the informal nature of the dialogue genre, which allowed for a personal rather than learned style, and the genre's openness to treating topics of concern to women all encouraged women to write their own dialogues.

Italian women followed the Ciceronian model, using real or plausibly real speakers. Isota Nogarola circulated her exchange of Latin letters with Lodovico Foscarini as a dialogue under the title *On the Equal or Unequal Sin of Adam and Eve* (1451–1453). Olympia Morata wrote two Latin dialogues between herself and a real female friend about humanist and religious pursuits (ca. 1550, published posthumously in 1562). Writing in Italian rather than Latin, Chiara Matraini's *Dialoghi spirituali* (1602) offer four days of conversation between Teophila and the son of Matraini's friend Cangenna, thus suggesting that women have a proper maternal role as educators. Even the courtesan Tullia d'Aragona, responding to Speroni's dialogue on love with her *L'infinità dell'amore* (1547), rejected the role of fleshly female, emphasizing instead her ability to hold her own in an intellectual discussion with one of the leading men of letters, Benedetto Varchi. Moderata Fonte's *Il Merito delle Donne* (posthumously, 1600) engages seven Venetian women from various stages of life in a debate on men's relations with women, advocating the right of women to education and to a more equal role.

Following Italian models, Marguerite de Navarre's *Heptameron* (posthumously, 1559) put its discussions on varied topics into the mouths of men and women from the French court. Influenced by Morata's work, Catherine des Roches in her *Secondes Œuvres* (1583) wrote an Italianate pair of dialogues in which two fathers and their two daughters debate the value of female education. Other French women's dialogues were influenced more by Lucian and the medieval *débat*: Helisenne de Crenne's *Songe* (1540) with its debates between Venus and Minerva, Sensuality and Reason; Louise Labé's *Débat de Folie et d'Amour* (1555); and the "Dialogues" among personifications in Catherine des Roches's *Œuvres* (1579). Marie Le Gendre's *Dialogue des Chastes Amours d'Eros et de Kalisti* (1595), despite its title, comes close to being a play, with characters combining realistic and symbolic qualities.

Most women dialogue writers were interested in persuading their readers, male and female, that women are rational and, given an education, quite capable of contributing to the broader cultural conversation.

Janet Smarr

Bibliography

Cox, Virginia. *The Renaissance Dialogue: Literary Dialogue in Its Social and Political Contexts, Castiglione to Galileo.* Cambridge Studies in Renaissance Literature and Culture. Cambridge: Cambridge University Press, 1992.

Cox, Virginia. "Seen But Not Heard: Women Speakers in Cinquecento Literary Dialogue." *Women in Italian Renaissance Culture and Society.* Edited by L. Panizza, 385–400. Oxford: European Humanities Research Centre, 2000.

Forni, Carla. *Il "Libro Animato": Teoria e Scrittura del Dialogo nel Cinquecento.* Turin: Tirrenia Stampatori, 1992.

Smarr, Janet. *Joining the Conversation: Renaissance Dialogues by Women.* Ann Arbor: University of Michigan Press, 2004.

Snyder, Jon. *Writing the Scene of Speaking: Theories of Dialogue in the Late Italian Renaissance.* Stanford, CA: Stanford University Press, 1989.

Vianello, Valerio. *Il "Giardino" delle Parole. Itinerari di scrittura e modelli letterari nel dialogo cinquecentesco.* Materiali e Ricerche N.S. 21. Rome: Jouvence, 1993.

Winn, Colette, ed. *The Dialogue in Early Modern France, 1547–1630: Art and Argument.* Washington, DC: Catholic University of America Press, 1993.

Sonnet Writing

Very much a part of sixteenth-century salon culture were the sonnets and verse epistles that women and men exchanged. In Italy, many women's sonnets and canzoni were published by the piece in the popular poetry anthologies the Venetian presses produced during the years 1540–1570. Italian women poets whose works were anthologized included, among others, Tullia d'Aragona, Francesca Baffa, Lucia Bertana, Vittoria Colonna, Laudomia Forteguerri, Veronica Gàmbara, Gaspara Stampa, Chiara Matraini, Isabella di Morra, Caterina Pellegrina, Virginia Martini Salvi, Maria Spinola, and Laura Terracina. Between 1538 and 1567, a smaller number of Italian women writers published solo authored volumes of their poetry: among this elite group were the Naples academy member Laura Terracina, the noblewoman Vittoria Colonna, the *virtuosa* singer and musician Gaspara Stampa, and the courtesan Tullia d'Ara-

gona. In 1559 in Lucca, the prominent editor Lodovico Domenichi published the first women's anthology of poetry in literary history; it featured fifty-three Italian female poets.

In France, the women poets Catherine des Roches, Christine de Pizan, Pernette du Guillet, Claude Bectone, and Marguerite de Navarre were frequently anthologized in poetry compilations published between 1545 and 1550. French women poets also participated in *tombeaux,* collections of funeral eulogies honoring a royal or literary figure. The solo authored poetry collections of Pernette du Guillet and Louise Labé were published in Lyon. Printers in Paris produced the solo collections of Anne de Marquets, Marie de Romieu, Antoinette de Loynes, and Camille de Morel. Numerous editions of Marguerite de Navarre's poetry were printed in Alençon, Lyon, and Paris in the sixteenth century.

Diana Robin

Bibliography

Broomhall, Susan. *Women and the Book Trade in Sixteenth-Century France.* Aldershot, UK: Ashgate, 2002.

Domenichi, Lodovico. *Rime diverse d'alcune nobilissimi, et virtuosissime donne raccolte. . . .* Lucca: Vincenzo Busdragho, 1559.

Robin, Diana. *Publishing Women: Salons, the Presses, and Religious Reform in Renaissance Italy.* Chicago: University of Chicago Press, 2007.

Letter Writing

Overview

For many years, women's letters were assessed as historical documents, useful only for the facts they provided about specific events described in them, rather than being evaluated stylistically as literature or interpreted in the context of women's lives, voices, and effects on their society. More recently, those who study women's letters have begun to cross the traditional disciplinary lines between literature and history and to examine letters for indications of social and linguistic interrelationships and of personal creativity within cultural conventions. Some scholars have argued that the letter was an established literary form in the Renaissance, a form we need to better understand and interpret. Others are exploring the connections between a woman's language and her understanding of herself and her power within her social situation. Some critics have challenged previously held assumptions that women's correspondence was largely domestic and argued that women were aware of and actively participated in major social and political events of the era. Because so many letters have been preserved and are now becoming available through print and online editions, we can expect to learn much more about early modern Englishwomen's lives, letters, and influence on their culture.

England

English women's letters are a vibrant source of information about women's daily lives, roles, forms of expression, and participation in the religious, political, social, and cultural aspects of the Renaissance. A large number of letters exist today: James Daybell has estimated that ten thousand Englishwomen's letters are extant from the years before 1642. The majority of writers were members of the middle and upper classes. As literacy increased during the early modern era, women from the gentry and aristocracy were more likely to have been educated than women of the lower classes and thus were capable of engaging in correspondence. Letters from such women also were more likely to have been saved, whether as a matter of family pride, political or historical interest, or simply available space in a home or on an estate. For some women, only one letter remains; for others, hundreds of letters offer windows into their ongoing activities, concerns, beliefs, and personal artistry.

The content of these women's letters is as wide-ranging as their lives and correspondents. Some letters treat personal and family issues. Women woo and are wooed; the letters of Lydia DuGard and Dorothy Osborne provide examples of sustained correspondence about romantic relationships. Women inquire about visits from friends and relatives; send useful meats and medicine; worry about or rejoice in their children's educations, marriages, and pregnancies; and update distant spouses, friends, and relatives about recent occurrences in the neighborhood and among the wider networks of kinship. They ask questions and offer advice. Other letters are directly associated with business and estate management. Women hire and dismiss workers, order timber and oxen, debate land leases and mortgages, engage in legal disputes, direct building construction, and work with foundries and mills. Many extant letters are petitions or suits. English society was based in patronage; personal and familial issues were intricately intertwined with broader social and political connections. Thus women engage in gift giving, the exchange of tokens to indicate alliance, and they sue for favors, positions, and promotions for husbands, friends, servants, and family members, becoming politically influential through their relationships. A letter accompanied by a New Year's gift to a lady-in-waiting of the queen, for example, might be reciprocated when the lady-in-waiting reminds the queen of how worthy one's nephew is to serve at court. Other women petition to free family members from prison, to have their children supported or debts paid, or to have someone restored to another's good graces, and sometimes women are powerful enough to assume that their requests will be granted. In an era before newspapers were widespread, women as well as men created networks of correspondents, collecting and circulating political intelligence. For example, Elizabeth Talbot, countess of Shrewsbury, received regular reports from men and women about activities across Europe and at the English court. Such news items were "gifts," as were the letters themselves. Other women, such as Dorothy Moore, debate religious and social issues. English women address letters to women and men, to those above them in the social hierarchy and those below, to people with whom they are close and those they have never met. Their styles vary from the formal and businesslike to the descriptive and expressive, from the barely literate to the linguistically sophisticated. Taken as a whole, the letters suggest emotions from anger and playfulness to annoyance, humor, despair, tenderness, confidence, anxiety, and joy.

Manuscript Letters: Material Aspects and Conventions

The majority of extant Englishwomen's letters have been preserved in manuscript, and the manuscripts themselves carry meaning. A letter might be in the handwriting of the author or of a secretary to whom the woman dictated her letter. Most literate women employed the italic style of handwriting rather than other forms popular in England. Italic, much like our modern cursive, was the style most often taught to women—what Malvolio in Shakespeare's *Twelfth Night* called "the sweet Roman hand"—because it was believed to be easier to learn. It was also easier to read and eventually replaced other forms. By the end of the sixteenth century, female and male signatures commonly appeared in the italic hand, even when the letter itself might have been written by a secretary or in another style of handwriting. Among aristocratic women like Lady Arbella Stuart, there might be more than one style of italic hand, a presentation hand for letters to superiors and an informal hand for letters to close family members and friends. Writing in one's own hand indicated affection or alliance. And because handwriting mattered and because early in the era women usually lacked the training and practice that men of the same social class had, women sometimes apologized to their friends and social superiors for the quality of their handwriting. A recent study of sixteenth-century Englishwomen's letters revealed that approximately one-quarter of them were physically written by a secretary and three-quarters by the authors. It would not be correct to assume, however, that having

a letter in a secretary's hand indicates illiteracy on the part of the author. A literate woman might choose to use a secretary for many reasons; she might be ill, she might prefer someone more skilled in Latin or French if the addressee were European, or the letter might be a routine business letter that did not require personal involvement. The use of secretaries does raise questions about the accuracy of the letter's transcription, about possible collaboration during the process, and about the author's level of openness and comfort. One well might censor oneself with a secretary present at the composition of a letter.

It is hard to tell whether women read the letter-writing manuals, such as Angel Day's *The English Secretary* (1599), or whether they absorbed the conventions of letter writing by active involvement in the process, but in general they understood the social hierarchies of letter writing. The amount of unfilled space on a page, for example, might suggest respect in an era in which most paper was expensive. Similarly, the distance between the body of the text and the signature, which was placed near the bottom edge of the paper, could suggest deference and indicate the relative social distance between the writer and an addressee from whom a favor was being requested. By contrast, in a letter to a friend, a writer well might fill the space with closely written text and even write up and down the margins or between previously written lines.

Until 1635, the royal postal system did not accept private letters. Through most of the Renaissance, when a letter was composed, the woman would entrust it to a private carrier, often a friend or relation or servant, to be delivered. Sometimes a passerby would be drafted into service. Letters often included phrases about the woman's having to write in haste when a carrier became available or having been unable to send a letter earlier because she had no messenger by whom to send it. Such a system meant delays were frequent, letters were often lost, and even letters carried by one's own servants had to be written with the knowledge that they could be lost or read by someone other than the intended recipient, whether curious neighbors or antagonists in a dispute. Letters also were read aloud to groups and enclosed in letters to friends who might be interested in the news they contained, an early modern equivalent of a distribution list, or to those who might better be able to respond to a request. Because of the uncertainties associated with mail delivery, trusted carriers sometimes were given oral messages that the writer felt uncomfortable putting into print: notes such as "this bearer will explain at more length" are common. Or a writer might indicate that the letter should be destroyed after being read. Anne Bacon, for example, hoping to restrict her potential readership, asks that her son not share one of her letters with his male servants or companions; she asks him to send it back or burn it.

Because the composition of letters frequently involved a secretary and letters often were read by people for whom they were not intended, our contemporary assumptions about the private and personal nature of correspondence should be reexamined. In the Renaissance, letter writing had a very public aspect.

Sara Jayne Steen

Bibliography

Primary Works

DuGard, Lydia. *Cousins in Love: The Letters of Lydia DuGard, 1665–1672*. Edited by Nancy Taylor. Tempe: Arizona Center for Medieval and Renaissance Studies, with Renaissance English Text Society, 2003.

Moore, Dorothy. *The Letters of Dorothy Moore, 1612–64: The Friendships, Marriage, and Intellectual Life of a Seventeenth-Century Woman.* Edited by Lynette Hunter. Aldershot, UK, and Burlington, VT: Ashgate, 2004.

Osborne, Dorothy. *Letters to Sir William Temple.* Edited by Kenneth Parker. London: Penguin, 1987.

Stuart, Arbella. *The Letters of Lady Arbella Stuart.* Edited by Sara Jayne Steen. New York and Oxford: Oxford University Press, 1994.

Thynne, Joan, and Maria Thynne. *Two Elizabethan Women: Correspondence of Joan and Maria Thynne, 1575–1611.* Edited by Alison D. Wall. Devizes, UK: Wiltshire Record Society, 1983.

Secondary Works

Couchman, Jane, and Ann Crabb, eds. *Women's Letters Across Europe, 1400–1700: Form and Persuasion.* Aldershot, UK: Ashgate, 2005.

Daybell, James, ed. *Early Modern Women's Letter Writing, 1450–1700.* Hampshire, UK, and New York: Palgrave, 2001.

Daybell, James, ed. *Women and Politics in Early Modern England, 1450–1700.* Aldershot, UK, and Burlington, VT: Ashgate, 2004.

Daybell, James. "Women's Letters and Letter-Writing in England, 1540–1603." Ph.D. dissertation, University of Reading, 1999.

Magnusson, Lynne. "Widowhood and Linguistic Capital: The Rhetoric and Reception of Anne Bacon's Epistolary Advice," *ELR,* 31 (2001): 3–33.

Stewart, Alan, and Heather Wolfe. *Letterwriting in Renaissance England.* Washington, DC: The Folger Shakespeare Library, 2004.

France

Women contributed to all of the many varieties of letter writing that were practiced during the Renaissance. Responding to the revival of classical epistolary models by Erasmus and other humanists, women published erudite "familiar letters." Women wrote and sometimes published *epistres en vers* (verse epistles). Pamphlet literature during the French Religious Wars could take the form of published letters, some of which were written by women. Women exchanged *lettres missives* (real letters, sent and received) with their families and their broader social and political networks and sometimes reworked letters from actual correspondences for publication. Letters in municipal archives offer glimpses of the epistolary activities of middle- and lower-class women.

As she did for other literary genres, Christine de Pizan (ca. 1363–ca. 1431) provided models of epistolary forms for French women writers. The philosophical verse *Epistre Othea* (The Letter of Othea [to Hector], written around 1400) was published in France before 1525. In it, Christine conflates words and images, Classical and Christian wisdom. Other epistolary works by Christine were known in manuscript: a verse epistle, *L'Epistre au Dieu d'Amour* (Cupid's Letter, 1399), and polemic prose letters in defense of women (1401–1403); an *Epistre à la Royne de France* (Epistle to the Queen of France, 1405) urging Isabelle of Bavaria to pursue peace at court and in war-torn France; and the consolatory *Epistre de la prison de vie humaine* (Letter on the Prison of Human Life, ca. 1416–1418).

Women's Published Letters

The first letter collection published in French was by a woman: the *Lettres familières et invectives* (Familiar and Invective Letters, 1539) of Hélisenne de Crenne (Marguerite Briet). Hélisenne's letters are Erasmian in their emphasis on *varietas* and in their erudition. They relate to her novel *Les Angoysses douloureuses qui procedent d'amour* (The Torments of Love, 1538), in which letters play a central role. The *Familiar Letters* offer thanks, advice, and intimate disclosures to various unnamed friends. In the *Invective Letters,* Hélisenne defends women's right to be educated and to publish their work. The second published collection of women's letters, *Les Missives* (1586) of Madeleine and Catherine des Roches, consists of letters selected from their private correspondence, twenty-six by Madeleine and seventy by her daughter Catherine. They deal with a wide range of subjects (illness, the Religious Wars, legal cases, love, literary style). Revised for publication, the *Missives* combine the immediacy and some of the epistolary conventions of *lettres missives,* the attention to style and variety of the humanist letter, and the sociability of their salon and their mutual affection.

Marguerite de Cambis applied another humanist activity, translation, to letters. She published her translations of two extended Italian humanist letters, the *Epistre du Seigneur Jean Trissin de la vie que doit tenir une Dame veuve* (Epistle by Lord Jean Trissin on How a Widowed Lady Should Live, 1554) and the *Epistre consolatoire de messier Jean Boccace, envoyée au Signeur Pino de Rossi* (Consolatory Epistle by

Boccaccio to Lord Pino de Rossi, 1556). Marie de Romieu prefaced both her published works, *Instruction pour les dames* (Instruction for Ladies, 1572) and *Premières oeuvres poétiques* (First Poetic Works, 1581), with letters defining her persona as an author, while Georgette de Montenay's *Emblèmes ou Devises Chrestiennes* (1571) open with a dedicatory epistle to Jeanne d'Albret and end with an allegorical epistle. Gaspar de Saillans included some of his wife Louise de Bourges's letters with his own in a beautifully bound volume (1569). These letters, affectionate and personal, also reflect the Erasmian familiar letter and Renaissance debates about the nature of love.

Verse Epistles

Verse epistles could be private or meant for publication. Louise de Savoie (1476–1531), her son Francis I, and her daughter Marguerite de Navarre (1492–1549) exchanged affectionate private letters in verse. In later life, Marguerite de Navarre wrote verse epistles to her daughter, Jeanne d'Albret, expressing her maternal love and the pain of her daughter's absence. Anne de Graville's *Beau Romant des deux amans* (Beautiful Story of Two Lovers, 1521) concludes with two verse epistles, "*De Clériande à Réginus*" and "*De Maguelonne à Pierre de Provence,*" which echo Ovid's popular *Heroides,* letter-poems of unrequited love and abandonment written in the female voice. *Les devotes epistres* (Devout Epistles, ca. 1545) of Catherine d'Amboise, prayers in the form of letters addressed to Jesus and to the Virgin, are preserved in a fine illuminated manuscript.

Pamphlet Literature

During the Religious Wars, pamphlet literature often took the form of published letters. Marie Dentières's *Epistre tresutile envoyée à la Royne de Navarre* (Epistle to the Queen of Navarre, 1539) is an eloquent plea to Marguerite de Navarre and to all women to rally to the Reformed cause. The anonymous *Epistre d'une demoiselle françoise . . . sur la mort de . . . Léonore de Roye . . .* (The Translation of a Letter . . . upon the Death of . . . Eléonore of Roye, . . .), published in French and English in 1564, exhorts women to follow Eléonore de Roye's example as faithful wife, tender mother, and pious Huguenot. The letters of Renée Burlamacchi (1568–1641) on the death of her husband Agrippa d'Aubigné express their shared Reformed faith. The Catholic position was firmly argued by Charlotte de Minut in two prefatory letters to works by her brother: *A Nostre Sainct Pere le Pape Sixte* (To Our Holy Father Pope Sixtus) and *Epistre à la Royne* (Letter to the Queen [Catherine de Médicis], both 1587).

Noblewomen's lettres missives

The correspondences of many royal and noble women (and men) survive in family or national archives and some have been published. Women's *lettres missives* reflect family networks that also operated politically. These letters are rich sources of historical information from women's points of view; they can also be added to the growing corpus of texts known to have been written by women during the Old Régime. Like their male relatives, women who had learned to read but not to write (reading was taught before writing) dictated their letters to secretaries or relatives. Noble letters followed letterbooks and manuals, the successors of the Medieval *ars dictaminis* (letter-writing manuals), including Gabriel Chappuys' *Secrétaire* (1568) and Étienne du Tronchet's *Lettres missives et familières* (Missives and familiar letters, 1569), both modeled on Italian sources. Women's *lettres missives* demonstrate a skillful use of epistolary conventions and rhetorical strategies. Even in letters written for women by scribes, the woman's voice is heard in the details she chooses to include and in the persuasive tactics adopted.

There is an illumination by Jean Bourdichon showing Anne de Bretagne, queen of France (1477–1517), writing a letter (ca. 1510, Russian National Library ms. Fr. F.v.XIV, 8, fol. 1v), and some 220 of her letters are said to be extant. The correspondence among Francis I, Louise de Savoie, and Marguerite de Navarre reflects the power of the "Trinity" this family group formed. We observe the rhetorical strategies Marguerite employed to negotiate complicated loyalties to her brother, her husband Henri d'Albret, king of Navarre, and her daughter Jeanne d'Albret (1528–1572). Marguerite also exchanged letters with her spiritual director, Guillaume Briçonnet. Letters from Diane de Poitiers (1500–1566), Henri II's mistress, deal with political matters as well as arrangements for Henri's children. Almost all the letters written by Louise de Clermont, duchess of Uzès (ca. 1504–ca. 1596) are lost, and the correspondence of Renée de France, duchess of Ferrara (1510–1570), has not yet been published. The most extraordinary woman's correspondence of the period, that of Catherine de Médicis (1519–1589), wife of Henri II, mother of the last three Valois kings, and regent during her sons' minorities, documents the networks she maintained and the brilliant rhetorical strategies she used to strengthen her sons' and her own position during the French Religious Wars. The rich correspondence of Catherine's daughter, Marguerite de Valois ("Queen Margot") (1553–1615), first wife of Henri IV, offers another fascinating view of these troubled times. Anne d'Este, duchesse de Guise et de Nemours (1531–1607), wrote as a bereaved wife and mother and a brilliant negotiator. There are a few extant letters from Catherine de Clermont, duchesse de Retz (1545–1603), a brilliant patron of the arts, and fifty of the letters of Louise de Lorraine, wife of Henri III, have been published. Huguenot noblewomen used their correspondences to maintain networks and to argue in defense of their faith. Jeanne d'Albret's letters reveal her political acuity as leader of the Huguenot party. Jeanne's daughter, Catherine de Bourbon (1559–1604), wrote to Huguenot leaders and to her brother Henri IV to ask in vain for a suitable husband; she also resisted Henri's pressure on her to convert to Catholicism. Eléonore de Roye (1535–1564) corresponded with Catherine de Médicis and Elizabeth I, arguing successfully, twice, for the liberation of her husband Louis, prince de Condé. Charlotte de Bourbon-Montpensier (1546/1547–1582) wrote from the court of her husband William of Orange, employing her rhetorical skills to seek reconciliation with her father, the Catholic Duke Louis de Bourbon-Montpensier. Louise de Coligny (1555–1620), fourth wife of William of Orange, crafted a correspondence that allowed her to play an important role as intermediary between Henri IV and her stepson, Maurice de Nassau, and between Henri IV and her sons-in-law, the dukes of Bouillon and of la Tremoille, estranged from the king after his conversion to Catholicism.

In letters from the late sixteenth and early seventeenth centuries, intimate details and words of affection among family members become even more prominent, as in the letters exchanged between Louise de Coligny and her stepdaughter, Charlotte-Brabantine de la Tremoille (1580–1631), and between Charlotte-Brabantine, her sister, Elizabeth de Bouillon (1577–1642), and members of the La Tremoille family, including young children.

Few letters written by French women in convents in this period appear to have survived, with the exception of four letters from Antoinette d'Orléans (1572–1618), who entered the religious life after the death of her husband Charles de Gondi, marquis de Belle-Isle.

Merchant and Pauper Letters

Municipal archives preserve some letters by middle-class and even lower-class women and men. In Lyon, the family and business correspondence of the merchant Guyot de Masso includes letters from several women, some dictated, some poorly written, and some skillfully composed, dealing with family matters and also with quite complicated business transactions. The Tours archives contain letters written for women seeking poor relief from the

city. Though written by curés or court scribes following a standard format, these letters show how pauper women constructed themselves as worthy of assistance and how they defined the mutually beneficial relationship between the poor and the donors.

Jane Couchman

See also entries for women named in this entry.
Bibliography
Primary Works
Coligny, Louise de. *Correspondance.* Geneva: Slatkine, 1970. (Originally printed in Paris, 1887.)
Crenne, Hélisenne de. *A Renaissance Woman: Helisenne's Personal and Invective Letters.* Translated by Marianna M. Mustacchi and Paul J. Archambault. Syracuse, NY: Syracuse University Press, 1986.
Dentières, Marie. *Epistle to Marguerite de Navarre.* Edited and translated by Mary B. McKinley. Chicago: University of Chicago Press, 2004.
Des Roches, Madeleine and Catherine. *Les Missives.* Edited by Anne R. Larsen. Geneva: Droz, 1999.
Goldsmith, Elizabeth C., and Colette H. Winn, eds. *Lettres de femmes: Textes inédits et oubliés du XVIe au XVIIIe siècle.* Paris: Champion, 2005.
Valois, Marguerite de. *Correspondance, 1569–1614.* Edited by Eliane Viennot. Paris: Champion, 1998.
Secondary Works
Berriot-Salvadore, Evelyne. *Les Femmes dans la société française de la Renaissance.* Geneva: Droz, 1990.
Couchman, Jane, and Ann Crabb, eds. *Women's Letters Across Europe, 1400–1700: Form and Persuasion.* Aldershot, UK: Ashgate, 2005.
Goldsmith, Elizabeth C., ed. *Writing the Female Voice: Essays on Epistolary Literature.* Boston: Northeastern University Press, 1989.
Stephenson, Barbara. *The Power and Patronage of Marguerite de Navarre.* Aldershot, UK: Ashgate, 2003.

Italy

Women's letters in Renaissance Italy exhibit both the Latin and vernacular styles current among male letter writers. Women wrote formal letters continuing the twelfth-century tradition of *ars dictaminis* (manuals on the art of letter writing); they penned letters using the relatively informal late medieval Italian merchant style; and, as humanist Latin trends moved into the Italian vernacular idiom, they addressed Ciceronian-style "familiar" letters to friends. Most of women's private letters have been lost over time, with those still in family archives surviving by deliberate selection or by chance, published only by later generations, if at all. Letters in the Ciceronian mode, which became popular after the widespread use of printing, were often written for publication. Taken together, these letters demonstrate an active culture of letter writing among Italian women in early modern Italy.

The Fourteenth and Fifteenth Centuries

The first woman's correspondence to be published in Italy was Saint Catherine of Siena's (Caterina di Giacomo di Benincasa da Siena, 1347–1380), a mystic and a semiliterate member of the mantellate, a group of lay Third Order women. Catherine's vernacular letters address kings, queens, popes, princes, prisoners, prostitutes, clergymen, family, and friends, all of whom she wrote because she believed that her mystical union with Christ obliged her to establish peace in the church and in Italy. Showing familarity with the patristic and Thomistic theology dominant in her time, her 382 surviving letters concern both public and private issues. Some of her letters attempt to convey her intense mystical experiences (Noffke 1994, 60); others resemble carefully constructed sermons. It is generally believed that Catherine's words, though later edited, were transcribed accurately by her scribes, who saw them as coming from God. Her collected letters entered the standard canon of Italian literature when they were published in 1500 by the Venetian scholar and printer, Aldo Manuzio (Aldus Manutius, 1449–1515), internationally known for the library of Greek and Latin classics he produced, among which were the first printed editions of Plato and Pindar.

An important epistolary style in the late Middle Ages and early Renaissance was the merchant letter. Written in the plain style of everyday speech, merchant correspondence assumed an ongoing exchange, with the body of the letter going point by point over letters received. Two outstanding women's letter collections exemplify the genre: those of Margherita Bandini Datini (1357–1423) of Prato, wife of the prominent merchant and banker, Francesco Datini, and the noblewoman Alessandra Macinghi Strozzi (1407–1471) of Florence, widow of the wealthy scion of the long-exiled Strozzi clan, Matteo Strozzi. Portraying an unhappy and childless marriage, Margherita Datini's letters also vividly depict her activities as her husband's agent. Although Datini depended on scribes to transmit her correspondence until the 1390s, she produced twenty-one substantial letters in 1399 in her own hand (now preserved in the Archivio di Stato di Prato). Alessandra Strozzi sent letters in her own hand to her sons when they were working abroad (1449–1471). Motivated by her desire to communicate rather than display her craft as a writer, Strozzi represents herself in her colorful, colloquial letters as a devoted mother who combined practical wisdom, religious belief, and a cynical outlook on politics and society.

Most fourteenth- and fifteenth-century middle- to upper-class girls in Florence, Venice, and other northern Italian cities received only cursory instruction in reading and writing. By the middle of the fifteenth century, however, a growing number of elite families sent their daughters to humanist tutors, who taught them to compose Latin letters in the style of Cicero and Seneca. Among the girls and women whose elegant Latin letters survive in manuscript are Maddalena Scrovegni of Padua (1356–1429), Battista da Montefelro Malatesta (1383–1450) of Urbino, Costanza Varano of Pesaro (1428–1487), and Ippolita Sforza of Milan (1445–1488). A few women, such as Isotta Nogarola (1418–1466) of Verona, Cassandra Fedele (1465–1558) of Venice, and Laura Cereta (1469–1499) of Brescia produced their own full-scale humanist letterbooks, a

genre de rigueur for male courtiers in the fifteenth century. These women's letterbooks,
which comprised from eighty to one hundred
and twenty letters written in Latin, were usually autobiographical.

Other fifteenth-century noblewomen at
the courts of Milan, Naples, Ferrara, and Mantua, including notably Eleonora d'Aragona,
duchess of Ferrara (1450–1493), and Isabella
d'Este, marchesa of Mantua (1474–1539), received a humanist education as well as one in
the Italian literary tradition. These ladies of the
courts lived in a world of diplomatic duties
and circulated their extensive correspondence
in Italian. Chancellery secretaries wrote many
of their letters, as they did for male nobles, although both women and men planned and
edited important letters themselves.

The Sixteenth and Seventeenth Centuries
A survey of letter collections by sixteenth- and
seventeenth-century Italian women indicates
the diverse forms the genre took in the late Renaissance. In 1544, the noblewoman Vittoria
Colonna (1492–1547), who played a leading
role in the evangelical movement in Italy and
was already a published poet, saw a slender volume containing three spiritual letters she addressed to Costanza d'Avalos go to press under
the title *Litere*. In 1558, the last major collection
of humanist Latin letters authored by a woman,
Olympia Morata (1526–1555) of Ferrara, was
published posthumously in Basel; Morata's book
also included some Greek letters and two Latin
dialogues she wrote. In 1580, the poet Veronica
Franco (1546–1591) published her prose *Lettere
familiari*. Franco, a Venetian courtesan introduced into the profession by her mother, built a
literary reputation on the material support and
verbal recommendations of her male patrons
and clients. In her letters, she wrote as a moral
and social counselor to a male elite, as a critic of
mercenary and cruel love, and as a defender of
women and courtesans. The poet Chiara Matraini (1515–1604) published two editions of
her collected correspondence under the title

Lettere della signora Chiara Matraini in 1595 and
1597, in Lucca. Whereas Franco's and Matraini's
letters came out in relatively small editions, the
collected *Lettere* of the Padua-born actress and
playwright Isabella Andreini (1562–1604) were
popular enough to be republished in Venice in
multiple editions between 1607 and 1663. Published posthumously by her actor-husband, her
letters address such themes as unrequited love,
fading beauty, and friendship between husband
and wife. In 1650, the Venetian nun Arcangela
Tarabotti (1604–1652) produced the last major
letter collection published by a woman in
seventeenth-century Italy, her *Lettere familiari e
di complimento* (Venice: Guerigli). Among Tarabotti's highly polemical and radically feminist
works, all of them autobiographical, Elissa
Weaver notes, "It is from her letters that we
learn the details of her life. She writes of her illnesses, her friendships, her enemies; she com-
plains about her own situation, her publishers,
and her critics" (Weaver 1994, 419).

While nuns were generally more literate
than laywomen, their letters changed under the
influence of the Council of Trent and its decrees
mandating strict enclosure. The contrast can be
seen in the letters of two Florentine mystics of
the late sixteenth century: like Catherine of
Siena, the Dominican nun Caterina de' Ricci
(Santa Caterina de' Ricci, 1522–1590) wrote as
a community advisor about moral and personal
issues as well as religious ones, whereas the
Carmelite Suor Maria Maddalena de' Pazzi
(1566–1607) wrote devotional letters solely directed to other nuns. Galileo's highly literate
daughter Suor Maria Celeste Galilei (1600–
1634), on the other hand, wrote only to her father using her correspondence with him as a
chance to communicate thoughts that she
could not expess in the convent.

Almost all upper-class women could write
and were involved in a familial and social exchange of letters in the late sixteenth century.
However, as Marina d'Amelia and Maria Pia
Fantini point out in their studies of noblewomen outside the courts, many of these

women wrote semiliterate family letters and social letters that depended on scribes or on formulas found in letter-writing manuals. By the seventeenth century a higher level of literacy was expected than in the previous century, and poorly written letters became an embarrassment.

Ann Crabb

See also entries for women named in this entry.

Bibliography

Primary Works

Catherine of Siena, Saint. *Letters.* Edited and translated by S. Noffke. Tempe: Arizona Center for Medieval and Renaissance Studies, 2000.

Cereta, Laura. *Collected Letters of a Renaissance Feminist.* Edited and translated by Diana Robin. Chicago: University of Chicago Press, 1997.

Datini, Margherita. *Per la tua Margherita: Lettere di una donna del '300 al marito mercante.* CD-ROM. Prato: Archivio di stato, 2002.

Fedele, Cassandra. *Letters and Orations.* Edited and translated by Diana Robin. Chicago: University of Chicago Press, 2000.

Franco, Veronica. *Poems and Selected letters.* Edited and translated by Ann R. Jones and Margaret F. Rosenthal. Chicago: University of Chicago Press, 1998.

Morata, Olympia. *The Complete Writings of an Italian Heretic.* Edited and translated by Holt N. Parker. Chicago: University of Chicago Press, 1998.

Nogarola, Isotta. *Complete Writings: Letterbook, Dialogue on Adam and Eve, Orations.* Chicago: University of Chicago Press, 2004.

Nogarola, Isotta, Cassandra Fedele, Laura Cereta, et al. *Her Immaculate Hand: Selected Works by and About the Women Humanists of Quattrocento Italy.* Edited by Margaret L. King and Albert Rabil, Jr. Binghamton, NY: Medieval and Renaissance Texts and Studies, 1992.

Strozzi, Alessandra. *Selected Letters: Bilingual Edition.* Edited and translated by Heather Gregory. Berkeley: University of California Press, 1997.

Secondary Works

Couchman, Jane, and Ann Crabb, eds. *Women's Letters Across Europe: Form and Persuasion.* Aldershot, UK: Ashgate, 2005.

Crabb, Ann. *The Strozzi of Florence: Widowhood and Family Solidarity in the Renaissance.* Ann Arbor: University of Michigan Press, 2000.

D'Amelia, Marina. "Lo scambio epistolare tra Cinque e Seicento: scene di vita quotidiana e aspirazioni segrete." In *Per Lettera: La scrittura epistolare femminile tra archivio e tipografia, secoli XV-XVII.* Edited by Gabriella Zarri, 79–110. Rome: Viella, 1999.

Doglio, Maria Luisa. "Letter writing, 1350–1650." In *A History of Women's Writing in Italy.* Edited by Letizia Panizza and Sharon Wood, 13–30. Cambridge: Cambridge University Press, 2000.

Fantini, Maria Pia. "Lettere alla Madre di Cassandra Chicgi (1535–1556): grafia, espressione, messaggio." In *Per Lettera: La scrittura epistolare femminile tra archivio e tipografia, secoli XV-XVII.* Edited by Gabriella Zarri, 111–150. Rome: Viella, 1999.

Noffke, Suzanne. "Catherine da Siena (Catherine of Siena, 1347–1380)." In *Italian Women Writers: A Bio-Bibliographical Sourcebook.* Edited by Rinaladina Russell, 58–66. Westport, CT: Greenwood Press, 1994.

Panizza, Letizia, and Sharon Wood, eds. *A History of Women's Writing in Italy.* Cambridge: Cambridge University Press, 2000.

Quondam, Amedeo. *Le "carte messaggiere": Rettorica e modelli di comunicazione epistolare: per un indice dei libri di lettere del Cinquecento.* Rome: Bolzoni, 1981.

Rosenthal, Margaret F. *The Honest Courtesan.* Chicago: University of Chicago Press, 1992.

Russell, Rinaldina, ed. *Italian Women Writers: A Bio-Bibliographical Sourcebook.* Westport, CT: Greenwood Press, 1994.

Sobol, Dava. *Galileo's Daughter.* New York and London: Penguin, 2000.

Weaver, Elissa. "Suo Arcangela Tarabotti (1604–1652)." In *Italian Women Writers: A Bio-Bibliographical Sourcebook.* Edited by Rinaladina Russell, 414–422. Westport, CT: Greenwood Press, 1994.

Zarri, Gabriella, ed. *Per Lettera: La scrittura epistolare femminile tra archivio e tipografia, secoli XV-XVII.* Rome: Viella, 1999.

Literary Patronage

Overview

To survive in early modern Europe, creative people who had no money of their own—artists, architects, poets, dramatists, philosophers, publishers, and printers—had to find a patron willing to commit to their support, sometimes in the form of an annual or monthly stipend. In return for the plays, orations, eulogies, dialogues, or poems a writer might compose at the request of her possibly royal and certainly wealthy patron, the patron would pay her protégé the going wage for such work, sometimes providing housing and other provisions for the writer and her family as well. With painters and sculptors, a contract was usually drawn up so that the artist could pay for materials in advance. In the case of literary patronage, the wealthy noblewoman or nobleman simply gave verbal assurances that she or he would take care of the poet's needs. Elite women who had little or no formal political power in the state found that they could derive considerable authority and influence both within and beyond their own cities from their roles as patrons of the arts and literature. Aristocratic women were aware that they were, as patrons and entrepreneurs, responsible for the culture on display when foreigners visited their cities or courts. Works that were exhibited or performed—masques, letters, epic poems, sonnets, portraits, frescoes, whether literary or visual—were seen as the measure of the patron's court, realm, or republic. In short, Renaissance patrons, women included, knew that their taste could leave its imprint on an entire age.

Italy

At the court of the Gonzaga, Isabella d'Este, marchesa of Mantua (1475–1539), supported a revolving coterie of poets including Boiardo, Equicola, Castiglione, Ariosto, Bibbiena, and Trissino, who wrote works in her honor. Purchasing books and manuscripts regularly from the Venetian scholar and publisher Aldo Manuzio and other booksellers, she assembled a collection of over a hundred rare codices in ancient Greek, Latin, and the vernacular, enriching the already notable library of the Gonzaga. Eleonora d'Aragona, duchess of Ferrara (1450–1493), provided funding for the writers Bartolomeo Goggio and Antonio Cornazzano,

each of whom wrote works praising women's capability as rulers. In Florence, Eleonora di Toledo, duchess and wife of Cosimo I de Medici (1522–1562), established her own literary academy, the *Elevati,* devoted to the promotion of Tuscan poetry and poets. She also supported two women poets working outside the all-male academy in Florence: Tullia d'Aragona and Laura Battiferra. In Naples, Giovanna d'Aragona, duchess of Tagliacozzo (1502–1577), who established literary salons in that city and on Ischia, was the dedicatee of a 525-page poetry anthology entitled *Il tempio alla divina signora Giovanna d'Aragona* (Venice 1555), in which many of the poets she had supported paid tribute to her generosity and commitment to literature. In Milan, Giovanna and her sister Maria d'Aragona d'Avalos, marchesa del Vasto (1502–1568), inaugurated their literary academy *Chiave d'Oro;* the historian and biographer Paolo Giovio and Girolamo Muzio were among their clientele.

France

The material support and protection that Marguerite de Navarre (Queen Marguerite d'Angoulême, 1492–1549) granted to poets and other writers cannot be separated from her patronage of the intellectuals who were active in the evangelical reform movement in France. Marguerite was a writer herself, having published not only a collection of her religious poetry but also a collection of tales titled the *Heptameron* based on Boccaccio's *Decameron.* She sheltered many Protestant writers and philosophers at her château in Nérac, including Marot and Calvin. Her support allowed the famous philologist Hellenist and the legal scholar Guillaume Budé to establish a center of humanist learning that eventually became the Collège of France.

Schooled in the classics in Italy, Catherine de Médicis, queen consort to the king of France (1519–1589), wrote poetry in Italian; she filled the Bibliothèque Royale with her many purchases of manuscript books of ancient as well as modern Italian works; and she was the principal patron of the Pléiade poets, a celebrated group of writers led by Ronsard and Du Bellay, who were committed to reviving the classical tradition. Educated at the court of King Henri II in France, Mary Stuart, queen of Scots (1542–1587), was another patron of Ronsard, whose books she helped publish. After her return to Scotland in 1561, Mary brought the French poets Pierre de Châtelard and Seignuer de Brantôme back to her court. She also hired the Scottish humanist George Buchanan to write the masques that provided courtly entertainment during the early years of her reign (Guy 1996, 73, 147).

England

Trained as a Protestant and a humanist, Elizabeth I (1533–1603), queen of England in 1558, presided over one of the most brilliant European courts in the Renaissance. Under her reign, the cultivation of poetry and the theater saw a golden age. Her tastes ran especially to tragedies, comedies, masques, and dialogues on Classical themes. Shakespeare, Christopher Marlowe, Thomas Nash, and George Peele were all writing and producing plays for the London theater during the last two decades of Elizabeth's reign. Thomas Hoby published his translation of Castiglione's influential *Il cortegiano* (The Book of the Courtier, 1561) under her aegis, and Edmund Spenser's *Faerie Queen* and Philip Sidney's *Arcadia* were two of the most important early works composed during her reign. The poet Mary Sidney, countess of Pembroke (1554–1586), was herself the patron of a circle of younger poets including Samuel Daniel, Abraham Fraunce, Thomas Moffatt, and Nicholas Breton. Sidney's niece Mary Wroth, countess of Montgomery (1586–1653?), was active in the writing, staging, and production of court masques. A poet herself and the author of a massive prose romance, *Urania,* she was the central figure in a circle of literary women and men for twenty years (1604–1620s), among whom was Shakespeare's friend and rival Ben

Jonson, who dedicated his popular play *The Alchemist* (1612) to Wroth. Anna of Denmark, queen consort of King James I of England (1574–1619), supported dramatists and frequently performed in court masques herself using the theater as a platform for her anti-Spanish politics.

The Renaissance courts, court masques, and salons served as safe havens for some literary women. Within them, a wealthy few assumed significant social and cultural roles as promoters of poetry, the theater, and the art of letter writing.

Debra Barrett-Graves

See also Aragona, Giovanna d'; Education, Humanism, and Women; entries for other women mentioned in this entry; Este, Isabella d'; Toledo, Eleonora di.

Bibliography

Brucker, Gene. *Florence: The Golden Age, 1138–1737.* Berkeley: University of California Press, 1998.

Campbell, Julie. *Literary Circles, Ritual, and Gender in Early Modern Europe: A Cross-Cultural Approach.* Aldershot, UK: Ashgate, 2006.

Eisenbichler, Konrad, ed. *The Cultural Politics of Duke Cosimo I de' Medici.* Aldershot, UK: Ashgate, 2001.

Eisenbichler, Konrad, ed. *The Cultural World of Eleonora di Toledo, Duchess of Florence and Siena.* Aldershot, UK: Ashgate, 2004.

Kent, Francis William, Marina Belozerkaya, Ted-Larry Pebworth, and Claude J. Summers. "Patronage: Patrons and Clients in Renaissance Society." In *Encyclopedia of the Renaissance.* Edited by Paul F. Grendler, 424–434. New York: Charles Scribner's Sons, 1999.

Levin, Carole, et al. *Extraordinary Women of the Medieval and Renaissance World: A Biographical Dictionary.* Westport, CT: Greenwood Press, 2000.

Mendelson, Sara, and Patricia Crawford. *Women in Early Modern England.* Oxford: Clarendon Press, 1998.

Locke, Anne Vaughan (1530–1590)

English scholar, religious writer, Calvinist

Anne Vaughan Locke was born into a pious Protestant household in London; her father, Steven Vaughan, was a diplomat in the service of King Henry VIII. Although Anne received no formal education, she was taught to read and write and she was particularly learned in theology.

In her early 1520s Anne married Henry Locke, who, like Anne, was committed to Protestant principles. In 1553 Scottish Protestant reformer John Knox lived with the Lockes in London before the accession of Catholic Mary Tudor led to his departure for the Continent. Knox, taken with Anne's piety, wrote her several letters from Switzerland and invited her to join the community of Protestants in exile there. In May 1557 Anne accepted Knox's invitation and moved to Geneva with her two small children; her husband joined them later. In Geneva, Anne began translating some of John Calvin's sermons into English. After the death of Queen Mary and the accession of Elizabeth, which made England safer for Protestants, Anne returned to England; in 1560 she published her *Sermons of John Calvin* and dedicated her work to Catherine, dowager duchess of Suffolk, who had herself been a Protestant in exile.

Anne's husband, Henry, died in 1571, and she remarried a preacher, Edward Dering. Anne's second husband, ten years younger than herself, was an outspoken and active preacher whose views were initially applauded by the queen but were eventually found too critical of the Church of England. In 1576 Dering died after a brief illness, leaving a strong legacy of Puritan criticism against what he and his circle perceived as Elizabeth's insufficient measures toward Protestant reform.

In 1583 Anne married again; her third husband was Richard Prowse, a cloth merchant and member of parliament who, like her first two husbands, demonstrated decidedly Puritan sympathies. At the end of her life, Anne published a translation from the French of Jean Taffin's religious treatise, *Of the markes of the children of God, and of their comfort in afflictions.*

In recent years scholars have attended to the work appended to Locke's translation of Calvin's sermons: *A Meditation Of A Penitent Sinner: Written in Maner of A Paraphrase upon the 51. Psalme of David.* This work, a reflection on the healing powers of faith, takes the form of twenty-six sonnets and is particularly notable as the first known sonnet sequence in English. Throughout her life, Locke remained within the domestic sphere circumscribed for sixteenth-century women but nonetheless made significant contributions to the religious writing of her period.

Jo Eldridge Carney

See also Religious Reform and Women; Translation and Women Translators.

Bibliography

Primary Works

Anne Locke. *A Meditation of a Penitent Sinner: Anne Locke's Sonnet Sequence with Locke's Epistle.* Edited and with an introduction by Kel Morin-Parsons. Waterloo, Ontario, Canada: North Waterloo Academic Press, 1997.

Anne Vaughan Lock. *The Collected Works of Anne Vaughan Lock.* Medieval and Renaissance Texts and Studies. Vol. 185. Edited by Susan Felch. Tempe: Arizona Center for Medieval and Renaissance Studies, Renaissance English Text Society, 1999.

Secondary Works

Collinson, Patrick. *Godly People: Essays on English Protestantism and Puritanism.* Pages 273–289. London: Hambledon Press, 1983.

Donawerth, Jane. "Women's Poetry and the Tudor-Stuart System of Gift Exchange." *Women, Writing, and the Reproduction of Culture.* Edited by Mary Burke, Jane Donawerth, Linda Dove, and Karen Nelson, 3–18. Syracuse, NY: Syracuse University Press, 2000.

Loynes, Antoinette de (1505–1568)

Humanist, translator, poet and patron

Antoinette de Loynes, a highly learned woman, descended from a noble family of parliamentarians. Her father, François de Loynes (d. 1524), was first regent of the University of Paris and then counselor at the Parisian parliament. Antoinette must have been initiated early on in the reading of Greek, Latin, and Italian authors. She competed with poets and entertained correspondences in Latin and French with renowned humanists.

From her first husband, Lubin d'Allier, a Norman patrician and lawyer at the parliament of Paris, Antoinette had a daughter, Marie d'Allier, born around 1529, who married Jean Mercier, the famous Hebrew scholar and the king's professor and public reader; their son, Josias Mercier (1572–1626), was to become famous for his learning as well. In 1546, Antoinette married Jean de Morel (1511–1581), a nobleman of Dauphiné and disciple of Erasmus, who was employed by the royal family first as squire, then as *maréchal des logis de la Reine* (1548, 1556, 1558), subsequently as *valet de chambre* of King Henri II (1558), and finally, chosen by Catherine de Médicis, as *maître d'hôtel, gouverneur,* and instructor of the duc d'Angoulême, Henri II's natural son. The Morel couple had a son, Isaac, and three daughters, Camille, Lucrèce, and Diane, who benefited from their parent's exceptional learning and stimulating intellectual environment, where Latin was spoken at home and literary conversations were a daily event. In fact, the Morel mansion was the foremost cultural meeting place of the time, and the family's patronage had a bearing on nearly all French intellectuals in the second half of the sixteenth century, including the poets of the Pléiade who were favored at court thanks to Morel's influence. Consequently, numerous writers dedicated their works to members of the Morel family and praised them in forewords or letter exchanges. Several sixteenth-century biographers mention Antoinette de Loynes and her daughters, among them the prodigy Camille de Morel, for their mastery of classical and foreign languages and their poetic compositions. The importance the Morels acquired in the royal circles is well illustrated by the fact that their children were to act in the play written by Du Bellay for the wedding of Francis I's daughter, Marguerite de France, herself a member of Antoinette's poetic cenacle. Even though this *Epithalame* was never performed (due to the tragic accident taking the life of the bride's brother Henry II), it attests to the high regard the poet and the entire court must have had for the exceptional training of these children.

Antoinette's familiarity with the court and taste for poetry allowed her to become well acquainted with Francis I's sister, Marguerite de Navarre, and to participate in the *Tombeau de Marguerite de Valois Royne de Navarre* (1551), a poetic collection to honor the deceased queen (d. 1549). After publishing a first Latin memorial (*Hecatodistichon,* 1550) featuring one hundred distiches written by the Seymour sisters and a few compositions by great Neolatin poets, Nicolas Denisot invited the poets of the Brigade (later known as Pléiade) to translate the distiches into French and Italian and to add other homage of their own. Unlike Ronsard and Du Bellay, who participated in this *recueil* mainly to highlight their reputation at court and please their new protector, Marguerite de France, Antoinette de Loynes writes a humble panegyric of her friend Marguerite de Navarre, whom she praises both for her spiritual example and literary talent. In her translation of eighteen Latin distiches and her French sonnet in memory of the queen, she also salutes Margaret, Anne, and Jane Seymour for their beautiful verses and fine understanding of Marguerite's poetry. Antoinette further participated in Charles de Sainte-Marthe's *Oraison funebre de l'incomparable Marguerite, royne de Navarre* (A Funeral Oration on the Incomparable Marguerite, Queen of Navarre) in which she translated a few of his Latin verses into French and wrote two sonnets in honor of the queen. She also composed a French epigram on the death of a female friend, the spouse of the Neolatin poet, Jean Salmon (Macrin), which was included in Salmon's *Neaniae* honoring his wife. Antoinette de Loynes's presence in these three collections is of great literary importance as the only extant example of female encomiastic literature in the French Renaissance.

Catherine M. Müller

See also Education, Humanism, and Women; Literary Culture and Women; Marguerite de Navarre; Morel, Camille de; Seymour, Jane; Translation and Women Translators.

Bibliography
Primary Works
Loynes, Antoinette de. *Annae, Margaritae, Janae, sororum virginum, heroidum Anglarum, In mortem Divae Margaritae Valesiae, Navarrorum reginae, Hecatodistichon. . . .* Paris: Regnaut Chauldiere et fils [Claude], 1550.

Loynes, Antoinette de. "Anne, Margaret, and Jane Seymour." Edited and introduction by Brenda M. Hosington. In *The Early Modern Englishwoman: A Facsimile Library of Essential Works.* I: Printed Writings, 1500–1640; Series II, vol. 6. Edited by Betty S. Travitsky and Patrick Cullen. Aldershot, UK: Ashgate, 2000.

Loynes, Antoinette de. *Le Tombeau de Marguerite de Valois Royne de Navarre faict premierement en Disticques Latins par les trois Sœurs Princesses en Angleterre. Depuis traduictz en Grec, Italien & François par plusieurs des excellents poëtes de la France. Avecques plusieurs Odes, Hymnes, Cantiques, Epitaphes, sur le mesme subiect.* Paris: Michel Fezandat, 1551.

Salmon, Jean. *Salmonii Macrini Iuliodunensis Cubicularii Regii Naeniarum libri tres, De Gelonide Borsala uxore carissima nuper defuncta.* Paris: apud Vascosanum, 1550. (Antoinette's Epigram is on p. 135.)

Secondary Works
Hosington, Brenda M. "England's First Female-Authored Encomium: The Seymour Sisters' *Hecatodistichon* (1550) to Marguerite de Navarre. Text, Translation, Notes, and Commentary." *Studies in Philology* 93, no. 2 (1996): 117–163.

Müller, Catherine M. "Éloges au féminin: la voix nouvelle d'Antoinette de Loynes (poétesse et traductrice) dans le *Tombeau* de Marguerite de Navarre (1551)." *Versants* 46 (La littérature au féminin, 2004): 49–63.

Nolhac, Pierre de. "Le premier salon littéraire de Paris." *La Revue Universelle* (1 June 1921): 537–552.

Stephens, Winifred. *Margaret of France, Duchess of Savoy, 1573–74, a Biography.* London: J. Lane, 1912. (Page 120 lists all women present in the literary circle of Antoinette de Loynes, among them Marguerite de France, daughter of King Francis I and primary patron of the Pléiade poets.)

Will, Samuel F. "Camille de Morel: A Prodigy of the Renaissance." *PMLA* 51 (1936): 83–119.

(A list of Antoinette de Loynes's writings is given on p. 116 in this pioneer article.)

Will, Samuel F. "The Dedication and Rededication of Ronsard's 'Hymne de la Mort.'" *PMLA* 46 (1931): 432–440. (Attribution and edition of Antoinette de Loynes's witty poetic response to Ronsard is on p. 438.)

Lumley, Jane (1537–1578)

Greek scholar, first translator of Euripides into English
One of the most highly educated women of her time, Lady Jane Lumley, daughter of Henry Fitzalan, the twelfth earl of Arundel (1512–1580), is best known for her translation of Euripides' tragedy *Iphigenia at Aulis* (*The Tragedie of Euripides called Iphigeneia translated out of the Greake into Englisse,* ca. 1554). This was the first translation of one of Euripides' plays into English. Scholars have suggested that Lumley made use of Erasmus's Latin translation of the *Iphigenia,* which included a Greek text. In any case, her edition of the *Iphigenia* is an adaptation rather than a complete translation, and some of the long choral odes have been omitted.

When Jane's mother died in 1542, her father, who was committed to the idea that she and her younger brother, Henry Fitzalan, should benefit equally from humanist studies in the classics, assumed sole care of her education. At the age of fifteen or sixteen, Jane received and accepted a proposal of marriage from John Lumley, a university friend of her brother's and a titled baron. Although her stepmother and her brother Henry were dead by 1557, Jane and her husband, who at the time was engaged in translating Erasmus's *Institutio Principis Christiani* from Latin into English, remained close to her father, united in their passion for learning and their commitment to Catholicism. In 1553, Lord Arundel had been active in installing Mary I on the throne of England, and the Lumleys took part in the coronation ceremony.

Jane Lumley died on 27 July 1578 after having two sons and a daughter, who all died in childhood. She was survived by her father and husband, who erected a tomb for her at Cheam in Surrey in 1596.

Carole Levin and Shannon L. Meyer

See also the subheading Greek Learning and Women (under Education, Humanism, and Women); Translation and Women Translators.

Bibliography

Primary Works

Child, Harold H., ed. *Iphigenia at Aulis translated by Lady Lumley.* Oxford: Malone Society, 1909.

Purkiss, Diane, ed. *Three Tragedies by Renaissance Women: Euripides and Others.* New York and London: Penguin, 1998.

Secondary Works

Beilin, Elaine V. *Redeeming Eve: Women Writers of the English Renaissance.* Princeton, NJ: Princeton University Press, 1987.

Findlay, Alison, and Stephanie Hodgson-Wright with Gweno Williams. "Translating the Text, Performing the Self." By Gweno Williams. *Women and Dramatic Production, 1550–1700.* Harlow, UK: Pearson Education Limited, 2000.

Hodgson-Wright, Stephanie. "Lumley, Jane Lady Lumley (1537–1578)." *Oxford Dictionary of Nation Biography.* Oxford: Oxford University Press, 2004.

M

Makeup and Cosmetics

Although the craft of cosmetic enhancement was known to women from the ancient times, it is in the Renaissance that its use became increasingly widespread. From Italy and France, beauty aids found their way to England, where women of all classes eagerly welcomed the new fashion. A look into a typical makeup box would reveal powders, ointments, paints, and dyes whose primary purpose was to achieve the brilliant colors of the ideal Renaissance beauty: a white and red face framed by blonde hair. Unfortunately, many of these cosmetics contained harmful ingredients: mercury-based paints for reddening women's cheeks and lips; ceruse (white lead), which was widely used in the bleaching concoctions; and compounds that included borax and alum. All these aids soon sapped the complexion of its vitality, produced wrinkles, and even affected the teeth. Poisonous belladonna was used to give the eyes a sparkling appearance and widen the pupils. Along with such injurious substances, contemporary recipe books invited women to reach for more wholesome ingredients such as egg whites, olive oil, bear's grease, and juices and dyes derived from certain trees or berries, but also recommended the use of such unsavory components as animal blood, snail shells, and ashes made from the crushed bones of various creatures.

The relative crudeness of cosmetics available to Renaissance women was probably responsible for such caustic remarks as the seventeenth-century English writer Thomas Tuke's pronouncement suggesting that women wear so much makeup on their cheeks that it looks like curds of cheesecake; however, while sometimes women flaunted their makeup by applying it liberally, they also knew how to paint themselves with skill and subtlety that deftly blended nature and art. Such skill of application caused a great deal of anxiety among men, who could not always readily discern whether a woman's beauty was natural or artificial. The issue was especially important because face painting provoked lively debate in the Renaissance. The opponents of the use of cosmetics lined up a battery of arguments rooted in the writings of the church fathers. The most important objection concerned a woman's appropriation of God's right to creation: in this view, a woman who used makeup heretically altered the sacred work of God—her face—and became, as Tuke put it, "her own creatrisse." Further criticism reminded women that, by painting themselves, they resembled the notorious users of makeup—courtesans and prostitutes. In addition, some economic objections were put forth: not only were cosmetics costly, but the hours spent in front of a mirror subtracted from the time a woman spent running her household.

Meanwhile, the supporters of the new fashion published collections of recipes for homemade cosmetics as well as treatments for the blemishes like freckles and acne. The prefaces to these books encouraged women to take charge of their appearance, emphasized the repulsiveness of facial imperfections, and explained that it was unfair to their souls to keep them imprisoned in the withering bodies that could be easily turned into palaces. The defenders of cosmetics argued that women who painted their faces sought to please their own husbands rather than other men. Perhaps the most persuasive statement in favor of cosmetics, however, was made by women themselves: face painting flourished in such powerful courts as those of Catherine de Médicis and Elizabeth I, and women of all classes across Europe followed this example, opening their makeup boxes every morning to create themselves anew.

Anna Riehl

Bibliography

Primary Works

Jeamson, Thomas. *Artificiall Embellishments; or, Arts Best Directions: How to Preserve Beauty or Procure It.* Oxford: William Hall, 1665.

Tuke, Thomas. *A Treatise Against Painting and Tincturing of Men and Women.* London: 1616.

Secondary Works

Carney, Jo Eldridge. " 'God hath given you one face, and you make yourselves another': Face Painting in the Renaissance." *Lamar Journal of the Humanities* 21, no. 2 (Fall 1995): 21–34.

Dolan, Frances E. "Taking the Pencil Out of God's Hand: Art, Nature, and the Face-Painting Debate in Early Modern England." *PMLA* 108, no. 2 (March 1993): 224–239.

Phillippy, Patricia. *Painting Women: Cosmetics, Canvases, and Early Modern Culture.* Baltimore, MD: Johns Hopkins University Press, 2006.

Makin, Bathsua (1600–1676?)

Educator, author, healer, linguist, and advocate of women's education

At language learning, Bathsua Makin (née Reginald) was a child prodigy. She could read in six languages, thanks to instruction from her schoolmaster father, Henry Reginald. She published her first book, the *Musa Virginea,* which included poems and passages praising King James I and his family in Latin, Greek, Spanish, French, and Hebrew, when she was sixteen. Another work, written with her father, gave an account of a shorthand system they had developed, called radiography. Her contemporary, Sir Simonds D'Ewes, said she was far more learned than her father and the greatest scholar of any woman in England.

After marrying Richard Makin in 1622, she had eight children. She also began her career as an educator of the aristocracy, with a strong avocation for healing the sick. Her most important pupil was Princess Elizabeth Stuart, daughter of Charles II, whom she taught in the 1640s. Later she taught the countess of Huntingdon and her children. Makin also maintained epistolary friendships with such notable individuals as James I's physician, George Eglisham, the London physician Baldwin Hamey, the Ralegh family, and, above all, the Dutch scholar and polymath, Anna Maria van Schurman.

In 1673 Makin wrote her most important work, *An Essay to Revive the Antient* [sic] *Education of Women,* in which she argued that educating girls was a sound practice, both because of the many precedents she cited of learned women from the classical period and the Bible, as well as from her own period, and because of the practical benefits to a woman's household. The pamphlet is witty, arguing strongly for educational reforms, and is certainly one of the first essays by an Englishwoman to defend the power of the female intellect and to recommend higher education for women.

Frances Teague

See also the subheadings Latin Learning and Women; Greek Learning and Women (under Education, Humanism, and Women); the subheading Letter Writing (under Literary Culture); Translation and Women Translators.

Bibliography

Primary Works

Makin, Bathsua. *An Essay to Revive the Antient Education of Gentlewomen.* London: 1673. Wing M309.

Makin, Bathsua. *Musa Virginea Graeco. Latino. Gallica.* London: 1616. STC 20835.

Makin, Bathsua, with Henry Reginald. *Ad Annam . . . Reginam.* London: no date. STC 20834.5.

Secondary Works

Brink, J. R. "Bathsua Reginald Makin: 'Most Learned Matron.'" *Huntington Library Quarterly* 54 (1991): 313–327.

Salmon, Vivian. "Bathsua Makin: A Pioneer Linguist and Feminist in Seventeenth-Century England." In *Neuere Forschungen zur Wortbildung und Histriographie der Linguistik: Festgabe für Herbert E. Brekle.* Edited by Brigitte Asbach-Schnitker and Johannes Rogenhofer, 303–318. Tübingen: Gunter Narr Verlag, 1987.

Teague, Frances. *Bathsua Makin, Woman of Learning.* Lewisburg, PA: Bucknell University Press, 1998.

Malatesta, Battista da Montefeltro (1383–1450)

Writer and orator from Urbino, dedicatee of Leonardo Bruni's De studiis et literis

Battista da Montefeltro Malatesta was the youngest daughter of Antonio da Montefeltro, count of Urbino, and Agnesina di Giovanni dei Prefetti di Vico. In 1405 she married Galeazzo Malatesta, lord of Pesaro from 1429 to 1431. She bore her husband a single daughter, Elisabetta. After the death of her husband, Battista returned to Urbino. She died almost twenty years later at the Monastero di Santa Lucia di Foligno, having taken the name Girolama as a sister of the Franciscan Order of Saint Clare. Battista was the grandmother of Cecilia Gonzaga and Costanza Varano, whose early education she oversaw, as well as the great-grandmother of Vittoria Colonna.

Battista's father encouraged her early education such that, by the time of her marriage, she was already widely known as an exceptionally learned woman. Her literary production was later supported by her father-in-law, Malatesta di Pandolfo Malatesta, with whom she exchanged letters and poems after her husband's assassination. Battista's erudition, her ability to negotiate shrewdly but prudently, and her Latin and vernacular writings were praised by her contemporaries as well as by later Quattrocento humanists and biographers, including Guiniforte Barzizza, Vespasiano da Bisticci, and Jacobus Philippus Bergomensis. She was also the dedicatee of Leonardo Bruni's letter, *De studiis et literis,* which was written in 1424 and detailed a program of humanist education for women, including the importance of good Latin, solid writing skills, and the need to explore the disciplines of religion, morals, history, and poetry.

Throughout her marriage, Battista exchanged numerous letters with her relatives in Urbino, including her sister, Anna, and sister-in-law, Paola Gonzaga. In 1418, she congratulated Martin V on his recent election as pope in a Latin oration, and in 1425 wrote requesting his aid on behalf of her sister-in-law, Clofe,

whose husband was threatening to abandon her. In 1433, Battista delivered a Latin oration to the Holy Roman Emperor Sigismund in which she begged, on behalf of her family, for the return of Pesaro and, on behalf of her daughter, for the freedom of her son-in-law, Pier Gentile Varano da Camerino, who was unjustly languishing in prison. Several of Battista's Latin letters and orations, sacred poems, and personal letters in the vernacular have been published, but more exist only in manuscript form at the Biblioteca Oliveriana, the Vatican, and the Chigi Libraries.

Amyrose Gill

See also Colonna, Vittoria; Education, Humanism, and Women; the subheading Letter Writing (under Literary Culture and Women); Varano, Costanza.

Bibliography

Fattori, A., and B. Feliciangeli. "Lettere inedite di Battista da Montefeltro." *Rendiconti della Reale Accademia dei Lincei, Classe di scienze morali, storiche e filologiche* Ser. 5 26 (1917): 196–215.

Franceschini, Gino. "Battista Montefeltro Malatesta, Signora di Pesaro." In *Figure del Rinascimento urbinate.* Pages 159–193. Urbino: S.T.E.U., 1959. (Includes poems and letters.)

King, Margaret L., and Albert Rabil, Jr., eds. *Her Immaculate Hand: Selected Works by and about the Women Humanists of Quattrocento Italy.* Binghamton: State University of New York Press, 1983. (Includes the oration to Holy Roman Emperor Sigismund in translation.)

Margaret of Parma (Margaret of Austria; 1522–1586)

Regent of the Netherlands; married Alessandro de Medici, duke of Florence (1536–1537), and Ottavio Farnese (1538–1586), duke of Parma and Piacenza

Margaret of Parma was born in Oudernaarde, Flanders, the natural daughter of Charles V, Holy Roman emperor and king of Spain (1519–1556), and Johanna von der Gheenst, a servant. Like her bastard half brother John of Austria, Margaret was legitimized by her father. Her childhood was spent at the Habsburg

Margaret of Parma, daughter of Emperor Charles V and regent of the Netherlands. Portrait by unknown artist. (Library of Congress)

court in Mechelen under the supervision of her namesake, Charles's aunt Margaret of Austria, regent of the Netherlands (1507–1515 and 1518–1530). With Margaret's death, she came under the care of her aunt, Mary of Hungary, who succeeded her guardian as regent of the Netherlands (1531–1555).

In 1530 Charles V helped Pope Clement VII restore the Medici family at Florence, naming Alessandro de' Medici (b. 1510/1511–1537) the first hereditary duke of the city (1532–1537). Alessandro, an illegitimate child himself, was betrothed to Margaret, then only eight years of age. They were married in 1536, when Margaret was fourteen, but Alessandro was murdered a year later. In 1538 she married again, this time to Ottavio Farnese (1521–1586), then duke of Camerino. He was the son of Pier Luigi Farnese and Girolama Orsini, and a grandson of Pope Paul III. In 1546 Pier Luigi became duke of Parma and Piacenza but was murdered the following year. Ottavio claimed his father's inheritance, ob-

taining the restitution of the duchy of Parma from Giulio III in 1550 and that of Piacenza from Margaret's half brother, Philip II of Spain (1556–1598), in 1556, thanks to the intervention of Henry II of France.

In 1556 Margaret and Ottavio returned to the Netherlands. Here, like her aunt and great-aunt before her, she was made regent (or "governess"). She served from 1559 to 1567, but Philip II reserved most of the executive power for himself. At this time the Spanish empire, over which "the sun never set," included Spain and its American colonies, Portugal and its colonies, the duchy of Milan, the kingdoms of Naples and Sicily, the Netherlands, the Franche-Comté, and the Philippines. As regent, Margaret was supported by three institutions created in 1531: a council of state (for foreign and domestic policy), a council of finance (for economic affairs), and a privy council (for judicial matters); she also counted on the advice of the respected if unpopular Bishop Antoine Perrenot of Arras (later Cardinal Granvelle) and several close Spanish advisors.

The regency of the Netherlands was to prove a most difficult task because of growing discontent with Spanish rule. Many Dutch were opposed to the prospect of the Low Countries becoming a mere Spanish colony, and linked to this was the growing popularity of Calvinism, which set large sectors of the local population against the Catholicism of their ruler, Philip II. Hence, between 1565 and 1568 Margaret was confronted with the beginning of the Dutch Revolt for Independence, which would in time become a key factor in the collapse of Spain as a global power. Several problems contributed to make Margaret's task of governing difficult: the proposal to augment the number of bishoprics in the Netherlands from four to fourteen and to establish the archbishop of Mechelen as primate, the project to introduce an Inquisition to combat Protestantism, and the presence of Spanish troops, who being irregularly paid were prone to bouts of mutinous looting. Most serious, an increasingly active struggle for independence pitted Dutch nobles, like William of Nassau, prince of Orange, the count of Egmont, and the duke of Aerschot, against Philip II and his representatives.

In the summer of 1556 Margaret was confronted by a revolt of the lower nobility, which was accompanied by rioting in the streets. In an attempt to settle the situation, in 1567 Philip II decided to act against those responsible and sent an army under the command of his most reputable general, Fernando Álvarez de Toledo, duke of Alba, who was appointed captain-general of the Netherlands. Margaret opposed the duke's aggressively repressive policies, which included the implementation of the Inquisition and the establishment of a Council of Troubles (known to the Dutch as the Council of Blood) to restore order. But, unable to restrain the captain, Margaret resigned her position as regent and returned to Italy that same year, leaving the duke of Alba as her successor.

Margaret's role in the Netherlands provides a further example of the participation of women in formal politics during the Renaissance. The ultimate failure of her mission was due to the difficulty of the assignment and the nature of the Spanish empire and the crises it faced, rather than any lack of ability on her part. Margaret had one son, Alessandro Farnese, who was raised at the court of Philip II and went on to become a well-reputed soldier before being appointed regent of the Netherlands (1578–1592) in a subsequent period of the Dutch Revolt. At this time Margaret returned to the Netherlands to assist her son for a short while until, because of their differences of opinion, she returned to Italy in 1583. Margaret died at Ortona in 1586.

Nuria Silleras-Fernandez

See also Forteguerri, Laudomia; Power, Politics, and Women.

Bibliography

Primary Work

Thiessen, J. S., and Enno van Gelder, H. A., eds. *Correspondence française de Marguerite d'Austriche, duchesse de Parme, avec Philipe II.* 3 vols. Utrech: 1925–1942.

Secondary Works

Dumont, Georges Henri. *Marguerite de Parme: Bâtarde de Charles Quint (1522–1586).* Brussels: Le Cri Éditions, 1999.

Lefèvre, Renato. *"Madama" Margarita d'Austria (1522–1586).* Rome: Newton Compton, 1986.

Martini, Silvia, ed. *Margherita d'Austria (1522–1586): costruzioni politiche e diplomazia, tra corte Farnese e monarchia spagnola.* Rome: Bulzoni, 2003.

Parker, Geoffrey. *The Dutch Revolt.* New York and London: Penguin, 1990.

Puaux, Anne. *Madama, fille de Charles Quint: régente des Pays-Bas.* Paris: Payot, 1987.

Margaret Tudor (1489–1541)

Queen consort of James IV of Scotland, sister of Henry VIII

The eldest daughter of Henry VII and Elizabeth of York, Margaret Tudor married James IV, king of Scotland on 8 August 1503. Margaret's marriage, though not a particularly happy one, brought a period of peace between Scotland and England that lasted until the early years of Henry VIII's reign and had the unforeseen consequence of leading to Stuart claims to the English throne.

By 1511, the young Henry VIII, wanting to prove his mettle, renewed hostilities with France, the traditional ally of Scotland. Seeking to aide his French allies, James IV invaded England, dying at the Battle of Flodden Field along with the majority of his nobility on 9 September 1513. With James IV's death, Margaret became queen regent for her seventeen-month-old son, James V. Regent though she may have been, a divided council ran the government of Scotland with Margaret, but her sudden and unwise marriage in 1514 to Archibald Douglas, earl of Angus, whom she chose to make coregent, weakened her political position. In 1516, parliament deposed her in favor of John Stuart, duke of Albany; Margaret, along with her husband, fled Scotland for a brief exile in England.

After lengthy negotiations, Albany allowed Margaret to return to Scotland in June 1517, simply to live there as the mother of the king. From 1518 to 1524, Margaret found herself caught between the pro-English Scottish and pro-French Scottish factions of the nobility. Margaret, to the detriment of her own reputation, played one side against the other in the hope of regaining control of her son and her finances. Finally, in 1524, Margaret regained her position as queen regent and continued to pursue a middle ground policy, much to the consternation of her brother, Henry VIII. Unfortunately, the feuding continued, with her own husband, aided by the English, usurping her authority and custody of James V, between 1527 and 1528.

In 1528, James, now sixteen, managed to escape from the control of the Douglas clan and asserted himself as king of Scotland. Margaret divorced Douglas, married Henry Stewart, lord Methven, and resumed her life as queen dowager. Though she continued to try to influence her son and never ceased to have financial difficulties, her political importance to either England or Scotland had long passed her by. Her death in 1541 went largely unnoticed.

Timothy G. Elston

See also Power, Politics, and Women.

Bibliography

Buchanan, Patricia Hill. *Margaret Tudor, Queen of Scots.* Edinburgh: Scottish Academic Press, 1985.

Harvey, Nancy Lenz. *The Rose and the Thorn: The Lives of Mary and Margaret Tudor.* New York: Macmillan, 1975.

Perry, Maria. *Sisters to the King: The Tumultuous Lives of Henry VIII's Sisters, Margaret of Scotland and Mary of France.* New York: St. Martin's Press, 1999.

Marguerite de Navarre (Marguerite d'Angoulême, Margaret of Navarre; 1492–1549)

Queen of Navarre; author of the Heptameron, *poetry, several collection of poems, and a play; literary patron; religious reform thinker and activist*

Marguerite de Navarre, duchess of Alençon and Berry and queen of Navarre, was born in Angoulême to Louise de Savoie and Charles d'Angoulême. Her brother Francis was born in 1494. Charles died in 1496, and his cousin Louis, the duke of Orleans, obtained guardianship of the children. Louise retained custody and provided a serious education for the children. Francis Demoulins, a humanist cleric and disciple of Erasmus and Lefèvre d'Etaples, was their preceptor. Marguerite took from her mother and her teacher a spiritual disposition that marked her entire life. Louis became king of France in 1498 and, having no male heir, designated Francis as his heir presumptive in 1505. As the sister of the heir to the French crown, Marguerite was a valuable pawn in the brokerage of royal marriages. She was the subject of negotiations with Henry VII of England for his son, the future Henry VIII, and even for himself. However, on 2 December 1509, in a match arranged to settle a territorial dispute, Marguerite married Charles d'Alençon. Louis XII died on 31 December 1514, and Francis became king of France on 1 January 1515. Francis quickly embarked on his first Italian campaign and won the Battle of Marignan in September. Marguerite and Louise traveled south to welcome the returning hero, stopping en route at Saint Maximin La Sainte Baume in Provence, a site revered as the burial place of Mary Magdalen. During this period Marguerite's interest in religious reform was already evident. While in the south she visited several convents, supporting reform in the convent of Hyères. Marguerite was soon recognized as an important member of her brother's inner circle. People referred to Francis, Louise, and Marguerite as the royal "trinity." In 1517 Francis gave her the duchy of Berry and made her a ducal peer, a highly unusual position for a woman. Letters from Italian and English ambassadors refer to her as an influential figure whose favor they courted. Marguerite remained a key figure in unofficial negotiations with English emissaries representing Henry

Marguerite de Navarre, queen of Navarre, author of the Heptameron, *poet and playwright. Anonymous portrait. Musée Condé, Chantilly, France. (Réunion des Musées Nationaux/Art Resource)*

VIII. Her name appears regularly in letters of Venetian ambassadors and papal nuncios. She also became known as a lover of letters and a patron of poets. Clement Marot, Bonaventure Des Périers, and Jean Bouchet were among the earliest writers to enjoy her protection.

It is uncertain when she began to write the religious poetry that established her own literary reputation. From 1521 to 1524 she corresponded with Guillaume Briçonnet, bishop of Meaux, disciple of Lefèvre, and leader of a movement to reform the Catholic Church from within. In his letters Briçonnet asked her support for his group, called *évangéliques,* because the Gospels, or *évangiles,* were their model for reformed Christianity. He urged Marguerite toward a mystical quest for God. Marguerite wrote of her grief at the deaths of her sister-in-

law Queen Claude and Claude's young daughter Charlotte in September 1524. One of Marguerite's earliest poems, *Dialogue in the Form of a Nocturnal Vision,* reflects that experience and echoes Briçonnet's counsel. During those years she composed a commentary on the Lord's Prayer, modeled on a work by Martin Luther. In the early 1520s the Parisian Faculty of Theology, known as the Sorbonne, had moved to prevent Luther's influence from spreading in France and had accused the Meaux group of heresy. Marguerite worked to protect the evangelical reformers. In February 1525, Francis was defeated at the Battle of Pavia and taken prisoner to Madrid by Charles V, the Hapsburg emperor. Marguerite's public role in the court became more prominent when she traveled to Madrid and participated in the negotiations to obtain her brother's release. Charles d'Alençon had died in the aftermath of Pavia, and, soon after Francis was ransomed, Marguerite married Henri d'Albret, King of Navarre, in January 1527. She gave birth to their daughter, Jeanne, in November 1528. A son, Jean, was born in July 1530 but died the following Christmas.

In 1531 the first of Marguerite's writings to be published, *The Mirror of the Sinful Soul,* was printed in Alençon, to be reprinted in 1533 in Paris by Antoine Augereau. By then she had aroused the ire of the Parisian theologians, who tried to censure the *Mirror* before Francis intervened. She had invited Gerard Roussel, a staunch evangelical, to preach Lenten sermons at the Louvre, sermons that criticized Lenten fasting. In October students at the University of Paris presented a play that ridiculed Marguerite as a mad heretic. Rising tensions exploded in October 1534 when placards attacking the mass appeared throughout Paris and in other cities. Francis, alarmed by the audacity of the conspirators, allowed the Paris Parlement to unleash a severe crackdown, executing over a dozen perceived heretics, including Augereau. Many of the evangelical group fled. Marguerite harbored Marot and John Calvin briefly at her château in Nérac before they moved on to

Italy. Although supporting the reformers became more difficult after the Placards Affair, Marguerite remained committed to their cause. She provided a home at Nérac for Lefèvre d'Etaples until his death in 1536, and that year she obtained a bishopric for Gérard Roussel at Oloron in the safety of her husband's territories. Calvin wrote a letter from Geneva criticizing Roussel and by implication Marguerite, for compromising his beliefs by accepting the post. Calvin continued his attacks on those who stayed "among the papists" and obliquely targeted Marguerite and her circle, calling them "Nicodemites" in a 1544 treatise. In a 1545 treatise he excoriated the Spiritual Libertines, a group that Marguerite protected, and wrote a letter to her defending himself and exhorting her not to abandon the "Church of God." Those years brought severe blows to the evangelical reformers. Several writers in Marguerite's circle died: Clément Marot in exile in Turin in 1544; Bonaventure Des Periers, apparently by suicide, the same year. The Counter-Reformation Council of Trent opened in 1545. In April of that year, Francis authorized the massacre of the Waldensians in Provence; some three thousand people were killed. Guillaume Farel reported to Calvin that Marguerite wept bitterly when she heard the news and swore to make life miserable for the baron d'Oppède, the massacre's leader. Perhaps as a result of those events, Rabelais dedicated his 1546 *Third Book of Pantagruel* to Marguerite.

In 1540 negotiations were under way to marry Marguerite's daughter, Jeanne d'Albret, to the duke of Cleves, a move calculated to strengthen Francis's alliance with the German Protestant Schmalkald princes against Emperor Charles V. Henri d'Albret opposed that union; he hoped to regain his kingdom of Spanish Navarre by marrying his daughter to Charles V's son. Marguerite was caught in the conflict between her brother and her husband, while her daughter, a willful twelve-year-old, vigorously resisted the marriage. Marguerite supported the union, and the wedding took place in June 1541. However, citing Jeanne's tender age, she delayed sending her daughter to live with Cleves, and eventually, following a breakdown of Francis's alliance with Cleves, the marriage was annulled. In October 1548 Jeanne d'Albret married Antoine de Bourbon, a disappointing marriage in Marguerite's eyes. She could not have known that the couple's son, Henri de Navarre, would become the king of France in 1589.

Marguerite maintained connections with many women, including Renée de France, duchess of Ferrara. She exchanged letters with Vittoria Colonna, Italian humanist and advocate of reform. Marie Dentière addressed an *Epistle* to her from Geneva in 1539. It was probably a copy of the *Mirror of the Sinful Soul* given by Marguerite to Anne Boleyn that Elizabeth I, then twelve years old, used to translate the work into English in 1544.

Marguerite was a prolific writer. She composed an impressive body of religious poetry, although she did not publish a collection until 1547, when *The Pearls of the Pearl of Princesses* appeared. It included *The Triumph of the Lamb, Spiritual Songs, The Coach,* and a cycle of nativity plays as well as the earlier *Mirror*. In 1545, Antoine le Maçon dedicated to her his translation of Boccaccio's *Decameron,* a work she had commissioned. Her own collection of one hundred stories, which acknowledges that model, remained unfinished at her death. An unauthorized version, *Stories of Fortunate Lovers,* appeared in 1558. Seventy-two tales with a prologue and frame story were published in 1559 with the title *Heptameron.* That work is remarkable for its narrative complexity as well as its portraits of contemporary society. During those later years she also completed major poetic works, all conveying her intense mysticism: *The Prisons, The Ship,* and *The Mirror of Jesus Christ Crucified,* as well as the *Comedy of Mont de Marsan* and other plays.

Francis died on 31 March 1547, leaving his sister in a long period of mourning. His son and successor, Henri II, showed animosity toward his aunt and her mission to reform the church. In the summer of 1548, Marguerite traveled from Navarre to Lyon to join Henri's court and accompanied him and the new queen, Catherine de Médicis, on their royal entry into that city. Marguerite returned to Pau at the end of the year and spent time there and at Cauterets in the spring with her daughter. For the last six months of her life she was in relative solitude in Odos, where she died on 21 December 1549.

Mary McKinley

See also Albret, Jeanne d'; Colonna, Vittoria; Literary Culture and Women; Religious Reform and Women; Renata di Francia.

Bibliography

Primary Works

Marguerite de Navarre. *Heptaméron*. Edited by Renja Salminen. Geneva: Droz, 1999.

Marguerite de Navarre. *The Heptameron*. Translated by Paul Chilton. Harmondsworth, UK: Penguin, 1984.

Marguerite de Navarre. *Œuvres complètes, sous la direction de Nicole Cazauran*. Paris: Champion, 2001.

Secondary Works

Cazauran, Nicole, and James Dauphiné, eds. *Marguerite de Navarre, 1492–1992. Actes du colloque internationale de Pau (1992)*. Mont-de-Marsan, France: InterUniversitaires, 1995.

Cottrell, Robert D. *The Grammar of Silence: A Reading of Marguerite de Navarre's Poetry*. Washington, DC: Catholic University of America Press, 1986.

Ferguson, Gary. *Mirroring Belief: Marguerite de Navarre's Devotional Poetry*. Edinburgh: Edinburgh University Press, 1992.

Jourda, Pierre. *Marguerite d'Angoulême, . . . Etude Biographique et Littéraire*. 2 vols. Paris: Champion, 1930.

Lyons, John, and Mary McKinley, eds. *Critical Tales: New Studies of the Heptameron and Early Modern Culture*. Philadelphia: University of Pennsylvania Press, 1993.

Reid, Jonathan A. *King's Sister, Queen of Dissent: Marguerite of Navarre (1492–1549) and Her Evangelical Network*. Ann Arbor: University of Michigan Press, 2001.

Sommers, Paula. *Celestial Ladders: Readings in Marguerite de Navarre's Poetry of Spiritual Ascent*. Geneva: Droz, 1989.

Thysell, Carol. *The Pleasure of Discernment: Marguerite de Navarre as Theologian*. Oxford: Oxford University Press, 2000.

Marguerite de Valois (1553–1615)

Queen and memorialist

The daughter of Henry II and Catherine de Médicis, sister of Charles IX and Henry III, Marguerite de Valois (1553–1615) was a member of the French royalty. She was qualified to be called Queen of France, both by birth and by marriage, as well as Queen of Navarre due to her marriage to the Protestant Henry of Navarre, who later became Henry IV (1593), after converting to Catholicism. Marguerite is also known as Queen Margot from the Alexander Dumas novel of the same name (1845), and more recently the French film directed by Patrice Chéreau (1994). The image of Queen Margot is an extremely fictionalized and sensationalized one. Still, it has served to make her better known than most French royal women of the sixteenth century. Although technically a queen, Marguerite could never rule in her own right, because the French Salic Law forbade it. This law did not permit women to rule (as was possible in England, for example), because it was feared that a queen could marry and thus put France under the power of a foreign king. After her marriage to Henry IV was annulled in 1599, she was known as Queen Marguerite until her death in 1615.

Marguerite was married to the Protestant Henry of Navarre in 1572, an event that hastened the Saint Bartholomew's Day Massacre the same year (one of the bloodiest incidents of the French Wars of Religion [1563–1598]), in which thousands of Protestants across France were slaughtered. The marriage did not produce children, and it was eventually annulled (1599), after Marguerite had been exiled (in 1586) to the remote fortress of Usson, in the Auvergne. There she wrote the bulk of her literary work, much of which has been lost. The *Memoirs*

Marguerite de Valois, queen of France during the religious wars. Painting by François Clouet. Chateaux de Versailles et de Trianon, Versailles, France. (Réunion des Musées Nationaux/Art Resource)

(written in the late 1590s but not published until 1628) describe events from her childhood, her marriage, and her separation from Henry of Navarre; but the work breaks off abruptly in 1582. There has been speculation that she did finish the *Memoirs,* but that the post-1582 material was either lost or censored in the early seventeenth century.

Marguerite also wrote many letters, mostly in a formal, rhetorical style and generally to ask for favors from royalty and other powerful figures (Catherine de Médicis, Henry III, Henry IV, his second wife Marie de Medici, as well as foreign royalty and members of the great families of France). Eliane Viennot, the foremost Marguerite scholar today, has recently edited the *Correspondence* (1569–1614). Many letters have been lost, but still almost 470 have survived. They concern war, peace, political negotiations, as well as financial and personal problems. There are several to a lover,

Jacques Harlay de Champvallon, lamenting his infidelity and suggesting that he read more as a consolation for the pain of love.

Viennot has also edited, with the *Memoirs,* the *Justificatory Memoir for Henry Bourbon* (1574), the *Learned and Subtle Discourse* (1614), as well as the *Poetry* (1580?–1614). The *Justificatory Memoir* (1574) is the first text we have by Marguerite. It was a speech some fifteen minutes long, which tried to free her husband, Henry of Navarre (Bourbon), from suspicion of involvement in a plot by the Malcontents, a sort of proto-Fronde that took place during the tumultuous two years following the St. Bartholomew's Day Massacre. The *Learned and Subtle Discourse* (1614) is on the other hand the last thing written by Marguerite. It takes the form of a long letter addressed to the Jesuit priest Loryot in response to a book of his that had appeared earlier the same year. What is unusual about the *Discourse* is the fact that feminist sentiments are expressed there, as well as that it was the only thing published during Marguerite's lifetime in her own name.

The poetry, none of which is signed, expresses contemporary themes, such as sorrow at death and neo-Platonic love, and is mostly limited to short genres like the sonnet. Poetry was a favorite genre of Marguerite's, and it is unfortunate that much of it has been lost. However, Viennot has found poems of Marguerite included with collections written by some of her close friends, such as Brantôme. Not included by Viennot is a humorous prose dialogue, *The Ill-Assorted Bedside,* which compares the pleasures of love and study, suggesting that her lover read neo-Platonic authors such as Agricola, Leone Hebreo, and Ficino. Most commentators now believe that this dialogue is not authentic, although as recently as 1986, Yves Cazaux included it with Marguerite's collected prose works.

The *Memoirs* are Marguerite's best-known work. They appear to constitute the first completely autobiographical book by a woman in

French and were imitated in several French women's memoirs during the seventeenth century. The memoir was a genre that had been practiced in France by males in the late Middle Ages and early Renaissance but was generally used to describe public and military events rather than private or personal ones. Marguerite's contribution to the genre is that, in addition to chronicling public events, she describes seemingly insignificant incidents from her childhood and adolescence, which had an impact on her personal development, rather than on the history of France. She apparently knew the essayist Michel de Montaigne (1533–1592), since his "Apology for Raymond Sebond" (*Essays, Book II, Chap. 12)* is believed to have been written for and dedicated to her (ca. 1576–1579). Although Marguerite's *Memoirs* are more conventional, chronological autobiography than are Montaigne's *Essays,* the emphasis on the subjective side of human experience may have been something she borrowed from him.

Her most productive intellectual friendship, however, was with the memorialist Pierre de Bourdeille, Abbé de Brantôme (1540–1614). Her *Memoirs* are dedicated to him and in fact claim to respond to the overly flattering picture of her he had painted in the *Illustrious Ladies* (1580s). She sent him her version of many of the events he had also described, asking him in turn to correct her book, and to give it shape. The fact that he did not do this attests to the power of her book to stand on its own. Like Brantôme, Marguerite does write extensively about details of public royal events, particularly about her clothing and jewelry. But in addition to these traditionally "feminine" topics, the *Memoirs* chronicle her developing introspective side, strong Catholic faith, and interest in classical literature and philosophy.

Like the sixteenth-century French women poets Pernette du Guillet and Catherine des Roches, Marguerite de Valois responds to a flattering male discourse that tends to objectify her and substitutes an authentically subjective version of herself and of events (such as the Saint Bartholomew's Day Massacre), which had previously been seen only from the outside and from a male point of view. She is certainly not independent of men, as the Des Roches mother and daughter (for example) strove to be, but, as one of the first women to write openly about herself, she is original in claiming the importance of "herstory" and of her version of events that had previously been chronicled only by male historians.

Cathleen M. Bauschatz

See also Dames des Roches; Guillet, Pernette du; Literary Culture and Women.

Bibliography

Primary Works

Cazaux, Yves, ed. *Mémoires de Marguerite de Valois.* Paris: Mercure de France, 1986.

Viennot, Eliane, ed. *Correspondance 1569–1614.* Paris: Champion, 1998.

Viennot, Eliane, ed. *Mémoires et autres écrits: 1574–1614.* Paris: Champion, 1999.

Secondary Works

Bauschatz, Cathleen M. " 'Plaisir et proffict' in the Reading and Writing of Marguerite de Valois." *Tulsa Studies in Women's Literature* 7, no. 1 (Spring 1988): 27–48.

Boucher, Jacqueline. *Deux Epouses et Reines à la fin du XVIe Siècle: Louise de Lorraine et Marguerite de France.* Saint-Etienne, France: Publications de L'Université Saint-Etienne, 1995.

Cholakian, Patricia E. "Marguerite de Valois and the Problematics of Self-Representation." In *Renaissance Women Writers, French Texts / American Contexts.* Edited by Anne Larsen and Colette Winn, 67–81. Detroit, MI: Wayne State University Press, 1994.

Dumas, Alexandre. *La Reine Margot.* Paris: "J'ai lu" (Flammarion), 1994.

Garrisson, Janine. *Marguerite de Valois.* Paris: Fayard, 1994.

Lazard, Madeleine, and J. Cubelier de Beynac, eds. *Marguerite de France, Reine de Navarre et son temps.* Agen, France: Presses de l'Imprimerie Coopérative, 1994.

Viennot, Eliane. *Marguerite de Valois, histoire d'une femme, histoire d'un mythe.* Paris: Payot, 1995.

Films

La Reine Margot. Jean Dréville: 1954.

La Reine Margot. Patrice Chéreau: 1994.

Marie of Guise (Mary of Guise; 1515–1560)

Queen consort of James V of Scotland, mother of Mary, Queen of Scots

Marie of Guise became the wife of James V of Scotland on 18 May 1538, thus sealing the Scottish-French alliance with King Francis I. Prudent, intelligent, and, as she would later prove, courageous, Marie journeyed to Scotland on 10 June 1538 to take up her duties as queen consort. On 8 December 1542, having already buried two sons, Marie gave birth to Mary, princess of Scotland. With James's death eight days later, her daughter became Mary, Queen of Scots, and Marie's role changed from consort to dowager and defender of her daughter's right to rule.

Between January 1543 and 29 July 1548, a period known as England's Rough Wooing because of Henry VIII's violent policy toward Scotland, Marie of Guise largely supported the governing council's idea of an independent Scotland. However, the Battle of Pinkie Cleugh in 1547 convinced her that Scotland could not stand alone against English aggression, so Marie made every effort to maintain the French alliance, ultimately guiding the ruling council in their decision to transport her daughter Mary Stuart to France for safety.

Meanwhile in Scotland, squabbles between nobles led to continued unrest. The governor of Scotland, James Hamilton, earl of Arran, finally proved himself inept by 1554, and Marie took control. As regent, Marie had to balance the desires of the vocal Protestant clergy and nobility, suspicious of a woman ruler, against the pressures placed upon her by the French king, Henri II, who was soon to be Mary Stuart's father-in-law. Though she naturally favored the French, Marie practiced tolerance and pursued a conciliatory policy with respect to her daughter's Protestant subjects. One reason she did so was to counter the Spanish-influenced government of Mary Tudor by encouraging the Protestants in England. In early 1559, however, faced with rebellion from Scottish Protestants after Elizabeth I succeeded her sister, Marie ended her policy of tolerance, opting for union with France since Mary Stuart had married the Dauphin the previous year. By the time of her death on 11 June 1560, though Marie of Guise had kept Scotland for her daughter, the Scots had undergone such a complete change in religion and government that, when Mary Stuart returned in 1562, they hardly knew her.

Timothy G. Elston

See also Mary Stuart; Religious Reform and Women.

Bibliography

Fleming, Arnold. *Marie de Guise.* Glasgow: McLellan, 1960.

Fraser, Antonia. *Mary, Queen of Scots.* New York: Delacorte Press; London: Weidenfeld and Nicolson, 1969.

Marshall, Rosalind K. *Mary of Guise.* London: Collins, 1977.

Marinella, Lucrezia (1571–1653)

Prolific writer and poet, author of a feminist treatise

In her half-century-long literary career, Venetian writer Lucrezia Marinella published a dozen original works in a vast array of genres, including devotional prose and poetry, the treatise, the pastoral, and the epic. Several of her works had considerable success and were repeatedly reprinted. The most famous of these is a treatise first published in 1600 that defended women from misogynist attacks and asserted their superiority to men. This work, *The Nobility and Excellence of Women and the Defects and Vices of Men,* has ensured Marinella's enduring fame and has earned her a place among Europe's most important protofeminists. It has also eclipsed the rest of her æuvre, which despite its diversity demonstrated a consistent interest in women. In the lives of female saints, in the creation of heroic female characters, in dedications to powerful women, and in explicit defenses of women, Marinella showed an unwavering allegiance to her sex.

Lucrezia was born in Venice in 1571. She was the daughter of a famous physician, Giovanni Marinelli, who authored numerous texts in Latin and the vernacular and penned two texts devoted to the women: *The Adornments of Women* (1562) and *Medicine for the Infirmities of Women* (1563). Lucrezia had at least two brothers, Curzio and Angelico, and a sister Diamantina; we know nothing of Marinella's mother. Curzio was, like his father, a physician and author, and he coedited with his father a seven-volume series of Aristotle's works. He also published several medical texts in Latin. The Marinelli family was from the upper level of the nonpatrician community and perhaps belonged to the citizen class. The family's status, as well as its scholarly tradition, certainly helped Lucrezia to write and publish successfully. Also important to Marinella were the other Venetian women who wrote and published during her lifetime, in particular the protofeminists Moderata Fonte (1555–1592) and Arcangela Tarabotti (1604–1652), whose texts, with Marinella's, created a remarkable feminist flowering in Venice in these years.

Probably after 1595 and possibly after 1601, Marinella married Girolamo Vacca, also a physician. She had two children, probably born late in the first decade of the 1600s. This dating is suggested by archival documents and by a ten-year lull in Marinella's publishing, which may have coincided with her children's births and young childhood. Indeed Marinella, who published an astounding eight books and a major revision of one of them in the first twelve years of her public literary career, from 1595 to 1606, published no new works from 1607 until 1616. In 1617 she began publishing again but issued only six new works over the next thirty years. Continuing familial responsibilities may have led her to publish more sporadically, but other factors may also have held sway. In a late work, the *Exhortations to Women* (1645), Marinella urged women to avoid the inevitable censure they would encounter in a public literary life. She herself encountered some difficulties—at least one charge of plagiary and seemingly other criticism—that, despite the extensive praise she also received, may have prompted her to retreat from the intense literary activity of her youth. She published her last work in 1648 and died in 1653 at the age of eighty-two.

In 1595, Marinella made her literary debut with a poem in ottava rima on the third-century virgin martyr, Saint Columba. The work, dedicated to Margherita Estense Gonzaga (1564–1618), was the first of Marinella's many lives of female saints, a genre that allowed the writer to combine her interest in women and her deep religious devotion. Two years later, Marinella published another devotional poem in *ottava rima,* her preferred verse form; the work, dedicated to Christine de Lorraine (1565–1636), grand duchess of Tuscany, traced the life of Saint Francis and was one of the few Marinella devoted to male saints. Religious themes were more oblique in her third work, *Cupid in Love and Insane,* published in 1598 and reissued in 1618 with a dedication to Catherine Medici Gonzaga (1593–1629), duchess of Mantua. The ten-canto work in ottava rima was an allegorical tale of the enamourment, madness, and redemption of Cupid. Marinella provided a Christian interpretation through brief versed summaries and prose allegories for each canto. She also criticized unrestrained male sexual passion and directed her sympathies toward women.

Marinella's advocacy for women came to center stage with her *La Nobiltà della Donne* (Nobility of Women), first published in 1600. Her first work in prose and extremely polemic in tone, the treatise represented a radical departure from her earlier production. With it, Marinella boldly entered into the *querelle des femmes,* the debates about women's worth that had raged in Europe for centuries. Marinella penned the work in response to Giuseppe Passi's misogynist *Defects of Women,* published in Venice in 1599. Passi's text, notably virulent if otherwise derivative, enumerated women's faults and detailed the ruin they caused men. Marinella split her response to this diatribe into two parts: in the first, to supplant Passi's grotesquely negative view of women, she demonstrated women's spiritual, intellectual, physical, and moral worth, which she insisted was superior to men's. In the second, she perfectly inverted Passi's catalog of women's vices by detailing men's many failings. But beyond deftly answering Passi, the *Nobiltà*, which was republished in a much expanded edition in 1601 and reprinted in 1621, responded to general misogyny in intellectual traditions, a misogyny Marinella traced back to Aristotle. In the expanded 1601 edition, she also argued against other influential antifeminism, including Giovanni Boccaccio's *Corbaccio*.

The *Nobility of Women* showed Marinella's deep knowledge of literary and philosophic traditions. She grounded herself on the authority of Classical authors, most notably Aristotle (even though she denounced his misogyny), and of vernacular authors, preeminently Petrarch and Ariosto. Marinella dedicated her controversial text to the doctor and well respected philosopher, Lucio Scarano, a friend of her father's and secretary of the second Accademia Veneziana. She perhaps hoped he would offer her and her text protection. Indeed the work seems not to have garnered direct hostile replies, despite its polemic tone and the general contentiousness of seventeenth-century Venetian literary society.

After the fiery *Nobiltà,* Marinella returned to the production of devotional works. In 1602 she published a life of Mary in poetry and prose (she was later accused of plagiarizing the work, which was repeatedly reprinted), and in 1603 she issued a book of religious poetry. Her 1605 pastoral novel *Happy Arcadia*—the only work of this genre she published—represented another brief departure from her devotional production. In fact, her narration, which centered on the arrival in Arcadia of the Roman emperor Diocletian after he abdicated power, did not even mention the bloody persecutions of Christians

attributed to him. Dedicated to Eleonora Medici Gonzaga (1567–1611), duchess of Mantua, the work was also noteworthy for the important presence of female characters, a presence that distinguished it from other works of the genre. Marinella's religious production returned to center stage in 1606: her 1597 life of Saint Francis, which had been republished in 1605, received new recognition by its inclusion in a collection of works honoring the saint; a life of Saint Peter was published that included her summaries and interpretations; and Marinella issued a life of the local virgin Saint Justine, born in Padova. This work was the last original one that Marinella published until 1617, when she issued her *Life of the Twelve Heroes of Christ and of the Four Evangelists.* Seven more years elapsed before publication of *The Heroic Deeds and Marvelous Life of the Seraphic Saint Catherine of Siena,* a prose tribute to one of the most powerful women in the history of Christianity. Marinella dedicated the text to Maria Magdalena (1589–1631), archduchess of Austria and grand duchess of Tuscany.

After another decade of public silence and well into her sixties, Marinella returned to the literary stage with the 1635 publication of the well-regarded epic poem *Henry, or Byzantium Gained.* The work, whose 1641 reprint indicates a measure of popularity, celebrated in twenty-seven cantos and more than two thousand *ottave* Christian victories in the fourth crusade and in particular the Venetian conquests under the leadership of Enrico Dandolo. With it, Marinella provided a hopeful model for the worrisome contemporary Venetian struggles against the Turks. The work recalled Tasso's *Jerusalem Delivered* in its form, historical inspiration, and focus on a religious crusade, but overturned the negative depiction of female characters that often marked the epic genre. Like the *Nobility of Women, Happy Arcadia,* and the *Exhortations to women,* the work stood apart from Marinella's largely devotional production and again showed the writer's remarkable versatility and ambition.

Amid several late devotional works was Marinella's last secular work and last major literary effort, her 1645 *Essortazioni alle donne* (Exhortations to Women). Marinella addressed women's and men's roles in society and recanted some of the statements from the *Nobility of Women*. While in the early work, for instance, she glorified women's public presence, in the *Essortazioni* she counseled women to stay at home because of the grief they would otherwise encounter. However reactionary this and other notions may seem, the work was not a fundamental disavowal of her earlier thought. Marinella indeed still insisted on female superiority and praised women's qualities and activities while disparaging those of men. It still argued for women's nobility and excellence and continued the allegiance to women that had marked her career from its inception.

Lynn Westwater

See also Education, Humanism, and Women; Feminism; Fonte, Moderata; Literary Culture and Women; Querelle des femmes.

Bibliography

Primary Works

Edited by Lavocat, Francoise, Marinella, Lucrezia. *Arcadia felice* (1605). Florence: L. S. Olschki, 1998.

Marinella, Lucrezia. *De' gesti eroici e della vita maravigliosa della serafica santa Caterina da Siena . . . libri sei. . . .* Venice: Barezzo Barezzi, 1624.

Marinella, Lucrezia. *Essortazioni alle donne e agli altri se saranno loro a grado . . . parte prima. . . .* Venice: Valvasense, 1645.

Marinella, Lucrezia. *La nobiltà e l'eccellenza delle donne co' diffetti e mancamenti degli uomini.* Venice: G. B. Ciotti, 1601.

Marinella, Lucrezia. *La vita di Maria Vergine imperatrice dell'universo, descritta in prosa & in ottava rima.* Venice: Appresso Barezo Barezi e compagni, 1602.

Marinella, Lucrezia. *L'Enrico, ovveroBizanzio acquistato. Poema eroico.* Venice: Appresso Gherardo Imberti, 1635.

Secondary Works

Chemello, Adriana. "La donna, il modello, l'immaginario: Moderata Fonte e Lucrezia Marinella." In *Nel cerchio della luna: Figure di donna in alcuni testi del XVI secolo.* Edited by Marina Zancan, 95–179. Venice: Marsilio, 1983.

Conti Odorisio, Ginevra. *Donna e società nel Seicento.* Rome: Bulzoni, 1979.

Cox, Virginia. "The Single Self: Feminist Thought and the Marriage Market in Early Modern Venice." *Renaissance Quarterly* 48, no. 3 (1995): 513–581.

Labalme, Patricia H. "Venetian Women on Women: Three Early Modern Feminists." *Archivio veneto* 5th ser., 117 (1981): 81–109.

Lavocat, Françoise. "Introduction." In *Arcadia felice.* By Lucrezia Marinella. Florence: L. S. Olschki, 1998.

Panizza, Letizia. "Introduction." In *The Nobility and Excellence of Women, and the Defects and Vices of Men of Lucrezia Marinella.* Edited by Anne Dunhill. Chicago: University of Chicago Press, 1999.

Westwater, Lynn. "Lucrezia Marinella: Life and Works" and "Lucrezia Marinella's *Essortazioni alle Donne.*" In "The Disquieting Voice: Women's Writing and Antifeminism in Seventeenth-Century Venice." Ph.D. dissertation, University of Chicago, 2003.

Marquets, Anne de (ca. 1533–1588)

Poet and Dominican nun

In all likelihood, Anne de Marquets was born in Marques near Eu in Normandy, into a family of the provincial nobility, and was sent at an early age to the priory of Saint-Louis in Poissy where she would spend the rest of her life. Saint-Louis was a royal foundation dating from 1304; it received primarily noblewomen and had a magnificent church, conventual buildings, and generous sources of revenue. The sisters thus enjoyed considerable material well-being, and, while certain aspects of their communal life were not wholly in accord with the spirit of monasticism, they were conducive to writing: the priory remained, for example, relatively open to the outside world; evidence also shows that many nuns were able to retain private incomes and property. At the priory school, Marquets received a solid cultural formation, apparently influenced by humanist tenets, studying Latin and probably some Greek. She would later teach in the school herself, earning the gratitude of a younger generation of women.

Marquets's first collection of poetry, *Sonets, prieres et devises* (Sonnets, Prayers, and Mottoes), was written in response to the Colloquy of Poissy (1561) that, at the instigation of Charles IX and Catherine de Médicis, brought together representatives of the Catholic and Protestant churches in the hope of effecting a reconciliation. This intervention by a woman in the domain of religious polemic was highly unusual: on the one hand, a Protestant riposte was drafted; on the other hand, the Catholic hierarchy arranged for the publication of Marquets's work, a crucial role in this process being almost certainly played by the noted theologian Claude d'Espence. Both d'Espence and Marguerite de Valois, who was also present at the colloquy, encouraged Marquets to continue writing, and her second major collection of verse, *Les Divines Poesies de Marc Antoine Flaminius* (The Sacred Poems of Marcantonio Flaminio), appeared a few years later. The translation of the Neolatin poet's *De rebus divinis carmina* (1550) is followed by a series of original compositions that accounts for the larger part of the volume.

Over the last twenty years of her life, Marquets composed her most substantial work, the *Sonets spirituels* (Spiritual Sonnets), published seventeen years after her death by Marie de Fortia, a fellow nun and former pupil of the poet. The four hundred and eighty sonnets lead the reader through the Sundays and feast days of the liturgical year; meditative and didactic in tone, they draw heavily on traditional religious and devotional texts, such as the Divine Office, the Bible, and the *Golden Legend*. Marrying the aesthetic possibilities of the lyric cycle with those of the liturgical cycle, the collection constitutes nothing less than a *canzoniere divino,* of a scope, richness, and unity unparalleled in the devotional poetry of the time. Nor does the spiritual nature of the collection prevent Marquets from intervening in some of the major debates of the day, such as the Reformation and the *querelle des femmes.* While the theological ideas and the "feminism" expressed in the *Sonets spirituels* are, in general, moderate and irenic, Marquets also defends both the Catholic church and women and has sharp criticism for their detractors. In addition, the sonnets present a number of characteristics that contribute to what is generally termed the "feminization" of devotion and that invite analysis in terms of gender: the use of images having to do with motherhood, child rearing, or the home; the valorization of female exemplars (women saints and biblical characters); the textual elaboration of a female community; the emphasis placed on qualities traditionally gendered as feminine (humility, patience, obedience, tenderness, compassion, pity, and so on).

Marquets was thus one of the key women writers of devotional and religious poetry of the second half of the sixteenth century in France. Appreciated in her own time, her poetry continues to attract readers interested in studying the modulations of a woman's poetic voice notable for the originality and diversity of its production as well as for its social and religious engagement.

Gary Ferguson

See also Convents; Education, Humanism, and Women; Literary Culture and Women; Marguerite de Valois; Religious Reform and Women; Querelle des Femmes.

Bibliography
Primary Works

Ferguson, Gary, ed. *Sonets spirituels . . . sur les dimanches et principales solennitez de l'année (Spiritual Sonnets . . . on the Sundays and Principal Solemnities of the Year).* Geneva: Droz, 1997. (Originally published in Paris: Claude Morel, 1605.)

Marquets, Anne de. *Les Divines Poesies de Marc Antoine Flaminius (The Sacred Poems of Marcantonio Flaminio).* Paris: Nicolas Chesneau, 1568.

Marquets, Anne de. *Sonets, prieres et devises en forme de pasquins, pour l'assemblée de Messieurs les Prelats et Docteurs, tenue à Poissy, M.D.LXI (Sonnets, Prayers, and Mottoes in the Form of Pasquills for the Assembly of Prelates and Doctors held in Poissy, 1561).* Edited by André Gendre. *Bibliothèque d'Humanisme et Renaissance* 62 (2000):

317–357. (Originally published in Paris: Guillaume Morel, 1562.)

Secondary Works

Ferguson, Gary. "Rules for Writing: The 'Dames de Poissey.'" In *Early Modern Convent Voices: The World and the Cloister.* Edited by Thomas M. Carr, Jr. *EMF: Studies on Early Modern France* 11 (forthcoming).

Ferguson, Gary. "The Feminisation of Devotion: Gabrielle de Coignard, Anne de Marquets, and François de Sales." In *Women's Writing in the French Renaissance: Proceedings of the Fifth Cambridge French Renaissance Colloquium, 7–9 July 1997.* Edited by Philip Ford and Gillian Jondorf, 187–206. Cambridge: Cambridge French Colloquia, 1999.

Fournier, Hannah S. "La Voix textuelle des *Sonets spirituels* d'Anne de Marquets." *Etudes littéraires* 20 (1987): 77–92.

Seiler, Mary Hilarine. *Anne de Marquets, poétesse religieuse du XVI*^e *siècle.* Washington DC: Catholic University of America, 1931; New York: AMS Press, 1969.

Marriage

Marital patterns and customs varied widely in Renaissance Europe. Though in most areas the vast majority of women and men married at least once—and many people several times—in some parts of Europe the number of women who remained unmarried was significant. Even in these areas, however, marriage was the clearest mark of social adulthood for both women and men, and marriage gave women authority over dependent members of the household, including not only children but also servants, slaves, and in craft households even apprentices and journeymen. Society was conceived of as a collection of households, with a marital couple, or a person who had once been half of a marital couple, as the core of each.

Marital patterns varied according to region, social class, and, to a lesser degree, religious affiliation. The most dramatic difference was between the areas of Northern and Western Europe (including the British Isles, Scandinavia, France, Germany, and much of Italy and Spain) and Eastern and Southern Europe. In most of Northwestern Europe, historians have identified a marriage pattern unique in the world, with couples waiting until their middle or late twenties to marry, long beyond the age of sexual maturity, and then immediately setting up an independent household. Husbands were likely to be only two or three years older than their wives at first marriage, and though households often contained servants, they rarely contained more than one family member who was not a part of the nuclear family. In most of the rest of the world, including most of Southern and Eastern Europe (and a few parts of Northwestern Europe, such as Ireland), marriage was between teenagers who lived with one set of parents for a long time or between a man in his late twenties or thirties and a much younger woman, with households again containing several generations. There were regional and class variations from these patterns—in southern Italy and southern Spain, nuclear families were more common than complex, which was also true among agricultural wage laborers in Hungary and Romania—but in large part the distinction holds.

Historians are not sure exactly why this pattern of delayed marriage developed, and its consequences are easier to trace than its causes: fewer total pregnancies per woman, though not necessarily fewer surviving children; a greater level of economic independence for newlyweds, who had often spent long periods as servants or workers in other households saving money and learning skills; more people who never married at all. The most unusual feature of this pattern was the late age of marriage for women. Women entered marriage as adults and took charge of running a household immediately. They were thus not as dependent on their husbands as were, for example, upper-class women in Italian cities, where the average age of marriage for men was over thirty and for women fifteen. They were not under the authority of their mothers-in-law the way women were in Eastern European households, where younger couples lived with the husbands' parents. Did this also mean that women had a greater say in whom they married? This has been a hotly debated question lately, particularly for England, which provides the most sources in the form of family letters, diaries, and statistics regarding marriage. Some historians have argued that kin networks and a woman's immediate family continued to play the major role, while others assert that. though couples may have received advice or even threats, they were largely free to marry whom they wished.

In some ways this debate sets up a false dichotomy, because both sides tend to focus on cases in which there was clear and recorded conflict between individuals and family or community. In the vast majority of marriages, the aims of the woman involved and her parents, kin, and community were the same; the best husband was the one who could provide security, honor, and status. Therefore even women who were the most free to choose their own husbands, such as widows or women whose parents had died, were motivated more by what might be seen as pragmatic concerns than romantic love. This is not to say that their choice was unemotional but that the need for economic security, the desire for social prestige, and the hope for children were as important emotions as sexual passion. The love and attraction a woman felt for a man could be based on any combination of these.

The link, rather than conflict, between social and emotional compatibility was recognized explicitly by Jewish authorities. Jewish marriages in most parts of Europe continued to be arranged throughout the Renaissance, and the spouses were both young. Authorities expected love to follow, however, and described the ideal marriage as one predestined in heaven. Jewish law allowed divorce (termed *get*) for a number of reasons, including incompatibility; in theory the agreement of both spouses was needed, and the economic division of the assets was to be based on each spouse's behavior. Divorce was then justified

on the grounds that the spouses had obviously not been predestined for each other.

One of the key ideas of the Protestant Reformation was the denial of the value of celibacy and the championing of married life as a spiritually preferable state. One might thus expect strong denominational differences in Christian marriage patterns, but this is very difficult to document, in large part because all the areas of Europe that became Protestant lie within Northwestern Europe. There were a number of theoretical differences. Protestant marriage regulations stressed the importance of parental consent more than Catholic ones and allowed the possibility of divorce with remarriage for adultery or impotence, and in some areas also for refusal to have sexual relations, deadly abuse, abandonment, or incurable diseases such as leprosy. Orthodox law in Eastern Europe allowed divorce for adultery or the taking of religious vows. The numbers of people of any Christian denomination who actually used the courts to escape an unpleasant marriage were very small, however, and apparently everywhere smaller than the number of couples who informally divorced by simply moving apart from one another. In parts of Europe where this has been studied, women more often used the courts to attempt to form a marriage, that is, in breach of promise cases, or to renew a marriage in which their spouse had deserted them, than to end one. The impossibility of divorce in Catholic areas was mitigated somewhat by the possibility of annulment and by institutions that took in abused or deserted wives; similar institutions were not found in Protestant areas.

Place of residence and social class had a larger impact than religion on marital patterns. Throughout Europe, rural residents married earlier than urban ones and were more likely to live in complex households of several generations or married brothers and their families living together. They also remarried faster and more often. Women from the upper classes married earlier than those from the lower, and the age difference between spouses was greater for upper-class women. Women who had migrated in search of employment married later than those who had remained at home and married someone closer to their own age.

Along with significant differences, there were also similarities in marriage patterns throughout Europe. Somewhere around one-fifth of all marriages were remarriages for at least one of the partners, with widowers much more likely to remarry—and to remarry faster—than widows. The reasons for this differ according to social class; wealthy or comfortable widows may have seen no advantage in remarrying, for this would put them under the legal control of a man again, and poor widows, particularly elderly ones, found it very difficult to find marriage partners.

Women of all classes were expected to bring a dowry to their marriage, which might consist of some clothing and household items (usually including the marriage bed and bedding) for poor women, or vast amounts of cash, goods, or property for wealthy ones; in Eastern Europe the dowry might even include serfs or slaves. The size of the dowry varied by geographic area and across time as well as by social class; in fifteenth- and sixteenth-century Florence, for example, dowries required for a middle- or upper-class woman to marry grew staggeringly large, and families placed many of their daughters in convents instead of trying to find husbands for them, because convent entrance fees were much lower than dowries. This dowry substituted in most parts of Europe for a daughter's share of the family inheritance and increasingly did not include any land, which kept land within the patrilineal lineage. Laws regarding a woman's control of her dowry varied throughout Europe, but in general a husband had the use, but not the ownership, of it during his wife's lifetime, though of course if he invested it unwisely this distinction did not make much difference. Women could sue their own husbands if they thought they were wast-

ing their dowries, however, and courts in many areas sided with the women, taking control of the dowry out of the husbands' hands. This was clearly something done only as a last resort, however, as it meant a woman had to admit publicly her husband was a wastral or spendthrift. During the late medieval period, women appear to have been able freely to bequeath their dowries to whomever they chose, but in many parts of Europe this right was restricted during the sixteenth century to prevent them from deeding property to persons other than the male heirs.

This increasing legal emphasis on the male lineage paralleled an increasing concern among male religious, literary, and political writers with the authority and role of the male head of household, though some writers also stressed the wife's authority over children and servants and the importance of mutual affection between spouses. But what about actual marital relations? Did husbands and wives show more or less affection for one another than modern couples? Which injunction was followed more in practice, that of husbandly authority or that of mutual respect? The earliest research on these questions tended to view the Renaissance family as patriarchal, authoritative, and unfeeling, but more recent work has discovered that spouses, particularly women, expected a marriage to include affection and companionship and were very distressed when it did not. Examples of both tyrannical husbands and of mutually caring relationships abound, with the safest generalization being the seemingly most obvious: marriages appear to have been most egalitarian when husband and wife were near in age or of the same (or relatively the same) social class, when the woman had brought some property or cash to the marriage as her dowry, and when her birth family supported her in disputes with her husband.

The majority of women in early modern Europe chose to marry. Single women remained notable exceptions in a culture that set a high premium on wedlock In Eastern and Southern Europe, with a much earlier average age at first marriage, the number of women who never married was small, and most of them were in convents. In 1552 in Florence, for example, there were 441 male friars and 2,786 nuns, out of a population of 59,000. In the cities of Northwestern Europe, however, demographers estimate that between 10 to 15 percent of the population from the fourteenth through the eighteenth centuries never married. Cities attracted unmarried women with the possibility of employment as domestic servants or in cloth production, a situation reflected in the gradual transformation of the word "spinster" during the seventeenth century from a label of occupation to one of marital status. City governments worried about how to keep unmarried women and widows from needing public support and about the fact that they were "masterless," that is, not members of a male-headed household. Laws were passed forbidding unmarried women to move into cities or women to live on their own, though such laws were difficult to enforce.

Women themselves, especially in Protestant areas, sometimes internalized the stigma attached to never being married. Funeral sermons of unmarried women, for which the women themselves often chose their own Biblical texts and wrote the biographical segment, explain that the deceased was not simply a person who had lost out in the marriage market, but one who had fulfilled her Christian duties in other ways than being a wife or mother, such as by taking care of elderly parents or serving the needy. Not all women agreed that marriage was preferable, however. Anna Bijns, a sixteenth-century poet from Antwerp, wrote:

> How good to be a woman, how much better to
> be a man!
> Maidens and wenches, remember the lesson
> you're about to hear
> Don't hurtle yourself into marriage far too
> soon . . .

> Though wedlock I do not decry:
> Unyoked is best! Happy the woman without a
> man. (Aercke 1987, 382)

Merry E. Wiesner-Hanks

See also Contraception and Birth Control; Convents; Power, Politics, and Women.

Bibliography

Aercke, Kristiaan P. G. "Anna Bijns: Germanic Sappho." In *Women Writers of the Renaissance and Reformation*. Edited by Katharina M. Wilson. Athens: University of Georgia Press, 1987.

Bennett, Judith M., and Amy M. Froide, eds. *Singlewomen in the European Past*. Philadelphia: University of Pennsylvania Press, 1998.

Brucker, Gene. *Giovanni and Lusanna: Love and Marriage in Renaissance Florence*. Berkeley: University of California Press, 1986.

Cavallo, Sandra, and Lyndan Warner, eds. *Widowhood in Medieval and Early Modern Europe*. London: Longman, 1999.

Chojnacki, Stanley. *Women and Men in Renaissance Venice: Twelve Essays on Patrician Society*. Baltimore, MD: Johns Hopkins University Press, 2000.

Cressy, David. *Birth, Marriage and Death: Ritual, Religion, and the Life-Cycle in Tudor and Stuart England*. Oxford: Oxford University Press, 1997.

Dean, Trevor, and K. J. P. Lowe, eds. *Marriage in Italy, 1300–1650*. Cambridge: Cambridge University Press, 1998.

D'Elia, Anthony F. *The Renaissance of Marriage in Fifteenth-Century Italy*. Cambridge, MA: Harvard University Press, 2004.

Harris, Barbara J. *English Aristocratic Women, 1450–1550: Marriage and Family, Property and Careers*. Oxford, New York: Oxford University Press, 2002.

Howell, Martha C. *The Marriage Exchange: Property, Social Place, and Gender in the Cities of the Low Countries, 1300–1500*. Chicago: University of Chicago Press, 1998.

Klapisch-Zuber, Christiane. *Women, Family, and Ritual in Renaissance Italy*. Chicago: University of Chicago Press, 1985.

Macfarlane, Alan. *Marriage and Love in England, Modes of Reproduction 1300–1840*. London: Basil Blackwell, 1986.

Mitterauer, Michael, and Reinhard Sieder. *The European Family: Patriarchy and Partnership from the Middle Ages to the Present*. Translated by Karla Oosterveen and Manfred Horzinger. Chicago: University of Chicago Press, 1982.

Wall, Richard, Tamara K. Hareven, and Josef Ehmer, eds. *Family History Revisited: Comparative Perspectives.* Newark, DE: University of Delaware Press, Associated University Presses, 2001.

Wunder, Heide. *He Is the Sun, She Is the Moon: Women in Early Modern Germany.* Translated by Thomas Dunlap. Cambridge, MA: Harvard University Press, 1998.

Mary I, queen of England and champion of Roman Catholicism (also known as "Bloody Mary"). Portrait by Anthonis Mor. Museo del Prado, Madrid, Spain. (Library of Congress)

Mary I (Queen of England; 1516–1558)

The first queen regnant of England; known as "Bloody Mary"; a devout papist embattled in a Protestant state; executed hundreds of suspected heretics; failed in her attempt to restore Catholicism to England

Born 18 February 1516, Mary was the sole surviving child of Henry VIII and Catherine of Aragon. Few births in English history were so anticipated and yet so disappointing. Her father had wanted a son to carry on the dynasty that his father, Henry VII, had started. Nevertheless, both Henry and Catherine doted upon Mary in her early years, providing her with a household befitting a princess and heir to the throne of England. Likewise, Catherine took a special interest in Mary's education and took advantage of the newest learning available, Christian humanism, which emphasized the study of the classics and theology, by employing a humanist scholar in England, Thomas Linacre, as Mary's tutor. She also commissioned the *Instruction of a Christian Woman* (Latin, 1523; English, 1529) from another humanist, Juan Luis Vives, a fellow Spaniard, who believed in the virtue of formally educating women so that they would become better wives and mothers. Mary excelled at her Latin, and she became quite adept at music, a skill inherited from her father.

As was the practice for all princesses of this period, Henry intended to use Mary in the dynastic marriage game. In 1522, wanting to eliminate France as a potential problem, Henry betrothed Mary, aged six, to her twenty-year-old cousin, Charles V, king of Spain and Holy Roman emperor, with the wedding to take place when she reached twelve. For his part, Charles wanted Henry's assistance in his territorial struggles with France, and the proposed marriage could secure his designs. However, in 1525, Charles, largely unaided by Henry, soundly defeated the French, making his alliance with Henry unnecessary. Consequently, Charles broke off the engagement and married Isabel, princess of Portugal, who was closer to his age and brought immediate strategic advantages.

Charles's abandonment of Mary was a hard blow to Henry's prestige, so he punished the only Spaniard in his control, Catherine, developing a pattern he would continue for the remaining years of their marriage. First, he elevated his bastard son, Henry Fitzroy, to the peerage, naming him duke of Richmond as if grooming him to be heir. Second, he separated mother from daughter by sending Mary away to Wales, ostensibly to take up her responsibilities as the princess of Wales. Though Henry never invested her with the actual title, Mary lived at Ludlow Castle in the full splendor of a royal governor and carried out the duties with the assistance of loyal advisors, remaining there until 1527.

That year marked a major change in Mary's life, when Henry decided to pursue an annulment of his marriage to Catherine of Aragon. Having convinced himself that his lack of a legitimate male heir was God's punishment for marrying his brother's widow, Henry sought freedom from his almost twenty-year marriage and soon received solace in the arms of his mistress, Anne Boleyn. Catherine, always maintaining that she was Henry's legal wife, enlisted the assistance of her Spanish and Holy Roman relations in her fight against her husband. Between 1527 and 1530, Mary's own relations with her father, though somewhat tenuous, remained civil. In 1531, however, in an attempt to crush Catherine's opposition, Henry ordered Catherine away from his presence, also separating her from Mary. Mary bravely supported her mother in the dispute, a decision that held lasting repercussions. With the assistance of parliament, Henry separated England from the authority of the Catholic Church and then had his marriage to Catherine annulled so that he could marry Anne in 1532. Later, Henry would order his subjects to no longer refer to Mary as the "Princess Mary" but rather as "Lady Mary," reflecting her illegitimate standing.

Mary's status as Henry's heir soon changed with the birth of Elizabeth Tudor on 7 September 1533, whom he recognized as his only legitimate child and heir. Life for Mary during this period remained difficult, with Henry repeatedly subjecting her to verbal threats if she did not surrender to his will. Mary's love for her mother and her devotion to her Catholic faith kept her from yielding to her father's desires, as did the support of representatives from Spain and the Holy Roman Empire, especially Eustace Chapuys, Charles V's ambassador, whom she used as a messenger to her mother and for emotional support when rumors suggested Henry would execute both mother and daughter. Her dependency upon these foreign advisors would have lasting consequences for her own reign.

Execution never came for Mary, and, after Catherine's death in January 1536 and Anne Boleyn's execution four months later, her situation changed dramatically. Catherine had served as a symbol and as moral support in the battle with Henry. With both wives dead and Henry quickly remarried to Jane Seymour, Mary had to consider how best to conduct her life. After weighing her options, Mary decided to yield to her father's authority, and, though not reinstated to the succession until 1544, Mary's remaining years with her father passed reasonably quietly.

With Henry's death in 1547, Mary's half brother from Henry's third marriage became Edward VI (1547–1553). As a minor, Edward could not directly rule; so a council, eventually led by John Dudley, duke of Northumberland, ruled for him. Heavily influenced by Reformed Protestantism, Edward's council repeatedly attempted to force Mary into abandoning her Catholic faith. Steadfastly, Mary refused, arguing that she had a right to worship according to her conscience and continued to hear mass in her private chapel. Edward was a convinced Protestant and, under the influence of Dudley, chose to change the order of succession in favor of Lady Jane Grey, Henry VIII's niece and Dudley's daughter-in-law.

Soon after Edward's death on 6 July 1553, the privy council, afraid of a return to Catholicism, proclaimed Lady Jane queen. Mary had already heard of the plot and quickly rode through the countryside, proclaiming herself queen and gaining an army from the public, sympathetic to her troubles. Though Dudley attempted to capture the queen, his supporters faded quickly, and nine days after Lady Jane became queen, the privy council deposed her.

Mary entered London on 24 July 1533 as the rightful queen of England.

From the outset of her reign, Mary demonstrated clemency toward her political enemies and set out to restore England to its ancient ways. Four days after her coronation in November, parliament reversed its previous decision and reinstated Henry and Catherine's marriage. Furthermore, parliament passed legislation that guaranteed that Mary, as queen, had all of the authority and privileges of any monarch to sit on the English throne.

As expected, Mary attempted to restore Catholicism to England. She made it her mission to reestablish the supremacy of the pope and to bring back the mass and the ecclesiastical system of Rome. Though she met with great opposition, by 1554 the pope restored England to the Catholic faith and sent Cardinal Reginald Pole to act as his representative in the further restoration in England. Mary also had the ancient heresy laws reinstated. These laws made it possible to punish with death any individual who failed to follow the religious practice of their sovereign. Unanimity of the faith was an essential, and those who chose a different path were thought of as traitors.

Mary faced further opposition on the domestic front when she made it clear that she intended to wed Philip II, king of Spain and son of Emperor Charles V. Her continued close ties with the Spanish ambassador and her dependence on him for advice in domestic matters made many uncomfortable. Furthermore, there was a legitimate fear that if Mary married Philip, then, according to the gender and religious standards of the day, Mary would turn the kingdom over to Philip and the Spanish. Soon opposition arose in England, including one rebellion led by Thomas Wyatt, who wanted to eliminate the Spanish control of England and possibly put Elizabeth on the throne, too.

With these challenges, Mary realized that she could no longer afford to be generous with her forgiveness. Consequently, she ordered the execution of Lady Jane Grey and her followers,

as well as Thomas Wyatt. Authorities even arrested Elizabeth Tudor because Mary believed Protestants would continue to threaten Mary's reign if the Protestant Elizabeth was free.

Having failed to produce an heir and feeling great political pressure from religious dissenters, Mary became increasingly hostile toward the Protestants as if, like her father, she believed God was punishing her. Therefore, she made active use of the heresy laws, ordering the arrest and later execution of many Protestants, including the Protestant archbishop of Canterbury, Thomas Cranmer. In all, Mary had about three hundred people burned at the stake for their religious beliefs and consequently earned the epithet "Bloody Mary."

Mary's own death finally arrived in November 1558 and came as a relief to many in England. Her unhappy life as the mistreated daughter of Henry VIII and the religiously persecuted sister of Edward VI set the stage for her own difficult reign. Mary would die believing she was an unloved monarch, distrustful of the Protestants and of the person they most rallied around, her successor Elizabeth Tudor.

Timothy G. Elston

See also Catherine of Aragon; Education, Humanism, and Women; Religious Reform and Women.

Bibliography
Loach, Jennifer. *Parliament and the Crown in the Reign of Mary Tudor.* Oxford: Clarendon Press; New York: Oxford University Press, 1986.
Loades, David. *Mary Tudor: A Life.* Oxford and Cambridge, MA: Blackwell, 1989.
Ridley, Jasper. *Bloody Mary's Martyrs: The Story of England's Terror.* New York: Carroll and Graf, 2001.

Mary Stuart (Mary, Queen of Scots; 1542–1587)

Catholic queen of Scotland, twice forced to abdicate her throne, pretender to the English throne, executed by her cousin Queen Elizabeth I

On 8 December 1542, Mary Stuart was born to Mary of Guise-Lorraine and James V of Scotland. Six days later, she succeeded her father and on 9 September 1543 was crowned queen. As her paternal grandmother was Margaret Tudor, Henry VIII's sister, Mary also possessed English succession rights. In July 1543, her governors approved the Treaties of Greenwich, which arranged for her marriage to Henry's heir, the future Edward VI, and her move to England at her tenth birthday. After Scotland repudiated the treaties in December, Henry and then Edward's Lord Protector, Edward, duke of Somerset, attempted to abduct Mary in raids called the "Rough Wooing." In 1548, she escaped to France as the betrothed of Henry II's son, Francis, leaving French forces occupying Scotland.

In France

In France, Mary received a humanist education, acquiring a basic grounding in Latin. She also became fluent in French and Italian and learned to sing, dance, play musical instruments, and embroider. Two favorite outdoor pastimes were horseback riding and hunting. On 24 April 1558, she wed Francis, to whom the Scottish parliament granted the title of king matrimonial. After Elizabeth I's accession as queen of England in November, Mary quartered the English arms with those of Scotland and France, signaling that her hereditary claims were superior to her cousin's, whom Catholics viewed as illegitimate.

In August 1559, Francis succeeded his father as king. Meanwhile, the Protestant Reformation garnered support in Scotland by denouncing the French domination that their queen's marriage to Francis legitimized. In 1560, English invaders in Scotland, supporting the reformers, signed the Treaty of Edinburgh with the French forces, arranging for both armies to depart and for Mary to cease bearing England's arms. Concerned that the treaty would negate her English claims, Mary never ratified it.

In Scotland

After Francis died on 5 December 1560, Mary quit bearing England's arms and decided to return home. When she reached Scotland in August 1561, Protestants controlled her government. Although refusing to validate the Reformation acts outlawing the mass and papal authority, she enforced them publicly while retaining Catholic services in her chapel.

During her short personal rule, she consulted with her privy councilors, summoned five parliaments or conventions, and governed competently. As Scottish sovereigns were expected to be seen dispensing justice throughout the realm, she went on several progresses and held a justice-ayre at Jedburgh. Her court was as culturally significant as her father's; it inspired the Bannatyne Manuscript, a collection of invaluable late medieval Scottish poetry, and attracted George Buchanan and other scholars.

In 1563 at Elizabeth's suggestion, Mary agreed to wed Robert Dudley, earl of Leicester, but only after gaining legislative validation of her English claims, which Henry VIII omitted from his will, limiting the succession. While negotiating this match, she was also secretly proposing to wed Don Carlos, Philip II of Spain's heir and hoping to move to the Netherlands, which he would rule as regent. In May 1565, upon learning that neither alliance could be arranged, she decided to marry Henry, Lord Darnley, an English citizen who came to Scotland to acquire his family's forfeited estates. A lukewarm Catholic born in December 1545, Darnley possessed claims to the English throne through his maternal grandmother, Margaret Tudor. After Elizabeth protested Mary's plans to wed Darnley, she postponed the wedding and asked for a conference concerning her marriage, a request Elizabeth refused. Having granted Darnley the title of king, Mary wed him on 29 July, apparently for his lineage and not for love. Her illegitimate brother, James Stewart, earl of Moray, orchestrated a failed rebellion to challenge her marriage, called the Chaseabout Raid.

That his royal status did not embody real governing powers troubled Darnley because he possessed strong succession rights as James II's

Mary, Queen of Scots, comforts a dying man after the Battle of Langside. Painting by F. Hartwich. (Library of Congress)

descendant. Without public authority, he also lacked the patriarch's position as head of his household. Having conspired to usurp Mary's throne and murder David Riccio, her secretary and rumored lover, on 9 March 1566 he introduced into his pregnant wife's chamber at Holyrood assassins, who imprisoned her and killed Riccio. Later, Mary somehow regained her husband's trust, and they escaped together. Afterward, he angered his allies by denying publicly any involvement in the conspiracy.

On 19 June, Mary gave birth to their son, James, and on 17 December, held a gala Roman Catholic christening for him at Stirling. Darnley absented himself from the ritual, primarily because the representatives of Elizabeth, his son's godmother, would not recognize his royal status. In late December, Darnley contracted smallpox en route to Glasgow. The next month,

Mary visited her estranged husband; they became reconciled, and she returned him to a lodge at Kirk o'Field to convalesce until he could safely interact with their son at Holyrood. On 10 February 1567 about 2:00 a.m., various individuals alienated by Darnley blew up the lodge. He escaped outside only to be smothered by assassins. One of the rumored murderers was James Hepburn, earl of Bothwell, who was tried for the crime but acquitted for lack of evidence. On 24 April, as Mary returned from visiting her son at Stirling, the married earl abducted and raped her. After his wife, Jane Gordon, obtained a divorce, Mary agreed to wed Bothwell in a Protestant service to protect her honor, thereby prompting some of her subjects to revolt against her authority. After Bothwell fled, she surrendered to the rebels, who imprisoned her at Lochleven, where she miscarried twins sired by

Bothwell and abdicated her throne to James. In May 1568, after she escaped, the army of Moray, her son's regent, defeated her forces and prevented her from taking refuge in Dumbarton Castle. She fled to England, seeking Elizabeth's aid to regain her authority.

English Captivity and Death

At an English inquiry in late 1568 concerning whether she colluded in her husband's death, Moray introduced the Casket Letters, reputedly copies of love messages she wrote to Bothwell before Darnley's death. The original French versions, if they ever existed, have not survived, and the copies are likely forgeries. Although the commissioners failed to find her guilty, she remained in captivity, dwelling until 1584 mostly at Sheffield Castle under George Talbot, earl of Shrewsbury's custodianship. After agreeing to wed Thomas Howard, duke of Norfolk, who supported her English claims, Mary attempted unsuccessfully to divorce Bothwell, who survived in a Danish prison until 1578. Meanwhile, in 1572, Norfolk was executed for treason following two abortive conspiracies favoring his marriage to her: the Catholic Rising in 1569 and the Ridolfi Plot in 1571.

The conspiracies led Shrewsbury to confine Mary to her quarters, although he later allowed her to go on walks and short rides under heavy guard. Indoors, she occupied herself with embroidering and reading. Shrewsbury denied her a priest, but in late 1584 a cleric secretly entered her household. Because she suffered from a chronic illness, perhaps porphyria, which she claimed her imprisonment exacerbated, she was allowed to visit Shrewsbury's Buxton medicinal baths several times. She never ceased longing for liberation and kept in contact with agents in France, who conspired with her Guise relatives and with Philip of Spain to invade England and free her. In 1581, she also began to negotiate successfully for a treaty to associate with her son, James VI, in the governance of Scotland be-

cause she anticipated that it might allow her greater freedom in England.

In 1584, Englishmen began endorsing a Bond of Association, which required its signatories to assassinate those who attempted to murder Elizabeth and the English claimants for whom they plotted. Although realizing she was the target, Mary signed it, convinced that her jailors would kill her when Elizabeth died, even of natural causes. Its later statutory form substituted a trial for the vigilantism.

After transferring Mary to Chartley in 1585, Sir Francis Walsingham, Elizabeth's principal secretary, who broke Mary's secret code, read and then forwarded her correspondence, including Sir Anthony Babington's proposal to free her first before assassinating Elizabeth. Mary's ciphered response, which is not extant, likely detailed the troops required for her liberation and ignored the plans for Elizabeth's murder. Walsingham had Mary's entire ciphered response copied and forwarded that version to Babington. The copier of Mary's letter probably added the phrases that made it appear she agreed to Elizabeth's murder to gain her freedom, thus altering Babington's original sequence. Walsingham hoped this altered timing would convince Elizabeth to consent to Mary's execution.

By authority of the Statute of Association, Elizabeth appointed a commission to try Mary at Fotheringhay. Initially, Mary refused to accept its jurisdiction but finally decided to appear before it to deny she agreed to Elizabeth's murder. After the commission found her guilty, Elizabeth reluctantly signed the death warrant. Despite the queen's withholding authorization for its delivery, William Davison, her secretary, secretly carried it to Fotheringhay. On 8 February 1587, Mary calmly entered the execution chamber supported by two soldiers, because her disease had crippled her. Before dying, she pardoned her enemies and prayed to Jesus Christ for absolution. It took two blows of the axe and the sawing of a sinew for the executioner to complete his task. She was buried at Peterborough, but James later transferred her corpse to Westminster Abbey.

Retha Warnicke

See also Elizabeth I; Grey, Jane; Marie of Guise; Power, Politics, and Women; Religious Reform and Women.

Bibliography

Fraser, Antonia. *Mary Queen of Scots.* New York: Delacorte, 1994.

Lynch, Michael, ed. *Mary Stewart in Three Kingdoms.* London: Blackwell, 1988.

Merriman, Marcus. *The Rough Wooings: Mary Queen of Scots, 1541–51.* Edinburgh: Tuckwell, 2000.

Warnicke, Retha M. *Mary Queen of Scots.* London: Routledge, forthcoming.

Watkins, Susan. *Mary Queen of Scots.* New York: Thames and Hudson, 2001.

Wormald, Jenny. *Mary Queen of Scots: Politics, Passion and a Kingdom Lost.* New York: Tauris Park, 2001.

Mary Tudor (Queen of France and Duchess of Suffolk; 1496–1533)

Wife of Louis XII, king of France, and sister of Henry VIII

In 1515, Henry VIII, looking to increase his prestige among European leaders, decided a marriage between his sister, Mary Tudor, and the widowed king of France, Louis XII, was in the best dynastic interest of England. However, Mary, born in 1496 and Henry's favorite sister, demonstrated intelligence, courage, and determination in her decision to avoid the fate of all princesses forced to play the dynastic marriage game.

For her part, Mary wanted to pick her own husband and had already set her heart upon Charles Brandon, duke of Suffolk, and Henry's best friend. Without revealing this to Henry, Mary used every means at her disposal to convince him to change his mind. Henry was as implacable as ever, and Mary finally compromised: she agreed to wed Louis, thirty-four years her senior, while Henry promised she could, if Louis died first, marry the man of her own choosing the next time.

In the fall of 1515, Mary became the queen of France, and the celebrations lasted three months. At the end of those celebrations, Louis, apparently worn out, died, leaving Mary a single woman determined to not play the dynastic marriage game again. Realizing she had to act quickly to hold Henry to his promise, Mary convinced Brandon, who had come to Paris to bring her home, to marry her, and with the aid of Francis I the couple wed at the Palais de Cluny in the spring of 1516. Though the marriage was technically a crime and Mary and Charles had to face Henry's full wrath, Henry agreed to forgive them after levying a heavy fine.

The marriage of Mary Tudor and Charles Brandon was successful, though her last years of life were somewhat difficult with respect to her relationship with her brother. Henry's decisions to divorce Catherine of Aragon and separate England from the Roman Catholic church strained their relationship. Mary openly opposed the divorce and absolutely refused to acknowledge Anne Boleyn as Henry's new wife, up to her death on 24 June 1533. As she had in her youth, Mary continued to demonstrate she had a will of her own and that, despite her powerful relative, she would do what she believed was right.

Timothy G. Elston

See also Marriage; Religious Reform and Women.

Bibliography

Harvey, Nancy Lenz. *The Rose and the Thorn: The Lives of Mary and Margaret Tudor.* New York: Macmillan, 1975.

Perry, Maria. *Sisters to the King: The Tumultuous Lives of Henry VIII's Sisters, Margaret of Scotland and Mary of France.* New York: St. Martin's Press, 1999.

Richardson, Walter Cecil. *Mary Tudor: The White Queen.* London: Owen, 1970.

Masculinity, Femininity, and Gender

The Renaissance was marked by a considerable preoccupation with gender, as is evidenced by the numerous tracts dedicated to the debates on women, the *querelle des femmes.* Feminist scholars such as Constance Jordan have opened the archives to show how gender was in great part perceived by Renaissance thinkers as a construct, and it is generally agreed that the construct of femininity involved a continuous regulation by institutions such as the church and government, as well as the promotion of pervasive cultural discourses by individuals. Feminist scholarship has more recently led to new studies on men sustaining that masculinity was constructed with much the same societal imperative, though it did not solicit the same type of open discussion—notably there is no *querelle des hommes.* In fact, the power claimed by men over women and other men required that their masculinity not be scrutinized, and consequently the denigration of nonmasculine behavior was an effective way for institutions to control the behavior of individuals. Interestingly, both discourses of masculinity and femininity were promoted above all through the creation of ideals.

The diffusion of models of ideal behavior can already be found in the Middle Ages. Beyond the Biblical examples of Christ and Mary, tales of saints' lives and romances depicting knights errant had created a mythology of figures to be emulated. Whereas women were confronted with the impossible contradiction of virgin mother, men were left to decipher the nebulous traits of honor and virtue and to reconcile acts of abstinence, sexual prowess, adventure, and domestication. With the advent of Florentine humanism, the literate Renaissance man could find treatises that provided new secular models of the ideal man based on the precepts of reason, social pragmatism, and decorum.

Reason, for the humanists, became the fundamental marker of masculine virtue. In Leon Battista Alberti's treatise on the family, *The Alberti of Florence* (1434, 1437), the head of the family tells his audience of young men that fathers must correct children's tendencies toward lust, sloth, and gluttony with "reason not anger"

and that above all a man must steer his life with the "rudder of reason." Alberti rehearses the well-known division of virtue (mind) and vice (body) inherited from Classical thought. Reason or the mind was for the neo-Platonists what separated humans from beasts, and these humanists found an essentialist gender split in Aristotle's *On the Generation of Animals,* in which masculinity became associated with rationality and femininity with the material body. Feminists have discussed the damaging and lasting effects of this division that denied women a claim to rational thought, but we should note that the early modern man was conversely faced with the predicament of negotiating a masculine existence in which his body was the betrayal of both beastly and feminine natures.

This tension of the gendering of the mind and body, along with the increasing emphasis placed on decorum (as laid out by Norbert Elias in his work *The Civilizing Process),* seems to have resulted in an intense policing of the male body—both by the individual himself as well as by other men. In his autobiography, Alberti tells how he must be attentive to how he rides, speaks. and walks since these above all communicate what type of man he is. Other writers across Europe such as Erasmus, Castiglione, Montaigne, and Della Casa express much the same concern. In fact, the regulation of gestures, speech, hairstyles, and clothing reflects the desire to express membership in a certain social class yet at times demonstrates a marked paranoia of appearing effeminate.

Studies on the early modern English gentleman suggest that men who belonged to polite society risked crossing the precarious and blurred line that separated refinement and effeminacy. The speakers in Castiglione's *Courtier* (1528) express much the same concern as they parse which qualities are the mark of a gentleman and which might make him too womanly. They state that a man should wear fine clothing, though not too many ruffles, be well groomed but not with an ostentatious hairstyle or plucked eyebrows, and they remain in disaccord on whether men should or should not be musicians. The imperative placed on decorum created the conundrum of a man dressing his class while still dressing his gender.

As the characters of Castiglione's text relate, there were no stable rules or laws that one could follow. The situation with women was much different; communities had created hundreds of statutes regulating women's dress in the so-called sumptuary laws, but, as Diane Owen Hughes has shown us, men's costume was not as frequently legislated. If one seeks to read history through law books, it would seem that men's dress was unproblematic, but as we find in narratives of the age, men regulated each other's dress and actions by means of a different social control—most frequently, using the shaming of effeminacy to prohibit what was seen as unacceptable. In nearly perfect unison, the voices of the Renaissance, from itinerant priests to courtiers, found effeminacy in men to be the cause of social degradation, where "effeminacy" was a remarkable social construct of arbitrary, often aesthetic criteria.

The fear of effeminacy is a critical focal point when studying the construction of masculinity, for it serves as a reminder that men in a certain sense had to "prove" their masculinity, again a condition arguably different from the construction of femininity. This process of confirming masculinity seems to be integrally linked to life stages, a commonplace in most texts on masculinity in the Renaissance and in our own contemporary culture. As is repeated by fathers in the Renaissance across Europe, boys were to be separated from females while still quite young to learn the art of being manly from other men. During this period, some fathers, such as Federico di Montefeltro, sought to expose their young sons to both learning and military training, as is artistically represented in the celebrated portrait by Pedro Berruguete (1477), which shows the duke dressed in armor and an academic robe reading to his young son. Other fathers believed exposure to classical learning would effeminize young boys, as we

see in a letter written by Francesco Gonzaga to his wife Isabella d'Este (1503) telling her that their son might be softened by humanists and their philosophical teaching.

After boys were separated from the influence of women, they were then professionally trained outside the family. Adolescent boys in most of early modern Europe were sent off at around age fourteen to be apprentices or servants depending on their social status, whereas girls would have been approaching marriageable age. These unmarried young men have a particularly interesting relationship to the societal structure of the period since they were expected to assert their masculine identities so that they could later integrate into the practical institutions of commerce or government.

In France, these young men were notoriously involved in gang rapes of young women in the community. Jacques Rossiaud suggests that up to 50 percent of the young men in Lyon had participated in a group rape. The rapes were a means of social control because the women chosen as victims were often concubines of their masters, abandoned wives, or mistresses of priests, but these acts were also a means of publicly demonstrating masculine behavior of sex and violence against women. Such public acts of sexual aggression are mirrored, in slightly different terms, in the Italian comedies of the period, where young males often participate in a publicly condoned sexual violation of the female space. The common aspect seems to be that the transition from boyhood youth to early manhood involves public demonstrations of sex, violence, or both. Finally, for men who did not enter the clergy, this phase ends when the young man marries and officially enters the stable position of either a tradesman or civic leader.

The traveling priest, San Bernardino da Siena, suggested that these young men should be married by at least age thirty-three. Marriage was the force that would mark the cooling of the youthful passions and an official entrance into rational male adulthood. San Bernardino was also in part concerned with the rampant practice of sexual relations between males in Florence. The study of Michael Rocke suggests that it is likely that a majority of the young men in Florence were involved in same-sex relations. The paradigm proposed by Rocke states that the Florentines condoned by custom if not by law the practice of sexual relations between young men and young boys. While adolescent boys would participate in a "feminine" sexual role, men in their twenties and thirties were still able to make claim to the masculine active role of penetration. However, after a certain age, somewhere in the early to midthirties, this practice was expected to stop as men married and began a family. The role of marriage as a means of controlling the irrational force of male sexual desire and thus controlling the potential danger of the lustful man was a pervasive discourse in both civic and religious contexts. Evidence of the rational force of marriage was echoed in priests' sermons, epic poetry, and even the governmental statutes of cities across Europe such as Florence, where unmarried men were denied access to public office.

The way boys "became" men was clearly not a stable or obvious process. For many males it would involve sexual aggression, military training, or marriage, and for all it would include a complex policing of behavioral traits. There are, however, various masculine models contingent on social classifications, including class, race, and profession. Scholars have given some attention to priests and castrati as examples of groups of men who challenged mainstream masculine values of sexual prowess and fatherhood respectively. Valeria Finucci, specifically, shows how the legal status of marriageable castrati in Counter-Reformation Rome was precarious since they were unable to father children. Similarly, priests had to negotiate their own positions of power and masculine identity without recourse to public sexual relations with women.

In sum, ideal models of masculinity were contradictory for the so-called Renaissance

man; sex was both a means to gain and lose one's masculinity, and politeness could mark a man's social rank or his effeminacy. Being called manly was without exception an expression of praise, and the description was used for both women and men: Vittoria Colonna and Isabella Andreini were termed manly because of their artistic production and (ironically) virtuous "feminine" lifestyles. On the other hand, when social crises such as war, pestilence, or economic depression befell a community, men were blamed for being effeminate, fearful of defending the *patria,* and unable to reproduce offspring. The ambiguous and unstable criteria of masculinity made it possible to praise or criticize individuals for their performance of manliness arbitrarily, and ultimately such critiques served as an effective means of social control. Thus men, caught up in a lifelong process of asserting their masculine identity, were also subject to the desires of institutions and other individuals—a dynamic suggesting again the centrality of gender in any discussion of early modern society.

Gerry Milligan

See also Androgyne; Hermaphrodite as Image and Idea; Querelle des Femmes; Transvestism.

Bibliography
Breitenberg, Mark. *Anxious Masculinity in Early Modern England.* Cambridge: Cambridge University Press, 1996.

Carter, Philip. *Men and the Emergence of Polite Society, Britain, 1600–1800.* New York: Pearson Education, 2001.

Finucci, Valeria. *The Manly Masquerade: Masculinity, Paternity, and Castration in the Italian Renaissance.* Durham, NC: Duke University Press, 2003.

Rocke, Michael. *Forbidden Friendships: Homosexuality and Male Culture in Renaissance Florence.* New York: Oxford University Press, 1996.

Rossiaud, Jacques. *Medieval Prostitution.* Translated by Lydia Cochrane. Oxford: Basil Blackwell, 1988.

Saslow, James. *Ganymede in the Renaissance: Homosexuality in Art and Society.* New Haven, CT: Yale University Press, 1986.

Sedgwick, Eve Kosofsky. *Between Men: English Literature and Male Homosocial Desire.* New York: Columbia University Press, 1985.

Shepard, Alexandra. *Meanings of Manhood in Early Modern England.* Oxford: Oxford University Press, 2003.

Smith, Bruce. *Shakespeare and Masculinity.* Oxford: Oxford University Press, 2000.

Matraini, Chiara (1515–1604?)

Self-identified "gentlewoman from Lucca"; prolific author of poems, letters, dialogues, and a discourse on the life of the Virgin Mary

Chiara Matraini spent most of her life in Lucca. At fifteen she married the aristocrat Vincenzo Cantarini but maintained the surname of her father's bourgeois family, which suffered for its participation a year later in the suppressed *straccioni* uprising (1531). She bore a son in 1533 and was widowed by 1542. A subsequent love affair with Bartolomeo Graziani ended with her lover's violent death. Love and loss became the subject of her early poetry. As with other literary women, her writing career flourished best during widowhood, although her economic independence was hampered by a long legal process over her son's refusal to return her dowry. Her intellectual contacts included Lodovico Domenichi above all, but also Benedetto Varchi and Lodovico Dolce, all three encouraging to women's intellectual aspirations.

A volume of her *Rime e Prose* (Poems and Prose) was published in Lucca in 1555—without her permission, according to the publisher's letter, although this may be a protective gesture. The prose includes her defense of women's writing, even about love. A year later, Lodovico Dolce's anthology *Rime di diversi signori napolitani, e d'altri* (Giolito, 1556) reprinted all ninety-nine of her poems, which include sonnets, madrigals, *canzoni,* octaves, and sestinas. Some poems reappeared in other sixteenth-century anthologies or were set to music by contemporaries such as Perissone. Her translation of a Latin letter of paternal counsel attributed to Isocrates was printed in 1556. After a few obscure years in Genoa (1562–1565), Matraini returned to Lucca in the post-Tridentine era as a newly pious writer, publishing her *Meditazioni spirituali* (Spiritual Meditations, 1581), *Considerationi sopra i sette salmi penitentiali del gran re & profeta Davit* (Considerations on the Seven penitential Psalms of the Great King and Prophet David, 1586), *Dialoghi spirituali* (Spiritual Dialogues, 1602 but probably written at least two decades earlier), and a *Breve discorso sopra la vita e laude della Beatissima Vergine* (Brief Discourse on the Life and Praise of the Blessed Virgin, 1590) that was reprinted six times during the seventeenth century. Matraini commissioned for her local church, Santa Maria Forisportam, a portrait of herself as a Sybil pointing to the Virgin Mary.

Another volume of *Lettere e rime* (Letters and Poems), published in 1595 with fifty-three new poems interspersed by two dozen of the earlier ones, reappeared in 1597 with an additional letter and ten more poems. Included are verses to a new—perhaps more platonic—love, the judge Cesare Coccopani, but the emphasis has shifted from earthly to spiritual devotion, as the poet contrasts the divine sun to her darker sensual love and prays to God for salvation. Matraini hopes also for fame, for a name that will remain *"chiara."* A few of Matraini's poems continued to appear in anthologies of later centuries.

Petrarch as usual influenced the narrative sequence and phrasing of the love sonnets; the *Rime* of the 1590s also introduces the division into two parts. But Dante too was an important model: Matraini's sestina, *Felice sasso,* imitates Dante's *Rime petrose;* one of the early sonnets echoes Francesca's line, *"Ch'amor a nullo amato amar perdona,"* and the *Vita Nuova* is discernible in the symmetrical ordering of poems framing the days of the *Dialoghi spirituali.* A general neo-Platonism pervades her poetry. While Bembo provided some of this influence, Vittoria Colonna was another important model from whom Matraini drew phrases or whole lines of verse along with the theme of turning from an earthly to a heavenly love. Matraini's admiration for Colonna and her friendship with Domenichi (accused of heresy) have provoked a questioning of her orthodoxy, although the *Spiritual Meditations* are quite orthodox discussions of sin and repentance.

The *Lettere* (1595, 1597) begin, like the *Dialoghi,* by explicating one of her own sonnets, revealed as a praise of intellectual beauty. Other letters argue for the superiority of intellectual over military prowess, exhort a youth to study philosophy, console friends for the loss of a husband or a son, discuss love, or describe a delightful picnic. A letter of advice to Matraini's son draws heavily from her translation of Isocrates. Rabitti argues from the lack of dating on the letters and from the array of topics that the text is more a literary artifact than a collection of real letters.

The *Dialoghi spirituali* contains three works, all related to themes of ascent through learning toward God and true self-knowledge. After the dialogue, which cites a shifting array of classical to ecclesiastical authors in its persuasion of her friend Cangenna's son to turn from commercial to intellectual and spiritual pursuits, comes a *Narratione* imitative of Dante's *Commedia* and *Sermoni* addressed to the possibly fictitious Academia dei Curiosi. Matraini, excluded because of her family's politics from Lucca's cultured gatherings in the Palazzo Buonvisi, may have sought to fashion an "academy" of her readers.

Most of her later books were dedicated to women: the *Dialoghi spirituali* to the noblewoman Marfisa da Este Cibò Malespina; the *Considerationi Sopra i Sette Salmi* to Lucrezia d'Este, duchess of Urbino; the *Vita della vergine* to a cousin who was the abbess of a convent in Pisa. The 1597 *Lettere* are framed by letters addressed first to her friend Cangenna Lipomeni (or Lipomanni) and last to the Virgin Mary.

Janet Smarr

See also Colonna, Vittoria; the subheadings Sonnet Writing; Letter Writing (under Literary Culture and Women).

Bibliography
Primary Works
Matraini, Chiara. *Breve discorso sopra la vita e laude della Beatiss. Verg. e Madre del Figliuol di Dio.* Lucca: Busdraghi, 1590.

Matraini, Chiara. *Considerazioni sopra i sette salmi penitenziali del gran re e profeta Davit.* Lucca: Busdraghi, 1586.

Matraini, Chiara. *Dialoghi spirituali.* Venice: Prati, 1602.

Matraini, Chiara. *Lettere della signora Chiara Matraini . . . con la prima e seconda parte delle sue Rime.* Lucca: Busdraghi, 1595.

Matraini, Chiara. *Meditazioni spirituali.* Lucca: Busdraghi, 1581.

Matraini, Chiara. *Orazione d'Isocrate a Demonico d'Ipponico, circa a l'essortazion de'costumi, che si convengono a tutti i nobilissimi giovani, do latino in volgare tradotta.* Florence: Torrentino, 1556.

Matraini, Chiara. *Rime e Lettere.* Edited by Giovanna Rabitti. *Scelta di Curiosità Letterarie Inedite o Rare dal Secolo XIII al XIX, Dispensa CCLXXIX.* Bologna: Commissione per i testi di lingua, 1989.

Matraini, Chiara. *Rime e prose di madonna Chiara Matraini gentildonna lucchese.* Lucca: Busdraghi, 1555.

Secondary Works
Bullock, Alan, and Gabriella Palange. "Per una edizione critica delle opere di Chiara Matraini." In *Studi in onore di Raffaele Spongano,* 235–262. Bologna: Boni, 1980.

Maclachlan, Elaine. "The Conversion of Chiara Matraini: The 1597 Rewriting of the *Rime* of 1555." *NEMLA Italian Studies* 16 (1992): 21–32.

Rabitti, Giovanna. "Chiara Matraini." In *Italian Women Writers. A Bio-Bibliographical Sourcebook,* 243–252. Edited by Rinaldina Russell. Westport, CT: Greenwood Press, 1994.

Rabitti, Giovanna. "Le lettere di Chiara Matraini tra pubblico e privato." In *Per lettera. La scrittura epistolare femminile.* Ed. Gabriella Zarri, 209–234. Rome: Viella, 1999.

Russell, Rinaldina. "Chiara Matraini nella tradizione lirica femminile." *Forum Italicum* 34, no. 2 (Fall 2000): 415–427.

Médicis, Catherine de. *See* Catherine de Médicis.

Medicine and Women
Overview

Women made important contributions to medical practice and theory during the Renaissance in Europe. Their work encompassed a broad range of areas of medical expertise, from nutrition and hygiene to gynecology and obstetrics. Moreover, outside of the health care fields, which were seen as "women's domain," they also participated in spheres where both men and women worked as medical providers, such as in surgery and optometry. During this period, therapeutic activities began to be sharply professionalized, and women's involvement could determine the recognition of medical practices, although not necessarily to the advantage of female practitioners. As well as more detailed examination of the work of female medical practitioners, in recent years historians have also reclaimed terms such as care and caregivers to recognize the full extent of women's medical labor. However, the use of these terms is also understood to be problematic since contemporary assumptions about the natural female caregiving role weakened other women's professional medical identities. Nine subheadings follow under the general heading of Medicine and Women: Home Care and Women Practitioners; Professionalization of Medicine and Women Practitioners; Legal Injunctions Against Women Practitioners; Women Religious Healers and Charges of Witchcraft; Hospital Administration and Nursing as Careers for Women; Childbirth and Reproductive Knowledge; Midwives and Licensing; Male Midwifery; and The Practice of Pharmacology and Laywomen.

Home Care and Women Practitioners

All women were acknowledged as providers of some forms of medical treatment, most commonly in the home. This could be both preventative as well as primary care. Although Monica H. Green has found little evidence of a strong tradition of university medical literature in women's libraries, women's commonplace books document a history of female transmission of a different kind of medical knowledge. Recipe books and housekeeping manuals handed down through generations taught female readers how to cultivate and cook health-preserving foods as well as how to prepare simple herbal medicinal compounds. Women's widespread application of culinary therapy was supported by contemporary Galenic preventative medical theories that demanded treatment for individual patients through holistic cures such as diet. These texts recorded not only treatments for female health issues such as ointments for sore nipples, drying up milk, or heavy menstruation, but also concerns of the entire household such as plague waters. Elite women such as Englishwoman Susanna Fontaineblew in 1510 and Flemish Anne de Croy in 1533 had manuscript medical compendiums compiled for them. Although women's practice of domestic medicine is well known, historians are only now attempting to historicize their contribution in a medical context. Questions are being asked of the development of women's medical thought charted through commonplace texts and investigating how it responded to changes in the pharmacopeia after the introduction of new products from overseas exploration and trade or after documented interactions with university medical practice. The assumption that women's domestic practice cannot be historicized since "women did what women had always done" is no longer accepted by those studying women's medical practice.

By the seventeenth century, women began to publish forms of commonplace books, intended for a broad female readership. At the same period, a division became discernible between pharmaceutical publications by apothecaries and physicians discussing the new Paracelsian chemical compounds and those by women and others that contributed to the long tradition of herbal simples and dietetic medicine. A number of women who were not medical practitioners but literate noblewomen managing large households represented this field by revealing the private world of women's manuscript commonplace texts to public scrutiny. In 1600 Eleonore Marie Rosalie of Jagersdorf and Troppau produced the much reprinted *Six Books of Medicines and Artificies, Chosen for All Human Bodily Weaknesses and Illnesses*. In England, Elizabeth Grey and her sister, Alathea Talbot, published *A Choice Manual of Rare and Select Secrets* (1653) and *Natura Exenterata* (1655) respectively. Even the queen, Henrietta Maria, was named as the author of *The Queen's Closet Opened* (1655).

Physicians too capitalized on public interest in women's home medicines and recipes and wrote texts teaching women how to tend minor injuries and common illnesses. These works assumed that women would have primary responsibility for the sick in their household. Elite women were expected to arrange medical care for those on their lands and were often praised by physicians for their charitable work in preparing herbal remedies and nursing their tenants in poor health. Jean Lyège expected that Antoinette de Bourbon would appreciate his 1557 medical text on fevers dedicated to her because of her keen charitable interest in nursing the poor and sick. However, the dedication of Sébastien Colin to Antoinette d'Aubeterre in his 1558 work on the same topic was followed by a second preface, in Latin, "to the reader." Physicians attempted to control domestic medical knowledge by their approval or rejection of women's household remedies, and increasingly university faculties absorbed botanical study into the syllabus.

Professionalization of Medicine and Women Practitioners

In practice, it is clear that many people, particularly outside of urban areas, had few means to access guild or university-trained care. They consulted local women who were reputedly knowledgeable in herbal medicine. These providers typically used the kinds of simple cures recommended in domestic handbooks of medicine and pharmacy. Others drew on their observations and experience to conduct surgical procedures such as bonesetting. When women conducted such work on a charitable basis, physicians and surgeons made few complaints. Indeed, some encouraged such female medical charity. Yet when women received payments for their practices, provided alternative remedies, or interfered with the client market of physicians and surgeons, the professional bodies of the latter groups prosecuted female healers regardless of their treatments' efficacy. When conflicts arose between rival practitioners, women often framed their medical contribution as a charitable service or situated it within the context of acceptable household primary care. In almost identical defenses, Jeanne Lescallier in her dispute with the physicians of Angers from 1567 to 1578 and Elizabeth Heyssin with the barber-surgeons of Memmingen from 1596 to 1602 argued that they only provided a few herbal "simples" for poor friends and neighbors with the assistance of God. This was a persuasive argument that convinced legal authorities to permit each to continue some forms of practice. Indeed Elizabeth I even ventured to defend the practice of one Margaret Kennix on the basis that she merely offered simples for the benefit of the poor. While compelling to the legal fraternity, this justification compromised the occupational medical identity of other women who felt that they were trained medical professionals with skills that should be remunerated.

Legal Injunctions Against Women Practitioners

By the time of the Renaissance, the rights of women to practice surgery, pharmacy, and medicine in their own right had been formally dissolved in most areas, mostly at the behest of university and guild-trained practitioners. In the effort to raise the status of medicine from a manual to a theoretical art, university-trained physicians sought to differentiate themselves from others on the basis of their knowledge. The reacquisition and interpretation of knowledge from classical texts during the Renaissance was to have profound effects on medicine. University medical knowledge was commonly transmitted in Latin. The increasingly text-based, classically derived syllabus of medical learning at universities alienated women as well as the unlearned generally. Female practitioners who competed for the clientele of physicians could find themselves before university authorities and examined about the basis of their medical knowledge. Irregular practitioners were often ridiculed if they claimed experience as their teacher, even in cases where their cures were as successful or more so than those of antiquated but authoritative texts.

Progressively other guild-trained providers such as barbers and apothecaries sought closer ties with the university medical faculties to increase the status of their own occupation. The medical guilds' adoption of an increasingly intellectual basis to their own knowledge and, on instruction from the medical faculties, barred many women from theory and practice. Women could not attend universities themselves in most parts of Europe. Over the same period, the regulation of medical guilds continued to restrict the rights of many women to practice. Some barred females from guild membership, and many more limited female practice to widowhood.

In France, women had been banned by law since 1271 from providing medical services that overlapped with university physicians, and after 1484 they could no longer practice surgery except as widows maintaining the business of their husbands. Laws in England saw women officially restricted in their medical work from 1421. Clearly such restrictions affected their public visibility in the medical records. By the late medieval period, only a handful of female physicians' names can be found in city archives as participating members of the Florentine guild of physicians, apothecaries, and grocers.

It is less clear that women suspended their medical practice because of the formal injunctions. In France, prosecutions for female practitioners are scattered through the Renaissance legal records. Jeanne Mabille, for example, was brought before the medical faculty in Paris in 1507 for her public medical work providing remedies based on uroscopy. In England, female surgeons were still able to obtain licenses from the ecclesiastical courts and could provide testimonies of their successful intervention, as did Isabel Warwicke in York in 1572. It seems likely that many other women continued their work informally without investing the time and costs associated with licensing. In 1560, a London surgeon, Thomas Gale, estimated that there were about sixty female practitioners operating in the city at that time. Between 1580 and 1610, at least twenty-nine female practitioners were prosecuted by the London-based College of Physicians. Some made no apology for their practice and demanded that physicians recognize their specialist knowledge. Examined in 1588, Mrs. Thomasina Scarlet refused to stop her treatments, some of which involved chemical preparations of mercury ointment. Mary Butler, investigated in 1637, claimed that she had learned her craft, including phlebotomy, from a fellow of the college itself. In Nuremberg in 1535, Catherine Koler was ordered by the city council to restrict herself to external treatments and not to provide internal remedies, the territory of the physicians. The Italian Inquisition's attempt to stamp out irregular beliefs revealed a range of specialist paid healers. In the southern Italian town of Guagnano, the 1565 investigation brought forth Sisters Avenia and Rosata who treated joint pains and headaches respectively.

By the seventeenth century, some female practitioners made no attempt to hide or excuse their paid medical work, but rather publicly celebrated their knowledge and skills. In 1606, Hester Langham of London advertised her sale of a powder against chlorosis. In the early seventeenth century, the celebrated surgeon and midwife Maria Colinetia, the wife of a surgeon, traveled throughout Germany demonstrating procedures and is credited with the technique of removing iron splinters from the eye with a magnet. Mary Trye, who trained under her father, published in 1675 one of the first medical manuals for women, her *Medicatrix, or the Woman-Physician.*

Women Religious Healers and Charges of Witchcraft

In ill health, many people also invested faith in the skills of mystical healers, female and male, who claimed expertise on the basis of divine intervention. Some women claimed to be born on days of particular religious significance. Barbe La Grosse Gorge, from Lorraine, explained that her healing powers, including the power to detect bewitching, stemmed from having been born on Good Friday during the reading of the Passion. Others claimed that their prayers to the saint on whose day they were born would prove decisive. Mystical healers derived authority from their ability to recognize a supernatural cause of an illness and to mediate the curative power of the saint working through them. A small number of these women were later recognized as saints themselves, usually after their death, for their miraculous thaumaturgic capabilities. Canonization procedures compiled lists of healing miracles by such women, which were attested to by both local and ecclesiastical communities. Even secular authorities accredited spiritual therapies of this kind. At the turn of the sixteenth century, the council records of the municipality of Lille reveal that they paid poor women to take sickly foundling children on pilgrimages to religious sites to cure them of a variety of illnesses.

The Renaissance was a time of deep religious anxiety, during which claims to any form of supernatural powers could prove dangerous for women. In regions that converted to Protestant beliefs, some customs of religious healing were dismissed as superstitions, disempowering the women and men who had provided them.

In regions that retained the Catholic faith, spiritual medicine became regulated through church officials, to the extent that only an exorcist was permitted to determine whether an illness was provoked by a supernatural cause. This allowed no role for Catholic women to practice a recognized form of mystical healing except as saints. In areas of the Italian peninsula, the Inquisition investigated what it perceived as superstitious beliefs, including female practitioners such as Camilla Nanni, examined in 1600 for her claims to cure headaches by prayers and incantations. Some female healers were tried as witches, particularly when their cures did not succeed. Ecclesiastical and secular courts attempted to establish, with the testimony of local witnesses, whether women's curative powers were divine or diabolical in origin. In 1577, Frenchwoman Barbe Dorée was examined for healing by her prayers and the placement of a pigeon on the stomach of a patient. She advised that a mass be celebrated for the following nine days in the local church. Authorities eventually determined that the source of her curative powers was diabolical and she was declared a witch. Often factors such as social status were vitally important in shaping how a magical therapeutic ability might be interpreted by local communities. The female healers prosecuted for witchcraft were frequently poor and socially isolated. When such women were perceived to harbor jealousy or ill will toward those more fortunate, their healing activities and the underlying cause of the illness could raise suspicions and fears in their neighborhood.

Some historians have drawn attention to the frequency with which midwives and lying-in maids were accused of witchcraft, and in seventeenth-century Germany a significant minority of witchcraft accusations involved these medical practitioners. Clearly childbirth was a time of great anxiety for the health of the mother and infant, and a point of tension at which the failure to succeed in the maternal role, whether through lack of breast milk or a cot death, might raise suspicions of the bewitching of the new mother. Early modern populations believed that the pregnant and parturient female body was particularly vulnerable to evil spirits and suggestions. Nevertheless, further investigations in France and England do not appear to bear out a strong connection between midwives and witchcraft accusations across Europe generally.

Hospital Administration and Nursing as Careers for Women

Women's involvement in religious medical care could take other forms as well. Some women embraced the active spiritual vocation of hospital nursing. However, the responsibilities for hospital structures were changing across Renaissance Europe. In some Protestant regions such as England, the Reformation signaled the end of the participation of religious women in nursing. Where laywomen replaced them, the work was so unappealing and poorly paid that it attracted only the most miserable or those who worked from a spirit of charity. In Catholic France, hospital governance transferred from ecclesiastical authorities to lay municipal administrators, but the everyday health care work of women continued to underpin medical services. In some towns, the nuns remained the nursing personnel, but in other cities they were replaced by laywomen. Jehanne de Tongrelou, a merchant's widow, governed the almshouse of Poitiers from 1535 until 1542 and donated many of her household utensils to it. By the seventeenth century, the dynamism of the Catholic Reformation saw a revival in female religious care, with new religious nursing orders developing under Saint Vincent de Paul and Louise de Marillac.

Hospital nursing often involved many thankless tasks of cooking, cleaning, and tending to the religious and medical needs of patients. Nuns undertook such an arduous life to secure their own and their patients' salvation. In larger charitable facilities, physicians and surgeons provided medical advice; in others, it was nuns who were responsible for the extent of care that the hospital could provide. Medical assistance in these organizations most commonly consisted of food, heat, and a bed, with occasional visits by physicians and surgeons. While nuns were frequently praised for their duty and dedication to the hard physical labor of running hospitals, rarely were they expected to provide input into the direction and organization of the facility; supervision and management of that kind usually lay with religious or secular authorities. Nuns knew, however, that increased funding and facilities could improve the general health care management of their patients, even if they had little training in diseases and specialized treatments. The nursing responsibilities of women were so naturalized that nuns struggled to have their voices heard as medical providers with knowledge and opinions about needs in the hospitals that they ran on a daily basis.

Municipal authorities often paid individual women for their care and cure of particular patients. In 1597, the Nuremberg city council paid one woman thirty-two guilden for treating eye diseases of the hospital's patients. St. Bartholomew's in London listed payments for Alice Gordon's surgical work in 1598. Some women were clearly recognized as specialist practitioners. In France, the Poitiers town hospital paid women throughout the sixteenth century for curing children of ringworm, and the Lyons hospital employed a number of female practitioners to treat patients with syphilis. In some French cities, councils arranged for women to treat patients from the town hospital in their home, when beds were in short supply. Barbe Gracieuse nursed three such patients in her Poitiers home in 1584. In 1532, the Strasbourg city council appointed community attendants, often poor widows, whom the sick could call upon.

Other women nursed their family, kin, and neighbors casually as part of a range of work activities. Parisian records show a number of women who worked intermittently as laundresses and sick nurses when the need arose.

Some were paid in small gifts and tokens by the patient or their family. This kind of work was similar to household medicine: every woman was expected to have some inherent nursing abilities, and their modes of treatment largely consisted of herbal and dietetic preparations, heating, and keeping the patient clean and comfortable. Sometimes the same palliative nurses also prepared the body for burial after death.

Childbirth and Reproductive Knowledge

For many women, childbirth and reproductive complaints would continue to be the domain of collective, usually local female advice and knowledge. Women generally understood the quickening at four months as the clearest sign of pregnancy. They identified both physical and emotional stress as causes of miscarriage. Traveling on horseback or by coach over bumpy roads was often feared by elite women during pregnancy. Catherine de Médicis rebuked the French ambassadors after hearing reports that Spanish courtiers were forcing her daughter, Elisabeth, to write her final testament and expressed concerns that she should not be disturbed emotionally during her pregnancy. Elite women exchanged ideas about their bodies in pregnancy and childbirth through correspondence. Sisters Elisabeth and Charlotte-Brabantine de Nassau exchanged remedies in their letters to make childbirth smoother, placing particular confidence in eagle stones, which were commonly believed to help the delivery. In 1602, Elisabeth also advised her sister to give birth standing, arguing that the labor was much shorter this way. Childbirth itself brought together midwives, relatives, and neighbors to assist the new mother and provided a forum for the dissemination and observation of knowledge and practices.

Yet in some circumstances, women's authority about their bodies was contested. Guild- and university-trained practitioners sought to instruct and advise about gynecology and obstet-

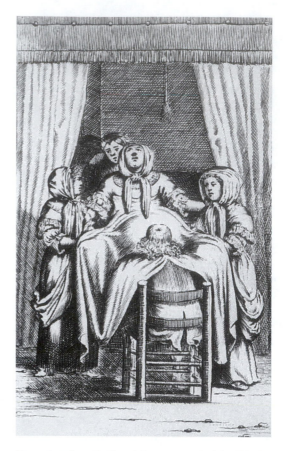

Engraving of a midwife assisting a woman in labor. Woodcut from Louise Bourgeois' Het begin en ingang van alle menschen in de wereld, Dutch trans. of Observations diverses sur la stérilité, perte de fruict, foecondité, accouchements et maladies des femmes et enfants nouveaux naiz, 1707, Leyden. (Courtesy of the National Library of Medicine, Bethesda, Md.)

rics in published textbooks. Physicians were increasingly present at the birth of elite and royal children, often in supervisory roles over female practitioners. Royal women, who were often in foreign courts and whose reproductive labor was of crucial national importance, found themselves surrounded by numerous medical advisors in such matters. Physicians, midwives, political advisors, ladies-in-waiting, and ambassadors were all involved in the exchange of reproductive knowledge and practices across national borders, promoting the medical customs of their country and the superiority of its practitioners.

Early historians of midwifery often accepted as fact the cartoonish images of the incompetent and illiterate midwives depicted by contemporary physicians, who had a vested interest in denigrating midwives' competitive services. An increasing body of evidence, however, suggests that midwives were widely respected by local communities as purveyors of expert reproductive care. Midwives themselves often emphasized their knowledge of learned theory.

Midwives and Licensing

The early modern trend toward the licensing of midwives was a double-edged sword for women and exposed the interests of a variety of community groups in reproductive medicine. In France, the first licensing regulations were established for Parisian midwives in 1560, and surgeons, not physicians, oversaw the apprenticeship of new midwives. In England and Italy, midwives continued to be licensed by ecclesiastical authorities, who focused attention on their religious and moral responsibilities rather than on their medical expertise. From the late Middle Ages, German municipal authorities took responsibility for licensing midwives, as did the Low Countries. Some women welcomed accreditation of their skills through licensing because of the status, financial security, and guild positions that it provided.

A few midwives even published texts in which they proudly related their professional experiences and advised on common reproductive and everyday illnesses. Louise Bourgeois, the most influential midwife in France, as midwife to the queen Marie de Médicis, claimed to have learned her craft from the study of learned surgical works. In 1609, she published her own observations on female reproductive illnesses. In later works, she gave advice on epilepsy, rabies, toothaches, headaches, chest problems, fevers, plague, and kidney and liver problems, among other illnesses beyond the domain of a midwife. In England, midwives would not publish their professional expertise until much later in the seventeenth century with Jane Sharp's *The Mid-* *wives Book* of 1671. When Elizabeth Cellier proposed plans for *A Scheme for the Foundation of a Royal Hospital . . . for the Maintenance of a Corporation of Skillful Midwives* (1687), she was attacked by the College of Physicians for her presumption. Despite the prominence of a number of midwives in Germany, the first midwifery book by a woman, Justine Siegemundin, was not published until 1700.

The Renaissance was thus for female practitioners a time of significant change in institutional and professional identities for medical work. In most cases, the change operated to the disadvantage of women, who were barred from long-held practice in certain medical fields that were seen as the exclusive domain of "qualified" university- and guild-trained men. For a small number of women, professionalization did bring, however, opportunities to be recognized as legitimate providers of medical services in a regulated structure, through the licensing of midwives. Overwhelmingly, though, the era of the Renaissance did little to alter perceptions about women's "natural" roles as caregivers in the domestic and local spheres, as providers of healthy food and environments, and as nurses to children, the sick, and elderly.

Susan Broomhall

See also Abortion and Miscarriage; Contraception.
Bibliography
Broomhall, Susan. *Women's Medical Work in Early Modern France.* Manchester, UK: Manchester University Press, 2004.

Crawford, Patricia. "Attitudes to Menstruation in Seventeenth-Century England." *Past and Present* 91 (1981): 47–73.

Evenden, Doreen. *The Midwives of Seventeenth-Century London.* Cambridge: Cambridge University Press, 2000.

Harley, David. "Historians as Demonologists: The Myth of the Midwife-Witch." *Social History of Medicine* 3, no. 1 (1990): 1–26.

Hunter, Lynette, and Sarah Hutton, eds. *Women, Science and Medicine, 1500–1700.* Stroud: Sutton, 1997.

Gentilcore, David. *Healers and Healing in Early Modern Italy.* Manchester, UK: Manchester University Press, 1998.

Green, Monica H. *Women's Healthcare in the Medieval West.* Aldershot, UK: Ashgate, 2000.

Klairmont Lingo, Alison. "Women Healers and the Medical Marketplace of Sixteenth-Century Lyon." *Dynamis* 19 (1999): 79–94.

Marland, Hilary, ed. *The Art of Midwifery: Early Modern Midwives in Europe.* London: Routledge, 1993.

McTavish, Lianne. *Childbirth and the Display of Authority in Early Modern France.* Aldershot, UK: Ashgate, 2005.

Rublack, Ulinka. "Pregnancy, Childbirth and the Female Body in Early Modern Germany." *Past and Present* 150 (1996): 84–110.

Wiesner, Merry E., *Working Women in Renaissance Germany.* New Brunswick, NJ: Rutgers University Press, 1986.

Male Midwifery

Throughout the early modern period, female midwives governed the birthing chamber, inviting men to assist at deliveries after days of unsuccessful labor, when the child was likely dead and the life of the mother in peril. These men were initially associated with both sexual impropriety and death, but slowly managed to attend even the uncomplicated deliveries of wealthy, urban French and English women by the eighteenth century. This transition has attracted attention from scholars determined to discover the complex medical, social, and cultural factors that encouraged men's taking a role in childbirth. During the 1970s and 1980s, the increased practice of male midwives was viewed as a battle of the sexes in which men prevailed. Feminists Barbara Ehrenreich and Deirdre English argued that women were systematically driven out of medical practice by men, with female midwives persecuted as witches because of their intimate understanding of women's bodies. Despite challenging the narrative, which featured men marching triumphantly into the lying-in chamber to save the lives of women and children, subsequent research by historians has disproved many of the arguments of Ehrenreich and English, particularly the idea that female midwives were identified as witches. Scholars continue to undermine the ideas that female midwives were incompetent, that women had no control over conception, and that birth itself was extremely dangerous, but now also focus on regional differences in midwifery practices, approaching birth as an important social event both shaped within and significant to early modern culture at large.

While in England childbirth became part of medicine between 1720 and 1770, in France male expansion into midwifery occurred at a slower rate and was always relatively rare in rural and southern areas. Eighteenth-century France even saw the revival of the female midwife, in the form of Madame du Coudray, hired by Kings Louis XV and Louis XVI to teach her methods throughout the country. The situation in Italy was in striking contrast to the rest of Europe, for there men never dominated the practice of childbirth. Historian Nadia Maria Filippini attributes this situation to the disapproval of both the Catholic church and the general populace, yet notes that by the eighteenth century the public role of the female midwife had been reduced to attending normal births. The material culture of childbirth in Italy was additionally unique, including Tuscan *deschi da parto,* painted wooden trays used to present food and drink to the newly delivered woman. Italian childbirth has nevertheless received less scholarly attention than childbirth in the rest of Europe, likely because of long-standing interest in the expansion of male midwifery.

Undermining the myth of the incompetent female midwife, historians Hilary Marland, Helen King, Doreen Evenden, and Nina Rattner Gelbart have shown that many midwives were not only well-educated, respected members of their communities, but also able to manage various complications in childbirth after undergoing lengthy apprenticeships with more experienced midwives. By studying famous midwives such as Louise Bourgeois and Jane Sharp as well as more typical practitioners, scholars have demonstrated that female midwives traditionally had a wide range of responsibilities, which included determining fertility and pregnancy; treating miscarriage; caring for women before, during, and after their delivery; and giving expert advice in legal cases involving rape or paternity. The regulation of female midwives varied according to region but generally began to increase toward the end of the fifteenth century. The earliest French statute, which appeared in 1560, dealt with the instruction, examination, licensing, and registration of midwives in addition to instituting a code of moral conduct. The regulation of midwives occurred somewhat later in England, during the sixteenth and seventeenth centuries. The moral character and religious affiliation of midwives continued to be of greater concern to the authorities than the women's medical competence. Historian David Harley has shown that the training of midwives was a rather informal affair in northern England, with women applying for a midwifery license only after they had been reported for practicing without one.

Although the forceps is no longer described as the key to the lying-in chamber, historian Adrian Wilson argues that British male midwives were tolerated only after improving their reputations by performing successful forceps deliveries of live children. He shows that forceps use was debated among male midwives in London during the first half of the eighteenth century and was apparently linked with political affiliations. According to Wilson, the expansion of male midwifery was aided by women's quest for increased social status. Contesting the belief that there was a unified women's culture, he argues that literate, wealthy Englishwomen sought to distinguish themselves from the lower orders during the eighteenth century by hiring more costly male midwives to assist at their deliveries.

Wilson's arguments cannot be transferred to France, for the forceps was invented by the Chamberlen family in England and was not widely used by French practitioners until after 1730. In France, male surgeons predominantly acted as male midwives (*chirurgiens accoucheurs*), whereas in England physicians often intervened in the lying-in chamber. When called to assist at difficult deliveries, French surgeons attempted to turn the child in the womb manually or used instruments, such as *crochets* (hooks), to perform craniotomies, a procedure that entailed crushing the infant's head and extracting its body piece by piece. They claimed such procedures were both highly skilled and strictly surgical, whereas activities normally undertaken by female midwives, such as cutting the navel string and ensuring the afterbirth was discharged, were unskilled. This disparagement of women's traditional occupation in the lying-in chamber was a standard feature in obstetrical treatises written by men in France as well as in England and Italy, though only a few such books were written by Italian physicians in contrast to the explosion of publications produced by French and English authors. French surgeons claimed their male hands were able to enter the womb and discern through touch the position of the unborn child. These men did not have visual access to the pregnant woman's body, which was draped both for warmth and to preserve feminine modesty. An eighteenth-century engraving of the lying-in chamber shows a laboring woman assisted by a male midwife with a sheet tied around his neck. Though none of the female figures in this the engraving are looking directly at the seated male figure, French obstetrical treatises indicate that women routinely scrutinized male midwives for signs of appropriate appearance and demeanor. These men strove to convey desirable qualities while disguising negative displays of fear and incompetence. Attending to the visual exchanges occurring in the lying-in chamber contributes to the growing belief that early modern European women were not simply passive victims of male midwives, but rather actively participated in their employment.

Lianne McTavish

Bibliography
Ackerknecht, Erwin H. "Midwives as Experts in Court." *Bulletin of the New York Academy of Medicine* 52 (1976), 1224–1228.

Cody, Lisa Forman. "The Politics of Reproduction: From Midwives' Alternative Public Sphere to the Public Spectacle of Man-Midwifery." *Eighteenth-Century Studies* 32, no. 4 (1999): 477–495.

Cressy, David. *Birth, Marriage, and Death: Ritual, Religion, and the Life-Cycle in Tudor and Stuart England.* Oxford: Oxford University Press, 1997.

Ehrenreich, Barbara, and Deirdre English. *Witches, Midwives, and Nurses: A History of Women Healers.* New York: The Feminist Press, 1973.

Evenden, Doreen. *The Midwives of Seventeenth-Century London.* Cambridge: Cambridge University Press, 2000.

Filippini, Nadia Maria. "The Church, the State and Childbirth: The Midwife in Italy During the Eighteenth Century." In *The Art of Midwifery: Early Modern Midwives in Europe.* Edited by Hilary Marland, 152–175. London: Routledge, 1993.

Gelbart, Nina Rattner. *The King's Midwife: A History and Mystery of Madame du Coudray.* Berkeley: University of California Press, 1998.

Harley, David. "Historians as Demonologists: The Myth of the Midwife-witch." *Journal of the Society for the Social History of Medicine* 3, no. 1 (1990): 1–26.

Harley, David. "Provincial Midwives in England: Lancashire and Cheshire, 1660–1760." Edited by Hilary Marland. *The Art of Midwifery: Early Modern Midwives in Europe.* Pages 27–48. London: Routledge, 1993.

King, Helen. " 'As if None Understood the Art that Cannot Understand Greek': The Education of Midwives in Seventeenth-Century England." Edited by Vivian Nutton and Roy Porter. *The History of Medical Education in Britain,* 184–198. Amsterdam: Rodopi, 1995.

McTavish, Lianne. *Childbirth and the Display of Authority in Early Modern France.* Aldershot, UK: Ashgate, 2005.

Perkins, Wendy. *Midwifery and Medicine in Early Modern France: Louise Bourgeois.* Exeter: University of Exeter Press, 1996.

Wilson, Adrian. *The Making of Man-Midwifery: Childbirth in England, 1660–1770.* Berkeley: University of California Press, 1995.

The Practice of Pharmacology and Laywomen

Women lay healers participated in medical practice in a variety of ways. The task of overseeing basic medical care for a household or estate generally fell to women, which meant that many women became experts in making medical remedies and in administering them to sick family members and acquaintances. These activities frequently overlapped with the activities of professional healers. It is important to remember that sick people in the Renaissance relied on many sources for their healing. Hence it was common for a patient to start with a household cure and seek the advice of a professional practitioner only if necessary or to use both household remedies and the advice of licensed practitioners concurrently. Even though university-trained physicians were the only healers legally permitted to administer internal medications, other practitioners, including laywomen, paid little heed to these regulations.

The Home Manufacture of Pharmaceuticals

A large number of laywomen were experts in the concoction of medical remedies. Like learned physicians, women used their medications to treat a wide variety of illnesses, including dysentery, ague, fevers, headaches, toothaches, and epilepsy. Many household remedies involved simple kitchen techniques such as chopping, pounding, boiling, and straining. Others required more specialized equipment, such as a scale for weighing and a pestle and mortar for grinding. Women made a wide variety of remedies in this manner, including salves, medicinal drinks, powders, plasters, electuaries, and herb- or flower-infused oils.

A more complicated, but common, technique women used to make medications was distillation. Physicians had lauded the medicinal value of distilled alcohol, or *aqua vitae* (literally, "water of life"), since the thirteenth century, and distillation became a widespread practice among laypeople by the sixteenth century. Some aristocratic estates possessed a separate house with extensive distillation equipment, but many smaller houses also owned at least one still. Not only was *aqua vitae* distilled, but also nonalcoholic oils and waters involving herbs, flowers, roots, and even animal parts. Women generally assisted in operating the stills, both at large noble manors and in more humble settings. In fact, in the sixteenth century it was quite common for German towns to employ female distillers, called *Wasserbrennerinnin*.

Ingredients for medicinal remedies varied widely based on location and social class. Local herbs, flowers, roots, and seeds represented the most common components of medical recipes. Animal ingredients also figured into many recipes, especially the milk, blood, eyes, heart, liver, and dung of animals such as pigs, cows, cats, wild boars, stags, and occasionally humans. Those who could afford them included expensive imported extravagances in certain remedies, including sugar, saffron, Tibetan rhubarb, and even ground pearls, precious gems, and gold. Sugar and honey were used to temper the taste of bitter herbs, and most medicinal powders and drinks were taken with wine, vinegar, beer, or water. Due to the close relationship between medicine and food in the Renaissance, women also made medicinal recipes using meat broths, eggs, bread, and fruits.

Women Healers' Guides to Home Remedies
Because the manufacture of medical remedies was so central to women's medical practice in the Renaissance, medical recipes played a significant role in women's healing. Physicians and some laymen had owned collections of medical recipes since the ninth or tenth century, and many female lay healers began to keep extensive handwritten medical recipe collections

from at least the late fifteenth century. The Milanese noblewoman Caterina Sforza (1469–1509) is one of the first women known to have possessed a medical recipe collection. She kept a volume full of 454 *experimenti,* of which 358 were recipes for medicine, 66 for cosmetics, and 30 for alchemy. Several of Caterina's medical recipes were written partially in code, a fairly common practice, especially in Italy and England, for recipes containing information perceived as especially valuable or secret.

Such attempts to safeguard certain recipes were prompted in part by the widespread interest in exchanging medical recipes. In a continual search for effective cures, people of all classes traded both individual remedies and entire recipe collections with family members, friends, and acquaintances. Many recipe collections recorded the name of the person from whom each recipe was obtained, and recipes originating from aristocrats and religious figures were especially prized. Both women and men exchanged medical recipes, and indeed recipe collections represent one area of Renaissance medicine in which women and men moved on relatively equal footing. German physician Oswald Gabelköver's recipe book, published as *The Boock of Physicke* in England in 1599, contained a number of recipes attributed to women, while Caterina Sforza's recipe collection contained entries attributed to Italian noblemen. The practice of collecting and exchanging medical recipes was especially extensive at the courts of Renaissance Europe. For example, Queen Elizabeth I of England (1533–1603) owned a collection of medical recipes, as did the Empress Maria of Spain (1526–1603) and Catherine de Médicis, queen of France (1519–1589).

Renowned Medicinewomen
The best-known female healers of the Renaissance were noblewomen. Far more than most women, noblewomen tended to be literate and to have both visibility vis-à-vis the outside

world and access to ingredients and prized recipes. Electress Anna of Saxony (1532–1585) became widely known for her skillfully distilled medicinal waters, even attracting the attention of the Holy Roman emperor and empress. Countess Dorothea of Mansfeld (1493–1578), one of the best-known lay healers of her time, ran an extensive hospice for the sick poor from her castle garden, caring for hundreds of patients a day during epidemics. In England, Lady Grace Mildmay (1552–1620) and Anne Howard, countess of Arundel (1557–1630), gained widespread renown for administering medicines to the poor.

Due to a lack of documentation, we know much less about nonaristocratic lay healers, but we do know that common women also made and administered remedies. Numerous recipes attributed to ordinary women appear in collections of medical recipes. Wives and daughters of physicians, barbers, and surgeons frequently became known as medical experts, and evidence shows that much medical knowledge was passed down from mothers to daughters. In rural areas, which generally had few licensed healers, women's household medicine likely represented most of the population's medical care.

Conclusion

Despite the large number of laywomen who practiced medicine in the Middle Ages and Renaissance, they have generally escaped the attention of historians. For a variety of social and cultural reasons, women were far less likely to print their medical works than were men, and even today most pharmacological recipe collections owned by laywomen exist only as handwritten manuscripts. The first medical books published by laywomen began to appear in the seventeenth century, notably the popular *A choice manuall, or, Rare and select secrets in physick and chirurgery* by Elizabeth Grey, countess of Kent (1581–1651), in 1654. Despite the late publication date, Grey's work reflected a long tradition of women as medical practitioners and medical authors.

Alisha Rankin

Bibliography

Primary Work

Grey, Elizabeth, Countess of Kent. *A Choice Manuall, or, Rare and Select Secrets in Physick and Chirurgery.* London: G. D., 1654.

Secondary Works

Broomhall, Susan. *Women's Medical Work in Early Modern France.* Manchester: Manchester University Press, 2004.

Fiumi, Fabrizia, and Giovanna Tempesta. "Gli 'esperimenti' di Caterina Sforza." In *Catarina Sforza: Una Donna del Cinquecento,* 139–146. Imola, Italy: La Mandrigora, 2000.

Hunter, Lynette. "Women and Domestic Medicine: Lady Experimenters, 1570–1620." In *Women, Science and Medicine, 1500–1700: Mothers and Sisters of the Royal Society.* Edited by Lynette Hunter and Sarah Hutton, 89–107. Stroud, UK: Sutton, 1997.

Pollock, Linda. *With Faith and Physic: The Life of a Tudor Gentlewoman Lady Grace Mildmay, 1552–1620.* London: Collins and Brown, 1993.

Rankin, Alisha. "Medicine for the Uncommon Woman: Experience, Experiment, and Exchange in Early Modern Germany." Ph.D. dissertation, Harvard University, 2005.

Stine, Jennifer. "Opening Closets: The Discovery of Household Medicine in Early Modern England." Ph.D. dissertation, Stanford University, 1996.

Stoudt, Debra L. "Medieval German Women and the Power of Healing." In *Women Healers and Physicians: Climbing a Long Hill.* Edited by Lilan R. Furst, 13–42. Lexington: University Press of Kentucky, 1997.

Midwives, Female and Male. *See* Medicine and Women.

Montenay, Georgette de (1540?–1607)

First author to publish a book of emblems in French Georgette de Montenay's *Emblemes ou Devises Chrestiennes,* published in 1571, made her not only the first author of emblems written in

French but also the first woman author of emblems. This elegant volume, illustrated with superb copper engravings by the famous artist Pierre Woeiriot, was so successful that it was repeatedly reedited and even translated into six languages in her lifetime. Yet for centuries after her death, she was generally listed as "an author of religious Emblems in imitation of Alciati," as one might casually describe Montaigne as having written essays or Marguerite de Navarre as having compiled short stories.

It seems certain that it is with the help and perhaps even subsidies from Jeanne d'Albret, the Protestant queen of Navarre and the daughter of Marguerite de Navarre, that the *Emblemes ou Devises Chrestiennes* were published in 1571. The privilege to print was granted for five years by Charles IX in 1566. Philippe de Castellas, the designated (Protestant) printer and the well-known artist Pierre Woeiriot, who was asked to design and engrave the one hundred and one copper plates illustrating the text, traveled from Lyon to Paris toward the end of 1566 or in early January 1567 and met Georgette de Montenay. While Montenay was not at any time a lady-in-waiting to Jeanne, both she and her husband Guyon du Gout had family ties to both Antoine de Bourbon-Vendôme and his queen, and they were part of their retinue. Queen Jeanne and her son, the future King Henri IV of France and Navarre, had been in Paris most of the year and left at the end of January 1567, to the great displeasure of Queen Catherine de Médicis, who would have preferred to keep them within reach. Woeiriot is bound to have read most of the hundred and one *huitains* and the legend to be inserted in each illustration before he began work on the copper engravings, a time-consuming and absorbing task. It can only be in Paris that he sketched the charming engraving of Georgette's portrait—pen in hand at her writing table, her lute at her elbow—bearing the date 1567. Below this portrait, she introduces herself to her readers as a devout Christian whose mind, heart, written words, and voice

are dedicated to the glory of God through Christ. The eighth line of this handwritten poem, *Gage d'or tot ne te meine,* an anagram of her name, invites the reader to eschew material possessions, and the three capital letters "GDM," inserted in the right margin, confirm her identity.

Woeiriot may have taken longer than anticipated to finish the project, but he probably completed it in 1568 at the latest, and the second civil war is the likely cause for the delay. The fortune of the Huguenots fluctuated greatly between 1566 and 1570. The queen of Navarre had barely escaped from Nérac in late August 1568, and she stayed in the Protestant city of La Rochelle for about two years, during which time she faced problems of a far more urgent nature. The author of the *Emblemes,* who does not appear to have followed Jeanne to La Rochelle, would have been unable to leave her small castle of Saint-Germier or to remain in touch with Castellas in Lyon. The Edict of Pacification of 8 August 1570 provided the needed lull in the religious conflict, and it is Jean Marcorelle, another Protestant printer from Lyon, who hastily published the volume in 1571 before its privilege expired. If Montenay had a chance to see the proofs of her work before it appeared in print—and it is doubtful she did—we may assume that the dedicatory epistle to Jeanne, queen of Navarre, in which a line is missing, was added before going to press. No errata sheet was included, and the error is corrected in none of the subsequent editions.

There are indeed one hundred emblems in the volume. Each includes a Latin motto (*inscriptio*), in most cases a direct quotation from Scriptures (and Montenay knew both quite well); a visual representation of its message (*pictura*) or of the ideas expressed in a poem; and a decasyllabic huitain (*susbscriptio*) that with few exceptions follows an ab–ab–bc–bc rhyme scheme.

Much misinformation was printed from the moment Montenay's name came to the attention of scholars. She was sometimes described as a Lyonnaise, but most sources, including *Annales,* the *Biographie Toulousaine,* the *Nouvelle Biographie Générale depuis les temps les plus reculés,* and the *Dictionnaire de la Noblesse,* state that she was born in Toulouse in 1540 or 1541 and died in 1581. In fact, Georgette de Montenay did not set foot in the southwest of France until 1563. She was the fourth and penultimate child born in Normandy to Jacques de Montenay, whose family had impeccable lines of nobility in that province, and Isabeau d'Estouteville, whose family, also from Normandy, enjoyed much prestige. Married in 1527, both of Georgette's parents died in late 1545 or early 1546. Mary, the third child, was married in 1550, and one may assume that she was born between 1532 and 1535, and while 1537 to 1541 cannot be dismissed outright for Georgette's birth, the dates of 1530–1540 more recently suggested seem unlikely. Most biographical texts mention Georgette's being reared at the house of Jeanne d'Albret, or her becoming a lady-in-waiting to the queen of Navarre. Additional research disproved both claims, but Georgette de Montenay was indeed related to both Jeanne d'Albret and her husband Antoine de Bourbon Vendôme. Since she had no descendants, she was also wrongly described as a spinster whose austere life was dedicated to her faith. In fact, she was married in 1562 to Guyon du Gout (the spelling he favored over De Goth, and De Gouth, found on various legal documents), a nobleman from Gascony. We know that du Gout was considerably older than his spouse for he is mentioned in 1524 as the eldest of four sons and one of his sisters had married in 1517. In 1539 he was listed as equerry to François de Bourbon, duke of Estouteville. It is unlikely that he would have been second in command to Marshall Du Biez at the siege of Boulogne in 1545 if he had been in his early twenties. After his last will was located, we can confirm that he died a devout Catholic in 1574. In spite of his spouse's having embraced the new religion, he was most generous toward his widow, and even made his sole legatee one

of his nephews who had also converted to the Protestant faith. Although she certainly had numerous contacts with the court of Navarre in Pau and in Nérac as early as 1563, Georgette de Montenay resided in the castle of Saint-Germier, where, in 1579, she received Prince Henri III of Navarre, the future Henri IV, king of France. She had known him as a child, and he may have stayed at Saint-Germier before this official visit. As to her death, the date of 1581 is premature: various letters, receipts, and quitclaims reproduced in a 1986 study had revealed that the "damoiselle de Montenay" was alive and in excellent spirits in early 1599, but the specific date of death itself remained elusive. Thanks to two documents of major importance found by the late Elisabeth Labrousse, we know at last that she died in late October or early November 1607.

Régine Reynolds-Cornell

See also Art and Women; Albret, Jeanne d';
    Catherine de Médicis.
Bibliography
Primary Works

Montenay, Georgette de. *Emblemes ou devises chrestiennes.* Lyon: Marcorelle, 1571. Montenay, Georgette de. *Emblemes ou devises chrestiennes.* Edited by C. S. Smith. Menston, UK: Scholars Press, 1973. (Facsimile edition of 1571 printing.)

Montenay, Georgette de. *Livre d'Armoiries en signe de fraternite contenant cent comparaisons de vertus et Emblemes chrestiens agences et ornes de belles figures gravees en cuivre.* Frankfurt: Peter Rollos, 1619.

Secondary Works

Adams, Allison. "Georgette de Montenay and the Device of the Dordrecht Printer François Bosselaer." *Bibliothèque d'Humanisme et Renaissance* 63 (2001): 63–71.

Adams, Allison. "Les Emblemes ou Devises Chrestiennes de Georgette de Montenay: Edition de 1567." *Bibliothèque d'Humanisme et Renaissance* 62 (2000): 637–629.

Labrousse, Elisabeth, and Jean-Philippe. "Georgette de Montenay et Guyon du Gout, son époux." *Bulletin de la Société archéologique, historique, littéraire et scientifique du Gers* (1990): 369–402.

Margolin, Jean-Claude. "Georgette de Montenay, ses Emblèmes ou Devises Chrestiennes, et

Anna Vischer." *Bibliothèque d'Humanisme et Renaissance* 51 (1989): 419–423.

Matthews Griego, Sara. "Georgette de Montenay: A Different Voice in Sixteenth-Century Emblematics." *Renaissance Quarterly* 47 (1994): 793–871.

Reynolds-Cornell, Régine. *Witnessing an Era, Georgette de Montenay and the Emblèmes ou Devises Chrestiennes.* Birmingham, UK: Summa, 1987.

Reynolds-Cornell, Régine. "Reflets d'une époque, les Devises ou Emblemes Chrestiennes de Georgette de Montenay." *Bibliothèque d'Humanisme et Renaissance* 48 (1986): 373–386.

Morata, Fulvia Olympia (1526/1527–1555)

Ferrarese writer of Latin and Greek letters, dialogues, and poems; convert to Protestantism who fled Italy to live in Germany

The eldest child of Fulvio Pellegrino Morato (Latinized from Moretto, ca. 1483–1548) and Lucrezia (possibly Gozi), Fulvia Olympia Morato, a talented teacher with considerable fame as a poet, served as a tutor in the Este court. During an exile from Ferrara between 1532 and 1539, she met Caelius Secundus Curio (1503–1569), who would become a life-long friend of the family. Through Curio and others, Morato was deeply influenced by the ideas of Erasmus, Melanchthon, Zwingli, and Luther, and by 1539 she was lecturing publicly on Calvin's *Institutes of Christian Religion*.

Morata was educated by her father. For Greek, she had the German Chilian Sinapius (1506–1563), brother of Johannes Sinapius (1505–1560) who was a friend of Calvin's. She was also influenced by Curio and by Celio Calcagnini (1479–1541). Between 1539 and 1541 (aged twelve to thirteen), Morata was brought to court as companion to Anna d'Este (1531–1607), eldest daughter of Duke Ercole II (1508–1559) and Renée de France (1510–1575). Renée established her own circle of French retainers and religious refugees filled with "Lutheran bandits from France." Visitors had included the Huguenot poet Clément Marot (1496?–1544), Vittoria Colonna (1492–1547), the preacher Bernardino Ochino (1487–1564), and Calvin himself. Morata showed her learning before Renée's heterodox court in Latin public lectures on Cicero's *Stoic Paradoxes* (1541) and a Greek "Defense of Scaevola." Lost works included a defense of Cicero, dialogues in Greek and Latin in imitation of Plato, and commentaries on Homer. Her poems "On True Virginity," "To Bembo," and "To Eutychus Pontanus Gallus" date from this period. The last is one of the few works in which Morata deals explicitly with feminist issues, treating the standard trope of the opposition of Parnassus and the Muses with women's work, "yarn, shuttle, loom-threads, and work-baskets." In this she seems very close to Cassandra Fedele. Morata asked Johannes Sinapius to present her poems to King Ferdinand I and to the great merchant Fugger, apparently in hope of securing some patronage, but nothing came of this.

Morata left court to care for her father at some point after 1546, and when he died in 1548, she stayed to help run the house and educate her sisters and brothers. She returned, but the marriage that same year of Anna d'Este to François de Lorraine, later duc de Guise (1519–1563), left her isolated at court and abandoned by Renée. Morata studied philosophy intensively and corresponded in Greek with Gasparo Sardi (1480–1564), who dedicated his work *De Triplici Philosophia* (On the Three-Fold Philosophy, 1549) to her.

During this period, she met Andreas Grunthler (Grundler, Gründler, ca. 1518–1555), a relative of Johannes Sinapius. He was famed as a Latin poet and took his laureate in medicine at Ferrara in 1549. Sometime in that year or early 1550, Morata and Grunthler were married, and she composed a Greek "Wedding Prayer." Their marriage was conceived by the couple themselves as a match between equals and looked upon by their friends as such. The lack of condescension in her contemporaries in speaking about the pair is striking.

Grunthler went ahead to Germany in summer 1550, eventually obtaining the post of municipal physician in his hometown of Schweinfurt (Protestant since 1541). During his absence, Morata wrote one of her two surviving dialogues. Using her friend Lavinia della Rovere (1521–1601) as interlocutor, Morata reveals her intellectual history, moving from a view of a random universe (under the influence of Lucretius), through a spiritual crisis precipitated in part by her loss of worldly position, to a recognition of the providence of God, and a decision to devote her powers to Biblical study. Grunthler returned to escort Morata and her brother Emilio over the Alps. They came first to Schwaz (12 June 1550), where they stayed with the royal councilor, Georg Hörmann, and then traveled with him to Kaufbeuren and Augsburg. They stayed for a period with Sinapius in Würzburg. Grunthler went on ahead to ready the house in Schweinfurt, where they were reunited at the end of the year. During all this time, Morata continued her biblical studies and worked on what her contemporaries regarded as her most brilliant creations, a series of translations of the Psalms (1, 2, 23, 34, 46, 70, 125, 151) into Greek hexameters and sapphics, which her husband set to music.

Settled in Schweinfurt, she corresponded with many of the leading Protestant theologians of the day, including Matthias Flacius Illyricus, Pietro Paulo Vergerio, Bernardino Ochino, Melanchthon, and Joachim Camerarius, and reestablished contact with Curio and Lavinia della Rovere, for whom she composed the *Dialogue Between Theophila and Philotima*. In this second dialogue Morata touched on many of her most important themes: Christian hope, faith in the promises of God, and the need for these to be strengthened by constant study of the Bible. In her emphasis on the transitory nature of this world, Morata integrated her early study of philosophy with the transcendent promise of Christian salvation. Morata also looked specifically at women's roles in times of trial and presented Queen Esther as a model for the wise woman who must keep faith with God in the world of affairs.

Morata and Grunthler were caught in the Siege of Schweinfurt (during the Margrave's War), which lasted from April 1553 to June 1554. Morata's letters are the most vivid witness to the intense suffering of the city. Morata and Grunthler narrowly escaped being burned alive in the church in which they had taken shelter. After harrowing adventures they made it safely to Heidelberg, but without any possessions. Morata's books and most of her writings were lost. In the course of her escape Morata contracted what was probably tuberculosis. At Heidelberg, Grunthler was appointed to the third professorship of medicine. Morata, despite constant illness, continued her studies. She also taught Greek as a tutor to students. This fact has given rise to a misunderstanding that Morata taught formally as a professor in the University of Heidelberg. Morata wrote to Anna d'Este, now duchesse de Guise, begging her to use her influence with her husband and the king to intercede for the victims of the Edict of Châteaubriant. Worn out by her illness, Morata died on 26 October 1555, something short of her thirtieth birthday, followed soon by Grunthler and her brother Emilio. After Morata's death, Curio gathered up whatever works and letters he could find. The first edition (1558) was dedicated to Isabella Manriquez Bresegna (1510–1567), an early follower of Erasmus and Italian evangelism. The work went through three later editions (1562, 1570, 1580), dedicated to Queen Elizabeth I.

Morata wrote in a brilliant, flexible, idiomatic Latin. Her letters are vivid documents not only of her life and times, but also to the troubles of early Protestantism. Morata wrestled with the doctrine of predestination, commended those who sought harmony over the nature of communion, and counseled peace. In a letter reproving a preacher for his dissolute life, Morata revealed not only her deep involvement in the life of the church but an astonishing boldness of preaching. When women were forbidden to teach men, Morata spoke from a position of power, which seemed to rest entirely on her known piety and admired erudition.

Morata was singled out as an inspiration and model to many of the learned women who followed her, including Catharine des Roches (1550–1587), Elizabeth Jane Weston (1582–1612), Bathsua Makin (1600–1674?), Anna Maria van Schurman (1607–1678), and Mary Robinson (1758–1800).

Holt Parker

See also Bresegna, Isabella; the subheadings Latin Learning and Women and Greek Learning and Women (under Education, Humanism, and Women); Religious Reform and Women; Renata di Francia.

Bibliography

Primary Works

Caretti, Lanfranco, ed. *Olimpia Morata. Epistolario (1540–1555)*. Ferrara: 1940.

Caretti, Lanfranco, ed. *Opere di Olympia Morata*. Ferrara: 1954.

Morata, Olympia Fulvia. *Olympiae Fulviae Moratae foeminae doctissimae ac plane divinae Orationes, Dialogi, Epistolae, Carmina tam Latina quam Graeca*. 2nd ed. Edited by Caelius Secundus Curio. Basel: Petrum Pernam, 1562. (Reprinted in microfilm, "History of Women," Reel 62, No. 396 [New Haven, 1975]. Available at: www.uni-mannheim.de/mateo/desbillons/olimp.html.)

Morata, Olympia Fulvia. *Olympiae Fulviae Moratae mulieris omnium eruditissimae Latina et Graeca, quae haberi potuerunt, monumenta*. Edited by Caelius Secundus Curio. Basel: Petrum Pernam, 1558. (This first edition is dedicated to Isabella Besegna.)

Secondary Works

Bainton, Roland H. "Learned Women in the Europe of the Sixteenth Century." In *Beyond Their Sex: Learned Women of the European Past*. Edited by Patricia H. Labalme, 117–128. New York: New York University Press, 1980.

Bainton, Roland H. *Women of the Reformation in Germany and Italy*. Pages 253–268. Minneapolis: Augsburg Publishing House, 1971.

Caretti, Lanfranco, ed. *Olimpia Morata. Epistolario (1540–1555)*. Ferrara: Deputazione di storia patria per l'Emilia e la Romagna. Sezione di Ferrara, 1940.

Caretti, Lanfranco, ed. *Opere di Olympia Morata*. Ferrara: Deputazione provinciale ferrarese di storia patria. Atti e memorie, n.s., v. 11, 1954.

Flood, John L. "Olympia Fulvia Morata." In *German Writers of the Renaissance, 1280–1580: Dictionary of Literary Biography*. Vol. 179. Edited by James Hardin and Max Reinhart, 178–183. Detroit, MI: Gale Research, 1997.

Parker, Holt. *Olympia Morata: The Complete Writings of an Italian Heretic*. Chicago: University of Chicago Press, 2003.

Rabil, Albert. "Olympia Morata (1526–1555)." In *Italian Women Writers: A Bio-Bibliographical Sourcebook*. Edited by Rinaldina Russell, 269–278. Westport, CT: Greenwood Press, 1994.

Morel, Camille de (1547–after 1611)

Child prodigy, poet, translator

A daughter of Antoinette de Loynes and Jean de Morel, the faithful protectors of numerous neo-Latin and French poets including the members of the Pléiade, Camille de Morel received a fine humanistic education, first by her learned mother, then (from 1557 to 1563) by Charles Uytenhove (1536–1600), the outstanding young tutor from Ghent that Antoinette chose for her, and finally by Uytenhove's pupil, Jean Dorat. Thanks to the impression she made on her former Flemish teacher, Camille's notoriety reached England, Germany, Switzerland, and, of course, Belgium, allowing for an interesting correspondence to take place between her and Johanna Otho, the talented daughter of an illustrious teacher of ancient languages, also born in Ghent.

A child prodigy, Camille was highly acclaimed by the writers who were conversing and competing with her at the Morel mansion, a literary circle open to great scholars of the time. When she was but ten years old, Du Bellay, Ronsard, Dorat, Scévole de Sainte-Marthe, Michel de l'Hospital, and Paul Melissus dedicated writings to her, praising her for her exceptional mastery of Greek, Latin, and Hebrew, as well as her unusual poetic talents.

Among these panegyric works, that of Dorat is particularly significant, for it shows how fascinating and yet disturbing such a learned female could be in the eyes of male humanists. Unfortunately only a small portion of Camille de Morel's childhood compositions survived, mostly translations from ancient languages, but also a few Latin (and more rarely French) verses honoring her parents and other contemporary intellectuals. When Antoinette de Loynes died in 1567, her daughter composed a touching poem in the form of an imaginary dialog between her parents. The next fourteen years offer very scarce biographical elements on Camille de Morel. We know, however, that she chose not to marry, that she was still corresponding with Uytenhove who had been appointed professor of Greek at the University of Basel, and that she seemed to have remained in the same literary circles as Jean Dorat.

At her father's death in 1581, Camille began to compile a vast collection in honor of Jean de Morel, asking all poets who benefited from his lifelong patronage to contribute. This *Tumulus* took two years to complete and included praises of her deceased mother and sisters (Lucrèce and Diane de Morel). In addition to the poetic contributions she wrote for this memorial project, her adult works include homage to personalities as different as the poet Du Bellay and the queen of England.

Little is known of her later years (much less the date of her death), but two entries in Pierre de l'Estoile's *Memoires-Journaux* in 1609 and 1611 allude to her spirituality and suggest that she may have been interested in the Reformation.

Catherine M. Müller

See also the subheadings Latin Learning and Women and Greek Learning and Women (under Education, Humanism, and Women); Translation and Women Translators.

Bibliography

Primary Works

Dorat, Jean. "Ad doctissimam virginem Camillam Morellam." In *Les Odes latines*. Edited by Geneviève Demerson, 182–183, v. 65–68.

Clermont-Ferrand: Publications de la Faculté des Lettres et Sciences Humaines, 1979.

Du Bellay, Joachim. *Epithalame sur le mariage de tresillustre prince Philibert Emanuel, duc de Savoie, et tresillustre princesse Marguerite de France, soeur unique du Roy et duchesse de Berry.* Paris: 1559.

Du Bellay, Joachim. *Xenia, seu ad illustrium aliquot Europae hominum nomina allusionum [. . .] liber primus. . . .* Basel: 1568. (Contains several verses by Camille, including her poem to the queen of England, "Ad sereniss. Angliae Reg.")

Secondary Works

Berriot-Salvadore, Evelyne. "Les femmes dans les cercles intellectuels de la Renaissance: de la fille prodige à la précieuse." In *Etudes corses, études littéraires. Mélanges Offerts au Doyen François Pitti-Ferrandi.* Pages 210–137. Paris: Cerf, 1989.

Müller, Catherine M. "Monstrum inter libros: la perception de la femme lettrée chez les humanistes de la Renaissance française." *Actes du colloque international "Livres et lectures des femmes entre moyen âge et Renaissance" de Lille (24–26 mai 2004).* Forthcoming.

Will, Samuel F. "Camille de Morel: A Prodigy of the Renaissance." *PMLA* 51 (1936): 83–119. (A list of Camille's writings is given on p. 116.)

Mornay, Charlotte Arbaleste Duplessis (Charlotte Duplessis-Mornay; 1550–1606)

Huguenot, author of monumental Mémoires et lettres

Best known for her *Mémoires* chronicling the life and times of her husband, the Huguenot diplomat Philippe Duplessis-Mornay, Charlotte Arbaleste Duplessis-Mornay began the work on her massive memoir in 1579, the same year her son Philippe was born: "so that you will not lack for a guide, here is one which I offer you with my own hand . . . ; it is the example of your father, which I urge you to have always before your eyes" (Mornay 1969, 3). She ceased writing when their son died in October 1606 at the age of twenty-six. The author herself is vividly present in this exemplary portrait of her husband. She incorporates the act of writing into her text ("as I was writing this . . . "; "I pick up my story again in 1601") and recounts her own life from the time she met her future husband, also filling in some of the details of their early lives. As well, Duplessis-Mornay's complete *Mémoires et lettres* include the letters they exchanged.

Because the couple played such a central role in the political and religious life of their country, the *Mémoires* are a precious source for an understanding of both public and private life at the time. Charlotte writes with energy and zest, and gives vivid accounts of the events in which she and her husband were involved (including a particulary striking first-person account of the St. Bartholemew's Day Massacre in August 1572). It is clear that she understood well the complexities of the political and religious situation through which she was living. The *Mémoires* were written under the aegis of "a single God, creator of Heaven and Earth, . . . who governs all things through his Providence" (Mornay 1969, 5). It is to Providence that Charlotte attributes her meeting with her future husband and indeed his entire career. Recently widowed, Charlotte had fully intended not to remarry when Philippe Duplessis-Mornay was introduced to her in 1574. She found his words "good and honest," and for eight months, they spent two or three hours a day together, in companionable intellectual discussions. Duplessis-Mornay proposed in 1575, on the eve of his departure to join the duke d'Alençon's army in the Netherlands. They were married when he returned in January 1576, but not before he had been taken prisoner and she had paid his ransom. Charlotte emphasizes the fact that her husband chose her, although she had no dowry, for her virtue, her fear of God, and her good reputation.

Charlotte often accompanied her husband on his travels as a negotiator and diplomat. In 1577 and 1578, they spent eighteen months in England, joining friends such as Sir Philip Sidney, Sir Francis Walsingham, and probably also Sydney's sister, Mary Sydney Herbert. She accompanied him to Anvers, where hostilities between the Spanish and the Dutch claimed his attention and where their son Philippe was born. Later, the family enjoyed a short period of tranquility in Nérac, but much of their time was spent in Paris or with the French court. Just as often, they were separated, as Duplessis-Mornay carried out his duties on behalf of Henri IV. They regularly exchanged letters, dealing with personal matters and also with political and religious issues. Duplessis-Mornay valued his wife's advice and counted on her to transmit important messages to and from him while he was away. Charlotte saw to the preparation and publication of his manuscripts and filed and concealed secret papers that she had deciphered. She was entirely responsible for their domestic and financial affairs; her husband gave her the legal means to manage them in his absence.

The couple had complete confidence in each other and also shared genuine affection. Sometimes the letters Duplessis-Mornay sent to his wife were written in cipher to prevent others from reading them. At least one of these conceals not diplomatic secrets but a message for Charlotte, telling her how much he missed her and what pleasure they would take in each other's company when they were reunited. Charlotte had one daughter from her first marriage and gave birth to four more daughters and four sons. Two daughters and three sons died in infancy. Her husband tried to be present for the births of their children; en route to Charlotte's bedside for the birth of their first daughter, he sensed the very moment at which she had given birth. Their shared anguish on the loss of their first and only surviving son was profound. Always in fragile health, Charlotte Duplessis-Mornay died only seven months later, in May 1606.

Jane Couchman

See also Literary Culture and Women; Sidney, Mary Herbert.

Bibliography

Primary Works

Mornay, Charlotte Duplessis. *A Huguenot Family in the XVIe Century. The Memoires of Philippe de*

Mornay . . . Written by his wife. Translated by L. Crumb. London: Routledge, 1926.

Mornay, Charlotte Duplessis. *Mémoires.* Edited and critiqued by Nadine Kuperty-Tsur. Paris: Champion, forthcoming.

Mornay, Charlotte Duplessis. *Mémoires de Madame de Mornay.* 2 vols. Edited by Mme. de Witt. Paris: Renouard, 1868–1869.

Mornay, Philippe de, seigneur du Plessis-Marly. *Mémoires et correspondance.* 12 vols. Geneva: Slatkine, 1969. (Reprint of Paris edition, 1824–1825.)

Secondary Works

Berriot-Salvadore, Evelyne. "Charlotte Arbaleste Du Plessis Mornay." In *Les Femmes dans la société française de la Renaissance.* Pages 127–133. Geneva: Droz, 1990.

Kuperty-Tsur, Nadine. "Rhétorique des témoignages protestants autour de la Saint-Barthélémy: le cas des *Memoires* de Charlotte Duplessis-Mornay." In *Se raconter, témoigner: Elseneur* 17 (September 2001): 159–178.

Morra, Isabella di (ca. 1520–1545)

Petrarchan poet, born and educated in the kingdom of Naples; murdered at the age of twenty-five

Isabella di Morra was born in 1520 to Luisa Brancaccio and Giovan Michele di Morra, the baron of Favale, a fief located in southernmost Basilicata but still within the jurisdiction of the kingdom of Naples. One of eight children, Morra, her siblings, and their mother were abandoned by their father, Giovan Michele, when he fled Spanish-ruled Naples in 1527 to settle at the French royal court under the protection of Francis I. Giovan Michele left the care of the fief and his family in the hands of his eldest son, Marcantonio. From the first, animosity marked the relationship between Isabella and her three younger brothers, Cesare, Decio, and Fabio, who resented their gifted sister and the attention lavished on her education. Having inherited her father's talent as a poet, Isabella was given a tutor who guided her in the study of Petrarchan lyric and the Latin poets. Chafing under the intense isolation she suffered in the Morra castle in Favale, she forged a friendship with her literary neighbors, Antonia Caracciolo and her husband Don Diego Sandoval di Castro. Morra could not have found a friend better connected to the Italian literary world than Sandoval di Castro. He had been inducted into Cosimo I de' Medici's Florentine Academy and his volume of *Rime* had recently been published in Rome (Valerio Dorico e Loigi fratelli, 1542). Moreover, with his ties to members of Naples's several literary academies, Castro was well situated to promote Morra's career as a poet.

Sometime in 1545, the Morra brothers heard talk that their sister might be having an affair with their married neighbor, Sandoval di Castro, and that her tutor was acting as the go-between. Though it was never clear that Morra and Sandoval were more than just friends, Cesare, Fabio, and Decio first went after the tutor. According to the testimony bound over to the viceroy at the inquest, after her brothers had murdered him, they hunted Isabella down, and, finding her with Castro's letters still unopened in her hands, they stabbed her to death. Castro proved more difficult to catch. Several months later, Isabella's three brothers and two of her uncles, Cornelio and Baldassino di Morra, ambushed him at Noia, not far from Favale, as he was returning from his fief in Taranto. He was left in the road to die of the multiple stab wounds he sustained, while his bodyguards were said to have run for their lives as soon as they saw the Morra men coming. Isabella's three brothers and their uncles got away safely to France before the viceroy could arraign them. But the eldest brother Marcantonio, who tesified in the case but had nothing to do with the murders, served a lengthy prison term in Taranto. The real killers remained in France for the duration of their lives. Their father, Giovan Michele, died in France soon after the murders.

A sample of sonnets from Morra's miniature canzoniere indicates how she packed an intense psychological self-portrait into the space of a few lines. Several themes are woven into a continuous lament in her ten sonnets: the loss of her father; her struggle with painful circumstances beyond her control (*crudele fortuna*); the ravaged country of her homeland mirroring her inner landscape (*fiume alpestre, rovinati sassi, valle inferna*); her desire to write and live among other poets; and finally her search for release from Favale, from her brothers, from her state of mind—and ultimately her life. Each of her poems plays on these themes in some way, giving a sense of cohesiveness and unity to the whole ensemble. While the themes are always the same and each poem in Morra's miniature canzoniere represents a drama for a solo actor, the constant changes of addressee and mis-en-scène provide both variety and a sense of progression. Given that her real life ended with her murder, the dominant theme of her work—the poet's search for a way out—had, and continues to have, a haunting resonance for modern as well as sixteenth-century readers. Each of her poems portrays a writer preoccupied with finding an exit from misery, one way or another.

According to the family history, entitled *Familiae nobilissimae de Morra historia,* which Isabella's nephew, Marcantonio, published in 1629, Morra's poems were posthumously discovered when the castle at Favale was searched during the investigation of the triple homicide. But given that Morra's alleged lover, Sandoval di Castro, had both powerful cultural and political allies in Naples (he was a protégé of the Viceroy Pedro di Toledo), we might speculate that he could have circulated Morra's poems among his literary friends in the city before she was murdered, though we have no evidence that he did so. In any case, six years after her murder, Lodovico Dolce published Morra's poems in two distinct groups in the four successive anthologies of Neapolitan poets he edited for the Giolito press in Venice (*Rime di diversi illustri signori napoletani e d'altri nobilissimi intelletti*). Volume 5 (1551/1552; 1552; 1555) contained eight of Morra's sonnets and one canzone; volume 7 (1556) contained two new sonnets of hers and three canzoni, two of which had not

appeared in volume 5. In 1559, the Venetian editor Lodovico Domenichi was the first to publish Morra's complete œuvre of ten sonnets and three canzoni, presenting them as a miniature canzoniere in his landmark anthology of fifty-three women poets. Marie-François Piejus has argued unconvincingly that Domenichi's "preoccupation" with religious ideas caused him to reorder Morra's poems in such a way as to paint her life as a religious journey (*un itinéraire,* Piejus 1982, 206–208). Domenichi, however, followed the order of Morra's first eight sonnets in Dolce's volume 5 to the letter, deviating only slightly in his positioning of the five remaining poems that Dolce had edited in volume 7.

Isabella di Morra was among the first of the Neapolitan poets, male or female, ever to be published by a prestigious commercial press in Venice. By the end of the 1550s, moreover, she numbered among the half dozen most frequently anthologized women authors in the sixteenth century, despite her obscure beginnings.

Diana Robin

See also the subheading Sonnet Writing (under Literary Culture and Women); Rape and Violence Against Women.

Bibliography
Primary Works
Bulifon, Antonio, ed. *Rime di cinquanta illustri poetesse.* Naples: Antonio Bulifon, 1695. (Verbatim reprint of Domenichi's *Rime diverse* [1559]) without acknowledgment or dedicatory letter.)
Dolce, Lodovico, ed. *Rime di diversi illustri signori napoletani, e d'altri nobilissimi ingegni. Nuovamente raccolte, et con nuova additione ristampate. Libro Quinto. Allo illust. S. F. Carrafa.* Venice: Gabriel Giolito, 1552. (Third revised edition printed in 1555.)
Dolce, Lodovico, ed. *Rime di diversi illustri signori napoletani e d'altri nobilissimmi intelletti; nouvamente raccolte, et non più stampate. Terzo Libro allo illus. S. Ferrante Carrafa.* Venice: Gabriel Giolito, 1551/1552.
Dolce, Lodovico, ed. *Rime di diversi signori napoletani, e d'altri. Nuovamente raccolte et impresse. Libro Settimo.* Venice: Gabriel Giolito, 1556.
Domenichi, Lodovico, ed. *Rime diverse d'alcune nobilissime et virtuosissime donne, raccolte per M. Lodovico Domenichi, e intitolate al S. Giannoto*

Castiglione gentil'huomo milanese. Lucca: Vincenzo Busdragho, 1559.

Morra, Isabella di. *Isabella di Morra con l'edizione del canzoniere.* Edited by Domenico Bronzini. Matera: Montemurro, 1975.

Morra, Isabella di. In *Rime delle signore Lucrezia Marinella, Veronica Gambara et Isabella della Morra.* Edited by Antonio Bulifon. Naples: Bulifon, 1693.

Stortoni, Laura Anna, ed. *Women Poets of the Italian Renaissance: Courtly Ladies and Courtesans.* Translated by Laura Anna Stortoni and Mary Prentice Lillie, 114–117. New York: Italica Press, 1997.

Secondary Works

Adler, Sara. "The Petrarchan Lament of Isabella di Morra." In *Donna: Women in Italian Culture,* 201–221. Ottawa: Dovehouse, 1989.

Caserta, Giovanni. *Isabella di Morra e la società meridionale del Cinquecento.* Matera: Mela, 1976.

Croce, Benedetto, ed. *Isabella di Morra e Diego Sandoval de Castro con l'edizione delle "Rime" della Morra e una scelta di quelle del Sandoval.* Bari: Laterza, 1929.

Finucci, Valeria. "Isabella di Morra." In *An Encyclopedia of Continental Women Writers.* Vol. 2. Edited by Katharina M. Wilson, 876–877. New York: Garland, 1991.

Piejus, Marie-Françoise. "La première anthologie de poèmes féminins: L'écriture filtrée et orientée." In *Le pouvoir et la plume. Incitations, contrôle et répression dans l'Italie du XVI siècle.* Pages 193–213. Paris: Université de la Sorbonne Nouvelle, 1982.

Russell, Rinaldina. "Intenzionalità artistica della 'disperata.'" In *Generi Poetici Medievali: Modelli e funzioni letterarie.* Pages 163–182. Naples: SEN, 1982.

Schiesari, Juliana. "The Gendering of Melancholia: Torquato Tasso and Isabella di Morra." In *Refiguring Women: Perspectives on Gender and the Italian Renaissance.* Edited by Marilyn Migiel and Juliana Schiesari, 232–262. Ithaca, NY: Cornell University Press, 1991.

Schiesari, Juliana. "Isabella di Morra (ca. 1520–1545)." In *Italian Women Writers: A Bio-Bibliographical Sourcebook.* Edited by Rinaldina Russell, 279–185. Westport, CT, and London: Greenwood Press, 1994.

Music and Women
Overview

During the Renaissance (ca. 1450–1650), women's music making flourished at the European courts, in convents, and in domestic spaces. Relatively few women earned income as musicians; rather, they participated in music making most often as a private recreational and devotional activity. Most female performances for an audience were limited to intimate gatherings. "Three Lady Musicians," a painting by the Flemish artist known as the Master of the Female Half-Lengths (or by his Antwerp workshop), offers a glimpse into women's musical practices in a genteel, secular milieu in the 1520s. The three well-dressed musicians are a singer, lutenist, and flutist. The music book on the table before them is open to an early sixteenth-century French chanson, "Jouissance vous donneray," which was popular at the time. Though the music and text were composed by men, this is a love song in a female voice.

Women were excluded from the systems of apprenticeship that trained professional instrumentalists and from choir schools and universities, where male singers and composers learned their craft. This relative lack of access to a formal musical education meant that few women composed music, and because of the Renaissance rhetoric of social grace and the equation of the public arena with immodesty, even fewer acknowledged their compositional activity. Exclusion from formal education, however, did not prevent women from acquiring musical expertise, for they learned to sing and play instruments from family members, private music teachers, and instruction books. Moreover, in the late Renaissance, the establishment of new types of educational institutions helped to make music training available to women. In late sixteenth-century Venice, state-run shelters for poor and homeless children provided formally organized music education for girls, as did the new boarding schools in early seventeenth-century England.

Much Renaissance music circulated in manuscript, but the advent of music printing at the beginning of the sixteenth century made available an ever-expanding repertoire of printed pieces as well. Print was a major impe-

Three Lady Musicians. *By the Flemish painter known as Master of the Female Half-Lengths. c.1520–1530. Harrach Gallerie, Rorhau. (Francis G. Mayer/Corbis)*

tus to the emergence of female composers in the late sixteenth century, allowing them to disseminate their work and allowing us to identify these women. An even greater factor, however, was the prominent role accorded to women in secular court culture, which increasingly replaced the church as the seat of political power in the Renaissance.

Four subheadings follow: Music at the Courts and Women Patrons; Music in the Churches and Convents; Professional Singers; Women Composers.

Music at the Courts and Women Patrons

Elite women were expected to be able to sing and to play at least one musical instrument, most often the harp, lute, or spinet, although flutes and recorders were also much in vogue and readily available for purchase in makers'

shops and at city fairs. Music making served as a means of displaying feminine beauty, but women were also expected to exhibit modesty about their musical accomplishments. On one occasion, Queen Elizabeth I of England (1533–1603), who was a skilled keyboardist, arranged to be overheard playing the virginal by the Scottish ambassador, but then informed him that she was not used to playing before men—only when she was alone, to avoid melancholy.

Participation in court festivals offered another avenue of musical expression for elite women. Costumed as goddesses, sirens, or nymphs, they could sing and dance to music that evoked ancient Greece or exotic lands. In Spain, court comedies even provided an opportunity for women to cross-dress and assume male roles, although these practices produced a backlash in contemporary literature.

Aristocratic women shaped musical culture through their roles as patrons of leading male musicians. The survival of numerous music manuscripts that belonged to Marguerite of Austria (1480–1530) testifies to the rich musical life at her Netherlandish court. In Mantua, Isabella d'Este (1474–1539) influenced the evolution of a specific type of Italian secular song, the *frottola,* through her support of its composers. In France, the regent and queen mother, Catherine de Médicis (1519–1589), maintained a large musical household and encouraged the development of court balls by importing a violin band from Italy to play dance tunes. Queen Elizabeth, although herself a Protestant, employed two prominent Catholic composers in her private chapel for many years, enabling them to produce exquisite sacred music. Elizabeth's namesake, Princess Elizabeth Stuart (1596–1662), later queen of Bohemia, was the inspiration for and performer of a major printed anthology of keyboard pieces.

Music in the Churches and Convents

Although women did not participate in public music making in churches and cathedrals, they did perform sacred music in convents. In Italy especially, many young women came to convents from wealthy families and therefore already had musical training. The nuns of San Vito in Ferrera presented semiprivate concerts in the late sixteenth century, which involved as many as twenty-three women playing all sorts of instruments. Musical nuns could be found elsewhere in Europe as well, and convent account books from Castile show that some Spanish nuns benefited from dowry waivers in exchange for musical service.

With the onset of the Reformation in the sixteenth century, women's sacred music making moved outside convent walls and into domestic spaces. Protestants in England and France developed new devotional practices that involved psalm and hymn singing in the home and in public squares. In England, a Puritan woman's daily routine might include playing and singing as well as Bible reading and prayer. In France, Huguenot women took part in group devotions in the city streets that involved choral singing.

Professional Singers

Women came to northern Italian courts in the late 1500s specifically to train for female vocal ensembles. The most renowned of these groups, the *Concerto delle dame,* performed at the court of Ferrara between 1580 and 1597, and included the virtuosi Laura Peverara (1550–1601), Anna Guarini (1563–1598), and Livia d'Arco (1563/1564?–1611). At first these "singing ladies" were gifted amateurs, but later they became highly trained professionals, whose musical practices had ramifications for the development of opera in the early seventeenth century. The singer-poet Tarquinia Molza (1542–1617) was an instructor and advisor to the group. Rival female *concerti* were founded in Florence, Mantua, and Rome, and although Venice did not establish such a group, that republic produced the most renowned woman singer-composer of the Renaissance, Barbara Strozzi (1619–1677).

The women employed as singers at Italian and French courts, such as the soprano Vittoria Archilei (1550–1620s or later), who worked for the Medici in Florence, were typically called "ladies-in-waiting" rather than "musicians." They were well remunerated, but treated differently from male singers in that they were not granted properties and therefore did not set up independent households. Sometimes these women were members of musical families, like the singer Adriana Basile (ca. 1590–ca. 1640), active in Naples, Mantua, and Rome, whose two sisters and daughter were also singers. The Genoese soprano Violante Doria, active in the second half of the sixteenth century, married a French musician and worked with him at the French royal court. Their daughter, Claude de Beaulieu, became a court musician too.

Less is known about music making among the lower classes, due to the lack of written sources documenting their activities, but there is evidence that similar professional situations existed, whereby women, trained by fathers or brothers, served in low-status jobs in traveling companies of minstrels or as household musicians. In England the theaters were all-male institutions, but in Italy there were theatrical opportunities for lower-class women: the actresses in the Italian *commedia dell'arte* troupes sang and danced for pay. Their music making, like that of courtesans and other marginal female figures, was largely improvisatory, and so their songs are known to us only through remnants of them found in elite written music.

Women Composers

The female singers of the Renaissance surely performed songs of their own creation. However, we do not think of them as composers because they did not write their music down. The first European woman who self-identified as a composer and saw her compositions into print was Maddalena Casulana (ca. 1544–after 1583), active in Vicenza. She had an international reputation and is known to have visited the French and imperial courts. Other important Italian women composers of the late Renaissance included Vittoria Aleotti (ca. 1575–after 1620), daughter of a Ferrarese architect, who was educated by the nuns at San Vito; Raffaella Elaotti (ca. 1570–after 1646), a member of San Vito and composer of the first printed collection of sacred music by a woman; and Francesca Caccini (1587–after 1641), the first woman to compose opera. The daughter of two singers, Caccini served the Medici family for nearly three decades, and in that capacity coached numerous aristocratic women and girls in their singing.

Outside of Italy we know of no women who wrote music for a living before the mid-seventeenth century. It may be that some of the anonymous Renaissance music that survives was written by women, who refrained from publishing or signing their pieces because they did not want to appear to be working for hire. Compositions by women probably circulated in manuscript in aristocratic social circles where many would have known the identities of the composers but would have playfully maintained the pretense of anonymity. Lastly, there was, of course, in every part of Europe a large repertoire of popular songs and dance tunes that could be learned by ear and used as a basis for improvisation.

In the history of women and music in Europe, the Renaissance emerges as the period in which women's voices came to be recognized as an aesthetically viable musical entity, separate from men's and boys voices. Elite female music making traditions that had begun in the Middle Ages, especially at courts and in convents, expanded in the Renaissance to include the middle classes. The new technology of music printing and the opportunities for music training provided by new types of educational institutions facilitated this democratization of women's music making and also made it possible for women to begin to gain greater visibility as musicians and composers. Most important, the Renaissance shift away from feudal and toward absolutist political structures, with the corresponding increasing role given to courts and courtly display, afforded women a new venue in which to exercise their musical talents. With the exception of nun musicians, many of whom came from court families anyway, all of the star female singers and composers of the Renaissance were located at large courts.

Carla Zecher

See also Art and Women; Literary Culture and Women; Stampa, Gaspara; Strozzi, Barbara.

Bibliography

Primary Works

Aleotti, Vittoria. *Ghirlanda de madrigal: a quatro voci.* Edited by C. Ann Carruthers. New York: Broude Trust, 1994.

Caccini, Francesca. *Francesca Caccini's Il primo libro delle musiche of 1618: A Modern Critical Edition of the Secular Monodies.* Edited by Ronald James Alexander and Richard Savino. Bloomington: Indiana University Press, 2004.

Casulana, Maddalena. *I madrigali di Maddalena Casulana.* Edited by Beatrice Fescerelli. Florence: L. S. Olschki, 1979.

Luzzaschi, Luzzasco. *Complete Unaccompanied Madrigals.* Edited by Anthony Newcomb. Madison, WI: A-R Editions, 2003.

Secondary Works

Austern, Linda Phyllis. " 'Singe Againe Syren': The Female Musician and Sexual Enchantment in Elizabethan Life and Literature." *Renaissance Quarterly* 42, no. 3 (1989): 420–448.

Bowers, Jane, and Judith Tick, eds. *Women Making Music: The Western Art Tradition, 1150–1950.* Urbana: University of Illinois Press, 1986.

Brooks, Jeanice. *Courtly Song in Late Sixteenth-Century France.* Chicago: University of Chicago Press, 2000.

Brooks, Jeanice. "*O quelle armonye:* Dialogue Singing in Late Renaissance France." *Early Music History* 22 (2003): 1–64.

Carter, Tim. "Finding a Voice: Vittoria Archilei and the Florentine 'New Music'." In *Feminism and Renaissance Studies.* Edited by Lorna Hutson, 450–467. Oxford: Clarendon Press, 1999.

Cusick, Suzanne G. "Of Women, Music, and Power: A Model from Seicento Florence." In *Musicology and Difference: Gender and Sexuality in Music Scholarship.* Edited by Ruth A. Solie, 281–304. Berkeley: University of California Press, 1993.

Cusick, Suzanne G. " 'Thinking from Women's Lives': Francesca Caccini after 1627." *The Musical Quarterly* 77, no. 3 (1993): 484–507.

Early Music 27, no. 3 (special issue on women's laments, 1999).

Kendrick, Robert L. *Celestial Sirens: Nuns and Their Music in Early Modern Milan.* Oxford: Clarendon Press, 1996.

LaMay, Thomasin, ed. *Musical Voices of Early Modern Women: Many-Headed Melodies.* Aldershot, UK: Ashgate, 2005.

Lindell, Robert. "Filippo, Stefano and Martha: New Findings on Chamber Music at the Imperial Court in the Second Half of the Sixteenth Century." In *Atti del XIV Congresso della Società Internazionale di Musicologia: Trasmissione et recezione delle forme di cultura musicale.* Edited by Angelo Pompilio, Donatella Restani, Lorenze Bianconi, and F. Albert Gallo, 869–875. Turin: Edizioni di Torino, 1990.

MacNeil, Anne. *Music and Women of the Commedia dell'arte in the Late Sixteenth Century.* Oxford: Oxford University Press, 2003.

Marshall, Kimberly, ed. *Rediscovering the Muses: Women's Musical Traditions.* Boston: Northeastern University Press, 1993.

Monson, Craig A. *Disembodied Voices: Music and Culture in an Early Modern Italian Convent.* Berkeley: University of California Press, 1995.

Pendle, Karin, ed. *Women and Music: A History.* Bloomington: Indiana University Press, 1991.

Piperno, Franco. "Diplomacy and Musical Patronage: Virginia, Guidubaldo II, Massimiliano II, 'Lo Streggino' and Others." *Early Music History* 18 (1999): 259–285.

Reardon, Colleen. *Holy Concord Within Sacred Walls: Nuns and Music in Siena, 1575–1700.* Oxford: Oxford University Press, 2002.

Sadie, Stanley, ed. *The New Grove Dictionary of Music and Musicians.* 29 vols. 2nd ed. London: Macmillan, 2001.

Slim, H. Colin. "Paintings of Lady Concerts and the Transmission of 'Jouissance vous donneray.'" In *Painting Music in the Sixteenth Century.* Vol. 7. Aldershot, UK: Ashgate, 2002.

Van Orden, Kate. "Female *Complaintes:* Laments of Venus, Queens, and City Women in Late Sixteenth-Century France." *Renaissance Quarterly* 54, no. 3 (Autumn 2001): 801–845.

N

Nelli, Plautilla (1523–1588)

One of the first known woman painters of extant large-scale religious works, Dominican nun, and teacher

Born in Florence in 1523 to a patrician family, Polissena Nelli entered the Dominican order in 1538 and took the name Plautilla. Her convent, Santa Caterina da Siena, now destroyed, was located near the church of San Marco in Florence and governed by the friars there. Serafino Razzi, a Dominican and brother of a sculptor at Santa Caterina, wrote in 1596 that Nelli served as prioress several times. He singled out three women as "students" of Nelli, and his account gives the impression that the convent was an active center of art education and production.

Nelli is the first woman artist in Florence who is more to us than just a name, and one of the first women in Europe we can identify as a painter of extant religious works on a large scale. Plautilla took advantage of the most accessible avenue of study for women, the convent. She became the primary "image maker" of the Dominicans in Tuscany, where she received important commissions and high praise from her contemporaries. Vasari's *Lives of the Artists* (1568) mentions more works by her than any other female artist, including large altarpieces, small devotional works, and miniatures, but only two of these paintings can be firmly identified. The *Lamentation with Saints,* from the outer (public) church of Santa Caterina, is now in the San Marco Museum, Florence; the *Last Supper,* from the refectory of Santa Caterina, where Nelli herself once ate, has been moved to the refectory still used by the Dominican friars at Santa Maria Novella, Florence.

In his *Life* of Fra Bartolomeo, Vasari noted that most of the drawings by the friar from San Marco then were at Santa Caterina, "with a nun who painted"; in 1727 the nuns there sold a large number of Fra Bartolomeo's drawings. These sheets, now in Rotterdam, must have provided the basis for study by Nelli, though she seems to have been largely self-educated. The composition of Fra Bartolomeo's *Lamentation with Saints* served as the prototype for the composition of Nelli's moving altarpiece, but she included two additional women next to the Virgin Mary. These figures and the men standing behind them openly express their grief through their gestures and visible tears. Significantly, many female figures also appear in the *Pentecost,* mentioned in Biliotti's obituary of Nelli (ca. 1588) and still in situ in the church of San Domenico, Perugia; clearly, the artist's fame extended beyond her native region. For this impressive work Nelli created a monumental architectural setting which, in its austerity and measured quality, compares to that in her *Last Supper.* Though this draws on Leonardo's fresco for some figures, Nelli chose to represent a tender intimacy between Christ and Saint John. The surprisingly detailed representation of the lamb, salad, and porcelain bowls on the table probably relate to the rituals and physical objects in Nelli's convent.

Sixteenth-century authors emphasized that Nelli demonstrated great artistic skill but also the most laudable moral virtues. Vasari, using an adjective that runs throughout Renaissance accounts of women artists, described her as *virtuosa.* With unusually high praise he observed that "she would have done marvelous things if, like men, she had been able to study and to devote herself to drawing and copying living and natural things"; nevertheless, she "carried out some works with such diligence that she has amazed our artists." Vasari noted that Nelli made many paintings for not only churches in Tuscany but also "the homes of the gentlemen of Florence," and Don Silvano Razzi gave one to the author Annibale Caro in Rome. The artist's gender and reputation for piety surely added to the appeal of these works. These count among the disparate group of forty-four paintings and eight drawings attributed to Nelli in Renaissance and modern sources.

Jonathan Katz Nelson

See also Anguissola, Sofonisba; Art and Women; Convents; Fetti, Lucrina; Fontana, Lavinia.

Bibliography
Primary Works
Biliotti, Modesto. *Chronica pulcherrimae aedis magnique coenobii S. Mariae Novellae Florentinae civitatis.* Florence: Convent of Santa Maria Novella, manuscript, ca. 1588. (Transcribed in Pierattini, 1938, pp. 29–30.)
Razzi, Fra Serafino. *Istoria de gli Huomini illustri, così nelle prelature, come nelle Dottrine, del sacro ordine de gli Predicatori,* 369–372. Lucca: Busdrago, 1596. (Republished in *Suor Plautilla,* 2000, pp. 115–116.)
Vasari, Giorgio. *Le vite de' più eccellenti pittori scultori e architettori nelle redazioni del 1550 e 1568.* Edited by Rosanna Bettarini, notes by Paola Barocchi, 403–405. Florence: S.P.E.S, IV, 1976. (Republished and translated in *Suor Plautilla,* 2000, pp. 111–112.)
Secondary Works
Jacobs, Fredrika H. *Defining the Renaissance Virtuosa: Women Artists and the Language of Art History and Criticism,* 111–121. Cambridge and New York: Cambridge University Press, 1997.
King, Catherine, "Plautilla Nelli." In *Dictionary of Women Artists.* 2 vols. Edited by Delia Gaze, vol. 2, 1010–1012. London and Chicago: Fitzroy Dearborn Publishers, 1997.
Marchese, Vincenzo. "Di suor Plautilla Nelli, pittrice Domenicana, e di altre Religiose dello stesso Istituto, che coltivarono la pittura, la miniatura, la plastica, in Firenze, in Prato, in Lucca e altrove." In *Memorie dei più insigni pittori, scultori e architetti domenicani.* 2 vols. Vol. 2, 326–350. Bologna: G. Romagnoli Libr., 1878–1879.
Pierattini, Giovanna. *Suor Plautilla Nelli pittrice domenicana.* Florence: 1938. (Offprint, with continuous numeration, from *Memorie domenicane,* LV, 1938, pp. 49–53, 82–85, 168–171, 221–227, 292–297.)

Suor Plautilla Nelli (1523–1588): The First Woman Painter of Florence. Edited by Jonathan Nelson. Florence: Cadmo, 2000

Nogarola, Isotta (1418–1466)
Veronese humanist, orator, and prolific writer of Latin letters

The first major female humanist in Europe, Isotta Nogarola was born in Verona to Bianca Borromeo and Leonardo Nogarola, both descendants of noble lines. She and her older sister Ginevra studied under Martino Rizzoni, a protégé of Guarino Veronese, the leading humanist scholar in Ferrara at midcentury and teacher of the Este princes. Nogarola first won fame when her letterbook—the bound volume of personal letters penned in Ciceronian Latin that constituted a humanist's signature work—circulated among Venice's literati in the late 1430s.

Nogarola's early letters (1434–1440) already displayed her extensive knowledge of Greek and Latin literature: in them she cites Cicero's *Brutus, De amicitia, De officiis,* and his *Pro Roscio;* Juvenal's *Satires;* Petronius's *Satyricon;* Aulus Gellius's *Attic Nights;* Philostratus's *Life of Appolonius of Tyana;* Plutarch's *Lives of Artaxerxes, Alexander, Aristides,* and *Demetrius;* Diogenes Laertius's *Lives of the Philosophers;* Valerius Maximus's *Memorabilia;* and Virgil's *Eclogues,* among other texts.

In 1438–1440/1441, the Nogarola family relocated to Venice, returning to Verona in 1441. While some previous studies hypothesized that, when Nogarola returned to Verona, she "renounced secular humanism" to attend solely to sacred study and religious works, living a reclusive life in her mother's house (King 1978, 1980), new research reveals Nogarola's continuing public prominence in northern Italy as a literary figure committed to the study of pagan antiquity as well as Christian theology. Her renown as a syncretic thinker, who combined Classical, Biblical, and patristic learning in her own writings and public lectures, in fact grew exponentially during her later years in Verona (Nogarola 2004, esp. 9–19, 138–201). The letters Nogarola exchanged in 1448 with the Venetian patrician, Lauro Quirini, who was then studying at the University of Padua, proved especially formative for her intellectual development. Quinrini recommended that she read Aristotle's *Moralia, Physics, Metaphysics, De interpretatione,* and the *Categories;* he also advised her to study the commentaries of Boethius, Aquinas, Averroes, and Avicenna on Aristotle as well as Cicero's philosophical works and Livy's histories, which she seems not to have known before the 1450s (Nogarola 2004, 106–113).

During the years 1550–1561, Nogarola put the finishing touches on a series of six important works, each designated for public performance and each demonstrating her expertise in one of the four of the principal humanist genres: the letterbook, the dialogue, the oration, and the funeral consolation (presented in written form or orally). In the Jubilee year of 1450, traveling to Rome with a delegation from Verona, she delivered an oration at the court of Pope Nicholas V (the only work among the six that is now lost; Nogarola 1886, 2.50). In 1451, Nogarola engaged the Venetian governor of Verona, Ludovico Foscarini, in a public debate on the question of original sin, the nature of woman, and gender difference itself. Circulating as the *Dialogue on the Equal or Unequal Sin of Adam and Eve,* Nogarola's work stands, after Christine de Pizan's, as the inaugural work in the European *querelle des femmes*— the controversy on gender and nature that would rage for the next four centuries (Nogarola 2004, 138–158). Splitting the blame for the Fall between the first man and first woman, Nogarola and Foscarini's dialogue, in effect, demonstrated Saint Augustine's proposition that Adam and Eve "sinned unequally in accord with their sexes, but equally in pride": *Contentio super Aureli Augustini sententiam videlicet: peccaverunt impari sexu sed pari fastu*—the subtitle of Nogarola's *Dialogue.* Weaving together

references to and paraphrases from Aristotle's *Nicomachean Ethics* and his *Posterior Analytics,* Saint Ambrose's *On paradise,* Saint Augustine's *The Literal Meaning of Genesis,* Boethius's *Consolation of Philosophy,* and the Bible, the character Isotta argues Eve's lesser guilt on the basis of the intellectual and moral inferiority of the female sex. But paradoxically, Isotta displays her formidable intellect in the course of the dialogue in such a way that she, though a woman, appears in no way inferior to her interlocutor, Ludovico, as the governor himself concedes in his closing statement in the dialogue.

In 1453, Nogarola presented two new orations honoring the incoming bishop of Verona, the Venetian Ermolao Barbaro. Making it clear that both orations were intended for public presentation, she began each speech with the classical rhetorician's stock disclaimer that she "had neither the skill nor the talent for oratory" (Nogarola 2004, 163, 169). The first of these speeches welcoming Barbaro to the city portrayed her own discomfort at speaking in public as the agony that plagued the great orators in antiquity—Theophrastus, Demosthenes, and Cicero. In her second oration, she told her audience that she had been invited by Barbaro to speak on the life of Saint Jerome, who famously preached and practiced the Christian virtue of sexual abstinence. But since Foscarini had informed Nogarola that Barbaro suspected her of having an adulterous affair with her former debating partner, she seized the opportunity to take high ground for herself in this second oration. Foregrounding the story of Saint Jerome's renunciation of worldly goods and his refusal of the cardinalate rather than dwelling on his celibacy, Nogarola implicitly warned the new bishop of Verona against squandering the city's scarce resources on ecclesiastical pomp (Nogarola 2004, 159–174). In 1459, Nogarola wrote her most emotional oration urging a crusade against the Turks. Though she clearly composed this work for public presentation at Pope Pius II's international Congress of Mantua, Nogarola did not travel to that city to deliver her oration (Nogarola 2004, 175–186). Her last major work was a funeral oration commissioned by the Venetian statesman Jacopo Antonio Marcello on the death of his eight-year-old son, Valerio. Her funeral elegy was published in 1461 in a deluxe manuscript edition, which included the contributions of some of the most famous humanists in Italy. Opening with a mythological tale from Plutarch's *Consolation for Apollonius,* Nogarola's elegy for Marcello followed the humanist consolatory tradition well established by Petrarch, Salutati, Marsuppini, and Giannozzo Manetti in her conflation of Classical and Biblical references (Nogarola 2004, 187–201).

On her death in 1466, her contemporary, Giammaria Filelfo, celebrated Nogarola not only as a Ciceronian public orator (*oratrix*), but for her more Horatian role as the public conscience (*vates*) of her city (see Filelfo's 1468 text in Nogarola 1886, 2.361–2.387). On the connection in Nogarola's work between the acquisition of knowledge and wisdom and the study of rhetoric and eloquence, Filelfo wrote: "Isotta devoted herself in her work to the study of oratory and she learned what poetic figures to employ to frame wisdom, what unknown territories she might conquer, and what knowledge she should deem worthy of attaining, following the reason of her own prudence" (Nogarola 1886, 2.366: lines 32–36).

Diana Robin

See also Cereta, Laura; Education, Humanism, and Women; Fedele, Cassandra; the subheading Letter Writing (under Literary Culture and Women); Querelle des Femmes.

Bibliography
Primary Works
Major manuscript collections of Nogarola's letters: Vienna (Vindobonensis 3481), Rome (Vaticanus 5127), Verona (Veronensis 256).
Kristeller, Paul Oskar. *Iter Italicum.* 6 vols. London: 1967–1997. (Locations of smaller collections and individual letters of Nogarola in Florence, Venice, Milan, Mantua, Munich, Paris, London, and Basel.)
Nogarola, Isotta. *Complete Writings: Letterbook, Dialogue on Adam and Eve, Orations.* Edited and translated by Margaret L. King and Diana Robin. Chicago: University of Chicago Press, 2004.
Nogarola, Isotta. *Isotae Nogarolae veronensis opera quae supersunt omnia, accedunt Angelae et Zenevrae Nogarolae epistolae et carmina.* Edited by Eugenius Abel. Vienna: apud Gerold et socios, and Budapest: apud Fridericum Kilian, 1886. (Contains Giammaria Filelfo's eulogy of her.)
Secondary Works
King, Margaret L. "Book-Lined Cells." In *Beyond Their Sex: Learned Women of the European Past.* Edited by Patrician Labalme, 66–90. New York: New York University Press, 1980.
King, Margaret L. *The Death of the Child Valerio Marcello.* Chicago: University of Chicago Press, 1994.
King, Margaret L. "The Religious Retreat of Isotta Nogarola (1418–1466)." *Signs* 3 (1978): 807–822.
King, Margaret L., and Albert Rabil, Jr., eds. *Her Immaculate Hand: Selected Works by and about the Women Humanists of Quattrocento Italy.* 2nd rev. ed. Binghamton, NY: Medieval and Renaissance Texts and Studies, 1991.

Nursing. *See* the subheading Hospital Administration and Nursing as Careers for Women (under Medicine and Women).

O

Obstetrics and Gynecology. *See* the subheading Childbirth and Reproductive Knowledge (under Medicine and Women).

Old Age and Women

Old age was as idiosyncratic as the woman who experienced it. Its onset was typically marked by changes in one's physical features, such as wrinkles or traits associated with menopause. Poor women aged earliest, around fifty, because of their strenuous lifestyles and poor diets. Wealthier women did not enter old age until some time in their sixth decade. Social standing, it appears, was a critical factor determining much of women's old age experience.

Spanning the breadth of Europe, the period of the Renaissance, and the whole social hierarchy, more women than men reached old age and lived longer once that milestone was achieved. Quattrocentro Italy was a notable exception, hosting more aged men than women. While figures for earlier centuries are unknown, as much as 8 percent of Europe during the sixteenth and seventeenth centuries was over the age of sixty.

Elderly women tended to live as part of their husbands' extended families in Italy and the Iberian peninsula, with a significant minority living in Roman Catholic religious communities as unmarried nuns. Northwestern Europe favored nuclear families, and, as long as her husband lived, the elderly woman remained, independent in her own home. Upon widowhood, she continued to function as an individual entity, although often as a subset of her adult child's household, her bed and board provided in her deceased husband's will as part of the passing on of the family property.

With the development of protocapitalism and a cash-and-credit economy, elderly widows tended to live apart from their children, paying their way via an annual annuity. France, which divided Northern and Southern Europe, was itself divided accordingly in its treatment of elderly women. Spain's lower orders were distinctive: an elderly mother's care and accommodation were rotated among her children.

Widowhood after the age of fifty virtually eliminated remarriage as a viable option. In Northwestern Europe widows tended to form independent households, cluster with other widows, or form composite households with distant relatives or nonkin. Among the poor, such households could contain an elderly woman and an orphaned child. Each helped the other, and their combined living arrangement eased the burden on the parish's poor relief. Only in advanced old age did the elderly widow join the household of an adult child. A significant minority, 40 percent in the seventeenth century, lived alone. Southern European and Iberian household patterns resulted in the elderly widow's continued residence in her deceased husband's extended household.

A significant minority of women in France and England would never marry, living in independent households. Among those over fifty years old, 15 percent of the aged women in seventeenth-century Lyon and Rheims were single. Widowhood in old age provided distinct legal benefits, such as the ability to make contracts and enter into legal proceedings. For some, it also allowed them the freedom to shape the course of their own lives.

Renaissance medical knowledge underpinned the greater responsibility and power of aged widows. Built on the Galenic four humors of hot, cold, dry, and moist—or blood, phlegm, yellow bile or choler, and black bile or melancholy—it was understood that aging and menopause (at roughly age fifty) caused a woman to dry up and become harder. Her body became more "male," and she was to be accorded respect on account of her years. However, the Galenic tradition also threatened her position. The postmenopausal woman was dangerous. Her polluting blood that had formerly been removed from her system monthly with menstruation was now considered "trapped" and increasingly dangerous. Therefore, it was medically possible for the aged woman to cause harm to those she touched or fixed with the evil eye.

In general, society expected old women to dress and act according to their age. Women who tried to look younger than their years became objects of ridicule among their friends and later on the stage in the figure of the "merry widow." Marriage after menopause or to a much younger man was held in low regard. Among the lower orders, communities across Europe expressed their ill feelings by engaging in a *charavari,* or "rough music," in which a mob rushed the residence of the new couple, singing and chanting their complaints. If the young bridegroom were captured, he might be castrated.

There was no retirement in Renaissance Europe, except perhaps at the closing of the seventeenth century and only among France's most aristocratic women. Instead, elderly women continued to do what they had previously done, be it a common spinner of wool or silk, or a patron to the arts. In all cases, their identities were derived from their occupations, and old women across Europe prided themselves on their ability to continue to perform them.

L. A. Botelho

See also Marriage; Work and Women.

Bibliography
Botelho, L., and P. Thane, eds. *Women and Ageing in British Society Since 1500.* Harlow, UK: Longmans, 2001.
Johnson, P., and P. Thane, eds. *Old Age from Antiquity to Post-Modernity.* London: Routledge, 1998.
Ottaway, S., L. A. Botelho, and K. Kittredge, eds. *Power and Poverty: Old Age in the Pre-Industrial Past.* Westport, CT: Greenwood Press, 2002.
Pelling, M., and R. M. Smith. *Life, Death, and the Elderly: Historical Perspectives.* London: Routledge, 1991.
Rosenthal, J. T. *Old Age in Late Medieval England.* Philadelphia: University of Pennsylvania Press, 1996.
Sharhar, S. *Growing Old in the Middle Ages.* London: Routledge, 1995.

O'Malley, Grace (Gráinne Uí Mháille; fl. 1577–1597)

Irish rebel and seafaring pirate captain

Grace O'Malley, or Gráinne Uí Mháille, was an Irish leader on the west coast of Ireland, notorious for her resistance to English colonial encroachment on Connaught and for her exploits at sea. She was known to the English as Grace O'Malley. During the latter part of the sixteenth century, England attempted to expand colonial efforts beyond the boundaries of the Pale to include O'Malley's domain in Connaught. Richard Bingham was the English colonial governor given jurisdiction over that area, and in 1584 he initiated a special campaign against O'Malley, intending to have her arrested and hanged if she refused to submit to English authority.

O'Malley had succeeded in maintaining her power by putting off the English with promises of fealty. Indeed, she sometimes arranged alliances with local English officials to better overcome her local Irish enemies. On other occasions, however, she formed alliances with neighboring Irish leaders to resist English colonial encroachments. She had considerable success playing each side against the other in this manner until 1593, when Bingham managed to capture one of O'Malley's sons and a cousin. Rather than submit to Bingham's demand for her submission in return for the lives of her kin, O'Malley chose to circumvent the English governor altogether by writing to the queen of England, Elizabeth I. In that letter,

O'Malley described her difficulties as a female leader, clearly hoping to appeal to Elizabeth's own experience, and she promised to fight against Elizabeth's enemies if Elizabeth would take up her cause. O'Malley then sailed to England and obtained an audience with Elizabeth. Although we do not have any documentation regarding what passed between the two women on that occasion, the result was gratifying for O'Malley: Elizabeth ordered Bingham to set free O'Malley's family and to allow O'Malley and her people to continue unmolested in lawful pursuits. Bingham was only temporarily hobbled; he and others later continued their pursuit of O'Malley. Though we do not know the exact date or manner of her death, we do know that O'Malley is mentioned in English documents as late as 1610, when she was still bedeviling vessels off the coasts of Aran Island.

Brandie Siegfried

See also Elizabeth I.

Bibliography

Chambers, Anne. *Granuaile: The Life and Times of Grace O'Malley.* Dublin: Wolfhound Press, 1988.

Siegfried, Brandie. "Queen to Queen at Check: Grace O'Malley, Elizabeth Tudor, and the Discourse of Majesty in the State Papers of Ireland." In *Elizabeth I: Always Her Own Free Woman.* Edited by Carole Levin, Jo Eldridge Carney, and Debra Barrett-Graves, 149–175. Aldershot, UK: Ashgate, 2003.

Oratory. *See* Rhetoric, Public Speaking, and Women.

P

Pamphlet Writing. *See* **Literary Culture and Women.**

Parr, Katherine (1512–1548)

Queen, religious writer, patron of artists and printers, musician

Katherine Parr, sixth queen of Henry VIII, was born in 1512, probably in August and probably in London. Named after Catherine of Aragon, her likely godmother, she had a close bond with her independent, widowed mother, Maud, a former devoted lady-in-waiting to Catherine. Parr received an education possibly based on the program laid out by Thomas More for his own children. She married four times, beginning in 1529 when she was a teen. Her husbands included Edward Borough, who was in his early twenties and died in 1533; John Neville, Lord Latimer, in 1534, aged forty (d. 1543); Henry VIII in 1543, aged fifty-two (d. 1547); and Thomas Seymour in 1547, aged about thirty-eight (d. 1549). When the king proposed marriage upon the death of her second husband, she could hardly refuse, although she was passionately in love with Thomas Seymour, brother of the former queen, Jane Seymour. She made her peace with the marriage by seeing it as the will of God.

Parr energetically exercised her fervent commitment to the new reformist religion. She supported projects such as the translation of Erasmus's *Paraphrases* and was involved in the publication of the *King's Primer*. She also participated in the founding of Trinity College, Cambridge, and at court influenced a number of women of the next generation who had outstanding intellectual accomplishments. She herself translated Bishop Fisher's *Psalms or Prayers* (1544), which included one of her own

Katherine Parr, queen, religious writer, and patron of artists and printers. Painting by English School. National Portrait Gallery, London. (Corel)

prayers. This was published many times after 1556 as *The King's Psalms* and attributed to Henry VIII. Her *Prayers and Meditations* (1545) was a collection of devotional materials, which also included four of her own prayers. Her final work, *The Lamentation of a Sinner,* was probably written in the winter of 1546–1547 but was kept secret until after the king's death and not published until 5 November 1547. This Lutheran work, with fragments of more radical thinking, revealed Parr's own voice and showed the influence of Marguerite of Navarre's *The Mirror of the Sinful Soul.* It may well have influenced the later lamentations by Isabella Whitney and Jane Grey. Parr was the first Englishwoman to publish in prose and the first queen of England to write and publish her own books and be acknowledged as an author during her lifetime.

Parr also was a significant patron of the arts in the budding English Renaissance. Her commissioning of an unusually large number of portraits of herself may have been a response to Henry's making former queen Jane Seymour his wife in portraits of the royal family. Parr also supported printing and bookbinding and maintained a company of players. She loved music and dancing as well as luxurious fabrics, fashionable clothing, and uniquely designed jewelry. The evidence of her accomplishments and of her taste contradicts the popular view of her as a lackluster queen.

By accommodating the king's need for sexual intimacy, nursing, and emotional support, Parr gained his trust. In 1544 she was named regent general while Henry was away and seems to have influenced his attempt to create a Protestant League in 1545. However, her success made her vulnerable to an attack by the conservative faction at court in 1546, which also encompassed the torture and execution for heresy of Anne Askew. Henry, having taken offense at what he came to consider Katherine's lecturing him on religion and encouraged by Bishop Stephen Gardiner to doubt her orthodoxy, ordered her arrest. Thinking quickly, Parr saved herself and regained the king's trust by reassuring and flattering him.

Parr also developed successful relationships with the king's three children and reconciled the king with his daughters, Mary and Elizabeth, ensuring their places in the succession. When Henry died in January 1546, Katherine was surprised and angered not to have been given a place on the regency council for the minor Edward VI. And she soon risked the new king's censure by marrying Thomas Seymour less than six months after Henry's death. She seemed at first not to fear Seymour's improper attention to the teenaged Princess Elizabeth, living with them in Chelsea. But by spring 1548, pregnant and cognizant of the

danger Seymour's attentions to the princess presented, she sent her away. Shortly after, Parr retired to Sudeley Castle in Gloucestershire and on 30 August 1548, gave birth to her only child, named after the Princess Mary. She died on 5 September of puerperal fever.

Martha Skeeters

See also Art and Women; Printers, the Book Trade, and Women; Religious Reform and Women.

Bibliography

Primary Work

Travitsky, Betty, Patrick Cullen, and Janel Mueller, eds. *The Early Modern Englishwoman: A Facsimile Library of Essential Works, Printed Writings, 1500–1640, Katherine Parr.* London: Scholars Press, 1996.

Secondary Works

Susan E. James. *Kateryn Parr/The Making of a Queen.* Aldershot, UK: Ashgate, 1999.

Antonia Fraser. *The Wives of Henry VIII.* New York: Vintage Books, 1994.

Alison Weir, *The Six Wives of Henry VIII.* New York: Grove Press, 1991.

Patronage and Women. *See* Art and Women; Literary Culture and Women; Music and Women; Religious Reform and Women; Theater and Women Actors, Playwrights, and Patrons.

Pharmacology. *See* the subheading The Practice of Pharmacology and Laywomen (under Medicine and Women).

Philips, Katherine (1631–1664)

Public literary figure, poet, leader of a group who formed the nucleus of a women's academy called the "Platonic Society of Friendship"

Daughter of a prosperous London cloth merchant, Katherine Fowler cultivated a love of literature and lasting friendships at a girls' boarding school from 1640 until 1646, when her widowed mother's third marriage took them to Wales. In 1648 Katherine married Colonel

James Philips, a kinsman of her stepfather and a moderate parliamentarian thirty-seven years her senior. Although raised and educated in Puritan circles, Philips espoused royalist sympathies as evidenced by the first poem in her published collections from about 1650, replying indignantly to a verse attacking the executed king, as if it were murdering him a second time. During the interregnum, Philips penned a considerable number of occasional poems commemorating marriages, deaths, and departures, which present an image of the poet diligently developing social, political, and literary connections. Although her elegies for her infant son and her stepdaughter betray deep maternal affection, her emotional focus seems to have been on her female friends with whom she established an ideal "society of friendship" (as she called it) by assigning literary nicknames, notably to her friends Mary Aubrey ("Rosania") and Anne Owen, who came from an influential Welsh family ("Lucasia"), and to herself ("Orinda"). Some of these passionate poems to Rosania and Lucasia evidence a poetic debt to John Donne's love poetry in Philips's use of extravagant metaphors, portraying love's bodily transcendence as a pure mingling of souls. Raising her friendships metaphorically to the level of a religion and circulating her poetry widely, Philips posed a delicate challenge to seventeenth-century gender expectations. She was apparently successful in balancing her familial obligations and friendships, her political leanings and her husband's parliamentarian involvement, and her social and literary ambitions.

With the restoration of the monarchy in 1660, Philips's royalism came to aid her husband's changed political and economic situation and allowed her to hazard public recognition as a writer. Encouraged by the noble friends of Anne Owen's husband in Ireland, where she accompanied her after her marriage, Philips completed a translation of Pierre Corneille's heroic play, *Pompey*, which was performed and published in Ireland and performed again in London in early 1663. Having become a public literary figure, Philips pined for the stimulating cultural life of London, though mindful of her duty to her husband in Wales. The unauthorized publication of her poetry in January 1664 threatened to upset the honorable role of private female poet she had negotiated, although several poems since 1660 and letters to Sir Charles Cotterell ("Poliarchus"), who had become Charles II's master of ceremonies, actively court the favor of aristocratic contacts but with an exceedingly deferential voice. She asked Cotterell to present a copy of her play to Charles II, but without inscribing her name. Finally allowed a stay in London in the spring of 1664, she died there of smallpox in June. Bolstered by the publication of her poems in 1667, which identified her on the title page as "the matchless Orinda," Philips's reputation of a virtuous and brilliant poet inspired a generation of women poets, notably Anne Killigrew and Anne Finch. Her poetry also inspired male poets, including Abraham Cowley and Henry Vaughn, to write praise poems during her lifetime and such poets as John Dryden to honor her poetic accomplishment after her death.

Nancy Hayes

See also Literary Culture and Women; Theater and Women Actors, Playwrights, and Patrons.
Bibliography
Primary Work
Philips, Katherine Fowler. *The Collected Works of Katherine Philips: The Matchless Orinda*. 3 vols. Edited by Patrick Thomas. Stump Cross, Essex, UK: Stump Cross Books, 1990.
Secondary Works
Barash, Carol. *English Women's Poetry, 1649–1714: Politics, Community, and Linguistic Authority*. Oxford: Clarendon Press, 1996.
Williamson, Marilyn. *Raising Their Voices: British Women Writers, 1650–1750*. Detroit, MI: Wayne State University Press, 1990.

Piscopia, Elena Lucrezia Cornaro (1646–1684)

First woman in Europe to earn a doctorate; scholar of theology; author of Latin and Italian letters, four philosophical discourses, eleven encomiastic orations, and poems in several genres

Elena Lucrezia Cornaro Piscopia was born on 5 June 1646, the fifth of seven children to the Venetian nobleman Giovanni Battista Cornaro Piscopia and the plebeian Zanetta Boni. Giovanni Battista married Boni only after fathering four of their children. This fact excluded Elena Cornaro Piscopia's elder siblings from the registry of Venetian nobility, though their father served the republic as procurator of Peschiera, as captain of Bergamo (1641–1642), and, from 1649 on, as one of nine procurators of San Marco in Venice, gaining this last position through a competition that required a donation of a substantial sum to the republic. In 1664 he paid an additional one hundred and five thousand ducats to acquire noble titles for his first two sons.

Noted for her erudition at an early age, Elena Cornaro Piscopia studied Greek with Giovanni Battista Fabris and Latin with Giovanni Valier, despite strong Venetian opposition to the serious education of girls. Following fifteen years of study with Fabris, she was tutored in both ancient and modern Greek by Alvise Grandenigo, premier Hellenist in Venice and librarian of San Marco. Her curriculum also included French, Spanish, mathematics, the natural sciences, astronomy, and geography—a program on the basis of which she was considered ready to undertake the study of philosophy and theology. For the former, she enrolled with Carlo Rinaldini, professor of philosophy at the University of Padua; the latter she studied with Father Felice Rotondi of the same university. To enrich her theological studies, she learned Hebrew from the renowned rabbi, Shemuel Aboaf. With organist Maddalena Cappelli she studied music.

By 1678, Cornaro Piscopia was deemed ready for the doctoral examination in either philosophy or theology. She chose theology. The university board (*Riformatori*) posed no opposition to the request, but the examining professors sought the consent of Cardinal Gregorio Barbarigo, bishop of Padua, who refused. Despite a prolonged campaign of letters, Barbarigo held firm, evidently on grounds of Catholic orthodoxy, which prohibited women from becoming expert instructors in the faith.

Cornaro Piscopia then applied for her doctoral examination in philosophy. On the appointed day, 25 June 1678, the assembled crowd was so large that proceedings had to be relocated in the chapel of the Madonna in the Paduan cathedral. The examiners, stupefied by her encyclopedic command of the material, dispensed with voting and granted her the Ph.D. by acclamation, presenting her with the traditional ermine robe, laurel crown, ring, and philosophy book. One immediate result of her success was renewed hostility toward women candidates for university degrees. The next request for examination, by Carla Gabriella, was never granted. It would be decades before any other woman would earn a doctorate.

Cornaro Piscopia was a celebrated member of the elite literary academies of five cities: the Ricovrati of Padua, the Infecondi of Rome, the Intronati of Siena, the Erranti of Brescia, and the Dodonea and Pacifici of Venice. She was also a secular oblate of the Benedictine order. When she died in Padua on 26 July 1684, thirty-seven members of the college of philosophers and doctors, together with the local religious orders and a crowd of citizens, marched through the city. Shops closed for a day of collective mourning. Her request that her sister destroy her writings was carried out immediately upon her death. The few that remain include four academic discourses in Italian, thirty letters in Latin and Italian, a short work translated from Spanish, two supplications to the pope, eleven encomia in various languages, five epigrams in Greek and Latin, one acrostic in French, six sonnets in various languages, and one ode in Italian. A funerary monument in her honor was torn down by her brother, Girolamo, in 1727. Memorials to Elena Lucrezia Cornaro Piscopia may be found today at the University of Padua, Vassar College, and the University of Pittsburgh. Her tomb lies in the Cornaro chapel in Padua's St. Giustina basilica.

Deanna Shemek

See also the subheadings Latin Learning and Women; Greek Learning and Women (under Education, Humanism, and Women); the subheadings Letter Writing; Sonnet Writing (under Literary Culture and Women).

Bibliography

Bruhns, E. Maxine. "The Cornaro and Her Impact in the United States and England." In *Elena Lucrezia Cornaro Piscopia. Prima donna laureata nel mondo. Terzo centenario del dottorato (1678–1978).* Edited by Maria Ildegarde Tonzig, 141–147. Vicenza: Università degli studi-Abbazia di S. Giustina (Padua), 1980.

Labalme, Patricia H. "Nobile e donna: Elena Lucrezia Cornaro Piscopia." In *Elena Lucrezia Cornaro Piscopia. Prima donna laureata nel mondo. Terzo centenario del dottorato (1678–1978).* Edited by Maria Ildegarde Tonzig, 163–167. Vicenza: Università degli studi-Abbazia di S. Giustina (Padua), 1980. (In English.)

Labalme, Patricia H. "Women's Roles in Early Modern Venice: An Exceptional Case." In *Beyond Their Sex: Learned Women of the European Past.* Edited by Patricia H. Labalme, 129–152. New York: New York University Press, 1980.

Maschietto, Francesco Ludovico. *Elena Lucrezia Cornaro Piscopia (1646–1684). Prima donna laureata nel mondo.* Padua: Antenore, 1978.

Maschietto, Francesco Ludovico. "Elena Lucrezia Cornaro Piscopia." In *Elena Lucrezia Cornaro Piscopia. Prima donna laureata nel mondo. Terzo centenario del dottorato (1678–1978).* Edited by Maria Ildegarde Tonzig, 108–138. Vicenza: Università degli studi-Abbazia di S. Giustina (Padua), 1980.

Pynsent, Mathilde. *The Life of Helen Lucretia Cornaro Piscopia, Oblate of the Order of St. Benedict and Doctor of the University of Padua.* Rome: St. Benedict's, 1896.

Pizan, Christine de
(1364/1365–ca. 1430)

First professional woman writer in Europe; early feminist; one of the inaugurators of the querelle des femmes (debate on women); prolific French author of treatises and dialogues on women, politics, war, and peace; also wrote an autobiography and a major collection of lyric poetry

Christine de Pizan, poet, historian, and dialogue-writer. Engraving by anonymous artist. (Gianni Dagli Orti / Corbis)

Born in Venice to the noted astrologer of Bologna, Tommaso da Pizzano, and the daughter of his elder colleague, Tommaso Mondino da Forlì, Christine Pizan moved to France with her family while still an infant (1368) after Thomas de Pizan was appointed to the court of the French king Charles V. Christine's correct patronym is thus Pizan, as she signed it, not Pisan, as was (and in some oddly resistant circles still is) believed. Although she had two younger brothers, her father displayed his special affection for her by educating her as an upper-echelon male: in Latin and the sciences. In contrast, Christine's mother seems to have envisioned a more conventional female role for her daughter, who never named her.

Thomas also arranged for Christine to marry, at about age fifteen, a bright young notary of good Picard (northern French) family, Étienne du Castel, who became a royal secretary and to whom she bore two sons and a daughter during an exceptionally happy union.

However, her family's idyll was soon disrupted, first by Charles V's premature death (1380), spelling professional uncertainty for Thomas, who died five years later, leaving many debts. A further blow came when Étienne died from an epidemic at Beauvais in 1390. Christine was now a widow at twenty-five and sole support not only of her children but also of her mother and a niece, her brothers having quickly left France to claim their Italian patrimony. Despite her social standing, the deceptive legalese customarily inflicted on widows at that time left her by herself, cheated out of much of her legacy and harassed by creditors' lawsuits.

Apart from some resources and possible employment as a sort of legal secretary in her first years of widowhood, Christine's financial and personal rescue lay in her rapid self-transformation from pampered royal notary's wife to workaday manuscript copyist, courtly poet, then militant moralist. She thereby reinvented herself as a professional and prolific author in an unparalleled variety of styles and topics.

Beginning as a lyric poet, she appears to have composed her first poems in about 1394. These deal mainly with the solitary sorrows of widowhood and lost love, sometimes wistfully evoking her bygone happiness and concomitant desire to "sing joyfully" despite her personal tragedies. During this formative phase, she composed hundreds of ballads and experiments in other "fixed-form" lyric genres: roundels, lays, virelays and "songs for sale"— obviously influenced by Guillaume de Machaut, Eustache Deschamps, and other fourteenth-century masters—which she then shaped into collections or sequences or wove into longer, mixed-genre narratives on love (like the *Duke of True Lovers*) over the years 1399–1405. Once published in high-quality illuminated manuscripts, such books of poems would soon win Christine the patronage of the most powerful and wealthy nobles in France, despite the complex politics often dividing them. She consequently became one of the first truly professional authors.

Significantly, even after she went on to compose weightier prose works, her lyric flair never left her; it was a mode to which she would return throughout her career with new insight and energy. Conversely, we also find numerous harbingers of her moral-political activism and learned encyclopedism complementing her early lyric themes, woven into her love lyrics and love debate poems. This involved, for example, taking episodes from ancient myth, usually from the Roman poet Ovid's *Metamorphosis* (CE 1–8, as transmitted via the fourteenth-century French collection known as the *Moralized Ovid*), describing tragic lovers and adventurous heroes in similar situations, as if seeking solace in what was then known of ancient lore and letters and universalizing her experience to benefit others. This amplifying, enumerative tendency, together with her didactic (educational) impulse as reflected in her popular *Moral Proverbs* and, for her son Jean, a future royal secretary, in *Moral Instructions* (both ca. 1400–1401), permeated her first nonpoetic work, the allegorized educational manual in the "mirror for princes" tradition, the *Epistle of the Goddess Othea to the Trojan Prince Hector* (1400–1401). In its best manuscripts (now in London's British Library and Paris's Bibliothèque nationale de France), this so-called "epistle" is a multileveled textual and visual marvel, in which a hundred episodes from history and myth (medieval notions of history blurred this distinction) are first related literally, then glossed allegorically and morally, often illustrated by an excellent miniature, to instruct a young prince. Christine's alternatingly personal-universal approach to history and politics then surfaced more fully in her *Path of Long Study* (1402–1403), a narrative verse pilgrimage inspired by Boethius's widely read *Consolation of Philosophy* (524) and Dante's *Divine Comedy* (1321), the latter's presence making Christine the first French author to incorporate him. Still more vast is her pseudoautobiography merged with world history, *Fortune's Mutations* (1403), which earned her the commission to write the official biography of

King Charles V, emphasizing his "good deeds and practices" and wisdom (1404). Her erudite, pedagogical approach also permeates her best-known work nowadays, the feminist revisionist *City of Ladies* (1404–1405), whose title's echo of St. Augustine's massive defense of Christianity, the *City of God* (422), straightaway sets the tone and purpose of Christine's use of history to defend women. Her chief source was Boccaccio's *Famous Women* (1361–1362), minus the Italian's irony.

The years 1399–1402 also witnessed Christine's feminist polemics, again in certain ballads, but most stirringly in her *Epistle of the God of Love* (1399), countering the male-centered idyll of joy and refinement in *fin' amors* (courtly love, love for love's sake outside marriage) as spelling certain destruction for women. She then confronted some leading Parisian intellectuals (Jean de Montreuil, Gontier and Pierre Col), via circulated letters comprising the debate on the *Romance of the Rose* (1401–1402), concerning their praise of Guillaume de Lorris's and Jean de Meun's seductive allegorical romance epic. For Christine and her ally, Sorbonne chancellor and theologian Jean Gerson, the *Rose*'s value as a monument to the richness of thirteenth-century thought was undermined by its misogyny (contempt for women), especially to unsuspecting readers. Although the debate ended unresolved and scarcely minimized the *Rose*'s popularity, Christine's courageously astute arguments in these letters and related poems position her as a credible intellectual reformer promoting an intellectualism devoid of misogyny, similar to her concept of love in her lyrics and debate poems—both ideals inspired by Dante. Overall, her feminism consists of a *viable* equality (i.e., women may have to endure some abuse for the good of domestic stability) between the sexes rather than female supremacy or even complete equality—a bit conservative for modern feminists.

Her piety also emerges during 1402–1403 in three devotional poems to Mary and Jesus.

Often laced with political concerns, these were public prayers—for France and its beloved but mentally unstable king, Charles VI, unfit to rule his kingdom beset by the Hundred Years' War—as much as personal outpourings. Later came her *Seven Allegorized Psalms* (1409), in apparent emulation of Petrarch, while her devotional writing, intensifying a decade later, would have her self-identify with Christ's suffering on the Cross and with Mary's grief (*Hours of Contemplation*).

Her densely written literary and political-spiritual autobiography, *Christine's Vision* (1405–1406), combining all the qualities of the previously cited works, heralds her middle phase (1405–1415). Her grave subject matter elicited an increasingly authoritative tone, as in the *City of Ladies* and its real-life, survival-manual version for women of all classes, the *Three Virtues* (1405, popularized by the printer Vérard as *Treasury of the City of Ladies* from 1497). Her voice is necessarily less personal in her military-political treatises: the *Body Politic* (1407), *Feats of Arms and Chivalry* (1410), and the *Book of Peace* (1412–1413). In the lyric vein, she penned her longer love complaints and more ballads, including *One Hundred Ballads of a Lover and Lady,* which ends dramatically on the theme of love and death. Her prose (with verse) *Epistle to the Queen of France* (1405) pleads with the French queen Isabel to act as "mediatrix," to foster peace among the warring French nobles.

Works from her last phase (1415–1429) emit an even greater sense of urgency and pathos because of France's worsening political situation, marked by English domination and civil war—a grimly appropriate backdrop for Christine's personal losses, particularly that of her son Jean (died ca. 1425). These laments and consolations advocate a kind of Christian stoicism, as in the *Prison of Human Life* (ca. 1418) for Marie de Berry. But then, after eleven years' resigned silence, she composed her last known work: a politically vital, (probably) eye-witness poem at the Abbey of Poissy during

Joan's triumphant passage through that area, the *Tale of Joan of Arc* (1429), celebrating new hope for France's expulsion of the English—thanks to a maiden. After this, Christine disappears, although her didactic works were widely copied, printed, and translated over the fifteenth and sixteenth centuries, especially in England. Arguably a humanist in her deployment of learning for civic good, she nevertheless always wrote in the vernacular (French) citing mostly French sources, thus guaranteeing her survival beyond her Latinate contemporaries expressing similar ideas. Her promotion of French over Italian and Latin may also be interpreted as patriotic during a time of fervent cultural rivalry. Although not an original thinker in the modern sense, Christine's talent for compilation, authoritative citation, and communication with men and women alike enable her work to surpass her sources.

Nadia Margolis

See also Education, Humanism, and Women; Literary Culture and Women.

Bibliography

Primary Works

Christine de Pizan. *Book of the Body Politic.* Translated by Kate Langdon Forhan. Cambridge, UK: Cambridge University Press, 1994.

Christine de Pizan. *Book of the City of Ladies.* Rev. ed. Translated by Earl Jeffrey Richards. Gainesville: University Press of Florida, 1998.

Christine de Pizan. *Chemin de longue estude.* Edited and translated into modern French by Andrea Tarnowski. Paris: 2000.

Christine de Pizan. *Epistre Othea.* Edited by Gabriella Parussa. Geneva: 1999.

Christine de Pizan. *L'Advision Cristine.* Edited by Christine Reno and Liliane Dulac. Paris: Champion, 2001.

Christine de Pizan. *Livre du corps de policie.* Edited by Angus J. Kennedy. Paris: Champion, 1998.

Christine de Pizan. *Livre du duc des vrais amans.* Edited by Thelma S. Fenster. Albany, NY: State University of New York Press, 1995.

Christine de Pizan. *Selected Writings of Christine de Pizan.* Edited by Renate Blumenfeld-Kosinski. Translated by R. Blumenfeld-Kosinski and Kevin Brownlee. New York: W. W. Norton, 1997.

Christine de Pizan. *Writings of Christine de Pizan.* Edited by Charity Willard. Translated by C. Willard et al. New York: Persea Books, 1994.

Secondary Works

Kennedy, Angus J. *Christine de Pizan: A Bibliography.* Woodbridge, Suffolk, UK, and Rochester, NY: Tamesis, 1984. (Two supplements in 1994 and 2004.)

Quilligan, Maureen. *The Allegory of Female Authority: Christine de Pizan's Cité des Dames.* Ithaca, NY: Cornell University Press, 1991.

Willard, Charity C. *Christine de Pizan: Her Life and Works.* New York: Persea Books, 1984.

Poitiers, Diane de (1499/1500–1566)

Royal mistress of Henri II of France and patron of the arts

Diane de Poitiers, one of the most powerful and best documented women of the French Renaissance, was the daughter of a rich heiress, Jeanne de Batarnay, and Jean de Poitiers, count of Saint-Vallier. Political ties probably led to her education at the Bourbon court under the astute former regent, Anne de France, who subsequently helped arrange Diane's marriage to Louis de Brézé (a *grand seneschal* like her father and older than him). Brézé's high rank at the royal court propelled his fifteen-year-old wife among the ladies serving Louise de Savoie, a remarkable role model and regent. Diane's mastery of the courtly skills of prudence and dissimulation was no doubt furthered by reflection on two tragic mistakes that marred the history of her clan: the execution for adultery of her husband's mother—daughter of Agnès Sorel, the first official royal mistress in French history—and her father's near execution in 1523, after he unadvisedly sided with the treasonous constable of Bourbon.

In 1531, Diane's having become the mistress of Henri d'Orléans (he was twenty years her junior) was openly acknowledged when the young knight honored his lady in a tournament. Henri's marriage to Diane's cousin, Catherine de Médicis, was contracted at Anet, a Brézé estate, and widowhood brought Diane

Diane de Poitiers, mistress of Henri II of France and patron of the arts. Painting by unknown artist. (Hulton Archive/Getty Images)

independence, with full control over her dynastic line. (Numerous contracts and the extent of the Brézé possessions at her death offer proof of her phenomenal management skills.) Aristocratic anxiety over reputation renders elusive the chronology of ensuing events: a secretive Diane choreographed her increasingly equivocal life. It was only in 1536 that she commissioned a funerary monument to her husband, casting herself in the role of eternally devoted widow and innovative patroness of the arts. While Diane briefly played the grieving widow, she showed herself ready to exchange her "honor" for the increased power that a sexual bond with Henri could afford when he became heir to the throne. By the time the remarkable Rouen Cathedral tomb was consecrated to her husband's memory (1544), her servant was sporting her colors of black and white; and the emblems (*H-D*), devices (arrows, bows, quivers), and the lives of

Henri and Diane were inextricably intertwined. A number of Diane's eminently political letters deal with the education of Henri and Catherine's children.

Henri's accession to the throne signaled Diane's triumph (1547), and the following year she received the title duchess of Valentinois. Positioned at the very heart of the courtly power structure, alongside Saint-André, Montmorency, and the Guise, she rendered herself indispensable to the king, even in affairs of state and war. Royal entries celebrated the companion "whose crescent [the king] wore"; Du Bellay, Mellin de Saint-Gelais, and Olivier de Magny sang her praise and that of Anet, the new "regal" realm of the goddess of the hunt, invented by Philibert Delorme. Diane realized that Renaissance power was grounded in the masterful staging of imagery, and her naturalistic and symbolic projections of self (of problematic authenticity today) are simultaneously elusive and fraught with meaning. Though dedicated to the king, Anet was Diane's ultimate creation, affording a key to her soul. Its wooded location and pool betray her athletic self. Her ultra-Catholic political stance dovetails with Delorme's masterpiece chapel. Content to acquire possessions confiscated from heretics, even in her will she militated for "the good and ancient and Catholic religion"; similarly, some of the works of art she acquired were "spoils of war." The HD monogram recurred from floor to ceiling, but pride of place at this feudally inflected château went to Louis de Brézé. As the brilliantly negotiated marriages of her daughters show, Diane was laboring in the name of her clan. The nudity of the marble *Diana* posed over a sarcophagus, from a fountain at Anet—a masterwork of the French Renaissance—reveals the risks this independent but traditional noblewoman took. Her will specified tellingly that, if she died in Paris, she wanted to be buried in the church of the Filles Repenties. She trespassed, however, in Anet, where her final image shows her kneeling alone, praying for salvation, fully clothed.

Kathleen Wilson-Chevalier

See also Beaujeu, Anne de; Catherine de
   Médicis.
Bibliography
Primary Work
Poitiers, Diane de. *Dianne de Poytiers. Lettres in-
   édites.* Edited by G. Guiffrey. Paris: 1866;
   Geneva: 1970.
Secondary Works
Cloulas, Ivan. *Diane de Poitiers.* Paris: Fayard, 1997.
Leloup, Daniel. *Le château d'Anet. L'amour de
   Diane de Poitiers et d'Henri II.* Paris: 2001.
Melchior-Bonnet, Sabine. *L'Art de vivre au temps
   de Diane de Poitiers.* Paris: Nil, 1998.
Zerner, Henri. "Diane de Poitiers, maîtresse de
   son image." In *Actes du colloque Le mythe de
   Diane en France au XVIe siècle, Albineana* 14
   (2002): 335–343.

Power, Politics, and Women

European societies during the period roughly
between 1350 and 1650 did not generally encourage women to demonstrate power or autonomy. With some exceptions, most women
could not own property, attend university, or
defend their rights in court. The majority lived
under the governance of their husbands, fathers, and, in the case of women who entered
convents, the church. Further, all of Europe
had political traditions that supported male
leadership.

For a variety of reasons during the fifteenth
and sixteenth centuries, however, a number of
elite women were able to gain not only personal but also political power, usually through
their positions as daughters, wives, or mothers.
Such women occupied thrones throughout
Europe, including countries with strong central governments such as England, France,
Scotland, and Spain, as well as areas of more
diversified government such as Italy. To gain
and hold onto political power, many women
had to take on roles uncharacteristic of most
females of their time: giving orders to men, an-
alyzing international relations, forging diplomatic alliances, and cultivating a strong public
persona. Conversely, other roles they assumed
were typically female, such as representing

themselves as steadfast wives and promoting
the status of their children. Three subheadings
follow: Women and Monarchy; Conjugal
Power; Maternal Power.

Women and Monarchy

A number of elite women held political power
in their own right by virtue of their birth. In
Spain, Isabella, queen of Castile (1451–1504),
married her cousin Ferdinand, king of Aragon
(1452–1516). She ruled Castile and Aragon together with Ferdinand in a relationship of mutual admiration and respect. Although Isabella
chose to share her rule with her husband, she
did not relinquish her power to him. Similarly,
although they were known throughout their
kingdom as joint monarchs and both their
faces appeared on their coinage, Isabella did
not allow her own identity to be subsumed by
her consort's. To this day, historians portray Isabella as a strong, pioneering monarch.

English queens Mary I and Elizabeth I, half
sisters and the daughters of Henry VIII, each
ruled their country as queens in their own right
after the death of their younger half brother,
Edward VI. Mary I (Bloody Mary, 1516–1558),
daughter of Catherine of Aragon, ruled from
1553 until her death. She chose not to rule
alone, however, and formed an alliance with
Spain by marrying Prince Philip (soon to be
Philip II, king of Spain). Many of the hallmarks
of her reign—her inability to bear an heir to the
throne; her loss of the last English city on the
continent; and her heartfelt but unsuccessful attempt to reunite English citizens with the
Roman Catholic Church—were distressing to
her. When Elizabeth I (1533–1603) took the
throne, she did not marry, though she played
with the idea of marriage and used courtship as
a political tool for the first twenty years of her
reign. Her rule endured for nearly half a century until her death in 1603, though she chose
to govern alone. Although many of her subjects
thought it unusual—even wrong—that a
woman should rule without the support and aid
of a husband, Elizabeth held firm. She insisted

that she was "married" to England and that her "children" were her many subjects. Further, in the latter part of her reign, she developed an image of herself as the Virgin Queen, which became an important aspect of her public persona. Elizabeth's reign was long and eventful, and even today she is regarded as one of England's strongest monarchs.

But having the right or entitlement to political power did not guarantee that a woman would be able to retain or exercise that power. Elizabeth I's cousin, Mary Stuart (queen of Scots, 1542–1587), daughter of James V and Mary of Guise, was raised at the French court from the time she was five years old. After the death of her young husband, Francis II, in 1562, Mary Stuart returned to Scotland to take her place as the country's ruler because her mother, Scotland's regent, had recently died. Although she was intelligent and charming, Mary eventually became the center of a number of scandalous events, not the least of which were accusations that she had conspired to kill her second husband, Henry Stuart, Lord Darnley. Because of this and other allegations and because she had not been able to gain support from powerful figures at court and elsewhere in the realm, she was forced to abdicate her Scottish crown to her infant son. In 1569, Mary fled to England where she remained as Elizabeth's enforced "guest," never regaining her former power. In 1587, Mary was tried and found guilty of involvement in a plot to assassinate Elizabeth. With great reluctance, Queen Elizabeth signed her cousin Mary Stuart's death warrant.

The Spanish Queen Juana of Castile (1479–1555), daughter of Ferdinand of Aragon and Isabella of Castile and heir to their crowns, struggled to keep her power under different circumstances. Those around her began, even before the death of her mother made her queen of Castile in her own right, to question her sanity. Indeed, she eventually acquired the sobriquet *Juana la Loca* (Mad Juana). Although scholars have debated the extent and nature of her mental instability, her political rivals—including her husband, father, and son—were able to use the queen's supposed madness to their advantage. In 1509, her father Ferdinand had her declared incompetent and ordered her incarcerated in a remote castle in Tordesillas. Yet even in jail, she held power. In 1518, her son, Emperor Charles V, was obliged to visit her in prison to compel her to delegate to him the authority to rule. Juana returned to the throne for a brief interim in 1520 when the people of Castile rebelled against Charles's absentee rule and set Juana free, but a year later she was locked up again when Charles's army suppressed the revolt and retook Spain. Ultimately, Juana died imprisoned and alone, clearly insane yet ignored by those in power, including her son.

Conjugal Power

Some elite women were able to share power with their husbands. Depending on the specific situation, this could involve varying degrees of political power, both official and unofficial. Many such women became trusted advisors and friends to their husbands, such as the English queen Catherine of Aragon (1485–1536). She acted for a number of years as her husband Henry VIII's friend, confidante, and political advisor. In addition to this private, unofficial role, Henry also granted Catherine some specific, official political jurisdiction; she ruled as governor of the realm in 1511 while Henry was away at war in France. Catherine lost whatever political authority she had when Henry divorced her, however, and married Anne Boleyn, whose power was brief.

In contrast, Caterina Sforza (1463–1509), daughter of the duke of Milan, Galeazzo Maria Sforza, first gained political power through her husband, but then continued to hold it herself. After her marriage in 1477 to Girolamo Riario, who was commander in chief of the papal army, Sforza proved her courage when she put down a citizens' revolt while her husband was away campaigning in Rome. After Riario's death, she governed her kingdom alone. Her reign was not tranquil, however, but plagued by assassination attempts, a popular rebellion, the incarceration of her children who were held as hostages, and, after her husband's death, invasion and occupation of her territories by the new papal captain, Cesare Borgia. Though she refused to surrender her lands to Borgia, even during the pope's yearlong internment of her in the Castel Sant'Angelo in Rome, she finally gave up her rights to her property and spent the rest of her days in Florence working to gain political advantage for her children.

Maternal Power

Many elite women gained political authority through their relationships with their children. The majority of these women already had some political power, or at least potential for power, through their husband's or their own birth. Although many were motivated by the desire to promote their children's advancement, others also saw such situations, at least in part, as a way to gain power themselves. In the Italian signory of Mantua, Isabella d'Este (1474–1539) was able to exercise considerable power and control through not only her marriage but also her children. Wed in 1490 to Francesco Gonzaga, lord of Mantua, Isabella cultivated good relations with her subjects, ruled during her husband's frequent absences, and helped to develop important alliances with surrounding powers. After Francesco's death, Isabella's eldest son, Federico II Gonzaga (1500–1540), was named first duke of Mantua, while her second son, Ercole (1505–1563), was elevated to the cardinalate by Pope Clement VII. In 1504, Isabella engineered the betrothal of her daughter, Eleonora (Leonora, 1494–1572), to the powerful duke of Urbino, Francesco Maria della Rovere.

In 1485, Margaret Beaufort acquired substantial political power by helping her son ascend the British throne as Henry VII and then by advising him once he was king. Although a previous act of parliament had declared that no one of Beaufort descent could take the throne,

Margaret was undeterred. She took advantage of her son's position in a disputed succession and as his advisor gained the power she would otherwise have been denied.

France was perhaps the most difficult region for women to gain political power because of Salic Law, a legal tradition mandating that the crown could not be transferred *to* or *through* a woman. Thus, a deceased king's daughter could never take the throne, even when there were no living sons. Even under this strict law, however, some women gained unofficial power. Catherine de Médicis (1519–1589) exercised considerable power as the mother of three kings of France. After the untimely deaths of her husband, Henry II (d. 1559), and her eldest son, Francis II (d. 1560), she became regent and advisor for her son, Charles IX. After his death in 1574 she helped secure the crown for her son, Henry III. In her role as regent, she was influential in the French Wars of Religion (1562–1598) and in the weakening of the conservative Catholic Guise family's authority in France.

Thus, through diverse means, some elite women of the Renaissance were able not only to access political power but to use it to the advantage of their states and their subjects. Whether or not public opinion about women and power began to change at this time as the result of their example remains an open question.

Amy Gant and Carole Levin

See also Catherine de Médicis; Catherine of Aragon; Elizabeth I; Este, Isabella d'; Mary I; Mary Stuart; Sforza, Caterina.

Bibliography

Primary Work

Marcus, Leah, Janel Mueller, and Mary Beth Rose, eds. *Elizabeth I: Collected Works.* Chicago: University of Chicago Press, 2002.

Secondary Works

Bucholz, Robert, and Newton Key. *Early Modern England, 1485–1714: A Narrative History.* Malden, MA: Blackwell, 2004.

Levin, Carole. *The Reign of Elizabeth.* New York: Palgrave, 2002.

Levin, Carole, et al. *Extraordinary Women of the Medieval and Renaissance World: A Biographical*

Dictionary. Westport, CT: Greenwood Press, 2000.

Liss, Peggy K. *Isabel the Queen: Life and Times.* Oxford: Oxford University Press, 1992.

Primrose, Diana (fl. 1630)

Author of the English poem, A Chaine of Pearle

Absolutely nothing is known about the poet Diana Primrose except that, in London in 1630 under her name, the printer Thomas Paine published the poem, *A Chaine of Pearle. Or a Memoriall of the peerles Graces, and Heroick Vertues of Queene Elizabeth, of Glorious Memory.* Evidence suggests that Primrose might have been either the daughter or wife of Gilbert Primrose, a minister in the French Protestant church who returned to England in 1622/1623. However, antiquarian John Nichols (1745–1826) proposed that Diana Primrose might be a pseudonym; certainly, the Latin epigraph to the poem, "*Dat rosa mel apibus qua sugit aranea virus*" ("the rose gives honey to the bees, from which the spider sucks venom") plays on the author's name, Primrose. The poem, composed in rhyming iambic pentameter, opens with a dedication to "All Noble Ladies, and Gentlewomen"; these lines are followed by a second dedicatory poem in praise of Diana by another unknown poet who signs herself as Dorothy Berry. A third dedicatory piece, the Induction, directly addresses Queen Elizabeth herself: "Thou English goddess, empresse of our Sex,/ O thou whose name still reigns in all our hearts." The poem goes on to celebrate the virtues of the queen (Eliza, she is called), and, associating her "empresse" with Diana, the virgin goddess, Primrose presents Elizabeth as an exemplar for all women to emulate in the realms of education, religion, and the intellect.

Some scholars have suggested a composition date much earlier than the print date, placing the work among poems written in remembrance of the recently deceased queen. Others who support a composition date closer to 1630 argue that the poem may have been intended either as a veiled criticism of Charles I or perhaps as a nostalgic look back on a more enlightened age.

Regardless of the identity of Diana Primrose, *A Chaine of Pearle* stands as an example of the ways in which some seventeenth-century women-centered poets evoked the image of Elizabeth I as a model of female erudition and autonomy.

Tara Wood

Bibliography
Primary Work

Primrose, Diana. *A Chaine of Pearle. Or, A Memoriall of the peerless Graces, and Heroick Vertues of Queene Elizabeth, of Glorious Memory.* London: Printed by J. Dawson for Thomas Paine, sold by Philip Waterhouse, 1630.

Secondary Works

Gim, Lisa. " 'Faire *Eliza's* Chaine': Two Female Writers' Literary Links to Queen Elizabeth I." In *Maids and Mistresses, Cousins and Queens.* Edited by Susan Frye and Karen Robertson, 183–198. New York and Oxford: Oxford University Press, 1999.

Wynne-Davies, Marion. *Women Poets of the Renaissance.* New York: Routledge, 1999.

Printers, the Book Trade, and Women

For centuries, scholars have placed women at the margins of the early modern book industry, this in sharp contrast to their contributions as illuminators and scribes in late medieval manuscript production. Knowledge of women's roles in the early book industry is hampered by scattered and incomplete sources. Chief among these are the books themselves. Even when she published a book, only rarely would a woman sign her name in the colophon. She remained anonymous. Social constraints also reinforced the notion that a woman was incapable of performing certain jobs, including working in a printer's shop. The nature of movable type technology conspired against her involvement. Presswork, being physically demanding, was considered "men's work." A woman's presence in the shop was a distraction (from the point of view of the master), one likely to compromise the efficiency and high levels of production expected from skilled artisans. Books were printed in cramped quarters, where pressmen, typesetters, proofreaders, and shop boys rubbed elbows, exchanged crude language, traded insults, and occasionally came to blows. The milieu was decidedly masculine, not suitable for what Renaissance culture generally considered a "gentle spirit." Jean Huchier, a typesetter who worked in the printing shops of the Parisian businesswoman Charlottte Guillard, praised her as "a woman of great courage" but added that his work was "beyond that of her sex."

Drawing on new information from documentary and printed sources, social historians and historians of early printing are revising the traditional picture of women as being on the fringes of the early book industry. We are learning, for example, that a printer's business—even that of a modest typographer—was not usually limited to one shop but rather included multiple shops (for the storage of supplies or purposes of accounting) attached to his place of residence. It was a printing house, where business and family often overlapped. Thus, though she might be barred from the printing shop itself, the wife or daughter of a printer could learn other facets of his business, such as bookkeeping, binding books, and preparing paper for printing. These last two skills, for example, were taken up by nieces of the wife of Bernardino Benali, a Venetian bookseller and printer who in his will (1517) left twenty ducats for their assistance in his business. Now and then, anecdotal evidence confirms a wife's involvement in her husband's printing operation. In a letter from 1506, Margarete, the eight-year-old daughter of Johann Amerbach, the eminent printer from Basel, addressed her mother as Frau Barbara Druckerin (Mrs. Barbara Printer). High rates of literacy among wives and daughters of printers also encouraged a strong feminine presence in the trade. While an exceptional case, the four eldest daughters of Christopher Plantin, the il-

lustrious Antwerp publisher, put their linguistic skills to good use proofreading copy in his shops. Also proficient in languages were Sisters Marietta and Rosarietta, who were hired by a monastic press—the Ripoli Press in Florence—to set pages of type for works by Augustine, Boccaccio, Petrarch, and Suetonius.

Even more directly—as when the wealth of her dowry passed to her husband—a woman could influence the success of a printing or publishing operation. The marriage of a printer or bookseller often coincided with a downturn in his business and the need to find additional capital. The dowry itself, usually consisting of cash and/or property (including presses and typographical tools, if her father was a printer), was usually reinvested by the husband or used to settle debts. However, he was required to return the dowry or the monetary value of the goods upon his death. Thus a printer or book merchant with large debts who died without having made legal restitution of the dowry could have his estate seized by the widow. Consider the case of Dorotea Scotto, wife of Andrea Calvo, a highly successful Milanese book merchant. From 1543 to 1546, Dorotea filed a series of lawsuits against her husband, claiming he had squandered away her livelihood (a substantial dowry of five thousand lire) to pay off his debts. Reduced to poverty and unable to support herself and seven children, Dorotea placed a lien (*apprehensio*) on Calvo's assets. These included large stocks of books in two shops and warehouses in Milan as well as books in Pavia, all of which she seized. One year before her husband's death in 1546, she took control of his business. Along with her brother, Girolamo (Calvo's erstwhile associate), she ran it successfully for the next ten years, nearly doubling the stocks of books found in Calvo's warehouses a decade earlier. During this period she conducted business with the Giolito firm in Venice, negotiated dowries for her daughters, and sold books to local merchants in Milan. Her case was not unusual. In 1596 Clara Somasca, the wife of the Milanese bookseller Antonio degli Antoni, also seized her late husband's estate because he too had failed to make restitution of her dowry. A similar case shows up in Florence as well, involving the heirs of the printer Giorgio Marescotti. When he died intestate in 1602, his wife, Agnoletta and son, Cristofano, entered into extended litigation over his estate. Though much of it was sold to pay off debts, Agnoletta continued to sell his books. Soon after Cristofano expired in 1611, his wife Margherita took over the business. However, with no family members to help her run the operation and unable to secure the monopoly her late husband had on printing official edicts, laws, and pronouncements in Florence, the business floundered. As Margherita's case shows, success for a woman in the early book trade depended largely on maintaining the continuity of a family firm, drawing on well-established family networks, and working with her husband's business connections.

The death of a husband and the need to maintain his printing and/or bookselling operation was the most compelling reason for a woman to continue working in the book trade. Not surprisingly, the difficulties of keeping the business running led numerous widows to remarry other printers and book merchants, including those who had worked in her husband's shops. If she had a son, who was usually the beneficiary of the business, she would provide him with adequate training in the craft before he took over the business. If she remained single, however, she might manage the operation with the help of siblings or a skilled artisan. For instance, when the Milanese bookseller Jacopo Corsico passed away in 1536, he left his wife Elisabetta Barechis with three children to raise and the added responsibility of running his bookshop. Within six months she had hired another bookseller, Pietro Antonio Sessa, to help manage the shop on the condition that he agree in writing to teach both Elisabetta and her eldest son (Giovanni Francesco) the art of bookselling ("*docere et instuere Elisabet*

et Iohannes Francisci in dicta arte librarie"). Similar cases are documented for widows of printers. When the Venetian printer Nicolo' Bevilacqua passed away in 1573, his widow, Teodosia, hired her son-in-law, Francesco Ziletti, to run Nicolo's press until her eight-year-old son and universal heir, Giovanni Battista, had reached maturity. A similar situation obtained for Luchina, wife of the Roman printer Pietro Ravani, who managed her husband's firm with the help of the printer Giovanni Varisco until her son, Vittorio, came of age. Even more revealing is the example of Veronica Sessa, who after the death of her husband, the large-scale Venetian publisher Melchior Sessa, hired her brothers to help her supervise the operation. The range and complexity of Veronica's business activities are striking. She bestowed power of attorney, arranged dowries, negotiated business contracts, and collected debts. She was not alone as a woman bookseller and publisher of extraordinary business talents, as the careers of Dorotea Scotto, Paola Blada, Lucrezia Dorico, and Cecilia Tramezzino also testify.

Why did women of the late Renaissance rarely sign the books they published? The answer has less to do with cultural constraints than with sound business practice—namely, the need to maintain the quality and proven reliability of an established publishing firm. Privileges were typically granted to a widow based on the longevity and reputation of her husband's business. Keeping his name, his mark, and his shop sign was essential for success. The career of Aurelia da Ponte, daughter of the printer Pacifico da Ponte, exemplifies this trend. Da Ponte had been the official typographer for the archbishop of Milan and the city's most prolific printer for nearly twenty-five years when he died without male issue in 1594. Aurelia, who inherited half of his business, continued its operation, publishing liturgical and religious texts for the archdiocese with a father-and-son team of printers who had worked in her father's shops. Colophons on the books they published read "*eredi di Pacifico Pontio*" or "*nella stamparia del*

quondam Pacifico da Ponte" (In the printing shop
of the former Pacifico da Ponte). There are,
however, a few exceptional women who did
sign their names to books, including Caterina
De Silvestro (in Naples), Elisabetta Rusconi (in
Venice), and Girolama Cartolari (in Rome).
When her husband, Sigismondo Mayr, died in
1517, De Silvestro took over the business and
added typographical innovations (such as italic
type and ornamental letters) to Mayr's stocks of
type. At first she signed her books "Madonna
Caterina who was [the] wife of master Sigismondo Mayr." By 1522, however, she preferred
to sign them as being printed "in the house of
Catherine de Silvestro," a clear indication of the
respect she had earned as a female printer.
Much the same can be said for Girolama Cartolari, who after the death of her husband, Baldassare, in 1543 directed his book operation for
the next sixteen years. A prolific printer, she followed Baldassare's publication program closely,
printing papal bulls, pronouncements issued by
the apostolic chamber, religious pamphlets,
anti-Lutheran tracts, and works of authors who
spent time at the court of Pope Paul III.

There were, of course, women outside Italy
who also led highly successful careers as printers,
publishers, and booksellers. Most notable among
these—Yolande Bonhomme, Charlotte Guillard
(who spent fifty years in the trade), Francoise de
Louvain, and Nicole Vostre in Paris; Madeleine
de Portunais and Jeanne Giunta in Lyon; Mar-
garethe Pruss in Strasbourg—overcame the
same financial hurdles and social constraints
faced by Italian women to break into the book
industry. Women north and south of the Alps
made significant contributions to the early modern book trade, even if their names appear infre-
quently on the books they manufactured and
sold. They were not marginal to this industry.
These "bookwomen" deserve the same recognition as their male counterparts in the scholarly
literature on early printing and publishing in
Europe.

Kevin M. Stevens

See also Work and Women.

Bibliography
Broomhall, Susan. *Women and the Book Trade in
    Sixteenth-Century France.* Burlington, VT: Ash-
    gate, 2002
Davis, Natalie Zemon. "Women in the Crafts in
    Sixteenth Century Lyon." In *Women and Work
    in Preindustrial Europe.* Edited by Barbara A.
    Hanawalt, 167–197. Bloomington: Indiana
    University Press, 1986.
Halpern, Barbara C. *The Correspondence of Johann
    Amerbach: Early Printing in its Social Context.*
    Ann Arbor: University of Michigan Press,
    2000.
Novati, Francesco. "Donne tipografe nel Cinque-
    cento." *Il libro e la stampa* 7 (1907): 41–49.
Parker, Deborah. "Women in the Book Trade in
    Italy, 1475–1620." *Renaissance Quarterly* 49
    (1996): 509–541.
Rouse, M. A., and R. H. Rouse. *Cartolai, Illumina-
    tors and Printers in Fifteenth-Century Italy.*
    Berkeley: University of California Press, 1988.
Stevens, Kevin M. "New Light on Andrea Calvo
    and the Book Trade in Sixteenth-Century
    Milan." *La Bibliofilia* 103, no. 1 (2001): 25–54.
Usher, Miriam Cushman. *Lay Culture, Learned
    Culture: Books and Social Change in Strasbourg,
    1480–1599.* New Haven and London: Yale
    University Press, 1982.
Zannini, Gian Ludovico Masetti. *Stampatori e librai
    a Roma nella seconda meta' del Cinquecento.*
    Rome: 1980.

Public Speaking and Women. *See* Rhetoric, Public Speaking, and Women.

Pulci, Antonia Tanini (1452/54–1501)

*Florentine writer of popular mystery and miracle
plays published in numerous editions in the fifteenth
and sixteenth centuries.*

Antonia Pulci was born sometime between
1452 and 1454, the daughter of Francesco
d'Antonio di Giannotto Tanini, a merchant;
her mother was a Roman woman, Jacopa di
Torello di Lorenzo Torelli, whose family was
from Trastevere. There were five sisters and a

brother as well as a half brother and sister (her father's natural children). Francesco died in 1467, and his eldest (and natural) son Guilio provided him with a splendid marble floor tomb in Santa Croce. Giuseppe Richa, who included a biography of Antonia in his history of the Florentine church, reported that four of the Tanini sisters married well, three in Florence and one in Pisa. Girolama, the firstborn, married Roberto Visdomini; Antonia married Bernardo di Jacopo Pulci. At least one Tanini sister entered a local convent. Antonia's brother Niccolò married Girolama di Battista di Francesco Strozzi.

Antonia's marriage took place in 1470 or 1471. Bernardo Pulci was a well-known literary figure and later an important administrator of the Florentine University. Antonia seems to have brought Bernardo a dowry of a thousand florins. The noble Pulci family had suffered serious financial difficulties and were ultimately bankrupted by the eldest brother Luca's unwise investments. Luca died in 1470, leaving his brothers in dishonor and responsible for his family. Antonia's dowry, very good at the time for a merchant's daughter, was a boon to the Pulcis.

Antonia's first play, a *sacra rappresentazione,* or miracle play, entitled the *Rappresentazione di Santa Domitilla* (The Play of Saint Domitilla), is dated 1483. She published it in the 1490s, if not before, together with two, possibly three others, in the important two-volume anthology of *sacre rappresentazioni* that has been called the "Raccolta Miscomini" because Antonio Miscomini is thought to be the publisher. The other plays attributed to "Antonia donna di Bernardo Pulci" in the anthology are the *Rappresentazione di Santa Guglielma* (The Play of Saint Guglielma) and the *Rappresentazione di San Francesco* (The Play of Saint Francis). The collection also includes another play possibly written by Antonia, the *Rappresentazione di Giuseppe figlio di Giacob* (The Play of Joseph, Son of Jacob), and Bernardo Pulci's *Rappresen-*

tazione di Barlaam e Giosafat (The Play of Barlaam and Josafat). Antonia's close friend, Fra Antonio Dolciati, attributed a play on the Joseph story to Antonia in a work written some years after her death. He also mentions that she wrote other plays, including one on the Prodigal Son and another on Saul and David. The plays to which Dolciati refers seem to have been the *Rappresentazione del figliuol prodigo* (The Play of the Prodigal Son), known today only in sixteenth- and seventeenth-century editions, and the *Destruzione di Saul e il pianto di Davit* (The Demise of Saul and the Tears of David), the only extant Florentine *sacra rappresentazione* on that biblical subject, and one whose earliest known edition was published in the 1490s.

In 1488, Bernardo died. The couple was childless, and Antonia became an *ammantellata,* a third-order sister living in secular society. She resided for a while at San Vincenzo, the Dominican convent known as Annalena, and also at her mother's home near Piazza della Signoria. She studied Latin with a student from the cathedral school, Francesco Dolciati, whom she convinced to enter the religious life. Francesco took Fra Antonio as his religious name in her honor and referred to her as his *maestra* (teacher), in religion. According to Dolciati, while waiting for her dowry to be returned, Antonia spent most of her time secluded on the upper floor of her home, studying Scripture and doing penance. She continued to write, but *laude,* religious poems of praise rather than plays, one on the *corpus domini,* of which Dolciati had an autographed copy that he treasured in her memory.

When she obtained her dowry from the Pulcis, Antonia purchased property outside the gate of San Gallo, between the monastery known as Lapo and the Mugnone River, to which she retired with a small group of Augustinian tertiaries to establish there a convent. Her will, written in 1501, the year she died, provided the funding for the house, to be known as the convent of Santa Maria della Misericordia (it was also called the Assunta). She built the chapel of Santa Monica in the church of San Gallo, where she wished to be buried. The church and friary of San Gallo, where Fra Antonio Dolciati was prior for several years, was destroyed in the 1530s. The nuns of Santa Maria della Misericordia soon moved from their dangerous position outside the city walls to the convent of San Clemente, just inside the wall in Via San Gallo.

Typical of many Florentine mystery and miracle plays of the time, Antonia's plays generally remain rather close to their sources. However, her *Destruzione di Saul e il pianto di Davit* contains an original episode, not found in the Bible, that depicts the martyrdom of the wife of Saul. Her Saint Francis play is also somewhat unusual and seems to contain autobiographical references to her family: for example, when Francis's good friend Jacopa da Settesoli, called Jacopa da Roma, appears at his deathbed, the scene is surely also an homage to Antonia's mother, another Jacopa from Rome.

Antonia plays are very well written in pleasant, recitable verse. They were published repeatedly throughout the sixteenth century and into the seventeenth, probably because they were texts that could serve nuns well for convent theater and devotional reading. Of the early editions, the *Santa Domitilla,* the *San Francesco,* and the *Santa Guglielma* were the most often published, and the latter two have been included in nineteenth- and twentieth-century anthologies.

There has been confusion regarding Antonia's name since the late nineteenth century, when the family's surname was erroneously thought to be Giannotti rather than Tanini. The error stems from a partial reading of archival documents. In the early fifteenth century Antonia's family had not yet assumed a surname and her father used two patronymics:

Francesco di Antonio di Giannotto. However, by midcentury the family had begun to use the surname Tanini, based on an earlier ancestor Tanino.

Elissa Weaver

See also Convents; Theater and Women Actors, Playwrights, and Patrons.

Bibliography

Primary Works

Ponte, Giovanni, ed. *Sacre rappresentazioni fiorentine del Quattrocento.* Milan: Marzorati Editore, 1974.

Pulci, Antonia. *Florentine Drama for Convent and Festival.* Translated by James Wyatt Cook and edited by James Wyatt and Barbara Collier Cook. Chicago: University of Chicago Press, 1996.

Pulci, Antonia Tanini. *La rappresentatione di Santa Domitilla,* a8–c4, *La rappresentatione di Santa Gugielma,* g8–i6, *La rappresentatione di San Francesco,* n8–p4. Florence: Antonio Miscomini?, ca. 1490–1495.

Secondary Works

Bryce, Judith. " 'Or altra via mi convien cercare': Marriage, Salvation, and Sanctity in Antonia Tanini Pulci's Rappresentazione di Santa Guglielma." In *Theatre, Opera, and Performance in Italy from the Fifteenth Century to the Present: Essays in Honour of Richard Andrews.* Edited by Brian Richardson, Simon Gilson, and Catherine Keen, 195–207. Leeds: Society for Italian Studies, 2004.

Martines, Lauro. *Strong Words: Writing and Social Strain in the Italian Renaissance.* Pages 64–69. Baltimore, MD: Johns Hopkins University Press, 2001.

Newbigin, Nerida. "Agata, Apollonia, and Other Martyred Virgins: Did Florentines Really See These Plays Performed?" In *European Medieval Drama 1997.* Edited by Sydney Higgins, 175–197. Camerino: Centro Audiovisivi e Stampa Universitá di Camerino, 1998.

Weaver, Elissa. *Convent Theatre in Early Modern Italy: Spiritual Fun and Learning for Women,* 97–104. Cambridge: Cambridge University Press, 2002.

Note: Weaver's biography of Pulci is available at http://www.lib.uchicago.edu/efts/IWW/BIOS/A0040.html. It is printed here in a revised version, courtesy of the author.

Q

Queens. *See* Power, Politics, and Women.

Querelle des Femmes (Controversy on Women)

Criticism of the vices and praise for the attractions of women are perennial topics in literature, but only at a few moments in history have writers in favor of women engaged in formal debate with misogynists to challenge fundamental negative assumptions about women. The European Renaissance was one such period. From the late fourteenth century through the seventeenth century, traditional misogynist assertions that women were naturally weak, tended to vice, and could not be trusted to behave well without male supervision in domestic or social situations were answered by carefully reasoned, innovative arguments in favor of women's capacity for moral virtue, physical endurance, and intellectual accomplishment and by proposals for changes in the organization of social and domestic life appropriate to the revised notion of women. During this period, the negative and the positive attitudes toward women were juxtaposed with each other in pairs or series of texts devoted exclusively to discussing womankind and also appeared in tracts dealing with other topics related to women, such as marriage and domestic economy. Scholars refer to this formal debate by the French term *querelle des femmes* (dispute about women), in part because the debate was very popular in France and in part because scholars first became aware of the debate when examining French texts, but interest in the topic was pan-European. Authors in every country participated in the debate, and well over one hundred texts on the subject were produced.

The Renaissance dispute about women was a development of an already active medieval *querelle* but differed from it in the prowoman texts' push toward a deep reconsideration of the nature of woman. The earlier debate was characterized by the production of matched sets of arguments that did not upset fixed ideas about women's natural inferiority. For example, antiwoman scriptural texts were confronted with prowoman scriptural texts; thus, Eve's guilt was balanced by Mary's virtue, but Mary was so exceptional a figure that misogynists could counter that her behavior revealed nothing positive about the nature of women in general. While retaining many of the medieval topics and continuing to rely heavily on scriptural quotation, the prowoman side of the Renaissance *querelle* introduced two innovations in method that made it possible to make a convincing case in favor of women: first, authors used biographical evidence drawn from myth, legend, and, most important, history and contemporary life to support revisionist claims about the nature of woman; second, they used the formal philosophical paradox to break down negative assumptions.

Biographical evidence was introduced into the defense of women by the humanists Petrarch and Boccaccio in Italy. The first extensive collection of female biographies since Plutarch, Boccaccio's *De Mulieribus Claris* was enormously popular and influential. Originally written in Latin, it was translated into most of the European vernaculars; it circulated widely in manuscript and was printed early and often; it was updated several times with additions of modern lives. In his book, Boccaccio shows himself to be at a turning point in conceptualizing women. Caught between his innovative assembly of copious evidence that women have performed many actions worthy of admiration in the arts and sciences, government, and war and his acceptance of the opinion of authorities who defined women as naturally incapable of heroic actions and as inclined to vice, he frequently interprets women's heroic behavior as being due to a miraculous infusion of male spirit that permits them to overcome their nature in extraordinary circumstances.

For the most part, later prowoman writers in the *querelle* accepted Boccaccio's evidence and rejected his interpretation; demonstrating that women are naturally capable of virtue, intellectual activity, and heroic feats and that cultural restraints rather than natural inability have held women back is at the heart of the Renaissance case for women. The French writer Christine de Pizan, one of the first authors to make this case and the first woman to enter the *querelle,* challenged Boccaccio on this very point in her collection of female biographies, *La Cité des dames* (The City of Ladies). She conspicuously borrowed Boccaccio's material but used it to demonstrate a notion of woman completely opposed to Boccaccio's extraordinary woman theory; she argued that, given the education and opportunity to act, women were the equals of men.

Though all Renaissance defenses of women incorporate biographical evidence of women's capacities, not all defenses are straightforward in their attack on misogyny. Many humanist and sixteenth-century defenses are written in a subtle and witty philosophical genre, the formal paradox. This has sometimes caused modern readers to perceive them as a frivolous intellectual game rather than recognizing them as making a serious challenge to the status quo. Like Erasmus's famous *Praise of Folly* (1511), these works discover valuable positive qualities in something apparently indefensible—in this case womankind. They do not necessarily reject conventional notions of woman's nature, but rather they challenge the negative valuation put on it. For example, in both the English Sir Thomas Elyot's brief dialogue *Defence of Good*

Women (1535) and the Italian Baldessare Castiglione's extended debate about woman and her role at court in Book III of *Il Cortegiano* (The Courtier, 1528, translated into English by Thomas Hoby in 1561), the prowoman speakers argue that woman's timidity, conventionally seen as a weakness, is a strength that adapts her for her domestic role of preserving the goods that the brave, but potentially profligate, husband brings home. Although the paradoxical strategy of finding strength in weakness (used by many in addition to Elyot and Castiglione) did not lead to the opening up of new fields of activity, as a modern feminist might wish, it did lend dignity and value to the domestic work that was the lot of most women in the period, and it provided a basis for writers on household management to advise that the wife be responsible for the direction of the household. Similarly, some Renaissance paradoxical texts do not take the obvious tack of defending Eve by arguing that Adam rather than she bears ultimate responsibility for the Fall but rather discover good in Eve's apparently bad action. For example, the unpublished early paradoxical text *De laudibus mulierum* (1487), by the Italian Bartolommeo Goggio, asserts that many benefits came from Eve's eating of the fruit—among them, the opening of the eyes of the intellect for mankind.

Some texts supplement the strategy of showing that qualities in woman that had previously been seen as weaknesses were actually strengths with proof that, at least in the quality of intelligence, the fundamental assumption that the two sexes are naturally different (a position now known as essentialism) is incorrect; they assert that differences have a cultural cause—some even positing a golden age of equality that ended when men began to oppress women. A few authors who make this claim are the German Agrippa von Nettesheim in his much translated and highly influential *De nobilitate et praecellentia foeminei sexus* (1529), the Italian Galeazzo Flavio Capella in his *Della eccellenza et dignità della donna,* Ludovico Ariosto in the *Orlando Furioso,* and Spenser in *The Faerie Queene.* Many authors, including the Italians Capella and Castiglione and the Englishmen Thomas More and the author of the *Dyalogue Defensive of Women* proposed that women could profit from education just as much as men if they were given the opportunity. In his dialogue *The Defence of Good Women,* the Englishman Sir Thomas Elyot uses logic to demonstrate that women are capable of the same virtues as men—they are not timid by nature but by upbringing—and, thus, if properly educated they are capable of playing the same roles in society that men play. Elyot goes further than most English authors, however, when he endorses the political consequences of education: the dialogue concludes with the entry of Queen Zenobia, who explains that education made her capable of participating in politics. Most support intellectual activity by women, including writing and publishing, but find that political action by women is desirable only in extraordinary circumstances, for example, when there is no male heir to the throne, as was the case when Elizabeth I became queen of England.

Although the vast majority of defenses of women were written by men, women authors participated in the Renaissance *querelle* from its earliest days, as is shown by Frenchwoman Christine de Pisan's *Cité des dames* (ca. 1405) and Italian humanist Isotta Nogarola's *Dialogue* (1451) on Saint Augustine's doctrine that Adam and Eve "sinned differently because of the inequality of the sexes, but that both sinned with equal pride" (*peccaverunt impari sexu sed pari fastu*). Women's greatest participation in the early modern *querelle* was during the late sixteenth century and early seventeenth centuries. The Frenchwoman Catherine des Roches (1542–1587) incorporated elements of the *querelle* into several of her dialogues. The year 1600 saw the publication of two Italian works. Lucrezia Marinella's *On the Nobility and Excellence of Women* touched on the standard topics of the querelle, in response to a specific misog-

ynist text, and Modesta Pozzo's (pen name, Moderata Fonte) much freer dialogue *Il Merito delle donne* (The Worth of Women, written ca. 1592) presented a group of women discussing a very wide range of practical issues—husbands' vices, the value of education, and domestic economy—as well as philosophical ones. The Englishwoman Rachel Speght responded to a virulent misogynist attack in her bitingly satiric but rational and substantial proof of "Womans excellency," *A Mouzell for Melastomus* (1617), and, most unusually, another Englishwoman, Aemilia Lanyer, incorporated elements of the *querelle,* including a defense of Eve, in the passion poem and other writings in the volume *Salve Deus Rex Judeorum* (1611). Though it might seem reasonable to assume that women would have argued clearly for women's equality or superiority, that is not so. Rather, in the tradition of the paradox, they often unsettle assumptions about women by setting their own skill as writers against the content of their works. In Nogarola's dialogue, the male sustainer of woman's inferiority makes the stronger case, but Nogarola, as author, simultaneously and paradoxically demonstrates a quality that he denies—women's wit and intelligence. Similarly, Lanyer defends Eve on the grounds that she was weaker and thus cannot be held responsible, at the same time that she demonstrates her own command of a complex literary genre and urges female readers to think for themselves.

An unusual feature of the English *querelle* is the popular tone of many of the texts from the mid-sixteenth century onward. Rather than, or in addition to, the formal paradox and dialogue, many English authors used older genres, such as the bird debate, the dream vision, and the invective. Such works offered down-to-earth praise for women's successful fulfillment of their roles as mothers and homemakers, and they featured in general *ad hominem* argument and disparagement of men nearly as often as praise of women for accomplishments in traditionally masculine fields. English publishers often artificially stimulated a sense of crisis in the definition of woman by commissioning texts on both sides of the debate. This is true of the pamphlets that form the Schoolhouse Controversy (1541–1542 and 1557–1560) and the Swetnam Controversy (1615–1620); each is named for a misogynist text that provoked numerous prowoman responses: Edwarde Gosynhyll's (?) *The Scholehouse of Women* (1541, 1560, 1572) and Joseph Swetnam's *The Araignment of lewd, idle, froward and unconstant Women* (1615 and many editions thereafter). As in the more highly philosophical texts, however, the popular misogynist texts were compendia of age-old arguments, while the companion prowoman publications, though full of entertaining invective, often exhibited original thinking and made a persuasive case for women's virtue. For example, *A Mouzell for Melastomus,* the young Englishwoman Rachel Speght's satiric defense of women, is noteworthy for its skillful deployment of scriptural evidence to refute the outrageous claims of the misogynist *Araignment of Women.* The popular appeal of the controversy in England can be seen in Shakespeare's *Taming of the Shrew,* in which the final speech by Katherine, the female protagonist, explores the most modern ideas about woman's social role.

Pamela Benson

See also Education, Humanism, and Women, particularly The Humanist Curriculum; entries for the women mentioned in this article; Feminism.

Bibliography

Primary Works

Benson, Pamela Joseph, ed. *Texts of the Querelle des femmes, 1521–1640.* The Early Modern Englishwoman: A Facsimile Library of Essential Works, 1500–1750, series 3. Aldershot, UK: Ashgate, 2006.

Boccaccio, Giovanni. *Famous Women.* The I Tatti Renaissance Library. Edited and translated by Virginia Brown. Cambridge, MA, and London: Harvard University Press, 2001.

Bornstein, Diane, ed. *The Feminist Controversy of the Renaissance: Guillaume Alexis, An Argument betwyxt Man and Woman (1525); Sir Thomas Elyot, The Defence of Good Women (1545); Henricus Cornelius Agrippa, Female Pre-Eminence (1670).* Delmar, NY: Scholars' Facsimiles and Reports, 1980.

Fonte, Moderata (Modesta Pozza). *The Worth of Women: Wherein Is Clearly Revealed Their Nobility and Their Superiority to Men.* Edited and translated by Virginia Cox. Chicago: University of Chicago Press, 1997.

Henderson, Katherine Usher, and Barbara F. McManus, eds. *Half Humankind: Contexts and Texts of the Controversy about Women in England, 1540–1640.* Urbana: University of Illinois Press, 1985.

Lanyer, Aemilia. *The Poems of Aemilia Lanyer: Salve Deus Rex Judaeorum.* Women Writers in English, 1350–1850. Edited by Susanne Woods. New York: Oxford University Press, 1993.

Marinella, Lucrezia. *The Nobility and Excellence of Women and the Defects and Vices of Men.* The Other Voice in Early Modern Europe. Edited and translated by Anne Dunhill. Introduction by Letizia Panizza. Chicago and London: University of Chicago Press, 1999.

Nogarola, Isotta. *Complete Writings: Letterbook, Dialogue on Adam and Eve, Orations.* The Other Voice in Early Modern Europe. Edited and translated by Margaret L. King and Diana Robin. Chicago and London: University of Chicago Press, 2003.

O'Malley, Susan Gushee, ed. *Defences of Women: Jane Anger, Rachel Speght, Ester Sowernam, and Constantia Munda.* The Early Modern Englishwoman, Part 1, Printed Writings, 1500–1640. Vol. 4. Aldershot, UK: Scholars Press; Brookfield, VT: Ashgate, 1996.

Pizan, Christine de. *The Book of the City of Ladies.* Translated by Earl Jeffrey Richards. New York: Persea Books, 1982.

Secondary Works

Benson, Pamela Joseph. *The Invention of the Renaissance Woman: The Challenge of Female Independence in the Literature and Thought of Italy and England.* University Park: Pennsylvania State University Press, 1992.

Fenster, Thelma, and Clare A. Lees, eds. *Gender in Debate from the Early Middle Ages to the Renaissance.* The New Middle Ages. New York: Palgrave, 2002.

Jones, Ann Rosalind. "Counterattacks on 'the Bayter of Women': Three Pamphleteers of the Early Seventeenth Century." In *The Renaissance*

Englishwoman in Print: Counterbalancing the Canon. Edited by Anne M. Haselkorn and Betty S. Travitsky. Amherst: University of Massachusetts Press, 1990.

Jordan, Constance. *Renaissance Feminism: Literary Texts and Political Models.* Ithaca, NY: Cornell University Press, 1990.

Larsen, Anne R. "Paradox and the Praise of Women: From Ortensio Lando and Charles Estienne to Marie de Romieu." *Sixteenth Century Journal* 28 (1997). 759–774.

Malcolmson, Cristina, and Mihoko Suzuki, eds. *Debating Gender in Early Modern England, 1500–1700.* New York: Palgrave Macmillan, 2002.

Mclean, Ian. *Woman Triumphant: Feminism in French Literature, 1610–1652.* Oxford: Clarendon Press, 1977.

Woodbridge, Linda. *Women and the English Renaissance: Literature and the Nature of Womankind, 1540–1620.* Urbana: University of Illinois Press, 1984.

R

Rape and Violence Against Women

Women of the Renaissance experienced violence in virtually all of their roles and vocations, across all socioeconomic classes, and at all ages. Forms of violence were many and varied, occurring in domestic, social, and political arenas, and they ranged from murder, rape, and incest to beatings, whippings, and other forms of torture. Domestic punishments were most common. While frowned upon, especially by Protestant ministers, wife beating was legal in England, France, and Italy; husbands could batter wives with impunity. Likewise, though parents and teachers were advised to use some restraint, the physical "correction" of girls was believed to be a critical component of education. Employers could and did beat their servants (many of whom were female) for insubordination or disobedience. Rape and violence against women were portrayed in a staggering number of stories, plays, and poems, indicating the culture's fascination with such matters.

Though it was a felony, rape was underreported, underprosecuted, and underpenalized. In England rapes represented less than 1 percent of criminal indictments. Rape accusations and convictions decreased for several reasons as the period progressed. First, in accordance with beliefs that female orgasm was essential for conception, if a raped woman became pregnant, her condition seemed to indicate that she had consented to the crime. Second, as legally defined, rape required penile penetration, which was very hard to prove; judges dismissed rape cases where bloodstains or torn clothing were unconvincing or lacking. Third, accusers, seen as revengeful or opportunistic, were open to charges of slander and other reprisals. Fourth, rape victims had to report graphic details before all-male officials, an act that was itself perceived as shameful. Fifth, it cost time and money to travel to court to testify against a culprit who was unlikely to be convicted.

Whereas in the Middle Ages rape was considered a crime against family property, in the Renaissance it began to be regarded as a personal crime. This shift resulted in an emphasis on the victim's consent, making it more likely that women from the laboring classes would bring up charges. But the focus on consent was sometimes beneficial for rapists in that it created the pregnancy loophole and gave the accused room to claim that consent had been granted. It also meant that, despite strict laws, rape began to be treated as a relatively minor crime.

Though rape was a capital crime, convicted rapists were most likely to be fined or briefly imprisoned, especially if the victim was a servant, a laborer, or without a family. In Venice, the median penalty for a rape was six months in jail or a fine of one hundred lire. The penalties were heavier if the rapist drew blood; if abduction, robbery, or breaking and entering also occurred; or if the victim was prepubescent (virginal) or wealthy. Rapists of young girls tended to receive harsh penalties, but if the victim had passed through puberty, the sentence was mild. Punishments for rape and attempted rape tended to be similar, indicating that the crime was not so much in the completion of the act but in the violence of it. Rapes and attempted rapes of married women were punished more severely, possibly because the word of a married woman, who had little to gain from accusing a man of rape, was taken more seriously than that of unmarried ones. Single women were sometimes encouraged to marry their rapists; in other cases, a portion of the fine was allocated for the victim's dowry.

A 1576 statute in England denied the benefit of clergy for convicted rapists. Before the statute, rapists could read some lines of Scripture and receive a branding rather than death by hanging. In closing one legal loophole, the statute opened another; it made the rape of a girl under the age of ten a felony, whether she consented or not. This had the auxiliary effect of reducing the age of consent from twelve to ten. The courts tended to doubt the rape accusations of children younger than seven, possibly because they believed penetration impossible in girls so young. Reports of incest, which presupposed intercourse, were rare; more frequent were cases of "incestuous abuse" (Ingram 2001, 64). Because of their vulnerability to masters, stepfathers, neighbors, bawds, workmen, and customers, a large number of girls under the age of sixteen were raped, and the consequences were grave. Victims often contracted infections. The abuse of a child would come to light when she had trouble urinating or walking or when there was a noxious discharge. The girls themselves were often blamed and had to endure subsequent physical chastisement from their parents.

Rape occurred most often to females of the laboring classes who had little protection from their employers and fellow workers. In France, gang rape appears to have been more common than in England and Italy; in fourteenth-century Dijon, 80 percent of rapes were group attacks. In Italy, rapes of servants and slaves by their employers were most frequent. Among the aristocracy, rape prosecutions were rare, and, because of the wealth and power of high-born rapists, generally there were no concomitant crimes of breaking and entering or robbery, which meant that penalties were light.

The rape of nuns was often prosecuted as fornication rather than rape, the assumption being that they had desired and invited the attention. Though they tended to be of the nobility, nuns were less valuable than heiresses, and so the penalties for raping them varied. In France, it was reported that, in various uprisings, the Huguenots invaded the convents and raped nuns.

Rape, of course, was only one form of violence against women. Girls vulnerable to rapists were also vulnerable to beatings, and, because of the imbalance of power between husbands and wives, parents and children, employers and servants, physical harm was common. Men were thought to be violent by nature, and, because most carried some form of weapon, their aggression could easily become deadly.

Criminalized women endured particular kinds of violence. Scolds (shrews), especially repeat offenders, were sometimes forced to wear painful bridles; they could be whipped or dunked into water, a practice called "cucking." Prostitutes could have their ears cut off or noses slit. For other crimes such as the watering of ale, women could be sentenced to the "thew," a pillory for women to which they were attached by a neck ring. Women convicted of capital crimes such as murder, heresy, and witchcraft could be buried alive, burned, drowned, or hanged. Tortures such as whippings and "prickings" were used to extract confessions from accused witches. Given the large number of witch executions, especially in France, it is likely that more witches than rapists were punished with death in this period.

Sid Ray

See also Courtesans and Prostitution, Italy; Gentileschi, Artemisia; Morra, Isabella di; Religious Persecution and Women; Witches, Witchcraft, and Witch-Hunting.

Bibliography

Bashar, Nazife. "Rape in England between 1550 and 1700." In *Sexual Dynamics of History.* Edited by London Feminist History Group, 28–42. London: Pluto Press, 1983.

Ingram, Martin. "Child Sexual Abuse in Early Modern England." In *Negotiating Power in Early Modern Society: Order, Hierarchy and Subordination in Britain and Ireland.* Edited by Michael J. Braddick and John Walter. Cambridge: Cambridge University Press, 2001.

Rossiaud, Jacques. *Medieval Prostitution.* Translated by Lydia G. Cochrane. London: Blackwell, 1988.

Ruggiero, Guido. *Violence in Early Renaissance Venice.* New Brunswick, NJ: Rutgers University Press, 1980.

Walker, Garthine. "Reading Rape and Sexual Violence in Early Modern England." *Gender and History* 10:1 (April 1998): 1–25.

Religious Persecution and Women

In the sixteenth century, as shock waves from the Reformation rocked the established church not only in Germany and the Netherlands but also in France, England, and Italy, officials strove to maintain doctrinal purity, whether Catholic or Protestant. Increasingly they targeted women, often repeating Saint Jerome's dictum that women tended to be the first to spread heresy.

As England underwent its dynastic swings between Catholicism and Protestantism, women of both faiths suffered for their beliefs. During the reign of Henry VIII, Anne Askew's refusal to acknowledge the doctrine of transubstantiation led to her arrest. During her imprisonment, she was tortured on the rack. Refusing to recant, she was burned for her beliefs. With the return to Catholicism under Mary I, many Protestant women, holding strongly to their religious faith, refused to worship as Catholics. Of the nearly three hundred people executed for their beliefs in the reign of Mary I, approximately one-fifth were women; however, not all women arrested for their religious beliefs under Mary were martyred. In 1558, officials arrested Elizabeth Young for smuggling Protestant literature into England. After enduring many interrogations, in which she was called a whore and accused of being a priest's concubine, Elizabeth was temporarily released to care for her children, and, fortunately for her, Mary soon died and was succeeded by her Protestant half sister. During the reign of Queen Elizabeth, several Catholic women were arrested and executed. For refusing to plead guilty or not guilty, Margaret Clitherow was pressed to death with stones. Margaret Ward, who sheltered a priest, refused to recant and receive the queen's pardon; she was executed.

There were conflict and violence in France as well. As John Calvin's writings and teachings were disseminated, a Protestant minority established itself in the largely Catholic country. Calvin actively formed relationships with many French noblewomen who either converted or displayed Calvinistic leanings. In 1557, a Calvinist communion service was forcibly invaded, and twenty-two women were arrested. Philippe de Luns, one of the arrested women, was imprisoned, tortured, and executed; she was one of the first female French martyrs. Madelein Mailly, comtesse de Roye, converted to Calvinism and tried to influence Queen Catherine de Médicis. Imprisoned by the court's Catholic party, she was later released and in 1563 helped negotiate a peace treaty to end the first French war of religion. Not all adherents to Calvinism were noblewomen, and Jean Crespin recorded their stories in his *History of True Testimonies.* Marguerite Le Riche, a wife of a Parisian bookseller, refused to attend mass and was arrested, interrogated, and burned.

In the Catholic strongholds of Italy and Spain, fewer women were arrested for holding explicitly Protestant beliefs than in England and France. Before the Inquisition was officially instituted in Italy by Pope Paul III in 1542, fewer than 5 percent of the women were accused of "Lutheranism." However, some Italian women were charged with heresy. Franceschina, the wife of a silk weaver, was charged with having visited various Catholic churches in Venice and having ripped the rosary beads out of women's hands. The tailoress Caterina was also brought before the Inquisition for heretical leanings: she had, it was alleged, discussed the writings of Saint Paul with men, and she had denigrated journeymen who followed Catholic ritual as ignorant or mad. In Spain, few women were arrested for Protestant beliefs since the country was more concerned with its *converso* Christians, or Christians with Muslim or Jewish heritage.

As society was torn apart and reconfigured during the time of the Reformation and Counter-Reformation, brave women of all faiths clung to their beliefs. Many refused to recant, even when faced with imprisonment, torture, or death. Women chose and witnessed about their faith, even to the point of martyrdom.

Kory Bajus

See also Religious Reform and Women.

Bibliography
Primary Work
Foxe, John. *Acts and Monuments of Matters Most Special and Memorable. . . .* London: Printed for the Company of Stationers, 1648.
Secondary Works
Crawford, Patricia. *Women and Religion in England, 1500–1720.* London and New York: Routledge, 1996.
Davis, Natalie Zemon. "City Women and Religious Change." *Society and Culture in Early Modern France.* Stanford, CA: Stanford University Press, 1975.
Giles, Mary E., ed. *Women in the Inquisition: Spain and the New World.* Baltimore, MD: Johns Hopkins University Press, 1999.
Greaves, Richard L., ed. *Triumph over Silence: Women in Protestant History.* Westport, CT: Greenwood Press, 1985.
Snyder, C. Arnold, and Linda A. Huebert Hecht. *Profiles of Anabaptist Women: Sixteenth-Century Reforming Pioneers.* Waterloo, ON: Wilfrid Lauier University Press, 1996.

Religious Reform and Women
Overview

As we look back on it, the sixteenth century seems to have been brimming with religious ferment, in clear contrast to the "secularization" of the papacy that in the previous century had worked to reinforce papal authority, both spiritual and temporal. Political and institutional conflicts between certain states and the church heightened tension between traditional religion and the new piety of the *devozio moderna* that developed out of a cultivated, predominantly secular humanism and led to a radicalization of ideas among the more alert cultural and religious leaders. Demand for reform of the church in Europe was supported by a number of social groups that were slowly moving away from Catholicism and embracing the Protestant Reformation, although in varying degree.

Women were present in this movement on several levels: as wives, mothers, and sisters who accepted and professed the new faith within the family, or as promoters and supporters of individual reformers or reform-minded groups. Obviously, a historical description of many women's participation in the Reformation presents difficulties. Accusations of Protestant tendencies in inquisitorial denunciations and the records of trials that often took place well after the deaths of the accused require careful evaluation. In distinguishing between membership in a Reform-minded "spiritual" group and in one of the groups that remained within the sphere of Catholic renewal, analogies are often neglected. The religious thought of both groups was rooted in Scripture, in particular in the reading of and meditating on the Epistles of St. Paul, and a full acceptance of a Reformed confession occurred gradually over time as doctrine became better defined on either side.

Eight subheadings follow: Forms of Religious Dissent; Women's Participation in the Religious Reform Movements; International Connections Among Religious Reform Activists; The Courts: An Arena for Reform Ideas; Naples, Valdesian Reform Thought, and Women; Women as Patrons of Religious Reform in Italy; The Reform Movement in France; The Reformation and Resistance in England.

Forms of Religious Dissent

Within a widespread sympathy for and an interest in a purified, evangelical religion, explicit acceptance of one or another of the Reformed confessions was expressed either by fleeing the homeland or by an implicit repudiation of Catholicism in words or deeds. When Emilia

Pio, the wife of Antonio da Montefeltro, refused the sacraments at the point of death in 1528, her refusal could be taken as a sign of detachment from the religion of the Roman papacy, held responsible for the ills that had befallen the duchy of Urbino, but it might also be explained by the sympathy that many Italian aristocrats, after the Sack of Rome, displayed toward a new doctrine that violently attacked papal authority. Nonparticipation in the sacraments and in religious ceremonies became the most common way for aristocrats—as well as ordinary people and members of the middle class—to manifest their sympathy toward the new religious confessions. Calvin's theorization of the legitimacy of Nicodemite practices makes it more difficult to prove historically the adhesion of persons or groups to the Protestant Reformation. When historians, in the absence of concrete testimony or documentary proof, appeal to Nicodemite practices, the explanation can seem arbitrary. Moreover, in the pre-Tridentine period there was no genuine definition of the Catholic confession, and many apparently ambiguous attitudes were common to "spirituals" of a variety of tendencies.

Women's Participation in the Religious Reform Movements

Women's participation in movements for religious reform in Italy and throughout Europe has been studied in two perspectives. In the first, Roland Bainton pointed in the direction of biographical investigation in the aim of creating a gallery of portraits of the women who had opted for the Reformation or displayed strong sympathies for it. In the second, Natalie Zemon Davis, adopting a more sociological viewpoint, asked whether religious change had favored social as well as religious change and which segments of society had joined the Reformed camp with the greatest enthusiasm. Davis also investigates what women lost or gained in terms of liberty and privileges in their shift from Catholicism to Protestantism. Her

answer, as far as the women of Lyons were concerned, is dual: they gained the ability to read and interpret Scripture along with their husbands and on a par with them, but they excluded themselves from a managerial role in the female communities devoted to contemplation or social assistance that provided Catholic women a way to counterbalance women's all-devouring role in the family. This duality seems to have been decisive as women weighed the advantages and disadvantages of joining a Reformed confession.

International Connections Among Religious Reform Activists

A brief survey of the women who embraced a Reformed religion in Italy and in Europe shows widespread support of the new ideas, but also international connections. The women who are best-known and have most often been studied are aristocrats or women with court connections. Among these are Olympia Morata and Isabella Bresegna, the only two Italian women who left their homeland to profess their new religion freely. But there were also merchants' wives who became acquainted with innovative ideas that their husbands had brought back to Italy, along with books printed in German lands, and who sometimes, after organizing domestic churches in their native cities, emigrated with their husbands to imperial lands or kingdoms bordering Italy. The wives of two Florentine merchants, Gismondo Pucci and Bartolomeo Panciatichi, are known to have supported the Reformation. Equally well-known is the case of entire families from Lucca—the Balbani, Burlamacchi, Arnolfini, and Diodati families—who transferred to Geneva. By the mid-sixteenth century, there were also women among the common people who began to question indulgences and purgatory or debate free will and justification by faith alone, as attested in city chronicles and surviving trial records. Even some nuns—the Poor Clares of Udine, for example—were not immune to

the fascination of the new doctrines after reading books introduced into the cloister by relatives or itinerant booksellers. Others, like the
Poor Clares of Reggio Emilia, absorbed some of
the principles of the evangelical religion or of
utopian religious thought from the sermons of
preachers or visionaries who had access to the
convents, or else from certain of the laity, such as
Basilio Albrisio, the convent's physician.

The Courts: An Arena
for Reform Ideas

An appeal to a purer religion, based on the
reading of the Holy Gospel and accentuating
salvation through Jesus' sacrifice on the cross
and God's mercy, first found a reception in the
cultivated atmosphere of the princely courts
and in intellectual circles that gathered around
high-born females, women accustomed to
conversing with humanists, poets, and men of
letters, but also with princes and cardinals, all
of whom belonged to the leading ruling
houses or the urban patriciate. The centers of
most intense penetration of ideas from north
of the Alps were the Milan area, the Valtellina,
and Venice and the other cities of the Most
Serene Republic. Naples, on the other hand,
was influenced by Erasmian tendencies tinged
with an *alumbrado* mysticism that came directly
from Spain. In north central Italy, one of the
major poles of attraction was Ferrara and the
court of Renée of France, the daughter of
Louis XII of Valois, who, as a woman, was excluded from succession to the French throne
by Salic Law and whose sister, Claude de
France, was the wife of Francis I. After Renée's
marriage to Ercole II d'Este, the son of Alfonso
I and Lucrezia Borgia, in France in June 1528,
the couple returned to the Po Valley duchy.
Since the new duchess spoke no Italian, for
some time she surrounded herself with a court
of French ladies. In 1534 she offered hospitality to a number of French exiles, among them
the poet Clément Marot, who was already suspected of sympathies for the Reformed cause.
At a later date Calvin himself visited her court.

Her entourage included such famous Ferrarese
intellectuals as Pellegrino Morato and Celio
Secondo Curione, respectively the father and
the tutor of Olympia Morata, both of whom
openly embraced the Reformation. Olympia
herself, who was well-known as an accomplished Greek and Latin scholar, married a
German and emigrated to Germany. After her
death Curione published her works, which included a vast collection of letters. Renée de
France had strong sympathies for the Calvinist
religion, and she protected Italians and French
people accused of heresy. She brought up her
daughters in the new religion, but her high social position prevented her from openly embracing Calvinism: in fact, in 1554 she was
forced to pronounce something resembling an
abjuration and to participate in the sacraments
of confession and communion. After the death
of her husband in 1559, she returned to
France, where she found herself in the thick of
the wars that history knows as the Wars of Religion, conflicts in which her own daughters
and her kin, whose families had joined the
ranks of the high aristocracy, took an active
part.

Naples, Valdesian Reform
Thought, and Women

If the court of Ferrara was a gathering place
for free spirits with Calvinist leanings, in the
city of Naples religious dissent was expressed
in the form of a spiritualistic religion with Reform leanings among a circle of humanists and
noblewomen gathered around Juan de Valdés, a
Spaniard and the author of a number of brief
spiritual works. Between 1531 and 1541 Valdés
lived in a villa between Rome and Naples,
where he often received others who hoped for
a religious life inspired by the knowledge of
and meditation on the Holy Scriptures and
who yearned for a reform of the church accompanied by a purification of exterior ceremonies and superstitions. Valdés's primary and
most dedicated disciple was Giulia Gonzaga,
the beautiful duchess of Fondi, a twenty-two-

year-old widow condemned to chastity by her husband's will, which stipulated that his wife would enjoy his vast patrimony only if and as long as she did not remarry. Giulia Gonzaga was at first struck by the vehement preaching of Bernardino Ochino, a Capuchin friar, but soon turned to the gentler spiritual direction of Valdés, who dedicated his catechetical dialogue, *Alfabeto cristiano,* to her and who guided her on the path to a faith founded on trust in the love of Christ crucified and the illumination of the Holy Spirit. Other women followed Valdés's teachings, among them Isabella Bresegna, who was Spanish and married to a Spanish nobleman who later became governor of Piacenza. Probably Caterina Cibo Varano and Vittoria Colonna also knew Valdés, although we do not yet have proof of their meeting. After Valdés's death, Giulia Gonzaga and those same noblewomen chose as their spiritual guide a young and high-born English prelate, Reginald Pole, later the papal legate at Viterbo. Pole welcomed into his circle intellectuals, members of the papal court, friars, priests, but also in a reform of the Church of Rome that might be open to some aspects of the new Protestantisms of northern Europe. The doctrinal orientation of Pole's group, whose members historians designate somewhat generically as *spirituali,* were reflected in a book that enjoyed great popularity in Italy, *Il beneficio di Cristo.* This work, which became the manifesto of religious dissent in Italy because it promoted the doctrine of salvation by faith alone, was written by the Cassino Benedictine Benedetto Fontanini and revised by the humanist Marcantonio Flaminio. It was placed on the Index of Forbidden Books and all known copies were destroyed.

How was religious dissent articulated by noblewomen who followed the teachings of Valdés and Pole and who aspired to a reform of the church that in ways would make it significantly different from the church of Rome? Among the women who have been mentioned, only Isabella Bresegna spoke openly in favor of the Protestant Reformation. In 1548, when her husband was transferred to Piacenza, she became a friend of Isabella di Capua, the wife of Ferrante Gonzaga, the governor of Milan. In 1557 Ferrante was accused of plotting against the Spanish rulers of Milan and fell into disgrace, thus casting suspicion on Bresegna. After taking careful measures to safeguard the administration of the family fortune and assure her children's well-being, Isabella moved to the Lutheran city of Tübingen, where she was welcomed by Paolo Vergerio, the former bishop of Capodistria. Resisting appeals from her husband and her children to return home, she then moved on, first to Zurich, then to Chiavenna, where she attracted many Italian exiles to her home. Celio Secondo Curione dedicated the first edition of the works of Olympia Morata to her.

Women as Patrons of Religious Reform in Italy

The other women who had frequented Valdesian circles in Naples and were part of the Viterbo coterie never openly opted for the Reformed religion: instead they acted as patrons to preachers and spiritually minded men who embraced the Reformation—the Cappuchin friar Bernardino Ochino, for example—and extended friendship and moral support to religious and prelates such as the protonotary Pietro Carnesecchi and Cardinal Giovanni Morone, both of whom were later accused of heresy. Caterina Cibo and Vittoria Colonna also offered support to Ochino and assiduously attended his sermons. Giulia Gonzaga was a genuine friend of Carnesecchi's, to the point that Pope Pius V, who sentenced the Florentine protonotary to death, declared that she would have been condemned as well if she had not died before Carnesecchi. Not only did these noblewomen protect religious figures accused of heresy, they worked to proselytize their beliefs by opening their houses and their salons to intellectual circles interested in problems of the faith and the reform of the church.

The Reform Movement in France

In the first half of the sixteenth century, the religious context in which French noblewomen sensitive to the problem of church reform moved was not markedly different from that of their Italian counterparts. Very often, ties of kinship and friendship encouraged similar aspirations and sentiments in the two groups. Marguerite d'Angoulême (Marguerite, queen of Navarre), a sister of Francis I and related to Renée de Valois, acted as godmother to Guillaume Briçonnet, the bishop of Meaux, in his experiment in religious reform. Some groups in Italy (the followers of Savonarola and the Este, for example), who were working for a renewal of the church linked to the politics of the king of France, viewed Briçonnet as an "angelic pastor," and he had enjoyed a certain fame in Italy in the period of the French occupation of Milan (1512–1525). Famous French humanists interested in a renewal of the faith gathered in Meaux. One of these was Jacques Lefèvre d'Étaples, the translator of the Bible into French. Perhaps thanks more to the generation in which she was born than for political reasons, Marguerite never openly abandoned the Catholic religion, even though she wrote verse clearly inspired by Reformed thought. She used her influential position to welcome and protect preachers and writers who had left France after the Sorbonne condemned their works. Her daughter, Jeanne d'Albret, princess of Navarre, openly professed the Calvinist religion, however. By 1560, when Jeanne converted, perhaps under the influence of the fervent preaching of Théodore de Bèze, the political and religious situation in France had changed radically. The imminent threat of the Wars of Religion had obliged the nobles of the kingdom to join the party of one religious confession or the other. Although proselytism among the gentlewomen of France might have been encouraged by didactic printed works and by Georgette de Montenay's refined collections of emblems, it was more likely the long and bloody wars, interrupted by pauses filled with ambushes and massacres, that forced aristocrats to take a stand.

The Reformation and Resistance in England

The subjects of the king of England faced a situation quite different from that of Italian and French women who opted, more or less openly, for religious reform. The English had to adapt to a sudden rupture with the established (Roman Catholic) church, which forced them to make choices that could have serious repercussions. For a few decades that were among the most portentous in European history, opting to save one's soul could mean losing one's life. It is clear that in the England of Henry VIII, as elsewhere, it was the women of the court who were the earliest and most active propagators of a religion more radical than the Anglicanism of the sovereign. From Anne Boleyn, who had been educated in France, to Catherine Parr, the kings' wives espoused a Puritanism later incorporated into the Book of Common Prayer as it was revised under Elizabeth I. Country noblewomen also became Puritans. One of these was Anne Askew, who left her husband to join Catherine Parr's ladies-in-waiting, and who professed a reformed religion. Anne Askew remained faithful to her religious ideas and to the companions who had welcomed her in their midst, accompanied her in her new faith, and stood by her as she was subjected to torture and led to the stake, clutching her Bible.

Martyrdom was the baptism of the new religion for many converts during the Protestant Reformation, but many English Catholics who refused to obey the king's decrees were executed as well. The mother of Reginald Pole, the high prelate who for a short time had aroused Italians' hopes and expectations of the advent of an angelic pastor, was among those Catholic martyrs.

Gabriella Bruna Zarri
(Translated by Lydia G. Cochrane)

See also Albret, Jeanne d'; Askew, Anne; Boleyn, Anne; Bresegna, Isabella; Cibo, Caterina; Colonna, Vittoria; Gonzaga, Giulia; Marguerite de Navarre; Parr, Katerine; Renata di Francia.

Bibliography

Adorni-Braccesi, Simonetta. " 'Una città infetta': La repubblica di Lucca nella crisi religiosa del Cinquecento." Florence: Olschki, 1994.

Bainton, Roland H. *Donne della Riforma in Germania, in Italia e in Francia.* With an introduction, "Per la storia delle donne nella Riforma," by Susanna Peyronel Rambaldi. Turin: Claudiana, 1992.

Bainton, Roland H. *Women of the Reformation in France and England.* Minneapolis, MN: Augsburg Publishing House, 1973.

Bainton, Roland H. *Women of the Reformation in Germany and Italy.* Minneapolis, MN: Augsburg Publishing House, 1971.

Beilin, Elaine V., ed. *The Examinations of Anne Askew.* Women Writers in English, 1350–1850. New York and Oxford: Oxford University Press, 1996.

Biondi, Albano, and Adriano Prosperi. "Il processo al medico Basilio Albrisio, Reggio 1559." *Contributi* 2, no. 4 (1978).

Caponetto, Salvatore. *La Riforma protestante nell'Italia del Cinquecento.* Turin: Claudiana, 1992.

Davis, Natalie Zemon. *Society and Culture in Early Modern France: Eight Essays.* Stanford, CA: Stanford University Press, 1975.

Firpo, Massimo. *Gli affreschi di Pontormo a San Lorenzo: Eresia, politica e culura nella Firenze di Cosimo I.* Turin: Einaudi, 1997.

Firpo, Massimo. *Inquisizione romana e controriforma: Studi sul Cardinal Giovanni Morone e il suo processo d'eresia.* Bologna: Il Mulino, 1992.

Firpo, Massimo. *Tra alumbrados e "spirituali": Studi su Juan de Valdés e il valdesianesimo nella crisi religiosa del '500 italiano.* Florence: Olschki, 1990.

Firpo, Massimo, and Dario Marcatto, eds. *Il processo inquisitoriale dl cardinal Giovanni Morone: Edizione critica.* 6 vols. Rome: Istituto storico italiano per l'età moderna e contemporanea, 1981–1995.

Fragnito, Gigliola. "Vittoria Colonna e il dissenso religioso." In *Vittoria Colonna e Michelangelo.* Catalog of an exhibition. Edited by Pina Ragionieri, 97–105. Florence: Mandragora, 2005.

Gregory, Brad S. *Salvation at Stake: Christian Martyrdom in Early Modern Europe.* Harvard Historical Studies, 132. Cambridge, MA, and London: Harvard University Press, 1999.

Grieco, Sara Matthews. "Georgette de Montenay: A Different Voice in Sixteenth Century Emblematics." *Renaissance Quarterly* 4 (1994): 283–370.

Marshall, Sherrin, ed. *Women in Reformation and Counter-Reformation Europe: Public and Private Worlds.* Bloomington: Indiana University Press, 1989.

On Isabella Bresegna, Caterina Cibo, Vittoria Colonna, and Giulia Gonzaga, *see* entries under their names in *Dizionario Biografico degli Italiani.* Rome: Istituto dell'Enciclopedia italiana.

Paolin, Giovanna. "L'eterodossia nel monastero delle Clarisse di Udine nella seconda metà del '500." *Collectanea franciscana* 50 (1980): 107–167.

Peters, Christine. *Patterns of Piety: Women, Gender and Religion in Late Medieval and Reformation England.* Cambridge and New York: Cambridge University Press, 2003.

Peyronel Rambaldi, Susanna. "Olimpia Morata e Celio Secondo Curione: Un dialogo dell'Umanesimo cristiano." In *La formazione storica della alterità: Studi di storia della tolleranza nell'età moderna offerti a Antonio Rotondò.* 3 vols. Organized by Henry Méchoulan, Richard H. Popkin, Giuseppe Ricuperati, and Luisa Simonutti. Vol. 1, *Secolo 16,* 93–133. Florence: Olschki, 2001.

Prosperi, Adriano. *L'eresia del Libro grande: Storia di Giorgio Siculo e della sua setta.* Milan: Feltrinelli, 2000.

Roelker, Nancy L. *Queen of Navarre: Jeanne d'Albret, 1528–1572.* Cambridge, MA: Belknap Press of Harvard University Press, 1968.

Roelkher, Nancy L. "The Role of Noblewomen in the French Reformation." *Archiv für Reformationsgeschichte* 48 (1972): 168–195.

Seidel Menchi, Silvana. *Erasmo in Italia, 1520–1580.* Turin: Bollati Boringhieri, 1987.

Wandel, Lee Palmer, ed. *History Has Many Voices.* Kirksville, MO: Truman State University Press, 2003.

Zahl, Paul F. M. *Five Women of the English Reformation.* Grand Rapids, MI: William B. Eerdmans, 2001.

Renata di Francia (Renée de France, 1510–1574)

Duchess of Ferrara, daughter of the king of France, leader of the evangelical circle at the Este court, friend and patron of John Calvin

Born in France to Louis XII and Anne of Brittany, sister-in-law of King Francis I, Renée de France married Ercole II d'Este, duke of Ferrara in 1528, becoming Renata di Francia. Arriving in Ferrara with all the prestige of a daughter of the king of France, Renata made the Este court a destination for artists, poets, and philosophers and a sanctuary for reform thinkers in the 1530s and 1540s. Encouraged by her older cousin and mentor, Marguerite de Navarre, who had supervised her religious education at the French court, Renata entertained her countryman John Calvin at the Este castle in the summer of 1536. Under the duchess's tutelage, Calvin's opus magnum, the *Institutes of the Christian Religion,* circulated at the Este court in two Latin editions (1536, 1539) and in 1541 in French. From the late 1530s on, the duchess gathered around her a circle of men and women who met regularly to discuss Scripture and translations of the Bible. Among the women who attended were the duchess's two daughters, Anna and Lucrezia, Giulia Gonzaga's protégée Isabella Bresegna, and the poet and reform thinker Vittoria Colonna, who had traveled from Rome to Ferrara and remained at Renata's court for several months in 1537–1538. The charismatic evangelical Bernardino Ochino was also preaching in the cathedral in Ferrara at the time.

Renata's friends and religious reformist activities deeply disturbed Duke Ercole, who was a devout Catholic. The duchess had instituted a reform salon that operated within the auspices of the Este court yet was not sanctioned by the duke. Books prohibited by the church as Protestant circulated freely at the Este court, and men and women the Catholic church would soon condemn as heretics were shown hospitality and welcomed by Renata, among them the professor and published poet Celio Secondo Curione and the writer Olympia Morata, both of whom subsequently fled Italy, the former to Switzerland and the latter to Germany. As if to stem the Protestant influence, Ercole at first expelled Renata's gov-

Renata di Francia, duchess of Ferrara and religious reform leader. Drawing by studio of Clouet. Musee Conde, Chantilly, France. (Giraudon/The Bridgeman Art Library)

erness, Michelle de Soubise, and then her secretary, Clément Marot, from the court, sending both back to France. In 1554, however, the duke confined Renata to the ducal palace and forced her to renounce her evangelical beliefs. Nonetheless, Renata continued to correspond with Calvin until his death, and, when Duke Ercole died in 1559, she returned to her birthplace in Montargis, France, where she lived the rest of her life as a Protestant, though not without turmoil since her daughter Anne's husband Francis of Guise sacked her castle at Montargis during the French Wars of Religion.

Diana Robin

See also Anne of Brittany; Bresegna, Isabella; Colonna, Vittoria; Gonzaga, Guilia; Marguerite de Navarre; Morata, Fulvia Olympia; Religious Reform and Women.

Bibliography

Bainton, Roland H. *Women of the Reformation in Germany and Italy.* Minneapolis, MN: Augsburg Publishing, 1971.

Baumgartner, Frederic J. "Renée of Ferrara." In *Encyclopedia of the Renaissance.* Edited by Paul F. Grendler. New York: Charles Scribner's Sons, 1999.

Caponetto, Salvatore. *The Protestant Reformation in Sixteenth-Century Italy.* Translated by Anne C. Tedeschi and John Tedeschi. Kirksville, MO: Truman State University Press, 1998.

Robin, Diana. *Publishing Women: Salons, the Presses, and the Counter-Reformation in Sixteenth-Century Italy.* Chicago: University of Chicago Press, 2007.

Rhetoric, Public Speaking, and Women

In Renaissance Europe, rhetoric—the art of persuasion—was the foundation of humanist education. Early modern women were generally excluded from training in classical rhetoric, oratory, and the art of public speaking. They had no need of such knowledge, it was argued, since they were forbidden to stand for public office; they could not hold appointments as professors or lecturers at universities; and they were not permitted to preach in the churches. If women were given a humanist education, they were trained in reading, writing, and ancient and modern languages; they were not expected to perform as orators.

Despite cultural prohibitions, some women did study rhetoric and the principles of oratory. Women destined to be rulers (such as Queen Elizabeth I of England) or brides of rulers (such as Mary Stuart, who married the French Dauphin) were schooled in rhetoric; their social roles as public figures outweighed the restrictions of gender. As a young girl at the French court, Mary Stuart (who became Mary, Queen of Scots) even gave a public oration defending rhetorical education for women.

Other women of the merchant and professional classes acquired some knowledge of rhetoric because their class status provided them leisure for study, because they worked with their brothers' tutors, and because their parents valued humanist education for women

as well as men. The female professor of rhetoric, Beatriz Galindo of Salamanca, taught Catherine of Aragon, the Spanish princess who became the wife of Henry VIII of England. The Italian Laura Cereta learned Latin at a convent, participated in humanist debates in Brescia, and perhaps lectured at literary salons. In England, Sir Thomas More's daughters, the Cooke sisters (Anna and Elizabeth), and the women of the Sidney family (Mary Sidney and Mary Wroth) received training in classical rhetoric.

In addition, many women writers used their training in rhetoric to defend women in pamphlet debates or to argue for the extension of humanist rhetorical education to women. Catherine des Roches wrote a defense of women's education, *Dialogues de placide et sévère* (1583), which nonetheless circumscribed women's learning within the bounds of feminine modesty. In *The Nobility and Excellence of Women* (1601), Lucrezia Marinella defended women in the Italian debate about women, basing her argument on rhetorical commonplaces, arguing for women's worth through the etymology of woman, woman's nature and essence, the causes of women's worth, women's actions and virtues, and the refutation of men who cast blame on women. Following the example of the renowned Dutch polymath Anna Maria van Schurmann, who wrote a defense of women's education in Latin, Bathsua Makin publicized the lives of ancient female orators, praising them as models for contemporary women in her *Essay to Revive the Antient Education of Gentlewomen* (1673).

Certainly many early modern women demonstrate the influence of classical rhetoric. The Venetian scholar Cassandra Fedele, who was taught Latin and Greek by the Servite friar Gasparino Borro, circulated her humanist letter book in manuscript, published an oration, and even delivered public Latin orations, one of them at the University of Padua. In *Jane Anger, Her Protection for Women* (1589), Anger employs an erudite rhetoric, elaborating her argument through copious amplification as recommended by Erasmus, using examples (Hiliogabalus, Chilperic, and Xerxes for unrestrained lust in men), comparisons (God made men out of "filthy clay" but women out of "man's flesh"), opposites ("Our good toward them is the destruction of ourselves"), and metaphor ("our body is a footstool to their vile lusts"). In *Les Femmes illustres* (1642) and in four volumes of *Conversations* (in the 1680s), Madeleine de Scudéry offered model speeches and conversations featuring women speakers, adapting concepts of classical rhetoric to salon conversation and letter writing. In *The Worlds Olio* (1655), a collection of short essays, Margaret Cavendish discussed women's and men's speech, conversation, the physiology of speech, and eloquence. In her *Orations* (1662), Cavendish presented sample speeches by male speakers on public political topics and by women speakers on "The Woman Question" (also known as the *Querelle des Femmes*), a topos that had become ubiquitous in European letters by the middle of the sixteenth century.

Another source of rhetorical influence on women during the Reformation and Counter-Reformation was biblical and sermon rhetoric. Employing a biblical style and citations to Scripture as their main means of argument, several women defended women's right to preach (at least in writing), thus entering religious debates: the German Argula von Grumbach in her 1523 letter to the divines of the University of Ingolstadt, the French Marie Dentière in her 1539 letter to Marguerite de Navarre, and the English Margaret Fell in her 1666 pamphlet defending women's preaching, and in many other Quaker pamphlets. During these centuries there were also many women preachers in the Protestant sects.

Did the study of rhetoric lead women to claim their rights? There is no consensus on the influence of humanist rhetoric in European society. Some argue that early modern rhetoric, unlike that of ancient Greece and re-

publican Rome, was adapted to the limitations of monarchy and the reinforcement of hierarchy. Others argue that the classical principles of republican rhetoric provided the Renaissance with models for participatory government and the tools to reform society. Women's rhetoric ranged across these purposes, with some women taking more conservative and some more radical positions.

Jane Donawerth

See also Education, Humanism, and Women; entries for the women mentioned in this article; Literary Culture and Women.

Bibliography

Primary Works

Anna Maria van Schurman. Edited and translated by Joyce L. Irwin, 1998.

Cassandra Fedele. Edited and translated by Diana Robin, 2000.

Isotta Nogarola. Edited and translated by Margaret L. King and Diana Robin, 2004.

King, Margaret L., and Albert Rabil, eds. The Other Voice in Early Modern Europe series. Chicago: University of Chicago Press. *See* translations of works:

Laura Cereta. Edited and translated by Diana Robin, 1997.

Lucrezia Marinella. Edited and translated by Anne Dunhill, 1999.

Madeleine de Scudéry. Edited and translated by Jane Donawerth and Julie Strongson, 2004.

Marie Le Jars de Gournay. Edited and translated by Richard Hillman and Colette Quesnel, 2002.

Tullia d'Aragona. Edited and translated by Rinaldina Russell and Bruce Merry, 1997.

Secondary Works

Donawerth, Jane, ed. *Rhetorical Theory by Women before 1900: An Anthology.* Lanham, MD: Rowman and Littlefield, 2002.

Glenn, Cheryl. *Rhetoric Retold: Regendering the Tradition from Antiquity Through the Renaissance.* Carbondale: Southern Illinois University Press, 1997.

Levin, Carole, and Patricia A. Sullivan, eds. *Political Rhetoric, Power, and Renaissance Women.* Albany: State University of New York Press, 1995.

Wertheimer, Molly Meijer, ed. *Listening to Their Voices: The Rhetorical Activities of Historical Women.* Columbia: University of South Carolina Press, 1997.

Romieu, Marie de (ca. 1545–1590)

Author and translator

The best-known and arguably most interesting works of Marie de Romieu are quasi translations of poems by Italian male authors. In keeping with the standards of her time, she translates them freely, incorporating modifications to suit her own sex, time, place, and station (which was presumably that of her audience). Romieu wrote mainly, though by no means exclusively, for women.

Marie de Romieu was born around the middle of the sixteenth century and died near its end. The uncertainty that surrounds her birth and death dates extends to other aspects of her biography as well. Exhaustive archival research in her native region, the Vivarais in eastern France, has failed to turn up any records pertaining to her and further suggests that the *de* in her name marks only geographical origin and perhaps also a desire for upward mobility rather than aristocratic forebears. In her works she speaks of a son and of the press of domestic duties, from which we can assume she was married. Poems celebrating the birth of Charles de Lorraine would likely have been written soon after that event in August 1571, at which time she was old enough to be writing poetry intended to attract the patronage of the most important noble family of the region. She had an older brother, Jacques de Romieu, secretary to the king's chamber, who declared himself her mentor. She probably shared his schooling since her poems include translations from Italian and Renaissance Neolatin poets, indicating that she could read both those languages, though competence in the former language was not unusual in a woman. Her poetry is marked by the influence of Pierre de Ronsard and Philippe Desportes, among the most important poets of her day, as well as of the ancient writers Hesiod, Ovid, and Virgil.

Inasmuch as some of her work was published, she is well ahead of the majority of her contemporaries, much of whose work circulated in manuscript, usually within a circle of friends and family. Romieu titled her published work *Premières Œuvres* (1581); the work contains short poems of praise and celebration and some love poems. In none of the fifteen love lyrics in this collection is it apparent that the writer is a woman. For this reason among others, some critics suggest that her brother might have written the poems using her name. It is just as likely that Marie de Romieu reflects poetic convention, or lending her voice, writing in place of someone else. Among her contemporaries, Guillaume Colletet defended her style as preferable to that of her brother. The *Premières Œuvres* also contains an adaptation of a translation from the Italian: *Brief Discourse: That Woman's Excellence Surpasses that of Man, As Recreative as it is Full of Fine Examples,* which is based on Charles Estienne's *Paradoxes* (1554), translating Ortensio Lando's *Paradossi*. The defense of women in the *Brief Discourse* seems heartfelt; Marie repeatedly elaborates on the claims her masculine models made on behalf of women.

L'Instruction pour les jeunes dames (Instruction for Young Ladies, 1572), based on Alessandro Piccolomini's *Dialogo della bella creanza delle donne* (Dialogue on Good Manners for Ladies, 1539), is signed *MDR* and has been generally attributed to Marie de Romieu. Systematically rejecting Piccolomini's burlesque tone and turning his protagonist, a Madam, into an apparently respectable bourgeoise, the work instructs young married women in adultery. Whether or not Romieu is its author, the *Instruction* must surely be read as a satire.

Marian Rothstein

See also Education, Humanism, and Women; Literary Culture and Women; Translation and Women Translators.

Bibliography

Primary Works

Romieu, Marie de. *Brief Discourse.* Translated by Marian Rothstein. *Writings by Pre-Revolutionary French Women.* Edited by Anne R. Larsen and

Colette H. Winn, 137–149. New York: Garland, 2000.

Romieu, Marie de. *Premières Œuvres poetiques*. Edited by André Winandy. Geneva: Droz, 1972.

Secondary Works

La Charité, Claude. "Le problème de l'attribution de *l'Instruction pour les jeunes dames* (1572) et l'énigmatique cryptonyme R.D.R." *Bibliothèque d'Humanisme et Renaissance* 62, no. 1 (2000): 119–128.

Larsen, Anne R. "Paradox and the Praise of Women: From Ortensio Lando and Charles Estienne to Marie de Romieu." *Sixteenth Century Journal* 2, no. 3 (1997): 759–774.

Roper, Margaret More (Margaret Roper, Margaret More; 1504–1544)

Humanist scholar and writer

The eldest of Sir Thomas More's children by his first wife, Jane Colt, Margaret More Roper enjoyed the fruits of her father's belief in making classical education available to both men and women. Educated with her brother, two sisters, and other dependent youth, Margaret received an early instruction at the hands of More and other tutors who shared his belief in humanist learning. In his household school, More had the children taught Latin, Greek, rhetoric, logic, mathematics, philosophy, astronomy, theology, and medicine. Margaret excelled as a student, particularly in Latin and Greek, and later as a scholar in her own right.

Margaret's abilities as a scholar gained the attention of other humanist scholars. Both Desiderius Erasmus and Juan Luis Vives, two of the most talented humanists of their day, praised Margaret and her sisters for their accomplishments in the sphere of learning. Vives's impressions of Margaret and her sisters were so favorable that when he published his *Instruction of a Christian Woman* (1523) he included them among a list of educated women from throughout history who he believed made a significant and positive difference to society. Even Henry VIII welcomed Margaret and her sisters to discuss scholarly arguments in his presence.

The formal education of sixteenth-century Englishwomen was, however, not the norm. The typical education for upper-class daughters was to learn what it took to run a household, so that they could run their future husbands' estates and leave them to duties that many believed were more within the realm of a man's world, like politics. Sir Thomas More believed a formal education, regardless of gender, would benefit a future husband and wife and sought through his daughter's education to demonstrate how successful a wife and mother she could ultimately be. Certainly, as he often reminded his daughter Margaret, More believed husbands would benefit from an educated spouse since she would be pious, humble, and a good advisor. Furthermore, their children would benefit from an educated mother's effective guidance and instruction.

Margaret More married William Roper, a member of another educated family, in 1521. Following the advice of her father, Margaret continued her studies and arranged for the humanist education of her own three daughters and two sons. During these years, Margaret also published some of her translations. In 1524, Margaret translated from Latin into English Erasmus's commentary on the Lord's Prayer, *A devout treatise upon the Pater Noster*. Margaret also wrote poetry, translated Eusebius from the Greek, and wrote many Latin letters. One of her works, which has not survived, was a treatise on the *Four Last Things*. This treatise discussed heaven, hell, death, and judgment and was, in the opinion of Sir Thomas More, better than his own rendition.

After 1532, with her father's resignation as lord chancellor due to his opposition to Henry VIII's religious and dynastic policies, Margaret, like the rest of the More family, faded from public view. During this time (1532–1535), Margaret devoted her time to her immediate family and to the situation surrounding her father, whom Henry arrested in 1534 and charged with treason for his refusal to swear to the Oath of Supremacy and thus make the pope powerless in England in spiritual matters. Thomas More remained in prison until July 1535. While there he wrote many letters, several addressed to Margaret, in which he defended his rights for obeying his conscience and not the king.

On 6 July 1535, the day of the Feast of St. Thomas, Henry VIII ordered the execution of Sir Thomas More. Margaret, always the loving and supportive daughter, along with her foster sister, Margaret Giggs Clement, oversaw the interment of More's corpse in the Chapel of St. Peter ad Vincula within the Tower grounds. Afterward, Margaret More Roper bribed a guard to receive her father's head, which she then preserved and protected until other family members later interred it in the Roper family vault in St. Dunstan's, Canterbury.

As for Margaret and the remaining More family, they found themselves watched and at times persecuted by members of Henry VIII's government. Her death in 1544 came only after she had taken to heart all that her father had trained her to be. She had become the perfect female humanist: loyal and devoted daughter, virtuous wife, educator of her children, and well-rounded scholar.

Timothy G. Elston

See also the subheadings Latin Learning and Women and Greek Learning and Women (under Education, Humanism, and Women); Religious Reform and Women.

Bibliography

King, Margaret L. *Women of the Renaissance.* Women in Culture and Society. Chicago: University of Chicago Press, 1991.

More, Sir Thomas. *The Last Letters of Thomas More.* Edited by and with an introduction by Alvaro de Silva. Grand Rapids, MI: William B. Eerdmans, 2001.

Reynolds, E. E. *Margaret Roper: Eldest Daughter of St. Thomas More.* New York: Kennedy, 1960.

Warnicke, Retha M. *Women of the English Renaissance and Reformation.* Contributions in Women's Studies, No. 38. Westport, CT: Greenwood Press, 1983.

Roye, Eléonore de (Princesse de Condé; 1535–1564)

Huguenot activist, skilled political negotiator, nursed the sick and wounded during the siege of Orléans

Eléonore de Roye was one of the Huguenot noblewomen who contributed to the establishment of Calvinism in France. Daughter of Charles, count de Roye, and Madeleine de Mailly, and wife of Louis de Bourbon, prince de Condé, she was related to prominent Catholics (Anne de Montmorency) and Huguenots (Antoine de Bourbon, Jeanne d'Albret, the Colignys) and used her network well. Eléonore's influence was particularly important when Condé was imprisoned, first as a suspect in the Conspiracy of Amboise in 1560 (Condé was accused, with other Protestant sympathizers, of plotting to kill Francis II) and subsequently in 1562–1563, after the Battle of Dreux during the first Religious War. In each case, Eléonore corresponded at length with Catherine de Médicis and rallied Condé's supporters, including Elizabeth I. In each case, Condé was freed. Catherine's and Eléonore's negotiations after the Battle of Dreux, through letters and when they met within earshot of the hostilites, led to an exchange of prisoners (Condé for Anne de Montmorency) and the Peace of Amboise.

Considered a model wife and mother, Eléonore bore eight children, nursed the sick and wounded during the siege of Orléans, travelled frequently to be with her husband, and remained faithful even when Condé's extramarital indiscretions inspired a stern letter from Calvin and Bèze (September 1563). Eléonore's death on 23 July 1564, surrounded by her children, her husband, and her mother, was recorded by a woman companion for an English friend as an example for young women in both countries.

Jane Couchman

See also Catherine de Médicis; the subheading Letter Writing (under Literary Culture and Women); Religious Reform and Women.

Bibliography

Primary Works

Delaborde, Jules. *Eléonore de Roye, princesse de Condé 1535–1564.* Paris: Sandoz and Fischbacher, 1876. (Includes examples of Eléonore's letters.)

Roye, Eléonore de. "The Translation of a letter . . . upon the death of . . . Elenor of Roye. . . ." In *Epistre d'une demoiselle françoise a une sienne amie dame estrangere, sur la mort d'excellente & vertueuse Dame Léonore de Roye, Princesse de Condé . . . .* [s.l.], 1564. Translated by Henry Myddelmore. London: John Daye, 1564.

Secondary Works

Bainton, Roland. "Eleonore de Roye." In *Women of the Reformation in France and England.* Pages 84–88. Boston: Beacon Press, 1973.

Couchman, Jane. "La vertu féminine et les relations franco-anglaises: la traduction anglaise de *l'Epistre [. . .] sur la mort d'excellente & vertueuse Dame, Léonore de Roye, Princesse de Condé.*" In *Femmes et Traduction.* Edited by Jean-Philippe Beaulieu. Ottawa: Presses de l'Université d'Ottawa, forthcoming.

S

Salons, Salonnières, and Women Writers. *See* the subheadings Virtual Salons: Women in Renaissance Dialogues; Sonnet Writing; Letter Writing; Literary Patronage (under Literary Culture and Women).

Sappho and the Sapphic Tradition

For French and English poets of the Renaissance, the Greek lyric poet Sappho (born ca. 612 BCE in the cultural center Eressos on the island of Lesbos) was the original poet of female desire as well as the original figure of same-sex female erotics. The basis of her reputation in Western culture was established by the transmission to early modern Europe of two of her poems and various fragments preserved in the works of other authors. Following the disappearance of her work during the early Christian era, the French led in the European recovery of it, when in 1566 the printer Henri Estienne published the two odes preserved by Dionysius of Halicarnassus and by "Longinus," as well as all known fragments. The French and English perpetuated her reputation during the sixteenth and seventeenth centuries by preserving and translating these poems and fragments of her work.

Sappho's poetic preeminence was made known to the Renaissance by Aristotle's comment that "Everybody honors the wise . . . and the Mytilineans honored Sappho although she was a woman" and by Plato's naming her "the Tenth Muse." While nothing whatever is known about Sappho's life, contradictory biographical fictions from antiquity to the Middle Ages perpetrated two Sapphos: a desexualized, chaste Sappho and a second polymorphously promiscuous Sappho—Sappho the poet and Sappho the whore. Ovid's tale in the *Heroides* of Sappho's love for the ferryman, Phaon, who abandoned her and on whose account she purportedly committed suicide, dominated sixteenth-century French interpretations of Sappho. But Sappho's best-known odes in the Renaissance—the *Ode to Aphrodite* and *Phainetai moi*—were recognized as early as the seventeenth century as poems addressing love and erotic relations between women. Moreover, the fiction that Sappho headed an academy or a salon for young women to whom she wrote poems and taught the lyric arts has been discredited by modern scholars as the invention of nineteenth-century German philologists (DeJean 1989; Parker 1996). Despite these ambiguities of her sexual reputation, Sappho's became the one name associated with female poetic excellence; she was the sole ancient model to whom early modern women writers might compare themselves and to whom they might be compared.

The complexities of Sappho's sexuality as they were represented in the ancient world were disseminated in England as early as the mid-sixteenth century in translations of Ovid's *Heroides* and *Tristia*. The three primary modes of representing Sappho in early modern England were (1) as a mythologized figure who acts the part of the suicidal abandoned woman in the Ovidian tale of Sappho and Phaon; (2) as the first example of female poetic excellence, most often with a disclaimer of any sexuality; and (3) as an early exemplar of "unnatural" or monstrous sexuality. Modes of representing Sappho were not always discrete but often functioned in ways that were interconnected and overlapping.

Ovid's influential defamation of Sappho in his version of the myth of Sappho and Phaon circulated throughout early modern England and Europe in numerous editions of the *Heroides*. In this work, Sappho is seduced away from both her art and her female companions by her self-destructive heterosexual obsession with Phaon and, lamenting her unrequited passion, finally ends her life by leaping to her death at sea from the White Rock of Leucas. Ovid rewrote Sappho's sexual reputation by appropriating her voice and ventriloquizing her grief in such a way that the *Heroides* provided an opportunity for misogyny: it offered a much emulated model for representing the destruction of Sappho's power as a poet/artist and reducing her to the status of a lover of women debilitated by an unrequited heterosexual passion.

Sappho's status as the first and preeminent female poet made her a model for early modern women poets. Following the French example of Madeleine de Scudéry (1607–1701), who presented herself as a second Sappho and composed her own biographical fiction of Sappho, male contemporaries referred to the English poet Katherine Philips (1632–1664) as "the new Sappho," making certain always to emphasize Philips's exemplary virtue. This encomium was later taken over by English women writers who used it among themselves, so much so that it became almost de rigueur in the commendatory poems that introduce work by, for example, the poets Anne Killigrew, Jane Barker, and Anne Finch, countess of Winchelsea, and the dramatists Delarivier Manley, Catharine Trotter, and Mary Pix. Sappho's literary reputation was well established in seventeenth-century England, though sometimes shadowed by her reputedly transgressive sexuality.

Sappho was also the most prominent exemplar of erotic behaviors between women, having been used to illustrate tribadism—the classical term for sexual relations between women. Notable is Thomas Bartholin's *Anatomical History* (1653), in which he incorporated Sappho as the embodiment of tribadism and so furnished a model for representations of transgressive female sexuality in the semipornographic medical treatises and other texts that followed in the eighteenth century. Tribades, with Sappho as their original, were regarded as "monstrous," "hateful," "wicked women," "worthily punished" for their "unnatural lusts"—a perspective that survives in some quarters even into the present.

In addition to various scholarly translations of the available—and fragmentary—corpus of Sappho's poetry, a broad range of fictions of Sappho has continued to be produced throughout Western culture. These fictions are usually motivated by the various nationalistic, political, and/or scholarly agendas operating at any particular historical moment, so that Sappho has not only continued to be the iconic female poet but the exemplary lesbian lover as well.

Harriette Andreadis

See also Killigrew, Anne; Philips, Katherine.
Bibliography
Primary Works
Barnstone, Willis, trans. *Sappho: Lyrics in the Original Greek.* New York: New York University Press, 1965.
Secondary Work
Andreadis, Harriette. *Sappho in Early Modern England: Female Same-Sex Literary Erotics, 1550–1714.* Chicago: University of Chicago Press, 2001.
DeJean, Joan. *Fictions of Sappho, 1546–1937.* Chicago: University of Chicago Press, 1989.
Greene, Ellen, ed. *Reading Sappho: Contemporary Approaches.* Berkeley: University of California Press, 1996.
Greene, Ellen, ed. *Re-Reading Sappho: Reception and Transmission.* Berkeley: University of California Press, 1996.
Parker, Holt N. "Sappho Schoolmistress." In *Re-Reading Sappho: Reception and Transmission.* Edited by Ellen Greene, 146–183. Berkeley: University of California Press, 1996.

Williamson, Margaret. *Sappho's Immortal Daughters.* Cambridge, MA: Harvard University Press, 1995.

Savoie, Louise de (1476–1531)

Queen of France, duchess of Anbouleme, mother of King Francis I of France and of Marguerite de Navarre

Louise de Savoie was born to Philip, count of Bresse, and his wife, Marguerite of Bourbon. When she lost her mother at the age of seven, Louise was sent to Amboise to be raised and educated by Anne de France. Intelligent and gifted, Louise was educated in the traditionally feminine domains of household management and Christian morality. But the lessons in court conduct that she learned at Anne's knee involved more than decorum, dress, and public demeanor. Louise was able to observe firsthand a powerful woman who effectively ruled France during the early years of the reign of her brother, Charles VIII.

At the age of twelve Louise was married to Charles de Valois, count of Angoulême, great-grandson of King Charles V of France. Louise had only a shaky grasp of Latin, but she possessed an ardent desire to read and had at her disposal her husband's impressive library. His collection included medieval classics, such as *Lancelot* and the *Romance of the Rose,* as well as Dante, Petrarch, Christine de Pizan, and Boccaccio.

Louise had two children: Marguerite, born in 1492, and Francis, born in 1494. In January 1496, when Louise was nineteen years old, her husband died. Louise never remarried; indeed, she refused a number of proposals that would have been advantageous to her. Instead, Louise devoted herself to her family, particularly to her son, Francis. He became heir presumptive to the throne of France because Anne de Bretagne had failed to produce a male child with either of her royal husbands, Charles VIII and Louis XII. While her son was still a child, Louise referred to him as her king, her lord, her Caesar.

Francis and Marguerite had a close and constant relationship with their mother, which was rare among early modern French nobility. Louise took charge of her children's education and appointed a tutor for her son. It is believed that this tutor, Francis Demoulins, ultimately edited the version of Louise's journal that exists today. Louise is due considerable credit for the significant contributions that Marguerite and Francis made to learning and letters. Both were patrons of the arts: Francis lent his support to many of the greatest writers and artists of his time, and Marguerite (later Marguerite de Navarre) wrote poems, plays, and the *Heptameron,* a highly regarded collection of novellas.

In January 1515, Louis XII died, and his cousin Francis inherited the throne. Now the mother of the French king, Louise was granted the courtesy title of *Madame,* and her son named her a duchess. The young king, ambitious to win glory for himself, sought to renew French claims in Italy and designated his mother to act as regent of France during this military expedition. Louise's first term as regent was brief. However, during Francis's absence, Louise filled the most important governmental offices with men devoted to her own interests. Although her official role ended early in 1516, Louise continued to exert considerable influence in her son's government.

When Francis once more went off to war in Italy in 1523, he again designated his mother regent. Louise's second regency lasted significantly longer than her first: in February 1525, Francis was defeated and taken prisoner at the Battle of Pavia. In Francis's absence, Louise found herself in the position of having to defend France against possible foreign invasion. She negotiated the 1525 Treaty of the Moore with King Henry of England and the 1526 League of Cognac with Pope Clement VIII and the Venetians.

Louise ultimately succeeded in securing Francis's release from captivity. She raised the money necessary to ransom her son and negotiated the Treaty of Madrid, signed by Francis on 14 January 1526. The provisions of the treaty were harsh. Francis was forced to renounce all claims to Italy, and his sons, François and Henry, would be held hostage by the emperor to ensure compliance with the treaty. Two months later Francis was exchanged for the young princes, but the French king, apparently on the advice of Louise, repudiated the treaty, claiming he had signed it under duress.

Peace between Francis I and Holy Roman Emperor Charles V was finally achieved in August 1529 with the signing of the Treaty of Cambrai. This "Ladies' Peace" was negotiated by Francis's mother, Louise, and Charles's aunt, Margaret of Austria. These two powerful women had a lifelong history. They had been educated together in the court of Anne of France, and they were relatives, Margaret having married Louise's brother, Philibert of Savoie. According to the terms of this treaty, a large sum was to be paid as ransom for the captive princes, Francis would definitively abandon any claims to Italian territory, and he would marry Eleanor of Austria, Charles V's older sister.

Louise was often criticized by her contemporaries and has not been treated well by most historians. She is frequently described as amoral, rapacious, and vindictive. She was at least partially responsible for the downfall of Charles de Bourbon, who, according to contemporary rumor, refused Louise's marriage proposal and renounced allegiance to the French crown following a dispute over his late wife's vast properties. She was also involved in the ruin of Jacques de Beaune, baron of Semblançay, Francis's superintendent of finances. Semblançay was condemned to death for having falsified Louise's accounts and having diverted money intended for the king. Louise was, however, an able and industrious ruler whose offspring ushered the Renaissance into France. She died on 22 September 1531.

Kathleen M. Llewellyn

See also the subheading Literary Patronage (under Literary Culture and Women); Power, Politics, and Women.

Bibliography

Henry-Bordeaux, Paule. *Louise de Savoie, "roi" de France.* Paris: Perrin, 1971.

Jansen, Sharon L. *The Monstrous Regiment of Women: Female Rulers in Early Modern Europe.* New York: Palgrave, 2002.

Matarasso, Pauline. *Queen's Mate: Three Women of Power in France on the Eve of the Renaissance.* Aldershot, UK, Burlington, VT: Ashgate, 2001.

McCartney, Elizabeth. "The King's Mother and Royal Prerogative in Early-Sixteenth-Century France." In *Medieval Queenships.* Edited by John Carmi Parsons. Stroud, UK: Sutton, 1994.

Scala, Alessandra (1475–1506)

Poet, Greek scholar who played Sophocles's Electra *in a salon performance of the tragedy*

Alessandra Scala was born in 1475, the fifth daughter of the chancellor of Florence, Bartolomeo Scala. The chancellor and Alessandra took part in the brilliant circle of Classical scholars and writers around Lorenzo (Il Magnifico) de Medici in the 1480s. In addition to Scala and his daughter, the learned group included the first important translator and interpreter of Plato in Europe, Marsilio Ficino; the poet Angelo Poliziano; and the renowned scholar of Jewish theology and Greek philosophy Giovanni Pico della Mirandola. Alessandra Scala studied Greek poetry with the Greek scholars in exile, Janus Lascaris and Demetrius Chalcondylas, who were then teaching at the University of Florence. When they left Florence, she continued her studies with Poliziano who was among the leading Hellenists in Italy at the time.

Only two of her writings survive, an epigram in Classical Greek addressed to Poliziano, and a Latin letter Scala sent to the Venetian humanist Cassandra Fedele. Scala's fame, however, stems from her salon performance of Sophocles's *Electra* at her father's villa in Florence, in which she played the title role. Poliziano published a Greek epigram in honor of Scala's "riveting" performance, and he fired off a review of the event to Fedele in Venice.

"Alessandra played the role of the young Electra," he wrote her, "with such art, finesse, and elegance that the entire audience was transfixed. So authentically Attic was the music of her voice, so well did her gestures suit the narrative, and so affecting was her emotional range, that the play, so long a fiction, was imbued with meaning and truth."

In February 1492, Scala wrote Cassandra Fedele asking her advice on whether she should choose marriage or a career as a writer and a scholar. Cagily refusing to commit herself, Fedele gave an answer worthy of her namesake. "You should follow your nature" was all the advice she offered Scala. In 1494, Scala did marry, and the mate she chose was the Greek poet Michele Marullo. Six years later Marullo drowned while fording the Cecina River. Abandoning her Greek studies and her home, Scala entered the convent of San Pier Maggiore in Florence. She died there in 1506.

Diana Robin

See also the subheading Greek Learning and Women (under Education, Humanism, and Women); Theater and Women Actors, Playwrights, and Patrons.

Bibliography
Primary Works

Fedele, Cassandra. *Clarissimae feminae Cassandrae Fidelis venetae epistolae et orationes.* Edited by Jacopo Filippo Tomasini, 164–167. Padua: Franciscus Bolzetta, 1636.

King, Margaret L., and Albert Rabil, Jr., eds. *Her Immaculate Hand: Selected Works by and about The Women Humanists of Quattrocento Italy.* Albany: State University of New York Press, 1983.

Pesanti, Giovanni. "Lettere inedite del Poliziano." *Athenaeum* 3 (1915): 284–304.

Scala, Alessandra. "Alexandra Scala Cassandrae Fideli. Epistola CVII." In Cassandra Fedele, *Clarissimae feminae Cassandrae Fidelis venetae epistolae et orationes.* Edited by Jacopo Filippo Tomasini, 163–164. Padua: Franciscus Bolzetta, 1636.

Scala, Alessandra. "Epigramma greco." In Angelo Poliziano, *Prose volgari inedite e poesie latine e greche.* Edited by Isidoro del Lungo. Florence: Barbera, 1867.

Secondary Works

Bignone, A. "A proposito di alcuni epigrammi greci di Poliziano." *Studi italiani di filologia classica* 4 (1927): 392–397.

Brown, Alison. *Bartolomeo Scala, 1430–1497, Chancellor of Florence.* Princeton, NJ: Princeton University Press, 1979.

Pesenti, Giovanni. "Alessandra Scala: una figurina di rinascenza fiorentina." *Giornale storico della letteratura italiana* 85 (1925): 241–267.

Schurman, Anna Maria van (1607–1678)

Polymath; fluent in Latin, Greek, Hebrew, Arabic, German, French, and Italian; exchanged letters with the French feminist Marie de Gournay, the philosopher René Descartes, and the religious reform thinker Jean de Labadie

In the middle of the seventeenth century, Anna Maria van Schurman was at the center of a far-flung network of intellectual women. From Scandinavia to Bohemia and from Ireland to Italy, a web of learning connected Schurman to other female scholars. Some were inspired by Schurman's *Dissertatio,* a formal discourse in Latin on the aptitude of the female mind for the study of science and letters. Seeking to connect with others like themselves, intellectual women throughout Europe wrote to Schurman in Latin, Hebrew, Greek, and French. Schurman in turn responded positively; as she wrote to one correspondent, she too was longing for some imaginary intellectual sanctuary, where they might work together in "a union of minds and studies." Schurman also corresponded with the English educator Bathsua Makin, the Anglo-Irish reformer Dorothy Moore, the French scholar Marie de Gournay, the Huguenot educator Marie du Moulin, and the Palatine Princess Elisabeth, who had an extensive philosophical correspondence with René Descartes. Some of these connections continued throughout Schurman's lifetime. For instance, Marie du Moulin became Schurman's "intellectual sister," and, when Schurman's religious community needed asylum in the 1670s, it was Princess Elisabeth who sheltered them.

Other female scholars encountered Schurman through mutual friends at the exile court of the queen of Bohemia in The Hague or through mutual correspondents in the Republic of Letters. And there were some intellectual women whom Schurman sought out herself—for instance, she made contact with the well-known French feminist and scholar, Marie de Gournay, who had responded by making Schurman her "intellectual daughter."

Beyond this core group of female scholars, the network of intellectual women extended even further. To the south, it reached into Italy; and in the *Dissertatio,* Schurman made it clear that she had been studying the work of Italian female scholars such as Lucrezia Marinella, whose *The Nobility and Excellence of Women* was a treatise she found to be too forceful. To the north, the network reached into Scandinavia. Schurman was in touch with the Danish scholar, Birgitte Thott, and contributed an epigram to Thott's 1658 translation of Seneca. Throughout Britain, France, Germany, and the Netherlands, these women were in turn connected with other female scholars. Thus this female Republic of Letters was a chain that eventually linked a very disparate group, including the French writer Madeleine de Scudéry, the learned Queen Christina of Sweden, and the Irish reformer Lady Ranelagh, the sister of the scientist Robert Boyle. Apart from their scholarship, then, the women of this intellectual commonwealth were characterized by a remarkable heterogeneity, cutting across barriers of religion, nation, social status, and intellectual allegiance.

The existence of their correspondence community serves to demonstrate that female scholars were neither anomalous nor invisible in the Intellectual Revolution. Because these scholars were women, however, they were not permitted to attend a university or to practice learned professions. Thus in addition to their connections to male scholars, their connec-

tions to each other created a unique web of female intellectual correspondence and patronage. The center of that web was Anna Maria van Schurman. Yet in spite of her collegial network, Schurman's reputation has always been one of singularity.

It is not difficult to understand how she garnered this reputation. Throughout the seventeenth century, the Dutch scholar Anna Maria van Schurman was renowned as an intellectual phenomenon. She was also highly praised as an artist and was adept in drawing, painting, sculpting, etching, and paper cutting. Moreover, her reputation for modesty, piety, and virtue was on a par with her reputation as a scholar. But it was her scholarship that astounded philosophers and men of learning. She was a linguist, rhetorician, poet, and classicist; she had an excellent command of mathematics, astronomy, theology, history, poetry, and music; she mastered the learned languages (Latin, Greek, and Hebrew); and she was proficient in Chaldaic, Arabic, Ethiopian, Flemish, German, French, and Italian.

As Schurman's fame spread, she corresponded with some of the foremost scholars of the age: René Descartes, Claude Saumaise, Daniel Heinsius, Constantijn Huygens, André Rivet, Caspar Barlaeus, and Pierre Gassendi, to name a few. She was "the Star of Utrecht" and "the Tenth Muse." It was said that "to have been in Utrecht without having seen Mademoiselle de Schurman was like having been to Paris without seeing the king." And yet it was also said that she was a "monster of nature" and partial to eating spiders. These praises placed her in a category not only beyond other women, but beyond nature itself.

Schurman was born in 1607 into a wealthy and staunchly Calvinist family in Cologne, one of four children. Although she briefly attended a French school, it was apparently far too worldly, and her father decided to educate Anna Maria along with her brothers at home. She quickly outstripped them, mastering German at the age of three and Latin at the age of eleven. When she was thirteen, she came to the notice of the Dutch poet Anna Roemers Visscher, and by the age of sixteen she was corresponding in Latin with scholars in the Republic of Letters. She also garnered two supportive yet conservative mentors, the Calvinist theologians André Rivet and Gisbert Voëtius, to whom she was devoted throughout her life.

In 1636, Schurman was asked to write a Latin ode for the opening of the new University of Utrecht. The poem was followed in 1639 by *De vitae termino*, a theological treatise on the end of human life. Then in 1641 she published her *Dissertatio,* which became her most important work and was quickly translated into French and English. In the *Dissertatio,* she argued that the entire encyclopedia of learning should be open to women—not all women, but certainly those not hampered by economic hardship or family responsibilities. This text remains difficult to assess. On the one hand, the formal discourse ended with her claim that she had proved her point. On the other hand, however, it was published together with letters in which Rivet critiques Schurman and apparently convinces her to retreat from her position. Rivet's argument was that Schurman was essentially a sample of one; thus those studies that had exalted her would be unnecessary, unwanted, and indeed spiritually perilous for other women. The *Dissertatio* was followed in 1648 by *Opuscula* (Little Works). This text reprinted the *Dissertatio,* along with over seventy other letters in Latin, Greek, Hebrew, and French, a small sampling of her correspondence with the Republic of Letters.

After this, the modest Schurman began to withdraw from the secular stage. In the mid-1660s, she began associating with the French cleric Jean de Labadie, a charismatic religious chameleon who was constantly running afoul of ecclesiastical authorities. Johan Godschalk van Schurman had been impressed by Labadie and had shared his enthusiasm with his younger sister, Anna Maria. From this point until her death in 1678, Anna Maria van Schurman's life was completely entwined with Labadie's pietistic faith, and she cofounded the Labadist community. As Labadie's preaching outraged authorities in one city after another, Schurman used her intelligence, influence, and reputation to secure a succession of temporary homes for their unwanted sect.

Schurman's final publication was *Eukleria* in 1673. *Eukleria* was partly an apology for Labadie and partly an explanation of why she had walked away from the secular limelight to join him. Many scholars in the Republic of Letters had been yearning for such an explanation. Perplexed and alarmed by what had seemed a sudden and ill conceived move, they were convinced that Schurman had come under the sway of a spiritual charlatan. Thus Schurman used *Eukleria* to review her childhood, her education, and her fame. In angry and condemnatory language, she problematized the intellectual renown of her youth, recounting how she was once swayed by the praises of "lying eulogists" and their "literary idolatry." She died five years later, in 1678, in the Labadist community at Wieuwerd.

Carol Pal

See also Education, Humanism, and Women; the subheading Letter Writing (under Literary Culture and Women); Religious Reform and Women.

Bibliography

Primary Sources

Koninklijke Bibliotheek, The Hague. MS. 133 B 8. Letters of Anna Maria van Schurman.

Schurman, Anna Maria van. *De vitae termino.* Leiden: Johannus Maire, 1639.

Schurman, Anna Maria van. *Eukleria seu Melioris Partis Electio. Tractatus Brevem Vitae ejus Delineationem Exhibens.* Altona, Germany: Cornelius van der Meulen, 1673.

Schurman, Anna Maria van. *Nobiliss. Virginis Annae Mariae a Schurman Dissertatio De Ingenii Muliebris ad Doctrinam, & meliores Litteras aptitudine. Accedunt Quaedam Epistolae eiusdem Argumenti.* Leiden: Elsevier, 1641.

Schurman, Anna Maria van. *Nobiliss. Virginis Annae Mariae à Schurman, Opuscula Hebraea, Graeca, Latina, Gallica: Prosaica & Metrica.* Leiden: Elsevier, 1648.

Schurman, Anna Maria van. *Whether a Christian Woman Should Be Educated: and other writings from her intellectual circle.* The Other Voice in Early Modern Europe. Edited and translated by Joyce L. Irwin. Chicago: University of Chicago Press, 1998.

Yvon, Pierre (1646–1707). "Abregé sincere de la vie & de la conduite & des vrais sentimens de feu Mr. De Labadie." In *Forsetzungen und Erläuterungen, Unpartheyische Kirchen- und Ketzerhistorie.* Edited by Gottfried Arnold, 1234–1270. Frankfurt am Main: 1715.

Secondary Sources

Baar, Mirjam de, Machteld Löwensteyn, Marit Monteiro, and A. Agnes Neller, eds. *Choosing the Better Part: Anna Maria van Schurman (1607–1678).* Dordrecht, The Netherlands: Martinus Nijhoff, Kluwer Academic Publishers, 1996.

Birch, Una [Constance Pope-Hennessy]. *Anna van Schurman: Artist, Scholar, Saint.* London and New York: Longmans, Green and Co., 1909.

Douma, Anna Margaretha Hendrika. *Anna Maria van Schurman en de Studie der Vrouw.* Ph.D. dissertation, University of Amsterdam. Amsterdam: H. J. Paris, 1924.

Schotel, G. D. J. *Anna Maria van Schurman.* Hertogenbosch, Netherlands: Gebroders Muller, 1853.

Stighelen, Katlijne van der. *Anna Maria van Schurman: of "Hoe hooge dat een maeght kan in de konsten stijgen."* Leuven, Belgium: Universitaire Pers Leuven, 1987.

Seymour, Jane (?–d. 1537)

Third wife and queen of Henry VIII, mother of King Edward VI of England

Descended from King Edward III of England on her mother's side and daughter of Sir John Seymour, a gentleman of the bedchamber under Henry VIII, Jane Seymour served in the households of Henry VIII's first two wives, Catherine of Aragon and Anne Boleyn. Following the execution of Anne Boleyn, Jane and Henry were betrothed and later married on 30 May 1536. Unlike other members of her family, Jane did not embrace Protestantism, and on at least one occasion she unsuccessfully attempted to use her influence with Henry VIII to stop the suppression of a Cistercian convent at Catesby. Jane was also instrumental in bringing about a reconciliation between Henry and his Catholic daughter, Mary I. On 12 October 1537, Jane Seymour gave birth to Henry VIII's long awaited and only male heir. Although she was well enough to receive guests after the baby's christening three days following the birth, her health then began to deteriorate. Jane Seymour died of puerperal fever twelve days after the birth of her son. She had been queen of England for less than eighteen months. Following the death of Henry VIII, her son would rule as Edward VI.

Shawndra Holderby

See also Elizabeth I; Mary I.
Bibliography
Fraser, Antonia. *The Wives of Henry VIII.* New York: Alfred A. Knopf, 1992.

Jansen, Sharon. *The Monstrous Regiment of Women: Female Rulers in Early Modern Europe.* New York: Palgrave, 2002.

Loades, David. *Henry VIII and His Queens.* Phoenix Mill, UK: Sutton, 2000.

Starkey, David. *Six Wives: The Queens of Henry VIII.* New York: Harper Collins, 2003.

Sforza, Caterina (1463–1476)

Ruler of Forlì, who famously defied rebel citizens who had taken her children hostage and stood her ground

Born in 1463 to Galeazzo Maria Sforza (1444–1476), future duke of Milan (1466–1476), and to his mistress, Lucrezia Landriani, Caterina grew up in the ducal palace and was educated under the tutelage of Bianca Maria Visconti Sforza, her paternal grandmother, and Bona of Savoy, her father's legitimate wife. In 1477, she married Girolamo Riario, the nephew of Pope Sixtus IV (1471–1484), who was commander in chief of the papal army and castellan of the Castel St. Angelo. Caterina Sforza brought Riario a dowry of ten thousand ducats and the town of Imola and its countryside. Her father, Duke Galeazzo, surrendered those lands to the church with the understanding that Riario, and after him his descendants, would rule it in the name of the

Caterina Sforza, ruler of Forlì who famously put down a citizens' revolt. Painting by Lorenzo di Credi. Pinacoteca Civica, Forlì, Italy. (Bettmann/Corbis)

pope. In 1480, the pope added the vicariate of Forlì to the towns and lands under Riario's control, after he had wrested them from the Ordelaffi family.

When Sixtus IV died on 12 August 1484, the Roman people sacked the papal apartments. Fearing they would attack her own properties next, she climbed to the battlements of the Castel St. Angelo where she appeared wearing armor over a satin dress, a hawk perched on her wrist. Although she was begged by her husband and the cardinals to surrender the castle, she refused to do so until the newly elected pontiff, Innocent VIII, confirmed the investiture of Imola and Forlì on her family. In the months spent at Forlì, the Riarios managed to administer the city finances so improvidently that they turned the townspeople against them. After two failed assassination attempts by members of the Orde-

laffi clan, a successful plot was organized by Checco Orsi, a prominent citizen of Forlì. Girolamo Riario was murdered in 1488, and Caterina and her six children were taken prisoner. In a matter of hours, all Forlì revolted and gave itself up to the pope. Leaving her children as hostages, Caterina escaped to the city's fortress of Ravaldino and refused to surrender, determined to wait for the scheme of her rebellious citizenry to collapse. The well-known story of the answer she gave those who threatened to kill her children if she did not give up the fortress is probably due to what Niccolò Machiavelli wrote in his *Discorsi* (book III, chap. 6): lifting her skirt and pointing to her genitals, she shouted that she still had the tools to make more children. Later, liberated by the troops sent by her uncle, Ludovico Sforza of Milan, and by Giovanni Bentivoglio of Bologna, she forbade the sack of Forlì and returned to rule it in the name of her son, Ottaviano.

Caterina Sforza became an important actor in Italian politics when, in 1494, Charles VIII of France invaded the peninsula and claimed to be the legitimate heir to the kingdom of Naples. Because of the strategic position of her territories in the Po Valley along the Via Emilia, the old Roman road, Caterina's alliance was sought by the French, the Sforzas of Milan, the Aragonese of Naples, the pope, and Florence. After lengthy and crafty delays, during which she seemed to lean toward the Aragonese, Caterina switched her allegiance to Florence and the French. The sack of Mordano and the surrender of Bubano to the foreign army in October 1494 persuaded her to let Charles's troops march south unopposed. In time, her alliance with Florentine republic became suspect, and in July 1499 a delegation headed by Niccolò Machiavelli was sent from Florence to assess her intentions and secure her loyalty to the republic.

Of all the turbulent events that engulfed Caterina's life the most famous is the conquest of her territories by Cesare Borgia, the natural son of Pope Alexander VI (1492–1503). It was Cesare's plan to carve a domain of his own out of the papal possessions of Romagna. He had been provided by Louis XII of France with three hundred lances led by Yves d'Alègre and with some four thousand Swiss and Gascon infantrymen under Bailly de Dijon. On 9 March 1499, the pontiff declared forfeited all the vicariates of Romagna, including those of the lords of Forlì and Imola, on the grounds of nonpayment of the yearly contribution due to the church. Caterina, who had lost the backing of the Sforzas, whose Milanese domain had been toppled by Louis, was now abandoned by the Florentines and left to defend herself against Cesare's lancers and the powerful French artillery. Borgia entered the Riario territory in November. The citizens of Imola surrendered to him on the twenty-fifth, soon followed by the other towns of the contado and then by the city of Forlì on December 19. Caterina withdrew again into the Rocca Ravaldino and from its ramparts looked down on the devastation and torture inflicted on the population by the Gascon soldiers. She went on resisting, however, bombarding both her citizens and the invading army as much as she might. When Cesare advanced to the brink of the moat of the fortress to come to terms with her, she tried to kill him by luring him onto the drawbridge and then raising it. The siege lasted until 12 January when the French artillery opened a breach in the wall of Ravaldino and entered it. In the fierce hand-to-hand fighting that took place inside the fortress, Caterina was seized by the soldiers of Bailly de Dijon. He wanted to hold her for ransom, but Yves d'Alègre wrenched her away and consigned her to Borgia. It was the general opinion of contemporaries that Caterina, then thirty-six years of age and a woman of great beauty, was raped, not necessarily forcefully, by Cesare, who was twenty-four and very handsome. The Venetian chronicler Marin Sanudo, in the report he made to the senate on 18 January, wrote that Borgia kept Caterina in his room and took his pleasure with her repeatedly.

When she finally arrived in Rome, Pope Alexander made a show of treating Caterina with all due cordiality and lodged her in the elegant Villa Belvedere in the Vatican gardens. But when she refused to sign away her rights to Imola and Forlì, she was thrown into a solitary dungeon in Castel St. Angelo. There she remained in miserable conditions for more than a year until 1501, when she was rescued again by the gallant Yves d'Alègre, who demanded her in name of the king of France. Compelled formally to renounce her domains and the tutelage of her children, Caterina took refuge in Florence. For the rest of her life she resided in the palazzo Medici, now Riccardi, in The Via Lata, and there she died on 28 May 1509.

After the death of Girolamo Riario, she fell in love with an undistinguished soldier by the name of Iacopo Feo and made him captain of the fortress of Ravaldino. Feo, much younger than she was, proved to be inept, arrogant, and demanding. When he was murdered before her eyes on 25 August 1495, she inveighed against the presumed killers relentlessly and with even more ferocity than she had displayed against the murderers of her husband, Girolamo, in 1488. Her choice of a mate improved greatly when, around 1496, she married into the former first family of Florence. Her new husband, Giovanni de Medici, was a grandnephew of Cosimo the Elder (1389–1464) and the grandson of Lorenzo de Medici, Cosimo's brother. In her tumultuous middle years, Sforza was almost continuously pregnant. At least eight children of hers are known to have reached maturity: Bianca, Ottaviano, Cesare, Giovanni Livio, Galeazzo Maria, and Francesco, whom she had from Girolamo Riario; Carlo, born from her relationship with Feo; and Giovanni, son of Giovanni de Medici. This last offspring became in time the famous condottiere, Giovanni delle Bande Nere (1498–1526), whose son, Cosimo I, would be duke of Florence (1437) and grand duke of Tuscany (1469–1474).

Caterina was a passionate hunter, an excellent dancer, and a charming conversationalist who dazzled with her intelligence and wit. She indulged in beautiful clothing and rich jewelry, and she took exacting care of her appearance and health throughout her life. Her notebook, by the title of *Experimenti,* is full of interesting information about beauty lotions, the care of hair and body, poisons, abortifacients, medical cures, and surgical practices.

Rinaldina Russell

See also subheadings Childbirth and Reproductive Knowledge; The Practice of Pharmacology and Laywomen (under Medicine and Women); Makeup and Cosmetics; Power, Politics, and Women.

Bibliography

Primary Works

Alberi, Eugenio. *Le relazioni degli ambasciatori veneti al Senato.* Florence: Società Editrice Fiorentina, 1839–1863.

Bernardi, Andrea. *Cronache forlivesi dal 1476 al 1517.* 2 vols. Edited by G. Mazzatinti. Bologna: Regia deputazione di storia patria, 1895–1897.

Buonaccorsi, Biagio. *Diario dei successi più importanti seguiti in Italia. . . . dall'anno 1498 in sino all'anno 1512.* Florence: Giunta, 1568.

Burchard, Johannes. *At the court of the Borgia, being an account of the reign of Pope Alexander VI, written by his master of ceremonies, Johann Burchard.* Edited and translated by Geoffrey Parker. London: The Folio Society, 1963.

Burchard, Johannes. *Liber notarum ab anno 1483 usque ad annum 1506.* Edited by Enrico Celani. Rerum italicarum scriptores, XXXII, 2. Città di Castello, Italy: S. Lapi, 1907.

Cattaneo, Gian Lucido. *Diario ferrarese 1409–1502.* Rerum italicarum scriptores, XXIV. Bologna, Italy: N. Zanichelli, 1934–1937.

Guicciardini, Francesco (1483–1540). *Storie fiorentine dal 1378 al 1509.* Edited by R. Palmarocchi. Bari, Italy: Laterza, 1931.

Machiavelli, Nicolò (1469–1527). *Legazioni, Commissarie, Scritti di Governo.* 2 vols. Edited by Fredi Chiapelli. Bari, Italy: Laterza, 1971.

Sanuto, Marino (Marin Sanudo; 1466–1536). *I diarii di Marino Sanuto (MCCCCXCVI–MDXXXIII) dall' autografo Marciano ital. cl. VII codd. CDXIX-CDLXXVII.* Edited by Rinaldo Fulin, Federico Stefani, Nicolò Barozzi, Guglielmo Berchet, and Marco Allegri. Venezia, Italy: F. Visentini, 1879–1903.

Sforza Riario, Caterina. *Experimenti de la Ex.ma S.ra Caterina da Furlj, matre de lo inllux.mo signor Giovanni de Medici copiati dagli autografi di lei dal Conte Lucantonio Cuppano; pubblicati da Pier Desiderio Pasolini.* Imola, Italy: Ignazio Galeati e Figlio, 1894.

Sforza Riario, Caterina. *Ricettario di bellezza.* Introduction by Luigi Pescasio. Castiglione delle Stiviere, Italy: Wella Italiana, 1971.

Secondary Works

Atti del Convegno di studi per il quinto centenario della nascita di Caterina Sforza: Imola, 29 giugno 1964, Forlì, 25 ottobre 1964. Bologna: Cassa dei Risparmi di Forlì, 1967.

Breisach, Ernst. *Caterina Sforza, a Renaissance Virago.* Chicago: University of Chicago Press, 1967.

Burrièl, Antonio. *Vita di Caterina Sforza Riario, contessa d'Imola, e signora di Forlì, descritta in tre libri.* Bologna: Stamperia di S. Tommaso d'Aquino, 1795.

Cian, Vittorio. "Caterina Sforza: a proposito della 'Caterina Sforza' di Pier Desiderio Pasolini." *Rivista storica italiana,* X, no. IV, a (1893). (Reprinted in Turin: F.lli Bocca, 1893.)

Hairston, Julia L. "Skirting the Issue: Machiavelli's Caterina Sforza." *Renaissance Quarterly* 53, 3 (2000): 686–712.

Graziani, Natale, and Gabriella Venturelli. *Caterina Sforza.* Milan: Dall'Oglio, 1987.

Kühner, Hans. *Caterina Sforza: Fürstin, Tyrannin, Büsserin.* Zürich: W. Classen, 1957.

Pasolini, Pier Desiderio. *Caterina Sforza.* 3 vols. Rome: Loescher, 1893.

Pasolini, Pier Desiderio. *Catherine Sforza . . . Authorized Edition, Translated and Prepared with the Assistance of the Author by Paul Sylvester. Illustrated with Numerous Reproductions from Original Pictures and Documents.* Chicago and New York: H. S. Stone and Co., 1898.

Rachet, Guy. *Catherine Sforza: la dame de Forlì.* Paris: Denoël, 1987.

Randi, Aldo. *Caterina Sforza.* Milan: Ceschina, 1951.

Santoro, Caterina. *Gli Sforza.* Milan: Dall'Oglio, 1968.

Sidney, Mary Herbert (Mary Sidney Herbert; 1521–1621)

Poet, patron, and center of an important circle of English poets

Mary Sidney, daughter of Mary Dudley Sidney and Sir Henry Sidney, lord president of the council of Wales and lord deputy of Ireland, was born 27 October 1561 at Tickenhall near Bewdley, Worcestershire, on the English border with Wales. Sidney came from a long line of well-educated women politically active in court circles. Jane Guilford Dudley, her maternal grandmother, was educated by the Spanish humanist Juan Vives, and her aunt, Katherine Dudley, had been a leader in the campaign for Protestant education. From tutors at home, Mary Sidney received a humanist education and was taught the classics, the church fathers, poetry, music, French, and Italian, and dedications to her in Latin and Greek indicate that she knew those languages as well (Hannay 1990, 27).

After Mary's sister, Ambrosia, died in 1575 in the damp climate of Wales, Elizabeth I suggested that Mary Sidney come to court. Within two years, her famous uncle, Robert Dudley, earl of Leicester, had arranged her marriage with the widower Sir Henry Herbert, second earl of Pembroke. Still childless, Henry needed an heir to his large estate. Mary Sidney became Mary Sidney Herbert, countess of Pembroke, when they married on 21 April 1577. Henry was in his midforties; Mary was fifteen. The couple produced four children: William (1580), Katherine (1581), Anne (1583), and Philip (1584).

In 1586, Mary Sidney lost her daughter Katherine and both her parents. But the most unbearable loss for her was the death that year of her brother and fellow poet, Philip Sidney. Most of the poem that would establish his reputation, *The Countesse of Pembrokes Arcadia,* had been written at her house and in collaboration with her (Hannay 1990, 70–71). After recovering from the shock of these deaths, she began to expand her own literary production and influence. She wrote a number of elegiac poems honoring Philip's work and promoting his image as a writer: "A Dialogue betweene two shepherds, Thenot and Piers, in praise of Astrea," "Even now that Care," "To the Angell spirit of the most excellent Sir Phillip Sidney," and "The Dolefull Lay of Clorinda," which was

Mary Herbert Sidney, English poet and patron of poets. Engraving from "Lodge's British Portraits." (Ken Welsh/ The Bridgeman Art Library)

published in Edmund Spenser's *Astrophel* (1595). She translated Robert Gardiner's "Marc Antoine" as *Antonius* (1592), providing Shakespeare with one of his sources for *Anthony and Cleopatra.* She also translated *A Discourse of Life and Death* by Philippe de Mornay (1592) and Petrarch's *The Triumph of Death* (1600).

In addition to her own poetry and translations, Sidney edited her brother Philip's poetry and prose after his death. Unhappy with Fulke Greville's 1590 edition of *The Countess of Pembroke's Arcadia,* she published her own edition in 1593, a composite of Philip's original version of the poem and the revisions he was making before he died. She brought together all of the Astrophil poems, *A Defence of Poetry,* and *Arcadia* in another edition in 1598. At the same time, Mary Sidney also completed the metrical English translation of the Psalms that Philip had started, adding one hundred and seven to his forty-three. These poetical translations were circulated in manuscript and prepared for presentation to Elizabeth.

In the 1590s, Mary Sidney assumed her brother Philip's role as the central figure in a circle of important young poets and as their patron. With the financial backing of her husband, she found support for such poets as Samuel Daniel, Abraham Fraunce, Thomas Moffatt, and Nicholas Breton. The poems they dedicated to her indicate the influence her various verse forms in the *Psalmes* had on their work. Daniel, for example, praised her for encouraging him to write "another kind" of poetry, one of "higher straine" (Daniel 1885, 24). Poets who dedicated works to her, paying tribute to her poetic legacy, include, among others, Michael Drayton, Aemilia Lanyer, and Edmund Spenser.

After her husband Henry's death in 1601, Mary Sidney administered the family properties, she negotiated her children's marriages, and she continued to play at least a limited role at court. She sought the return of her brother Robert from the Netherlands and, unsuccessfully, the pardon of Walter Ralegh during the reign of James I. At the same time, she encouraged her niece, Mary Sidney Wroth, to write poetry.

Sidney died in her Aldersgate Street home of smallpox, on 25 September 1621. She was buried in Salisbury Cathedral.

Joy Currie

See also Education, Humanism, and Women; Lanyer, Aemilia Bassano; Wroth, Mary.

Bibliography
Primary Works
Carlton, Dudley. *Dudley Carlton to John Chamberlain, 1603–1624: Jacobean Letters.* Edited by Maurice Lee, Jr. New Brunswick, NJ: Rutgers University Press, 1972.
Daniel, Samuel. *The Complete Works in Verse and Prose of Samuel Daniel.* Vol. 3. Edited by Alexander B. Grosart. London: Hazell, Watson, and Viney, 1885.
Herbert, Mary Sidney. *The Collected Works of Mary Sidney Herbert Countess of Pembroke.* 2 vols. Edited by Margaret P. Hannay, Noel J. Kinnamon, and Michael G. Brennan. Oxford: Clarendon, 1998.
Sidney, Philip. *The Countess of Pembroke's Arcadia.* Edited by Maurice Evans. London: Penguin, 1987.

Secondary Work
Hannay, Margaret P. *Philip's Phoenix: Mary Sidney, Countess of Pembroke.* New York and Oxford: Oxford University Press, 1990.

Sonnet Writing. *See* Literary Culture and Women.

Speght, Rachel (b. 1597– death date unknown)

English Protestant poet, best-known for her feminist polemical tract, A Mouzell for Melastomus *(1617)*

Born in London, Rachel Speght was the daughter of the Calvinist minister and author James Speght. Speght's father oversaw her humanist education, which included biblical and religious studies, Latin grammar, logic, and the classical authors, and he promoted her writing and publication. A member of the English middle class, she dedicated her texts to women, among whom was her godmother, Mary Moundford, the wife of Thomas Moundford, a physician and also a writer.

Speght became a public figure when she entered the *querelle des femmes,* the debate on women's rights that was already raging on the continent, with her publication of the feminist tract, *A Mouzell for Melastomus, The cynicall Bayter of, and foule mouthed Barker against Evahs Sex* (1617), a work in prose. The first Englishwoman to publish a feminist tract under her own name, Speght wrote her work in response to Joseph Swetnam's *The Arignment of Lewde, idle, froward and unconstant women* (1615). It is unclear whether she first presented the *Mouzell* to publisher and bookseller Thomas Archer (who had also published Swetnam's text), or if Archer approached Speght and solicited her manuscript to increase his sales. Speght's learned references to the classics and the Bible in her response to Swetnam's misogynist work betray both her Protestant learning and her humanist education in rhetoric. Speght dismisses King Solomon's inability to find one virtuous woman among one thousand, for example, claiming it points more to Solomon's unfortunate choices regarding women than it does the nature of the female sex. Her sense of humor is also apparent in an addendum to the *Mouzell,* in which, labeling Swetnam an "Asse," she mocks the flaws in grammar and logic that appear in his tract.

Inspired by the death of her mother, Speght's second and final poem, *Mortalities Memorandum with a Dreame Prefixed* (1621), stands as a meditation on death and the transience of human life. "No less feminist because couched in metaphors and rhetorical flourishes," Marion Wynne Davies writes of the *Mortalities,* Speght's dream vision "is re-sexed to display a woman's point of view, while her account of death commences with a vigorous defence of Eve" (1996, 360–361). Reasserting her authorship of the *Mouzell,* which apparently had been contested, Speght writes in her preface to the *Mortalities* that a motive for this publication is to "divulge this spring of my endeavor, to [those] . . . who have formerly deprived me of my due" (Speght 1996, 45).

Little is known of the remainder of Speght's life. She married William Procter, a cleric who became a Calvinist minister like her father, on 6 August 1621. Baptism records of two children, Rachel (26 February 1627) and William (15 December 1630), identify Minister William Procter as their father. There is no reference to the children's mother, but their Christian names point to the Speght-Procter union. William Procter published the sermon, *The Watchman Warning,* in 1624 and died in 1653; there is no record of Rachel Speght's death.

Michele Osherow

See also Education, Humanism, and Women; Feminism; Querelle des Femmes.

Bibliography
Primary Sources
O'Malley, Susan Gushee, ed. *The Early Modern Englishwoman: A Facsimile Library of Essential Works, Part 1, Printed Writings, 1500–1640, Volume 4, Defences of Women, Jane Anger, Rachel Speght, Ester Sowernam, and Constantia Munda.* Hants, NS, and Brookfield, UK: Scolar Press Series, 1996.
Speght, Rachel. *The Polemics and Poems of Rachel Speght.* Edited by Barbara Kiefer Lewalski. Oxford: Oxford University Press, 1996.
Secondary Sources
Walker, Kim. *Women Writers of the English Renaissance.* New York: Twayne Publishers, 1996.
Wynne-Davies, Marion, ed. *Women Poets of the Renaissance.* New York: Routledge, 1999.

Stampa, Gaspara (1523–1554)

Prolific Petrarchan lyric poet, virtuosa (professional singer), and salonnière

Because relatively little is known about the life of the Padovan poet Gaspara Stampa, scholars have been tempted to recreate that life from her three hundred and eleven posthumously published poems. And the fact that the poems, as Benedetto Croce remarked almost a century ago, tease us with their intimate, epistolary nature has led readers like Croce to assume that the task is not necessarily a difficult one and the artistic nature of the poetry not particularly subtle: "Her collection . . . is nothing other than the letters and diary of her great love that ravished her for three years and . . . gave her, along with grief, joy greater than she could have imagined, joy in which she found the only meaning and value of her life." Croce's contemporary, Rainer Maria Rilke, made Stampa the primary example of unrequited love in the first of his *Duino Elegies,* and the early twentieth-century editor of Stampa's works, Abdelkader Salza, concluded from the amorous affairs that Stampa charts in her poems (not one, but two) that Stampa must have been one of Venice's many infamous courtesans who profited from their beauty, education, and cultural versatility.

While Salza's characterization of Stampa as a courtesan has been amply challenged, it is also the case that it is difficult to categorize her. She does not fit comfortably into early modern norms: an acclaimed and unmarried virtuosa who sang and played the lute, she frequented

Venice's most elegant social circles and carried on a very public affair with one of the city's leading aristocrats, to the extent that she chose for her academic pseudonym the Latinized name of the river on his estate. Her first biographer, Alessandro Zilioli, wrote of her in the late 1500s, "having given herself to converse freely with well-educated men, she brought such scandal to herself that had not her great talents and the honor of her poetry concealed and almost cancelled her failings, it would be necessary to cover her with blame rather than include her here within this temple of honor among such valorous women." Blame aside, Zilioli manages to capture, as Marina Zancan comments, the "transgressive nature" of Stampa's figure—a figure who eludes those who would understand her. Certainly her writing conveys far more intimacy than that of female contemporaries, such as Vittoria Colonna and Veronica Gàmbara, despite the fact that all three were shaped by Petrarch's *Canzoniere* and in turn Pietro Bembo's *petrarchismo*. There are many pangs of unrequited love in the *Rime,* although pace Rilke, there are also moments of consummation, as in the famous sonnet (104) in which Stampa calls the night her friend and wishes that she was like Alcmene, Jupiter's lover, for whom the rising sun had been stayed by Apollo.

What is known about her life as pieced together from correspondence and civic records is that Stampa's father, a well-off jewel merchant, was anxious to have her educated in Latin and Greek, along with her sister Cassandra and brother Baldessar, and hired a tutor for that purpose. When her mother became widowed in the early 1530s, she moved her three children from Padova to Venezia, and by the mid-1540s the sisters were both acclaimed for their musical skills; one singer called Gaspara a "divine siren," and the organist Gerolamo Parabosco asks in his *Lettere amorose* of 1545, "who has ever heard such sweet and elegant words? . . . and what will I say of that angelic voice that struck the air with its divine accents and made such sweet harmony that it awakened spirit and life in the coldest stones?" The death of Gaspara's brother at age nineteen prompted from his friends the outpouring of works dedicated to Gaspara, including an edition of Boccaccio's *Ameto*. Such attention in Venice's elite circles suggests that the Stampa home had become something of a salon or *ridotto,* at which the sisters performed for their guests. Stampa seems to have participated in the meetings of one of Venice's literary academies, the *Dubbiosi* (doubtful ones), and attended the salons of others, including that of the powerful if bedridden Domenico Venier, who in his old age patronized Veronica Franco. Stampa's collection, in fact, includes sonnets to Venier, the Florentine poet Luigi Alamanni, the critic and cultural arbiter Sperone Speroni, and numerous *petrarchisti*—as well as Catherine de Médicis, only a few years older than herself, and Catherine's husband, Henri II of Valois. These largely occasional verses suggest that Stampa was a familiar figure in Venetian cultural life, and they also, of course, show her embracing the life of poet as well as musician.

But it is with Stampa's emergence as a poet that her biography becomes entangled with her writing. At one of Venier's salons she met Count Collaltino di Collalto, a knight who was to fight for the king of France on several occasions and a member of a prestigious family. The liaison, which initially sparked hopes of marriage, was punctuated by Collalto's lengthy visits to his estates and his service to Henri II. Well over two hundred poems in the collection are focused on Collalto, who seems to have definitively broken off the affair by 1552. Another romantic attachment with a Venetian patrician, Bartolomeo Zen, seems to have followed; some sixteen poems are dedicated to Zen, including one in which his name is spelled out using the first letters of each line. Virtually nothing is known of this affair, but shortly after it ended, fever claimed the apparently fragile Gaspara, and she died, thirty years old, in April 1554.

Her sister Cassandra published a volume of Gaspara's poems six months later, with a dedication to the poet and future cardinal, Giovanni della Casa, a frequent visitor to the Stampa home, and a letter by Gaspara herself to Collalto. But the book seems to have passed largely unnoticed. While three of Stampa's sonnets had been included in an anthology of 1553 entitled *Il sesto libro delle rime di diversi eccelenti autori,* the *Rime* marked the first and, for almost two centuries, the only edition of Stampa's collected writings. The rediscovery and reedition of the text by a descendant of Collalto in 1738, featuring portraits of Stampa and Collalto himself (and a selection of his poems revealing his poetic talents as mediocre at best, despite Gaspara's claims to the contrary), helped launch the romantic reception of Stampa as the passionate woman whose love for the haughty Collalto was, as Croce would later say, the great joy of her life. Salza's early twentieth-century edition, as has been noted, made of the passion a profession, citing among other things a letter by the gadfly Pietro Aretino as proof (and ignoring the fact that Aretino had also accused that paragon of female virtue, Vittoria Colonna, of being a whore).

Yet Salza's more damaging legacy was the rearrangement of the 1554 edition into two sections: the love poetry to Collalto and Zen, and *rime varie*—verses in various meters to Henri, Alamanni, Venier, and, at the end, God, the "Lord who hangs on the cross." In ending the *Rime* with what could be called Stampa's penitential poems ("Crestfallen and repentant for my serious lapses, / for so much raving— so much of it thoughtless— / for having spent the little time/ our fugitive lives give us in vainly loving" opens the final sonnet in Salza's edition), Salza created a narrative of passion and repentance. His and all subsequent editions of Stampa's poems take us from Stampa's Christmas Day encounter with Collalto that (sacrilegiously?) turns her into Mary and Collalto into the lord who has found his *nido* within her, to the lover's belated turn to God

and confession of her errors. The 1554 version contains no such narrative, since its divisions are based on differing metrical forms. The sonnets are followed by *capitoli* and madrigals, and the collection ends with an attack on the god Amore, who pitilessly leaves the narrator without recompense—even, she says, without life (poem 240 in Salza). Returning to the 1554 volume demands that we confront the fact that Stampa's own version of the Petrarchan *canzoniere* offers us not a life that moves from uncontrollable love to penitence, but a rich, sometimes bewildering array of feelings, poetic voices, and literary and mythological personae. The original edition may not have been authorized by Stampa, but one can speak of it as a kind of collaboration between Gaspara and her sister, who was persuaded by "many gentlemen of intellectual gifts" to publish the results of Gaspara's "honored labors."

These are labors that went against the tide of mid-sixteenth-century poetry even as they bore the stamp of Petrarch—including an opening modeled on Petrarch's valedictory poem: "You who hear in these troubled rhymes, / in these troubled, in these dark accents, / the sound of my amorous laments / and my sufferings that vanquish all others': // wherever valor is prized and esteemed, / I hope to find glory among the well-born: / glory, and not only pardon. . . ." Yet even these opening lines suggest a difference: Petrarch had sought "pity" from his well-heeled reader, while Gaspara seeks the *gloria* and fame that the 1554 edition's engraving of her, perhaps a rendering of a painting by Titian, proleptically bestows: she is seated with books to her left and a laurel wreath on her head. And it is the *pena* (pain) that she suffers for a beautiful but cruel Collalto that she hopes will find an outlet in her *penna* (her pen), thus enabling her to write in a "new style." The style, as Croce, however, dismissively noted, is often colloquial and conversational, as Stampa frequently soliloquizes, addressing alternately her "happy heart," courtesy, love, an unnamed friend, the *donne* who read her poems, and, of course, Collalto himself, whom she addresses in one of her most lacerating sonnets not as the formal *voi* but as an equal: *tu*. Conventions abound, some of them tiring, but the majority of the verse is notable for its directness and avoidance of the pedantic. This "new style" in turn finds its parallel in the poems' startling content. Collalto may be a handsome and worthy knight, but he is cruel in love; and, as we hear of his prolonged absences and infidelities, we realize he is no idealized beloved but a human with considerable foibles, some of them unforgivable. Thus not only does Stampa present us with a poetic sequence in which she takes on the role of the desiring woman in pursuit of a reluctant male (one sonnet opens, "he flees me; / I follow him, while others destroy themselves for me") but the male himself is finally unworthy of her love. In the sonnet where she first addresses Collalto as *tu,* she calls him "cruel, uncivilized, disdainful, inhuman and unkind"— but only to her, as he turns his "spirit, thoughts, heart, soul, and gaze" to others. Shakespeare's dark lady, it would seem, has made her first appearance in the figure of Collalto. And given the wide range of emotions that the speaker expresses as she identifies herself with Echo, the shepherdess/river Anasilla, and, after falling in love with Zen, as Dido (there are hints of "I recognize the trace of an old flame" in several poems), she seems an interesting precursor for Shakespeare's Will.

And a persona, of course, is what Stampa creates in her poetry, despite the *Rime*'s convincing production of intimacy as Stampa indulges her readers' desire for the authentic voice of the virtuosa in an age of *sprezzatura* and the emergence of professional women artists. Yet it is a production. The poet's voice conceals as much as it conveys through its superb control of and challenge to the period's conventions and its play with the musicality and suspenseful rhythms of the newly legitimized *volgare.*

Jane Tylus

See also Morra, Isabella di; the subheadings Salons, Salonnières, and Women Writers; Sonnet Writing (under Literary Culture and Women).

Bibliography

Primary Works
Stampa, Gaspara. *Rime*. Edited by Maria Bellonci. Milan: R.C.S., 2002.
Stampa, Gaspara. *Rime di Gaspara Stampa e di Veronica Franco*. Edited by A. Salza. Bari: 1913.
Stampa, Gaspara. *Rime di Madonna Gaspara Stampa*. Venice: Pietrasanta, 1554.
Secondary Works
Bassanese, Fiora. *Gaspara Stampa*. Boston: Twayne, 1982.
Jones, Ann Rosalind. "Bad Press: Modern Editors Versus Early Modern Women Poets (Tullia d'Aragona, Gaspara Stampa, Veronica Franco)." In *Strong Voices, Weak History: Early Women Writers and Canons in England, France, and Italy.* Edited by Pamela Joseph Benson and Victoria Kirkham, 287–313. Ann Arbor: University of Michigan Press, 2005.
Jones, Ann Rosalind. *The Currency of Eros.* Bloomington: Indiana University Press, 1990.
Zancan, Marina. "Gaspara Stampa: Rime." In *Letteratura Italiana: Le Opere.* Vol. II. Edited by Aldo Asor Rosa, 407–436. Milan: Einaudi, 1992.

Strozzi, Alessandra Macinghi (1407–1471)

Florentine noblewoman and prolific letter writer

Born in the first decade of the fifteenth century into the elite Macinghi family, Alessandra Strozzi is known for her seventy-three extant letters, written in her own hand in the Italian merchant script of the day; these letters are housed in the Archivio di Stato in Florence. All but one are addressed to her sons, all of whom would become bankers in Naples, Spain, and Bruges. Like most women of the upper class in Florence, Strozzi learned to read and write in the venacular, though she had no schooling in the humanist studies for which her husband Matteo and other members of the Strozzi clan were noted.

Alessandra married Matteo Strozzi when she was fourteen. By the time she was twenty-eight, in 1435, she had lost three of the eight children she bore to the plague. That year, her husband also died in the epidemic. Her earliest surviving letters, which begin when she had been a widow for twelve years, show her establishing her sons in merchant careers and finding husbands for her daughters. Later letters document her efforts to obtain the repeal of her sons' exile and to find them wives. Spanning a twenty-three-year period (1447–1470), Strozzi's letters leave a portrait of a woman who was religious and a devoted mother, serious in her desire for her sons to become successful but morally just men. They also suggest that Strozzi was a woman of strong will but considerable tact, an astute judge of family and business matters, and a keen but cynical observer of the Florentine scene. Letters written by Alessandra's relatives reinforce this self-portrait and depict her as a guiding force in family decisions until the end of her life.

Ann Crabb

See also the subheading Letter Writing (under Literary Culture and Women).

Bibliography

Primary Work

Strozzi, Alessandra. *Selected Letters: Bilingual Edition*. Translated by Heather Gregory. Berkeley: University of California Press, 1997.

Secondary Works

Crabb, Ann. "How to Influence Your Children: Persuasion and Form in Alessandra Macigni Strozzi's Letters to Her Sons." In *Women's Letters Across Europe, 1400–1700*. Edited by Jane Couchman and Ann Crabb. Aldershot, UK: Ashgate, 2005.

Crabb, Ann. *Widowhood and Family Solidarity in the Renaissance: The Strozzi of Florence*. Ann Arbor: University of Michigan Press, 2000.

Strocchia, Sharon. "Strozzi, Alessandra Macinghi." In *Encyclopedia of the Renaissance*. Edited by Paul F. Grendler, 93. New York: Scribners, 1999.

Strozzi, Barbara (1619–1677)

Venetian singer, musician, composer, and salonnière

Barbara Strozzi was one of the first secular female composers in Western Europe. Celebrated as a *virtuosissima cantatrice* (consummate vocalist)

in her native city of Venice, seven of Barbara's eight known opus numbers, comprising well over one hundred and fifty musical compositions, are extant. Scholars are optimistic that more of Barbara's compositions may await discovery. As the evidence now stands, however, her last published compositions were issued in 1664. Details of Barbara's early life are hazy, but she was almost certainly the illegitimate daughter of the renowned poet Giulio Strozzi (1583–1652) and his maid, Isabella Garzoni. Giulio saw to Barbara's training, named her in his final will as both universal heir and "elective daughter" and unquestionably served as the father of her musical career.

Giulio's high stature among the Venetian intellectual elite assured Barbara connections and opportunities for patronage. He arranged her singing debut at a gathering of Venetian literary and musical notables, an event that inspired the composer Niccolò Fontei to write two volumes of songs for her. Heartily supporting this project, her father gave Fontei his own poetry to use as text. Noting Barbara's early interest in composition, moreover, he arranged for her to study with the preeminent Venetian composer, Francesco Cavalli. And Giulio again presented his poetry to serve as *libretti* (lyrics) for her first published volume of compositions.

Most important, Giulio established in Barbara's honor the *Accademia degli Unisoni* (fl. 1638), a literary and musical society that convened in the Strozzi home. This salon atmosphere proved an ideal venue for Barbara to impress the cultural elite. She served not only as performer, but also as hostess and arbiter of debate, roles that highlighted her wit and erudition. In the published descriptions of the academy's meetings, the secretary wrote that "Your Ladyship [Barbara] has the greater part of the glory in this New Academy, you who are the prime mover in this Heaven." Barbara chose the subjects on which members were to debate, judged them, and awarded prizes of flowers for the best disquisitions on a learned theme. On one occasion (1638), she herself delivered two opposing speeches that debated the respective merits of tears or song, concluding in favor of song with the remark to her audience of gentlemen: "well do I know that I would not have received the honor of your presence at our last session had I invited you to see me cry rather than to hear me sing." The publications from the academy also provide ample testimony concerning Barbara's role as a singer, both in transcribing the songs that she performed and in comparing the beauty of her voice favorably with celestial harmony.

In 1534, Barbara also sang for another illustrious Venetian intellectual society, of which her father was a member, the *Accademia degli Incogniti*. Another prominent member of this academy, the nobleman Giovanni Loredano, praised the quality of Barbara's music with the words: "had she been born in another era, she would certainly either have usurped or enlarged the place of the muses."

Given her talent as a singer, it appears incongruous that Barbara never performed in opera. Keeping instead to drawing rooms and academies, she avoided the predominant musical interest of seventeenth-century Venice and a venue in which many female singers of her era enjoyed great success. Her own compositional style may, however, suggest an explanation. Barbara experimented with musical forms, but her work on the whole constituted pieces that suited her own singing style and soprano range. In addition, although her corpus includes a few works of wide dramatic scope, it is otherwise devoted to more intimate meditations on the theme of unrequited love, perhaps best conveyed within close proximity to the audience.

Barbara's æuvre consists largely of secular songs that she dedicated to powerful members of the European political elite. Opus 1 (*The First Book of Madrigals for Two, Three, Four and Five Voices,* 1644) honored Vittoria della Rovere, the grand duchess of Tuscany. Emperor Ferdinand III of Austria was the dedicatee of Opus 2 (*Cantatas, Arias and Duets,* 1651). Anna de Medici, archduchess of Austria, was the dedicatee of Opus 5 (*Sentimental Sacred Music,* 1655), and Francesco Caraffa, prince of the Belvedere, was celebrated in opus 6 (*Ariettas for Solo Voice,* 1657). The only Venetian among Barbara's dedicatees, Niccolò Sagredo—an important government official and later doge—received opus 7 (*Amusements of Euterpe or Cantatas and Ariettas for Solo Voice,* 1659). Barbara's final opus (number 8, *Arias,* 1664) went to Sophie, duchess of Brunswick.

Opus 3 (*Cantatas for One, Two and Three Voices,* 1654) lacks a single dedication, but in its place one finds the trademark of the *Incogniti,* "*Ignotae Deae,*" a feminized version of the Academy's motto, "*Ignoto Deo.*" Because it was the first of her works to be published after Giulio Strozzi's death in 1652, Opus 3 suggests that Barbara attempted to substitute her father's academic connections for his own sponsorship. Indeed, among the poets who supplied *libretti* for her works after Opus 2, one finds several who were also members of the *Incogniti.*

Barbara's rhetorically sophisticated dedications evince her substantive training in letters as well as in music, and the influence of her poet father. To the grand duchess of Tuscany, she wrote: "I must reverently consecrate this first work, which as a woman, I publish all too anxiously, to the Most August Name of Your Highness, so that under an oak of gold it may rest secure against the lightning bolts of slander prepared for it." One should not make too much of the humility tropes that Barbara employed in this instance, which any contemporary patronage seeker would have employed. It is noteworthy, however, that by the dedication of Opus 5 Barbara felt sufficiently sure of her professional stature to write, "since my feminine weakness restrains me no more than any indulgence of my sex impels me, on the lightest leaves do I fly, in devotion, to bow before you." The remaining three dedications, two of them to men, make no reference either to femininity or weakness.

Reputation, Children, and Legacy

Most of the contemporary comment on Barbara consisted of praise. Yet there was a prevalent connection between music and courtesans in the early modern period, and at least one anonymous satirist published some biting remarks concerning what other "functions" Barbara may have performed for the members of the *Unisoni*. Modern scholars have suggested the possibility that Barbara was a courtesan, a notion based largely on the evidence of one portrait of a partially unclad female musician painted by Bernardo Strozzi—who was no relation to the Strozzis discussed here but who did paint a portrait of Giulio.

Music historian Beth Glixon, however, has presented new evidence that challenges the courtesan label. Barbara seems to have engaged in a long-term sexual liaison with Giovanni Paolo Vidman, a close friend of her father. Of her four illegitimate children, three (Giulio Pietro, Isabella, and Laura) were in all probability Vidman's: among other pieces of evidence, the children received extensive financial support from his family, presumably in accordance with Vidman's final will. In light of Glixon's findings, it now seems best to characterize Barbara's life as (possibly) unconventional for her era, but far more complex than the term "courtesan" suggests.

The most important point concerning Barbara's legacy is that she set a precedent for women's careers as published composers. Her ability to do so depended on her father's support and the connections he fostered between his daughter and the Venetian cultural elite, coupled with Barbara's own talent and, hardly less important, her shrewd financial strategies that produced the resources necessary for publishing her work. While there were a number of female singers in seventeenth-century Venice who may well have composed informally, we have no record of their work apart from con-

temporary references to their beauty and talent. The particular achievement of Barbara Strozzi was thus to leave for posterity a securely attributable corpus of compositions that gives substance to an important figure who would otherwise be known only as a beautiful singer.

Sarah Gwyneth Ross

See also Music and Women; Stampa, Gaspara.
Bibliography
Primary Work
Veglie de' Signori Unisoni. Venice: Farfinas, 1638.
Secondary Works
Berdes, Jane. *Women Musicians of Venice.* Oxford: Oxford University Press, 1993.
Glixon, Beth L. "More on the Life and Death of Barbara Strozzi." *The Musical Quarterly* 83, no. 1 (1999): 134–141.
Glixon, Beth L. "New Light on the Life and Career of Barbara Strozzi." *The Musical Quarterly* 81, no. 2 (1997): 311–335.
Rosand, Ellen. "Barbara Strozzi, 'virtuosissima cantatrice': The Composer's Voice." *Journal of the American Musicological Society* 31, no. 2 (1978): 241–281.
Rosand, Ellen. "The Voice of Barbara Strozzi." In *Women Making Music.* Edited by Name M. Bowers and Judith Tick. Urbana: University of Illinois Press, 1986.
Rosand, Ellen, and David Rosand. " 'Barbara di Santa Sofia' and 'Il Prete Genovese': On the Identity of a Portrait by Bernardo Strozzi." *The Art Bulletin* 63, no. 2 (1981): 249–258.
Website
http://www.barbarastrozzi.org

Stuart, Arbella (1575–1615)

Woman of letters and royal cousin

Arbella Stuart was a niece of Mary, Queen of Scots, and daughter of Charles Stuart (earl of Lennox) and Elizabeth Cavendish. As the granddaughter of Henry VIII's older sister, Margaret, Arbella was a possible heir to Queen Elizabeth I. It was Arbella's royal blood that brought about the twists, turns, and standstills of her life, making it a tragic sequence of great expectations, frustration, rise to favor, disobedience, and punishment.

Arbella's shrewd grandmother, Bess of Hardwick, undertook the risky business of

Arbella Stuart, woman of letters and royal cousin. Painting by unknown artist, ca. 1589. (Library of Congress)

marrying her daughter into a royal family to produce her "jewel Arbella." Raised in anticipation of grandeur, Arbella realized full well her singular proximity to the throne. This overconfidence never found favor in the court of Elizabeth I, and Arbella had to live in the country until her cousin, James I, came to the throne of England and made her a favorite in his court. Before she got to shine in court, however, Arbella spent years in confinement in Hardwick, under Bess's watchful eye: Arbella's royal blood made her an attractive prize in nu-

merous plots. Bess made sure that Arbella received a fine education. Particularly during her years at Hardwick Arbella read extensively and wrote many letters.

Throughout Arbella's life, marriage plans surfaced and burst like bubbles. Indeed, the choice of her husband was a matter of such importance that, it seemed, she would never marry at all. Even after James I became king and Arbella no longer had a strong claim to succession, the king preferred to keep her unwed. Arbella, however, took the matters into her own hands. In 1610, she secretly married William Seymour, who as grandson of Tudor cousin Katherine Grey was also a distant cousin of the king. As a result, the outraged James I separated Arbella from her husband and put her under house arrest. In 1611, the couple's plans of escape to France went awry, and Arbella found herself imprisoned in the Tower of London. There she remained till her death in 1615, her husband out of her reach in France.

To an extent, some of Arbella's imprudent behavior was related to recurrent periods of mental instability. However, ultimately, this witty, educated, and fashionable woman tried to find a way to shape her own life but was forced to succumb to the royal power that regarded her as kin and rival at the same time.

Anya Riehl

See also Bess of Hardwick; Elizabeth I; the subheading Letter Writing (under Literary Culture and Women); Mary Stuart.

Bibliography

Primary Work

Steen, Sara Jayne, ed. *The Letters of Lady Arbella Stuart.* New York: Oxford University Press, 1994.

Secondary Works

Cooper, Elizabeth. *The Life and Letters of Lady Arbella Stuart.* 2 vols. London: Hurst and Blackett, 1866.

Durant, David N. *Arbella Stuart: A Rival to the Queen.* London: Weidenfeld and Nicolson, 1978.

Nottington, Ruth. *In the Shadow of the Throne: The Lady Arbella Stuart.* London and Chester Springs, PA: Peter Owen Publishers, 2002.

T

Tarabotti, Arcangela (1604–1652)

Benedictine nun, feminist, polemicist, and public voice of protest

Arcangela Tarabotti was a born rebel. All of her writings articulate her anger at life's injustices to women in general, at the injustices of the seventeenth-century Venetian family, marriage, and religious life in particular, and at the injustices perpetrated upon herself. Tarabotti is hard to place in any conventional literary slot. Her writings both elude the usual genres and mix features of many of them; what unites them is her overriding voice of protest.

Her life was scarred by three traumatic events. First, she inherited from her father a physical deformity of the spine and leg, which rendered her unmarriageable in the eyes of her family and Venetian society. Tarabotti remained acutely self-conscious about her physical appearance. When someone insulted her, she registered the hurt but also engaged in counterattack. Her mocker might be "sound of body" but was "crippled in soul" and would be excluded from Christ's great feast in the next life.

Second was her enforced enclosure as a nun in the Benedictine convent of Sant'Anna in Castello in Venice. At the age of eleven, she was sent as a boarder to Sant'Anna in the area of Venice near the famous shipyards, called the Arsenale. When she was sixteen, in 1620, she took her solemn vows of poverty, chastity, obedience, and stability—the latter characteristic of Benedictines, who were bound to remain in the same convent for life and be buried there. Nonetheless she was already a rebel, refusing to wear the religious habit or to cut her hair. Tarabotti saw the religious life in the darkest light, as a dumping ground for a family's unwanted, maimed, mentally retarded, and illegitimate offspring. She was appalled at the lack of adequate education in the convent and linked it, whether inside the convent or outside in contemporary society, to women's general subjection. Fathers made sure that from an early age their daughters' minds were stunted by ignorance and then took advantage of women's lack of literacy to attack them mercilessly, knowing they could not answer back. Tarabotti never came to terms with this rejection by her own parents and relatives. She was the only one of two brothers and four other sisters to suffer such a fate. Two of her sisters married, and the other two were allowed to remain single and stay at home, just what Tarabotti wanted for herself. She kept in touch with her sister Lorenzina, who married Giacomo Pighetti, mentioned several times in her correspondence. She never speaks of her father, Stefano, who died an old man in 1642. When her mother, Maria Cadena, died in 1649, she recorded her death in a letter to her friend, Betta Polani, to whom she turned for comfort.

The third traumatic event of Tarabotti's life was her tumultuous relationship with Gian Francesco Loredan, one of the most distinguished, talented, and powerful aristocrats of the age. Loredan founded the prestigious Venetian Academy of the Incogniti in 1627 and remained its leading light until his death in 1661. The academy's reputation for promoting anticlerical if not anti-Catholic sentiments was well-known, and some of its members, including Loredan himself and the academy's secretary, Ferrante Pallavicino, became known as "libertines." Tarabotti was the only woman writer in Venice to enjoy the company, support, and financial support of Loredan, an incongruous attachment for a Benedictine nun, however rebellious. Her brother-in-law, Giacomo Pighetti, a lawyer and art collector from

Brescia and a member of the Incogniti, may have first introduced her to him and other illustrious members of the academy. It was a remarkable achievement for Tarabotti to have Loredan's letter to another Venetian patrician, Giovanni Polani, singing her praises in the front of her first published book, *Paradiso monacale,* of 1643. Equally prestigious was the dedication of her own correspondence, *Lettere familiari e di complimento* of 1650, to Loredan, who acted as her editor and benefactor. But he would also be her chief adversary. In his own collected correspondence are found letters in which he vilified her.

Her *Paternal Tyranny*—in addition, more than any other book her "manifesto"—denounces at least two works of the Incogniti: first and foremost, Loredan's own *Vita d'Adamo* (The Life of Adam) and then Ferrante Pallavicino's *Corriero svaligiato* (The Postboy Robbed of His Bag). Guglielmo Oddoni, the printer of Tarabotti's *Paradiso monacale* (The Convent as Paradise) of 1643, had cheerfully told the reader to "Expect in a short while other compositions from the same very famous hand, more spicy, perhaps, as they are far better suited to worldly tastes: I hope that *Paternal Tyranny* will be the first." The second was to be her *L'Inferno monacale* (Convent Life as Inferno)—a work she said would show that in convents "reign all the pains of Hell." But *Paternal Tyranny* was not published until after her death, and then outside Italy in a Protestant country. Despite her revisions and title change to *La semplicità ingannata* (Innocence Betrayed), *Inferno monacale* was not published until 1990. Reading *Paternal Tyranny,* one can understand why Loredan—let alone the Catholic Church—could not agree to its publication. Tarabotti admitted as much: "I realize the subject matter is scandalous because it goes against our political as well as against our Catholic way of life." It severely censured the Venetian state that condemned girls to the convent to remove them from the marriage market and reproduction, policies requiring the collusion of the church. Most of the time, Tarabotti

delivers an invective against the oppressions of patriarchy and on the evil consequences in this life and the next of forcing young girls into a life they are not suited for. She recounts the torments of childhood and adolescence in the Venetian family of her day, and she takes apart major texts of contemporary misogyny. She enters boldly into the forbidden territory of theology with a feminist commentary on the Bible and, finally, argues as a lawyer might for women's inalienable rights to liberty and universal education. Daughters, she shows, were made to feel responsible for the financial survival of the family, as overbearing fathers preached that it was "much better for one woman to be shut up to serve God than for a whole family to be ruined." Greed spreads throughout the family as brothers brag to their sisters that they alone will inherit the family's wealth. Mothers stay silent in their obligation as wives to obey their husbands.

When *Paradiso monacale* came out in 1643, Tarabotti was almost forty and had been in the convent for over twenty-five years. She had become painfully aware of the contrast between the "true" nun, who gladly embraces the religious life, for whom Tarabotti was full of praise, and the "false" one, a nun only in appearance. Where does Tarabotti place herself? Certainly not among the former. In the eyes of the Catholic Church and society she had consented to vows; in her heart of hearts she had not. She even refuses to call herself a nun: "Even when it comes to the modern condition of girls forced to take religious vows," she writes, "I am only able to have an imperfect and shadowy knowledge, as I am a lay person."

Tarabotti's dismantling of the structures supporting paternal tyranny takes place on many overlapping planes: theological, political, social, and psychological. In response to Giuseppe Passi's misogynistic *I donneschi diffetti* (The Defects of Women, 1599), Loredan's encomium for Adam before the unwanted arrival of Eve, and Pallavicino's offensive satires, Tarabotti lines up the Bible itself (in particular, the Book of

Genesis and the New Testament), Dante's *Divine Comedy,* an anonymous Italian translation of Cornelius Agrippa's *The Nobility and Preeminence of the Female Sex,* the writings of contemporary Venetian women such as Lucrezia Marinella and Moderata Fonte, and vernacular poets like Ariosto, Tasso, and Guarino. Tarabotti's original uniting of Genesis with Dante's proclamation on free will as God's greatest gift to humans gives Tarabotti grounds to proclaim that both Adam and Eve were created equal by God in a state of innocence with choice and free will. Fathers and other patriarchal authorities who force daughters either to take religious vows or marry disobey God's will and commit a grave sin. When God spoke to Adam of Eve as "a help like unto himself" (Gen. 2:18), he was not giving Adam a servant subject to him, but a companion. Tarabotti shifts blame for the Fall from Eve to Adam since he failed to take responsibility for his deed when God called him to account and, like a coward, "excused himself by accusing his wife."

Turning her attention to the social and political aspects of patriarchy that harm women, the injustices of the double sexual standard in adultery laws come under Tarabotti's scrutiny. For abusive fathers, Tarabotti invokes a vindictive God who will not fail to smite sinners. For abusive husbands who betray their wives, she draws on Saint Paul. According to one of her targets, Passi's *Defects of Women,* an adulterous married woman was more "justly" condemned, punished, and even put to death than the lover, married or not. But Tarabotti reminds husbands that both husbands and wives have equal sexual rights over one another, that it takes two to commit adultery and produce an illegitimate child, and that men are far more to blame as they put more pressure on women to commit adultery than the other way around.

Paternal Tyranny was the only one of Tarabotti's books to be condemned by the Holy Office, in 1660.

Her search for liberty and her interpretations of Scripture were silenced with a heavy hand. She was suspected of Lutheranism. The description of convent life as hell elaborated on aspects of *Paternal Tyranny.* Although Tarabotti does not use the first person "I," she describes a young girl's entry into the convent, her novitiate, and profession of vows as the acts of an unfolding tragedy. The details could only have been recorded by someone who had lived through them. This is an astonishingly original work of psychological and sociological observation; Tarabotti depicts the mental suffering— anxiety, depression, compulsiveness, hysteria bordering on madness—brought on by the rejection of young girls by their own parents, brothers, and sisters and by the refusal of these same parents to listen to the pleas of their own flesh and blood. Convent life is shown to be unnatural and repulsive. Parents haggle over the dowry for their daughters, and convent superiors try to extract a larger amount for the room and board of the future nun. It would be better if these daughters, treated as economic "burdens," had never been born, Tarabotti judges. She highlights parents' meanness by contrasting not only the nun's dowry with that of the exorbitant sum paid out for the privileged daughter marrying her earthly groom, but also the ceremonies themselves. Convent communities, she then shows, are riven by cliques backbiting and bullying one another, by snobbishness deriving from different standards of living, with some nuns enjoying better food and amenities and others surviving near starvation. The utter boredom of the daily routine and the lack of mental stimulation, added to the demands of *clausura* by which nuns may never step outside to enjoy a change of scenery and company, produce a sickly torpor. We do not know to what extent *L'Inferno monacale* circulated. Soon after her "repentent" *Paradiso monacale* of 1643, Tarabotti laid herself open once again to the charge of controversial worldliness. In 1644, she brought out a short tract in direct answer to an earlier one published in Venice in 1638, *Contro 'l lusso donnesco, satira menippea* (Against Women's Luxury,

Menippean Satire), by Francesco Buoninsegni of Siena, friend of Loredan. In her *Antisatira,* she dons the persona of the confidante of married women who turn to her as their advocate, begging her to answer the ridicule poured on women by Buoninsegni for their seemingly excessive love of clothes, hairstyles, and adornments. Tarabotti resorted to her favourite principle of equal standards: if men ridiculed women, women could exercise the corresponding right to ridicule men for their love of luxury displayed in items like fancy lace collars and cuffs, padded stockings, and expensive wigs. Indeed, if men first divested women of ignorance by educating them, women would soon give up worldly vanities.

Her last work to come out during her lifetime was published under the pseudonym Galerana Barcitotti in 1651, a year before her death, titled *Che le donne siano della spezie degli uomini* (Women Do Belong to the Species Mankind), subtitled *Difesa delle donne.* This work confronted a treatise attributed to Orazio Plata Romano, *Che le donne non siano della spezie degli uomini. Discorso piacevole* (Women Do Not Belong to the Species Mankind. An Amusing Speech, 1647). The tract quoted Scripture to "prove" that women do not have a rational soul, cannot make ethical choices, and cannot therefore be saved by Christ. In her counterattack, Tarabotti dismantles the sophistries of the original tract like an expert logician spotting the misreadings of passages from Scripture as a theologian would. In addition, she attacks the author by a series of animal metaphors that invert the misogynistic opposition of (rational) male versus (irrational) female. It is the anonymous (male) author, not his female adversary, who ends up stripped of a human soul.

By the time Tarabotti died, she had achieved her goal as a woman who had successfully entered into dialogue with members of the Venetian aristocracy, the clergy, and the literary elite of her day as their equal in every sense. Her overturning of the assumptions of patriarchy, her call for greater personal freedoms for women, her insistence on education as the only way to gender equality, and her contempt for social convention constitute a unique voice.

On 28 February 1652, after prolonged bouts of fever and illness, the signs most probably of tuberculosis, Arcangela Tarabotti died. She was forty-eight.

Letizia Panizza

See also Convents; Feminism in the Renaissance; Fonte, Moderata; Marinella, Lucrezia; Querelle des Femmes; Religious Reform and Women.

Bibliography

Primary Sources

Loredan, Gian Francesco. *The Life of Adam.* Gainesville, FL: Scholar Facsimiles and Reprints, 1967. (Facsimile reproduction of English translation of 1659.)

Passi, Giuseppe. *I donneschi difetti.* Venice: I. A. Somasco, 1599.

Tarabotti, Arcangela. *Che le donne siano degli spezie degli uomini* (Women Are No Less Rational Than Men). Edited and with an introductory essay by Letizia Panizza. London: Institute of Romance Studies, University of London, 1994.

Tarabotti, Arcangela. *Che le donne siano della spetie degli uomini. Difesa delle Donne di Galerana Barcitotti contro Horatio Plata, il traduttore di quei fogli che dicono: Le donne non essere della spetie degli huomini.* Nuremberg: I. Cherchenbergher, 1651.

Tarabotti, Arcangela. *Contro il lusso donnesco. Satira Menippea del Sig. Fran. sBuoninsegni. Con l'Antisatira D. A. T.* [di Arcangela Tarabotti]. Venice: F. Valvasense, 1644.

Tarabotti, Arcangela. *F. Buoninsegni e Suor A. Tarabotti. Satira e Antisatira.* Edited and with an introduction by Elissa Weaver. Rome: Salerno, 1998.

Tarabotti, Arcangela. *Il Paradiso monacale con un soliloquio a Dio.* Venice: G. Oddoni, 1643.

Tarabotti, Arcangela. *La semplicità ingannata.* Leiden: G. Sambix (Elzevier), 1654.

Tarabotti, Arcangela. *Lagrime per la morte dell'Illustrissima signora Regina Donati.* Venice: Guerigli, 1650.

Tarabotti, Arcangela. "Letter to the Reader" from *Paradiso monacale* and Ferrante Pallavicino's Letter 5, "To an Ungrateful Woman" from *Corriero svaligiato.* In *Paternal Tyranny.* Edited and translated by Letizia Panizza. Chicago: University of Chicago Press. 2004.

Tarabotti, Arcangela. *Lettere familiari e di compli-mento.* Venice: Guerigli, 1650.

Tarabotti, Arcangela. *Lettere familiari e di compli-mento.* Edited by Meredith Ray and Lynn Westwater. Foreword by Gabriella Zarri. Turin: Rosenberg and Sellier, 2005.

Tarabotti, Arcangela. *L'Inferno monacale.* Edited by Francesca Medioli. Turin: Rosenberg and Sellier, 1990.

Tarabotti, Arcangela. *"Women Are Not Human." An Anonymous Treatise and Responses.* Translated by Teresa M. Kenney. New York: Crossroad Publishing Co., 1998.

Secondary Sources

Costa-Zalessow, Natalia. "La condanna all'*Indice* della *Semplicità ingannata* di Arcangela Tarabotti alla luce di manoscritti inediti." *Nouvelles de la République des Lettres* 1 (2000): 97–113.

Medioli, Francesca. "Alcune lettere autografe di Arcangela Tarabotti: autocensura e imagine di sé." *Rivista di storia e letteratura religiosa* 32 (1996): 135–141, 146–155.

Spini, Giorgio. *Ricerca dei libertini: la teoria dell'im-postura delle religioni nel Seicento veneziano.* 2nd ed., revised and amplified. Florence: La Nuova Italia, 1983.

Weaver, Elissa, ed. *Arcangela Tarabotti: A Literary Nun in Baroque Venice.* Ravenna: Longo Editore, 2006.

Zanette, Emilio. *Suor Arcangela Tarabotti monaca del Seicento veneziano.* Venice-Rome: Istituto per la Collaborazione Culturale, 1960.

Teerlinc, Levina (Teerling; ca. 1510–1576)

Professional miniaturist, manuscript illuminator, and painter

The Flemish miniature painter Levina Teerlinc was born sometime between 1510 and 1520 in Bruges. The eldest of five daughters, she received training from her father, Simon Benninck, the internationally renowned miniaturist, book illuminator, and leading artist in the School of Ghent-Bruges. Recruited by Henry VIII, Levina began a distinguished thirty-year career in 1545 as "paintrix" at the English court. She enjoyed the royal patronage of Henry VIII, Edward VI, Mary I, and Elizabeth I, as well as prominent women such as Anne Parr, sister of Catherine Parr, Henry VIII's sixth wife. Her place in the royal household was guaranteed by a substantial salary granted first by Henry VIII and then paid annually throughout the subsequent three reigns. She is described as a "gentle-woman" in court records. In 1556, her husband, George Teerlinc of Blankenbergh, was granted the lease to a property in Stepney, where he built a house. In 1566, she, her husband, and her son, Marcus, became English subjects. She died at her house in Stepney on 23 June 1576 and was buried in the parish church of St. Dunstan.

Teerlinc arrived in England in 1545 with her husband, who was appointed gentleman pensioner in the royal household. Initially, she received a fee of forty pounds a year, which was converted on 10 October 1559 to a permanent annuity of the same amount. Her annuity exceeded that of any painter of the early Tudor period, including Henry VIII's superb court artist, Hans Holbein. It was not until 1599, twenty-three years after Levina's death and thirty years into his professional life, that Nicholas Hilliard was to receive an annuity of forty pounds from Elizabeth I. Generous support from the crown guaranteed Teerlinc a comfortable financial and social situation. She had no need to seek commercial commissions. The first record of a warrant for payment to Levina is dated 1551; this was a request from Edward VI for a portrait of Elizabeth when she was a young princess. For this portrait, Teerlinc was paid the considerable sum of ten pounds. According to the New Year's Roll of 1556, Levina gave Mary I a small picture of the Trinity, for which she received a gilded salt cellar. The New Year's Gift Rolls record and briefly describe nine limnings presented to Elizabeth I, which include images of the queen alone, on progress, at court, and with her Knights of the Garter. In return for these limnings, Teerlinc was given costly presents, such as a pair of gilded spoons.

Identifying Teerlinc's work has proved vexing. Her signature does not appear on any extant limning. Twentieth-century scholars have attributed a handful of extant miniatures and woodcut designs to Teerlinc, though there has been much dispute about most of the attributions. Tudor art scholar Erna Auerbach has argued that *An Elizabethan Maundy Ceremony* (ca. 1560–1565) appears to be an authentic Teerlinc, and subsequent scholars have agreed with this attribution. The limning of Elizabeth I participating in the Maundy Thursday ceremony at which she washed the feet of the poor was most likely a New Year's gift presented to the queen. Other strong possible attributions include miniature portraits of the young Elizabeth, Countess Katherine Grey, Lady Hunsdon, and an unidentified young woman. The portrait of Katherine Grey holding her child (ca. 1560–1563) portrays her wearing a miniature around her neck, which serves as early documentary evidence that limnings were worn as jewelry. Art scholar Roy Strong suggests that Teerlinc was also responsible for designing the Great Seal and pattern images of Elizabeth I for official documents, as well as woodcut portraits of the queen for books, such as George Turbervile's *Booke of Hunting* (1575) and *Booke of Falconrie* (1575).

Roy Strong also believes that Teerlinc instructed Nicholas Hilliard, her great successor at court, in limning. Whether she gave instruction to young painters or not, Levina clearly possessed the authority, knowledge, and skill in the art of limning to do so. Working at court after Hans Holbein and before Hilliard, she was the most significant miniaturist active in England during the years 1545–1576. Given this time span and the responsibilities an annuity entailed, she undoubtedly produced a sizable body of work. Elizabeth I did not replace Levina after her death. Teerlinc deserves recognition as the prominent court artist that she was; a greater effort on the part of art scholars is needed, however, to verify her *œuvre*.

Marguerite Tassi

See also Art and Women; Elizabeth I; Fontana, Lavinia; Gentileschi, Artemisia; Inglis, Esther; Killigrew, Anne; Mary I; Work and Women.

Bibliography

Auerbach, Erna. *Nicholas Hilliard.* London: Routledge and Kegan Paul, 1961.

Auerbach, Erna. *Tudor Artists: A Study of Painters in the Royal Service and of Portraiture on Illuminated Documents from the Accession of Henry VIII to the Death of Elizabeth I.* London: The Athlone Press, 1954.

Bergmans, Simone. "The Miniatures of Levina Teerling." *Burlington Magazine* 64 (1934): 231–234.

Edmond, Mary. *Hilliard and Oliver: The Lives and Works of Two Great Miniaturists.* London: Robert Hale, 1983.

Harris, Ann Sutherland, and Linda Nochlin. *Women Artists: 1550–1950.* New York: Alfred A. Knopf, 1976.

Strong, Roy. *Artists of the Tudor Court: The Portrait Miniature Rediscovered, 1520–1620.* Exhibition catalogue, The Victoria and Albert Museum, 9 July–6 November 1983. London: The Victoria and Albert Museum, 1983.

Strong, Roy. *The English Renaissance Miniature.* New York: Thames and Hudson, 1983.

Strong, Roy. *Gloriana: The Portraits of Queen Elizabeth I.* New York: Thames and Hudson, 1987.

Tufts, Eleanor. *Our Hidden Heritage: Five Centuries of Women Artists.* New York: Paddington Press, 1974.

Terracina, Laura Bacio (Bacio-Terracina; 1519–ca. 1577)

Naples-born writer, member of the Neapolitan Academy of the Incogniti, one of the most frequently published poets in sixteenth-century Italy

Author of eight volumes of poetry published between 1548 and 1567 and a ninth unpublished collection in the Biblioteca Nazionale of Florence, Laura Bacio Terracina was honored in her lifetime for her lyric poems and her *Discorsi,* as she called her verse commentary on Ariosto's *Orlando furioso.* The most prolific woman poet of her century, she exhorted other women to put down the needle and thread and take up the pen so as to win fame on a par with men, who doubted their ability. Among the many sixteenth-century women who heeded the call to letters, Terracina was less proficient technically than the best of her peers. Nevertheless, her work, promoted by booksellers and praised by fellow writers and poets, reached a large and appreciative audience. After her death, both her poetic ambition and her personal virtue were subject to literary satire, and only recently has her work begun to receive due attention. Full recognition awaits a modern edition of her work along with further study of her place in the culture she observed and criticized with skillful acumen.

Born in 1519 into the noble Bacio Terracina family, Laura lived in the comfortable district of Chiaia on the Neapolitan coast where she with her family and other members of Naples' aristocracy were loyal to the Spanish monarchy. Her siblings, addressed in her verses, include two brothers, Mariano (later Abbate) and Giacomo, and a sister, Dionira. Her mother's name, Diana Anfora of Sorrento, may be reflected in the name Phoebea (Diana) that Laura took when she entered the Neapolitan Academy of the Incogniti in 1545. Although she left the academy in 1547, a year before the Spanish viceroy suppressed all Neapolitan academies, throughout her life she stayed in contact with many of its members, among them the writers Angelo di Costanzo, Marco Antonio Epicuro, Antonio Minturno, and her friend Luigi Tansillo, dedicating poems to fellow former academy members and signing her volumes of verse with her academic name. Lacking a formal education, she was assisted in writing by Marcantonio Passero, bookseller and editor, whom she acknowledges with gratitude in her first volume of verse published in Venice in 1548. A woodcut image of the poet appears at the front of the volume, and Ludovico Domenichi, writer, editor, and general consultant to the publishing industry, wrote a dedication to Vincenzo Belprato, count of Aversa, with whom Laura had a romantic interest. Laura did not marry, however, until she was close to forty when she wed Polidoro Terracina, a relative. Poems addressed to her husband indicate anger and jealousy in the relationship.

Terracina's first volume of lyrics is a collection in the Petrarchan tradition ending with a poem to the Virgin, although she makes little use of Petrarchan tropes in the poems. When she does imitate Petrarch directly, she adopts a male poetic voice in literal imitation of her model. The poet whom Terracina follows assiduously is Ludovico Ariosto. Four *lamenti* in her first volume, in the voices of Sacripante, Rodomonte, Isabella, and Bradamante, signaled an early interest in Ariosto and the practice of setting Ariosto's stanzas to music. In further imitation of Ariosto and mindful, no doubt, of an audience seeking moral lessons in *Orlando furioso,* Terracina composed a forty-two-canto poem ingeniously linked to Ariosto's epic, her *Discorso sopra il Principio di Tutti I Canti di Orlando Furioso* (1559). While Ariosto's cantos vary in length, each of Terracina's cantos has seven octaves preceded by an original stanza dedicated to an illustrious individual, Pope Julius III (Canto XIV) for example, or to categories of persons such as *Le Magnifiche Donne* (Splendid Women) in Canto XXII. Each of her next seven stanzas ends with a verse taken in sequence from Ariosto's first stanza in the corresponding canto, except that her seventh stanza ends with Ariosto's verses seven and eight. Thus her seven octaves echo Ariosto's first octaves for the entire poem (she omitted Ariosto's five additional cantos because she considered them inferior to the original text). Terracina's cantos, however, tell no story. Although characters from *Orlando furioso* appear in her verses, her cantos for the most part castigate betrayers of friendship, the prideful, the fraudulent, the avaricious, the libidinous, courtiers, usurers, and prostitutes. Her publisher affirmed her poem's relation to *Orlando furioso* by decorating her volumes with the same woodcut illustrations depicting chivalric scenes that appear in the first edition of *Orlando furioso.* Her "commentary" provided at least one sixteenth-century classroom with a morally safe substitute for Ariosto's masterpiece.

Publication of the *Discorso* established Laura Terracina as a leading figure among the women poets whom publishers cultivated, printed, and anthologized. Her *Seconde Rime* was published in 1549 in Florence, and that same year Ludovico Domenichi cited Laura among other noblewomen of fame and virtue in his *La Nobiltà delle Donne,* calling her a "Laura among Lauras," not only celebrated by others but author of her own fame. The *Discorso* was reprinted and corrected in 1550, 1551, 1554, 1557, and 1559; ten additional printings are listed in the bibliography.

In 1550 Terracina published a fourth book of poems and a fifth book in 1552, both in Venice with G. A. Valvassori. Her sixth volume was published first in Lucca in 1558 with a diatribe against Doralice based on *Orlando furioso* XXVII. 118 and two new *lamenti* in the voices of Zerbino and Orlando. Her later rhymes increasingly deplore political turmoil and social disturbances, Terracina's personal familiarity with public life and the vanities of public figures resonating in her condemnation of their failings. Her religious meditations look inward to personal suffering. and she despairs of achieving her artistic goals. A seventh volume published in Naples in 1561 contains poems addressed to the widowed women of Naples, titled and not titled. A few years later, encouraged by her husband and by a Venetian publisher happy, no doubt, to print new *Discorsi* by a best-selling author, she published a second commentary on *Orlando furioso* with G. A. Valvassori in 1567. The stanzas in her second *Discorsi* follow a plan similar to her first book, except that the stanzas in her *Ottave rime* are based on Ariosto's second stanzas in a pattern slightly varied from that of the first book. A ninth collection remains unpublished, although its contents, including the author's dedicatory Epistle to Don Ferrante Cardinal de Medici dated November 1577 and a representative sampling of verses, was published in 1993 by Luigi Montella, who notes that many of the poems in this last collection had already appeared in earlier volumes. Terracina presumably died soon after dedicating her ninth vol-

ume, having acted all her life on her belief in women's need to pursue the laurel crown of fame. Championing and chiding her sex toward that end, she wrote with a passion that has been likened to the *furore* of Orlando in her quest to gain women equal opportunity with men in that pursuit.

Nancy Dersofi

See also Feminism in the Renaissance; the subheadings Sonnet Writing and Literary Patronage (under Literary Culture and Women).

Bibliography

Primary Works

Terracina, Laura Bacio. *Rime della Signora Laura Terracina.* Venice: G. Giolito de' Ferrari, 1548, 1549, 1550, 1553, 1554, 1560; Venice: D. Farri, 1565; Naples: Boulifon, in 2 volumes, anthologized with the *Rime terze, quarte and quinte.*

Terracina, Laura Bacio : *Rime seconde della Signora Laura Terracina di Napoli et di diversi a lei.* Florence: L. Torrentino, 1549.

Terracina, Laura Bacio : *Discorso sopra tutti li primi canti d'Orlando Furioso. Fatti per la Signora Laura Terracina.* Venice: G. Giolito de Ferrari, 1549, 1550, 1551, 1554, 1557, 1559; Venice: G. Giolito, 1565; Venice: Frazzaria, Al Segno della Regina, 1579; Venice: Godini, 1577; Venice: Frezzari al segno della Regina, 1581.

Terracina, Laura Bacio : *Quarte rime della Signora Laura Terracina detta Phebea nel' Accademic degl'Incogniti.* Venice: G. A. Valvassori, 1550; Lucca: V. Busdrago, 1551; Venice: D. Farri, 1560.

Terracina, Laura Bacio : *Quinte rime della Signora Laura Terracina detta Phebea nel' Accademia degl'Incogniti.* Venice: G. A. Valvassor, 1552; Venice: D. Farri, 1558, 1560.

Terracina, Laura Bacio : *Le seste rime della Signora Laura Terracina di Napoli nuovamente stampate.* Lucca: V. Busdrago, 1558; Naples: R. Amato, 1560.

Terracina, Laura Bacio : *Settime Rime sovra tutte le donne vedove di questa nostra città di Napoli titolate et non titolate. Fatte per la Signora Laura Terracina.* Naples: M. Cancer, 1561.

Terracina, Laura Bacio : *La seconda parte de' discorsi sopra le seconde stanze de' canti d'Orlando Furioso della S. Laura Terracina detta nell'Accademia degl'Incogniti Febea. Nuovamente mandate in luce.* Venice: Valvassori, 1567.

Secondary Works

Borzelli, Angelo. *Laura Terracina, poetessa napoletana del Cinquecento.* Naples: M. Marzano, 1924.

Dersofi, Nancy. "Laura Terracina." In *Italian Women Writers: A Bio-Bibliographical Sourcebook*. Edited by R. Russell, 423–430. Westport, CT: Greenwood Press, 1994.

Jaffe, Irma B., with Gernando Colombardo. *Shining Eyes, Cruel Fortune*. New York: Fordham University Press, 2002.

Maroi, Lucia. *Laura Terracina napolitana del secolo XVI*. Naples: Francesco Perella, 1913.

Mazzarella di Cerreto, A. "Laura Terracina." In *Biografia degli uomini illustri del Regno di Napoli*. Edited by D. Martuscelli. Naples: 1814.

Montella, Luigi. *Una Poetessa del rinascimento, Laura Terracina*. Salerno: Edisud-Salerno, ca. 1993.

Mutini, C. In *L'autore e l'opera*. Rome: Bulzoni, 1973.

Russell, Rinaldina. In *An Encyclopedia of Continental Women Writers*. Edited by K. M. Wilson, 2:1227–1229. New York: Garland Publishing, 1991.

Shemek, Deanna. *Ladies Errant*. Durham, NC: Duke University Press, 1998.

Theater and Women Actors, Playwrights, and Patrons

Long overlooked and underrated, women's contributions to European Renaissance theater have only recently been acknowledged and valued by scholars. European women of the fifteenth through early seventeenth centuries participated in both public and private theatrical activities not only as audience members, but also as playwrights, translators, actresses, patrons, shareholders, employees of theaters, and leaders of acting troupes. Monarchs such as Elizabeth I, Anne of Denmark, Catherine de Médicis, and Marie de Médicis were instrumental in cultivating a theatrical culture at their courts. These and other noblewomen commissioned dramatic works, sponsored acting troupes, and functioned as honored spectators, all of which lent social legitimacy to theater as a private enterprise. The professional or public theater, however, was perceived as morally compromising, especially for women. Yet Renaissance women of all classes defied social conventions and moral restrictions not only by attending theatrical productions, but also by pursuing professional writing and acting opportunities.

During the English Renaissance, women were banned from public and university stages, yet, like their aristocratic female counterparts throughout Europe, they played significant roles behind the scenes at court and in aristocratic households as patrons, writers, and masque performers. Queen Elizabeth I was the most prominent English patron of playing companies; the Queen's Men gained great popularity in the 1580s, playing at court and in English public playhouses. Following the queen's lead, other aristocratic women gave patents and lent their names to companies. Mary Sidney, the countess of Pembroke, was one of the most influential female patrons of the arts. Not only was she at the center of a productive artistic circle, Sidney also sponsored a small acting troupe, Pembroke's Men, and translated Robert Garnier's drama, *The Tragedy of Antonie* (1595, original 1578), which was most likely intended for household performance. Other Englishwomen produced translations of dramatic texts, the first known one being Lady Jane Lumley's version (ca. 1553) of Euripides' *Iphigenia at Aulis*. A fragment from a translation of Seneca's *Hercules Oetaeus* has been attributed to Queen Elizabeth. Mary Wroth and Elizabeth Cary have both been recognized by recent scholars as dramatists in their own right, Wroth for *Love's Victory* (ca. 1621) and Cary for *The Tragedy of Miriam* (1613).

While Englishwomen were not licensed to perform with theater troupes, women of the Stuart court (early seventeenth century) had occasion to play silent, yet physically expressive, roles in masques commissioned by Queen Anne of Denmark (James I's wife). Female courtiers and in some cases the queen herself danced in no fewer than eight masques alongside professional male actors. Just as significant as a female presence on an English stage was Anne's deep involvement in the production of some of these masques and her working relationship with Ben Jonson, her favored playwright. She was the

Engraving showing Shakespeare performing before Queen Elizabeth I and her court. (Library of Congress)

visionary force behind the masquing culture at the early Stuart court, which fostered noble-women's access to the Renaissance stage. Not until 1660 were women allowed by patent to pursue acting as a profession, and, with the rise of female playwrights such as Aphra Behn, En-glishwomen finally became theater professionals in their own right.

In Italy, Antonia Pulci was the earliest ver-nacular playwright, the author of three *sacre rappresentazioni* on the lives of saints and the possible author of at least four other plays. Her plays were most likely performed in convents for Florentine nuns, with the possibility that the nuns performed the parts. Her works were printed in the 1490s and reprinted throughout the sixteenth century. Later female dramatists include the Roman courtesan, Margherita Costa, who produced songs, operas, and dra-

mas, the most famous of them the *comedia ridi-cola, Li buffoni* (1641).

More visible than female dramatists, who were primarily nonprofessionals during this period, were actresses who rose to fame (and some degree of infamy) in the Italian profes-sional troupes during the sixteenth and seven-teenth centuries. In the early Renaissance, Ital-ian female courtesans were private entertainers who sang and danced in spectacles and *inter-mezzi;* in the religious community, nuns per-formed in cloistered dramatic rituals. Early professional actresses were most likely courte-sans who were skilled in performance arts. By 1565, a shift from women's functioning in pri-vate entertainments to public theatrical activ-ity can be noted with the first record, which appeared in Rome, of a professional actress (a woman named Lucrezia from Siena). From this time on, Italian women began to achieve a degree of professional prominence as members of acting troupes, which played not only in Italy but also across the continent. Italian actresses were acclaimed in Paris and made their mark on the French court as well as in the emerging acting troupes in Italian cities, which began to include women only later in the century. Furthermore, records demonstrate that in 1567 two women, known as Vincenza and "the Roman Flaminia," led companies of *commedia* players. Other entrepreneurial women directed troupes in later years.

A handful of actresses, such as Vittoria Piissimi and Isabella Andreini, became famous as brilliant, versatile performers of *commedia dell'arte*. Their trademark, or most notable innovation, was improvisation, which had not been associated with the earlier male troupes. Piisimi was the leader of the Confidenti troupe, and Andreini was the female lead of the Gelosi traveling players, who received patronage from the duke of Mantua for a time. She wrote a pastoral play, *La Mirtilla* (1588), stage dialogues, lyrics, and letters, and she was elected to the Pavian academy, the *Intendi*.

Records of professional French actresses began to appear at the end of the sixteenth century in conjunction with the famous actor Valleran le Conte and his acting troupe. Not until the 1630s, however, did Frenchwomen gain a degree of social acceptance and centrality in public performances. Marie Champmeslé became the reigning actress of the seventeenth century. By the latter part of the seventeenth century, Frenchwomen performed regularly both at court and in the public theaters. They also served as theater professionals of another kind: as costumers, ushers, and box office managers. More important, talented actresses earned a share or quarter share in companies and therefore gained a voice and a percentage of the profit. French female dramatists emerged later than their English and Italian counterparts with the works of Marie-Catherine Desjardins (known also as Mme. de Villedieu) and Cather-

ine Bernard in the later seventeenth and early eighteenth centuries. According to recent scholarship, approximately thirty-three plays were written by Frenchwomen before 1700; some of these works have been lost, and some were never performed.

Women of the European Renaissance clearly influenced and participated in the theatrical culture of their time, whether they were showcasing new acting techniques onstage, as were the Italian *commedia* actresses, or writing, commissioning, and patronizing dramatic activity, as were the aristocratic and noblewomen of the great houses and families of Europe. Despite moral censure, women frequented the public theaters throughout Europe and were considered by playwrights to be a critical audience mass to which they needed to appeal. Even though traditional scholarship is accurate in its assumption that European Renaissance theater was dominated by male artists and businessmen, the contributions of women were far too numerous and significant to be overlooked.

Marguerite A. Tassi

See also Andreini, Isabella; Behn, Aphra; Cary, Elizabeth Tanfield; Literary Culture and Women; Lumley, Jane; Pulci, Antonia Tanini; Scala, Alessandra; Sidney, Mary Herbert; Wroth, Mary.

Bibliography

Bryce, Judith. "Adjusting the Canon for Later Fifteenth-Century Florence: The Case of Antonia Pulci." In *The Renaissance Theatre: Texts Performance, Design*. Vol. 1. Edited by Christopher Cairns, 133–145. Aldershot, UK: Ashgate, 1999.

Cerasano, S. P., and Marion Wynne-Davies. *Renaissance Drama by Women: Texts and Documents*. London and New York: Routledge, 1996.

McGill, Kathleen. "Women and Performance: The Development of Improvisation by the Sixteenth-Century Commedia dell-Arte." *Theatre Journal* 43 (1991): 59–69.

McManus, Clare. *Women on the Renaissance Stage: Anna of Denmark and Female Masquing in the Stuart Court (1590–1619)*. Manchester, UK, and New York: Manchester University Press, 2002.

Woodrough, Elizabeth, ed. *Women in European Theatre*. Oxford, UK: Intellect Books, 1995.

Toledo, Eleonora di
(ca. 1522–1562)

Duchess of Florence; commodities trader in iron, coal, wood, livestock, wine, salt, sugar, grain; dealer in foreign exchange; proxy head of state; protector of the Franciscan and Jesuit orders in Florence; and patron of poets, painters, sculptors, and architects

Eleonora di Toledo, second duchess of Florence, is almost exclusively renowned for her wealth and powerful family connections. Most histories of sixteenth-century Florence largely ignore her, except for speculations about her death in Pisa on 17 December 1562. Having followed so soon after the deaths of two of her children, this gave rise almost immediately to fantastic stories about fratricide and poisoning, although she had suffered from some form of "consumption" for years and died of a malarial fever contracted while hunting with her husband and children in the Maremma, then a mosquito-filled swamp on the Tuscan coast. While Eleonora's fondness for jewels, her generosity to religious orders, and her provision of dowries to poor Florentine girls have also been noted, her role as patron has been neglected, unless it is to say that it was her money that was used to buy the Pitti Palace and that she kept Benvenuto Cellini and the other court goldsmiths busy with commissions. Eleonora, by and large, employed the same artists that her husband, Cosimo I de Medici, second duke of Florence, later first grand duke of Tuscany, did, many of whom received a regular annual stipend, although there are important distinctions between their acts of patronage that cannot be explained merely by gender differences. Eleonora's Spanish and Neapolitan heritage provided her with important role models for strong, educated, active women: she expected to play an important role in public life as duchess of Florence and did so. Her wealth, power, and importance as a patron were all noted by contemporaries.

Eleonora's recorded history and public life coincide with her arrival in Italy in 1534, two years after her father, Pedro Álvarez de Toledo, a

Eleonora di Toledo, duchess of Florence and Siena and patron of the arts. Portrait by Bronzino. Uffizi, Florence, Italy. (Library of Congress)

younger son of Don Fadrique, the second duke of Alba, arrived in Naples to assume his role as Charles V's viceroy there. She was one of seven children, possibly the youngest of the three sons and four daughters born to Pedro and his wife, Maria Osorio Pimentel. Like that of her sisters, the precise date of her birth remains unknown, although it probably took place in 1522, since her funerary epitaph and other contemporary sources refer to her as having died at the age of forty in 1562. She was thus about thirteen or fourteen years old when Naples temporarily became the principal social center for the imperial world during the autumn and winter of 1535–1536, when Charles V made his triumphal entry into the city following his military victory in Tunisia. Splendid festivities were mounted for the emperor and his court, and foreign visitors traveled to Naples to pay homage to him. Among these were Alessandro de Medici, the first duke of Florence, betrothed from 1529 to Charles's illegitimate daughter, Margaret of Austria. It is often stated that

Eleonora saw her future husband, Cosimo, at this time. A sixteen-year-old page in the Florentine court of his distant cousin, Cosimo did indeed travel to Naples in 1535. However, it is possible that the future consorts did not even see each other on this occasion, given the care exercised during Charles's visit to limit the public appearance of noblewomen, presumably to avoid the possibility of scandalous incidents with so many foreign dignitaries in the city; for example, women were permitted to view processions only from the windows of their palaces. This was an exception, however, as Naples was a city in which women played a decidedly public role throughout the fifteenth and sixteenth centuries.

Upon the assassination of Alessandro on 6 January 1537 and his own unlikely ascension to the ducal throne, Cosimo began seeking a suitable consort. With every indication that he would be confirmed by the emperor as duke, Elisabetta, daughter of the erudite Francesco Guicciardini, apparently Cosimo's intended, was no longer an expedient match. Through his ministers at the imperial court he requested the hand of Margaret of Austria. It seems unlikely that he actually expected this request to be granted, but it was an immediate sign to Charles V that he wanted to cement ties to Spain and the Empire. Margaret, however, had already been promised to Ottavio Farnese, Pope Paul III's grandson. Correspondence between Cosimo and Giovanni Bandini, his envoy to the imperial court, reveals that the bridal candidates discussed were as varied as Charles V's niece, Cristina of Denmark, a sister of the duke of Alba, and even one of the Tudor princesses.

It was Pedro de Toledo himself who came forward at the imperial court to offer the hand of one of his daughters to the young duke. Charles favored the project and negotiations were begun. Pedro had apparently intended to give Cosimo the elder of his two unmarried daughters, Isabella, offering as an added enticement the enormous dowry of eighty thousand scudi, but Cosimo had already been warned by

one of his secretaries then in Naples, Angelo Niccolini, to insist absolutely on the younger daughter, Eleonora, since Isabella was "of an ugly age and her brain the scorn of Naples." The copious correspondence that survives from Cosimo's agents in Naples regarding the two sisters argues against the often stated hypothesis that his and Eleonora's was a love match; if he had met her in Naples in 1535, let alone loved her, this would have been unnecessary. Furthermore, if he had hoped to marry her, his ambassador could have suggested this at the imperial court immediately after negotiations for Margaret's hand had failed.

Negotiations between Cosimo and Pedro were eventually concluded, and a dowry of fifty thousand scudi was agreed upon, thirty thousand to be paid by Pedro and twenty thousand to be paid as a counterdowry by Cosimo; apparently, neither of these amounts was ever disbursed. On 29 March 1539, Jacopo de Medici and Luigi Ridolfi acted as Cosimo's proxies in a marriage ceremony in Naples. The couple was not united until June of that year when Eleonora left Naples with a large entourage of Spanish courtiers, including her brother García, and sailed for Livorno. A week following her arrival in Tuscany, on 29 June, Eleonora made her triumphal entry into Florence to find an extravagant display of ephemeral decorations, many of them created by artists who would continue to be employed by both the duke and the duchess throughout their reign. The celebrations that followed concluded on 11 July with the performance of Il Commodo, a comedy by Antonio Landi, with spectacular costumes and stage effects by Niccolò Tribolo and Aristotile da Sangallo.

Cosimo and Eleonora's marriage proved to be remarkably felicitous. Vincenzo Fedeli, the Venetian ambassador to the Florentine court in 1561, observed that Cosimo, "after becoming prince, never conversed with any woman other than the duchess his wife." In 1565, Lorenzo Priuli, the new Venetian ambassador to the Florentine court for the wedding of Francesco I de Medici to Joanna of Austria, noted that, after the death of the duchess, the duke's admirable morality ceased to exist entirely. Priuli's report is of special interest as he singles out Eleonora's wise council as the sole font of Cosimo's early prudence and "a major contributing factor to his greatness." Along with her dowry, an alliance with the Spanish house of Alba, and imperial goodwill, Eleonora brought her education, her observations of her father's method of rule, and the expectation, formed in the Neapolitan court environment that had permitted women to accede to the throne, that after marriage she would enter public life and exercise power; all of these proved immensely valuable to Cosimo.

Another important factor for the success of the ducal couple's union was the duchess's remarkable fecundity. In the first fifteen years following her arrival in Florence, Eleonora gave birth to eleven children, eight of whom survived to maturity, but only four of whom outlived their mother. Three of these four were male children, ensuring the survival of the line, even after the sole male child born to Cosimo and Eleonora's heir, Francesco I, predeceased his father. Francesco was therefore succeeded by another child of Eleonora's, Ferdinando I, whose descendants ruled the grand duchy of Tuscany into the eighteenth century.

Eleonora's devotion to religious orders can be documented primarily in regard to the Franciscans and the Jesuits. During her second pregnancy, she traveled to the Tuscan shrine of La Verna, where Francis had received the stigmata, and prayed to the saint to give birth to a son; when the child was born male, he was named Francesco in recognition of this pilgrimage. Both Cosimo and Eleonora remained devoted to the Franciscan sanctuary, sponsoring the construction of the Foresteria there, where the Medici-Toledo arms are prominently visible over the portals. Later, the duchess would also be influential in assisting the recently founded Jesuit order to establish a presence in Florence. She is particularly credited with ob-

taining the church of San Giovannino and the adjacent building for the foundation of their college. From the arrival of the Society of Jesus in Florence, her personal confessor was exclusively chosen from among their number: the first of these was Diego Laínez, among the original founders of the order, who eventually succeeded Ignatius of Loyola as its second general; the last was Francisco Strada, present at her death in Pisa.

A major influence on Eleonora's early life appears to have been her childhood tutor, Bienvenida Abrabanel, described by Cecil Roth as having "played in Jewish life a part not unlike that of the great noblewomen of the age in secular affairs." Two years after Eleonora's departure for Tuscany in 1539, the expulsion of the Jews from the kingdom of Naples forced Bienvenida's family to move from Naples to Ferrara. The duchess and her former governess appear to have remained in contact following these peregrinations. Important evidence in this regard is provided by the contract for the betrothal of Lucrezia de Medici to Alfonso II d'Este in 1558; Eleonora provided at least half of the enormous dowry of two hundred thousand scudi established for her daughter, while the rest of the sum was guaranteed in part by Bienvenida's son Jacob. Bienvenida may therefore have been an important conduit for information about the activities of the Este court during these years in which the Florentines and the Ferrarese were engaged in fierce diplomatic, social, and artistic rivalry. In addition, Eleonora's early contact with the highest levels of hispano-Jewish society in the Italian peninsula may in part account for the protection she reputedly offered to the Jewish community in Florence after her arrival there.

As part of her responsibilities as duchess, Eleonora was charged with controlling the household finances, a significant undertaking given the extent of the Medici estates and the quantity of goods required by the court. She proved to be not only a capable but an astute estate manager. She derived income from mining, beekeeping, and cultivating silkworms, and she dealt in all the principal commodities of the day, including wood, livestock, cheeses, meat, wine, salt, sugar, and other goods. Above all, the duchess raised and sold substantial quantities of grain, for which she maintained her own galleons for export as far away as her native Spain; indeed, three years after her death, Priuli reported that the commerce of grain had been restricted in Florence and could be bought or sold only through Eleonora. Another significant expense managed by her was the clothing of the ducal family and the livery of their courtiers. Many of these commercial activities can be linked to economic reforms undertaken by Cosimo and all ultimately led to Eleonora amassing significant capital. By the time Fedeli visited the Florentine court in 1561, she reputedly earned an annual income of forty thousand scudi. With her liquid funds, she borrowed and lent money and dealt in foreign exchange. Among her principal debtors was Cosimo; by 1553, he was forced to grant her an annual income of ten thousand gold scudi out of the Florentine salt tax to repay her. She vastly augmented the extent of her husband's land holdings by reinvesting her money in real estate; among her more important purchases were the marquisate of Castiglione della Pescaia and the Isola del Giglio, for which she paid thirty thousand scudi to the Piccolomini in 1558. No other ducal or grand ducal consort would contribute so extensively to developing the Medici patrimony.

That the duchess was a shrewd administrator and intelligent investor is evident from a letter written by her husband to their eldest son on 18 December 1562, the day following her death. Francesco was at the Spanish royal court as part of a diplomatic mission and a failed attempt to secure an illustrious bride, Philip II's recently widowed sister Maria, when his younger brothers Giovanni and Garzia and his mother all died. Cosimo wrote from Pisa that Eleonora, weakened from consumption and malarial fever, "confessed, took extreme unction, wrote a most honorable testament in my presence, thus thinking first of her soul and then of her servants, and then, one might say, in my arms, gave up her soul to God" three days later, "having spent two days waiting for death in complete control of her faculties, almost always with a crucifix in her hand and seated on the bed, reasoning in a mundane fashion about death as if it were negotiable." Being an able negotiator was most clearly a key element of her personality or her husband would not have mentioned it to their son in this tender description of her passing.

Eleonora was required to act as head of state during her husband's absences and in times of war, a role she assumed on more than one occasion. The first of these regencies occurred less than two years after their marriage. In 1541, Cosimo availed himself of Charles V's arrival at Genoa to travel there to personally negotiate for the return of the fortresses of Florence and Livorno, still under imperial control following the assassination of Duke Alessandro. To undertake this diplomatic mission, he left Eleonora in charge of the government of Florence. The negotiations in Genoa were prolonged, and Cosimo remained there for much of the year, except for a brief return to Florence to celebrate the baptism of his heir Francesco on 1 August. For much of the year, therefore, Eleonora served as Florentine head of state; she evidently proved herself because Cosimo continued to confirm her as head of state during his absences.

For the first half of 1543 we find her performing this role again while her husband returned to Genoa to meet with Charles V, finally succeeding in obtaining the return of the fortresses. From May 1544 to February 1545, Cosimo was deathly ill with malaria, and once again she was called upon to run the government of Florence. By far, her longest period of rule occurred during the war with Siena, officially taken over from the imperial forces by Cosimo in 1554 but certainly a major concern for the Florentine state from its outbreak in

1551. Whatever the outcome of the Sienese uprising, it was certain to have important consequences for the duke's territories; the prospect of Charles V and the king of France engaging in a war for hegemony over Tuscany must have been terrifying. Forced to direct most of his attention to military and foreign affairs, Cosimo left the everyday functions of his state to his consort. When the Sienese finally capitulated, it was to the duchess, not the duke, that their ministers made their address; this may be seen as a token of the very real power that she wielded in Florence.

Following her entry into Florence as Cosimo's bride in 1539, most of the state ceremonies in which she participated were for her children's baptisms or weddings. In the autumn of 1560, however, she participated in two significant triumphal entries, into Siena and the Vatican. In Siena, splendid ephemeral decorations were created by Bartolomeo Ammannati and Francesco Tomasi, some of which specifically celebrated the duchess. In Rome, a measure of her importance is provided by the fact that she and her husband were each received by Pope Pius IV with separate entries. Eleonora's entry is described by various contemporaries, including the diarist Agostino Lapini and the Florentine ambassador Averardo Serristori. This was organized to occur shortly after sunset, when the copious jewels worn by the duchess and employed in her livery were apparently intended to achieve maximal brilliance as they reflected the light of the torches carried by the attendants in her retinue. While the pope showered Cosimo with gifts of antiquities, he gave Eleonora the marquisate of Marignano, a measure of her political stature.

Eleonora's most active periods of patronage appear to coincide with her terms as acting head of state; with Cosimo away, court artists would have been somewhat freer to execute works for her. These commissions required vast sums of money, which came directly out of her personal income, raised through her own financial activities and recorded in separate accounts.

By far, her most significant act of patronage was the purchase of the Pitti Palace, its subsequent adaptation, and the development of the adjacent Boboli Gardens. Eleonora also commissioned numerous portraits of herself and her children, primarily from the painter Agnolo Bronzino, whose most important work for the duchess is the fresco cycle and altarpiece for her private chapel in the Palazzo Vecchio. The other two artists most closely associated with her are the sculptor, Baccio Bandinelli, and Tribolo, the polymath sculptor, architect, and hydraulic engineer. In addition, the duchess was also the direct patron of Ammannati, Francesco Ubertini (called il Bachiacca), Santi Buglioni, Cellini, Giulio Clovio, Giovanni Fancelli (called Nanni di Stocco), Davide Fortini, Ridolfo del Ghirlandaio and Michele Tosini (called Michele di Ridolfo del Ghirlandaio), Giampaolo and Domenico Poggini, Francesco Salviati, Jan van der Straet (called Giovanni Stradano), and Giorgio Vasari. Eleonora also engaged in literary patronage, sponsoring the Accademia degli Elevati, a literary academy dedicated to poetry, and was the subject of poems by such contemporaries as Tullia d'Aragona, Laura Battiferri, Bronzino, Giambattista Gelli, and Benedetto Varchi. Significantly, the first edition of Tullia's *Rime* was dedicated to the duchess, who had personally interceded to gain an exemption from local sumptuary laws for the courtesan-poet during her residence in Florence in 1546–1548.

Bruce L. Edelstein

See also Art and Women; the subheading Literary Patronage (under Literary Culture and Women); Margaret of Parma.

Bibliography

Primary Works

Baldini, Baccio. *Vita di Cosimo Medici, primo gran duca di Toscana, discritta da M. Baccio Baldini suo protomedico.* Florence: Sermartelli, 1578.

Cellini, Benvenuto. *Vita.* Edited by Ettore Camesasca. Milan: Rizzoli, 1985.

Cini, Giovambattista. *Vita del serenissimo signor Cosimo de Medici primo gran duca di Toscana.* Florence: Giunti, 1611.

Cirni Corso, Anton Francesco. *La reale entrata dell'ecc.mo signor duca et duchesa di Fiorenza, in Siena, con la significatione delle latine inscrittioni, e con alcuni sonetti.* Rome: Blado, 1560.

Coppi, Enrico, ed. *Cronaca fiorentina 1537–1555.* ("Diario del Marucelli"). Florence: Olschki, 2000.

Giambullari, Pierfrancesco. *Apparato et feste nelle noze dello illustrissimo signor duca di Firenze, et della duchessa sua consorte, con le sue stanze, madriali, comedia, & intermedij, in quelle recitate.* Florence: Giunta, 1539.

Giovio, Paolo. *Dialogi et descriptiones.* Edited by Ernesto Travi and Mariagrazia Penco. Rome: Istituto Poligrafico dello Stato, 1984.

Giovio, Paolo. *Lettere.* 2 vols. Edited by Giuseppe Guido Ferrero. Rome: Istituto Poligrafico dello Stato, 1956–1958.

Ignatius of Loyola, Saint (1960). *Letters to Women.* Edited by Hugo Rahner. Freiburg: Herder, 1960.

Lapini, Agostino. *Diario fiorentino dal 252 al 1596.* Edited by Giuseppe Odoardo Corazzini. Florence: Sansoni, 1900.

Medici, Cosimo I de'. *Lettere.* Edited by Giorgio Spini. Florence: Vallecchi, 1940.

Vasari, Giorgio. *Der Literarische Nachlass Giorgio Vasaris.* 2 vols. Edited by Karl Frey. Munich: Müller, 1923–1930.

Vasari, Giorgio. *Le vite de' più eccellenti pittori scultori ed architettori.* 9 vols. Edited by Gaetano Milanesi. Florence: Sansoni, 1878–1882.

Vettori, Piero. *Laudatio Eleonorae, Cosmi Medicis, Floren. ac Senens. ducis, uxoris: quae habita est IIII. k. ian. Florentiae, à Pietro Victorio, in aede divi Laurentii.* Florence: Torrentino, 1562.

Secondary Works

Arrighi, Vanna. "Eleonora de Toledo." In *Dizionario biografico degli italiani* 42. Edited by Fiorella Barroccini e Mario Caravale, 437–441. Rome: Enciclopedia Italiana, 1993.

Baia, Anna. *Leonora di Toledo, Duchessa di Firenze e di Siena.* Todi, Italy: Foglietti, 1907.

Cantini, Lorenzo. *Vita di Cosimo de' Medici Primo Granduca di Toscana.* Florence: Albizziniana, 1805.

Cox-Rearick, Janet. *Bronzino's Chapel of Eleonora in the Palazzo Vecchio.* Berkeley: University of California, 1993.

Cox-Rearick, Janet, and Mary Westerman Bulgarella. "Public and Private Portraits of Cosimo de' Medici and Eleonora di Toledo: Bronzino's Paintings of his Ducal Patrons in Ottawa and Turin." *Artibus et Historiae* 49 (2004): 101–159.

Edelstein, Bruce. "Bronzino in the Service of Eleonora di Toledo and Cosimo I de' Medici: Conjugal Patronage and the Painter-Courtier." In *Beyond Isabella: Secular Women Patrons of Art in Renaissance Italy.* Edited by Sheryl E. Reiss and David G. Wilkins, 225–261. Kirksville, MO: Truman State University Press, 2001a.

Edelstein, Bruce. "The Early Patronage of Eleonora di Toledo: The Camera Verde and its Dependencies in the Palazzo Vecchio." 2 vols. Ph.D. dissertation, Harvard University, 1995.

Edelstein, Bruce. "Janet Cox-Rearick, Bronzino's Chapel of Eleonora in the Palazzo Vecchio" (Review). *The Art Bulletin* 76 (1994): 171–175.

Edelstein, Bruce. "Nobildonne napoletane e committenza: Eleonora d'Aragona ed Eleonora di Toledo a confronto." *Quaderni storici* 104 (2000): 295–329.

Edelstein, Bruce. "Observations on the Genesis & Function of Bronzino's Frankfurt *Modello* for the Vault Decoration in the Chapel of Eleonora." In *Coming About . . . A Festschrift for John Shearman.* Edited by Lars R. Jones and Louisa C. Matthew, 157–163. Cambridge, MA: Harvard University Art Museums, 2001b.

Eisenbichler, Konrad, ed. *The Cultural World of Eleonora di Toledo: Duchess of Florence and Siena.* Aldershot, UK: Ashgate, 2004.

Kaufmann, Henry W. "Art for the Wedding of Cosimo de' Medici and Eleonora of Toledo (1539)." *Paragone* 21 (1970): 52–67.

Minor, Andrew C., and Bonner Mitchell. *A Renaissance Entertainment: Festivities for the Marriage of Cosimo I, Duke of Florence in 1539.* Columbia: University of Missouri Press, 1968.

Parigino, Giuseppe Vittorio. *Il Tesoro del Principe: funzione pubblica e privata del patrimonio della famiglia Medici nel Cinquecento.* Florence: Olschki, 1999.

Tornabuoni de Medici, Lucrezia (1425–1482)

Art patron, diplomat, businesswomen, writer of sacred poems on biblical themes, prolific letter writer

Lucrezia Tornabuoni de Medici, mother of Lorenzo the Magnificent and grandmother of two popes, was the most prominent woman in fifteenth-century Florence. During her city's golden age—the era of Botticelli, Poliziano, Fra Angelico, and Filippo Brunelleschi—she presided over the Medici dynasty from the haven of the family palazzo on the Via Larga, and, as her almost fifty extant letters attest, she was as at home negotiating with noble Roman families for a bride for Lorenzo as she was collecting rents from Pisan storeowners. A descendant of a noble line herself (unlike her husband Piero de Medici), Tornabuoni was crucial for cementing alliances between Florence's leading upstart family and its more established clans. She seems to have been highly respected not only for her political and social acumen but also for her many charitable endeavors. When she died, she was lamented by Francesco da Castiglione, canon at the Medici church of San Lorenzo, as a wise and compassionate leader: "She advised the most important persons as well as the magistrates, and she also admitted the humblest to her presence, and all she sent away happy and contented. She knew how to manage the most important affairs with wise counsel, and to succor the citizens in time of calamity."

Such calamities were varied, extending from Florence's varying hostilities with Rome and moments of internal unrest, such as the assassination of Lucrezia's younger son, Giuliano, in the Duomo of Florence of 1478 (Lorenzo, the other target of the conspiracy, was wounded but escaped). Tornabuoni's influence and talents, however, were not limited to her role in the city's public life (albeit much of what she did was necessarily behind the scenes). Probably some time after Piero's death in 1469, she began writing a series of *laudi,* or sacred poems, a genre in which Savonarola and Lorenzo were also fluent. She also launched a more ambitious literary project in her five *storie sacre,* or sacred narratives, extensive poems based on biblical stories. Supple translations and revisions of the Latin Vulgate into vernacular Italian in both *terzine* and the more challenging *octave,* the poems range across Old Testament (primarily Apocryphal) and New Testament traditions to embrace the tales of Esther, Judith, Susanna, Tobias, and John the Baptist, Florence's patron saint.

That three of the stories focus on Hebrew heroines is surely significant, particularly given Lucrezia's own status in Florence. (The fact that she may have written her poems for her granddaughters has prompted a few scholars to treat them as slight domestic affairs; but if this were the case, Tornabuoni would not have given drafts to Florence's leading humanist, Angelo Poliziano, or to the poet Luigi Pulci, who dedicated his playful epic *Morgante* to Tornabuoni.) Esther is the wife of powerful King Ahasuerus, who successfully pleads with him on behalf of her people; Susanna is unjustly accused of adultery by two elders who are ultimately stoned to death; Judith becomes the powerful savior of her city, Bethulia, when she seduces the Assyrian general, Holoferness, and then cuts off his head. Even the story of Tobias, a tale about charitable deeds and their rewards in the time of the Babylonian captivity, features a strong and passionate believer in Sara, who prays to God to release her from a curse that has killed her first seven husbands. And the tale of John the Baptist gives us an antiheroine who nonetheless steals the show: Herodias, who baits her daughter into asking for John's head. But she too is balanced by the serene Mary of the story's opening pages, who in Tornabuoni's translation calmly receives her gift from Gabriel: "I am his handmaiden; let what you have just revealed so clearly and so openly be done to me" (Tylus 2001).

All of the figures to which Tornabuoni turned in her poetic narratives—Herodias, of course, excepted—demonstrate fierce loyalty to their people and a selflessness that enables them to challenge social convention and local custom. In particular, Judith, Esther, and the elderly Tobias exemplify a sanctity that is directed toward a larger community, and they thus exemplify virtues of an active and social kind. While one would not wish to treat the *storie sacre* as autobiographical, it is useful to ask in what ways Tornabuoni might have herself wrestled with justifying both her political and literary activities to a Florentine republican ideology grounded in the inequality of the sexes. A figure such as Judith thus becomes a tempting paradigm for a Tornabuoni anxious to legitimize her own interventions into Florentine cultural life: as she says in her exordium to "The Story of Judith," "I found her story written in prose/ and I was greatly impressed by her courage:/ a fearful little widow,/ she had your [God's] help, and she knew what to do and say;/ Lord, you made her bold and helped her plan succeed./ Would that you could grant such favor to me,/ so that I may turn her tale into rhyme,/ in a manner that might please" (Tylus 2001).

Critics have not always looked kindly at Tornabuoni, and her poems have never been published in their entirety in Italian. In particular, her works have been dismissed as "merely" religious literature, following in the tradition of the *cantari* or singers of both sacred and secular tales in Florence's little piazza of San Martino. Yet recent reevaluations of Tornabuoni's poems and of the flourishing Quattrocento religious tradition as a whole lead one to hope that Tornabuoni too will enjoy a renaissance as a poet who no doubt influenced her son Lorenzo's own innovations in the vernacular. And one also hopes that, thanks to the recent publication of her letters, her undeniably important roles as patron, diplomat, businesswoman, and advisor will come to be more deeply appreciated and understood.

Jane Tylus

See also Art and Women; the subheading Letter Writing (under Literary Culture and Women).

Bibliography

Primary Works

Medici, Lucrezia Tornabuoni de. *I poemetti sacri di Lucrezia Tornabuoni.* Edited by Fulvio Pezzarossa. Florence: Olschki, 1978.

Medici, Lucrezia Tornabuoni de. *Lettere.* Edited by Patrizia Salvadori. Florence: Olschki, 1993.

Tylus, Jane, ed. and trans. *Sacred Narratives.* Chicago: University of Chicago Press, 2001.

Secondary Works

Kent, F. William. "Sainted Mother, Magnificent Son: Lucrezia Tornabuoni and Lorenzo de'

Medici." *Italian History and Culture* 3 (1997): 3–34.

Maguire, Yvonne. *The Women of the Medici.* London: Routledge, 1927.

Martelli, Mario. "Lucrezia Tornabuoni." In *Les femmes écrivains en Italie au Moyen Âge et à la Renaissance.* Pages 51–86. Aix-en-Provence, France: Publications de l'Université de Provence, 1994.

Plebani, Elenora. *I Tornabuoni: una famiglia fiorentina alla fine del medioevo.* Milan: Franco Angeli, 2002.

Tomas, Natalie. *The Medici Women: Gender and Power in Renaissance Florence.* Aldershot, UK, and Burlington, VT: Ashgate, 2003.

Note: Quotations taken from Lucrezia Tornabuoni de' Medici, Sacred Narratives, *edited and translated by Jane Tylus.*

Translation and Women Translators

Overview

The importance of translation in the Renaissance cannot be overestimated. It brought the newly discovered classical texts to a wider audience; it helped circulate the currents of religious debate throughout the Reformation and Counter-Reformation; and it made vernacular works available to a new readership. Both humanism and the Reformation were made possible by the dissemination of translations of important texts from the ancient world, including the Bible, which were made available to a mass readership for the first time by the new printing presses. National languages were enriched with new words and thereby acquired respectability, while knowledge of the great literary works of antiquity was viewed as a means to enrich the vernacular literatures. Mastery of Latin and Greek being indispensable tools for this, translation from and to Classical languages was regarded as important intellectual work in the colleges, universities, academies, and new publishing houses of early modern Europe.

Brenda Hosington and Hannah Fournier

Women Translators in England

Women played a formative role in the translation movement in early modern England, but
their work as translators has not always been
accurately represented by critics. The following
are some of the false claims that have been
made: that translation was an ideal activity for
women since it was a secondary and even "degraded" activity, passive and silent in nature, and
that women translated more closely and literally than men did. It was also said that religious
translation was the sole mode of discourse considered appropriate for women and that therefore such works far outnumbered both secular
translations and original compositions by
women. Finally, it was alleged that the great
majority of women's translations were from
modern vernaculars because women seldom
studied the classical languages.

In fact, each of these views is erroneous.
Translation was not perceived as "degraded,"
passive, and silent. The sheer number of translations executed by men and the views they
express in their accompanying paratexts (prefaces, dedications, epistles to the reader, and so
on) concerning the usefulness of their work to
the state or to religion demonstrate exactly the
opposite. Nor is translation passive and silent.
All translation entails interpretation of the
original and recreation in rewriting it. The
translator can therefore leave her stamp on her
work (Trill 1996). In terms of religious versus
secular translations, our corpus of fifty-two
translations comprises thirty-one religious
works and twenty-one secular. The difference
is not overwhelming. As for women's translations versus original compositions, they are approximately the same in number (White
1999). The way in which women translated is
as difficult to categorize as men's because it is
varied. Some worked literally or closely, adher-
ing to the original in form as far as linguistic
constraints would allow and reproducing as
much of the original's content as possible.
Others took liberties with the texts, omitting
and adding elements as they saw fit. Very few,

as is the case with male translators in the period, especially in the early sixteenth century,
discussed or even alluded to their method of
translating in their paratexts. Finally, this body
of translations represents a variety of languages, and, while it is true that the translations
from European vernaculars (French, Italian,
Spanish, Dutch, and Scottish) outnumber
those from Greek and Latin, they do so by
only twenty-nine to twenty-two. This hardly
points to a "great majority."

The Translators

The twenty-eight women translators consid-
ered in this article represent a wide social spectrum, thereby also putting into question an earlier belief that educated women in Renaissance
England came almost exclusively from royalty
and the aristocracy. True, four are queens (Margaret Beaufort, Katherine Parr, Mary Tudor, and
Elizabeth I) and four aristocrats (Elizabeth
Cary, Helen Livingston, Joanna Lumley, and
Mary Sidney), while the three Cooke sisters
(Anne Bacon, Mildred Cecil, and Elizabeth
Russell), whose father was tutor to Edward VI,
all married men highly placed at court. How-
ever, others came from well-connected human-
ist families (Margaret Roper and her daughter
Mary Basset) or modest scholarly homes (Anna
Hume and Rachel Jevon). The gentry pro-
duced two women translators (Judith Man and
Elizabeth Melville, Lady Culcross) and the
fairly prosperous trades class produced four
(Anne Locke, Dorcas Martin, Elizabeth
Grymeston, and Anne Jenkinson). Five were
nuns in Continental convents (Prudentia Deacon, Elizabeth Evelinge, Alexia Gray, Catherine
Greenbury, and Mary Percy). Only two remain
largely unaccounted for (Susan Du Verger and
Margaret Tyler), but both came from fairly
modest families.

A similar range is represented in the ages of
the women whose dates of birth, death, and
compositions are known. Three constitute a familiar Renaissance figure, the female prodigy.
Princess Elizabeth, at eleven, and Elizabeth

Cary, at twelve, translated from French while Joanna Lumley, as a young teenager, translated from Greek. Three women published translations at age nineteen (Cecil, Roper, and Man), four while in their twenties (Bacon, Basset, Evelinge, and Gray), and three in their thirties (Jevon, Mary Tudor, and Sidney). Four attained their fifties before their work appeared (Beaufort, Deacon, Hume, and Russell).

Although religious works do not outnumber secular ones as dramatically as was once believed, no fewer than nineteen out of our twenty-eight translators can be identified as religious in inclination or actively involved in religious issues. They are fairly evenly divided between Protestants and Catholics, with ten in the former group and nine in the latter. For example, the three Cooke sisters were all involved in the Protestant cause in various ways, Locke was a Genevan exile who later became a leading figure in the Elizabethan Protestant community, while her kinswoman, Martin, was a model of Protestant godliness. Katherine Parr's and Elizabeth I's roles in promoting and establishing Protestantism in England need no rehearsal. On the other side, among the early generation of women translators were Roper and Basset, of impeccable Catholic pedigree as daughter and granddaughter of Thomas More, and four nuns who through their translations furthered the English recusant cause and the spiritual reach of the Counter-Reformation. Du Verger introduced the moral fictions of a French bishop and Cary, who underwent untold suffering for her faith, the polemical treatise of a French cardinal. Religion therefore loomed large on the horizon for many of these women.

English Translations

The various interests of these women are reflected in the range of genres and subjects found in their translations, both religious and secular. Within the body of religious texts there are Protestant sermons translated by Bacon (Barnardino Ochino, *Fouretene sermons of Barnardine Ochyne*, 1551) and Locke (John

Calvin, *Sermons of John Calvin*, 1560; Jean Taffin, *Of the markes of the children of God*, 1586). Polemical and theological works are translated by Bacon (John Jewel, *An apologie or answere in defence of the Churche of England*, 1564), Cary (Cardinal Perron, *The reply of the most illustrious cardinall of Perron*, 1630), and Russell (John Poynet, *A way of reconciliation of a good and learned man*, 1605). There are translations of biblical commentary like Cecil's (*An homilie or sermon of St Basile the great . . . upon Deuteronomie [XV.9]*, 1545), Jenkinson's (*Meditations upon the Lamentations of Ieremy*, 1609), Mary Tudor's (Erasmus' *Paraphrase of the Gospel of St John*, 1548), and Margaret Roper's (Erasmus' *A deuout treatise vpon the Pater noster*, 1526). The only book of the Bible that women were allowed to translate was the Psalms. They did so with fervor, using as intermediary texts French vernacular translations and verse paraphrases (Sidney, *The Psalmes of David*, 1598) as well as the Vulgate Psalter (Parr, Psalm 51 and possibly *John Fisher's Psalms*, n.d.; Locke, *A Meditation of a Penitent Sinner, Written in maner of a Paraphrase upon the 51. Psalme of David*, 1560). One translation, Basset's, is of a text on church history (Eusebius's *Ecclesiastical History*, 1550–1553), while another, Melville's self-translation, is visionary (*A godly dreame*, 1604?). Three saints' lives are translated by the nuns Evelinge (*The History of the angelical virgin gloriuos S. Clare*, 1635; *The life of St Catherine of Bologna*, 1621) and Greenbury (*A Short relation of the life of S. Elizabeth*, 1628). The monastic rules of Saint Clare and Saint Benedict are also translated by two nuns, Evelinge (*The declarations and ordinances made upon the Rule of our holy Mother, s. Clare*, 1622) and Gray (*The rule of the most blessed father saint Benedict Patriarke of all Munkes*, 1632). The largest group of religious texts, however, is meditative. Margaret Beaufort translates two (*The fourthe boke of the folowynge Jesu cryst out of the contemninge of the worlde*, 1504; *The mirroure of golde for the synfull soule*, 1506?). The young Princess Elizabeth translates Marguerite de Navarre (*A godly medytacyon of the christen sowle,* 1548), and Basset translates Thomas More (*Of the sorowe, weriness, feare, and prayer of Christ before hys taking,* 1557). Sidney renders Philippe de Mornay's 1576 meditation into English (*A Discourse of life and death,* 1592). One Protestant work on spiritual exercises for the Christian is translated by Martin (*An Instruction for Christians,* n.d.), and two Catholic ones are Englished by Percy (*An Abridgment of Christian Perfection,* 1626) and Deacon (*Delicious entertainments of the sovle,* 1632).

A similar variety of subject and genre is demonstrated in the secular texts. Du Verger translated selections from two of Jean-Pierre Camus's collections of moral tales (*Admirable Events,* 1639; *Certain Moral Relations,* 1639) as well as one of his novels (*Diotrephe,* 1641), while Tyler translated a Spanish novel by Diego Ortuñez de Calahorra (*The mirrour of princely deedes and Knighthood,* 1578). Two women turned their interest to Petrarch, with Sidney translating part of, and Hume all of, *I Trionfi* (*The triumph of death,* n.d.; *The Triumphs of love: chastity: death,* 1644). Classical authors in several genres are well represented. Elizabeth I rendered parts of Seneca's *Hercules oetaeus* (ms., n.d.), Plutarch's *De curiosite* (1598), and Horace's *De arte poetica* (1598), as well as the whole of Boethius's *De consolatione philosophiae* (1593). Lumley translated six of Isocrates' orations (ms., n.d). In a different mode, Jevon self-translated her Latin encomium to Charles II (*Carmen tpiambeyikon regiae maiestati Caroli II,* 1660). Drama is also represented by Lumley's translation of Euripides' *Iphigenia* (ms., n.d.) and Sidney's rendering of Robert Garnier's play, *Antonie* (1595). Lastly, the young Elizabeth Cary translated a French version of Ortelius's *Theatrum orbis terrarium* (ms., n.d.).

The Paratexts

Prefaces, dedications, epistles, and epilogues written by the translator, editor, or publisher accompany a great many Renaissance translations, including those penned by women. Eighteen have dedications and/or epistles to the reader written by the translators themselves, and seven have similar paratexts written by men. The choice of dedicatees is often revealing. With only four exceptions (Russell dedicates her work to her daughter and Tyler hers to her employer Lord Thomas Howard, while Jenkinson and Lumley dedicate theirs to their fathers), they choose women of higher standing and, in the majority of cases, champions of their particular faith. For example, the Protestants choose Parr (Princess Elizabeth); Anne Stanhope, duchess of Somerset (Cecil); the countess of Warwick and duchess of Suffolk (Locke); and Queen Elizabeth (Sidney). Three Catholics choose Queen Henrietta Maria (Cary, Du Verger, Evelinge), and one (Basset) honors Mary Tudor. The various epistles, with the exception of Basset's dedicatory epistle to Mary Tudor prefacing the Eusebius translation, say little about their translating practices but several address questions of gender. Tyler's outspoken defense of a woman's right to read and translate secular texts is no doubt the best-known, but Cary's defense of her translation on the grounds of her gender and religion is also bold. Locke says she will help "build the walls of Jerusalem" with her "poor basket of stones" (her translation of Taffin) since her sex prevents her from doing "great things." The male-authored paratexts present things differently. Richard Hyrde, editing Roper's translation, paints a portrait of an ideal humanist woman, learned, modest, virtuous. Learned women also have their defenders in five other male editors (Father San Martino of Cary; Matthew Parker and "G. M." of Bacon; Bale and Chancellor of the Princess Elizabeth; Udall of Mary Tudor), yet some comments do not rise above the overworked topoi found in Renaissance writings about women while others are undermined by negative observations on women in general.

The translations penned by Renaissance Englishwomen offered a means by which they could make their own voices heard, even if the original texts were, with one exception (Marguerite de Navarre's *Miroir de l'âme pécheresse*), written by men. Their paratexts, on the other hand, were channels through which those voices could become louder and more distinct. Together, translations and paratexts constituted a contribution to the world of learning and religion, one that their authors must have hoped would have some impact.

Brenda Hosington

See also Bacon, Anne Cooke; Cary, Elizabeth Tanfield; Cecil, Mildred Cooke; Locke, Anne Vaughan; Lumley, Jane; Roper, Margaret More; Sidney, Mary Herbert; entries for women translators mentioned in this article.

Bibliography

Hannay, Margaret P. "Introduction." In *Silent But for the Word: Tudor Women as Patrons, Translators, and Writers of Religious Works.* Edited by Margaret P. Hannay, 4–9. Kent, OH: Kent State University Press, 1985.

Lamb, Mary Ellen. "The Cooke Sisters: Attitudes Toward Learned Women in the Renaissance." In *Silent But for the Word: Tudor Women as Translators, Patrons, and Writers of Religious Works.* Edited by Margaret P. Hannay, 107–125. Kent, OH: Kent State University Press, 1985.

Trill, Suzanne. "Sixteenth-Century Women's Writing: Mary Sidney's *Psalmes* and the 'Femininity' of Translation." In *Writing and the English Renaissance.* Edited by William Zunder and Suzanne Trill, 140–158. London and New York: Longman, 1996.

White, Micheline. "Renaissance Englishwomen and Religious Translations: The Case of Anne Lock's *Of the Markes of the Children of God* (1590)." *ELR* 29 (Autumn, 1999): 375–400.

Women Translators in France

Of the approximately one hundred early modern French women writers whose works we know, over 10 percent published translations of ancient or modern vernacular texts, either in manuscript or printed editions. Also, at least one woman, Marie de Gournay, took part in the discussion of translation theory inaugurated in France by such eminent literary men of the day as Dolet, Sébillet, du Bellay, and Pelletier. Although they were excluded from the colleges, universities, and academies, where translation was a standard part of the curriculum, the works of these women translators reflect the various approaches to translation current in Renaissance France. While such women writers as Anne de Graville, Marie de Cotteblanche, Claudine Scève, Anne de Marquets, Marguerite de Cambis, and Marie de Romieu translated popular Italian and English works into French, others like Hélisenne de Crenne, Madeleine de L'Aubespine, Catherine Des Roches, Camille Morel, Marie de Brabant, and Marie de Gournay made translations from classical Latin and, more rarely, Greek texts as well as from the Vulgate Bible. The number of women involved in adaptations or paraphrases of ancient and modern works is even greater; among these writers were Hélisenne de Crenne and Anne de Marquets. Still others may have used already existing translations as the sources for their adaptations: Jeanne Flore, Marguerite de Navarre, Louise Labé, or Marie de Gournay, among them. The intertextuality of Renaissance texts frequently involved substantial, unattributed passages from other authors whose works were originally in other languages; this practice was as common among female as among male writers.

Translators and Translations

The translations of Marie de Cotteblanche, Marie de Romieu, and Anne de Marquets made available in French works on current religious, social, and scientific themes, while Anne de Graville, Marguerite de Cambis, and Claudine Scève translated works by the very popular Italian writers, Trissino and Boccacio. Hélisenne de Crenne and Marie de Gournay translated books of the *Aeneid,* and both Madeleine de L'Aubespine and Gournay translated Ovid. The latter also translated selections from Tacitus, Sallust, Cicero, Ausonius, and Horace, as well as selections from the Bible and a fragment of the neo-Latin of Daniel Heinsius. Catherine Des Roches paraphrased Pythagoras probably by using texts already translated from the Greek and translated Claudian as well as texts from the Bible, and Marie de Brabant did a versified version of the Biblical Song of Songs.

In accordance with the full range of views on freedom in translation, some writers, such as Cotteblanche, Romieu, and Gournay, translated with great attention to fidelity to the original text, making only minor modifications to enable the French reader to understand better the original, while others, such as L'Aubespine and Des Roches, paraphrased the original texts more freely to suit the tastes of the time.

In the two key texts, *De la façon d'escrire de Messieurs l'eminentissime cardinal du Perron, et Bertaut* and *Sur la Version de deux Oraisons Latines,* Gournay articulated her own theory of translation. Based on the Horatian precept *nec verbum verbo curabis reddere fidus interpres* (As a faithful translator, you will take care not to translate word for word), freedom and fidelity to the source text are the watchwords of her approach. In these two essays, she states that, in the interests of clarity and an attractive style, the translator needs to avoid slavish translation, but modifications of literal meaning can be done sparingly and reverently, in a way that remains faithful to the source text. Gournay points out that, while translation is a long and difficult undertaking, it is also a noble and creative one.

Participating in the mainstream activity of translation was not obviously acceptable as an activity for women in early modern France. In addition to the difficulty they all faced in acquiring the skills necessary, they also suffered from general skepticism about their ability as women to carry out scholarly tasks. Marie de Gournay, probably the outstanding case representing the issues facing a woman, who, among other intellectual pursuits, undertook the translation of ancient Latin texts, was accused of basing her work on that of other translators. Even though some women were the first to translate a text into French (Cotteblanche, Romieu, Des Roches), so deep was the skepticism about women having the competence to write an acceptable translation that Claude de Gruget, for instance, got away with publishing Cotteblanche's version as his own by incorporating it into his more extensive translation.

In early modern France, the affirmation (or the self-affirmation) of the authority of a woman writer to speak in a published text caused early writers and their biographers considerable anxiety. This anxiety of authority was expressed (and diffused) not only by early female authors in the "modesty" topos, but by their commentators in various ways, including what might be called the "amazement" topos. Rabelais' observation in *Pantagruel* (chapter viii) typifies the attitude of numerous commentators, male and female, who expressed wonder over the growing number of erudite and writing women. While only 1 percent of male writers were engaged in translation at the time, about 10 to 15 percent of the known French women writers did so. Translation was a route to demonstrating the legitimacy of one's claim to intellectual equality and worth, as Tilde Sankovitch has pointed out. Beginning in the Renaissance, the translation of the works of others, especially the great authors of antiquity and Italy, was a recognized and accepted route to intellectual respectability and even equality for women who, in France as elsewhere, had few other ways of attaining these goals.

Hannah Fournier

See also Cambis, Marguerite de; Cotteblanche, Marie de; Dames des Roches; Romieu, Marie de; entries for others mentioned in this article.

Bibliography

Primary Works

Cambis, Marguerite de. *Epistre consolatoire de l'exil, envoyée par Jean Boccace au Seigneur Pino de Rossi.* Edited by Colette H. Winn. Paris: Champion, 2003. (Originally printed in Lyon: Guillaume Rouillé, 1556.)

Cambis, Marguerite de. *Epistre du Seigneur Jean-Georges Trissin. . . .* Lyon: Guillaume Rouillé, 1554.

Cotteblanche, Marie de. *Trois dialogues de M. Pierre Messie.* Paris: Frédéric Morel, 1571.

Crenne, Hélisenne de. *Les Œuvres.* Paris: Charles Langelier, 1543.

Des Roches, Madeleine and Catherine. *Les Missives.* Edited by Anne R. Larsen. Geneva: Droz, 1999.

Des Roches, Catherine and Madeleine. *Les Secondes Œuvres.* Edited by Anne R. Larsen. Geneva: Droz, 1998.

Gournay, Marie de. *Les Advis ou les presens de la demoiselle de Gournay.* Paris: Jean Du Bray, 1641.

Gournay, Marie de. *Les Advis, ou, les Presens de la Demoiselle de Gournay 1641.* 2 vols. Edited by Jean-Philippe Beaulieu and Hannah Fournier. Amsterdam: Rodopi, 1997 (vol. 1), 2002 (vol. 2).

Gournay, Marie de. *Œuvres completes.* 2 vols. Edited by Jean Claude Arnould. Paris: Champion, 2002.

Graville, Anne Malet de. *Le Beau Romant des deux amans Palamon & Arcita. . . .* Edited by Yves Le Hir. Paris: Presses Universitaires de France, 1965.

L'Aubespine, Madeleine de. *Les Chansons de Callianthe.* Edited by Roger Sorg. Paris: L. Pichon, 1926.

Marquets, Anne de. *Les divines poesies de Marc Antoine Flaminius.* Paris: Nicolas Chesneau, 1568.

Romieu, Marie de. *Les Premières Œuvres poétiques.* Edited by André Winandy. Geneva: Droz, 1972.

Secondary Works

Berriot-Salvadore, Evelyne. *Les Femmes dans la société française de la Renaissance.* Geneva: Droz, 1990.

Broomhall, Susan. *Women and the Book Trade in Sixteenth-Century France.* Aldershot, UK: Ashgate, 2002.

La Charité, Claude. "Le *Dialogo de la bella creanza de le donne* (1539) d'Alessandro Piccolomini et ses adaptateurs français." *Renaissance and Reformation/Renaissance et Réforme* 23, no. 1 (1999): 43–57.

Sankovitch, Tilde. "Translation (Renaissance)." In *The Feminist Encyclopedia of French Literature.* Edited by Eva Martin Sartori, 532–535. London and Westport, CT: Greenwood Press, 1999.

Transvestism

Transvestism was acceptable and widely practiced in very particular and limited forms in the Renaissance. At the level of popular culture, in the cities, carnivals and other festive occasions, such as the Feast of Fools, which often included parades in which men dressed as women, appeared prominently in a figuration of the "world turned upside down." Some examples of this are Mère Folle in Lyon and Mère Sotte in Paris, in which celebrants led their boisterous children through the streets at carnival time. *Charivaris,* or "rough music," were village events in which men disguised themselves, often as women, to shame individuals who might not be behaving according to social expectations. In these instances, it was rare for women to dress as men.

At the courts of England and France, a certain amount of gender play was tolerated. During the reign of Francis I of France, for example, a number of representations of the myth of Hercules and Omphale were produced. In the myth, Hercules was assigned to be Omphale's slave; she donned his lion's skin, making him wear her robes. Later, in the court of Henri III of France (ruled 1574–1589), refined, almost feminine, clothing was favored. This fashion extended even into the reign of Henri IV and spread to the court of King James in England. It should be noted that in these cases, the full adoption of female attire was not necessary for a charge of "dressing as a woman" to be leveled; Henri wore breeches, but a very unmasculine open doublet, with ropes of pearls around his neck. In royal masques, both in England and in France, some transvestism was tolerated.

Theater was another site of transvestism, most particularly in England, where boy actors flourished in the Elizabethan and Jacobean periods. The practice of using boys to play feminine roles was denounced even during the Elizabethan era, but also with increasing severity as the Revolution approached in the mid-seventeenth century. Renaissance sumptuary laws (the most famous being Elizabeth I's proclamation of 1597) were primarily focused on distinctions of rank, but had implications for gender as well. At the same time, popular pamphlets portrayed transvestite women (and men, although to a lesser degree) as a serious threat to the social order. The most famous denunciations of cross-dressing are the pamphlets *Hic Mulier: Or, the Man-Woman* and *Haec Vir: Or, the Womanish Man,* both published in 1620. Women wearing broad-brimmed hats and doublets are taken to task, as are effeminately dressed men. In both works, the full adoption of the opposite sex's attire was not necessary for a charge of cross-dressing. In Venice, prostitutes often wore breeches and men's shirts and vests, and the higher-class courtesans often wore breeches under their long skirts, but they were also denounced for this practice.

The most severe condemnation was reserved for women who dressed as men to improve their social status, as is evident from the case of the "hermaphrodite" Marin le Marcis (France, 1610), at first condemned to death as a woman wearing man's clothes and saved only by the "discovery" that s/he possessed a penis. This case echoes the more complex one of Elena de Céspedes (Toledo, 1587), accused of being a woman living as a man. Such cross-dressing, along with the adoption of social roles normally signaled by this clothing, was considered a usurpation of elevated social status on the part of these "women." Transvestism was clearly not acceptable in everyday situations, particularly among the lower classes, and even less so in France and Spain than in England.

In the literary and theatrical realms in which transvestism was conceptually permissible, male transvestism and female transvestism served very different purposes. This is particularly evident in the romance tradition. In Italian, French, Spanish, and English versions of this genre, particularly in the many versions and continuations of *Amadis de Gaule,* male protagonists dress up as women for a number of reasons: to escape danger and, most frequently, to gain access to and seduce a woman (that is, paradoxically, they dress as women to impose their manliness). Women dress to save themselves, their family, their friends, or a beloved; Spenser's Britomart is exemplary in this category. Women's transvestism is thus portrayed as exceptional and necessary. Women dress as men in English theater as well; the most evident examples of this being Rosalind in *As You Like It,* and Viola/Cesario in *Twelfth Night,* whose situation echoes that of Boccaccio's cross-dressed

heroine, Zinevra (*Decameron,* II, 9). While these women dress as men mainly to reinforce social order, Middleton's *Roaring Girl* (1611) is clearly a more threatening figure, but this is a rarity in the mostly idealizing literary tradition. The frequency of women characters cross-dressed as men increased in English theater only when female actors were allowed on stage.

In an echo of the female warriors of romance and of the mythological Amazons, a number of French noblewomen disguised themselves as soldiers before and during the period of the Fronde (1648–1653). Catherine Meurdrac de La Guette was the first of these "Amazons," literally living a soldier's life. Barbe d'Ernecourt, comtesse de Saint-Baslemont, dressed as a man so that she could go to battle to defend her property and that of her neighbors throughout the 1620s and 1630s, because her husband was constantly away at war. La Grande Mademoiselle (Anne-Marie Louis d'Orléans, duchesse de Montpensier, 1627–1693) and the duchesse de Longueville (Anne Geneviève de Bourbon, 1619–1679) also dressed frequently in military fashion and behaved in a martial manner. While some praised the bravery of these women, these practices were also strongly denounced, particularly in the pamphlet literature, and could be seen as contributing to a backlash against strong women in politics (DeJean).

Eventually, male transvestism becomes a mark of the corruption and decadence of the nobility, most particularly the court, and is linked to excessive spending and taxation. Henri III is at first compared favorably by Philippe Desportes to the transvestite Achilles, disguised as a girl by Thetis so that he will not be pressed into service for the Trojan War and revealed by Odysseus, himself disguised as a peddler selling feminine trinkets—and swords. Later, he is criticized for his feminine attire and accused of having a weak and emotional temperament to match his clothing.

The public perception of male transvestism, outside the realm of literature and carnival practices, was thus very negative. Dressing in women's clothing and behaving in a stereotypically feminine fashion weakened a man both physically and morally. But within the realm of romance in particular, such attire did not diminish sexual or physical prowess. Thus, symbolic transvestism in literary fantasies, ritual, and theater could foster social cohesion and even conformity; on the other hand, it might also suggest new forms of freedom. These were acceptable forms of transvestism in the Renaissance; an individual's attempt to cross gender barriers through transvestism was not.

The case of the enigmatic Abbé de Choisy (1644–1724) demonstrates the intrusion of once imaginary forms of transvestism, which literary characters use to master a social situation, into the political realm. In the late seventeenth century, he wore female attire as a means of distinguishing himself at court rather than as a disguise. This was both a continuation of socially permissible forms of deviance in Renaissance France, particularly those of Henri III and his courtiers, and a new direction for transvestism, which in this case deconstructed gender identity into multiple, less stable possibilities and was accepted for the freedom it offered, though only under carefully circumscribed conditions.

Kathleen Long

See also Androgyne; Hermaphrodite as Image and Idea; Masculinity, Femininity, and Gender; Querelle des Femmes; Sappho and the Sapphic Tradition.

Bibliography

Primary Works

Choisy, François Timoléon de. *Mémoires de l'Abbé de Choisy*. Edited by Georges Mongrédien. Paris: Mercure de France, 1983.

Desportes, Philippe. "Pour Monseigneur le Duc d'Anjou." In *Cartels et masquerades. Epitaphes.* Edited by Victor Graham, 30–31. Geneva: Droz, 1958.

Haec Vir: Or the Womanish Man: Being an Answere to a Late Booke Intituled Hic-Mulier. London: 1620. Exeter: Scolar Press, 1973. (Facsimile reprint.)

Hic Mulier: Or, the Man-Woman: Being a Medicine to Cure the Coltish Disease of the Staggers in the Masculine-Feminines of Our Times. London: 1620. Facs. Rpt. Exeter: Scolar Press, 1973.

Le huitiesme livre d'Amadis de Gaule. Lyon: 1575.

L'Estoile, Pierre de. *Registre-journal du regne de Henri III.* Edited by Madeleine Lazard and Gilbert Schrenck. Geneva: Droz, 1997–2003.

L'Isle des hermaphrodites. Edited by Claude-Gilbert Dubois. Geneva: Droz, 1996.

Middleton, Thomas, and Thomas Dekker. *The Roaring Girl.* Edited by Andor Gomme. London: Ernest Benn, 1976.

Spenser, Edmund. *The Faerie Queene.* Edited by A. C. Hamilton. London: Longman, 1977.

Secondary Works

Burshatin, Israel. "Interrogating Hermaphroditism in Sixteenth-Century Spain." In *Hispanisms and Homosexualities.* Edited by Sylvia Molloy and Robert McKee Irwin, 3–18. Durham, NC: Duke University Press, 1998.

Davis, Natalie Zemon. *Society and Culture in Early Modern France.* Stanford, CA: Stanford University Press, 1975.

DeJean, Joan. "Violent Women and Violence Against Women: Representing the 'Strong' Woman in Early Modern France." *Signs: Journal of Women in Culture and Society.* 29, no. 1 (2003): 117–147.

Garber, Marjorie. *Vested Interests: Cross-Dressing and Cultural Anxiety.* New York: Routledge, 1992.

Gilbert, Ruth. "Mingle-Mangle: Masculine Women and Feminine Men." In *Early Modern Hermaphrodites.* Pages 77–103. New York: Palgrave, 2002.

Jones, Ann Rosalind, and Peter Stallybrass. "Transvestism and the 'Body Beneath': Speculating on the Boy Actor." In *Renaissance Clothing and the Materials of Memory.* Pages 207–219. Cambridge, New York: Cambridge University Press, 2000.

Kates, Gary. *Monsieur d'Eon Is a Woman: A Tale of Political Intrigue and Sexual Masquerade.* Baltimore, MD: Johns Hopkins University Press, 2001.

Marino, Virginia M. "A Curious Study in 'Parallel Lives': Louis XIV and the Abbé de Choisy." In *High Anxiety: Masculinity in Crisis in Early Modern France.* Edited by Kathleen Long, 165–182. Kirksville, MO: Truman State University Press, 2002.

Schleiner, Winfred. "Male Cross-Dressing and Transvestism in Renaissance Romances." *Sixteenth Century Journal* 19, no. 4 (1988): 605–619.

V

Varano, Costanza (b. 1426, Camerino–d. 1447, Pesaro)

Humanist scholar and writer

Costanza Varano was an active participant in the fifteenth-century revivification of Classical Latin as an intellectual medium. Her corpus of Latin writings, while somewhat modest in comparison to other humanists, nonetheless attests her mastery of the epistolary, oratorical, and poetic genres. A member of the hereditary nobility, Varano corresponded with some of the most important political figures of the day—many of whom were her relatives either by birth or by marriage. She married Alessandro Sforza (brother of Francesco Sforza, duke of Milan) on 8 December 1444 and had a daughter, Battista (b. 1446); she died giving birth to another child the following year.

The violent power struggles in Varano's birth town of Camerino resulted in the execution of her father (Pier Gentile da Varano) in 1433. Varano's mother, Elisabetta, immediately fled with her daughter Costanza and son Rodolfo, as well as two other children, and sought refuge in Pesaro, where she was born and where her mother, Battista da Montefeltro Malatesta, resided. Good fortune followed tragedy: Malatesta was a brilliant scholar in her own right, and she gave her granddaughter a thorough education in the humanities.

References in Varano's writings display her familiarity with many of the Classical and patristic authors that boys read, especially Aristotle (in Latin translation), Cicero, Virgil, Quintillian, and Lactantius. More than a passive reader of Latin, however, her compositional skills compare favorably with those of her male contemporaries (Parker 2002, 31). Among Varano's admirers was Guarino Guarini, a famous humanist pedagogue, who sent her a lengthy letter of praise in 1444. Guarino considered Varano's erudition to be proof that the eloquence attributed to the learned women of antiquity had returned, and he exhorted her to continue her studies. He also addressed her as a colleague. It was natural, he reasoned, that fellow intellectuals should write to each other, "since 'equals mix freely with equals,' as the old proverb goes and as Cicero says" (*Pares enim cum paribus veteri proverbio, ut est apud Ciceronem, facillime congregantur;* Feliciangeli 1894, 58).

Varano most often used her learning to serve the interests of her family. Among her best-known works is a 1442 oration to Bianca Maria Visconti, wife of Francesco Sforza and duchess of Milan, in which she requested that Visconti intercede with her husband to return Camerino to the Varano family. She wrote an eloquent epistle to King Alfonso of Aragon with this same end in view. Varano's oration and letter obtained the desired result. She delivered a celebratory oration (1443) to the people of Camerino, which inaugurated her family's return to sovereignty, but also flattered her auditors and assured them that the Varano family would rule with justice and equanimity. Her marriage the following year to Francesco Sforza's brother solidified the peaceful conclusion to these long-standing and bloody conflicts. Varano demonstrated her continued dedication to family interests in 1447/1448, when she wrote to Pope Eugenius IV, begging him to revoke the excommunication placed on her grandfather, Galeazzo.

Varano's letters and poems to her fellow women humanists show an altogether different rhetorical program. Her encomia of Cecilia Gonzaga (ca. 1443) and Isotta Nogarola (ca. 1443/1444) celebrate the presence of learned women in her own day, in conjunction with their ancient Roman foremothers. In eulogizing women intellectuals, she put her Latin in the service of protofeminism. The importance of erudite women like Costanza Varano, however, does not rest on her literary legacy alone. Varano was a widely admired intellectual, who provoked contemporaries and later observers to think in new ways about female capability. The catalogues of famous women popular in Italy from the fifteenth century onward continually recalled her life and achievements, and she often served as a point of reference in the related genre of "defenses of women." One such text lauded Varano, her grandmother, Battista Malatesta, and the learned Veronese sisters, Isotta and Ginevra Nogarola, as important members of a new community of knowledge: "scholarly women, embellished with most beautiful letters" (*donne studiose, e di bellissime lettere adornate;* Garzoni 1586, 171–172).

Sarah Gwyneth Ross

See also Cereta, Laura; Education, Humanism, and Women; Fedele, Cassandra; Literary Culture and Women; Nogarola, Isotta.

Bibliography

Feliciangeli, B. "Notizie sulla vita e sugli scritti di Costanza Varano-Sforza." *Giornale storico della letteratura italiana* 23 (1894): 1–75.

Garzoni, Tommaso. "Discorso . . . sopra la nobiltà delle donne." In *Le Vite delle Donne Illustri della Scrittura Sacra.* Venice: Domenico Imberti, 1586.

Jardine, Lisa. " 'O Decus Italiae Virgo': The Myth of the Learned Lady in the Renaissance." *The Historical Journal* 28, no. 4 (December 1985): 799–819.

King, Margaret, and Albert Rabil, eds. "Book-Lined Cells: Women and Humanism in the Early Italian Renaissance." In *Beyond Their Sex: Learned Women of the European Past.* Edited by Patricia Labalme, 91–116. New York: New York University Press, 1984.

King, Margaret, and Albert Rabil, eds. *Her Immaculate Hand: Selected Works By and About the Women Humanists of Quattrocento Italy.* New York: Center for Medieval and Early Renaissance Studies, State University of New York at Binghamton, 1983.

Parker, Holt N. "Costanza Varano (1426–1447): Latin as an Instrument of State." In *Women*

Writing Latin from Roman Antiquity to Early Modern Europe. 3 vols. Vol. 3. Edited by Laurie Churchill et al., 31–54. New York: Routledge, 2002.

Vere, Anne Cecil de (1556–1588)

Poet, patron, and member of a faction hostile to Mary and Philip Sidney and their circle at court

Anne Cecil de Vere, countess of Oxford, was the eldest (and favorite) daughter of William Cecil (Lord Burghley) and his second wife, Mildred Cooke. She married (1571) Edward de Vere, seventeenth earl of Oxford, a match considered advantageous on both sides because Oxford was a significant matrimonial prize and Cecil's fortune would rescue the unstable finances of the de Vere family. It seems, at least on her side, to have been a love match. The marriage did not prosper, mostly on account of de Vere's famously uncertain temper, which caused him in 1576 to repudiate his wife, slander her virtue (by disclaiming paternity of their daughter, born in 1575), and go on a ruinous spending spree, reputedly because Cecil failed to save de Vere's uncle (Thomas Howard, fourth duke of Norfolk) from execution. Reconciled in 1582, Anne bore de Vere a son, Lord Bulbeck (May 1583), who lived only hours, and three more daughters.

Four sonnets and two quatrains were published in John Southern's *Pandora* (1584), which he claims were "made by the Countes of Oxenford, after the death of her young Sonne" (Moody 1989, 154). This authorship has been contested, it being suggested after stylistic analysis that the verse is Southern's and the exercise one of *prosopopoeia* (May 1992, 15). It has been further noted that the poems contain translations from Desportes, to whose work Southern's own poetry is deeply indebted (Smith 1994, 446). A British Library manuscript (Landsdowne MS 104, ff.195v–214r) contains elegiac verses preceded by Latin notes on Anne's character (my translation): "Very much beloved by a Prince, parents, brothers and the whole royal court for her piety, prudence, patience, modesty and outstanding affection in marriage." She died at Greenwich on 6 June 1588.

Teresa Grant

See also Cecil, Mildred Cooke; Literary Culture and Women; Sidney, Mary Herbert.

Bibliography

Primary Work

de Vere, Anne Cecil. "Four Epitaphs." In *Women Poets of the Renaissance*. Edited by Marion Wynne-Davies. London: J. M. Dent, 1998.

Secondary Works

May, Steven W. "The Countess of Oxford's Sonnets: A Caveat." *English Language Notes* 29, no. 3 (March 1992): 9–18.

Moody, Ellen. "Six Elegiac Poems, Possibly by Anne Cecil de Vere, Countess of Oxford." *English Literary Renaissance* 19, no. 2 (Spring 1989): 152–170.

Payne, Helen. "The Cecil Women and Court." In *Patronage, Culture and Power: The Early Cecils.* Edited by Pauline Croft. New Haven, CT, and London: Yale University Press, 2002.

Smith, Rosalind. "The Sonnets of the Countess of Oxford and Elizabeth I: Translations from Desportes." *Notes and Queries* 41, no. 4 (1994): 446–450.

Ward, Mary (1585–1645)

English gentlewoman and recusant Catholic, founder of schools for women based on the Jesuit model despite strenuous opposition from within the Catholic Church

Born in Yorkshire in 1585, Mary Ward left England, as did many Catholic Englishwomen of her time, seeking the religious life; she entered a Poor Clare convent in the Spanish Netherlands in 1606. Between 1609 and 1610, she founded a religious institute and school for women and girls at St. Omer based on Jesuit traditions; the curriculum of the English Ladies included preparation for religious or secular life through study in reading, writing, religion, Latin, and the acting of plays to improve speaking. Like the Jesuits, Mary Ward envisioned an unenclosed order that combined the contemplative life with active service and that was ruled not by local church authorities but that was directly overseen by the pope. The Englishwomen of the institute also took vows of poverty, chastity, and obedience. On one occasion, a Jesuit minister commented that "fervour will decay; and when all is done, they are but women!" Mary Ward, an outspoken advocate of women's education, responded that "there is no such difference between men and women that women may not do great things . . . ," and she insisted that "women in time will do much."

Mary Ward constantly found her mission in financial hardship because, without papal approval, her novices had difficulty providing their dowries for the institute. There was also stringent opposition to her undertaking from adversaries who were resistant to nonenclosure for women and who feared the institute's association with the Jesuits. Nevertheless, she established schools in Flanders, Germany, Italy, Austria, and Hungary. However, in 1631, Pope Urban VIII signed a Bull of Suppression, which effectively ended Mary Ward's work. In a letter from Cardinal San'Onofrio, Pope Urban VIII's brother, she was declared "a heretic, schismatic, and rebel to the Holy Church" and imprisoned at a Poor Clare convent in Munich for over two months (Littlehales 1998, 204). Finally exonerated, Mary Ward's institute never received papal approval in her lifetime, although she devoted the rest of her life to safeguarding it in Rome and England for her companions to rebuild in subsequent years.

Marlo Belschner

See also Convents; Religious Reform and Women.

Bibliography
Fraser, Antonia. "Mary Ward: A 17th Century Reformer." *History Today* 31, no. 5 (1981): 14–18. Available at: http://www.historytoday.com.
Littlehales, Margaret Mary. *Mary Ward: Pilgrim and Mystic, 1585–1645.* Kent: Burns and Oates, 1998.
McClory, Robert. *Faithful Dissenters: Stories of Men and Women Who Loved and Changed the Church.* Maryknoll, NY: Orbis, 2000.

Weston, Elizabeth Jane (1582–1612)

Poet and political exile

Elizabeth Jane Weston was born in England, but during her early childhood she moved to Prague with her brother, mother, and stepfather, Edward Kelley. Weston maintained ties to England, but her personal and professional life was in Bohemia.

Weston's stepfather, Kelley, was an occultist and alchemist and an assistant to the famed

English magician Dr. John Dee. In the early 1580s, Kelley accompanied Dee to Europe, but after Dee returned to England, Kelley remained behind in Prague and entered the court of Emperor Rudolf II; Kelley convinced the emperor that he could manufacture gold, and the emperor rewarded him with a knighthood and property. However, Kelley eventually fell out of favor with Rudolf, either because of his failed alchemical attempts or his involvement in various court scandals, and he was arrested and imprisoned in 1591. Throughout these tumultuous years, Kelley and Weston's mother still ensured that Elizabeth Jane and her brother received an excellent education. By her teens, Weston was fluent in Czech, German, and Italian as well as English and Latin. She was also a skilled calligrapher.

In 1597 Kelley died and his property was confiscated, leaving Weston and her mother destitute. In an attempt to provide support for herself and her mother, Weston wrote poetry, seeking patronage from nobles at Rudolf's court. In 1603, Weston married Johann Leo, a lawyer at the imperial court. Leo actively supported both Weston's appeal to regain her stepfather's estate and her writing career. They had seven children in the nine years of their marriage. Weston died in 1612 at the age of 30.

Weston, known as both Westonia and the English Maiden in literary circles, first published her neo-Latin poems in a two-volume edition in 1602 with the help of one of her patrons, George Martin von Baldhoven. In 1608 she published a revised and expanded edition, *Parthenica*. Her facility in writing Latin verse demonstrates her learnedness as well as her understanding that it was the language most accessible to an international audience of humanist readers. Weston's poems are characterized by their epigrammatic neatness, formalistic versatility and sophistication, and wide range of classical and contemporary allusions. Her subjects include religious meditations, colorful accounts of personal experiences, addresses to her mother and brother, and revi-

sions of Aesop's fables. Beyond their specific literary purpose, many of Weston's poems are intended as appeals for patronage support; they also demonstrate the challenges that early modern women writers faced entering the public realm.

Jo Eldridge Carney

See also Education, Humanism, and Women; Literary Culture and Women.

Bibliography
Primary Work
Cheney, Donald, and Brenda M. Hosington, eds. and trans. *Elizabeth Jane Weston: Collected Writings*. Toronto: University of Toronto Press, 2000.
Secondary Work
Schleiner, Louise. *Tudor & Stuart Women Writers*. Bloomington: Indiana University Press, 1994.

Whitney, Isabella (fl. 1567–1573)

Poet and first professional woman writer in England
Arguably the first professional Englishwoman writer, Isabella Whitney wrote for publication without the subterfuge or apology characteristic of many early modern women whose works found their way into print. The author of works included in two collections and probably an epitaph, Whitney adopted a sensible and forthright voice through which she critiqued the gender and also financial relations of her time. Unlike many Englishwomen writers before her, Whitney did not enjoy the privileges of wealth and rank, and her position as a domestic worker in London of the 1560s provides a valuable window into the difficulties confronting working women of that time. Written in the highly regular metrics characteristic of midcentury verse, Whitney's verse remains lively and expressive.

Most information about Whitney's life derives from autobiographical statements in her own poetry and from facts known about her eldest brother, Geoffrey Whitney, who published a book of emblems in 1586. Isabella Whitney was born to parents of gentry or lower gentry rank. While her poem "Manner of Her Will" refers to a stay in Smithfield, her parents' primary residence seems to have been in Cheshire. Sometime in the 1560s, Whitney arrived in London to enter domestic service, apparently as a companion to an unidentified gentlewoman. At that time, her two younger sisters and a brother, Brooke, were also in service, while a married sister, Anne Baron, was set up in her own household. By the time Whitney wrote *A Sweet Nosegay* (1573), she was no longer employed. Whitney is thought to have left London around 1573, presumably to return to her family's house. Names appearing in the will of her brother Geoffrey suggest she may have married an Eldershae or Evans, although it is also possible that she predeceased her brother.

Isabella Whitney signed her initials "Is. W." to two of the four verse epistles published by Richard Jones in 1567 in a collection usually referred to as *The Copy of a Letter*, whose full descriptive title reads: *The Copy of a letter, lately written in meeter, by a yonge Gentilwoman: to her unconstant Lover, With an Admonition to al yong Gentilwomen, and to all other Mayds in general to beware of menns flattery. By Is. W. Newly ioyned to a Loveletter sent by a Bacheler, (a most faithfull Lover) to an unconstant and faithles Mayden.* While the word "copy" in the title suggests secondhand transmission to the printer, Whitney's invitation to her inconstant lover to read her second letter reveals her assumption that her letters would reach print: "And now farewel, for why at large/ my mind is here exprest?/ The which you may perceive, if that/ you do peruse the rest?" Whitney's first poem in this collection agreeably turns the tables on her former betrothed, who has recently married another woman. Rather than scolding him or berating her misfortune, Whitney positions his betrayal of her in a rereading of classical literature as a succession of betrayals of women by epic heroes such as Aeneas, Theseus, and Jason. Adopting the tone of a marriage counselor, Whitney catalogues the traits that an ideal wife should possess, pointing out

that she, in fact, possesses most of them. In her following letter, "The Admonition," she draws on her disappointing experience to advise young women to beware of the promises made by suitors. Probably influenced by the popularity of the complaints of abandoned women available in Turberville's recent translation from Ovid's *Heroides,* Whitney draws on classical literature for examples of male betrayals of women who love them. Whitney urges her female readers to exercise caution, to "always trie before ye trust." Written not only to "Gentilwomen" but also to "all other Maids being in Love," Whitney's verse epistle may speak directly to the dilemmas confronted by young women who enter service to find a suitable husband, only to be confronted by predatory sexual attentions by faithless suitors. This collection balances Whitney's accusations against men with two verse epistles by male personae who lament the infidelities of their female beloveds.

In 1573 Jones published *A Sweet Nosegay, Or pleasant Posye: contayning a hundred and ten Phylosophicall Flowers.* These philosophical flowers refer to Whitney's versifications of one hundred and ten of the commonplaces or wise proverbs translated in Hugh Plat's *The Flowres of Philosophie* (1572) from writings attributed to Seneca. Following these commonplaces is a section titled *Certain familier Epistles and friendly Letters by the Auctor: with Replies,* including ten verse epistles written by Whitney to family members and friends, with three responses. *A Sweet Nosegay* concludes with her most anthologized poem, alternatively titled "The Manner of Her Will" and Whitney's "Wyll and Testament." Prefaced with a short poem describing the financial difficulties requiring her departure, this poem appears with the heading, "The maner of her Wyll, and what she left to London: and to all those in it: at her departing."

Like her poems in the previous collection, the versified commonplaces of *Sweet Nosegay* represent useful advice, in this case on a series of topics from the right conduct of friendship, to caution in love affairs, to the careful management of goods. In her prefatory letter to the readers, Whitney develops the nosegay metaphor by describing these "flowers" gathered from Plat's translation as protection against the infections of London's streets. Whitney's most innovative contribution to the commonplace tradition is her personalization of its use in her own experience. Earlier "harvestlesse and servicelesse also" (Whitney 1982, 1.1-2 l.1–2), she had attempted to alleviate her dejection by reading Scripture, histories, and classical literature. Finding consolation only in Plat's collection, she generously offers her versifications to readers to protect their moral health. More information regarding her personal history emerges in Whitney's verse epistles to family members and friends, from whom she requests emotional or financial relief. Her letter to her brother G. W. avows her continued loyalty to her former mistress: "A vertuous Ladye, which / tyll death I honour wyll: / The losse I had of service hers, / I languish for it styll." Entitled "An Order prescribed by Is.W." with the running title "A modest meane for Maides," Whitney's versified advice to her younger sisters in service cautions against the special dangers of believing groundless slander and, as experience has taught her, the use of contentious or reproachful speech referred to as "fleetyng" or "flyting." Her letter to her married sister, Anne, represents her writing as enabled by her freedom from marriage and its household responsibilities. Reminding her that Christ himself was subject to slander, her friend C. W. expresses confidence that those who know Whitney will continue to believe in her virtue. Taken together, these letters seem to represent an attempt to repair damage to Whitney's reputation, perhaps to gain another position. In addition to providing insights into the experience of her service in London of the 1560s, these letters invite a close personal relationship between the poets and readers, as vicarious members of an intimate social network.

Whitney's concluding long poem, "The Manner of her Will," in which she wills the goods of London to itself, well deserves the recent critical attention it has elicited. The poem falls generally into two parts. In the first, Whitney maps the commodities of London onto the city streets in an inventory that incites consumer desires for foods, weapons, plate ("with Purle of Silver and of Golde"), and especially clothing ("Hoods, Bungraces, Hats or Caps"; "French Ruffes, high Purles, Gorgets, and Sleeves/ of any kind of Lawne"; "Boots, shoes or Pantables"; and "sweeping Cloakes,/ with Gardes beneth the Knee"). Remarkably, the second part of the poem maps the prisons and other places where criminals, including debtors, are punished: Newgate Bedlam, Holborn Hill, the Fleet, Ludgate, Bridewell. Identifying herself with debtors, Whitney claims that, if she had gained enough credit to accrue debt, she would herself have died in Ludgate. Taking nothing from London, she requests only a shroud and modest burial. The tone of this poem is complex, mixing unrequited love for the city, desire for goods, a lively sense of social injustice, with a resignation to an imminent departure represented as impending death. Few poems so successfully express the complicated responses of an early modern to the pleasures and pressures of a protocapitalist economy.

Finally, Whitney has also been claimed as the author of an epitaph, "The Lamentation of A Gentlewoman upon the Death of Her Late-Deceased Friend, William Gruffith," collected in *A Gorgeous Gallery of Gallant Inventions* (1578) after publication in broadside form (Fehrenbach 1981). As the female persona observes, her mourning for her lover must remain anonymous "for feare of flying fame." Whitney may well be the author of various anonymous poems in the numerous collections of the time.

Mary Ellen Lamb

See also Literary Culture and Women; Work and Women.

Bibliography

Primary Works

Martin, Randall, ed. *Women Writers in Renaissance England.* New York: Longman, 1997.

Stevenson, Jane, and Peter Davidson, eds. *Early Modern Women Poets (1520–1700): An Anthology.* Oxford: Oxford University Press, 2001.

Walker, Kim. *Women Writers of the English Renaissance.* Twayne English Authors Series, 521. Pages 152–162. New York: Twayne, 1996.

Whitney, Isabella. *A Sweet Nosegay and The Copy of a Letter.* Edited by Richard J. Panofsky. Delmar, NY: Scholars' Facsimiles and Reprints, 1982.

Secondary Works

Beilin, Elaine. "Writing Public Poetry: Humanism and the Woman Writer." *MLQ* 51 (1990): 249–259.

Bell, Ilona. "Women in the Lyric Dialogue of Courtship: Whitney's *Admonition to al yong Gentilwomen* and Donne's *The Legacie.*" In *Representing Women in Renaissance England.* Edited by Claude J. Summers and Ted-Larry Pebworth, 76–92. Columbia: University of Missouri Press, 1997.

Berry, Boyd. " 'We are not all alyke nor of complexion one': Truism and Isabella Whitney's Multiple Readers." *Renaissance Papers* (2000): 13–23.

Brace, Patricia. "Isabella Whitney, *A Sweet Nosegay.*" In *A Companion to Early Modern Women's Writing.* Edited by Anita Pacheo, 97–109. Oxford: Blackwell, 2002.

Fehrenbach, R. J. "Isabella Whitney (fl. 1565–75) and the Popular Miscellanies of Richard Jone." *Cahiers Elisabethains* 19 (1981): 85–87.

Fehrenbach, R. J. "Isabella Whitney, Sir Hugh Plat, Geoffrey Whitney, and 'Sister Idershae.' " *English Language Notes* (1983): 7–11.

Hutson, Lorna. *The Usurer's Daughter: Male Friendship and Fictions of Women in Sixteenth-Century England.* London and New York: Routledge, 1994.

Jones, Ann Rosalind. "Maidservants of London: Sisterhoods of Kinship and Labor." In *Maids and Mistresses, Cousins and Queens: Women's Alliances in Early Modern England.* Edited by Susan Frye and Karen Robertson, 21–32. Oxford: Oxford University Press, 1999.

Philippy, Patricia. "The Maid's Lawful Liberty: Service, the Household, and 'Mother B' in Isabella Whitney's *Sweet Nosegay.*" *Modern Philology* 95 (1997–1998): 439–462.

Travitsky Betty. "Isabella Whitney, 'The 'Wyll and Testament.' " *English Literary Renaissance* 10 (1980): 76–95.

Wall, Wendy. *The Imprint of Gender: Authorship and Publication in the English Renaissance.* Ithaca: Cornell University Press, 1993.

Widows and Guardianship

Guardianship law was contradictory in regard to women in early modern Europe. While even adult women often had to be represented before the law by a guardian, widows were frequently appointed the legal guardians of their children. The legal concept of guardianship could, therefore, deprive a woman of her individual legal identity or make a woman the temporary head of her family, giving her all the rights, obligations, powers, and responsibilities that were traditionally reserved for her husband or son. In spite of the limitations that guardianship could impose on women, studies across Europe have found that in practice widows often took on the male role within the political, economic, and social worlds they occupied, and that even women of lower status could have substantial power within their own families and communities in their roles as legal guardians. The amount of power a female guardian had depended on her ability to receive the guardianship of the heir whether she was the sole guardian, and her ability to negotiate her remarriage.

The possibility that women could be chosen as guardians of their children and the amount of power female guardians actually possessed was affected by both the formal and customary laws of their countries. Throughout Renaissance Europe law codes were in the process of being codified, recorded, and formalized, so almost any legal matter was still affected both by local, customary law and by law codes that were being written and compiled by royal governments that were trying to unify and assert control over their domains. For example, Roman law and Lombard law existed side by side in fifteenth-century Florence, and legal disputes in Renaissance Spain were affected by local law codes, known as *fueros,* as well as a series of royal law codes that dated back to the Visigoths in the seventh century. One of those royal law codes, the *Siete Partidas,* exemplifies the contradictions in the early modern attitude toward female guardians. Dealing rather grudgingly with the possibility of women guardians, the *Siete Partidas* states, "A person appointed the guardian of minors should be neither dumb, deaf, nor destitute of understanding, nor a spendthrift of his property, nor of bad morals. The party should be over twenty-five years of age, a man and not a woman . . ." The law goes on, however, to say that women can be appointed guardians of their children or grandchildren, and indeed a mother who wants guardianship of her children should have it "in preference to any other of their relatives, provided she is a good and prudent woman."

Guardianship was also powerfully affected by the way early modern laws were actually practiced. In Florence, Lombard customary law required a woman to have a male legal guardian, or *mundualdus,* to consent to her legal transactions and make them valid. Women could choose their own *mundualdus,* but the choice had to be confirmed by a judge, thereby officially equating women's status with that of minors who also had to have a judge-appointed guardian to approve their legal transactions. However, as Thomas Kuehn notes in *Law, Family, and Women,* even in Florence widows were occasionally guardians for their children or were able to stand as sureties for their children's actions (Kuehn 1991, 213–214). This discrepancy between the text of the law and the practice of the community seems to have existed in various forms throughout Europe. Breton customary law made fathers the automatic guardians of their children. In *The Practice of the Patriarchy,* however, Julie Hardwick finds that in almost 90 percent of cases in the families of notaries, after the death of the father the extended kin network chose the children's mothers as their guardians (Hardwick 1998, 123).

Throughout Renaissance Europe, husbands routinely chose their wives as guardians. Spanish noblemen stated in their wills that they appointed their wives guardians because their wives were the people they trusted the most, the people who knew the most about the property and had the most experience running it, and the people who were closest to their children. García Fernández's study of inheritance practices in Castile from 1650 to 1834 reveals that more than 84.4 percent of men named their wives as guardians of their young children, even if those wives were not the children's mothers (García Fernández 1994, 296). In his introduction to *Jewish History,* (vol. 16, 2002), Julius Kirshner notes that Renaissance Italian men accepted the power of a mother's natural love for her children while simultaneously recognizing that a mother made a safe guardian because she could not inherit if her children died intestate (Kirshner 2002, 2). Rebecca Lynn Winer's article, "Family, Community, and Motherhood," highlights the important role that Jewish widows played in thirteenth-century Perpignan in managing family property and businesses, thereby making them well qualified to be guardians.

In England, feudal custom complicated guardianship by letting the king retain control over all minors, their wardships, and their land. English monarchs exploited this custom for all it was worth by selling the wardships of young noble heirs and heiresses to the highest bidders among the nobility. Sometimes widowed mothers were able to buy back the wardships of their inheriting children or could be granted those wardships as a mark of favor from the monarch, but often the wardships were purchased by other nobles who anticipated profits from running the estates or saw the heir or heiress as a potential marriage partner for one of their own children. Non-inheriting children, however, occupied a different category, and in

English Aristocratic Women Barbara Harris notes that 86 percent of her sample of male testators who wrote wills between 1450 and 1550 appointed their wives as guardians of their younger, non-inheriting, minor children (Harris 2002, 279).

Guardianship could be a heavy responsibility and often involved financial risks, so early modern communities sometimes tried to protect the women who were routinely appointed as guardians. Rebecca Lynn Winer finds that the Jewish community in thirteenth-century Perpignan appointed widows as members of a guardianship committee, a move that minimized a woman's financial risk but must also have limited her ability to make autonomous decisions. Among the Breton notaries, as Julie Hardwick points out, guardianship was usually seen as an expensive and time-consuming burden that many family members tried hard to avoid. In an attempt to ease this burden and to prove that a guardian had the resources necessary to do the job, the family members who were not guardians usually served as guarantors for the guardian (Hardwick 1998, 121; 124). However, Julius Kirshner reports that the laws in Aragon prohibited joint guardianship (Kirshner 2002, 2). Archival records from the high nobility of Castile and Aragon prove that when widowed mothers were appointed in a joint guardianship along with several male guardians, it was the widows who most frequently signed the documents and initiated decisions about the property.

Remarriage of the widowed guardian complicated the ability of women to retain guardianship of their children, but the split between theory and practice continued to give most remarried women at least some power in the matter of guardianship. Julius Kirshner notes that husbands in Italy often appointed their wives guardians and provided them with support from the estate on the explicit condition that the wives not remarry or request the return of their dowries. This strategy gave the husband's family the advantage of not having to return the (often large) dowries of widows (Kirshner 2002, 3). In Breton, widows lost their guardianships if they remarried, but they could petition to have their new husbands take over the office of guardianship. The extended family had to scrutinize and approve this new arrangement, giving them the chance to express their disapproval of a widowed guardian's remarriage by removing from her the guardianship of the children (Hardwick 1998, 123–124). In England, aristocratic widows often protected their guardianship of their children and their roles as executors of their first husbands' wills by signing extensive prenuptial agreements with their second husbands (Harris 2002, 167). In Spain, women legally lost the right to hold a guardianship when they remarried. Aristocratic widows of high rank who could enlist the help of their male kin were often able to raise their children themselves after their remarriage and could sometimes even retain legal guardianship of the children's property (Coolidge 2001, 108; 164).

In Renaissance Spain the law required that to function as a guardian, a woman must take on the legal characteristics of a male. Family archives reveal the traditionally male activities that women guardians regularly performed. These activities varied from the mundane to the dramatic. Female guardians oversaw business deals, repaired houses, looked after the stock, appointed officials to run the courts of the towns they controlled, oversaw the huge trade fairs that occurred on their estates, and settled lawsuits. In 1663 the widowed duchess of Béjar (guardian of her son) repaired the city walls of Béjar against an attack, and Elvira de Ayala (widow of Alvaro de Guzmán and guardian of two daughters) fought a war with the counts of Medinaceli between 1399 and 1401 over two towns that she claimed as part of her minor daughters' inheritances. All of this business falls into the traditionally male jurisdiction of "outside" matters such as defense, government, courts, agriculture, and industry.

Female guardians are most visible in Spanish estate records of lawsuits, in which a widow's control over her family's lands and property, or political privileges and status traditionally accorded to her family, came under threat. In 1763 the duchess of Medina de Rioseco (guardian of her daughter) defended her family's right to appoint the mayor of the city of Medina de Rioseco, while Leónor de la Vega, widow of the Admiral of Castile fought furiously throughout the early fifteenth century to keep her husband's relatives from stealing her children's land and assets. Female guardians also faced legal challenges over their handling of the guardianship itself. The Duchess of Béjar was accused in court of alienating an important part of her ward's inheritance to provide a dowry for her own daughter.

The power that women had as guardians is only one example of the practical power that they held across Europe. Spanish noblemen clearly indicated that they chose their wives as guardians because these women were the most experienced and trustworthy people they could find to accomplish a task on which the future of the dynasty hinged. Archival records support this belief, as the accounts of female guardians show that they were sometimes more skilled than their deceased husbands at running and improving the noble estates. As a role for women, guardianship signaled a state of emergency, seen as a way to hold together the patriarchy until another man could assume control of the family. Women could not count on the role of guardianship the way their brothers could count on a career that involved managing, owning, creating, or controlling property. However, the percentage of women chosen as guardians is so high that it is clear from a historian's perspective that women often did exercise power over land, valuables, lives, and family strategies in the role of guardians, and it is also clear that men expected their wives, mothers, and daughters to prepare for this contingency. The widespread practice of allocating guardianship to women in early modern Europe had an impact on the social and political status of women not anticipated or determined by the formal legal codes of the period.

Grace E. Coolidge

Bibliography
Primary Work
Las Siete Partidas, trans. Samuel Parsons Scott. Philadelphia: University of Pennsylvania Press, 2001.
Secondary Works
Calvi, Giulia. "Reconstructing the Family: Widowhood and Remarriage in Tuscany in the Early Modern Period." In *Marriage in Italy, 1300–1650.* Edited by Trevor Dean and K. J. P. Lowe. Cambridge: Cambridge University Press, 1998.
Coolidge, Grace E. "Families in Crisis: Women, Guardianship, and the Nobility in Early Modern Spain." Ph.D. diss., Indiana University, 2001.
García Fernández, Máximo. *Herencia y Patrimonio Familiar en la Castilla del Antiguo Régiment (1650–1834): Efectos Socioeconómicos de la Muerte y la Partición de Beienes.* Valladolid: Universidad de Valladolid, 1994.
Hardwick, Julie. *The Practice of Patriarchy: Gender and the Politics of Household Authority in Early Modern France.* University Park: Pennsylvania State University Press, 1998.
Harris, Barbara J. *English Aristocratic Women, 1450–1550: Marriage and Family, Property and Careers.* Oxford: Oxford University Press, 2002.
Kirshner, Julius. "Introduction." *Jewish History* 16, no. 1 (2002): 1–14.
Kuehn, Thomas. *Law, Family, and Women: Toward a Legal Anthropology of Renaissance Italy.* Chicago: University of Chicago Press, 1991.
Winer, Rebecca Lynn. "Family, Community, and Motherhood: Caring for Fatherless Children in the Jewish Community of Thirteenth-Century Perpignan." *Jewish History* 16, no. 1 (2002): 15–48.

Witchcraft, Witches, and Witch-Hunting

From 1435 to 1750, between one hundred and ten thousand and two hundred thousand Europeans were accused of witchcraft, and sixty thousand to one hundred thousand were executed by burning or hanging. Nearly 80 percent of the accused were women. This was not the work of irrational mobs, but rather involved all ranks of society, including the educated elite, who feared that witches, in league with Satan, were threatening their Christian way of life. Prosecution peaked in the decades from 1580 to 1650, and some 75 percent of prosecutions occurred in Western and West Central Europe, i.e., the Germanic states, France, Switzerland, and the Low Countries. For the most part, the prosecution of witches ended in the mid-eighteenth century when elites, who controlled the judiciary, abandoned their belief in diabolic witchcraft.

Causes

A number of factors contributed to witch-hunting, and historians debate their relationship and relative importance. The development of the idea of the diabolical witch and legal changes that fostered torture were preconditions, while religious change and conflict, socioeconomic change, and political crises made it more likely by creating a mood of anxiety, which was expressed and relieved in witch-hunting. Traditional misogyny and the defense of patriarchy at a time of great social change also played a substantial role. But the triggers for accusations were usually personal or communal misfortune. such as illness or the death of family or livestock, the loss of crops through a hailstorm, and occasionally episodes of demonic possession. Thus, while many conditions conducive to hunting witches might be in place, varying local circumstances and actions were decisive.

The Concept of the Witch

Although the definition of a witch had been unstable, by the beginning of the fifteenth century a cumulative concept of the witch had emerged. This joined the idea long held by the common people of a witch as someone who practiced low, black magic (*maleficia*) to that of the elite who focused on witches' service to the

Engraving of a witch riding backward on a goat accompanied by putti. Albrecht Dürer. (Library of Congress)

Devil (*diabolism*) and the pact in which the witch gave her soul to the Devil in return for his help. Her body was marked with the Devil's mark, called in England the witch's teat, from which demons sucked blood. Witches were said to fly on broomsticks, fence posts, spits, animals, or of their own accord to attend meetings called Sabbaths, where they worshipped the Devil in a black mass, participated in a sexual orgy, practiced cannibalism, and created magical ointments from the bodies of dead infants. In some areas of Europe ideas about the Sabbath were not prominent, and in England demons, known as familiars or imps, tended to replace Satan as the diabolic feature. As the idea of the witch as a sorcerer came to be linked more strongly with the Devil, it became more feminized. This was particularly true after 1550, when the idea of the witch became more sexualized and witchcraft came to be defined as a secular crime rather than heresy.

The Significance of Gender

A majority of those who were accused of witchcraft were women who were poor, old, and unmarried. However, not all witches fell into these categories; over 20 percent were men. Many men were charged when witchcraft was closely related to heresy or to political sorcery, during panics, or when their wives were already charged. A number of men, however, were accused under circumstances similar to women. So it is clear from this angle, at least, that witch-hunting was not the same as woman hunting. However, that accusations of women at times constituted over 90 percent of all those indicted for witchcraft testifies to the targeting of women. Even though the idea of the witch was not limited to one gender, witch-hunting was used to attack women, especially women who in some way threatened gender hierarchy.

Beliefs about both women and witches made witch-hunting a powerful tool against women. Long-standing misogynistic beliefs that women were inferior to men physically, intellectually, morally, and emotionally and were sexually insatiable were crucial. Reflected in early modern witchcraft treatises, such as the intensely misogynistic *The Hammer of the Witches* and in the works of reformers such as Martin Luther, these beliefs indicated that women were more susceptible to the Devil's temptations. Additionally, witches, like women, were socially constructed as vengeful, lusty, and full of pride.

A second reason for the focus of accusations on women was patriarchy, the gender hierarchy, which misogynistic ideas supported. Because women's access to power was limited, people believed women would more readily use witchcraft. This, too, would be even more true for poor, unmarried, older women. In-

deed, the threat of black magic could command respect from neighbors who otherwise showed disdain.

Additionally, a number of accusations arose in the context of women's relationships with women, still in a patriarchal context. In early modern Augsburg, the mothers accused the lying-in servants who cared for them and their newborns, projecting their socially unacceptable negative feelings about motherhood onto the poor, older, and unmarried servant rather than acknowledging these negative feelings to themselves. A mother's hostility to her older servant may also have been linked to her position of authority in the household during this time and the new mother's unresolved ambivalence toward her own mother. Anxieties incurred by the vulnerability of women's bodies and their households may also have been related to women's accusing other women when their household duties went awry rather than admitting to incompetence in areas that marked their social identities.

Finally, the primacy of witchcraft accusations against women may have been part of a backlash against changes in the early modern period that threatened patriarchy. Beginning in the sixteenth century, the number of unmarried women, both widows and never-marrieds, grew significantly. Moreover, the age of a women at her first marriage also rose, increasing the overall number of single women. In Protestant areas, the closing of convents added to what was perceived as a social problem related to poverty and the maintenance of the social order. While the situations of widows and never-married women were not identical and the class status among those in either group could vary considerably, these women symbolized independence from patriarchal control. That this was a paramount concern is reflected not only in witch-hunting but also in urban regulations against women's living together, outside male control, even though this was obviously one solution to the social problem of poverty. In New England witch-hunting was connected to women's inheritance of land, but whether this holds true in Europe has yet to be examined.

Threats to gender hierarchy also came with the Reformation as both Protestant and Catholic women sought to participate publicly in spite of the gendered social restrictions that religious leaders continued to favor. Moreover, Protestants' ambiguous view of women as spiritually equal but socially subordinate to men added to the general mood of anxiety that encouraged witch-hunting. The Protestant emphasis on a woman's role as subordinate wife and mother in the godly household partly answered this anxiety and may have indirectly contributed to witch-hunting as well. Carol Karlsen argues that in New England the contradiction between women as godly wives and as daughters of the disobedient and proud Eve created psychic tension that found expression in witch-hunting (1998, 173–180). Both Protestant and Catholic leaders campaigned for restricting sexuality to patriarchal marriage, which may have created guilt that men projected in witch-hunting and which contributed to the growing number of prosecutions of women for fornication and infanticide.

There is no question that many accusations were leveled against women who in some way got out of their place. This is also an element in Keith Thomas's theory that witchcraft accusations developed from the growing contradiction between the traditional Christian dictate of helping a neighbor in need and the new demands of capitalist competition and institutionalized poor relief. When uncharitable neighbors refused to grant their needy neighbors' requests, they projected guilt onto them rather than feeling it themselves (Thomas 1971, 553–560). These needy neighbors were usually female and often expressed anger when their requests were not met. Thus, the developing contradiction in values also entailed a further contradiction between the Christian duty to help a poor, weak woman and the desire to punish a woman whose assertiveness was improper to her gender, class, and age.

Confessions

If only a few of the accused were actually practicing witchcraft, why did so many women confess? Many of the accused confessed only after horrendous torture at the hands of their interrogators. Others believed promises that they would be granted a quick dismissal if they confessed. In some cases, personal tragedies had unhinged the accused emotionally. Some of the accused came to believe that they were witches when interrogations brought to mind the myriad ways they had not lived up to the womanly ideal of the faithful and submissive wife and mother. The witch was not simply a diabolic sorcerer but also the mirror image of a good woman. Thus, the woman identified as a witch was an object onto which women as well as men could project the elements that no "good" woman could admit in herself or allow society to perceive in her. Contrarily, however, a number of women claimed the identity of witch and asserted their pact with the devil and their use of sorcery. For them, the witch was a cultural resource in a society that placed severe constraints on women's power.

While all the accused, even those who practiced witchcraft or chose the identity of witch, were victims, their agency also is evident in the records. Even within the horror of trials, torture, forced confession, and execution, many accused continued to assert themselves by strategizing, resisting, and preserving a sense of self. Thus, while the story of witch-hunting is a sad testament to the human potential for cruelty and the strength of patriarchy, it also demonstrates the historicity of these elements and the strength of individuals confronted with them.

Martha Skeeters

See also Rape and Violence Against Women; Religious Persecution and Women.

Bibliography

Primary Works

Gibson Marion, ed. *Early Modern Witches: Witchcraft Cases in Contemporary Writing*. London and New York: Routledge, 2001.

Kramer, Heinrich, and James Sprenger. *The Malleus Maleficarum*. Translated and edited by M. Summers. London: John Rodker, 1928. (Reprinted in Escondido, CA: The Book Tree, 2000.)

Secondary Works

Apps, Lara, and Andrew Gow. *Male Witches in Early Modern Europe*. Manchester, UK: Manchester University Press; Palgrave, 2003.

Barstow, Anne Llewellyn. *Witchcraze: A New History of the European Witch Hunts*. New York: Pandora/Harper Collins, 1994.

Karlsen, Carol F. *The Devil in the Shape of a Woman: Witchcraft in Colonial New England*. New York and London: W. W. Norton and Company, 1998.

Klaits, Joseph. *Servants of Satan: The Age of the Witch Hunts*. Bloomington: Indiana University Press, 1985.

Levack, Brian. *The Witch-Hunt in Early Modern Europe*. 2nd ed. London and New York: Longman, 1995.

Purkiss, Diane. *The Witch in History: Early Modern and Twentieth-Century Representations*. London and New York: Routledge, 1996.

Roper, Lyndal. *Oedipus and the Devil: Witchcraft, Sexuality and Religion in Early Modern Europe*. London and New York: Routledge, 1994.

Thomas, Keith. *Religion and the Decline of Magic*. New York: Scribner's, 1971.

Work and Women

Though the actual work that men and women performed in the Renaissance economy was often very similar or the same, their relationship to work and work identities were very different. Male work rhythms and a man's position in the economy were to a large degree determined by age, class, and training, with boys and men often moving as a group from one level of employment to the next. Female work rhythms were also determined by age and class, but even more so by individual biological and social events such as marriage, motherhood, and widowhood, all of which were experienced by women individually and over which they might have little control. Women often changed occupations several times during their lives or performed many different types of jobs

at once, so that their identification with any one occupation was not strong.

Women rarely received formal training in a trade, and during the Renaissance many occupations were professionalized, with the setting up of required amounts of formal training and a licensing procedure before one could claim an occupational title. Thus in the Middle Ages both male and female practitioners of medicine were often called physicians, but by the sixteenth century, despite the fact that some specializations within medicine such as gynecology and obstetrics remained the province of female midwives, only men who had attended university medical school could be called physicians. This professionalism trickled down to occupations that did not require university training; women might brew herbal remedies, but only men could use the title "apothecary." Professionalization affected not only titles but also the fees people could charge for their services; a university-trained physician, for example, earned many times the annual salary of a female medical practitioner.

In the cities and the courts, a few women worked as painters, miniaturists, composers, musicians, singers, and printers. Many such women worked in the ateliers and shops of their fathers. Other women plied their trades as artists and composers under the auspices of a convent.

During the Renaissance, gender also became an important factor in separating what was considered skilled from what was considered unskilled work. Women were judged to be unfit for certain tasks, such as glass cutting, because they were too clumsy and "unskilled," yet those same women made lace or silk thread jobs that required an even higher level of dexterity than glass cutting. The gendered notion of work meant that women's work was valued less and generally paid less than men's. All economies need both structure and flexibility, and during the early modern period these qualities became gender-identified: male labor provided the structure for work that was regulated, tied to a training process, and lifelong; female labor provided the flexibility for work that was discontinuous, alternately encouraged or suppressed, not linked to formal training, and generally badly paid. Women's work was thus both marginal and irreplaceable.

Rural Areas

Despite enormous economic changes during the Renaissance, the vast majority of people in almost all parts of Europe continued to live in the countryside, producing agricultural products for their own use and for the use of their landlords. Agricultural tasks were highly, though not completely, gender-specific, though exactly which tasks were regarded as female and which as male varied widely throughout Europe. These gender divisions were partly the result of physical differences, with men generally doing tasks that required a great deal of upper body strength, such as cutting grain with a scythe; they were partly the result of women's greater responsibility for child care, so that women carried out tasks closer to the house, which could be more easily interrupted for nursing or tending children; they were partly the result of cultural beliefs, so that women in parts of Norway, for example, sowed all grain because people felt this would ensure a bigger harvest. Whatever their source, gender divisions meant that the proper functioning of a rural household required at least one adult male and one adult female; remarriage after the death of a spouse was much faster in the countryside than in the cities.

Women's labor changed as new types of crops and agricultural products were introduced and as agriculture became more specialized. Women in parts of Italy, for example, tended and harvested olive trees and grapevines, and carried out most of the tasks associated with the production of silk: gathering leaves from mulberry trees, raising the silk cocoons, and processing cocoons into raw silk by reeling and spinning. Women also worked as day laborers in agriculture, and from wage regulations we can see that female agricultural laborers were paid about half of what men were and were given less and poorer-quality food.

Women also found work in rural areas in nonagricultural tasks, particularly in mining, and by the sixteenth century in domestic industry. In mining, women carried ore, wood, and salt, sorted and washed ore, and prepared charcoal briquettes for use in smelting. In domestic industry, they produced wool, linen, and later cotton thread or cloth (or cloth that was a mixture of these), and they were hired by capitalist investors as part of a household or as an individual. In areas of Europe where whole households were hired, domestic industry often broke down gender divisions, for men, women, and children who were old enough all worked at the same tasks; labor became a more important economic commodity than property, which led to earlier marriage, weaker parental control over children, and more power to women in family decision making. In parts of Europe where women were hired as individuals, men's agricultural tasks were more highly paid, so men continued to make most of the decisions in the family, and there was little change in women's status.

Urban Areas

In the cities, domestic service was probably the largest source of employment for women throughout the period. Girls might begin service as young as seven or eight, traveling from their home village to a nearby town. Cities also offered other types of service employment on a daily or short-term basis. Many of these jobs were viewed as extensions of a woman's functions and tasks in the home— cleaning, cooking, laundering, caring for children and old people, nursing the sick, preparing bodies for burial, mourning the dead. Women combined part-time work in laundering and sewing with selling sex for money— what later became known as prostitution— which many cities tried to regulate, setting up official city brothels with rules for the women and their customers. In the late fifteenth century, cities began to limit brothel residents' freedom of movement and require them to wear clothing that would mark them as "dishonorable." Such restrictions increased dramatically after the Protestant Reformation, with most Protestant and then Catholic cities in Northern Europe closing their municipal brothels, while major Italian cities favored regulation over suppression.

Women were important providers of health care and charity. The hospitals, orphanages, and infirmaries run by the Catholic Church were largely staffed by women, as were the similar secular institutions that many cities set up beginning in the fifteenth century. Women continued to dominate midwifery in most parts of Europe, the one female occupation whose practitioners developed a sense of work identity nearly as strong as that of men. In many cities women distributed poor relief to families in their own homes, with the city governments relying on women's knowledge of their own neighborhoods to prevent fraud.

The city marketplace, the economic as well as geographic center of most cities, was filled with women; along with rural women with their agricultural and animal products were city women with sausage, pretzels, meat pies, cookies, candles, soap, and wooden implements that they had made. Women sold fresh and salted fish that their husbands had caught or that they had purchased from fishermen, game and fowl they had bought from hunters, and imported food items such as oranges, and by the seventeenth century tea and coffee bought from international merchants. Pawnbrokers sold used clothing and household articles, and female money changers exchanged travelers' money for the type of coinage accepted in the city. Because there was no way to preserve food easily, women or their female servants had to shop every day, and the marketplace was where they met their neighbors, exchanged information, and talked over recent events.

Women also ran small retail establishments throughout the city. They made beer, mead, and hard cider, and ran taverns and inns to dispense their beverages and provide sleeping quarters for those too poor to stay in the more established inns. These taverns also provided employment for serving women, though there were perils with such a job; inn servants in France were the one group of women denied the right to sue their seducer if they became pregnant. Women's work as producers and distributors of alcohol changed somewhat during the period, for they often left or were pushed out of certain occupations, such as brewing beer, once these became larger scale, requiring more capital investment but also producing more profit.

Domestic industry provided employment for increasing numbers of urban as well as rural women, particularly in spinning. Renaissance techniques of cloth production necessitated up to twenty carders and spinners per weaver, so that cloth centers like Florence, Augsburg, or Antwerp could keep many people employed. The identification of women and spinning became very strong in the early modern period, and by the seventeenth century unmarried women in England came to be called spinsters.

Women increasingly turned to spinning as other employment avenues were closed to them, particularly in craft guilds, which continued to dominate the production and distribution of most products into the eighteenth century. There were a few all-female guilds in cities with highly specialized economies, such as Cologne, Paris, and Rouen, but in general the guilds were male organizations and followed the male life cycle. One became an apprentice at puberty, became a journeyman four to ten years later, traveled around learning from a number of masters, then settled down, married, opened one's own shop, and worked at the same craft full-time until one died or got too old to work any longer. Women fit into guilds much more informally, largely through their relationship to a master as his wife, daughter, or domestic servant. Masters' widows ran shops after the death of their husbands and were expected to pay all guild fees, though they could not participate in running the guild. Even this informal participation began to be restricted in the fifteenth century on the continent, however, and women largely lost this relatively high-status work opportunity.

The Renaissance has been viewed as a time of tremendous economic change, with the expansion of commercial capitalism, the beginning of domestic production, and the creation of a world market system because of European colonization. When we evaluate women's economic role during this period, however, we find that continuities outweigh the changes. Women were increasingly pushed out of craft guilds, but they had only rarely been full members in the first place. They took over new types of agricultural tasks, but continued to be paid half of what men were paid no matter what types of work they did. They dominated the urban marketplace, but only rarely were able to amass much profit. Women's legal dependence on fathers or husbands, their unequal access to family resources, and their inability to receive formally acknowledged training had adversely affected their economic position in the Middle Ages and would continue to do so through the Renaissance and into the twentieth (or in many cases twenty-first) century. The vast majority of women's work continued to be low status, badly paid or unpaid, frequently shifting, and perceived as marginal, but essential to the operation of all rural and urban economies. These were also qualities that marked the work of many men in the Renaissance, but they had the comfort of knowing that, however dismal their actual working conditions, their labor was valued higher than that of the women who worked beside them.

Merry E. Wiesner-Hanks

See also Anguissola, Sofonisba; Art and Women; Fontana, Lavinia; Inglis, Esther; the subheadings Home Care and Women Practitioners; Professionalization of Medicine and Women Practitioners; Legal Injunctions against Women Practitioners; Hospital Administration and Nursing as Careers for Women; Childbirth and Reproductive Knowledge; Midwives and Licensing; and The Practice of Pharmacolgy and Laywomen (under Medicine and Women); Music and Women; Nelli, Plautilla; Printers, the Book Trade, and Women; Strozzi, Barbara.

Bibliography
Bennett, Judith. *Ale, Beer and Brewsters in England: Women's Work in a Changing World, 1300–1600.* New York: Oxford University Press, 1996.

Charles, Lindsey, and Duffin, Lorna, eds. *Women and Work in Pre-Industrial England.* London: Croom Helm, 1985.

Desan, Philippe, ed. "Work in the Renaissance." *Journal of Medieval and Renaissance Studies* (Special issue) 25, no. 1 (1995).

Fairchilds, Cissie. *Domestic Enemies: Servants and Their Masters in Old Regime France.* Baltimore, MD: Johns Hopkins University Press, 1984.

Goldberg, P. J. P. *Women, Work and Life Cycle in a Medieval Economy: Women in York and Yorkshire c. 1300–1520.* Oxford: Clarendon Press, 1992.

Hafter, Daryl, ed. *European Women and Preindustrial Craft.* Bloomington: Indiana University Press, 1995.

Hanawalt, Barbara, ed. *Women and Work in Preindustrial Europe.* Bloomington: Indiana University Press, 1986.

Howell, Martha. *Women, Production and Patriarchy in Late Medieval Cities.* Chicago: University of Chicago Press, 1986.

Murray, Mary. *The Law of the Father: Patriarchy in the Transition from Feudalism to Capitalism.* London: Routledge, 1995.

Ogilvie, Sheilagh C. *A Bitter Living: Women, Markets and Social Capital in Early Modern Germany.* Oxford: Oxford University Press, 2003.

Sharpe, Pamela. *Adapting to Capitalism: Working Women in the English Economy, 1700–1850.* New York: St. Martin's, 1996.

Wiesner, Merry E. *Women and Gender in Early Modern Europe.* Cambridge: Cambridge University Press, 1993.

Wiesner, Merry E. *Working Women in Renaissance Germany.* New Brunswick, NJ: Rutgers University Press, 1986.

Wroth, Mary (ca. 1587–1653)

Poet, playwright, actor, courtier, and author of the roman à clef, Urania

Noteworthy as the first woman writer of a sonnet sequence, *Pamphilia to Amphilanthus,* of the first prose romance, *The Countess of Montgomery's Urania,* and of an early pastoral drama, *Love's Victory,* Lady Mary Wroth née Sidney was born into a socially elite family of poets and patrons: most notably, her illustrious uncle, Philip Sidney, but also her father, Robert Sidney, and her aunt, Mary Sidney, countess of Pembroke. While the first modern critics of her work generally dismissed it as a poor imitation of her uncle and as undistinguished exercises in Petrarchan tradition, in the last twenty years, increasing critical attention has illuminated her innovative use of female voices and her distinctly female revisions of male literary traditions.

The eldest daughter of Robert Sidney and Barbara Gamage, Mary Wroth spent most of her early life at the family estate, Penshurst, at Baynards Castle in London, and in the Lowlands where her father served as governor of Flushing. Barbara Gamage took special care with her children's education, and Rowland Whyte, who managed Penshurst in Robert Sidney's absence, wrote her father that Mary "is very forward in her learning, writing and other exercises she is put to" (*HMC,* De L'Isle, II, 176).

Mary Sidney married Robert Wroth on 27 September 1604 at Penshurst, but shortly after the marriage, Robert Wroth complained to her father that "hee cannot take any exceptions to his wife, nor her cariage towards him" (*HMC,* De L'Isle, III, 140). Ben Jonson, an admirer of Lady Mary, also believed that the marriage was unhappy and in part because of her husband's jealousy. Through her husband's and father's connections at court, Lady Mary became a courtier and performed with Queen Anne in Jonson's *The Masque of Blackness* (1605) and *The Masque of Beauty* (1608).

Although Lady Mary and her husband were on good terms when he died on 14 March 1614, she was left with a one-month-old son, James, and a debt of twenty-three thousand pounds. With her son's death on 5 July 1616, the estate reverted to her husband's family, and she was left to struggle with her husband's debt for much of her life. Lady Mary did maintain some contact with Anne Clifford and other courtiers, but she was no longer part of Queen Anne's inner circle. Mary Wroth's social status continued to decline, possibly as a result of her affair with her married first cousin, William Herbert, third earl of Pembroke, with whom she had two children, William and Catherine. A patron of Jonson, a dedicatee of Shakespeare's first folio, and a womanizer, William Herbert had been banished from Elizabeth's court in 1601 for his refusal to marry Mary Fitton, a courtier of Queen Elizabeth, when she became pregnant.

The Countess of Montgomery's Urania (1621)

Unlike most women writers before her who penned religious texts or translations, Wroth's works focus on the secular topics of love and romance. Often regarded as an autobiographical roman à clef, Wroth's prose romance, *Urania,* exists in two parts and includes over three hundred characters. The first part, published in 1621, received much censure from those who saw their scandals reflected in its pages, including Lord Edward Denny, who in a vitriolic poem entitled "To Pamphilia from the father-in-law of Seralius," advises Wroth to "leave idle bookes alone / For wise and worthyer women have writte none" (Wroth 1995, 25–26). Despite her forceful response—"Your spitefull words against a harmless booke / Shows that an ass much like the sire doth looke" (Wroth 1995, 3–4)—Wroth was forced to ask for aid from influential friends to avoid the displeasure of James I. She promised to recall her romance, and she refrained from further publication. Thus, the second part exists only in autograph manuscript form. Like both Sidney's *New Arcadia* and the first part of the *Urania,* it ends in midsentence. In addition to her acute observations of her social world, Wroth's commentary in the *Urania* extends to politics, including James I and the Stuart court in Part Two of the *Urania;* for example, she claims, "the Government in Monarchi is the sweetest, Noblest, and gentlest of all" (Robert, Gossett, Mueller 1999, II, fol. 14).

In the *Urania,* like the rest of Wroth's œuvre, constancy and faithlessness are overarching issues between the faithful Pamphilius and her inconstant lover, Amphilanthus. Secondary couples attempt to overcome familial obstacles, and ultimately the romance argues for a more companionate marriage freely chosen. Throughout the first part of the *Urania,* Pamphilia virtuously upholds the ideal of constancy, but when confronted with Amphilanthus's marriage in the second part, she marries Rodomantro, the king of Tartaria, although she vows "to bee constant to inconstancy" (Roberts, Gossett, Mueller 1999, I, fol. 8ᵛ) and continue to love Amphilanthus despite his infidelity and in spite of her marriage. Although many comparisons have been made between Wroth's *Urania* and her uncle's *New Arcadia,* a more significant influence is Spenser's *Faerie Queen,* a source for the *Urania* both through allusions to the love story of Britomart and Arthegall and through its iconography and episodic structure.

Pamphilia to Amphilanthus (ca. 1620)

Pamphilia to Amphilanthus is the first secular Petrarchan sonnet sequence written by an Englishwoman. Because of thematic similarities to *The Countess of Montgomery's Urania* as well as recurring character names, most of Wroth's work is assumed to have been written around 1620. There are two extant versions of *Pamphilia to Amphilanthus:* the Folger Library's holograph manuscript includes one hundred and ten poems, and following the Newberry Library's printed version of *Urania* is a version of the sonnet sequence with eighty-three sonnets and twenty songs. The key innovations of the sequence result from the revision of the Petrarchan tradition by the use of a female speaker, Pamphilia ("all loving"), who be-

moans the inconstancy of her lover, Amphilanthus ("lover of two").

Although Wroth ostensibly employs the Petrarchan tradition of a melancholic male lover who bemoans the cruelty of his unobtainable beloved, the sequence focuses on her inner turmoil rather than the object of her love. Tension arises between the female protagonist and the personifications of love and passion, Cupid and Venus. In a dream vision, Pamphilia attempts to resolve tensions between overpowering, passionate love and love as a personal choice. She resents love's unpredictability, personified by Cupid as a putto, and her own resulting jealousy and despondency. Sonnets 77–90 create an Italian *corona* of fourteen interwoven poems—a form practiced by both Philip and Robert Sidney—that praise Cupid as monarch, but ultimately this cannot do justice to her conflicting emotions. In sonnets filled with ominous imagery of "huge clouds of smoke" and "thickest mists" (Wroth 1983, 99.1, 100.5), she acknowledges and accepts the complex intermingling of pleasure and jealous despair caused by love. In the final two sonnets, she comments: "eternall goodnes . . . / Injoying of true joye, the most, and best" (Wroth 1983, 103.6–7).

Love's Victory (ca. 1621)

Existing only in two manuscripts (one complete and one partial), *Love's Victory* is a pastoral tragicomedy with four pairs of lovers representing true, neo-Platonic, comic, and imperfect love. Primarily written in heroic couplets, the five-act drama also contains songs and poems. In a *deus ex machina* frame, Venus and Cupid, ignored and disdained, decide to raise havoc on a group of shepherds and shepherdesses to "grow our greatness to respect" (Wroth 1996, 1.1.4). This frame foreshadows Wroth's continuing focus on the relationship between carnality and love. Although Philisses and Musella are the central couple, the other three couples—Lissius and Simeana, Forester and Silvesta, and Rustic and Dalina—have nearly as many lines. Similar to Wroth's other protagonists, they struggle with inconstancy and jealousy, miscommunication and distrust, but the play's title assures a comic ending. Empowered by her chastity, Silvestra, the self-avowed servant of Diana, plays an active role while the other shepherdesses are constrained by their gender not to speak their love: "A woman woo?/ The most unfittest, shameful'st thing to do!" (Wroth 1996, 3.1.187–8). In act five as Musella, accompanied by Philisses, prepares to kill herself with a dagger in the Temple of Love, Silvestra offers them poison instead, which Venus later reveals to be a sleep-inducing drug. Like Wroth's other works, *Love's Victory* is often read as a personal as well as a familial autobiography with Musella as Wroth herself and Philisses as William Herbert, while within the Sidney family, Philisses represents Philip Sidney and Musella is Penelope Rich, the Stella of Philip Sidney's *Astrophil and Stella*.

With these three works, recently made available to modern readers, Wroth's writings represent some of the richest finds of the considerable literary treasures written by early modern women and rediscovered by scholars of the late twentieth century.

Marlo Belschner

> **See also** Clifford, Anne; Literary Culture and Women; Sidney, Mary Herbert; Theater and Women Actors, Playwrights, and Patrons.
> **Bibliography**
> *Primary Works*
> Historical Manuscript Commission (cited as HMC), De L'Isle, II, 176; III, 140.
> Wroth, Mary. "The First Part of the Countess of Montgomery's Urania." In *Medieval and Re-*

naissance Text and Studies. Vol 140. Edited by Josephine Roberts. Binghamton, NY: Renaissance English Text Society, 1995.

Wroth, Mary. *Love's Victory.* In *Renaissance Drama by Women, Texts and Documents.* Edited by S. P. Cerasano and Marion Wynne-Davies. London: Routledge, 1996.

Wroth, Mary. *The Poems of Lady Mary Wroth.* Edited by Josephine Roberts. Baton Rouge: Louisiana State University Press, 1983.

Wroth, Mary. "The Second Part of the Countess of Montgomery's Urania." In Renaissance English Text Society. Vol. 211. Edited by Josephine Roberts, Suzanne Gossett, and Janel M. Mueller. Tempe: Arizona Center for Medieval and Renaissance Studies, 1999.

Secondary Works

Cerasano, S. P., and Marion Wynne-Davies, eds. *Renaissance Drama by Women: Texts and Documents.* London: Routledge, 1996.

King, Sigrid, ed. "Pilgrimage for Love: Essays in Early Modern Literature in Honor of Josephine A. Roberts." In *Medieval and Renaissance Texts and Studies.* Vol. 213. Tempe: Arizona Center for Medieval and Renaissance Studies, 1999.

Lamb, Mary Ellen. *Gender and Authorship in the Sidney Circle.* Madison: University of Wisconsin Press, 1990.

McLaren, Margaret Anne. "An Unknown Continent: Lady Mary Wroth's Forgotten Pastoral Drama, *Loves Victorie.*" In *Readings in Renaissance Women's Drama: Criticism, History and Performance, 1594–1998.* Edited by S. P. Cerasano and Marion Wynne-Davies, 219–233. London: Routledge, 1998.

Miller, Naomi J., and Gary Waller, eds. *Reading Mary Wroth: Representing Alternatives in Early Modern England.* Knoxville: University of Tennessee Press, 1991.

Bibliography

Primary Sources

Agrippa, Henricus Cornelius. *Declamation on the Nobility and Preeminence of the Female Sex.* Translated and edited by Albert Rabil, Jr. Chicago: University of Chicago Press, 1996.

Albret, Jeanne d'. *Lettres d'Antoine de Bourbon et de Jehanne d'Albret.* Edited by Mis de Rochambeau. Paris: Renouard, 1877.

Albret, Jeanne d'. *Mémoires et poésies.* Edited by Alphonse de Ruble. Geneva: Slatkine, 1970. (Originally published in Paris, 1893.)

Aleotti, Vittoria. *Ghirlanda de madrigal: a quatro voci.* Edited by C. Ann Carruthers. New York: Broude Trust, 1994.

Andreini, Isabella. *La Mirtilla: A Pastoral.* Translated by Julie Campbell. Tempe: Arizona Center for Medieval and Renaissance Studies, 2002.

Andreini, Isabella. *Lettere.* Edited by Francesco Andreini. Venice, 1607. (Published many times after 1607.)

Andreini, Isabella. *The Madness of Isabella.* In *Scenarios of the Commedia dell'Arte.* Translated by Henry Salerno. New York: Limelight Editions, 1996.

Andreini, Isabella. *Mirtilla, favola pastorale.* Verona, 1588; Ferrara, 1590; Venice, 1590; Milan, 1605.

Andreini, Isabella. *Rime.* Milan, 1601; Paris, 1603; Milan, 1605.

Anne de France. *Les Enseignements d'Anne de France, duchesse de Bourbonnois et d'Auvergne, à sa fille Susanne de Bourbon.* Edited by A. M. Chazaud. Moulins: Desrosiers, 1878.

Anne Locke. *A Meditation of a Penitent Sinner: Anne Locke's Sonnet Sequence with Locke's Epistle.* Edited and with an introduction by Kel Morin-Parsons. Waterloo, Ontario, Canada: North Waterloo Academic Press, 1997.

Anne Vaughan Lock. *The Collected Works of Anne Vaughan Lock.* Medieval and Renaissance Texts and Studies. Vol. 185. Edited by Susan Felch. Tempe: Arizona Center for Medieval and Renaissance Studies, Renaissance English Text Society, 1999.

Aragona, Tullia d'. "Dialogo della infinità di amore." *Trattati d'amore del Cinquecento.* Edited by Giuseppe Zonta, 185–248. Bari: Laterza, 1912.

Aragona, Tullia d'. *Dialogo della signora Tullia d'Aragona della Infinità di Amore.* Venice: Gabriel Giolito de' Ferrari, 1547.

Aragona, Tullia d'. *Dialogue on the Infinity of Love.* Translated by Rinaldina Russell and Bruce Merry. Chicago: University of Chicago Press, 1997.

Aragona, Tullia d'. *Il Meschino, altramente detto il Guerrino. Fatto in ottava rima dalla signora Tullia d'Aragona. Opera nella quale si veggono e intendono le parti principali di tutto il mondo, e molte altre dilettevolissime cose, da essere sommamente care ad ogni sorte di persona di bello ingegno.* Venice: G. B. and M. Sessa, 1560.

Aragona, Tullia d'. *Il Meschino detto il Guerrino.* 12 vols. Parnaso Italiano. Edited by Francesco Zanotto, vol. 5. Venice: Giuseppe Antonelli, 1839.

Aragona, Tullia d'. *Le rime di Tullia d'Aragona cortigiana del secolo XVI.* Edited by Enrico Celani. Bologna: Commissione per i testi di lingua, 1968. (Originally published in 1891.)

Aragona, Tullia d'. *Rime della Signora Tullia di Aragona; et di diversi a lei.* Venice: Gabriele Giolito, 1547.

Arlier, Antoine. *Correspondance d'Antoine Arlier, humaniste languedocien, 1527–1545.* Edited by E. J. N. Pendergrass. Geneva: Droz, 1990. (A few of Claude de Bectoz's letters on pp. 114, 177, 198.)

Artus, Thomas. *Description de l'Isle des Hermaphrodites, nouvellemement descouverte.* Edited by Claude Gilbert Dubois. Geneva: Droz, 1996.

Astell, Mary. *The First English Feminist: Reflections on Marriage and Other Writings.* Edited and with an introduction by Bridget Hill. New York: St. Martin's Press, 1986.

Atherton, Margaret, ed. *Women Philosophers of the Early Modern Period.* Indianapolis, IN: Hackett Publishing, 1994.

Aughterson, Kate, ed. *Renaissance Woman: Constructions of Femininity in England. A Source Book.* London and New York: Routledge, 1995.

Bacon, Lady Anne Cooke. *Anne Cooke Bacon.* Edited by Valerie Wayne. Burlington, VT: Ashgate, 2000.

Backus, Irena. "Les clarisses de la rue Verdaine/The Poor Clares of the Rue Verdaine." In *Le guide des femmes disparues* (Forgotten Women of Geneva). Edited by Anne-Marie Käppeli, 20–39. Geneva: Metropolis, 1993.

Baker, L. M., ed. *The Letters of Elizabeth, Queen of Bohemia*. London: The Bodley Head, 1953.

Barbaro, Francesco. *On Wifely Duties*. In *The Earthly Republic. Italian Humanists in Government and Society*. Translated by Benjamin Kohl. Edited by Benjamin Kohl and R. G. Witt, 179–228. Philadelphia: Unversity of Pennsylvania Press, 1978.

Barnstone, Willis, trans. *Sappho: Lyrics in the Original Greek*. New York: New York University Press, 1965.

Battiferra, Laura. *I sette salmi penitenziali di David con alcuni sonetti spirituali*. Edited by Enrico Maria Guidi. Urbino: Accademia Raffaello, 2005.

Battiferra, Laura. *Il primo libro delle opere toscane*. Edited by Enrico Maria Guidi. Urbino: Accademia Raffaello, 2000.

Battiferra, Laura. *Lettere di Laura Battiferri Ammannati a Benedetto Varchi*. Edited by Carlo Gargiolli. Bologna: Commissione per i testi di lingua, 1968. (Originally printed in 1879.)

Battiferra, Laura degli Ammannati. *Laura Battiferra and Her Literary Circle*. Edited and translated by Victoria Kirkham. Chicago: University of Chicago Press, 2006.

Bauhin, Caspar. *De hermaphroditorum monstrosorumque partuum natura ex Theologorum, Jureconsultorumque, Medicorum, Philosophorum, et Rabbinorum sententia libri duo*. Oppenheim: Galleri, De Bry, 1614. (Reprint of the 1600 Frankfurt edition.)

Behn, Aphra. *The Works of Aphra Behn*. 7 vols. Edited by Janet Todd. Columbus: Ohio State University Press, 1992–1996.

Beilin, Elaine V., ed. *Protestant Translators: Anne Lock Prowse and Elizabeth Russell*. The Early Modern Englishwoman: The Printed Writings. Aldershot, UK: Ashgate, 1998.

Beilin, Elaine V., ed. *The Examinations of Anne Askewe*. New York and Oxford: Oxford University Press, 1996.

Bembo, Pietro. *La grande fiamma: lettere 1503–1517*. Edited by Giulia Raboni. Milano: R. Archinto, 1989.

Bembo, Pietro. *The Prettiest Love Letters in the World: Letters Between Lucrezia Borgia and Pietro Bembo, 1503–1519*. Translation and preface by Hugh Shankland. Wood engravings by Richard Shirly Smith. Boston: D. R. Godine, 1987.

Benson, Pamela Joseph, ed. *Texts of the Querelle des femmes, 1521–1640*. The Early Modern Englishwoman: A Facsimile Library of Essential Works, 1500–1750, series III. Aldershot, UK: Ashgate, 2006.

Berriot-Salvadore, Evelyne. *Les femmes dans la société française de la Renaissance*. Geneva: Droz, 1990.

Berriot-Salvadore, Evelyne. "Les femmes et les pratiques de l'écriture de Christine de Pisan à Marie de Gournay." *Réforme, Humanisme, Renaissance* 16 (1983): 52–69.

Biblioteca Estense di Modena. *Autografoteca Campori, Giulia Gonzaga*. (Letters dated 25 February, 25 March, 25 April, 26 May, and 10 June, 1553.)

Blasi, Jolanda de'. *Le scrittrici italiane dalle origini al 1800*. Florence: Nemi, 1930.

Bruni, Leonardo. "On the Study of Literature (1405) to Lady Battista Malatesta of Montefeltro." In *The Humanism of Leonardo Bruni: Selected Texts*. Translated with an introduction by Gordon Griffiths, James Hankins, and David Thompson, 240–251. Binghamton, NY: Medieval and Renaissance Studies and Texts, 1987.

Boccaccio, Giovanni. *Famous Women*. Edited and translated by Virginia Brown. I Tatti Renaissance Library. Cambridge, MA, and London: Harvard University Press, 2001.

Book of Prayers of Claude de France. New York: private collection.

Bornstein, Diane, ed. *The Feminist Controversy of the Renaissance: Guillaume Alexis, An Argument betwyxt Man and Woman (1525); Sir Thomas Elyot, The Defence of Good Women (1545); Henricus Cornelius Agrippa, Female Pre-Eminence (1670)*. Delmar, NY: Scholars' Facsimiles and Reports, 1980.

Bourbon, Catherine de. *Lettres et poésies de Catherine de Bourbon (1570–1603)*. Edited by Raymond Ritter. Paris: Champion, 1927.

Bourbon, Gabrielle de. *Œuvres spirituelles (1510–1516)*. Textes de la Renaissance, vol. 26. Edited by Evelyne Berriot-Salvadore. Paris: Champion, 1999.

Bourgeois, Louise (dite Boursier). *Observations diverses, sur la sterilité, perte de fruict, foecondité, accouchements, et maladies des femmes, et enfans nouveaux naiz / Amplement traittées, et heureusement practiquées par L. Bourgeois dite Boursier sage femme de la Roine / Oeuvre util et necessaire à toutes personnes / Dedié à la Royne*. Paris: Abraham Saugrain, 1609.

Bourgeois, Louise (dite Boursier). *Recueil des Secrets, de Louyse Bourgeois dite Boursier, sage-femme de la Royne Mere du Roy, Auquel sont continués ses plus rares experiences pour diverses maladies, principalement des femmes avec leurs embelissemens*. Paris: Melchior Mondiere, 1635.

Bréghot Du Lut, Claude. *Mélanges biographiques et littéraires pour servir l'histoire de Lyon*. Geneva: Slatkine, 1971. (Originally printed in Lyons: J.-M. Barret, 1828.)

Brézé, Jacques de. *La Chasse, Les Dits du Bon Chien Souillard et Les Louanges de Madame Anne de France.*

Edited by Gunnar Tilander. Lund, Sweden: Carl Bloms, 1959.

Bulifon, Antonio, ed. *Rime di cinquanta illustri poetesse*. Naples: Antonio Bulifon, 1695. (Verbatim reprint of Domenichi's *Rime diverse* [1559] without acknowledgment or dedicatory letter.)

Burchard, Johannes. *At the court of the Borgia, being an account of the reign of Pope Alexander VI, written by his master of ceremonies, Johann Burchard*. Edited and translated by Geoffrey Parker. London: The Folio Society, 1963.

Caccini, Francesca. *Francesca Caccini's Il primo libro delle musiche of 1618: A Modern Critical Edition of the Secular Monodies*. Edited by Ronald James Alexander and Richard Savino. Bloomington: Indiana University Press, 2004.

Cambis, Marguerite de. *Epistre consolatoire de l'exil, envoyée par Jean Boccace au Seigneur Pino de Rossi*. Edited by Colette H. Winn. Paris: Champion, 2003. (Originally printed in Lyon: Guillaume Rouillé, 1556.)

Cambis, Marguerite de. *Epistre consolatoire de messire Jean Boccace, envoyée au Signeur Pino de Rossi*. Lyons: Guillaume Rouillé, 1556.

Cambis, Marguerite de. *Epistre consolatoire de messire Jean Boccace, envoyée au Signeur Pino de Rossi (1556)*. Edited by Colette H. Winn. Paris: Champion, 2003.

Cambis, Marguerite de. *Epistre du Seigneur Jean Trissin de la vie que doit tenir une Dame veuve*. Lyons: Guillaume Rouillé, 1554.

Campiglia, Maddalena. *Flori, favola boscareccia*. Vicenza: 1588. (Some editions include an appendix with celebratory verse.)

Campiglia, Maddalena. *Flori, A Pastoral Drama*. Edited by Virginia Cox and translated by Virginia Cox and Lisa Sampson. Chicago: University of Chicago Press, 2004.

Cary, Elizabeth. *The Lady Falkland: Her Life*. Edited by Barry Weller and Margaret Ferguson. Berkeley: University of California Press, 1994.

Cary, Elizabeth. *The Tragedy of Mariam. Renaissance Drama by Women: Texts and Contexts*. Edited by S. P. Cerasano and Marion Wynne-Davies, 43–75. London: Routledge, 1996.

Castiglione, Baldessare. *The Book of the Courtier*. Translated by George Bull. New York: Penguin, 1967.

Casulana, Maddalena. *I madrigali di Maddalena Casulana*. Edited by Beatrice Fescerelli. Florence: L. S. Olschki, 1979.

Caterina da Siena, S. *Le lettere*. Edited by D. Umberto Meattini. Milan: Edizioni Paoline, 1987.

Catherine of Siena, Saint. *Letters*. Edited and translated by S. Noffke. Tempe: Arizona Center for Medieval and Renaissance Studies, 2000.

Cavendish, Margaret, duchess of Newcastle. *The Convent of Pleasure and Other Plays*. Edited by Anne Shaver. Baltimore: Johns Hopkins University Press, 1999.

Cavendish, Margaret, duchess of Newcastle. *The Description of a New World, Called the Blazing World and Other Writings*. Edited by Kate Lilley. New York: New York University Press, 1992.

Cazaux, Yves, ed. *Mémoires de Marguerite de Valois*. Paris: Mercure de France, 1986.

Cebà, Ansaldo. *Lettere a Sarra Copia*. Genoa: Pavoni, 1623.

Ceresano, S. P., and Marion Wynne-Davies, eds. *Readings in Renaissance Women's Drama: Criticism, History, and Performance*. London and New York: Routledge, 1998.

Cerasano, S. P., and Marion Wynne-Davies, eds. *Renaissance Drama by Women: Texts and Documents*. London and New York: Routledge, 1996.

Cereta, Laura. *Collected Letters of a Renaissance Feminist*. Edited and translated by Diana Robin. Chicago: University of Chicago Press, 1997.

Cereta, Laura. *Laura Ceretae Brixiensis Feminae Clarissimae Epistolae iam primum e MS in lucem productae*. Edited by Jacopo Filippo Tomasini. Padua: Sebastiano Sardi, 1640.

Chapman, Hester W. *Lady Jane Grey*. Boston: Little Brown and Company, 1962.

Charpentier, Françoise. *Louise Labé: Œuvres poétiques, précédées des Rymes de Pernette du Guillet*. Paris: Gallimard, 1983.

Cheney, Donald, and Brenda M. Hosington, eds. and trans. *Elizabeth Jane Weston: Collected Writings*. Toronto: University of Toronto Press, 2000.

Chiesa, Franceso Agostino della. *Theatro delle donne letterate, con un breve discorso della preminenza, e perfettione del sesso donnesco*. Mondovi, Italy: Giovanni Gislandi e Gio, Tomaso Rossi, 1620.

Child, Harold H., ed. *Iphigenia at Aulis translated by Lady Lumley*. Oxford: Malone Society, 1909.

Christine de Pizan. *Book of the Body Politic*. Translated by Kate Langdon Forhan. Cambridge: Cambridge University Press, 1994.

Christine de Pizan. *Book of the City of Ladies*. Rev. ed. Translated by Earl Jeffrey Richards. Gainesville: University of Florida Press, 1998.

Christine de Pizan. *Epistre Othea*. Edited by Gabriella Parussa. Geneva: Droz, 1999.

Christine de Pizan. *L'Advision Cristine*. Edited by Christine Reno and Liliane Dulac. Paris: Champion, 2001.

Christine de Pizan. *Livre du corps de policie.* Edited by Angus J. Kennedy. Paris: Champion, 1998.

Christine de Pizan. *Livre du duc des vrais amans.* Edited by Thelma S. Fenster. Albany, NY: State University of New York Press, 1995.

Christine de Pizan. *Writings of Christine de Pizan.* Edited by Charity Willard. Translated by C. Willard et al. New York: Persea Books, 1994.

Churchill, Laurie J., Phyllis R. Brown, and Jane E. Jeffrey, eds. *Women Writing Latin from Roman Antiquity to Early Modern Europe.* 3 vols. Vol. 3: *Early Modern Women Writing Latin.* New York and London: Routledge, 2002.

Clarke, Daniel, ed. *Isabella Whitney, Mary Sidney and Aemilia Lanyer: Renaissnce Women Poets.* New York: Penguin Books, 2000.

Coignard, Gabrielle de. *Œuvres chrestiennes.* Edited by Colette H. Winn. Geneva: Droz, 1995.

Coignard, Gabrielle de. *Spiritual Sonnets: A Bilingual Edition.* Edited and translated by Melanie E. Gregg. Chicago: University of Chicago Press, 2004.

Coligny, Louise de. *Correspondance de Louise de Coligny, princesse d'Orange.* Edited by Paul Marchegay and Léon Marlet. Geneva: Slatkine, 1970. (Originally published in Paris, 1887.)

Colonna, Vittoria. *Carteggio.* 2nd ed. Edited by Ermanno Ferrero and Giuseppe Müller with a supplement by Domenico Tordi. Turin: Ermanno Loescher, 1892.

Colonna, Vittoria. *Dichiaratione fatta sopra la seconda parte delle Rime della Divina Vittoria Collonna* [sic] *Marchesana di Pescara. Da Rinaldo Corso. . . .* Bologna: Gian battista de Phaelli, 1543.

Colonna, Vittoria. *Litere della Divina Vettoria* [sic] *Colonna Marchesana di Pescara alla Duchessa de Amalfi, sopra la vita contemplativa di santa Catherina, Et sopra della attiva santa Maddalena non più viste in luce.* Venice: Alessandro de Viano, Ad instantia di Antonio detto il Cremaschino, 1544.

Colonna, Vittoria. *Pianto della Marchesa di Pescara sopra la passione di Christo. Oratione della medesima sopra l'Ave Maria . . . etc.* Bologna: Manutio, 1557.

Colonna, Vittoria. *Rime.* Edited by Alan Bullock. Rome: Laterza, 1982.

Colonna, Vittoria. *Sonetti in morte di Francesco Ferrante d'Avalos, marchese di Pescara: edizione del ms. XIII. G. 43 della Biblioteca Nazionale di Napoli.* Edited by Tobia R. Toscano. Milan: Mondadori, 1998.

Colonna, Vittoria. *Sonnets for Michelangelo: A Bilingual Edition.* The Other Voice in Early Modern Europe. Edited and translated by Abigail Brundin. Chicago: University of Chicago Press, 2005.

Coppi, Enrico, ed. *Cronaca fiorentina 1537–1555.* ("Diario del Marucelli"). Florence: Olschki, 2000.

Cortese, Isabella. *I secreti della signora Isabella Cortese, de'qvali si contengono cose minerale, medicinali, artefiose, & alchimiche, & molte de l'arte profumatoria . . . Con altri bellissimi secret aggiunti. . . .* Venice: Giovanni Variletto, 1561.

Cotteblanche, Marie de. *Trois dialogues de M. Pierre Messie.* Paris: Frédéric Morel, 1571.

Couchman, Jane. "Lettres de Louise de Coligny aux membres de sa famille en France et aux Pays-bas." In *Lettres de femmes XVIe-XVIIe siècle.* Edited by Elizabeth Goldsmith et Colette Winn. Paris: Champion, forthcoming.

Couchman, Jane, trans. "Charlotte de Bourbon, Princess of Orange: Lettres et documents (1565–1582)." In *Writings by Pre-Revolutionary French Women.* Pages 107–121. New York: Garland, 2000.

Couchman, Jane, and Ann Crabb, eds. *Women's Letters Across Europe, 1400–1700: Form and Persuasion.* Aldershot, UK: Ashgate, 2006.

Crawford, Patricia, and Laura Gowing, eds. *Women's Worlds in Seventeenth-Century England: A Source Book.* London and New York: Routledge, 2000.

Crenne, Hélisenne de. *Les angoysses douloureuses qui procèdent d'amours.* Edited by Christine de Buzon. Textes de la Renaissance 13. Paris: Champion, 1997.

Crenne, Hélisenne de. *Les Epistres familieres et invectives de ma dame Hélisenne.* Edited by Jean-Philippe Beaulieu and Hannah Fournier. Montreal: Presses de l'Université de Montréal, 1995.

Crenne, Hélisenne de. *Les Œuvres.* Paris: Charles Langelier, 1543.

Crenne, Hélisenne de. *Le Songe.* Edited by Jean-Philippe Beaulieu. Paris: Indigo and Côté-femmes, 1995.

Crenne, Hélisenne de. "Le Songe de Madame Hélisenne." Translated by Lisa Neal. In *Writings by Pre-Revolutionary French Women. From Marie de France to Elizabeth Vigée-Le Brun.* Edited by Anne R. Larsen and Colette H. Winn, 63–105. New York: Garland, 2000.

Crenne, Hélisenne de. *Les quatre premiers liures des eneydes.* Paris: Denis Janot, 1541.

Crenne, Hélisenne de. *A Renaissance Woman. Hélisenne's Personal and Invective Letters.* Translated and edited by Marianna M. Mustacchi and Paul J. Archambault. Syracuse, NY: Syracuse University Press, 1986.

Crenne, Hélisenne de. *The Torments of Love.* Translated by Lisa Neal and Steven Rendall. Minneapolis: University of Minnesota Press, 1996.

Datini, Margherita. *Per la tua Margherita: Lettere di una donna del '300 al marito mercante.* Prato: Archivio di stato, 2002. CD-ROM, with handwriting images.

Daybell, James, ed. *Early Modern Women's Letter Writing, 1450–1700.* Houndmills, UK, and New York: Palgrave, 2001.

De Gournay, Marie Le Jars de. *Apology for the Woman Writing and Other Works.* Translated and edited by Richard Hillman and Colette Quesnel. Chicago: University of Chicago Press, 2002.

Delaborde, Jules. *Eléonore de Roye, princesse de Condé 1535–1564.* Paris: Sandoz and Fischbacher, 1876. (Includes examples of Eléonore's letters.)

de la Ferrière, Hector, and Gustave Basguenault de Puchesse, eds. *Lettres de Catherine de Médicis.* 10 vols. Paris: Imprimerie Nationale, 1880–1909.

D'Ennetières, Marie. *Œuvres.* Critical edition by Diane Desrosiers-Bonin, William Kemp, Isabelle Crevier-Denommé, et al. Forthcoming.

Dentière, Marie. *Epistle to Marguerite de Navarre and Preface to a Sermon by John Calvin.* Edited and translated by Mary B. McKinley. Chicago: University of Chicago Press, 2004.

Dentière, Marie. *Épistre tresutile faicte et composee par une femme Chrestienne de Tornay, Envoyée à la Royne de Navarre seur du Roy de France [. . .].* Antwerp: M. Lempereur; Geneva: J. Girard, 1539, 32 ff.

Dentière, Marie. *Un Sermon de la modestie des Femmes en leurs habillemens.* 1561.

Des Roches, Madeleine and Catherine. *From Mother and Daughter: Poems, Dialogues, and Letters by Les Dames des Roches. A Bilingual Edition.* Other Voice Series. Edited with critical introductions and translations by Anne R. Larsen. Chicago: University of Chicago Press, 2006.

Des Roches, Madeleine and Catherine. *Histoire et Amours pastoralles de Daphnis et de Chloe escrite premierement en grec par Longus et maintenant mise en françois. Ensemble un debat judiciel de Folie et d'Amour, fait par dame L. L. L. (Loyse Labé Lyonnoise). Plus quelques vers françois, lesquels ne sont pas moins plaisans que recreatifs, par M.D.R., Poictevine (Madame des Roches).* Paris: Jean Parent, 1578.

Des Roches, Madeleine and Catherine. *La Puce de Madame des Roches. Qui est un recueil de divers poemes Grecs, Latins et François, composez par plusieurs doctes personnages aux Grands Jours tenus à Poitiers l'an M.D.LXXIX.* Paris: Abel l'Angelier, 1582, 1583.

Des Roches, Madeleine and Catherine. *Les Missives.* Edited by Anne R. Larsen. Geneva: Droz, 1999.

Des Roches, Madeleine and Catherine. *Les Secondes Œuvres.* Edited by Anne R. Larsen. Geneva: Droz, 1998.

de Vere, Anne Cecil. "Four Epitaphs." In *Women Poets of the Renaissance.* Edited by Marion Wynne-Davies. London: J. M. Dent, 1998.

Dolce, Lodovico, ed. *Rime di diversi illustri signori napoletani, e d'altri nobilissimi ingegni. Nuovamente raccolte, et con nuova additione ristampate. Libro Quinto. Allo illust. S. F. Carrafa.* Venice: Gabriel Giolito, 1552. (Third revised edition printed in 1555.)

Dolce, Lodovico, ed. *Rime di diversi illustri signori napoletani e d'altri nobilissimmi intelletti; nouvamente raccolte, et non più stampate. Terzo Libro allo illus. S. Ferrante Carrafa.* Venice: Gabriel Giolito, 1551/1552.

Dolce, Lodovico, ed. *Rime di diversi signor napoletani. . . .* Venice: Gabriel Giolito, 1552, 1555.

Dolce, Lodovico, ed. *Rime di diversi signori napoletani, e d'altri. Nuovamente raccolte et impresse. Libro Settimo.* Venice: Gabriel Giolito, 1556.

Domenichi, Lodovico, ed. *Rime diverse d'alcune nobilissime et virtuosissime donne, raccolte per M. Lodovico Domenichi, e intitolate al S. Giannoto Castiglione gentil'huomo milanese.* Lucca: Vincenzo Busdragho, 1559.

Du Bellay, Joachim. *Epithalame sur le mariage de tresillustre prince Philibert Emanuel, duc de Savoie, et tresillustre princesse Marguerite de France, soeur unique du Roy et duchesse de Berry.* Paris: 1559.

Du Bellay, Joachim. *Xenia, seu ad illustrium aliquot Europae hominum nomina allusionum [. . .] liber primus. . . .* Basel: 1568. (Contains several verses by Camille, including her poem to the Queen of England, "Ad sereniss. Angliae Reg.")

DuGard, Lydia. *Cousins in Love: The Letters of Lydia DuGard, 1665–1672.* Edited by Nancy Taylor. Tempe: Arizona Center for Medieval and Renaissance Studies, with Renaissance English Text Society, 2003.

Duval, Jacques. *Des Hermaphrodits, accouchemens de femmes, et traitement qui est requis pour les relever en santé.* Rouen: David Geuffroy, 1612.

Elizabeth I: Collected Works. Edited by Marcus, Leah, Janel Mueller, and Mary Beth Rose. Chicago: University of Chicago Press, 2000.

Elyot, Thomas. *Defence of Good Women: The Feminist Controversy of the Renaissance.* Facsimile Reproductions. Edited by Diane Bornstein. Clifton Park, NY: Delmar, 1980.

Erasmus, Desiderius. *Erasmus on Women.* Edited by Erika Rummel. Toronto: University of Toronto Press, 1996.

Estienne, Nicole. *Les Misères de la femme mariée: où se peuvent voir les peines et tourmens qu'elle reçoit durant sa vie. Mis en forme de Stances, par Madame Liebaut.* In Ilana Zinguer, *Misères et grandeur des femmes au XVIe siècle,* 32–40. Geneva: Slatkine, 1982.

Estienne, Nicole. "A liminary quatrain." In François Béroalde de Verville, *Les Apprehensions Spirituelles, Poemes et autres Oeuvres Philosophiques, avec Les Recherches de la pierre philosophale*. Paris: Timothee Joüan, 1584.

Estienne, Nicole. "A liminary sonnet." In Baptiste Badere, *Devotes meditations chrestiennes, sur la Mort et Passion de nostre Seigneur Jésus Christ*. Paris: Guyon Giffard, 1588. (With "N.E." and signature anagram.)

Eusebius. *Ecclesiastical History*. Translated by Mary Bassett. London: British Library MS Harley, 1860.

Fedele, Cassandra. *Clarissimae feminae Cassandrae Fidelis venetae epistolae et orationes*. Edited by Jacopo Filippo Tomasini, 164–167. Padua: Franciscus Bolzetta, 1636.

Fedele, Cassandra. *Letters and Orations*. Edited and translated by Diana Robin. Chicago and London: University of Chicago Press, 2000.

Fedele, Cassandra. *Oratio pro Bertucio Lamberto*. Modena: 1487; Venice: 1488; Nuremberg: 1489.

Ferguson, Gary, ed. *Sonets spirituels . . . sur les dimanches et principales solennitez de l'année (Spiritual Sonnets . . . on the Sundays and Principal Solemnities of the Year)*. Geneva: Droz, 1997. (Originally published in Paris: Claude Morel, 1605.)

Flore, Madame Jeanne. *Comptes amoureux par Madame Jeanne Flore, touchant la punition que faict Venus de ceulx qui condemnent & mesprisent le vray Amour*. Lyon: Denis de Harsy, 1542?; Paris: Arnoul L'Angelier, 1543; Paris: Poncet le Preux, 1543; Lyon: Benoist Rigaud, 1574; Turin: Gay and Sons, 1870 (reprint of the 1574 edition); Geneva: Slatkine, 1971 (reprint of the 1870 edition); University of Saint-Etienne Press: Spring 2005.

Flore, Madame Jeanne. *Histoire de la belle Rosemonde et du preux chevalier Andro, par Jeanne Flore*. Edited by Albert de Rochas d'Aiglun. Paris: Marchand, 1888.

Flore, Madame Jeanne. *La Pugnition de l'Amour contempné, extrait de l'Amour fatal de Madame Jeanne Flore*. Lyon: François Juste, 1540; Paris: Denys Janot, 1541.

Foigny, Gabriel de. *La Terre Australe Connue*. Edited by Pierre Ronzeaud. Paris: Société des textes français modernes, 1990.

Folger Collective on Early Women Critics, ed. *Women Critics, 1600–1820: An Anthology*. Bloomington: Indiana University Press, 1995.

Fonte, Moderata. *Il Merito delle donne, ove chiaramente si scuopre quanto siano elle degne e più perfette de gli uomini*. Edited by Adriana Chemello. Venice: 1988.

Fonte, Moderata. *Tredici Canti del Floridoro*. Venice: 1581.

Fonte, Moderata (Modesta Pozza). *The Worth of Women: Wherein Is Clearly Revealed Their Nobility and Their Superiority to Men*. Edited and translated by Virginia Cox. Chicago: University of Chicago Press, 1997.

Foxe, John. *The Acts and Monuments of John Foxe; with a Life of the Martyrologist, and Vindication of the Work*. Edited by George Townsend. New York: AMS Press, 1965.

Fraioli, Deborah A. *Joan of Arc and the Hundred Years War*. Westport, CT, and London: Greenwood Press, 2005.

Franco, Veronica. *Lettere dall'unica edizione del MDLXXX*. Edited by B. Croce. Naples: Ricciardi, 1949.

Franco, Veronica. *Lettere familiari a diversi della s. Veronica Franca all'illustriss. et reverendiss. monsig. Luigi d'Este Cardinale*. Venice: 1580.

Franco, Veronica. *Poems and Selected letters*. Edited and translated by Ann R. Jones and Margaret F. Rosenthal. Chicago: University of Chicago Press, 1998.

Franco, Veronica. *Rime*. Edited by S. Bianchi. Milan: Mursia, 1995.

Franco, Veronica. *Terze rime di Veronica Franca al serenissimo signor Duca di Mantova et di Monferrato*. Venice: 1575.

Gaillarde, Jeanne (?). *Faintises du monde*. Paris: Bibliothèque Nationale de France fr. 14979 (f. 32v and 33r indicate that this manuscript was owned by Jeanne Gaillarde).

Galilei, Suor Maria Celeste. *Letters to Father. Suor Maria Celeste to Galileo, 1623–1633*. Translated and annotated by David Sobel. New York: Penguin, 2001.

Gàmbara, Veronica. *Rime*. Edited by Alan Bullock. Florence: Perth, 1995.

Gàmbara, Veronica. *Rime e lettere*. With a *Vita* by B. C. Zamboni. Edited by Francesco Rizzardi. Brescia: Rizzardi, 1759.

Gibson Marion, ed. *Early Modern Witches: Witchcraft Cases in Contemporary Writing*. London and New York: Routledge, 2001.

Giovio, Paolo. *Dialogi et descriptiones*. Edited by Ernesto Travi and Mariagrazia Penco. Rome: Istituto Poligrafico dello Stato, 1984.

Giovio, Paolo. *Lettere*. 2 vols. Edited by Giuseppe Guido Ferrero. Rome: Istituto Poligrafico dello Stato, 1956–1958.

Goldsmith, Elizabeth C., and Colette H. Winn, eds. *Lettres de femmes: Textes inédits et oubliés du XVIe au XVIIIe siècle*. Paris: Champion, 2005.

Gournay, Marie de. *Adieu de l'Ame du Roy de France et de Navarre, Henry le Grand à la Royne, avec la De-*

fence des Peres Jesuistes, par la damoiselle de G. Paris: Fleury Bourriquant, 1610.

Gournay, Marie de. *Le Proumenoir de M. de Montaigne, par sa fille d'alliance.* Paris: Abel L'Angelier, 1594.

Gournay, Marie de. *Marie le Jars de Gournay, Les Advis ou les presens de la Demoiselle de Gournay.* Vols. 1 and 2. Edited by Jean-Philippe Beaulieu and Hannah Fournier. Amsterdam: Rodopi, 2001 and 2002.

Gournay, Marie de. *L'Ombre de la Damoiselle de Gournay. Oeuvre composé de meslanges.* Paris: Jean Libert, 1623.

Gournay, Marie de. *Œuvres completes.* 2 vols. Edited by Jean-Claude Arnould. Paris: Champion, 2002.

Gournay, Marie de. "Préface à l'édition des *Essais* de Montaigne." Edited by François Rigolot. *Montaigne Studies* I (1989): 7–60. (Originally published in Paris: Abel L'Angelier, 1595.)

Gournay, Marie Le Jars de. *Apology for the Woman Writing and Other Works.* Edited by Richard Hillman and Colette Quesnel. Chicago: University of Chicago Press, 2002.

Graville, Anne Malet de. *Le beau Romant des deux amans Palamon & Arcita et de la belle et saige Emilia.* Edited by Yves Le Hir. Paris: Presses Universitaires de France, 1965.

Graville, Anne Malet de. *La Belle dame sans mercy. En Fransk dikt författad.* Edited by Carl Wahlund. Uppsala, Sweden: Almqvist & Wiksells Boktryckeri-Aktiebolag ("Skrifter utgifna af K. Humanistika Vetenskapssamfundet"), 1897.

Green, Mary Anne Everett, ed. *Letters of Queen Henrietta Maria, including Her Private Correspondence with Charles the First.* History of Women Microfilm Series. New Haven, CT: Research Publications, 1975. (Originally published in 1857.)

Grey, Elizabeth, countess of Kent. *A Choice Manuall, or, Rare and Select Secrets in Physick and Chirurgery.* London: G. D., 1654.

Guicciardini, Francesco. *Storie fiorentine dal 1378 al 1509.* Edited by R. Palmarocchi. Bari: Laterza, 1931.

Guillet, Pernette du. *Poésies de Pernette du Guillet, Lyonnaise.* Lyon: Louis Perrin, 1830.

Guillet, Pernette du. *Poètes du XVIe Siècle.* Edited by Albert-Marie Schmidt. Paris: Gallimard/Pléiade, 1953.

Guillet, Pernette du. *Rymes.* Critical edition by Victor Graham. Geneva: Droz, 1968.

Guillet, Pernette du. *Rymes de Gentile, et Vertueuse Dame D. Pernette du Guillet Lyonnoise.* Lyon: Jean de Tournes, 1545.

Haec Vir: Or the Womanish Man: Being an Answere to a Late Booke Intituled Hic-Mulier. London: 1620. Exeter: Scolar Press, 1973. (Facsimile reprint.)

Heale, William. *An Apologie for Women.* Oxford: 1609.

Henderson, Katherine Usher, and Barbara F. McManus, eds. *Half Humankind: Contexts and Texts of the Controversy about Women in England, 1540–1640.* Urbana: University of Illinois Press, 1985.

Hensley, Jeannine, ed. *The Works of Anne Bradstreet.* Cambridge, MA: Harvard University Press, 1967.

Herbert, Mary Sidney. *The Collected Works of Mary Sidney Herbert, Countess of Pembroke.* 2 vols. Edited by Margaret P. Hannay, Noel J. Kinnamon, and Michael G. Brennan. Oxford: Clarendon, 1998.

Heroick Vertues of Queene Elizabeth, of Glorious Memory. London: Printed by J. Dawson for Thomas Paine, sold by Philip Waterhouse, 1630.

Hic Mulier: Or, the Man-Woman: Being a Medicine to Cure the Coltish Disease of the Staggers in the Masculine-Feminines of Our Times. London: 1620. Facs. Rpt. Exeter: Scolar Press, 1973.

Historical Manuscript Commission (cited as HMC), De L'Isle, II, 176; III, 140.

Hobbins, Daniel, trans. *The Trial of Joan of Arc.* Cambridge, MA: Harvard University Press, 2005.

Ignatius of Loyola, Saint. *Letters to Women.* Edited by Hugo Rahner. Freiburg: Herder, 1960.

Jeamson, Thomas. *Artificiall Embellishments; or, Arts Best Directions: How to Preserve Beauty or Procure It.* Oxford: William Hall, 1665.

Jodelle, Etienne. *Œuvres Complètes.* 2 vols. Edited by Enea Balmas, vol. 1, 379. Paris: Gallimard, 1965–1968.

Jussie, Jeanne de. *Petite chronique.* Edited by Helmut Feld. Mainz: Von Zabern, 1996.

Kempe, Margery. *The Book of Margery Kempe.* Translated and edited by Lynn Staley. New York: W. W. Norton, 2001.

Khanna, Lee Cullen, ed. *Early Tudor Translators: Margaret Beaufort, Margaret More Roper and Mary Basset.* The Early Modern Englishwoman: The Printed Writings. Aldershot, UK: Ashgate, 1998.

Killigrew, Anne. *Poems.* Introduction by Richard Morton. Gainesville, FL: Scholars' Facsimiles and Reprints, 1967.

King, Margaret L., and Albert Rabil, Jr., eds. *Her Immaculate Hand: Selected Works by and About the Women Humanists of Quattrocento Italy.* Binghamton, NY: Medieval and Renaissance Texts and Studies, 1983. (A second revised paperback edition was published in 1991.)

Kirkham, Victoria, ed. and trans. *Laura Battiferra degli Ammannati and Her Literary Circle: An Anthology.* Chicago: University of Chicago Press, 2006.

Koninklijke Bibliotheek, The Hague. MS. 133 B 8. Letters of Anna Maria van Schurman.

Kors, Alan C., and Edward Peters, eds. *Witchcraft in Europe, 400–1700: A Documentary History.* Philadelphia: University of Pennsylvania Press, 2000.

Kramer, Heinrich, and James Sprenger. *The Malleus Maleficarum.* Translated and edited by M. Summers. London: John Rodker, 1928. (Reprinted in Escondido, CA: The Book Tree, 2000.)

Kristeller, Paul Oskar. *Iter Italicum.* 6 vols. London: Warburg Institute, 1967–1997.

Labé, Louise. *Complete Poetry and Prose. A Biligual Edition.* Edited with critical introductions and prose translations by Deborah Lesko Baker. Poetry translations by Annie Finch. Chicago: University of Chicago Press, 2006.

Labé, Louise. *The Debate of Folly and Love.* Translated by Anne-Marie Bourbon. New York: Peter Lang, 2000.

Labé, Louise. *Œuvres Complètes.* Edited by François Rigolot. Paris: Flammarion, 1986.

La Croix du Maine et Du Verdier. *Les bibliothèques françoises* (1584, 1585). 6 vols. Edited by Rigoley de Juvigny, vol. 1, 88. Graz, Austria: Academische Druck, 1969. (Originally printed in 1772–1773.)

Lanyer, Aemilia. *The Poems of Aemilia Lanyer: Salve Deus Rex Judaeorum.* Women Writers in English, 1350–1850. Edited by Susanne Woods. New York: Oxford University Press, 1993.

Lapini, Agostino. *Diario fiorentino dal 252 al 1596.* Edited by Giuseppe Odoardo Corazzini. Florence: Sansoni, 1900.

Larsen, Anne R., and Colette H. Winn, eds. *Writings by Pre-Revolutionary French Women: From Marie de France to Elizabeth Vigée-Le Brun.* New York and London: Garland Publishing, 2000.

L'Aubespine Madeleine de. *Cabinet des saines affections.* Edited by Colette H. Winn. Paris: Champion, 2001.

L'Aubespine Madeleine de. *Cabinet des saines affections. Derniere edition, nentee de XII. Discours et quelques Stances sur le mesme sujet. Par Madame de Rivery.* Paris: Antoine du Breuil, 1595.

L'Aubespine Madeleine de. *Les chansons de Callianthe.* Edited by Roger Sorg. Paris: L. Pichon, 1926.

Laurent, Marie-Hyacinthe, ed. *Il Processo Castellano. Fontes vitae s. Catharinae Senensis historici.* Milan: Bocca, 1942.

Lavocat, Francoise, ed. Marinella, Lucrezia. *Arcadia felice* (1605). Florence: L. S. Olschki, 1998.

Le Gendre, Marie. *L'Exercice de l'ame vertueuse, dedié à tres-haute, tres-illustre, et tres-vertueuse Princesse, Madame de Conty, par Marie Le Gendre, Dame de Rivery: Reveu, corrigé, & augmenté par elle-mesme d'un Dialogue des chastes Amours d'Eros, & Kalisti.* Paris: Jean Le Blanc, 1596.

Le Gendre, Marie. *L'exercice de l'âme vertueuse.* Edited by Colette H. Winn. Paris: Champion, 2001.

Lesko Baker, Deborah, and Annie Finch, eds. and trans. *Louise Labé. Collected Poetry and Prose: A Bilingual Edition.* Other Voice Series. Edited with critical introductions and prose translation by Deborah Lesko Baker. Poetry translation by Annie Finch. Chicago: University of Chicago Press, 2006.

L'Estoile, Pierre de. *Memoires pour servir à l'histoire de France* (1515–1611). Vol. 1. Cologne: 1719.

L'Estoile, Pierre de. *Registre-journal du regne de Henri III.* Edited by Madeleine Lazard and Gilbert Schrenck. Geneva: Droz, 1997–2003.

Levati, Ambrogio. *Dizionario biografico cronologico, divido per classe, degli uomini illustri V: donne illustre.* 3 vols. Milan: Nicolò Bettoni, 1821–1822.

Loftis, John, ed. *The Memoirs of Anne, Lady Halkett and Ann, Lady Fanshawe.* Oxford: Clarendon Press, 1979.

Loredan, Gian Francesco. *The Life of Adam.* Gainesville, FL: Scholar Facsimiles and Reprints, 1967. (Facsimile reproduction of English translation of 1659.)

L'Orme, Philibert de and Pierre Bontemps. *Tomb of François Ier and Claude de France.* Vendée, France: Basilica of Saint Denis.

Lorris, William de, and Jean de Meun. *The Romance of the Rose.* Translated by Charles Dahlbert. Princeton, NJ: Princeton University Press, 1971.

Loynes, Antoinette de. *Annae, Margaritae, Janae, sororum virginum, heroidum Anglarum, In mortem Divae Margaritae Valesiae, Navarrorum reginae, Hecatodistichon. . . .* Paris: Regnaut Chauldiere et fils [Claude], 1550.

Loynes, Antoinette de. "Anne, Margaret, and Jane Seymour." Edited and introduction by Brenda M. Hosington. In *The Early Modern Englishwoman: A Facsimile Library of Essential Works.* (I: Printed Writings, 1500–1640; Series II, vol. 6.) Edited by Betty S. Travitsky and Patrick Cullen. Aldershot, UK: Ashgate, 2000.

Loynes, Antoinette de. *Le Tombeau de Marguerite de Valois Royne de Navarre faict premierement en Disticques Latins par les trois Sœurs Princesses en Angleterre. Depuis traduictz en Grec, Italien & François par plusieurs des excellents poëtes de la France. Avecques plusieurs Odes, Hymnes, Cantiques, Epitaphes, sur le mesme subiect.* Paris: Michel Fezandat, 1551.

Madeleine de Scudéry: Selected Letters, Orations, and Rhetorical Dialogues. Edited and translated by Jane Donawerth and Julie Strongson. Chicago: University of Chicago Press, 2004.

Makin, Bathusa. *An Essay to Revive the Antient Education of Gentlewomen.* London: 1673. Wing M309.

Makin, Bathusa. *Musa Virginea Graeco. Latino. Gallica.* London: 1616. STC 20835.

Makin, Bathusa, with Henry Reginald. *Ad Annam . . . Reginam.* London: no date. STC 20834.5.

Marguerite d'Angoulême, Queen of Navarre. *The Heptameron.* Translated by P. A. Chilton. New York: Viking Penguin, 1984.

Marguerite de Navarre. *The Heptameron.* Translated by Paul Chilton. Harmondsworth, UK: Penguin, 1984.

Marguerite de Navarre. *Heptaméron.* Edited by. Renja Salminen. Geneva: Droz, 1999.

Marguerite de Navarre. *Les Prisons.* Edited by Simone Glasson. Geneva: Droz, 1978.

Marguerite de Navarre. *Œuvres complètes, sous la direction de Nicole Cazauran.* Paris: Champion, 2001.

Marguerite de Navarre. *Prisons.* Translated by Claire Lynch Wade. New York: Peter Lang, 1989.

Marinella, Lucrezia. *De' gesti eroici e della vita maravigliosa della serafica santa Caterina da Siena . . . libri sei. . . .* Venice: Barezzo Barezzi, 1624.

Marinella, Lucrezia. *Essortazioni alle donne e agli altri se saranno loro a grado . . . parte prima. . . .* Venice: Valvasense, 1645.

Marinella, Lucrezia. *La nobiltà e l'eccellenza delle donne co' diffetti e mancamenti degli uomini.* Venice: G. B. Ciotti, 1601.

Marinella, Lucrezia. *La vita di Maria Vergine imperatrice dell'universo, descritta in prosa & in ottava rima.* Venice: Appresso Barezo Barezi e compagni, 1602.

Marinella, Lucrezia. *L'Enrico, ovvero Bizanzio acquistato. Poema eroico.* Venice: Appresso Gherardo Imberti, 1635.

Marinella, Lucrezia. *The Nobility and Excellence of Women and the Defects and Vices of Men.* The Other Voice in Early Modern Europe. Edited and translated by Anne Dunhill. Introduction by Letizia Panizza. Chicago and London: University of Chicago Press, 1999.

Marot, Clément. *Œuvres poétiques complètes.* 2 vols. Edited by Gérard Defaux. Paris: Classiques Garnier, 1990. (The exchange between the poet and Jeanne Gaillarde is reproduced in vol. 1, 143–144.)

Marquets, Anne de. *Les Divines Poesies de Marc Antoine Flaminius (The Sacred Poems of Marcantonio Flaminio).* Paris: Nicolas Chesneau, 1568.

Marquets, Anne de. *Sonets, prieres et devises en forme de pasquins, pour l'assemblée de Messieurs les Prelats et Docteurs, tenue à Poissy, M.D.LXI (Sonnets, Prayers, and Mottoes in the Form of Pasquills for the Assembly of Prelates and Doctors held in Poissy, 1561).* Edited by André Gendre. *Bibliothèque d'Humanisme et Re-*naissance 62 (2000): 317–357. (Originally published in Paris: Guillaume Morel, 1562.)

Martin, Randall, ed. *Women Writers in Renaissance England.* New York: Longman, 1997.

Matraini, Chiara. *Breve discorso sopra la vita e laude della Beatiss. Verg. e Madre del Figliuol di Dio.* Lucca: Busdraghi, 1590.

Matraini, Chiara. *Considerazioni sopra i sette salmi penitenziali del gran re e profeta Davit.* Lucca: Busdraghi, 1586.

Matraini, Chiara. *Dialoghi spirituali.* Venice: Prati, 1602.

Matraini, Chiara. *Lettere della signora Chiara Matraini . . . con la prima e seconda parte delle sue Rime.* Lucca: Busdraghi, 1595.

Matraini, Chiara. *Meditazioni spirituali.* Lucca: Busdraghi, 1581.

Matraini, Chiara. *Orazione d'Isocrate a Demonico d'Ipponico, circa a l'essortazion de'costumi, che si convengono a tutti i nobilissimi giovani, do latino in volgare tradotta.* Florence: Torrentino, 1556.

Matraini, Chiara. *Rime e Lettere.* Edited by Giovanna Rabitti. *Scelta di Curiosità Letterarie Inedite o Rare dal Secolo XIII al XIX, Dispensa CCLXXIX.* Bologna: Commissione per i testi di lingua, 1989.

Matraini, Chiara. *Rime e prose di madonna Chiara Matraini gentildonna lucchese.* Lucca: Busdraghi, 1555.

May, Steven W. "The Countess of Oxford's Sonnets: A Caveat." *English Language Notes* 29, no. 3 (March 1992): 9–18.

Medici, Cosimo I de'. *Lettere.* Edited by Giorgio Spini. Florence: Vallecchi, 1940.

Menzio, Eva, ed. *Lettere/Artemisia Gentileschi; precedute da Atti di un processo per stupro.* Milan: Abscondita, 2004.

Montenay, Georgette de. *Emblemes ou devises chrestiennes.* Lyon: Marcorelle, 1571.

Montenay, Georgette de. *Emblemes ou devises chrestiennes.* Edited by C. S. Smith. Menston, UK: Scolar Press, 1973. (Facsimile edition of 1571 printing.)

Montenay, Georgette de. *Livre d'Armoiries en signe de fraternite contenant cent comparaisons de vertus et Emblemes chrestiens agences et ornes de belles figures gravees en cuivre.* Frankfurt: Peter Rollos, 1619.

Moody, Ellen. "Six Elegiac Poems, Possibly by Anne Cecil de Vere, Countess of Oxford." *English Literary Renaissance* 19, no. 2 (Spring 1989): 152–170.

Moore, Dorothy. *The Letters of Dorothy Moore, 1612–64: The Friendships, Marriage, and Intellectual Life of a Seventeenth-Century Woman.* Edited by Lynette Hunter. Aldershot, UK, and Burlington, VT: Ashgate, 2004.

Morata, Olympia. *The Complete Writings of an Italian Heretic.* Edited and translated by Holt N. Parker. Chicago: University of Chicago Press, 2003.

Morata, Olympia Fulvia. *Olympiae Fulviae Moratae foeminae doctissimae ac plane divinae Orationes, Dialogi, Epistolae, Carmina tam Latina quam Graeca.* 2nd ed. Edited by Caelius Secundus Curio. Basel: Petrum Pernam, 1562. (Reprinted in microfilm, "History of Women," Reel 62, No. 396 [New Haven, 1975]. Available at: www.uni-mannheim.de/mateo/desbillons/olimp.html.)

Morata, Olympia Fulvia. *Olympiae Fulviae Moratae mulieris omnium eruditissimae Latina et Graeca, quae haberi potuerunt, monumenta.* Edited by Caelius Secundus Curio. Basel: Petrum Pernam, 1558. (This first edition is dedicated to Isabella Bersegna.)

Morata, Olympia Fulvia. *Olimpia Morata. Epistolario (1540–1555).* Edited by Lanfranco Caretti. Ferrara: Deputazione di storia patria per l'Emilia e la Romagna. Sezione di Ferrara, 1940.

Morata, Olympia Fulvia. *Opere di Olympia Morata.* Edited by Lanfranco Caretti. Ferrara: Deputazione provinciale ferrarese di storia patria. Atti e memorie, n.s., v. 11, 1954.

Mornay, Charlotte Duplessis. *A Huguenot Family in the XVIe Century. The Memoires of Philippe de Mornay . . . Written by his wife.* Translated by L. Crumb. London: Routledge, 1926.

Mornay, Charlotte Duplessis. *Mémoires.* Edited and critiqued by Nadine Kuperty-Tsur. Paris: Champion, forthcoming.

Mornay, Charlotte Duplessis. *Mémoires de Madame de Mornay.* 2 vols. Edited by Mme. de Witt. Paris: Renouard, 1868–1869.

Mornay, Philippe de, seigneur du Plessis-Marly. *Mémoires et correspondance.* 12 vols. Geneva: Slatkine, 1969. (Reprint of Paris edition, 1824–1825.)

Morra, Isabella di. *Isabella di Morra con l'edizione del canzoniere.* Edited by Domenico Bronzini. Matera: Montemurro, 1975.

Morra, Isabella di. In *Rime delle signore Lucrezia Marinella, Veronica Gambara et Isabella della Morra.* Edited Antonio Bulifon. Naples: Bulifon, 1693.

Mush, John. "Life of Margaret Clitherow." [1586] In *The Troubles of Our Catholic Forefathers.* Edited by John Morris, SJ, 331–440. London: Burns and Oates, 1877.

Nichols, J. G., ed. *The Chronicle of Queen Jane and Queen Mary.* New York: AMS Press, 1968.

Noffke, Suzanne, trans. *The Dialogue of Catherine of Siena.* New York: Paulist Press, 1980.

Noffke, Suzanne, trans. *The Letters of Catherine of Siena.* Tempe: Arizona Center for Medieval and Renaissance Studies, 2001.

Nogarola, Isotta. *Complete Writings: Letterbook, Dialogue on Adam and Eve, Orations.* Edited and translated by Margaret L. King and Diana Robin. Chicago: University of Chicago Press, 2004.

Nogarola, Isotta. *Isotae Nogarolae veronensis opera quae supersunt omnia, accedunt Angelae et Zenevrae Nogarolae epistolae et carmina.* Edited by Eugenius Abel. Vienna: apud Gerold et socios, and Budapest: apud Fridericum Kilian, 1886. (Contains Giammaria Filelfo's eulogy of her.)

Ochino, Bernardino. *I "dialogi sette" e altri scritti del tempo della fuga.* Ed. U. Rozzo, 147–152. Turin: Claudiana, 1985.

O'Malley, Susan Gushee, ed. *Defences of Women: Jane Anger, Rachel Speght, Ester Sowernam, and Constantia Munda.* The Early Modern Englishwoman, Part 1, Printed Writings, 1500–1640. Vol. 4. Aldershot, UK: Scholars Press; Brookfield, VT: Ashgate, 1996.

O'Malley, Susan Gushee, ed. *The Early Modern Englishwoman: A Facsimile Library of Essential Works, Part 1: Printed Writings, 1500–1640, Volume 4, Defences of Women: Jane Anger, Rachel Speght, Ester Sowernam, and Constantia Munda.* Hants, NS, and Brookfield, UK: Scholar Press Series, 1996.

Osborne, Dorothy. *Letters to Sir William Temple.* Edited by Kenneth Parker. London: Penguin, 1987.

Paré, Ambroise. *On Monsters and Marvels.* Translated by Janis L. Pallister. Chicago: University of Chicago Press, 1982.

Pasquier, Étienne. "A Madame la duchesse de Retz." *Lettres Familières.* Edited by D. Thickett. Geneva: Droz, 1974.

Passi, Giuseppe. *I donneschi difetti.* Venice: I. A. Somasco, 1599.

Patrizi, Francesco. *The Philosophy of Love.* Translated by Daniela Pastina and John L. Crayton. Philadelphia: Xlibris, 2003

Payne, Helen. "The Cecil Women and Court." In *Patronage, Culture and Power: The Early Cecils.* Edited by Pauline Croft. New Haven, CT, and London: Yale University Press, 2002.

Pesanti, Giovanni. "Lettere inedite del Poliziano." *Athenaeum* 3 (1915): 284–304.

Philips, Katherine Fowler. *The Collected Works of Katherine Philips: The Matchless Orinda.* 3 vols. Edited by Patrick Thomas. Stump Cross, Essex, UK: Stump Cross Books, 1990.

Piccolominio, Alessandro. *Lettura del S. Alessandro Piccolomini Infiammato fatta nell'Accademia degli Infiammati.* Bologna: Bartolomeo Bonardo e Marc'Antonio da Carpi, 1541.

Plato, *Symposium.*

Poitiers, Diane de. *Dianne de Poytiers. Lettres inédites.* Edited by G. Guiffrey. Paris: 1866; Geneva: 1970.

Ponte, Giovanni, ed. *Sacre rappresentazioni fiorentine del Quattrocento.* Milan: Marzorati Editore, 1974.

Primer of Claude de France. Cambridge, UK: Fitzwilliam Museum.

Primrose, Diana. *A Chaine of Pearle, or, A Memoriall of the Peerless Graces, and Heroick Vertues of Queen Elizabeth, of Glorious Memory.* Providence, RI: Brown University Women Writers Project, 1999–.

Pryor, Felix. *Elizabeth I: Her Life in Letters.* Berkeley: University of California Press, 2003.

Pulci, Antonia. *Florentine Drama for Convent and Festival.* Translated by James Wyatt Cook and edited by James Wyatt and Barbara Collier Cook. Chicago: University of Chicago Press, 1996.

Pulci, Antonia Tanini. *La rapresentatione di Santa Domitilla,* a8–c4, *La rapres Xentation di Santa Gugielma,* g8–i6, *La rapresentatione di San Francesco,* n8–p4, s.n.t. Florence: Antonio Miscomini, ca. 1490–1495.

Purkiss, Diane, ed. *Three Tragedies by Renaissance Women: Euripides and Others.* New York and London: Penguin, 1998.

Queen Elizabeth I: Selected Works. Edited by Steven May. New York: Washington Square Press, 2004.

Raymond of Capua. *The Life of Saint Catherine of Siena.* Translated by Conleth Kearns. Wilmington, DE: Michael Glazier, Inc., 1980.

Ribera, Pietro Paolo de. *Le glorie immortali de'trionfi, et heroiche imprese d'ottocento quarantacinque Donne Illustri antiche, e moderne.* Venice: Evangelista Deuchino, 1609.

Romieu, Marie de. *Brief Discourse.* Translated by Marian Rothstein. *Writings by Pre-Revolutionary French Women.* Edited by Anne R. Larsen and Colette H. Winn, 137–149. New York: Garland, 2000.

Romieu, Marie de. *Les Premières Œuvres poétiques.* Edited by André Winandy. Geneva: Droz, 1972.

Ronsard, Pierre de. *Elegies, mascarades et bergerie (1565).* In *Œuvres Complètes.* Edited by Paul Laumonier, 13: 170–176. Paris: Didier, 1948.

Rosarium philosophorum. Edited by Joachim Telle. Weinheim: VCH, 1992. (Originally printed in Frankfurt, 1550.)

Roye, Eléonore de. "The Translation of a letter . . . upon the death of . . . Elenor of Roye. . . ." In *Epistre d'une demoiselle françoise a une sienne amie dame estrangere, sur la mort d'excellente & vertueuse Dame Léonore de Roye, Princesse de Condé. . . .* [s.l.], 1564. Translated by Henry Myddelmore. London: John Daye, 1564.

Sanuto, Marino (Marin Sanudo; 1466–1536). *I diarii di Marino Sanuto (MCCCCXCVI-MDXXXIII) dall' autografo Marciano ital. cl. VII codd. CDXIX-CDLXXVII.* Edited by Rinaldo Fulin, Federico

Stefani, Nicolò Barozzi, Guglielmo Berchet, and Marco Allegri. Venezia: F. Visentini, 1879–1903.

Scala, Alessandra. "Alexandra Scala Cassandrae Fideli. Epistola CVII." In Cassandra Fedele, *Clarissimae feminae Cassandrae Fidelis venetae epistolae et orationes.* Edited by Jacopo Filippo Tomasini, 163–164. Padua: Franciscus Bolzetta, 1636.

Scala, Alessandra. "Epigramma greco." In Angelo Poliziano, *Prose volgari inedite e poesie latine e greche.* Edited by Isidoro del Lungo. Florence: Barbera, 1867.

Schurman, Anna Maria van. *De vitae termino.* Leiden: Johannus Maire, 1639.

Schurman, Anna Maria van. *Eukleria seu Melioris Partis Electio. Tractatus Brevem Vitae ejus Delineationem Exhibens.* Altona, Germany: Cornelius van der Meulen, 1673.

Schurman, Anna Maria van. *Nobiliss. Virginis Annae Mariae a Schurman Dissertatio De Ingenii Muliebris ad Doctrinam, & meliores Litteras aptitudine. Accedunt Quaedam Epistolae eiusdem Argumenti.* Leiden: Elsevier, 1641.

Schurman, Anna Maria van. *Nobiliss. Virginis Annae Mariae à Schurman, Opuscula Hebraea, Graeca, Latina, Gallica: Prosaica & Metrica.* Leiden: Elsevier, 1648.

Schurman, Anna Maria van. *Whether a Christian Woman Should Be Educated: and other writings from her intellectual circle.* The Other Voice in Early Modern Europe. Edited and translated by Joyce L. Irwin. Chicago: University of Chicago Press, 1998.

Sforza Riario, Caterina. *Experimenti de la Ex.ma S.ra Caterina da Furlj, matre de lo inllux.mo signor Giovanni de Medici copiati dagli autografi di lei dal Conte Lucantonio Cuppano; pubblicati da Pier Desiderio Pasolini.* Imola, Italy: Ignazio Galeati e Figlio, 1894.

Sforza Riario, Caterina. *Ricettario di bellezza.* Introduction by Luigi Pescasio. Castiglione delle Stiviere, Italy: Wella italiana, 1971.

Sidney, Philip, *The Countess of Pembroke's Arcadia.* Edited by Maurice Evans. London: Penguin, 1987.

Smith, Rosalind. "The Sonnets of the Countess of Oxford and Elizabeth I: Translations from Desportes." *Notes and Queries* 41, no. 4 (1994): 446–450.

Speght, Rachel. *A Mouzell for Melastomus.* London: 1617.

Speght, Rachel. *The Polemics and Poems of Rachel Speght.* Edited by Barbara Kiefer Lewalski. Oxford: Oxford University Press, 1996.

Spenser, Edmund. *The Faerie Queene.* Edited by A. C. Hamilton. London: Longman, 1977.

Stampa, Gaspara. *Gaspara Stampa: Selected Poems.* Edited and translated by Laura Anna Stortoni and Mary Prentice Lillie. New York: Italica, 1994.

Stampa, Gaspara. *Rime.* Edited by Maria Bellonci. Milan: R.C.S., 2002.

Stampa, Gaspara. *Rime di Gaspara Stampa e di Veronica Franco.* Edited by A. Salza. Bari: 1913.

Stampa, Gaspara. *Rime di Madonna Gaspara Stampa.* Venice: Pietrasanta, 1554.

Steen, Sara Jayne, ed. *The Letters of Lady Arbella Stuart.* New York: Oxford University Press, 1994.

Stevenson, Jane, and Peter Davidson, eds. *Early Modern Women Poets, 1520–1700: An Anthology.* Oxford and New York: Oxford University Press, 2001.

Stortoni, Laura Anna. *Women Poets of the Italian Renaissance. Courtly Ladies and Courtesans.* Translated by Laura Anna Stortoni and Mary Prentice Lillie. New York: Italica Press, 1997.

Strozzi, Alessandra. *Selected Letters: Bilingual Edition.* Edited and translated by Heather Gregory. Berkeley: University of California Press, 1997.

Strype, John. *Annals of the Reformation and Establishment of Religion and Other Various Occurrences in the Church of England.* 2nd ed. 4 vols. London: Thomas Edlin, 1725.

Stuart, Arbella. *The Letters of Lady Arbella Stuart.* Edited by Sara Jayne Steen. New York and Oxford: Oxford University Press, 1994.

Sullam, Sara Copio. *Manifesto.* Venice: Giovanni Alberti, 1621.

Tarabotti, Arcangela. *Che le donne siano degli spezie degli uomini* (Women Are No Less Rational Than Men). Edited and with an introductory essay by Letizia Panizza. London: Institute of Romance Studies, University of London, 1994.

Tarabotti, Arcangela. *Che le donne siano della spetie degli uomini. Difesa delle Donne di Galerana Barcitotti contro Horatio Plata, il traduttore di quei fogli che dicono: Le donne non essere della spetie degli huomini.* Nuremberg: I. Cherchenbergher, 1651.

Tarabotti, Arcangela. *Contro il lusso donnesco. Satira Menippea del Sig. Fran. sBuoninsegni. Con l'Antisatira D. A. T.* [di Arcangela Tarabotti]. Venice: F. Valvasense, 1644.

Tarabotti, Arcangela. *F. Buoninsegni e Suor A. Tarabotti. Satira e Antisatira.* Edited and with an introduction by Elissa Weaver. Rome: Salerno, 1998.

Tarabotti, Arcangela. *Il Paradiso monacale con un soliloquio a Dio.* Venice: G. Oddoni, 1643.

Tarabotti, Arcangela. *Lagrime per la morte dell'Illustrissima signora Regina Donati.* Venice: Guerigli, 1650.

Tarabotti, Arcangela. *La semplicità ingannata.* Leiden: G. Sambix (Elzevier), 1654.

Tarabotti, Arcangela. *Lettere familiari e di complimento.* Venice: Guerigli, 1650.

Tarabotti, Arcangela. *Lettere familiari e di complimento.* Edited by Meredith Ray and Lynn Westwater. Foreword by Gabriella Zarri. Turin: Rosenberg and Sellier, 2005.

Tarabotti, Arcangela. "Letter to the Reader" from *Paradiso monacale* and Ferrante Pallavicino's Letter 5, "To an Ungrateful Woman" from *Corriero svaligiato.* In *Paternal Tyranny.* Edited and translated by Letizia Panizza. Chicago: University of Chicago Press. 2004.

Tarabotti, Arcangela. *L'Inferno monacale.* Edited by Francesca Medioli. Turin: Rosenberg and Sellier, 1990.

Tarabotti, Arcangela. *Paternal Tyranny.* Edited and translated by Letizia Panizza. Chicago: University of Chicago Press, 2004.

Tarabotti, Arcangela. *"Women Are Not Human." An Anonymous Treatise and Responses.* Translated by Teresa M. Kenney. New York: Crossroad Publishing Co., 1998.

Taylor, Craig, ed. and trans. *Joan of Arc, La Pucelle: Selected Sources.* Manchester, UK, and New York: Manchester University Press, 2006.

Terracina, Laura Bacio. *La seconda parte de' discorsi sopra le seconde stanze de' canti d'Orlando Furioso della S. Laura Terracina detta nell'Accademia degl' Incogniti Febea. Nuovamente mandate in luce.* Venice: Valvassori, 1567.

Terracina, Laura Bacio. *Rime della Signora Laura Terracina.* Venice: G. Giolito de' Ferrari, 1548, 1549, 1550, 1553, 1554, 1560; Venice: D. Farri, 1565; Naples: Boulifon, in 2 volumes, anthologized with the *Rime terze, quarte and quinte.*

Terracina, Laura Bacio. *Quarte rime della Signora Laura Terracina detta Phebea nel' Accademic degl'Incogniti.* Venice: G. A. Valvassori, 1550; Lucca: V. Busdrago, 1551; Venice: D. Farri, 1560.

Terracina, Laura Bacio. *Quinte rime della Signora Laura Terracina detta Phebea nel'Accademia degl'Incogniti.* Venice: G. A. Valvassor, 1552; Venice: D. Farri, 1558, 1560.

Terracina, Laura Bacio. *Rime seconde della Signora Laura Terracina di Napoli et di diversi a lei.* Florence: L. Torrentino, 1549.

Terracina, Laura Bacio. *Le seste rime della Signora Laura Terracina di Napoli nuovamente stampate.* Lucca: V. Busdrago, 1558; Naples: R. Amato, 1560.

Terracina, Laura Bacio. *Settime Rime sovra tutte le donne vedove di questa nostra città di Napoli titolate et non titolate. Fatte per la Signora Laura Terracina.* Naples: M. Cancer, 1561.

Terracina, Laura Bacio. *Discorso sopra tutti li primi canti d'Orlando Furioso. Fatti per la Signora Laura Terracina.* Venice: G. Giolito de Ferrari, 1549, 1550, 1551, 1554, 1557, 1559; Venice: G. Giolito, 1565; Venice: Frazzaria, Al Segno della Regina, 1579; Venice: Godini, 1577; Venice: Frezzari al segno della Regina, 1581.

Thiessen, J. S., and Enno van Gelder, H. A., eds. *Correspondence française de Marguerite d'Austriche, duchesse de Parme, avec Philipe II.* 3 vols. Utrech: Kemink et fils 1925–1942.

Thynne, Joan, and Maria Thynne. *Two Elizabethan Women: Correspondence of Joan and Maria Thynne, 1575–1611.* Edited by Alison D. Wall. Devizes, UK: Wiltshire Record Society, 1983.

Tornabuoni de' Medici, Lucrezia. *I poemetti sacri di Lucrezia Tornabuoni.* Edited by Fulvio Pezzarossa. Florence: Olschki, 1978.

Tornabuoni de' Medici, Lucrezia. *Lettere.* Edited by Patrizia Salvadori. Florence: Olschki, 1993.

Tornabuoni de' Medici, Lucrezia. *Sacred Narratives.* Edited and translated by Jane Tylus. Chicago: University of Chicago Press, 2001.

Travitsky, Betty, Patrick Cullen, and Janel Mueller, eds. *The Early Modern Englishwoman: A Facsimile Library of Essential Works: Printed Writings, 1500–1640: Katherine Parr.* London: Scholars Press, 1996.

Travitsky, Betty, and Anne Lake Prescott, eds. *Female and Male Voices in Early Modern England: An Anthology of Renaissance Writing.* New York: Columbia University Press, 2000.

Tuke, Thomas. *A Treatise Against Painting and Tincturing of Men and Women.* London: 1616.

Valdés, Juan de. *Alfabeto christiano.* Translated and edited by Marco Antonio Magno. Venice: Nicolò Bacarini, 1545.

Valdés, Juan de. "The Christian Alphabet Which Teaches the True Way to Acquire the Light of the Holy Spirit." In *Spiritual and Anabaptist Writers. Documents Illustrative of the Radical Reformation and Evangelical Catholicism as Represented by Juan de Valdés.* Translated by Angel M. Mergal. Philadelphia, PA: Westminster Press, 1957.

Valois, Marguerite de. *Correspondance, 1569–1614.* Edited by Eliane Viennot. Paris: Champion, 1998.

Vasari, Giorgio. *Le vite de' più eccellenti pittori scultori e architettori nelle redazioni del 1550 e 1568.* Edited by Rosanna Bettarini, notes by Paola Barocchi, 403–405. Florence: S.P.E.S, IV, 1976.

Vettori, Piero. *Laudatio Eleonorae, Cosmi Medicis, Floren. ac Senens. ducis, uxoris: quae habita est IIII. k. ian. Florentiae, à Pietro Victorio, in aede divi Laurentii.* Florence: Torrentino, 1562.

Vives, Juan Luis. *The Instruction of a Christen Woman.* Edited by Virginia Walcott Beauchamp, Elizabeth H. Hageman, and Margaret Mikesell. Urbana and Chicago: University of Illinois Press, 2002.

Walker, Kim. *Women Writers of the English Renaissance.* Twayne English Authors Series, 521. Pages 152–162. New York: Twayne, 1996.

Watt, Diane. *Secretaries of God: Women Prophets in Late Medieval and Early Modern England.* Woodbridge, UK, and Rochester, NY: D. S. Brewer, 1997.

Whitney, Isabella. *A Sweet Nosegay and The Copy of a Letter.* Edited by Richard J. Panofsky. Delmar, NY: Scholars' Facsimiles and Reprints, 1982

Wilson, Katharina M., ed. *Medieval Women Writers.* Athens: University of Georgia Press, 1984.

Wilson, Katharina M., ed. *Women Writers of the Renaissance and Reformation.* Athens: University of Georgia Press, 1987.

Wilson, Katharina M., and Frank J. Warnke, eds. *Women Writers of the Seventeenth Century.* Athens: University of Georgia Press, 1989.

Wroth, Lady Mary. *The Countess of Montgomery's Urania.* 2 parts. Edited by Josephine A. Roberts. Tempe, AZ: Medieval and Renaissance Texts and Studies, 1995, 1999.

Wroth, Lady Mary. *Lady Mary Wroth's "Love's Victory: The Penshurst Manuscript.* Edited by Michael G. Brennan. London: The Roxburghe Club, 1988.

Wroth, Lady Mary. *The Poems of Lady Mary Wroth.* Edited by Josephine A. Roberts. Baton Rouge: Louisiana State University Press, 1983.

Wroth, Mary. *Love's Victory.* In *Renaissance Drama by Women, Texts and Documents.* Edited by S. P. Cerasano and Marion Wynne-Davies. London: Routledge, 1996.

Wynne-Davies, Marion, ed. *Women Poets of the Renaissance.* New York: Routledge, 1999.

Secondary Sources

Ackerknecht, Erwin H. "Midwives as Experts in Court." *Bulletin of the New York Academy of Medicine* 52 (1976): 1224–1228.

Adams, Allison. "Georgette de Montenay and the Device of the Dordrecht Printer François Bosselaer." *Bibliothèque d'Humanisme et Renaissance* LXIII (2001): 63–71.

Adams, Allison. "Les Emblemes ou Devises Chrestiennes de Georgette de Montenay: Edition de 1567." *Bibliothèque d'Humanisme et Renaissance* 62 (2000): 637–629.

Adelman, Howard. "The Literacy of Jewish Women in Early Modern Italy." In *Women's Education in Early Modern Europe, A History, 1500–1800.*

Edited by Barbara J. Whitehead, 133–158. New York: Garland, 1999.

Adler, Sara. "The Petrarchan Lament of Isabella di Morra." In *Donna: Women in Italian Culture,* 201–221. Ottawa: Dovehouse, 1989.

Adler, Sara Maria. "Veronica Franco's Petrarchan Terze Rime: Subverting the Master's Plan." *Italica* 65 (1988): 213–233.

Adorni-Braccesi, Simonetta. " 'Una città infetta' : La repubblica di Lucca nella crisi religiosa del Cinquecento." Florence: Olschki, 1994.

Aercke, Kristiaan P. G. "Anna Bijns: Germanic Sappho." In *Women Writers of the Renaissance and Reformation.* Edited by Katharina M. Wilson. Athens: University of Georgia Press, 1987.

Åkerman, Susanna. *Queen Christina of Sweden and Her Circle: The Transformation of a Seventeenth-Century Philosophical Libertine.* Leiden and New York: E. J. Brill, 1991.

Alexandre-Bidon and Didier Lett. *Children in the Middle Ages, 5th–15th Centuries.* Translated by Jody Gladding. Notre Dame, IN: University of Notre Dame, 1999.

Allaire, Gloria. "Tullia d'Aragona's *Il Meschino* as Key to a Reappraisal of Her Work." *Quaderni d'Italianistica* 16, no. 1 (1995): 33–50.

Allen, Sister Prudence, R.S.M. *The Concept of Woman. Volume II. The Early Humanist Reformation, 1250–1500.* Grand Rapids, MI, and Cambridge, UK: William B. Eerdmans, 2002.

Almond, Philip C. *Adam and Eve in Seventeenth-Century Thought.* Cambridge: Cambridge University Press, 1999.

Alonso, Béatrice, and Eliane Viennot, eds. *Louise Labé 2005.* Collection "L'école du genre," special publication no. 1. Saint-Eienne, France: Publications Universitaires de Saint-Etienne, 2004.

Alsop, J. D. "William Welwood, Anne of Denmark and the Sovereignty of the Sea." *Scottish Historical Review* 59 (1980): 155–159.

Altman, Janet Gurkin. "The Letter Book as a Literary Institution 1539–1789: Toward a Cultural History of Published Correspondences in France." *Yale French Studies* 71 (1986): 17–62.

Altman, Janet Gurkin. "Women's Letters in the Public Square." In *Going Public: Women and Publishing in Early Modern France.* Edited by Elizabeth Goldsmith and Dena Goodman, 99–115. Ithaca, NY: Cornell University Press, 1995.

Amante, Bruto. *Giulia Gonzaga, contessa di Fondi e il movimento religioso femminile nel secolo XVI.* Bologna: Zanichelli, 1896. (The appendix contains several letters to Giulia [pp. 407–419] and others by her to friends and relatives, among them Vittoria Colonna, Pietro Carnesecchi, and Cardinal Seripando [pp. 421–82].)

Amante, Bruto. *Memorie storiche e statutarie del Ducato, della Contea e dell'Episcopato di Fondi in Campania dalle origini fino ai tempi più recenti.* Fondi, Italy: Emidio Quadrino [s.n.], 1971. (Originally printed in Rome: Ermanno Loescher, 1903.)

Andreadis, Harriette. *Sappho in Early Modern England. Female Same-Sex Literary Erotics, 1550–1714.* Chicago: University of Chicago Press, 2001.

Antinoro-Polizzi, Joseph. *Lady of Asolo: A Pictorial History of the Life and Times of Caterina Cornaro.* Rochester, NY: Ayers Printing Co., 1985.

Apps, Lara, and Andrew Gow. *Male Witches in Early Modern Europe.* Manchester, UK: Manchester University Press; Palgrave, 2003.

Armaille, Marie Celestine Amélie, Comtesse de. *Catherine de Bourbon: soeur d'Henri IV.* Paris: Didier et Cie., 1865.

Armstrong, Elizabeth. *Robert Estienne, Royal Printer.* Cambridge: Cambridge University Press, 1954.

Askew, P. "Lucrina Fetti." In *Women Artists: 1550–1950.* Edited by A. Sutherland Harris and L. Nochlin, 124–130. New York: Knopf, 1977.

Atti del Convegno di studi per il quinto centenario della nascita di Caterina Sforza: Imola, 29 giugno 1964, Forli, 25 ottobre 1964. Bologna: Cassa dei Risparmi di Forlì, 1967.

Auerbach, Erna. *Tudor Artists: A Study of Painters in the Royal Service and of Portraiture on Illuminated Documents from the Accession of Henry VIII to the Death of Elizabeth I.* London: The Athlone Press, 1954.

Austern, Linda Phyllis. " 'Singe Againe Syren': The Female Musician and Sexual Enchantment in Elizabethan Life and Literature." *Renaissance Quarterly* 42, no. 3 (1989): 420–448.

Avril, François, and Nicole Reynaud. *Les manuscrits à peintures en France 1440–1520,* 319 and nos. 176, 177, 178. Paris: Bibliothèque nationale de France, 1993.

Baar, Mirjam de, Machteld Löwensteyn, Marit Monteiro, and A. Agnes Neller, eds. *Choosing the Better Part: Anna Maria van Schurman (1607–1678).* Dordrecht, the Netherlands: Martinus Nijhoff, Kluwer Academic Publishers, 1996.

Backus, Irena. "Marie Dentière: un cas de féminisme théologique à l'époque de la Réforme?" *Bulletin de la Société d'Histoire du Protestantisme Français,* 137 (1991): 177–195.

Baglione, G. *Le vite de' pittori, scultori, architetti, ed intagliatori, dal ponitificato di Gregorio XIII del 1572, in fino a' tempi di Papa Urbano VIII nel 1642.* Rome: 1935. (Originally published in Rome, 1642.)

Baia, Anna. *Leonora di Toledo, Duchessa di Firenze e di Siena*. Todi, Italy: Foglietti, 1907.

Bailey, Michael D. "Religious Poverty, Mendicancy, and Reform in the Late Middle Ages." *Church History* 72, no. 3 (September 2003): 457–483.

Bainton, Roland. "Charlotte de Bourbon." In *Ladies of the Reformation in France and England*. Pages 89–111. Boston: Beacon Press, 1973.

Bainton, Roland H. *Donne della Riforma in Germania, in Italia e in Francia*. With an introduction, "Per la storia delle donne nella Riforma," by Susanna Peyronel Rambaldi. Turin: Claudiana, 1992.

Bainton, Roland H. *Women of the Reformation in France and England*. Minneapolis, MN: Augsburg Publishing House, 1973.

Bainton, Roland H. *Women of the Reformation in Germany and Italy*. Minneapolis, MN: Augsburg Publishing House, 1971.

Bal, Mieke. *The Artemisia Files: Artemisia Gentilechi for Feminist and Other Thinking People*. Chicago: University of Chicago Press, 2005.

Baldinucci, F. *Notizie dei professori del disegno, da Cimabue in qua*. Vol. IX. Florence: 1846.

Balsamo, Jean. "Abel L'Angelier et ses dames: les Dames des Roches, Madeleine de l'Auspepine, Marie le Gendre, Marie de Gournay." In *Des femmes & des livres, France et Espagnes XIVᵉ–XVIIᵉ siècle*. Edited by Dominique de Courcelles and Carmen Val Julian, 117–136. Paris: Ecole des Chartes, 1999.

Balsamo, Jean. "Traduire de l'italien: ambitions sociales et contraintes éditoriales à la fin du XVIᵉ siècle." In *Traduire et adapter à la Renaissance*. Edited by Dominique de Courcelles and Carmen Val Julian, 89–98. Paris: Publication de L'Ecole des Chartes, 1999.

Barash, Carol. *English Women's Poetry, 1649–1714: Politics, Community, and Linguistic Authority*. Oxford: Clarendon Press, 1996.

Barroll, Leeds. *Anna of Denmark, Queen of England: A Cultural History*. Philadelphia: University of Pennsylvania Press, 2000.

Barstow, Anne Llewellyn. *Witchcraze: A New History of the European Witch Hunts*. New York: Pandora/Harper Collins, 1994.

Barzaghi, Antonio. *Donne o Cortigiane? La prostituzione a Venezia. Documenti di costume dal XVI al XVII secolo*. Verona: Bertani, 1980.

Bashar, Nazife. "Rape in England between 1550 and 1700." In *Sexual Dynamics of History*. Edited by London Feminist History Group, 28–42. London: Pluto Press, 1983.

Bassanese, Fiora. *Gaspara Stampa*. Boston: Twayne, 1982.

Bassanese, Fiora A. "Private Lives and Public Lies: Texts by Courtesans of the Italian Renaissance." *Texas Studies in Language and Literature* 30, no. 3 (1988): 295–319.

Battigelli, Anna. *Margaret Cavendish and the Exiles of the Mind*. Lexington: University Press of Kentucky, 1998.

Bauschatz, Cathleen. "Cebille/Sebille: Jeanne Flore Reader of Christine de Pisan?" *Women in French Studies* (2000): 86–96.

Bauschatz, Cathleen M. " 'Plaisir et profict' in the Reading and Writing of Marguerite de Valois." *Tulsa Studies in Women's Literature* 7, no. 1 (Spring 1988): 27–48.

Bausi, Francesco. " 'Con agra zampogna'. Tullia d'Aragona a Firenze (1545–48)." *Schede umanistiche* 2 n.s. (1993): 61–91.

Bazzotti, U. "Margherita Gonzaga e il convento di Sant'Orsola." In *Domenico Fetti, 1588/89–1623*. Edited by E. A. Safarik, 45–50. Milan: 1996.

Beaulieu, Jean-Philippe, and Diane Desrosiers-Bonin, eds. *Hélisenne de Crenne. L'Ecriture et ses doubles*. Etudes et Essais sur la Renaissance 54. Paris: Champion, 2004.

Beaune, Colette. *Jeanne d'Arc*. Paris: Perrin, 2004.

Beilin, Elaine V. "Anne Dowriche." In *Dictionary of Literary Biography*. Vol. 172. Edited by James K. Bracken and Joel Silver. Detroit, MI: Gale Research Co., 1996.

Beilin, Elaine V. *Redeeming Eve: Women Writers of the English Renaissance*. Princeton, NJ: Princeton University Press, 1987.

Beilin, Elaine. "Writing Public Poetry: Humanism and the Woman Writer." MLQ 51 (1990): 249–259.

Beilin, Elaine V., ed. *The Examinations of Anne Askew*. Women Writers in English, 1350–1850. New York and Oxford: Oxford University Press, 1996.

Bell, Ilona. "Women in the Lyric Dialogue of Courtship: Whitney's *Admonition to al yong Gentilwomen* and Donne's *The Legacie*." In *Representing Women in Renaissance England*. Edited by Claude J. Summers and Ted-Larry Pebworth, 76–92. Columbia: University of Missouri Press, 1997.

Bell, Rudolph. *How to Do It: Guides to Good Living for Renaissance Italians*. Chicago and London: University of Chicago Press, 1999.

Belladonna, Rita. "Gli Intronati, Le Donne, Aonio Paleario e Agostino Museo in un Dialogo Inedito di Marcantonio Piccolomini. Il sodo Intronato (1538)." *Bullettino senese di storia patria* 99 (1994): 48–90.

Bellany, Alastair. "Carr, Robert, Earl of Somerset (1585/6?–1645)." *Oxford Dictionary of National*

Biography. Oxford University Press, 2004. Available at: http://0-www.oxforddnb.com.library.unl .edu:80/view/article/4754. Accessed 1 April 2006.

Bellany, Alastair. "Howard, Frances, Countess of Somerset (1590–1632)." *Oxford Dictionary of National Biography*. Oxford University Press, 2004. Available at: http://0-www.oxforddnb.com.library.unl .edu:80/view/article/53028. Accessed 21 Feb 2006.

Bellonci, Maria. *The Life and Times of Lucrezia Borgia*. Translated by Bernard and Barbara Wall. New York: Harcourt Brace, 1939.

Bellonci, Maria. *Lucrezia Borgia; la sua vita e i suoi tempi*. Milano: A. Mondadori, 1939.

Bellonci, Maria. *Private Renaissance*. Translated by William Weaver. New York: Morrow, 1989.

Bennett, Judith. *Ale, Beer and Brewsters in England: Women's Work in a Changing World, 1300–1600*. New York: Oxford University Press, 1996.

Bennett Judith M., and Amy M. Froide, eds. *Single-women in the European Past*. Philadelphia: University of Pennsylvania Press, 1998.

Benrath, Karl. *Julia Gonzaga. Ein Lebensbild aus der Geschichte der Reformation in Italien*. Halle, Germany: Verein für Reformationsgeschichte, 1900.

Benson, Pamela Joseph. *The Invention of the Renaissance Woman: The Challenge of Female Independence in the Literature and Thought of Italy and England*. University Park: Pennsylvania State University Press, 1992.

Benson, Pamela Joseph, and Victoria Kirkham, eds. *Strong Voices, Weak History: Early Modern Writers and Canons in England, France, and Italy*. Ann Arbor: University of Michigan Press, 2005.

Berdes, Jane. *Women Musicians of Venice*. Oxford: Oxford University Press, 1993.

Bergmans, Simone. "The Miniatures of Levina Teerling." *Burlington Magazine* 64 (1934): 231–234.

Berriot, Karine. *Louise Labé: La Belle Rebelle et le François nouveau, siuvi des Œuvres complètes*. Paris: Seuil, 1985.

Berriot-Salvadore, Evelyne. "Charlotte Arbaleste Du Plessis Mornay." In *Les Femmes dans la société française de la Renaissance*. Pages 127–133. Geneva: Droz, 1990.

Berriot-Salvadore, Evelyne. "Evocation et représentation du mariage dans la poésie féminine." In *Le Mariage au temps de la Renaissance*. Edited by M. T. Jones-Davies, 215–216. Paris: Klincksieck, 1993.

Berriot-Salvadore, Evelyne. *Les femmes dans la société de la société française de la Renaissance*. Geneva: Droz, 1990.

Berriot-Salvadore, Evelyne. *Les femmes dans la sociéte française de la Renaissance*. Geneva: Droz, 1990.

Berriot-Salvadore, Evelyne. "Les femmes dans les cercles intellectuels de la Renaissance: de la fille prodige à la précieuse." In *Etudes corses, études littéraires. Mélanges Offerts au Doyen François Pitti-Ferrandi*. Pages 210–137. Paris: Cerf, 1989.

Berriot-Salvadore, Evelyne. "Les héritières de Louise Labé." In *Louise Labé: Les voix du lyrisme*. Edited by Guy Démerson, 93–106. Saint-Etienne, FR: Publications de l'Université de Saint-Etienne, Editions du CNRS, 1990.

Berriot-Salvadore, Evelyne. "Louise de Coligny." In *Les Femmes dans la société française de la Renaissance*. Pages 134–139. Geneva: Droz, 1990.

Berriot-Salvadore, Evelyne. "Marie Le Gendre et Marie de Gournay à la manière de. . . ." In *Le lecteur, l'auteur et l'écrivain: Montaigne 1492–1592–1992*. Actes du Colloque International de Haïfa, April–May 1992. Edited by Ilana Zinguer, 237–245. Paris: Champion, 1993.

Berruti, Aldo. *Patriziato veneto—I Cornaro*. Turin: La Nuova Grafica, 1953.

Berry, Boyd. "Of the Manner in Which Anne Askew 'Noised It.'" *Journal of English Germanic Philology* 96, no. 2 (April 1997): 182–203.

Berry, Boyd. "'We are not all alyke nor of complexion one': Truism and Isabella Whitney's Multiple Readers." *Renaissance Papers* (2000): 13–23.

Besami, O., J. Hauser, and G. Sopranzi, eds. *Concordances to Vittoria Colonna e Galeazzo di Tarsia: Le rime*. Archivio tematico della lirica italiana. Vol. IV. Hildesheim, Germany, Zürich, and New York: Georg Olms Verlag, 1997.

Betteridge, Thomas. "Anne Askew, John Bale, and Protestant History." *The Journal of Medieval and Early Modern Studies* 27, no. 2 (Spring 1997): 265–284.

Bianco, Monica. "Le due redazioni del commento di Rinaldo Corso alle *Rime* di Vittoria Colonna." *Studi di filologia italiana* 56 (1998): 271–295.

Bignone, A. "A proposito di alcuni epigrammi greci di Poliziano." *Studi italiani di filologia classica* 4 (1927): 392–397.

Biondi, Albano, and Adriano Prosperi. "Il processo al medico Basilio Albrisio, Reggio 1559." *Contributi* 2, no. 4 (1978).

Birch, Una [Constance Pope-Hennessy]. *Anna van Schurman: Artist, Scholar, Saint*. London and New York: Longmans, Green and Co., 1909.

Bissel, R. Ward. *Artemisia Gentileschi and the Authority of Art*. University Park: Pennsylvania State University Press, 1999.

Bissel, R. Ward. "Artemesia Gentileschi: A New Documented Chronology." *Art Bulletin* 50, no. 2 (1968): 153–168.

Boccato, Carla. "Sara Copio Sullam, la poetessa del ghetto di Venezia: episodi della sua vita in un manoscritto del secolo XVII." *Italia* 6, nos. 1–2 (1987): 104–218.

Boillet, Danielle, and Marziano Guglielminetti. *Anthologie Bilingue de la poésie italienne.* Paris: Gallimard/Pléiade, 1994.

Bongi, Salvatore. "Rime della Signora Tullia di Aragona; et di diversi a lei." In *Annali di Gabriel Giolito de' Ferrari.* Vol. 1, 150–199. Rome: Principali Librai, 1890.

Borzelli, Angelo. *Laura Terracina, poetessa napoletana del Cinquecento.* Naples: M. Marzano, 1924.

Boswell, John. *The Kindness of Strangers: The Abandonment of Children in Western Europe from Antiquity to the Renaissance.* New York: Pantheon, 1988.

Botelho, L. and P. Thane, eds. *Women and Ageing in British Society Since 1500.* Harlow, UK: Longmans, 2001.

Bouchard, Mawy. "Anne de Graville (1492–1544) et la tradition épique au XVIe siècle." In *Littératures* 18 (*L'Écriture des femmes à la Renaissance française,* 1998): 31–63.

Boucher, Jacqueline. *Deux Epouses et Reines à la fin du XVIe Siècle: Louise de Lorraine et Marguerite de France.* Saint-Etienne, France: Publications de L'Université Saint-Etienne, 1995.

Bowerbank, Sylvia. "The Spider's Delight: Margaret Cavendish and the 'Female' Imagination." *English Literary Renaissance* 14, no. 3 (1984): 392–408.

Bowers, Jane, and Judith Tick, eds. *Women Making Music: The Western Art Tradition, 1150–1950.* Urbana: University of Illinois Press, 1986.

Boyer, Hippolyte. *Un ménage littéraire en Berry au XVIe siècle. (Jacques Thiboust et Jeanne de La Font).* Bourges: Impr. de la Veuve Jollet-Souchois, 1859.

Bozzetti, C., P. Gibellini, and E. Sandal, eds. *Veronica Gàmbara e la poesia del suo tempo nell'Italia settentrionale. Atti del convegno Brescia-Correggio, 17–19 ottobre 1985.* Florence: Olschki, 1989.

Brace, Patricia. "Isabella Whitney, *A Sweet Nosegay.*" In *A Companion to Early Modern Women's Writing.* Edited by Anita Pacheo, 97–109. Oxford: Blackwell, 2002.

Bradford, Sarah. *Lucrezia Borgia: Life, Love and Death in Renaissance Italy.* New York: Viking Penguin, 2004.

Breisach, Ernst. *Caterina Sforza, a Renaissance Virago.* Chicago: University of Chicago Press, 1967.

Breitenberg, Mark. *Anxious Masculinity in Early Modern England.* Cambridge: Cambridge University Press, 1996.

Bridenthal, Renate, and Claudia Koonz, eds. *Becoming Visible: Women in European History.* Boston: Houghton Mifflin, 1977.

Brink, J. R. "Bathsua Reginald Makin: 'Most Learned Matron.'" *Huntington Library Quarterly* 54 (1991): 313–327.

Brooks, Jeanice. *Courtly Song in Late Sixteenth-Century France.* Chicago: University of Chicago Press, 2000.

Brooks, Jeanice. "*O quelle armonye:* Dialogue Singing in Late Renaissance France." *Early Music History* 22 (2003): 1–64.

Broomhall, Susan. *Women and the Book Trade in Sixteenth Century France.* Aldershot, UK: Ashgate, 2002.

Broomhall, Susan. *Women's Medical Work in Early Modern France.* Manchester, UK: Manchester University Press, 2004.

Brown, Alison. *Bartolomeo Scala, 1430–1497, Chancellor of Florence.* Princeton, NJ: Princeton University Press, 1979.

Brown, Clifford M. *Per dare qualche splendore a la gloriosa cita di Mantua.* Documents for the Antiquarian Collection of Isabella d'Este. Rome: Bulzoni, 2002.

Brown, Clifford M., and Anna Maria Lorenzoni. *Isabella d'Este and Lorenzo da Pavia.* Documents for the History of Art and Culture in Renaissance Mantua. Geneva: Droz, 1982.

Brown, David Alan, ed. *Virtue & Beauty: Leonardo's Ginevra de' Benci and Renaissance Portraits of Women.* Washington, DC: National Gallery of Art, 2001.

Brown, Judith, and Robert C. Davis, eds. *Gender and Society in Renaissance Italy.* London and New York: Longman, 1998.

Brucker, Gene. *Florence: The Golden Age, 1138–1737.* Berkeley: University of California Press, 1998.

Brucker, Gene. *Giovanni and Lusanna: Love and Marriage in Renaissance Florence.* Berkeley: University of California Press, 1986.

Bruhns, E. Maxine. "The Cornaro and Her Impact in the United States and England." In *Elena Lucrezia Cornaro Piscopia. Prima donna laureata nel mondo. Terzo centenario del dottorato (1678–1978).* Edited by Maria Ildegarde Tonzig, 141–147. Vicenza: Università degli studi-Abbazia di S. Giustina (Padua), 1980.

Brundin, Abigail. *Vittoria Colonna.* Aldershot, UK: Ashgate, forthcoming.

Brundin, Abigail. "Vittoria Colonna and the Poetry of Reform." *Italian Studies* 57 (2002): 61–74.

Brundin, Abigail. "Vittoria Colonna and the Virgin Mary." *Modern Language Review* 96 (2001): 61–81.

Bryce, Judith. "Adjusting the Canon for Later Fifteenth-Century Florence: The Case of Antonia Pulci." In *The Renaissance Theatre: Texts Performance, Design*. Vol. 1. Edited by Christopher Cairns, 133–145. Aldershot, UK: Ashgate, 1999.

Bryce, Judith. " 'Or alra via mi convien cercare': Marriage, Salvation, and Sanctity in Antonia Tanini Pulci's Rappresentazione di Santa Guglielma." In *Theatre, Opera, and Performance in Italy from the Fifteenth Century to the Present: Essays in Honour of Richard Andrews*. Edited by Brian Richardson, Simon Gilson, and Catherine Keen, 195–207. Leeds: Society for Italian Studies, 2004.

Bryson, David. *Queen Jeanne and the Promised Land: Dynasty, Homeland, Religion and Violence in Sixteenth-Century France*. Boston: Brill, 1999.

Buchanan, Patricia Hill. *Margaret Tudor, Queen of Scots*. Edinburgh: Scottish Academic Press, 1985.

Bucholz, Robert, and Newton Key. *Early Modern England, 1485–1714: A Narrative History*. Malden, MA: Blackwell, 2004.

Bullock, Alan, and Gabriella Palange. "Per una edizione critica delle opere di Chiara Matraini." In *Studi in onore di Raffaele Spongano*, 235–262. Bologna: Boni, 1980.

Burke, Mary, Jane Donawerth, Linda Dove, and Karen Nelson, eds. *Women, Writing, and the Reproduction of Culture*. Syracuse, NY: Syracuse Univeristy Press, 2000.

Burrièl, Antonio. *Vita di Caterina Sforza Riario, contessa d'Imola, e signora di Forlì, descritta in tre libri*. Bologna: Stamperia di S. Tommaso d'Aquino, 1795.

Burshatin, Israel. "Interrogating Hermaphroditism in Sixteenth-Century Spain." In *Hispanisms and Homosexualities*. Edited by Sylvia Molloy and Robert McKee Irwin, 3–18. Durham, NC: Duke University Press, 1998.

Caccia, Ettore. "Cultura e letteratura nei secoli XV e XVI." In *Storia di Brescia, II. La dominazione Veneta (1426–1575)*. Pages 477–527. Edited by Giovanni Trecanni degli Alfieri. Brescia: Morcelliana, 1961.

Cadioli, G. *Descrizione delle pitture, sculture ed architetture che si osservano nella città di Mantova, e ne' suoi contorni*. Mantua: 1763; Bologna: A. Forni, 1974.

Cameron, Keith. *Henri III: A Maligned or Malignant King? (Aspects of the Satirical Iconography of Henri de Valois)*. Exeter, UK: University of Exeter, 1978.

Cameron, Keith. *Louise Labé: Feminist and Poet of the Renaissance*. Women's Series. New York: Berg, 1990.

Cameron, William. *New Light on Aphra Behn*. Auckland: University of Auckland Press, 1961.

Campanini Catani, Magda. *L'immagine riflessa. La riscrittura delle fonti nei Contes amoureux di Jeanne Flore*. Venice: Supernova, 2000.

Campbell, Julie. *Literary Circles and Gender in Early Modern Europe: A Cross-Cultural Approach*. Aldershot, UK: Ashgate, 2006.

Campbell, Stephen. *The Studiolo of Isabella D'este: Reading, Collecting and the Invention of Mythological Painting*. New Haven and London: Yale University Press, forthcoming.

Cantini, Lorenzo. *Vita di Cosimo de' Medici Primo Granduca di Toscana*. Florence: Albizziniana, 1805.

Capelli, Adriano. "Cassandra Fedele in relazione con Lodovico Il Moro." *Archivio Storico Lombardo* 3, no. 4 (1895): 387–391.

Capello, Sergio. "Le Corps dans les Comptes amoureux: Pyralius le jaloux." Udine, *Forum* (2001): 23–42.

Caponetto, Salvatore. *La Riforma protestante nell'Italia del Cinquecento*. Turin: Claudiana, 1992.

Caponetto, Salvatore. *The Protestant Reformation in Sixteenth-Century Italy*. Translated by Anne C. Tedeschi and John Tedeschi. Kirksville, MO: Truman State University Press, 1998.

Carney, Jo Eldridge. " 'God hath given you one face, and you make yourselves another': Face Painting in the Renaissance." *Lamar Journal of the Humanities* 21, no. 2 (Fall 1995): 21–34.

Carter, Philip. *Men and the Emergence of Polite Society, Britain, 1600–1800*. New York: Pearson Education, 2001.

Carter, Tim. "Finding a Voice: Vittoria Archilei and the Florentine 'New Music'." In *Feminism and Renaissance Studies*. Edited by Lorna Hutson, 450–467. Oxford: Clarendon Press, 1999.

Cartwright, Julia. *Isabella d'Este Marchioness of Mantua 1474–1539. A Study in the Renaissance*. London: John Murray, 1907.

Casadei, Alfredo. "Donne della Riforma italiana: Isabella Bresegna." *Religio* 13 (1937): 6–63.

Caserta, Giovanni. *Isabella di Morra e la società meridionale del Cinquecento*. Matera: Mela, 1976.

Catalano, Michele. *Lucrezia Borgia, duchessa di Ferrara; con nuovi documenti, note critiche e un ritratto inedito*. Ferrara: Taddei, 1920.

Cavallo, Sandra, and Lyndan Warner, eds. *Widowhood in Medieval and Early Modern Europe*. London: Longman, 1999.

Cavazzana, Cesira. "Cassandra Fedele erudita veneziana del Rinascimento." *Ateneo Veneto* 29, no. 2 (1906): 73–79, 249–275, 361–397.

Cave, Terence. *Devotional Poetry in France, c. 1570–1613*. Cambridge: Cambridge University Press, 1969.

Cazauran, Nicole, and James Dauphiné, eds. *Marguerite de Navarre, 1492–1992. Actes du colloque internationale de Pau (1992)*. Mont-de-Marsan, France: InterUniversitaires, 1995.

Cerreta, Florindo. *Alessandro Piccolomini. Letterato e Filosofo Senese del Cinquecento*. Siena: Accademia Senese degli Intronati, 1960.

Chadwick, Whitney. *Women, Art, and Society*. London: Thames and Hudson, 2002.

Chambers, Anne. *Granuaile: The Life and Times of Grace O'Malley*. Dublin: Wolfhound Press, 1988.

Chambers, D., and J. Martineau, eds. *Splendours of the Gonzaga* (exhibition catalog). London: Victoria & Albert Museum, 1981.

Charles, Lindsey, and Duffin, Lorna, eds. *Women and Work in Pre-Industrial England*. London: Croom Helm, 1985.

Chavy, Paul. *Traducteurs d'autrefois. Moyen Age et Renaissance. Dictionnaire des traducteurs et de la literature traduite en ancien et moyen français (842–1600)*. 2 vols. Paris: Champion; Geneva: Slatkine, 1988.

Chemello, Adriana. "La donna, il modello, l'immaginario: Moderata Fonte e Lucrezia Marinella." In *Nel cerchio della luna: Figure di donna in alcuni testi del XVI secolo*. Edited by Marina Zancan, 95–179. Venice: Marsilio, 1983.

Cheney, Liana. "Lavinia Fontana, Boston *Holy Family*." *Woman's Art Journal* 5, no. 1 (1984): 12–15.

Chiappini, Luciano. *Eleonora d'Aragona, prima duchessa di Ferrara*. Rovigo: S.T.E.R., 1956.

Chiappini, Luciano. *Gli Estensi*. Milan: Dall'Oglio, 1967.

Chojnacki, Stanley. *Women and Men in Renaissance Venice: Twelve Essays on Patrician Society*. Baltimore, MD: Johns Hopkins University Press, 2000.

Cholakian, Patricia E. "Marguerite de Valois and the Problematics of Self-Representation." In *Renaissance Women Writers, French Texts/American Contexts*. Edited by Anne Larsen and Colette Winn, 67–81. Detroit, MI: Wayne State University Press, 1994.

Christiansen, Keith, and Judith W. Mann, eds. *Orazio e Artemisia Gentileschi*. Milan: Skira, 2001.

Church, Frederic C. *The Italian Reformers, 1534–1564*. New York: Octagon Books, 1974.

Cian, Vittorio. "Caterina Sforza: a proposito della 'Caterina Sforza' di Pier Desiderio Pasolini." *Rivista storica italiana*, X, no. IV, a (1893). (Reprinted in Turin: F.lli Bocca, 1893.)

Claremont, Francesca. *Catherine of Aragon*. London: Robert Hale Limited, 1939.

Claridge, Mary (aka Katharine Longley). *Margaret Clitherow*. London: Burns and Oates, 1966.

Clarke, Danielle. *The Politics of Early Modern Women's Writing*. London: Longman, 2001.

Clarke, Danielle, and Elizabeth Clarke, eds. *"This Double Voice": Gendered Writing in Early Modern England*. New York: St. Martin's Press, 2000.

Clough, Cecil H. "Daughters and Wives of the Montefeltro: Outstanding Bluestockings of the Quattrocento." *Renaissance Studies* 10, no. 1 (1996): 31–55.

Cloulas, Ivan. *Diane de Poitiers*. Paris: Fayard, 1997.

Cloulas, Yvan. *Catherine de Médicis*. Paris: Fayard, 1981.

Cody, Lisa Forman. "The Politics of Reproduction: From Midwives' Alternative Public Sphere to the Public Spectacle of Man-Midwifery." *Eighteenth-Century Studies* 32, no. 4 (1999): 477–495.

Cohen, Elizabeth S. "Courtesans and Whores: Words and Behavior in Roman Streets." *Women's Studies* 19 (1991): 201–208.

Cohen, Elizabeth S. "The Trials of Artemisia Gentileschi: A Rape as History." *Sixteenth Century Journal* 31, no. 1 (2000): 46–75.

Collinson, Patrick. *Godly People: Essays on English Protestantism and Puritanism*. Pages 273–289. London: Hambledon Press, 1983.

Conti Odorisio, Ginevra. *Donna e società nel Seicento*. Rome: Bulzoni, 1979.

Cooper, Elizabeth. *The Life and Letters of Lady Arabella Stuart*. 2 vols. London: Hurst and Blackett, 1866.

Costa-Zalessow, Natalia. "La condanna all'*Indice* della *Semplicità ingannata* di Arcangela Tarabotti alla luce di manoscritti inediti." *Nouvelles de la République des Lettres* 1 (2000): 97–113.

Cottrell, Robert D. *The Grammar of Silence: A Reading of Marguerite de Navarre's Poetry*. Washington, DC: Catholic University of America Press, 1986.

Couchman, Jane. "Charlotte de Bourbon's Correspondence: Using Words to Implement Emancipation." In *Women Writers in Pre-Revolutionary France*. Edited by Colette H. Winn and Donna Kuizenga, 101–117. New York: Garland, 1990.

Couchman, Jane. "La lecture et le lectorat dans la correspondance de Louise de Coligny." In *Lectrices d'Ancien Régime*. Edited by Isabelle Brouard-Arends, 399–408. Rennes, France: PUR, 2003.

Couchman, Jane. "La vertu féminine et les relations franco-anglaises: la traduction anglaise de *l'Epistre [. . .] sur la mort d'excellente & vertueuse Dame, Léonore de Roye, Princesse de Condé*." In *Femmes et Traduction*. Edited by Jean-Philippe Beaulieu. Ottawa: Presses de l'Université d'Ottawa, forthcoming.

Couchman, Jane, and Ann Crabb, eds. *Women's Letters Across Europe, 1400–1700: Form and Persuasion*. Aldershot, UK: Ashgate, 2005.

Cox, Virginia. "Women Writers and the Canon in Sixteenth-Century Italy: The Case of Vittoria Colonna." In *Strong Voices, Weak History: Early Women Writers and Canons in England, France, and Italy*. Edited by Pamela Joseph Benson and Victoria Kirkham, 14–31. Ann Arbor: University of Michigan Press, 2004.

Cox, Virginia. *The Renaissance Dialogue: Literary Dialogue in Its Social and Political Contexts, Castiglione to Galileo*. Cambridge Studies in Renaissance Literature and Culture. Cambridge: Cambridge University Press, 1992.

Cox, Virginia. "The Single Self: Feminist Thought and the Marriage Market in Early Modern Venice." *Renaissance Quarterly* 48, no. 3 (1995): 513–581.

Cox-Rearick, Janet. *Bronzino's Chapel of Eleonora in the Palazzo Vecchio*. Berkeley: University of California Press, 1993.

Cox-Rearick, Janet, and Mary Westerman Bulgarella. "Public and Private Portraits of Cosimo de' Medici and Eleonora di Toledo: Bronzino's Paintings of his Ducal Patrons in Ottawa and Turin." *Artibus et Historiae* 49 (2004): 101–159.

Crabb, Ann, "How to Influence Your Children: Persuasion and Form in Alessandra Macigni Strozzi's Letters to Her Sons." In *Women's Letters Across Europe, 1400–1700*. Edited by Jane Couchman and Ann Crabb. Aldershot, UK: Ashgate, 2005.

Crabb, Ann. *The Strozzi of Florence: Widowhood and Family Solidarity in the Renaissance*. Ann Arbor: University of Michigan Press, 2000.

Craveri, Benedetta. *The Age of Conversation*. Translated by Teresa Waugh. New York: NYRB Collections, 2005.

Crawford, Patricia. "Attitudes to Menstruation in Seventeenth-Century England." *Past and Present* 91 (1981): 47–73.

Crawford, Patricia. "Sexual Knowledge in England, 1500–1750." In *Sexual Knowledge, Sexual Science: The History of Attitudes to Sexuality*. Edited by Roy Porter and Mikuláš Teich, 82–106. Cambridge: Cambridge University Press, 1994.

Crawford, Patricia. *Women and Religion in England, 1500–1720*. London and New York: Routledge, 1993.

Cremona, Virginio. "L'umanesimo Bresciano." In *Storia di Brescia, II. La dominazione Veneta (1426–1575)*. Pages 542–66. Edited by Giovanni Trecanni degli Alfieri. Brescia: Morcelliana, 1961.

Cressy, David. *Birth, Marriage, and Death: Ritual, Religion, and the Life-Cycle in Tudor and Stuart England*. Oxford: Oxford University Press, 1997.

Crevier-Denommé, Isabelle. "La vision théologique de Marie d'Ennetières et le 'Groupe de Neuchâtel.'" In *Le Livre évangélique en français avant Calvin*. Edited by Jean-François Gilmont, and William Kemp, 179–197. Turnhout, Netherlands: Brepols, 2004.

Croce, Benedetto, ed. *Isabella di Morra e Diego Sandoval de Castro con l'edizione delle "Rime" della Morra e una scelta di quelle del Sandoval*. Bari: Laterza, 1929.

Curtis-Wendlandt, Lisa. "Conversing on Love: Text and Subtext in Tullia d'Aragona's *Dialogo della infinità d'amore*." *Hypatia* 19, no. 4 (2004): 75–96.

Cusick, Suzanne G. "Of Women, Music, and Power: A Model from Seicento Florence." In *Musicology and Difference: Gender and Sexuality in Music Scholarship*. Edited by Ruth A. Solie, 281–304. Berkeley: University of California Press, 1993.

Cusick, Suzanne G. " 'Thinking from Women's Lives': Francesca Caccini after 1627." *The Musical Quarterly* 77, no. 3 (1993): 484–507.

da Fonseca-Wollheim, Corinna. "Faith and Fame in the Life and Works of the Venetian Jewish Poet Sara Copio Sullam (1592?–1641)." Ph.D. dissertation, University of Cambridge, 2000.

D'Amelia, Marina. "Lo scambio epistolare tra Cinque e Seicento: scene di vita quotidiana e aspirazioni segrete." In *Per Lettera: La scrittura epistolare femminile tra archivio e tipografia, secoli XV-XVII*. Edited by Gabriella Zarri, 79–110. Rome: Viella, 1999.

Daston, Lorraine, and Katharine Park. "The Hermaphrodite and the Orders of Nature: Sexual Ambiguity in Early Modern France." *Gay and Lesbian Quarterly* 1 (1995): 419–438.

Daston, Lorraine, and Katharine Park. "Hermaphrodites in Renaissance France." *Critical Matrix* 1 (1985): 1–19.

Davis, Natalie Zemon. "City Women and Religious Change." *Society and Culture in Early Modern France*. Stanford, CA: Stanford University Press, 1975.

Davis, Natalie Zemon. *Society and Culture in Early Modern France*. Stanford, CA: Stanford University Press, 1965.

Davis, Natalie Zemon. "Women in the Crafts in Sixteenth-Century Lyon." In *Women and Work in Preindustrial Europe*. Edited by Barbara A. Hanawalt, 167–197. Bloomington: Indiana University Press, 1986.

Daybell, James. "Women's Letters and Letter-Writing in England, 1540–1603." Ph.D. dissertation, University of Reading, 1999.

Daybell, James, ed. *Early Modern Women's Letter Writing, 1450–1700*. Hampshire, UK, and New York: Palgrave, 2001.

Daybell, James, ed. *Women and Politics in Early Modern England, 1450–1700*. Aldershot, UK, and Burlington, VT: Ashgate, 2004.

Dean, Trevor, and K. J. P. Lowe, eds. *Marriage in Italy, 1300–1650*. Cambridge: Cambridge University Press, 1998.

DeJean, Joan. *Fictions of Sappho. 1546–1937*. Chicago: University of Chicago Press, 1989.

DeJean, Joan. *Tender Geographies. Women and the Origins of the Novel in France*. New York: Columbia University Press, 1991.

DeJean, Joan. "Violent Women and Violence Against Women: Representing the 'Strong' Woman in Early Modern France." *Signs: Journal of Women in Culture and Society*. 29, no. 1 (2003): 117–147.

D'Elia, Anthony F. *The Renaissance of Marriage in Fifteenth-Century Italy*. Cambridge, MA: Harvard University Press, 2004.

De Marco, Giuseppe. *Maddalena Campiglia: La figura e l'opera*. Vicenza: 1988. (Includes some verse.)

Demerson, Guy, ed. *Louise Labé: Les voix du lyrisme*. Paris: Éditions du CNRS, 1990.

Desan, Philippe, ed. "Work in the Renaissance." *Journal of Medieval and Renaissance Studies* (Special issue) 25, no. 1 (1995).

Desrosiers-Bonin, Diane, and Eliane Viennot. *Actualité de Jeanne Flore. Dix-sept études réunies par Diane Desrosiers-Bonin et Eliane Vienno avec la collaboration de Régine Reynolds-Cornell*. Paris: Champion, 2004.

Dezon-Jones, Elyane. *Fragments d'un discours féminin*. Paris: José Corti, 1998.

Diller, George E. *Les Dames des Roches. Étude sur la vie littéraire à Poitiers dans la deuxième moitié du XVIe siècle*. Paris: Droz, 1936.

Dionisotti, Carlo. "Appunti sul Bembo e su Vittoria Colonna." In *Miscellanea Augusto Campana*. Edited by Rino Avesani et al., 257–286. Padua: Antenore, 1981.

Doglio, Maria Luisa. "Letter writing, 1350–1650." In *A History of Women's Writing in Italy*. Edited by Letizia Panizza and Sharon Wood, 13–30. Cambridge: Cambridge University Press, 2000.

Doglio, Maria Luisa. "Scrittura e 'offizio di parole' nelle *Lettere familiari* di Veronica Franco." In *Lettera e donna. Scrittura epistolare al femminile tra Quattro e Cinquecento*. Pages 33–48. Rome: Bulzoni, 1993.

Dolan, Frances E. "Taking the Pencil Out of God's Hand: Art, Nature, and the Face-Painting Debate in Early Modern England." *PMLA* 108, no. 2 (March 1993): 224–239.

Donawerth, Jane. "Women's Poetry and the Tudor-Stuart System of Gift Exchange." *Women, Writing, and the Reproduction of Culture*. Edited by Mary Burke, Jane Donawerth, Linda Dove, and Karen Nelson, 3–18. Syracuse, NY: Syracuse University Press, 2000.

Donawerth, Jane, ed. *Rhetorical Theory by Women before 1900: An Anthology*. Lanham, MD: Rowman and Littlefield, 2002.

Doran, Susan. *Elizabeth I and Foreign Policy, 1558–1608*. London and New York: Routledge, 2000.

Douma, Anna Margaretha Hendrika. *Anna Maria van Schurman en de Studie der Vrouw*. Ph.D. dissertation, University of Amsterdam. Amsterdam: H. J. Paris, 1924.

Dubois, Claude Gilbert. *L'Utopie hermaphrodite: La Terre Australe Connue de Gabriel de Foigny*. Marseille: Publications de C.M.R., 17, 1981.

Dumas, Alexandre. *La Reine Margot*. Paris: "J'ai lu" (Flammarion), 1994.

Dumont, Georges Henri. *Marguerite de Parme: Bâtarde de Charles Quint (1522–1586)*. Brussels: Le Cri Éditions, 1999.

Dunstan, G. R., ed. *The Human Embryo: Aristotle and the Arabic and European Traditions*. Exeter, UK: University of Exeter Press, 1990.

Durant, David N. *Arbella Stuart: A Rival to the Queen*. London: Weidenfeld and Nicolson, 1978.

Durant, David N. *Bess of Hardwick: Portrait of an Elizabethan Dynasty*. London: Peter Owen, 1999. (Originally printed in 1977.)

Eamon, William. "Science and Popular Culture in Sixteenth Century Italy: The 'Professors of Secrets' and Their Books." *Sixteenth Century Journal* 16 (Winter 1985): 471–485.

Eamon, William. *Science and the Secrets of Nature: Books of Secrets in Medieval and Early Modern Culture*. Princeton, NJ: Princeton University Press, 1994.

Early Music 27, no. 3 (special issue on women's laments, 1999).

Eckenstein, Lina. *Women Under Monasticism: Chapters on Saint-Lore and Convent Life Between A.D. 500 and A.D. 1500*. New York: Russell and Russell, 1963.

Edelstein, Bruce. "Bronzino in the Service of Eleonora di Toledo and Cosimo I de' Medici: Conjugal Patronage and the Painter-Courtier." In *Beyond Isabella: Secular Women Patrons of Art in Renaissance Italy*. Edited by Sheryl E. Reiss and David G. Wilkins, 225–261. Kirksville, MO: Truman State University Press, 2001a.

Edelstein, Bruce. "The Early Patronage of Eleonora di Toledo: The Camera Verde and Its Dependencies in the Palazzo Vecchio." 2 vols. Ph.D. dissertation, Harvard University, 1995.

Edelstein, Bruce. "Janet Cox-Rearick, Bronzino's Chapel of Eleonora in the Palazzo Vecchio" (Review) *The Art Bulletin* 76 (1994): 171–175.

Edelstein, Bruce. "Nobildonne napoletane e committenza: Eleonora d'Aragona ed Eleonora di Toledo a confronto." *Quaderni storici* 104 (2000): 295–329.

Edelstein, Bruce. "Observations on the Genesis & Function of Bronzino's Frankfurt *Modello* for the Vault Decoration in the Chapel of Eleonora." In *Coming About . . . A Festschrift for John Shearman*. Edited by Lars R. Jones and Louisa C. Matthew, 157–163. Cambridge, MA: Harvard University Art Museums, 2001b.

Edmond, Mary. *Hilliard and Oliver: The Lives and Works of Two Great Miniaturists*. London: Robert Hale, 1983.

Ehrenreich, Barbara, and Deirdre English. *Witches, Midwives, and Nurses: A History of Women Healers*. New York: The Feminist Press, 1973.

Eisenbichler, Konrad, ed. *The Cultural Politics of Duke Cosimo I de' Medici*. Aldershot, UK: Ashgate, 2001.

Eisenbichler, Konrad, ed. *The Cultural World of Eleonora di Toledo: Duchess of Florence and Siena*. Aldershot, UK: Ashgate, 2004.

Eisenbichler, Konrad, ed. "Laudomia Forteguerri Loves Margaret of Austria." In *Same-Sex Love and Desire Among Women in the Middle Ages*. Edited by Francesco Canadé Sautman and Pamela Sheingorn, 277–280. New York: Palgrave, 2001.

Eisenbichler, Konrad, ed. *The Premodern Teenager: Youth in Society, 1150–1650*. Toronto: Centre for Reformation and Renaissance Studies, 2002.

Elaborde, Jules. *Louise de Coligny, Princesse d'Orange*. Geneva: Slatkine, 1970. (Originally printed in Paris, 1890.)

Erdmann, Axel. *My Gracious Silence: Women in the Mirror of Sixteenth-Century Printing in Western Europe*. Luzern: Gilhofer and Ruschberg, 1999.

Evenden, Doreen. *The Midwives of Seventeenth-Century London*. Cambridge: Cambridge University Press, 2000.

Ezell, Margaret J. M. *Writing Women's Literary History*. Baltimore: Johns Hopkins University Press, 1993.

Fairchilds, Cissie. *Domestic Enemies: Servants and Their Masters in Old Regime France*. Baltimore, MD: Johns Hopkins University Press, 1984.

Fantini, Maria Pia. "Lettere alla Madre di Cassandra Chigi (1535–1556): grafia, espressione, messaggio." In *Per Lettera: La scrittura epistolare femminile tra archivio e tipografia, secoli XV-XVII*. Edited by Gabriella Zarri, 111–150. Rome: Viella, 1999.

Farinelli Toselli, Alessandra, ed. *Lucrezia Borgia a Ferrara*. Ferrara: Liberty House, 2002.

Fattori, A., and B. Feliciangeli. "Lettere inedite di Battista da Montefeltro." *Rendiconti della Reale Accademia dei Lincei, Classe di scienze morali, storiche e filologiche* Ser. 5 26 (1917): 196–215.

Favretti, Elena. "Rime e lettere di Veronica Franco." *Giornale storico della letteratura italiana* 163, no. 523 (1986): 355–382.

Fawtier, Robert. *Sainte Catherine de Sienne: Essaie de citique des sources, I. Sources hagiographiques*. Paris: De Boccard, 1921.

Fawtier, Robert. *Sainte Catherine de Sienne: Essaie de citique des sources, II. Les oeuvres de Sainte Catherine de Sienne*. Paris: De Boccard, 1930.

Fehrenbach, R. J. "Isabella Whitney (fl. 1565–75) and the Popular Miscellanies of Richard Jone." *Cahiers Elisabethains* 19 (1981): 85–87.

Fehrenbach, R. J. "Isabella Whitney, Sir Hugh Plat, Geoffrey Whitney, and 'Sister ldershae.'" *English Language Notes* (1983): 7–11.

Feliciangeli, B. "Notizie sulla vita e sugli scritti di Costanza Varano-Sforza." *Giornale storico della letteratura italiana* 23 (1894): 1–75.

Fenster, Thelma, and Clare A. Lees, eds. *Gender in Debate from the Early Middle Ages to the Renaissance*. The New Middle Ages. New York: Palgrave, 2002.

Ferguson, Gary. "The Feminisation of Devotion: Gabrielle de Coignard, Anne de Marquets, and François de Sales." In *Women's Writing in the French Renaissance: Proceedings of the Fifth Cambridge French Renaissance Colloquium, 7–9 July 1997*. Edited by Philip Ford and Gillian Jondorf, 187–206. Cambridge: Cambridge French Colloquia, 1999.

Ferguson, Gary. *Mirroring Belief: Marguerite de Navarre's Devotional Poetry*. Edinburgh: Edinburgh University Press, 1992.

Ferguson, Gary. "Writing at a Royal Priory: The 'Dames de Poissy.'" *EMF: Studies on Early Modern France* 11 (2005).

Ferguson, Margaret W., Maureen Quilligan, and Nacy Vickers, eds. *Rewriting the Renaissance: The Discourses of Sexual Difference in Early Modern Europe*. Chicago: University of Chicago Press, 1986.

Ferino-Pagden, Silvia, ed. *"La prima donna del mondo": Isabella d'Este, Fürstin und Mäzenatin der Renaissance*. Vienna: Ausstellungskatalog des Kunsthistorisches Museum, 1994.

Ferino-Pagden, Silvia, ed. *Vittoria Colonna: Dichterin und Muse Michelangelos*. Catalogue for the exhibition at the Kunsthistorisches Museum, Vienna, 25 February–25 May 1997. Vienna: Skira, 1997.

Ferino-Pagden, Sylvia, and Maria Kusche. *Sofonisba Anguissola, a Renaissance Woman*. Washington, DC: National Museum of Women in the Arts, 1995.

Ferrari, D. "Domenico Fetti: note archivistiche." In *Domenico Fetti, 1588/89–1623*. Edited by E. A. Safarik, 63–67. Milan: 1996.

Filippini, Nadia Maria. "The Church, the State and Childbirth: The Midwife in Italy During the Eighteenth Century." In *The Art of Midwifery: Early Modern Midwives in Europe*. Edited by Hilary Marland, 152–175. London: Routledge, 1993.

Findlay, Alison, and Stephanie Hodgson-Wright with Gweno Williams. "Translating the Text, Performing the Self." By Gweno Williams. *Women and Dramatic Production, 1550–1700*. Harlow, UK: Pearson Education Limited, 2000.

Findlay, Alison, Stephanie Hodgson-Wright, and Gweno Williams. *Women and Dramatic Production: 1550–1700*. Harlow, UK: Longman, 2000.

Finucci, Valeria. "Isabella di Morra." In *An Encyclopedia of Continental Women Writers*. Edited by Katharina M. Wilson, 2: 876–877. New York: Garland, 1991.

Finucci, Valeria. *The Manly Masquerade: Masculinity, Paternity, and Castration in the Italian Renaissance*. Durham, NC: Duke University Press, 2003.

Firpo, Massimo. *Gli affreschi di Pontormo a San Lorenzo: Eresia, politica e culura nella Firenze di Cosimo I*. Turin: Einaudi, 1997.

Firpo, Massimo. *Inquisizione romana e controriforma: Studi sul Cardinal Giovanni Morone e il suo processo d'eresia*. Bologna: Il Mulino, 1992.

Firpo, Massimo. *Tra alumbrados e "spirituali": studi su Juan de Valdés e il valdesianesimo nella crisi religiosa del '500 italiano*. Florence: L. S. Olschki, 1990.

Fiumi, Fabrizia, and Giovanna Tempesta. "Gli 'experimenti' di Caterina Sforza." In *Catarina Sforza: Una Donna del Cinquecento*, 139–146. Imola, Italy: La Mandrigora, 2000.

Fleming, Arnold. *Marie de Guise*. Glasgow: McLellan, 1960.

Flood, John L. "Olympia Fulvia Morata." In *German Writers of the Renaissance, 1280–1580. Dictionary of Literary Biography*. Vol. 179. Edited by James Hardin and Max Reinhart, 178–183. Detroit, MI: Gale Research, 1997.

ffolliott, Sheila. "Catherine de'Medici as Artemisia: Figuring the Powerful Widow." In *Rewriting the Renaissance: The Discourse of Sexual Difference in Early Modern Europe*. Edited by Margaret W. Ferguson, Maureen Quilligan, and Nancy J. Vickers, 227–241. Chicago: University of Chicago Press, 1986.

Forni, Carla. *Il "Libro Animato": Teoria e Scrittura del Dialogo nel Cinquecento*. Turin: Tirrenia Stampatori, 1992.

Forster, Leonard. *Janus Gruter's English Years*. Leiden: Leiden University Press, 1967.

Fortis, Umberto. *La "bella ebrea": Sara Copio Sullam, poetessa nel ghetto di Venezia del '600*. Turin: Silvio Zamorani editore, 2003.

Fournier, Hannah S. "La Voix textuelle des *Sonets spirituels* d'Anne de Marquets." *Etudes littéraires* 20 (1987): 77–92.

Fragnito, Gigliola. "Vittoria Colonna e il dissensio religioso." In *Vittoria Colonna e Michelangelo*. Catalog of an exhibition. Edited by Pina Ragionieri, 97–105. Florence: Mandragora, 2005.

Franceschini, Gino. "Battista Montefeltro Malatesta, Signora di Pesaro." In *Figure del Rinascimento urbinate*. Pages 159–193. Urbino: S.T.E.U., 1959. (Includes poems and letters.)

Fraser, Antonia. *Mary Queen of Scots*. New York: Delacorte, 1994.

Fraser, Antonia. "Mary Ward: A 17th Century Reformer." *History Today* 31, no. 5 (1981): 14–18. Available at: http://www.historytoday.com.

Fraser, Antonia. *The Six Wives of Henry VIII*. London: Weidenfeld and Nicolson, 1992.

Freeman, Thomas S., and Sarah Elizabeth Wall. "Racking the Body, Shaping the Text: The Account of Anne Askew in Foxe's 'Book of Martyrs.'" *Renaissance Quarterly* 54, no. 4.1 (Winter 2001): 1165–1196.

Frye, Susan. "Materializing Authorship in Esther Inglis's Books." *Journal of Medieval and Early Modern Studies* 32, no. 3 (2002): 469–491.

Frye, Susan, and Karen Robertson, eds. *Maids and Mistresses, Cousins and Queens*. New York and Oxford: Oxford University Press, 1999.

Furst, Lilan R, ed. *Women Healers and Physicians: Climbing a Long Hill*. Lexington: University Press of Kentucky, 1997.

Garber, Marjorie. *Vested Interests: Cross-Dressing and Cultural Anxiety*. New York: Routledge, 1992.

Gardner, Edmund. *Dukes and Poets in Ferrara*. New York: Haskell House Publishers, 1968.

Garrard, Mary D. *Artemisia Gentileschi: The Image of the Female Hero in Italian Baroque Art*. Princeton, NJ: Princeton University Press, 1991.

Garrard, Mary D. *Artemisia Gentileschi around 1622: The Shaping and Reshaping of an Artistic Identity*. Berkeley: University of California Press, 2001.

Garrard, Mary D. "Here's Looking at Me: Sofonisba Anguissola and the Problem of the Woman Artist." *Renaissance Quarterly* 47, no. 3 (Autumn 1994): 556–622.

Garrisson, Janine. *Catherine de Médicis. L'impossible har-monie.* Paris: Payot, 2002.

Garrisson, Janine. *Marguerite de Valois.* Paris: Fayard, 1994.

Gelbart, Nina Rattner. *The King's Midwife: A History and Mystery of Madame du Coudray.* Berkeley: University of California Press, 1998.

Gentilcore, David. *Healers and Healing in Early Modern Italy.* Manchester, UK: Manchester University Press, 1998.

Getto, Giovanni. *Saggio letterario su S. Caterina da Siena.* Florence: Sansoni, 1939.

Geybels, Hans. *Vulgariter Beghinae: Eight Centuries of Beguine History in the Low Countries.* Turnhout, Belgium: Brepols, 2004.

Ghirardi, A. "Dipingere in lode del Cielo: Suor Orsola Maddalena Caccia e la vocazione artistica delle orsoline di Moncalvo." In *Vita artistica nel monastero femminile.* Edited by V. Fortunati, 115–129. Bologna: 2002.

Gilbert, Ruth. *Early Modern Hermaphrodites: Sex and Other Stories.* New York: Palgrave, 2002.

Gilbert, Ruth. "Mingle-Mangle: Masculine Women and Feminine Men." In *Early Modern Hermaphrodites.* Pages 77–103. New York: Palgrave, 2002.

Giles, Mary E., ed. *Women in the Inquisition: Spain and the New World.* Baltimore, MD: Johns Hopkins University Press, 1999.

Gim, Lisa. " 'Faire *Eliza's* Chaine': Two Female Writers' Literary Links to Queen Elizabeth I." In *Maids and Mistresses, Cousins and Queens.* Edited by Susan Frye and Karen Robertson, 183–198. New York and Oxford: Oxford University Press, 1999.

Gladen, C. A. "A Painter, a Duchess, and the *Monastero di Sant'Orsola:* Case Studies of Women's Monastic Lives in Mantua, 1599–1651." Ph.D. dissertation, University of Minnesota, 2003.

Gladen, C. A. "Suor Lucrina Fetti: pittrice in una corte monastica seicentesca." In *I monasteri femminili come centri di cultura fra Rinascimento e Barocco.* Edited by G. Pomata and G. Zarri. Rome: forthcoming.

Glenn, Cheryl. *Rhetoric Retold: Regendering the Tradition from Antiquity Through the Renaissance.* Carbondale: Southern Illinois University, 1997.

Glixon, Beth L. "More on the Life and Death of Barbara Strozzi." *The Musical Quarterly* 83, no. 1 (1999): 134–141.

Glixon, Beth L. "New Light on the Life and Career of Barbara Strozzi." *The Musical Quarterly* 81, no. 2 (1997): 311–335.

Goffen, Rona. *Titian's Women.* New Haven, CT, London: Yale University Press, 1997.

Gold, Barbara, Paul Allen Miller, and Charles Platter. *Sex and Gender in Medieval and Renaissance Texts: The Latin Tradition.* Albany: State University of New York Press, 1997.

Goldberg, P. J. P. *Women, Work and Life Cycle in a Medieval Economy: Women in York and Yorkshire c. 1300–1520.* Oxford: Clarendon Press, 1992.

Goldsmith, Elizabeth. *Exclusive Conversations: The Art of Interaction in Seventeenth-Century France.* Philadelphia: University of Pennsylvania Press, 1988.

Goldsmith, Elizabeth C., ed. *Writing the Female Voice: Essays on Epistolary Literature.* Boston: Northeastern University Press, 1989.

Goldsmith, Elizabeth, and Dena Goodman, eds. *Going Public: Women and Publishing in Early Modern France.* Ithaca, NY: Cornell University Press, 1995.

Gowing, Laura. "Secret Births and Infanticide in Seventeenth-Century England." *Past and Present* 156 (1997): 87–115.

Gray, Floyd. *Gender, Rhetoric, and Print Culture in French Renaissance Writing.* Cambridge: Cambridge University Press, 2000.

Gray, Floyd. "Jeanne Flore and Erotic Desire: Feminism or Male Fantasy?" In *Gender, Rhetoric, and Print Culture in French Renaissance Writing.* Pages 30–46. Cambridge: Cambridge University Press, 2000.

Graziani, Natale, and Gabriella Venturelli. *Caterina Sforza.* Milan: Dall'Oglio, 1987.

Greaves, Richard L., ed. *Triumph over Silence: Women in Protestant History.* Westport, CT: Greenwood Press, 1985.

Green, Monica H. *Women's Healthcare in the Medieval West.* Aldershot, UK: Ashgate, 2000.

Greene, Ellen, ed. *Reading Sappho: Contemporary Approaches.* Berkeley: University of California Press, 1996.

Greene, Ellen, ed. *Re-Reading Sappho: Reception and Transmission.* Berkeley: University of California Press, 1996.

Gregori, M., ed. *Pittura a Mantova dal Romanico al Settecento* (exhibition catalogue). Milan: 1989.

Gregorovius, Ferdinand. *Lucretia Borgia: According to Original Documents and Correspondence of Her Day.* Translated from the third German edition by John Leslie Garner. New York: Appleton, 1903.

Gregory, Brad S. *Salvation at Stake: Christian Martyrdom in Early Modern Europe.* Harvard Historical Studies, 132. Cambridge, MA, and London: Harvard University Press, 1999.

Grendler, Paul. F. *Schooling in Renaissance Italy: Literacy and Learning, 1300–1600.* Baltimore, MD: Johns Hopkins University Press, 1989.

Grendler, Paul. F., ed. *Encyclopedia of the Renaissance,* 6 vols. New York: Charles Scribner's Sons, 1999.

Grieco, Sara Matthews. "Georgette de Montenay: A Different Voice in Sixteenth-Century Emblematics." *Renaissance Quarterly* 4 (1994): 283–370.

Gringore, Pierre. *Les Entrées royales à Paris de Marie d'Angleterre (1514) et Claude de France (1517).* Edited by Cynthia J. Brown. Geneva: Droz, 2005.

Gundersheimer, Werner I. *The Style of a Renaissance Despotism.* Princeton, NJ: Princeton University Press, 1973.

Guy, John. *Tudor England.* Oxford: Oxford University Press, 1990.

Haas, Louis. *The Renaissance Man and His Children: Childbirth and Early Childhood in Florence, 1300–1600.* New York: Saint Martin's Press, 1998.

Hafter, Daryl, ed. *European Women and Preindustrial Craft.* Bloomington: Indiana University Press, 1995.

Hairston, Julia L. "Out of the Archive: Four Newly-Identified Figures in Tullia d'Aragona's *Rime della Signora Tullia di Aragona et di diversi a lei (1547).*" *MLN* 118 (2003): 257–263.

Hairston, Julia L. "Skirting the Issue: Machiavelli's Caterina Sforza." *Renaissance Quarterly* 53, 3 (2000): 686–712.

Halpern, Barbara C. *The Correspondence of Johann Amerbach: Early Printing in Its Social Context.* Ann Arbor: University of Michigan Press, 2000.

Hamburger, Jeffrey. *Nuns as Artists: The Visual Culture of a Medieval Convent.* Berkeley: University of California Press, 1997.

Hanawalt, Barbara. "Medievalists and the Study of Childhood." *Speculum* 77, no. 2 (2002): 440–460.

Hanawalt, Barbara A. *Women and Work in Preindustrial Europe.* Bloomington: Indiana University Press, 1986.

Hannay, Margaret Patterson, ed. *Philip's Phoenix: Mary Sidney, Countess of Pembroke.* New York and Oxford: Oxford University Press, 1990.

Hannay, Margaret Patterson, ed. *Silent But for the Word: Tudor Women as Patrons, Translators, and Writers of Religious Works.* Kent, OH: Kent State University Press, 1985.

Hardwick, Julie. *The Practice of Patriarchy: Gender and the Politics of Household Authority in Early Modern France.* University Park: Pennsylvania State University Press, 1998.

Hare, Christopher (pseudonym of Marian Andrews). *A Princess of the Italian Reformation: Giulia Gonzaga, 1513–1566, Her Family and Her Friends.* London, New York: Harper, 1912.

Harley, David. "Historians as Demonologists: The Myth of the Midwife-Witch." *Journal of the Society for the Social History of Medicine* 3, no. 1 (1990): 1–26.

Harley, David. "Provincial Midwives in England: Lancashire and Cheshire, 1660–1760." Edited by Hilary Marland. *The Art of Midwifery: Early Modern Midwives in Europe.* Pages 27–48. London: Routledge, 1993.

Harris, Ann Sutherland. "Artemisia Gentileschi: The Literate Illiterate or Learning from Example." *Docere, delectare, movere: affetti, devozione e retorica nel linguaggio artistico del primo barocco romano.* Rome: Edizioni De Luca, 1998.

Harris, Ann Sutherland, and Linda Nochlin. *Women Artists: 1550–1950.* New York: Alfred A. Knopf, 1976.

Harris, Barbara J. *English Aristocratic Women, 1450–1550: Marriage and Family, Property and Careers.* Oxford, New York: Oxford University Press, 2002.

Harth, Erica. *Cartesian Women. Versions and Subversions of Rational Discourse in the Old Regime.* Ithaca, NY: Cornell University Press, 1992.

Harvey, Nancy Lenz. *The Rose and the Thorn: The Lives of Mary and Margaret Tudor.* New York: Macmillan, 1975.

Head, Thomas. "A Propagandist for the Reform: Marie Dentière." In *Women Writers of the Renaissance and the Reformation.* Edited by Katharina M. Wilson, 260–283. Athens: University of Georgia Press, 1987.

Hendricks, Margo, and Patricia Parker, eds. *Women, "Race," and Writing in the Early Modern Period.* London: Routledge, 1994.

Henry-Bordeaux, Paule. *Louise de Savoie, "roi" de France.* Paris: Perrin, 1971.

Hillman, David, and Carla Mazzio. *The Body in Parts: Fantasies of Corporeality in Early Modern Europe.* New York: Routledge, 1997.

Hochman, Michel. "Les dessins et les peintures de Fulvio Orsini et la collection Farnèse." *Mélanges de l'école française de Rome* (CV 1993): 49–83.

Hodgson-Wright, Stephanie. "Lumley, Jane Lady (1537–1578)." *Oxford Dictionary of Nation Biography.* Oxford: Oxford University Press, 2004.

Hogrefe, Pearl. *Women of Action in Tudor England: Nine Biographical Sketches.* Ames: Iowa State University Press, 1977.

Hosington, Brenda M. "England's First Female-Authored Encomium: The Seymour Sisters' *Hecatodistichon* (1550) to Marguerite de Navarre. Text, Translation, Notes, and Commentary." *Studies in Philology* 93, no. 2 (1996): 117–163.

Howell, Martha. *Women, Production and Patriarchy in Late Medieval Cities.* Chicago: University of Chicago Press, 1986.

Howell, Martha C. *The Marriage Exchange: Property, Social Place, and Gender in the Cities of the Low Countries, 1300–1500.* Chicago: University of Chicago Press, 1998.

Hubbard, Kate. *A Material Girl: Bess of Hardwick 1527–1608.* London: Short Books, 2001.

Hughes, Derek. *The Theatre of Aphra Behn.* London: Palgrave, 2001.

Hull, Suzanne. *Women According to Men: The World of Tudor-Stuart Women.* Walnut Creek, CA: AltaMira Press, 1996.

Hunter, Lynette, and Sarah Hutton, eds. *Women, Science and Medicine, 1500–1700: Mothers and Sisters of the Royal Society.* Thrupp, Stroud, Gloucestershire, UK: Sutton Publishing, 1997.

Hutson, Lorna. *Feminism and Renaissance Studies.* Oxford: Oxford University Press, 1999.

Hutson, Lorna. *The Usurer's Daughter: Male Friendship and Fictions of Women in Sixteenth-Century England.* London and New York: Routledge, 1994.

Ilsley, Marjorie. *A Daughter of the Renaissance: Marie le Jars de Gournay, Her Life and Works.* The Hague: Mouton, 1963.

Ingram, Martin. "Child Sexual Abuse in Early Modern England." In *Negotiating Power in Early Modern Society: Order, Hierarchy and Subordination in Britain and Ireland.* Edited by Michael J. Braddick and John Walter. Cambridge: Cambridge University Press, 2001.

Ives, Eric. *Anne Boleyn.* Oxford: Blackwell, 1986.

Jacobs, Fredrika. "Woman's Capacity to Create: The Unusual Case of Sofonisba Anguissola." *Renaissance Quarterly* 47, no. 1 (1994): 74–101.

Jacobs, Fredrika H. *Defining the Renaissance* Virtuosa: *Women Artists and the Language of Art History and Criticism.* Cambridge: Cambridge University Press, 1997.

Jaffe, Irma B., with Gernando Colombardo. *Shining Eyes, Cruel Fortune.* Bronx, NY: Fordham University Press, 2002.

James, Karen Simroth. "On veult responce avoir: Pernette du Guillet's Dialogic Poetics." In *A Dialogue of Voices: Feminist Theory and Bakhtin.* Pages 171–197. Minneapolis: University of Minnesota Press, 1994.

James, Susan E. *Kateryn Parr / The Making of a Queen.* Aldershot, UK: Ashgate, 1999.

Jansen, Sharon. *The Monstrous Regiment of Women: Female Rulers in Early Modern Europe.* New York: Palgrave Macmillan, 2002.

Jardine, Lisa. " 'O Decus Italiae Virgo': The Myth of the Learned Lady in the Renaissance." *The Historical Journal* 28, no. 4 (December 1985): 799–819.

Johnson, Geraldine, and Sara F. Matthews-Grieco. *Picturing Women in Renaissance and Baroque Italy.* Cambridge: Cambridge University Press, 1997.

Johnson, P., and P. Thane, eds. *Old Age from Antiquity to Post-Modernity.* London: Routledge, 1998.

Jondorf, Gillian. "Petrarchan Variations in Pernette du Guillet and Louise Labé." *Modern Language Review* 71, no. 4 (October 1976): 766–778.

Jones, Ann Rosalind. "Assimilation with a Difference: Renaissance Women Poets and Literary Influence." *Yale French Studies* 62 (1981): 135–153.

Jones, Ann Rosalind. "Counterattacks on 'the Bayter of Women': Three Pamphleteers of the Early Seventeenth Century." In *The Renaissance Englishwoman in Print: Counterbalancing the Canon.* Edited by Anne M. Haselkorn and Betty S. Travitsky. Amherst: University of Massachusetts Press, 1990.

Jones, Ann Rosalind. *The Currency of Eros: Women's Love Lyric in Europe, 1540–1620.* Bloomington: Indiana University Press, 1990.

Jones, Ann Rosalind. "Enabling Sites and Gender Difference: Reading City Women with Men." *Women's Studies: An Interdisciplinary Journal* 19, no. 2 (1991): 239–49.

Jones, Ann Rosalind. "Maidservants of London: Sisterhoods of Kinship and Labor." In *Maids and Mistresses, Cousins and Queens: Women's Alliances in Early Modern England.* Edited by Susan Frye and Karen Robertson, 21–32. Oxford: Oxford University Press, 1999.

Jones, Ann Rosalind. "Surprising Fame: Renaissance Gender Ideologies and Women's Lyric." In *The Poetics of Gender.* Edited by Nancy K. Miller, 74–95. New York: Columbia University Press, 1986.

Jones, Ann Rosalind, and Peter Stallybrass. "Transvestism and the 'Body Beneath': Speculating on the Boy Actor." In *Renaissance Clothing and the Materials of Memory.* Pages 207–219. Cambridge, UK: Cambridge University Press, 2000.

Jones, Ann Rosalind, with Peter Stallybrass, eds. *Renaissance Clothing and the Materials of Memory.* Cambridge: Cambridge University Press, 2000.

Jones, Michael K., and Malcolm G. Underwood. *The King's Mother, Lady Margaret Beaufort, Countess of Richmond and Derby.* Cambridge: Cambridge University Press, 1992.

Jordan, Constance. *Renaissance Feminism: Literary Texts and Political Models.* Ithaca, NY and London: Cornell University Press, 1990.

Jourda, Pierre. *Marguerite d'Angoulême, . . . Etude Bi-ographique et Littéraire.* 2 vols. Paris: Champion, 1930.

Kale, Steven. "Women, the Public Sphere, and the Persistence of Salons." *French Historical Studies* 25.1 (2002): 115–48.

Kalisch, Philip A., Margaret Scobey, and Beatrice J. Kalisch. "Louyse Bourgeois and the Emergence of Modern Midwifery." *Journal of Nurse Midwifery* 26, no. 4 (1981): 3–17.

Karlsen, Carol F. *The Devil in the Shape of a Woman: Witchcraft in Colonial New England.* New York and London: W. W. Norton and Company, 1998.

Kates, Gary. *Monsieur d'Eon Is a Woman: A Tale of Po-litical Intrigue and Sexual Masquerade.* Baltimore, MD: Johns Hopkins University Press, 2001.

Kaufmann, Henry W. "Art for the Wedding of Cosimo de' Medici and Eleonora of Toledo (1539)." *Paragone* 21 (1970): 52–67.

Keating, L. Clark. *Studies on the Literary Salon in France, 1550–1615.* Cambridge, MA: Harvard University Press, 1941.

Kelly, Joan. *Women, History, Theory: The Essays of Joan Kelly.* Chicago: University of Chicago Press, 1984.

Kemp, William. "L'épigraphe 'Lisez et puis jugez' et le principe de l'examen dans la Réforme française avant 1540." In *Le Livre évangélique en français avant Calvin.* Edited by Jean-François Gilmont and William Kemp, 241–274. Turnhout, Netherlands: Brepols, 2004.

Kemp, William, and Diane Desrosiers-Bonin. "Marie d'Ennetières et la petite grammaire hébraïque de sa fille d'après la dédicace de l'*Epistre* à Mar-guerite de Navarre (1539)." *Bibliothèque d'Human-isme et Renaissance* 51 (1998): 117–134.

Kendrick, Robert L. *Celestial Sirens: Nuns and Their Music in Early Modern Milan.* Oxford and New York: Clarendon Press, 1996.

Kennedy, Angus J. *Christine de Pizan: A Bibliography.* Woodbridge, Suffolk, UK, and Rochester, NY: Tamesis, 1984. (Two supplements in 1994 and 2004.)

Kennedy, William J. *Authorizing Petrarch.* Ithaca, NY: Cornell University Press, 1994.

Kent, F. William. "Sainted Mother, Magnificent Son: Lucrezia Tornabuoni and Lorenzo de' Medici." *Italian History and Culture* 3 (1997): 3–34.

King, Catherine. "Plautilla Nelli." In *Dictionary of Women Artists.* 2 vols. Edited by Delia Gaze, vol. 2, 1010–1012. London and Chicago: Fitzroy Dear-born Publishers, 1997.

King, Catherine. *Renaissance Women Patrons: Wives and Widows in Italy, c. 1300–c. 1500.* Manchester, UK, New York: Manchester University Press, 1998.

King, Helen. " 'As If None Understood the Art That Cannot Understand Greek': The Education of Midwives in Seventeenth-Century England." In *The History of Medical Education in Britain.* Edited by Vivian Nutton and Roy Porter. 184–198. Ams-terdam: Rodopi, 1995.

King, Helen. *Hippocrates' Woman: Reading the Female Body in Ancient Greece.* London: Routledge, 1998.

King, Margaret L. "Book-Lined Cells: Women and Humanism in the Early Italian Renaissance." In *Beyond Their Sex: Learned Women of the European Past.* Edited by Patricia H. Labalme, 66–90. New York: New York University Press, 1980.

King, Margaret L. *The Death of the Child Valerio Mar-cello.* Chicago: University of Chicago Press, 1994.

King, Margaret L. "The Religious Retreat of Isotta Nogarola (1418–1466)." *Signs* 3 (1978): 807–822.

King, Margaret L. *Women of the Renaissance.* Chicago: University of Chicago Press, 1991.

King, Margaret, and Albert Rabil, eds. *Her Immaculate Hand: Selected Works By and About the Women Hu-manists of Quattrocento Italy.* Binghamton: Center for Medieval and Early Renaissance Studies, State University of New York at Binghamton, 1983. (A second revised edition was published in 1991.)

King, Sigrid, ed. "Pilgrimage for Love: Essays in Early Modern Literature in Honor of Josephine A. Roberts." In *Medieval and Renaissance Texts and Studies.* Vol. 213. Tempe: Arizona Center for Me-dieval and Renaissance Studies, 1999.

Kirkham, Victoria. "Creative Partners: The Marriage of Laura Battiferra and Bartolomeo Ammannati." *Renaissance Quarterly* 55, no. 2 (2002): 498–558.

Kirkham, Victoria. "Dante's Fantom, Petrarch's Specter: Bronzino's Portrait of the Poet Laura Battiferra." In *"Visibile parlare": Dante and the Art of the Italian Renaissance.* Edited by Deborah Parker, 22–23. *Lectura Dantis* (Special issue) (1998): 63–139.

Kirkham, Victoria. "La poetessa al presepio: Una meditazione inedita di Laura Battiferra degli Am-mannati." *Filologia e critica* 27, no. 2 (2002): 258–276.

Kirkham, Victoria. "Laura Battiferra degli Ammannati benefattrice dei Gesuiti fiorentini." In *Commit-tenza artistica femminile.* Edited by Sara F. Matthews and Grieco and Gabriella Zarri. *Quaderni storici* 104, no. 2 (2000): 331–354.

Kirkham, Victoria. "Laura Battiferra's 'First Book' of Poetry: A Renaissance Holograph Comes Out of Hiding." *Rinascimento* 35 (1996): 351–391.

Kirkham, Victoria. "Poetic Ideals of Love and Beauty." In *Virtue and Beauty: Leonardo's* Ginevra de' Benci *and Renaissance Portraits of Women.*

Edited with an Introduction by David Alan Brown, 49–62. Princeton, NJ: Princeton University Press, 2001.

Kirshner, Julius. "Family and Marriage: A Socio-Legal Perspective." In *Italy in the Age of the Renaissance, 1300–1550.* Edited by John Najemy, 82–102. Oxford: Oxford University Press, 2004.

Kirschner, Julius. "Introduction." *Jewish History* 16, no. 1 (2002): 1–14.

Kirshner, Julius. "*Li Emergenti Bisogni Matrimoniali* in Renaissance Florence." In *Society and Individual in Renaissance Florence.* Edited by W. J. Connell, 79–109. Berkeley: University of California Press, 2002.

Kirshner, Julius, and Suzanne F. Wemple, eds. *Women of the Medieval World.* London: Blackwell, 1985.

Klairmont Lingo, Alison. "Women Healers and the Medical Marketplace of Sixteenth-Century Lyon." *Dynamis* 19 (1999): 79–94.

Klaits, Joseph. *Servants of Satan: The Age of the Witch Hunts.* Bloomington: Indiana University Press, 1985.

Klapisch-Zuber, Christiane. *Women, Family and Ritual in Renaissance Italy.* Translated by Lydia Cochrane. Chicago: University of Chicago Press, 1985.

Knecht, R. J. *Catherine de' Medici.* London: Longman, 1998.

Kuehn, Thomas. *Law, Family, and Women: Toward a Legal Anthropology of Renaissance Italy.* 2nd ed. Chicago: University of Chicago Press, 1994.

Kühner, Hans. *Caterina Sforza: Fürstin, Tyrannin, Büsserin.* Zurich: W. Classen, 1957.

Kuperty-Tsur, Nadine. "Rhétorique des témoignages protestants autour de la Saint-Barthélémy: le cas des *Memoires* de Charlotte Duplessis-Mornay." In *Se raconter, témoigner: Elseneur* 17 (September 2001): 159–178.

Labalme, Patricia H. "Nobile e donna: Elena Lucrezia Cornaro Piscopia." In *Elena Lucrezia Cornaro Piscopia. Prima donna laureata nel mondo. Terzo centenario del dottorato (1678–1978).* Edited by Maria Ildegarde Tonzig, 163–167. Vicenza: Università degli studi-Abbazia di S. Giustina (Padua), 1980.

Labalme, Patricia H. "Venetian Women on Women: Three Early Modern Feminists." *Archivio veneto* 5th ser., 117 (1981): 81–109.

Labalme, Patricia, ed. *Beyond Their Sex: Learned Women of the European Past.* New York: New York University Press, 1980.

Labrousse, Elisabeth, and Jean-Philippe. "Georgette de Montenay et Guyon du Gout, son époux." *Bulletin de la Société archéologique, historique, littéraire et scientifique du Gers* (1990): 369–402.

La Charité, Claude. "Le *Dialogo de la bella creanza de le donne* (1539) d'Alessandro Piccolomini et ses

adaptateurs français." *Renaissance and Reformation/Renaissance et Réforme* 23, no. 1 (1999): 43–57.

La Charité, Claude. "Le problème de l'attribution de *l'Instruction pour les jeunes dames* (1572) et l'énigmatique cryptonyme R.D.R." *Bibliothèque d'Humanisme et Renaissance* 62, no. 1 (2000): 119–128.

La Charité, Claude. "Marie de Cotteblanche, traductrice de Pierre Messie, ou l'espagnol en filigrane de l'italien." In *D'une écriture à l'autre: les femmes et la traduction sous l'Ancien Régime.* Edited by Jean-Philippe Beaulieu, 211–227. Ottowa: Presses de l'Université d'Ottowa ("Regards sur la traduction"), 2004.

LaMay, Thomasin, ed. *Musical Voices of Early Modern Women: Many-Headed Melodies.* Aldershot, UK: Ashgate, 2005.

Lamb, Mary Ellen. *Gender and Authorship in the Sidney Circle.* Madison: University of Wisconsin Press, 1990.

Lambert, Malcolm D. *Medieval Heresy: Popular Movements from Bogomil to Hus.* London: Edward Arnold, 1977.

Lapierre, Alexandra. *Artemisia. Un duel pour l'immortalité.* Paris: Robert Laffont, 1998.

Laqueur, Thomas. *Making Sex: The Body and Gender from the Greeks to Freud.* Cambridge, MA: Harvard University Press, 1990.

Larivaille, Paul. *La Vie quotidienne des courtisanes en Italie au temps de la Renaissance.* Paris: Hachette, 1975.

Larsen, Anne R. "The French Humanist Scholars: Les Dames des Roches." In *Women Writers of the Renaissance and Reformation.* Edited by Katharina Wilson, 232–259. Athens: University of Georgia Press, 1987.

Larsen, Anne R. "Marie de Cotteblanche: préfacière et traductrice de trois dialogues de Pierre Messie." In *Écrits de femmes à la Renaissance.* Edited by Anne R. Larsen and Colette H. Winn, 111–119. *Etudes littéraires* 27, no. 2 (1994).

Larsen, Anne R. "Nicole Estienne." In *Encyclopedia of Continental Women Writers.* Edited by Katharina M. Wilson. New York and London: Garland, 1991.

Larsen, Anne R. "Paradox and the Praise of Women: From Ortensio Lando and Charles Estienne to Marie de Romieu." *Sixteenth Century Journal* 2, no. 3 (1997): 759–774.

Larsen, Anne R. "Writing in the Margins: Marie de Cotteblanche's Preface to Her Translation of Pierre Messie (1566)." *Allegorica* 19 (1998): 95–103.

Larsen, Anne R., and Colette H. Winn, ed. *Renaissance Women Writers: French Texts/American Con-*

texts. Detroit, MI: Wayne State University Press, 1994.

Laurence, Anne. *Women in England, 1500–1760: A Social History.* New York: St. Martin's Press, 1994.

Lavaud, Jacques. "Quelques poésies oubliées de N. Estienne." *Revue du seizième siècle* 18 (1931): 341–351.

Lavocat, Françoise. "Introduction." In *Arcadia felice.* By Lucrezia Marinella. Florence: L. S. Olschki, 1998.

Lawner, Lynn. *Lives of the Courtesans: Portraits of the Renaissance.* New York: Rizzoli, 1987.

Lazard, Madeleine. "Deux sœurs ennemis, Marie Dentière et Jeanne de Jussie: Nonnes et Réformées à Genève." In *Les Réformes: enracinement socio-culturel.* Edited by Bernard Chevalier and Robert Sauzet, 239–249. Paris: Éditions de la Maisnie, 1985.

Lazard, Madeleine. *Images littéraires de la femme à la Renaissance.* Paris: PUF, 1985.

Lazard, Madeleine. *Les avenues de Fémynie: les femmes et la Renaissance.* Paris: Fayard, 2001.

Lazard, Madeleine. *Louise Labé.* Paris: Fayard, 2004.

Lazard, Madeleine, and J. Cubelier de Beynac, eds. *Marguerite de France, Reine de Navarre et son temps.* Agen, France: Presses de l'Imprimerie Coopérative, 1994.

Lecoq, Anne-Marie. *François Ier imaginaire. Symbolique et politique à l'aube de la Renaissance française.* Paris: Macula, 1987.

Lefèvre, Renato. *"Madama" Margarita d'Austria (1522–1586).* Rome: Newton Compton, 1986.

Leloup, Daniel. *Le château d'Anet. L'amour de Diane de Poitiers et d'Henri II.* Paris: Belin-Herscher, 2001.

Leonard, Amy. *Nails in the Wall: Catholic Nuns in Reformation Germany.* Chicago and London: University of Chicago Press, 2005.

Lesko Baker, Deborah. *The Subject of Desire: Petrarchan Poetics and the Female Voice in Louise Labé.* West Lafayette, IN: Purdue University Press, 1996.

Levack, Brian. *The Witch-Hunt in Early Modern Europe.* 2nd ed. London and New York: Longman, 1995.

Levin, Carole. *The Heart and Stomach of a King: Elizabeth I and the Politics of Sex and Power.* Philadelphia: University of Pennsylvania Press, 1994.

Levin, Carole. *The Reign of Elizabeth I.* New York: Palgrave, 2003.

Levin, Carole, Debra Barrett-Graves, Jo Eldridge Carney, W. M. Spellman, and Stephanie Witham. *Extraordinary Women of the Medieval and Renaissance World: A Biographical Dictionary.* Westport, CT: Greenwood Press, 2000.

Levin, Carole, and Patricia A. Sullivan, eds. *Political Rhetoric, Power, and Renaissance Women.* Albany: State University of New York Press, 1995.

Levin, Carole, and Jeanie Watson, eds. *Ambiguous Realities: Women in the Middle Ages and Renaissance.* Detroit: Wayne State University Press, 1987.

Lewalski, Barbara K. "Enacting Opposition: Queen Anne and the Subversion of Masquing." In *Writing Women in Jacobean England,* 15–43. Cambridge, MA: Harvard University Press, 1993.

Lewalski, Barbara Kiefer, "Imagining Female Community: Aemilia Lanyer's Poems." *Writing Women in Jacobean England.* Pages 212–241. Cambridge: Harvard University Press, 1993.

Lewalski, Barbara Kiefer. *Writing Women in Jacobean England.* Cambridge, MA: Harvard University Press, 1993.

Lindell, Robert. "Filippo, Stefano and Martha: New Findings on Chamber Music at the Imperial Court in the Second Half of the Sixteenth Century." In *Atti del XIV Congresso della Società Internazionale di Musicologia: Trasmissione et recezione delle forme di cultura musicale.* Edited by Angelo Pompilio, Donatella Restani, Lorenze Bianconi, and F. Albert Gallo, 869–875. Turin: Edizioni di Torino, 1990.

Lindley, David. *The Trials of Frances Howard: Fact and Fiction at the Court of King James.* New York: Routledge, 1993.

Lindsey, Charles, and Lorna Duffin. *Women and Work in Pre-Industrial England.* London: Croom Helm, 1985.

Lindsey, Karen. *Divorced, Beheaded, Survived: A Feminist Reinterpretation of the Wives of Henry VIII.* Reading, MA: Addison-Wesley, 1995.

Liss, Peggy K. *Isabel the Queen: Life and Times.* Oxford: Oxford University Press, 1992.

Littlehales, Margaret Mary. *Mary Ward: Pilgrim and Mystic, 1585–1645.* Kent, UK: Burns and Oates, 1998.

Loach, Jennifer. *Parliament and the Crown in the Reign of Mary Tudor.* Oxford: Clarendon Press; New York: Oxford University Press, 1986.

Loades, David. *Henry VIII and His Queens.* Gloucester, UK: Sutton, 2000.

Loades, David. *Mary Tudor: A Life.* Oxford and Cambridge, MA: Blackwell, 1989.

London Feminist History Group, ed. *The Sexual Dynamics of History.* London: Pluto Press, 1983.

Longhi, Roberto. "Gentileschi, padre e figlia." *L'Arte* 19 (1916): 245–314.

Longley, Katharine. *Saint Margaret Clitherow.* Wheathampstead: Anthony Clarke, 1986.

Looney, Dennis, and Deanna Shemek, ed. *Phaeton's Children: The Este Court and Its Culture in Early Modern Ferrara*. Tempe: Arizona State University Press, 2005.

Lougee, Carolyn C. *Le Paradis des Femmes: Women, Salons, and Social Stratification in Seventeenth-Century France*. Princeton, NJ: Princeton University Press, 1976.

Louviot, Louis. "Cabinet des Saines affections (1595)." In *Revue des Livres Anciens,* vol. 2. Edited by Fontemoing et C ie, 274–282. Paris: 1917.

Luzio, A. *La Galleria dei Gonzaga venduta all'Inghilterra nel 1627–28*. Rome: 1974.

Luzio, Alessandro. *I precettori di Isabella d'Este. Appunti e documenti per le nozze Renier-Campostrini*. Ancona, Italy: A. Gustavo Morelli, 1887.

Luzio, Alessandro, and Rodolfo Renier. "La cultura e le relazioni letterarie d'Isabella d'Este Gonzaga. 3. Gruppo lombardo." *Giornale storico delle letteratura italiana* 36 (1900): 325–349.

Luzio, Alessandro, and Rodolfo Renier. *Mantova e Urbino: Isabella d'Este ed Elisabetta Gonzaga nelle relazioni familiari e nelle vicende politiche*. Turin: Roux and Co., 1893.

Lynch, Michael, ed. *Mary Stewart in Three Kingdoms*. London: Blackwell, 1988.

Lyons, John, and Mary McKinley, eds. *Critical Tales: New Studies of the Heptameron and Early Modern Culture*. Philadelphia: University of Pennsylvania Press, 1993.

MacCaffrey, Wallace T. *Elizabeth I*. New York: Arnold, 1993.

MacDonald, Joyce Green. *Women and Race in Early Modern Texts*. Cambridge: Cambridge University Press, 2002.

Macfarlane, Alan. *Marriage and Love in England: Modes of Reproduction, 1300–1840*. London: Basil Blackwell, 1986.

Maclachlan, Elaine. "The Conversion of Chiara Matraini: The 1597 Rewriting of the *Rime* of 1555." *NEMLA Italian Studies* 16 (1992): 21–32.

Maclean, Ian. *The Renaissance Notion of Woman: A Study in the Fortunes of Scholasticism and Medical Science in European Intellectual Life*. Cambridge: Cambridge University Press, 1980.

Macneil, Anne. *Music and Women of the Commedia dell'Arte in the Late Sixteenth Century*. Oxford: Oxford University Press, 2003.

Magnusson, Lynne. "Widowhood and Linguistic Capital: The Rhetoric and Reception of Anne Bacon's Epistolary Advice." *English Literary Renaissance* 31, no. 1 (2001): 3–33.

Maguire, Yvonne. *The Women of the Medici*. London: Routledge, 1927.

Malcolmson, Cristina and Mihoko Suzuki, eds. *Debating Gender in Early Modern England, 1500–1700*. New York: Palgrave Macmillan, 2002.

Manca, Joseph. "Constantia et forteza: Eleonora d'Aragon's Famous Matrons." *Source: Notes in the History of Art* 19, no. 2 (Winter 2000): 13–20.

Manca, Joseph. "Isabella's Mother: Aspects of the Patronage of Eleonora d'Aragona." *Aurora: The Journal of the History of Art* 4 (2003): 79–94.

Mantese, Giovanni. "Per un profilo storico della poetessa vicentina Maddalena Campiglia: Aggiunte e rettifiche." *Archivio veneto* 81 (1967): 89–123.

Marchese, Vincenzo. "Di suor Plautilla Nelli, pittrice Domenicana, e di altre Religiose dello stesso Istituto, che coltivarono la pittura, la miniatura, la plastica, in Firenze, in Prato, in Lucca e altrove." In *Memorie dei più insigni pittori, scultori e architetti domenicani*. 2 vols. Vol. 2, 326–350. Bologna: G. Romagnoli Libr., 1878–1879.

Marczuk-Szwed, Barbara. "Le thème du péché et son expression poétique dans les *Oeuvres chrestiennes* de Gabrielle de Coignard et dans *Le mespris de la vie et consolation contre la mort* de J. B. Chassignet." *Zeszyty Naukowe Uniwersyteru Jagiellónskiego* 154 (1992): 51–71.

Margolin, Jean-Claude. "Georgette de Montenay, ses Emblèmes ou Devises Chrestiennes, et Anna Vischer." *Bibliothèque d'Humanisme et Renaissance* 51 (1989): 419–423.

Margolis, Nadia. *Joan of Arc in History, Literature and Film: A Select, Annotated Bibliography*. New York and London: Garland, 1990.

Marino, Virginia M. "A Curious Study in 'Parallel Lives': Louis XIV and the Abbé de Choisy." In *High Anxiety: Masculinity in Crisis in Early Modern France*. Edited by Kathleen Long, 165–182. Kirksville, MO: Truman State University Press, 2002.

Marland, Hilary, ed. *The Art of Midwifery: Early Modern Midwives in Europe*. London: Routledge, 1993.

Maroi, Lucia. *Laura Terracina napolitana del secolo XVI*. Naples: Francesco Perella, 1913.

Marsh, David. *Lucian and the Latins: Humor and Humanism in the Early Renaissance*. Ann Arbor: University of Michigan Press, 1998.

Marshall, Kimberly, ed. *Rediscovering the Muses: Women's Musical Traditions*. Boston: Northeastern University Press, 1993.

Marshall, Rosalind K. *Mary of Guise*. London: Collins, 1977.

Marshall, Sherrin, ed. *Women in Reformation and Counter-Reformation Europe: Public and Private Worlds*. Bloomington: Indiana University Press, 1989.

Martelli, Mario. "Lucrezia Tornabuoni." In *Les femmes écrivains en Italie au Moyen Âge et à la Renaissance.* Pages 51–86. Aix-en-Provence, France: Publications de l'Université de Provence, 1994.

Martin, Daniel. *Signes(s) d'Amante: L'agencement des Evvres de Louize Labé Lionnoize.* Paris: Honoré Champion, 1999.

Martin, Randall, ed. *Women Writers in Renaissance England.* London: Longman, 1997.

Martin, Wendy. "Anne Bradstreet." In *Dictionary of Literary Biography,* vol. 24. Edited by Emory Elliott. Detroit, MI: Gale Research Co., 1984.

Martines, Lauro. *Power and Imagination: City-States in Renaissance Italy.* New York: Random House, Vintage Books, 1979.

Martines, Lauro. *Strong Words: Writing and Social Strain in the Italian Renaissance.* Pages 64–69. Baltimore, MD: Johns Hopkins University Press, 2001.

Martini, Silvia, ed. *Margherita d'Austria (1522–1586): costruzioni politiche e diplomazia, tra corte Farnese e monarchia spagnola.* Rome: Bulzoni, 2003.

Martin-Ulrich, Claudie. *La "persona" de la princesse au XVIe siècle: personnage littéraire et personnage politique.* Paris: Champion, 2004.

Maschietto, Francesco Ludovico. "Elena Lucrezia Cornaro Piscopia." In *Elena Lucrezia Cornaro Piscopia. Prima donna laureata nel mondo. Terzo centenario del dottorato (1678–1978).* Edited by Maria Ildegarde Tonzig, 108–138. Vicenza: Università degli studi-Abbazia di S. Giustina (Padua), 1980.

Maschietto, Francesco Ludovico. *Elena Lucrezia Cornaro Piscopia (1646–1684). Prima donna laureata nel mondo.* Padua: Antenore, 1978.

Masson, Georgina. *Courtesans of the Italian Renaissance.* London: Secker and Warburg, 1975; New York: St. Martin's Press, 1976.

Matarasso, Pauline. *Queen's Mate: Three Women of Power in France on the Eve of the Renaissance.* Aldershot, UK: Ashgate, 2001.

Matter, E. Ann, and John Coakley, eds. *Creative Women in Medieval and Early Modern Italy: A Religious and Artistic Renaissance.* Philadelphia: University of Pennsylvania Press, 1994.

Matthews Griego, Sara. "Georgette de Montenay: A Different Voice in Sixteenth-Century Emblematics." *Renaissance Quarterly* 47 (1994): 793–871.

Matthieu-Castellani, Gisèle. *La quenouille et la lyre.* Paris: José Corti, 1998.

Mattingly, Garrett. *Catherine of Aragon.* Boston: Little, Brown and Company, 1941.

Maulde, M. de. *Anne de France, Duchesse de Bourbonnais, et Louis XII.* Paris: Imprimerie Nationale, 1885.

Mazzarella di Cerreto, A. "Laura Terracina." In *Biografia degli uomini illustri del Regno di Napoli.* Edited by D. Martuscelli. Naples: 1814.

McCartney, Elizabeth. "The King's Mother and Royal Prerogative in Early-Sixteenth-Century France." In *Medieval Queenships.* Edited by John Carmi Parsons. Stroud, UK: Sutton, 1994.

McClive, Cathy. "The Hidden Truths of the Belly: The Uncertainties of Pregnancy in Early Modern Europe." *Social History of Medicine* 15, no. 2 (2002): 209–227.

McClory, Robert. *Faithful Dissenters: Stories of Men and Women Who Loved and Changed the Church.* Maryknoll, NY: Orbis, 2000.

McColley, Diane Kelsey. *Milton's Eve.* Urbana: University of Illinois Press, 1983.

McGill, Kathleen. "Women and Performance: The Development of Improvisation by the Sixteenth-Century Commedia dell-Arte." *Theatre Journal* 43 (1991): 59–69.

McKinley, Mary B. "Les fortunes précaires de Marie Dentière au XVIe et au XIXe siècle." In *Royaume de fémynie. Pouvoirs, contraintes, espaces de liberté des femmes, de la Renaissance à la Fronde.* Edited by Kathleen Wilson-Chevalier and Éliane Viennot, 27–39. Paris: Champion, 1999.

McLaren, Angus. *A History of Contraception: From Antiquity to the Present Day.* Oxford: Blackwell, 1990.

McLaren, Angus. *Reproductive Rituals: The Perception of Fertility in England from the Sixteenth Century to the Nineteenth Century.* London: Methuen, 1984.

McLaren, Margaret Anne. "An Unknown Continent: Lady Mary Wroth's Forgotten Pastoral Drama, *Loves Victorie.*" In *Readings in Renaissance Women's Drama: Criticism, History and Performance, 1594–1998.* Edited by S. P. Cerasano and Marion Wynne-Davies, 219–233. London: Routledge, 1998.

Mclean, Ian. *Woman Triumphant: Feminism in French Literature, 1610–1652.* Oxford: Clarendon Press, 1977.

McManus, Clare. *Women on the Renaissance Stage: Anna of Denmark and Female Masquing in the Stuart Court (1590–1619).* Manchester, UK, and New York: Manchester University Press, 2002.

McTavish, Lianne. *Childbirth and the Display of Authority in Early Modern France.* Aldershot, UK: Ashgate, 2005.

Medioli, Francesca. "Alcune lettere autografe di Arcangela Tarabotti: autocensura e imagine di sé." *Rivista di storia e letteratura religiosa* 32 (1996): 135–141, 146–155.

Medioli, Francesco, Paola Vismara Chiappa, and Gabriella Zarri. "*De Monialibus* (secoli XVI-XVII-

XVIII)." *Revista di Storia e Letteratura Religiosa* 33 (1997): 643–715.

Melchior-Bonnet, Sabine. *Catherine de Bourbon, l'insoumise.* Paris: Nil Éditions, 1999.

Melchior-Bonnet, Sabine. *L'Art de vivre au temps de Diane de Poitiers.* Paris: Nil Éditions, 1998.

Mendelson, Sara. *The Mental World of Stuart Women: Three Studies.* Chapter 3. Amherst: University of Massachusetts Press, 1987.

Mendelson, Sara, and Patricia Crawford. *Women in Early Modern England.* Oxford: Clarendon Press, 1998.

Merlet, Agnès. *Artemisia.* Miramax Films, 1998.

Merrill, Robert Valentine, and Robert J. Clements. *Platonism in French Renaissance Poetry.* New York: New York University Press, 1957.

Merriman, Marcus. *The Rough Wooings: Mary Queen of Scots, 1541–51.* Edinburgh: Tuckwell, 2000.

Migiel, Marilyn, and Juliana Schiesari, eds. *Refiguring Woman: Gender Studies and the Italian Renaissance.* Ithaca, NY: Cornell University Press, 1991.

Milani, Marisa. "Da accusati a delatori: Veronica Franco e Francesco Barozzi." *Quaderni veneti* 26 (1996): 12–34.

Milani, Marisa. "Quattro donne fra i pavani." *Museum Patavinum* 1 (1983): 387–412.

Miller, Naomi J., and Gary Waller, eds. *Reading Mary Wroth: Representing Alternatives in Early Modern England.* Knoxville: University of Tennessee Press, 1991.

Minois, Georges. *Anne de Bretagne.* Paris: Fayard, 1999.

Minor, Andrew C., and Bonner Mitchell. *A Renaissance Entertainment: Festivities for the Marriage of Cosimo I, Duke of Florence in 1539.* Columbia: University of Missouri Press, 1968.

Mitterauer, Michael, and Reinhard Sieder. *The European Family: Patriarchy and Partnership from the Middle Ages to the Present.* Translated by Karla Oosterveen and Manfred Horzinger. Chicago: University of Chicago Press, 1982.

Monson, Craig A. *Disembodied Voices: Music and Culture in an Early Modern Italian Convent.* Berkeley: University of California Press, 1995.

Montella, Luigi. *Una Poetessa del rinascimento, Laura Terracina.* Salerno: Edisud-Salerno, ca. 1993.

Montmorand, Maxime de. *Une femme poète au XVIᵉ siècle. Anne de Graville, sa famille, sa vie, son œuvre, sa postérité.* Paris: A. Picard, 1917.

More, Sir Thomas. *The Last Letters of Thomas More.* Edited with and introduction by Alvaro de Silva. Grand Rapids, MI: William B. Eerdmans, 2001.

Morrill, John. "Devereux, Robert, Third Earl of Essex (1591–1646)." *Oxford Dictionary of National Biography.* Oxford: Oxford University Press, 2004. Available at: http://0-www.oxforddnb.com.library .unl.edu:80/view/article/7566. Accessed 21 Feb 2006.

Morsolin, Bernardo. *Maddalena Campiglia, poetessa vicentina del secolo XVI: Episodio biografico.* Vicenza: 1882.

Mulhauser, Ruth. *Maurice Scève.* Boston: Twayne Publishers, 1977.

Müller Catherine M. "Anne de Graville lectrice de 'Maistre Allain:' pour une récriture stratégique de la *Belle Dame sans Mercy.*" In *Lectrices d'Ancien Régime.* Edited by Isabelle Brouard-Arends, 231–241. Rennes: Presses Universitaires de Rennes, 2003.

Müller, Catherine M. "Éloges au féminin: la voix nouvelle d'Antoinette de Loynes (poétesse et traductrice) dans le *Tombeau* de Marguerite de Navarre (1551)." *Versants* 46 (La littérature au féminin, 2004): 49–63.

Müller, Catherine M. "*En donnant lieu à la main feminine:* lecture de quelques dialogues poétiques des XVᵉ et XVIᵉ siècles." In *De vrai humain entendement: études sur la littérature française à la fin du Moyen Age, hommage à Jacqueline Cerquiglini-Toulet.* Recherches et Rencontres, Vol. 21. Edited by Yasmina Foehr-Janssens and Jean-Yves Tilliette, 65–82. Geneva: Droz, 2004.

Müller, Catherine M. "Jeanne de la Font et Anne de Graville, translatrices de la Théséïde de Boccace au XVIᵉ siècle." *Les Femmes et traduction du Moyen Âge au XVIIIᵉ siècle.* Edited by Jean-Philippe Beaulieu. Montréal: Presses de l'Université d'Ottawa, 2004.

Müller, Catherine M. "Monstrum inter libros: la perception de la femme lettrée chez les humanistes de la Renaissance française." *Actes du colloque international "Livres et lectures des femmes entre moyen âge et Renaissance" de Lille (24–26 mai 2004).* Forthcoming.

Murk-Jansen, Saskia. *Brides in the Desert: The Spirituality of the Beguines.* Maryknoll, NY: Orbis Books, 1998.

Murphy, Caroline P. *Lavinia Fontana: A Painter and Her Patrons in Sixteenth-Century Bologna.* New Haven, CT: Yale University Press, 2003.

Murray, Mary. *The Law of the Father: Patriarchy in the Transition from Feudalism to Capitalism.* London: Routledge, 1995.

Mutini, C. In *L'autore e l'opera.* Rome: Bulzoni, 1973.

Nelson, Jonathan, ed. *Suor Plautilla Nelli (1523–1588): The First Woman Painter of Florence.* Fiesole: Cadmo, 2000.

Néret, Jean-Alexis. *Claude de France femme de François Ier—1499–1524*. Paris: Les Éditions de France, 1942.

Newbigin, Nerida. "Agata, Apollonia, and Other Martyred Virgins: Did Florentines Really See These Plays Performed?" In *European Medieval Drama 1997*. Edited by Sydney Higgins, 175–197. Camerino: Centro Audiovisivi e Stampa Universitá di Camerino, 1998.

Niccolini, Benedetto. "Una Calvanista Napoletana Isabella Bresegna." In *Ideali e passioni nell'Italia religiosa del Cinquecento*. Pages 5–23. Bologna: Libreria Antiquaria Palmaverde, 1962.

Nieto, José C. *Juan de Valdés and the Origins of the Spanish and Italian Reformation*. Geneva: Droz, 1970.

Noffke, Suzanne. *Catherine of Siena: Vision Through a Distant Eye*. Collegeville, MN: Liturgical Press/Michael Glazier, 1996.

Noiset, Marie-Thérèse. *Marie de Gournay et son œuvre*. Namur: Editions Namuroises, Presses Universitaires de Namur, 2004.

Nolhac, Pierre de. "Le premier salon littéraire de Paris." *La Revue universelle* 5 (1 June 1921): 537–552.

Norris, Pamela. *Eve: A Biography*. New York: New York University Press, 1999.

Nottington, Ruth. *In the Shadow of the Throne: The Lady Arbella Stuart*. London and Chester Springs, PA: Peter Owen Publishers, 2002.

Novati, Francesco. "Donne tipografe nel Cinquecento." *Il libro e la stampa* 7 (1907): 41–49.

Nulli, Siro Attilio. *Giulia Gonzaga*. Milan: Fratelli Treves, 1938.

Nummedal, Tara. "Alchemical Reproduction and the Career of Anna Maria Zieglerin." *Ambix* 48 (July 2001): 56–68.

O'Donnell, Anne M. "Contemporary Women in the Letters of Erasmus." *Erasmus of Rotterdam Society Yearbook* 9 (1989): 34–72.

O'Donnell, Mary Ann. *Aphra Behn: An Annotated Bibliography of Primary and Secondary Sources*. 2nd ed. Burlington, VT: Ashgate, 2004.

Ogilvie, Sheilagh C. *A Bitter Living: Women, Markets and Social Capital in Early Modern Germany*. Oxford: Oxford University Press, 2003.

Oliva, Mario. *Giulia Gonzaga Colonna: tra rinascimento e controriforma*. Milan: Mursia, 1985.

Olson, Todd. "'La Femme à la Puce et la Puce à l'Oreille': Catherine des Roches and the Poetics of Sexual Resistance in Sixteenth-Century French Poetry." *Journal of Medieval and Early Modern Studies* 32, no. 2 (2002): 327–342.

Origo, Iris. *Merchant of Prato*. Boston: David R. Godine, 1986. (Originally published in New York: Alfred A. Knopf, 1957.)

Orth, Myra D. "Dedicating Women: Manuscript Culture in the French Renaissance, and the Case of Catherine d'Amboise and Anne de Graville." *Journal of Early Book Society for the Study of Manuscript and Printing History* 1, no. 1 (1997): 17–47.

Otis, Leah. *Prostitution in Medieval Society: The History of an Urban Institution in Languedoc*. Chicago: University of Chicago Press, 1985.

Ottaway, S., L. A. Botelho, and K. Kittredge, eds. *Power and Poverty: Old Age in the Pre-Industrial Past*. Westport, CT: Greenwood Press, 2002.

Pagden, Sylvia Ferino. *Sofonisba Anguissola: A Renaissance Woman*. Exhibition catalog. Washington, DC: National Museum of Women in the Arts, 1995.

Panizza, Letizia, ed. *Women in Italian Renaissance Culture and Society*. Oxford: European Humanities Research Center, 2000.

Panizza, Letizia, and Sharon Wood, eds. *A History of Women's Writing in Italy*. Cambridge: Cambridge University Press, 2000.

Paolin, Giovanna. "L'eterodossia nel monastero delle Clarisse di Udine nella seconda metà del '500." *Collectanea franciscana* 50 (1980): 107–167.

Parigino, Giuseppe Vittorio. *Il Tesoro del Principe: funzione pubblica e privata del patrimonio della famiglia Medici nel Cinquecento*. Florence: Olschki, 1999.

Parker, Deborah. "Women in the Book Trade in Italy, 1475–1620." *Renaissance Quarterly* 49 (1996): 509–541.

Parker, Geoffrey. *The Dutch Revolt*. New York and London: Penguin, 1990.

Parker, Holt. "Costanza Varano (1426–1447): Latin as an Instrument of State." In *Women Writing Latin from Roman Antiquity to Early Modern Europe*. 3 vols. Vol. 3. Edited by Laurie Churchill et al., 31–54. New York: Routledge, 2002.

Parker, Holt. "Sappho Schoolmistress." In *Re-Reading Sappho: Reception and Transmission*. Edited by Ellen Greene, 146–183. Berkeley: University of Calfornia Press, 1996.

Pasolini, Pier Desiderio. *Caterina Sforza*. 3 vols. Rome: Loescher, 1893.

Patai, Raphael. "Maria the Jewess—Founding Mother of Alchemy." *Ambix* 29 (November 1982): 177–197.

Pecchiai, Pio. *Donne del Rinascimento in Roma. Imperia. Lucrezia figlia d'Imperia. La misteriosa Fiammetta*. Padua: CEDAM, 1958.

Pecchiai, Pio. *Roma nel Cinquecento*. Bologna: Licinio, 1948.

Pélicier, P. *Essai sur le Gouvernement de la Dame de Beaujeu: 1483–1491.* Chartres: Imprimerie Edouard Garnier, 1882.

Pelling, M., and R. M. Smith. *Life, Death, and the Elderly: Historical Perspectives.* London: Routledge, 1991.

Pendle, Karin, ed. *Women and Music: A History.* Bloomington: Indiana University Press, 1991.

Perkins, Wendy. *Midwifery and Medicine in Early Modern France: Louise Bourgeois.* Exeter: University of Exeter Press, 1996.

Perlingieri, Ilya Sandra. *Sofonisba Anguissola: The First Great Woman Artist of the Renaissance.* New York: Rizzoli, 1992.

Pernetti, Jacques. *Recherches pour servir à l'histoire de Lyon ou Les Lyonnois dignes de mémoire.* 2 vols. Lyon: Chez les frères Duplain, libraires, 1757.

Perrone, Carlachiara. *"So che donna ama donna": La Calisa di Maddalena Campiglia.* Galatina: Congedo, 1996. (Includes an edition of *Calisa.*)

Perry, Maria. *Sisters to the King: The Tumultuous Lives of Henry VIII's Sisters, Margaret of Scotland and Mary of France.* New York: St. Martin's Press, 1999.

Pesenti, Giovanni. "Alessandra Scala: una figurina di rinascenza fiorentina." *Giornale storico della letteratura italiana* 85 (1925): 241–267.

Peters, Christine. *Patterns of Piety: Women, Gender, and Religion in Late Medieval and Reformation England.* Cambridge and New York: Cambridge University Press, 2003.

Petrettini, Maria. *Vita di Cassandra Fedele.* Venice: 1814. (Reprinted in 1842.)

Peyronel Rambaldi, Susanna. "Olimpia Morata e Celio Secondo Curione: Un dialogo dell'Umanesimo cristiano." In *La formazione storica della alterità: Studi di storia della tolleranza nell'età moderna offerti a Antonio Rotondò.* 3 vols. Organized by Henry Méchoulan, Richard H. Popkin, Giuseppe Ricuperati, and Luisa Simonutti. Vol. 1, *Secolo 16,* 93–133. Florence: Olschki, 2001.

Philippy, Patricia. "The Maid's Lawful Liberty: Service, the Household, and 'Mother B' in Isabella Whitney's *Sweet Nosegay." Modern Philology* 95 (1997–1998): 439–462.

Phillippy, Patricia. *Painting Women: Cosmetics, Canvases, and Early Modern Culture.* Baltimore, MD: Johns Hopkins University Press, 2006.

Piejus, Marie-Françoise. "La première anthologie de poèmes féminins: L'écriture filtrée et orientée." In *Le pouvoir et la plume. Incitations, contrôle et répression dans l'Italie du XVI siècle.* Pages 193–213. Paris: Université de la Sorbonne Nouvelle, 1982.

Pierattini, Giovanna. *Suor Plautilla Nelli pittrice domenicana.* Florence: 1938. (Offprint, with continuous numeration, from *Memorie domenicane,* 55, 1938, pp. 49–53, 82–85, 168–171, 221–227, 292–297.)

Pinessi, Orietta. *Sofonisba Anguissola: un "pittore" alla corte di Filippo II.* Milan: Selene, 1998.

Piovesan, Luciana. *Storia di Asolo: Il Barco della Regina Cornaro ad Altivole.* Asolo: 1980.

Piperno, Franco. "Diplomacy and Musical Patronage: Virginia, Guidubaldo II, Massimiliano II, 'Lo Streggino' and Others." *Early Music History* 18 (1999): 259–285.

Plebani, Elenora. *I Tornabuoni: una famiglia fiorentina alla fine del medioevo.* Milan: Franco Angeli, 2002.

Plowden, Alison. *Henrietta Maria: Charles I's Indomitable Queen.* Gloucestershire, UK: Sutton, 2001.

Plowden, Alison. *Lady Jane Grey: Nine Days Queen.* Phoenix Mill, UK: Sutton, 2003.

Plowdon, Alison. *Tudor Women: Queens and Commoners.* New York: Atheneum, 1979.

Poirier, Guy. *L'Homosexualité dans l'imaginaire de la Renaissance.* Paris: Champion, 1996.

Pollock, Griselda. "Review of Mary Garrard's *Artemisia Gentileschi." Art Bulletin* 72, no. 3 (1990): 499–505.

Pollock, Linda. "Childbearing and Female Bonding in Early Modern England." *Social History* 22, 3 (1997): 286–306.

Pollock, Linda. *With Faith and Physic: The Life of a Tudor Gentlewoman Lady Grace Mildmay, 1552–1620.* London: Collins and Brown, 1993; New York: St. Martin's Press, 1995.

Pommerol, Madame Michel Jullien de. *Albert de Gondi, Maréchal de Retz.* Geneva: 1953.

Porter, Roy, and Mikulás Teich, eds. *Sexual Knowledge, Sexual Science: The History of Attitudes to Sexuality.* Cambridge: Cambridge University Press, 1994.

Poss, Richard. "Veronica Gambara: A Renaissance Gentildonna." In *Women Writers of the Renaissance and Reformation.* Edited by Katharina M. Wilson, 47–65. Athens: University of Georgia Press, 1987.

Power, Eileen. *Medieval English Nunneries, c. 1275–1535.* New York: Biblo and Tannen, 1964.

Pradel, Pierre. *Anne de France, 1461–1522.* Paris: Publisud, 1986.

Prizer, William F. "Una 'Virtù Molto Conveniente a Madonne': Isabella d'Este as a Musician." *The Journal of Musicology* 17, no. 1 (1999): 10–49.

Prosperi, Adriano. *L'eresia del Libro grande: Storia di Giorgio Siculo e della sua setta.* Milan: Feltrinelli, 2000.

Puaux, Anne. *Madama, fille de Charles Quint: régente des Pays-Bas.* Paris: Payot, 1987.

Purkiss, Diane. *The Witch in History: Early Modern and Twentieth-Century Representations.* London and New York: Routledge, 1996.

Pynsent, Mathilde. *The Life of Helen Lucretia Cornaro Piscopia, Oblate of the Order of St. Benedict and Doctor of the University of Padua.* Rome: St. Benedict's, 1896.

Quentin Bauchart, Ernest. *Les Femmes bibliophiles de France (XVIᵉ, XVIIᵉ, XVIIIᵉ siècles).* 2 vols. 2: 380. Geneva: Slatkine Reprints, 1993. (A list of Anne de Graville's own books is on p. 385. Originally printed in Paris: D. Morgand, 1886.)

Quilligan, Maureen. *The Allegory of Female Authority: Christine de Pizan's Cité des Dames.* Ithaca, NY: Cornell University Press, 1991.

Quondam, Amedeo. *Le "carte messaggiere": Rettorica e modelli di comunicazione epistolare: per un indice dei libri di lettere del Cinquecento.* Rome: Bolzoni, 1981.

Rabil, Albert, Jr. *Laura Cereta: Quattrocento Humanist.* Binghamton, NY: Medieval and Renaissance Texts and Studies, 1981.

Rabitti, Giovanna. "Le lettere di Chiara Matraini tra pubblico e privato." In *Per lettera. La scrittura epistolare femminile.* Edited by Gabriella Zarri, 209–234. Rome: Viella, 1999.

Rabitti, Giovanna, "Lyric Poetry, 1500–1650." In *A History of Women's Writing in Italy.* Translated by Abigail Brundin. Edited by Letizia Panizza and Sharon Wood, 37–42. Cambridge: Cambridge University Press, 2000.

Rachet, Guy. *Catherine Sforza: la dame de Forlì.* Paris: Denoël, 1987.

Randall, Catharine. "A Surplus of Significance: Hermaphrodites in Early Modern France." *French Forum* 19 (1994): 17–35.

Randi, Aldo. *Caterina Sforza.* Milan: Ceschina, 1951.

Ranft, Patricia. *Women and the Religious Life in Premodern Europe.* New York: St. Martin's Press, 1996.

Rankin, Alisha. "Medicine for the Uncommon Woman: Experience, Experiment, and Exchange in Early Modern Germany." Ph.D. dissertation, Harvard University, 2005.

Reardon, Colleen. *Holy Concord Within Sacred Walls: Nuns and Music in Siena, 1575–1700.* Oxford: Oxford University Press, 2002.

Reid, Jonathan A. *King's Sister, Queen of Dissent: Marguerite of Navarre (1492–1549) and Her Evangelical Network.* Ann Arbor: University of Michigan Press, 2001.

Reiss, Sheryl E., and David G. Wilkins, eds. *Beyond Isabella: Secular Women Patrons of Art in Renaissance Italy.* Kirksville, MO: Truman State University Press, 2001.

Renouard, Antoine-Augustin. *Annales de l'imprimerie des Estienne ou Histoire de la famille des Estienne et de ses éditions.* Geneva: Slatkine, 1971. (Originally published in Paris: J. Renouard, 1843.)

Rex, Richard. *Henry VIII and the English Reformation.* New York: St. Martin's Press, 1993.

Reynolds, E. E. *Margaret Roper: Eldest Daughter of St. Thomas More.* New York: Kennedy, 1960.

Reynolds-Cornell, Régine. "*Les Misères de la femme mariée:* Another Look at Nicole Liébault and a Few Questions About the Woes of the Married Woman." *BHR* 64 (2002): 37–54.

Reynolds-Cornell, Régine. "Reflets d'une époque, les Devises ou Emblemes Chrestiennes de Georgette de Montenay." *Bibliothèque d'Humanisme et Renaissance* 48 (1986): 373–386.

Reynolds-Cornell, Régine. *Witnessing an Era, Georgette de Montenay and the Emblèmes ou Devises Chrestiennes.* Birmingham, UK: Summa, 1987.

Rickard, Peter. "Le rôle des traducteurs." In *La langue française au seizième siècle. Etude suivie de textes,* 6–14. Cambridge: Cambridge University Press, 1968.

Riddle, John M. *Contraception and Abortion from the Ancient World to the Renaissance.* Cambridge, MA: Harvard University Press, 1992.

Riddle, John M. *Eve's Herbs: A History of Contraception and Abortion in the West.* Cambridge, MA: Harvard University Press, 1997.

Ridley, Jasper. *Bloody Mary's Martyrs: The Story of England's Terror.* New York: Carroll and Graf, 2001.

Rigolot, François. "Clément Marot Imports into French the Petrarchan Sonnet." *A New History of French Literature.* Edited by Denis Hollier, 171–174. Cambridge: Harvard University Press, 1989.

Ritter, Raymond. *Catherine de Bourbon 1559–1604: La soeur d'Henri IV.* Paris: J. Touzot, 1985.

Rigolot, François. *Louise Labé Lyonnaise, ou: La Renaissance au féminin.* Paris: Champion, 1997.

Robin, Diana. "Cassandra Fedele's *Epistolae* (1488–1477): Biography as Effacement." In *The Rhetorics of Life-Writing in Early Modern Europe: Forms of Biography from Cassandra Fedele to Louis XIV.* Edited by T. Mayer and D. Woolf. Ann Arbor: University of Michigan Press, 1995, pages 187–203.

Robin, Diana. "Courtesans, Celebrity, and Print Culture in Renaissance Venice: Tullia d'Aragona, Gaspara Stampa, and Veronica Franco." In *Italian Women and the City.* Edited by Janet Smarr and Daria Valentini. Fairleigh Dickinson University Press, 2003.

Robin, Diana. "Culture, Imperialism, and Humanist Criticism in the Italian City-States." In *The Cam-*

bridge History of Literary Criticism, Volume 3: The Renaissance. 1500–1700. Edited by Glyn P. Norton, 355–363. Cambridge: Cambridge University Press, 1999.

Robin, Diana. Filelfo in Milan: Writings, 1451–1477. Princeton, NJ: Princeton University Press, 1991.

Robin, Diana. "Humanism and Feminism in Laura Cereta's Public Letters." In Women in Italian Renaissance Culture and Society. Edited by Letizia Panizza, 368–384. Oxford: Legenda, University of Oxford, 2000.

Robin, Diana. Publishing Women. Salons, the Presses, and the Counter-Reformation in Sixteenth-Century Italy. Chicago: University of Chicago Press, 2007.

Robin, Diana. "Space, Woman, and Renaissance Discourse." In Sex and Gender in Medieval and Renaissance Texts: The Latin Tradition. Edited by Barbara K. Gold, Paul Allen Miller, Charles Platter, 165–187. Albany: State University of New York Press, 1997.

Robin, Diana. "Women and Humanism (Italy); "Querelle des Femmes: Renaissance (Italy)." In The Feminist Encyclopedia of Italian Literature. Edited by Rinaldina Russell, 153–157; 270–273.

Rocke, Michael. Forbidden Friendships: Homosexuality and Male Culture in Renaissance Florence. New York: Oxford University Press, 1996.

Rodini, Elizabeth, and Elissa B. Weaver. A Well-Fashioned Image: Clothing and Costume in European Art, 1500–1850. Chicago: The David and Alfred Smart Museum of Art, University of Chicago, 2002.

Roelker, Nancy L. Queen of Navarre: Jeanne d'Albret, 1528–1572. Cambridge, MA: Belknap Press of Harvard University Press, 1968.

Roelker, Nancy L. "The Role of Noblewomen in the French Reformation." Archiv für Reformationsgeschichte 48 (1972): 168–195.

Roelker, Nancy Lyman. "The Appeal of Calvinism to French Noblewomen in the Sixteenth Century." Journal of Interdisciplinary History 2 (Spring 1972): 391–418.

Roper, Louis H. "Unmasquing the Connections between Jacobean Politics and Policy: The Circle of Anna of Denmark and the Beginning of the English Empire, 1614–18." In High and Mighty Queens of Early Modern England. Edited by Debra Barrett-Graves, Jo Eldridge Carney, and Carole Levin, 45–59. New York: Palgrave Macmillan, 2003.

Roper, Lyndal. Oedipus and the Devil: Witchcraft, Sexuality and Religion in Early Modern Europe. London and New York: Routledge, 1994.

Rosand, Ellen. "Barbara Strozzi, 'virtuosissima cantatrice': The Composer's Voice." Journal of the American Musicological Society 31, no. 2 (1978): 241–281.

Rosand, Ellen. "The Voice of Barbara Strozzi." In Women Making Music. Edited by Jane Bowers and Judith Tick. Urbana: University of Illinois Press, 1986.

Rosand, Ellen, and David Rosand. " 'Barbara di Santa Sofia' and 'Il Prete Genovese': On the Identity of a Portrait by Bernardo Strozzi." The Art Bulletin 63, no. 2 (1981): 249–258.

Rose, Mary Beth. Women in the Middle Ages and Renaissance: Literary and Historical Perspectives. Syracuse, NY: Syracuse University Press, 1986.

Rosenberg, Charles. The Este Monuments and Urban Development in Renaissance Ferrara. Cambridge: Cambridge University Press, 1997.

Rosenthal, J. T. Old Age in Late Medieval England. Philadelphia: University of Pennsylvania Press, 1996.

Rosenthal, Margaret F. The Honest Courtesan. Veronica Franco, Citizen and Writer in Sixteenth-Century Venice. With a foreword by Catharine R. Stimpson. Chicago: University of Chicago Press, 1992.

Ross, Josephine. The Winter Queen: The Story of Elizabeth Stuart. New York: St. Martin's Press, 1979.

Rossiaud, Jacques. Medieval Prostitution. Trans. Lydia Cochrane. London: Blackwell, 1988.

Roth, Henri. "Une femme auteur du 16e siècle: Jeanne de Jussie." Revue du Vieux Genève 19 (1989): 5–13.

Rothstein, Marian. "The Mutations of the Androgyne: Its Functions in Early Modern France." Sixteenth Century Journal 34, no. 2 (2003): 409–437.

Rothstein, Marian. "Pernette du Guillet (1520?–1545)." French Women Writers. Pages 143–152. Lincoln, NE, and London: University of Nebraska Press, 1994.

Rouget, Francois. "De la sage-femme à la femme sage: Réfléxion et réfléxivité dans les Observations de Louise Boursier." Papers on French Seventeenth-Century Literature 25, no. 49 (1998): 483–496.

Rouse, M. A., and R. H. Rouse. Cartolai, Illuminators and Printers in Fifteenth-Century Italy. Berkeley: University of California Press, 1988.

Routh, E. M. G. Lady Margaret: A Memoir of Lady Margaret Beaufort, Countess of Richmond and Derby, Mother of Henry VII. Oxford: Oxford University Press, 1924.

Rublack, Ulinka. "Pregnancy, Childbirth and the Female Body in Early Modern Germany." Past and Present 150 (1996): 84–110.

Ruggiero, Guido. *Violence in Early Renaissance Venice.* New Brunswick, NJ: Rutgers University Press, 1980.

Russell, H. Diane, with Bernadine Barnes. *Eva/Ave: Woman in Renaissance and Baroque Prints.* Washington, DC: National Gallery of Art, 1990.

Russell, Rinaldina. "Chiara Matraini nella tradizione lirica femminile." *Forum Italicum* 34, no. 2 (Fall 2000): 415–427.

Russell, Rinaldina, "Intenzionalità artistica della 'disperata.'" In *Generi Poetici Medievali: Modelli e funzioni letterarie.* Pages 163–182. Naples: SEN, 1982.

Russell, Rinaldina. "The Mind's Pursuit of the Divine: A Survey of Secular and Religious Themes in Vittoria Colonna's Sonnets." *Forum Italicum* 26 (1992): 14–27.

Russell, Rinaldina, ed. *The Feminist Encyclopedia of Italian Literature.* Westport, CT, and London: Greenwood Press, 1997.

Russell, Rinaldina, ed. *Italian Women Writers. A Biobibliographical Sourcebook.* Westport, CT, and London: Greenwood Press, 1994.

Rütten, Thomas. "Receptions of the Hippocratic Oath in the Renaissance: The Prohibition of Abortion as a Case Study in Reception." *Journal of the History of Medicine and Allied Sciences* 51, no. 4 (1996): 456–483.

Ryley, M. Beresford. *Queens of the Renaissance.* Williamstown, MA: Corner House Publishers, 1982.

Saaler, Mary. *Anne of Cleves: Fourth Wife of Henry VIII.* London: Rubicon Press, 1995.

Sadie, Stanley, ed. *The New Grove Dictionary of Music and Musicians.* 29 vols. 2nd ed. London: Macmillan, 2001.

Salies, Pierre. "Gabrielle de Coignard: Poétesse toulousaine du XVIe siècle." *Archistra* 79 (March–April 1987): 33–43.

Salmon, Vivian. "Bathsua Makin: A Pioneer Linguist and Feminist in Seventeenth-Century England." In *Neuere Forschungen zur Wortbildung und Histriographie der Linguistik: Festgabe für Herbert E. Brekle.* Edited by Brigitte Asbach-Schnitker and Johannes Rogenhofer, 303–318. Tübingen: Gunter Narr Verlag, 1987.

San Juan, Rose Marie. "The Court Lady's Dilemma: Isabella d'Este and Art Collecting in the Renaissance." *Oxford Art Journal* 14, no. 1 (1991): 67–78.

Sankovitch, Tilde. *French Women Writers and the Book: Myths of Access and Desire.* Syracuse, NY: Syracuse University Press, 1988.

Sankovitch, Tilde. "Translation (Renaissance)." In *The Feminist Encyclopedia of French Literature.* Edited by Eva Martin Sartori, 532–535. London and Westport, CT: Greenwood Press, 1999.

Santoro, Caterina. *Gli Sforza.* Milan: Dall'Oglio, 1968.

Sartori, Diana. "Maddalena Campiglia." In *Le stanze ritrovate: Antologia di scrittrici venete dal Quattrocento al Novecento.* Edited by Antonia Arslan, Adriana Chemello, and Gilberto Pizzamiglio, 57–68. Mirano-Venice: 1991.

Saslow, James. *Ganymede in the Renaissance: Homosexuality in Art and Society.* New Haven, CT: Yale University Press, 1986.

Saulnier, Verdun-Louis. "Etude sur Pernette du Guillet et ses *Rymes.*" *Bibliothèque d'Humanisme et de Renaissance* 4 (1944): 7–119.

Scarabello, G. "Per una storia della prostituzione a Venezia tra il XIII e il XVIII sec." *Studi veneziani* 47 (2004): 15–101, especially 57–61.

Scaraffia, Lucetta, and Gabriella Zarri, eds. *Women and Faith: Catholic Religious Life in Italy from Late Antiquity to the Present.* Cambridge, MA: Harvard University Press, 1999.

Scarisbrick, J. J. *Henry VIII.* Berkeley: University of California Press, 1968.

Scarpari, Gianfranco. *Le ville venete.* Rome: Newton-Compton Editori, 1980.

Schaefer, Jean Owens. "A Note on the Iconography of a Medal of Lavinia Fontana." *Journal of the Warburg and Courtauld Institutes* 47 (1984): 232–234.

Schiavon, Antonia. "Per la biografia di Veronica Franco. Nuovi docuemnti." *Atti dell'Istituto veneto di Scienze, lettere ed Arti* 137 (1978–1979): 243–256.

Schleiner, Louise. *Tudor & Stuart Women Writers.* Bloomington: Indiana University Press, 1994.

Schleiner, Winfred. "Male Cross-Dressing and Transvestism in Renaissance Romances." *Sixteenth Century Journal* 19, no. 4 (1988): 605–619.

Schotel, G. D. J. *Anna Maria van Schurman.* Hertogenbosch, Netherlands: Gebroders Muller, 1853.

Schutte, Anne Jacobson. *Aspiring Saints: Pretense of Holiness, Inquisition, and Gender in the Republic of Venice, 1618–1750.* Baltimore, MD: Johns Hopkins University Press, 2001.

Schutte, Anne Jacobson. "Irene di Spilimbergo: The Image of a Creative Woman in Late Renaissance Italy." *Renaissance Quarterly* 1 (1991): 42–61.

Schutte, Anne Jacobson, Silvana Seidel Menchi, and Thomas Kuehn, eds. *Time, Space, and Women's Lives in Early Modern Europe.* Sixteenth Century Essays and Studies, 57. Kirksville, MO: Truman State University Press, 2001.

Schwartz, Kathryn. *Tough Love: Amazon Encounters in the English Renaissance.* Durham, NC: Duke University Press, 2000.

Scott, Joan Wallach. *Gender and the Politics of History.* Rev. ed. New York: Columbia University Press, 1999.

Scott, Karen. "*Io Catarina:* Ecclesastical Politics and Oral Culture in the Letters of Catherine of Siena." In *Dear Sister: Medieval Women and the Epistolary Genre.* Edited by Karen Cherewatuk and Ulrike Wiethaus, 87–121. Philadelphia: University of Pennsylvania Press, 1993.

Sedgwick, Eve Kosofsky. *Between Men: English Literature and Male Homosocial Desire.* New York: Columbia University Press, 1985.

Seidel Menchi, Silvana. *Erasmo in Italia, 1520–1580.* Turin: Bollati Boringhieri, 1987.

Seiler, Mary Hilarine. *Anne de Marquets, poétesse religieuse du XVIe siècle.* Washington, DC: Catholic University of America, 1931; New York: AMS Press, 1969.

Seward, Desmond. *The Wars of the Roses: Through the Lives of Five Men and Women of the Fifteenth Century.* London: Constable; New York: Viking, 1995.

Sharhar, S. *Growing Old in the Middle Ages.* London: Routledge, 1995.

Sharpe, Pamela. *Adapting to Capitalism: Working Women in the English Economy, 1700–1850.* New York: St. Martin's Press, 1996.

Shemek, Deanna. "Getting a Word in Edgewise: Laura Terracina's *Discorsi* on the Orlando furioso." In *Ladies Errant Wayward Women and Social Order in Early Modern Italy,* 126–157. Durham, NC, and London: Duke University Press, 1998.

Shemek, Deanna. "In Continuous Expectation: Isabella d'Este's Epistolary Desire." In *Phaethon's Children: The Este Court and Its Culture in Early Modern Italy.* Edited by Dennis Looney and Deanna Shemek, 269–300. Tempe: Arizona Medieval and Renaissance Texts and Studies, 2005.

Shemek, Deanna. "Isabella d'Este and the Properties of Persuasion." In *Form and Persuasion in Early Modern Women's Letters Across Europe.* Edited by Ann Crabb and Jane Couchman, 108–134. Brookfield, VT: Ashgate, 2005.

Shemek, Deanna. *Ladies Errant: Wayward Women and Social Order in Early Modern Italy.* Durham, NC, and London: Duke University Press, 1998.

Shemek, Deanna. " 'Mi mostrano a dito tutti quanti': Disease, Deixis, and Disfiguration in the *Lamento di una cortigiana ferrarese.*" In *Italiana 11: Essays on Gender, Literature, and Aesthetics in the Italian Renaissance, in Honor of Robert J. Rodini.* Edited by Paul A. Ferrara, Eugenio Giusti, and Jane Tylus, 49–64. Lafayette, IN: Bordighera, 2004.

Shepard, Alexandra. *Meanings of Manhood in Early Modern England.* Oxford: Oxford University Press, 2003.

Shepherd, Simon. *Amazons and Warrior Women: Varieties of Feminism in Seventeenth-Century Drama.* New York: St. Martin's Press, 1981.

Siegfried, Brandie. "Queen to Queen at Check: Grace O'Malley, Elizabeth Tudor, and the Discourse of Majesty in the State Papers of Ireland." In *Elizabeth I: Always Her Own Free Woman.* Edited by Carole Levin, Jo Eldridge Carney, and Debra Barrett-Graves, 149–175. Aldershot, UK: Ashgate, 2003.

Simon, Linda. *Of Virtue Rare: Margaret Beaufort, Matriarch of the House of Tudor.* Boston: Houghton Mifflin, 1982.

Simons, Walter. *Cities of Ladies: Beguine Communities in the Medieval Low Countries, 1200–1565.* Philadelphia: University of Pennsylvania Press, 2001.

Skenazi, Cynthia. "Marie Dentière et la prédication des femmes." *Renaissance et Réforme* 21, no. 1 (1997): 5–18.

Slim, H. Colin. "Paintings of Lady Concerts and the Transmission of 'Jouissance vous donneray.'" In *Painting Music in the Sixteenth Century.* Vol. 7. Aldershot, UK: Ashgate, 2002.

Smarr, Janet Levarie. "A Dialogue of Dialogues: Tullia d'Aragona and Sperone Speroni." *Modern Language Notes* 113 (1998): 204–212.

Smarr, Janet Levarie. *Joining the Conversation: Dialogues by Renaissance Women.* Ann Arbor: University of Michigan Press, 2005.

Smarr, Janet Levarie, and Daria Valentini, eds. *Italian Women and the City.* Madison, NJ: Fairleigh Dickinson University Press: Associated University Presses, 2003.

Smith, Bruce. *Shakespeare and Masculinity.* Oxford: Oxford University Press, 2000.

Snyder, C. Arnold, and Linda A. Huebert Hecht. *Profiles of Anabaptist Women: Sixteenth-Century Reforming Pioneers.* Waterloo, ON: Wilfrid Laurier University Press, 1996.

Snyder, Jon. *Writing the Scene of Speaking: Theories of Dialogue in the Late Italian Renaissance.* Stanford, CA: Stanford University Press, 1989.

Sobol, Dava. *Galileo's Daughter.* New York and London: Penguin, 2000.

Solterer, Helen. *The Master and Minerva: Disputing Women in French Medieval Culture.* Berkeley: University of California Press, 1995.

Somerset, Anne. *Unnatural Murder: Poison at the Court of James I.* London: Weidenfeld and Nicolson, 1997.

Sommers, Paula. *Celestial Ladders: Readings in Marguerite de Navarre's Poetry of Spiritual Ascent.* Geneva: Droz, 1989.

Sommers, Paula. "Gendered Distaffs: Gabrielle de Coignard's Revision of Classical Tradition." *Classical and Modern Literature* 18, no. 3 (Spring 1998): 203–210.

Sonnet, Martine. "A Daughter to Educate." In *A History of Women in the West: Renaissance and Enlightenment Paradoxes.* Edited by Natalie Zemon Davis and Arlette Farge, 101–131. Cambridge, MA: Harvard University Press, 1993.

Sorg, Roger. "Une fille de Ronsard, la bergère Rosette." *Revue des Deux Mondes* 13 (1923): 128–144.

Souchal, G. "Le Mécénat de la famille d'Amboise." *Bull. Soc. Antiq. de l'Ouest et des Musées de Poitiers* part 2, 13, no. 4 (1976): 567–612.

Spear, Richard. "Artemisia Gentileschi: Ten Years of Fact and Fiction." *Art Bulletin* 82 (2000): 568–577.

Spence, Richard T. *Lady Anne Clifford, Countess of Pembroke, Dorset and Montgomery (1590–1676).* Phoenix Mill, Thrupp, Stroud, Gloucestershire, UK: Sutton, 1997.

Sperling, Jutta Gisela. *Convents and the Body Politic in Late Renaissance Venice.* Chicago and London: University of Chicago Press, 1999.

Spini, Giorgio. *Ricerca dei libertini: la teoria dell'impostura delle religioni nel Seicento veneziano.* 2nd ed., revised and amplified. Florence: La Nuova Italia, 1983.

Stanford, Ann. "Anne Bradstreet: Dogmatist and Rebel." *The New England Quarterly* 39 (1966): 373–389.

Stanford, Ann. *Anne Bradstreet: The Worldly Puritan. An Introduction to Her Poetry.* New York: Burt Franklin and Co., 1974.

Starkey, David. *Six Wives: The Queens of Henry VIII.* New York: Harper Collins, 2003.

Stephens, Winifred. *Margaret of France, Duchess of Savoy, 1573–74, a Biography.* London: J. Lane, 1912.

Stephenson, Barbara. *The Power and Patronage of Marguerite de Navarre.* Aldershot, UK: Ashgate, 2003.

Sterling, Charles. *The Master of Claude, Queen of France: A Newly Defined Miniaturist.* New York: H. P. Kraus, 1975.

Stevens, Kevin M. "New Light on Andrea Calvo and the Book Trade in Sixteenth-Century Milan." *La Bibliofilia* 103, no. 1 (2001): 25–54.

Stevenson, Jane. "Female Authority and Authorization Strategies in Early Modern Europe." In *"This Double Voice": Gendered Writing in Early Modern England.* Edited by Danielle Clarke and Elizabeth Clarke, 16–40. New York: St. Martin's Press, 2000.

Stevenson, Jane. "Mildred Cecil, Lady Burleigh: Poetry, Politics and Protestantism." In *Early Modern Women's Manuscript Writing: Selected Papers of the Trinity/Trent Colloquium.* The Early Modern Englishwoman: The Printed Writings. Edited by Victoria Burke and Jonathan Gibson, 51–73. Aldershot, UK: Ashgate Publishing, 2004.

Stevenson, Jane. "Women and Classical Education in the Early Modern Period." In *Pedagogy and Power. Rhetorics of Classical Learning.* Edited by Yun Lee Too and Niall Livingstone, 83–109. Cambridge: Cambridge University Press, 1998.

Stevenson, Jane. *Women Latin Poets: Language, Gender, and Authority from Antiquity to the Eighteenth Century.* Oxford: Oxford University Press, 2005.

Stewart, Alan. "The Voices of Anne Cooke, Lady Anne and Lady Bacon." In *"This Double Voice": Gendered Writing in Early Modern England.* Edited by Danielle Clarke and Elizabeth Clarke, 88–102. New York: St. Martin's Press, 2000.

Stewart, Alan, and Heather Wolfe. *Letterwriting in Renaissance England.* Washington, DC: The Folger Shakespeare Library, 2004.

Stighelen, Katlijne van der. *Anna Maria van Schurman of "Hoe hooge dat een maeght kan in de konsten stijgen."* Leuven, Belgium: Universitaire Pers Leuven, 1987.

Stine, Jennifer. "Opening Closets: The Discovery of Household Medicine in Early Modern England." Ph.D. dissertation, Stanford University, 1996.

St-John, Christie Ellen. "The *Salon Vert* of the Maréchale de Retz: A Study of a Literary Salon in Sixteenth-Century France." Ph.D. dissertation, Vanderbilt University, 1999.

Stock, Phyllis. *Better Than Rubies: A History of Women's Education.* New York: Capricorn and G. P. Putnam's Sons, 1978.

Stone, Lawrence. *The Family, Sex, and Marriage in England, 1500–1800.* New York: Harper and Row, 1977.

Stoudt, Debra L. "Medieval German Women and the Power of Healing." In *Women Healers and Physicians: Climbing a Long Hill.* Edited by Lilan R. Furst, 13–42. Lexington: University Press of Kentucky, 1997.

Strasser, Ulrike. *State of Virginity: Gender, Politics and Religion in Early Modern Germany.* Ann Arbor: University of Michigan Press, 2003.

Straznicky, Marta. "Reading the Stage: Margaret Cavendish and Commonwealth Closet Drama." *Criticism* 37, no. 3 (1995): 355–390.

Strong, Roy. *Artists of the Tudor Court: The Portrait Miniature Rediscovered, 1520–1620.* Exhibition catalogue, The Victoria and Albert Museum, 9 July–6 November 1983. London: The Victoria and Albert Museum, 1983.

Strong, Roy. *The English Renaissance Miniature.* New York: Thames and Hudson, 1983.

Strong, Roy. *Gloriana: The Portraits of Queen Elizabeth I.* New York: Thames and Hudson, 1987.

Summit, Jennifer. *Lost Property: The Woman Writer and English History, 1380–1589.* Chicago: University of Chicago Press, 2000.

Tarabotti, Arcangela. *Paternal Tyranny.* Edited and translated by Letizia Panizza. Chicago and London: University of Chicago Press, 2004.

Teague, Frances. *Bathsua Makin, Woman of Learning.* Lewisburg, PA: Bucknell University Press, 1998.

Tedeschi, John. *The Italian Reformation of the Sixteenth Century and the Diffusion of Renaissance Culture: A Bibliography of the Secondary Literature, ca. 1750–1997, Compiled by John Tedeschi in Association with James M. Lattis; with a Historiographical Introduction by Massimo Firpo.* Modena: F. C. Panini; Ferrara: Istituto di studi rinascimentali, 2000.

Therault, Suzanne. *Un cénacle humaniste de la Renaissance autour de Vittoria Colonna châtelaine d'Ischia.* Paris: Didier; Florence: Sansoni Antiquariato, 1968.

Thomas, Keith. *Religion and the Decline of Magic.* New York: Scribner's, 1971.

Thompson, E. P. "Eighteenth-Century English Society: Class Struggle Without Class." *Social History* 3 (1978): 133–165.

Thysell, Carol. *The Pleasure of Discernment: Marguerite de Navarre as Theologian.* Oxford: Oxford University Press, 2000.

Timmermans, Linda. *L'accès des femmes à la culture (1598–1715). Un débat d'idées de Saint François de Sales à la Marquise de Lambert.* Paris: Champion, 1993.

Tinagli, Paola. *Women in Italian Renaissance Art: Gender, Representation, Identity.* Manchester, UK, New York: Manchester University Press, 1997.

Todd, Janet. "Aphra Behn." In *Oxford Dictionary of National Biography.* Oxford: Oxford University Press, 2004.

Tomas, Natalie. *The Medici Women: Gender and Power in Renaissance Florence.* Aldershot, UK, and Burlington, VT: Ashgate, 2003.

Tosi, Lucia. "Marie Meudrac: Paracelsian Chemist and Feminist." *Ambix* 48 (July 2001): 69–82.

Traub, Valerie, M. Lindsay Kaplan, and Dympna Callaghan, eds. *Feminist Readings of Early Modern Culture.* Cambridge: Cambridge University, 1996.

Travitsky Betty. "Isabella Whitney, The 'Wyll and Testament.'" *English Literary Renaissance* 10 (1980): 76–95.

Travitsky, Betty S., and Adele F. Seef. *Attending to Women in Early Modern England.* Newark, DE: Associated Presses, 1994.

Trexler, Richard C. *The Women of Renaissance Florence: Power and Dependence in Renaissance Florence.* Binghamton, NY: Medieval and Renaissance Texts and Studies, 1993.

Trible, Phyllis. *God and the Rhetoric of Sexuality.* London: SCM Press, 1992. (Originally published in 1978.)

Trill, Suzanne. "Feminism Versus Religion: Towards a Re-Reading of Aemilia Lanyer's *Salve Deus Rex Judaeorum.*" *Renaissance and Reformation* 25, no. 4 (2001): 67–80.

Trill, Suzanne. "Sixteenth-Century Women's Writing: Mary Sidney's *Psalmes* and the 'Femininity' of Translation." In *Writing and the English Renaissance.* Edited by William Zunder and Suzanne Trill, 140–158. London and New York: Longman, 1996.

Tucoo-Chala, Pierre. *Catherine de Bourbon: Une calviniste exemplaire.* Biarritz, France: Atlantica, 1997.

Tufts, Eleanor. *Our Hidden Heritage: Five Centuries of Women Artists.* New York: Paddington Press, 1974.

Tuohy, Thomas. *Herculean Ferrara: Ercole d'Este 1471–1505, and the Invention of the Ducal Capital.* Cambridge: Cambridge University Press, 1996.

Turner, James Grantham. *One Flesh: Paradisal Marriage and Sexual Relations in the Age of Milton.* Oxford: Clarendon Press, 1987, 1993, 2004.

Turner, James Grantham, ed. *Sexuality and Gender in Early Modern Europe: Institutions, Texts, Images.* Cambridge: Cambridge University Press, 1993.

Tylus, Jane. "Caterina da Siena and the Legacy of Humanism." In *Perspectives on Early Modern and Modern Intellectual History.* Edited by Joseph Marino and Melinda Schlitt, 116–144. Rochester, NY: University of Rochester Press, 2001.

Tylus, Jane. "Women at the Windows: Commedia dell'arte and Theatrical Practice in Early Modern Italy." *Theatre Journal* no. 49 (1997): 323–342.

Ultsch, Lori J. "Epithalamium Interruptum: Maddalena Campiglia's New Arcadia." *MLN* 120 (2005): 1.

Ultsch, Lori J. "Maddalena Campiglia, 'dimessa nel mondano cospetto'?: Secular Celibacy, Devotional Communities, and Social Identity in Early Modern Vicenza." *Forum Italicum* no. 2 (Fall 2005): 350–377.

Usher, Miriam Cushman. *Lay Culture, Learned Culture: Books and Social Change in Strasbourg,*

1480–1599. New Haven, CT and London: Yale University Press, 1982.

Van de Walle, Etienne. " 'Marvellous Secrets': Birth Control in European Short Fiction, 1150–1650." *Population Studies* 54 (2000): 321–330.

Van Orden, Kate. "Female *Complaintes:* Laments of Venus, Queens, and City Women in Late Sixteenth-Century France." *Renaissance Quarterly* 54, no. 3 (Autumn 2001): 801–845.

Vassalli, Donata Chiomenti. *Giovanna d'Aragona, fra baroni, principi e sovrani del Rinascimento.* Milan: Mursia, 1987.

Vianello, Valerio. *Il "Giardino" delle Parole. Itinerari di scrittura e modelli letterari nel dialogo cinquecentesco.* Materiali e Ricerche N.S. 21. Roma: Jouvence, 1993.

Viennot, Eliane. *Marguerite de Valois, histoire d'une femme, histoire d'un mythe.* Paris: Payot, 1995.

Viennot, Eliane. "Une Nouvelle d'Anne de France: L'Histoire du Siège de Brest." In *Devis d'amitié. Mélanges offerts à Nicole Cazauran.* Edited by Jean Lecointe, Catherine Magnien, Isabelle Pantin, and Marie-Claire Thomine, 139–150. Paris: Champion, 2002.

Vray, Nicole. *La guerre des religions dans la France de l'Ouest. Poitou, Aunis, Saintonge 1534–1610.* LaCrèche: Geste Editions, 1997.

Walker, Claire. *Gender and Politics in Early Modern Europe: English Convents in France and the Low Countries.* New York: Palgrave, 2003.

Walker, Garthine. "Reading Rape and Sexual Violence in Early Modern England." *Gender and History* 10:1 (April 1998): 1–25.

Walker, Kim. *Women Writers of the English Renaissance.* New York: Twayne Publishers, 1996.

Wall, Richard, Tamara K. Hareven, and Josef Ehmer, eds. *Family History Revisited: Comparative Perspectives.* Newark, DE: University of Delaware Press, Associated University Presses, 2001.

Wall, Wendy. *The Imprint of Gender: Authorship and Publication in the English Renaissance.* Ithaca, NY: Cornell University Press, 1993.

Wallwork, Jo, and Paul Salzman, eds. *Women Writing, 1550–1750.* Bundorra, Victoria: Meridian, 2001.

Wandel, Lee Palmer, ed. *History Has Many Voices.* Kirksville, MO: Truman State University Press, 2003.

Waquet, Françoise. *Latin, or the Empire of a Sign.* Translated by John Howe. London and New York: Verso, 2000.

Warnicke, Retha M. *The Marrying of Anne of Cleves: Royal Protocol in Early Modern England.* Cambridge: Cambridge University Press, 2000.

Warnicke, Retha M. *Mary Queen of Scots.* London: Routledge, forthcoming.

Warnicke, Retha M. *The Rise and Fall of Anne Boleyn: Family Politics at the Court of Henry VIII.* Cambridge, UK: Cambridge University Press, 1989.

Warnicke, Retha. *Women of the English Renaissance and Reformation.* Contributions in Women's Studies, No. 38. Westport, CT: Greenwood Press, 1983.

Watkins, Susan. *Mary Queen of Scots.* New York: Thames and Hudson, 2001.

Watson, Foster. *Luis Vives: El Gran Valenciano.* Oxford: Oxford University Press, 1922.

Watt, Diane. *Secretaries of God: Women Prophets in Late Medieval and Early Modern England.* Woodbridge, UK, and Rochester, NY: D. S. Brewer, 1997.

Weaver, Elissa. "Convent Comedy and the World: The Farces of Suor Annalena Odaldi (1572-1638)." In *Women's Voices in Italian Literature.* Edited by Dino S. Cervigni and Rebecca West. *Annali d'Italianistica* 7 (1989): 182–192.

Weaver, Elissa. *Convent Theatre in Early Modern Italy: Spiritual Fun and Learning for Women.* Cambridge: Cambridge University Press, 2001.

Weaver, Elissa, ed. *Arcangela Tarabotti: A Literary Nun in Baroque Venice.* Ravenna: Longo Editore, 2006.

Weber, Alison. *Teresa of Avila and the Rhetoric of Femininity.* Princeton, NJ: Princeton University Press, 1990.

Weir, Alison. *The Six Wives of Henry VIII.* New York: Grove Weidenfeld, 1992.

Wengler, Elizabeth M. "Women, Religion, and Reform in Sixteenth-Century Geneva." Ph.D. dissertation, Department of History, Boston College, 1999.

Wertheimer, Molly Meijer, ed. *Listening to Their Voices: The Rhetorical Activities of Historical Women.* Columbia: University of South Carolina Press, 1997.

Westwater, Lynn. "Lucrezia Marinella: Life and Works" and "The Disquieting Voice: Women's Writing and Antifeminism in Seventeenth-Century Venice." Ph.D. dissertation, University of Chicago, 2003.

Whitaker, Katie. *Mad Madge: The Extraordinary Life of Margaret Cavendish, Duchess of Newcastle, the First Woman to Live by Her Pen.* New York: Basic Books, 2002.

White, Elizabeth Wade. "The Tenth Muse—A Tercentenary Appraisal of Anne Bradstreet." *William and Mary Quarterly* 8 (1951): 355–377.

White, Micheline. "Renaissance Englishwomen and Religious Translations: The Case of Anne Lock's *Of the Markes of the Children of God* (1590)." In *ELR* 29 (Autumn, 1999): 375–400.

White, Micheline. "A Woman with Saint Peter's Keys: Aemilia Lanyer's *Salve Deus Rex Judaeorum* (1611) and the Priestly Gifts of Women." *Criticism* 45, no. 3 (2003): 323–341.

Whitehead, Barbara J. *Women's Education in Early Modern Europe: A History, 1550–1800.* New York: Garland, 1999.

Wiesner, Merry E. "Women and the Creation of Culture." In *Women and Gender in Early Modern Europe.* 2nd ed. Pages 177–185. Cambridge: Cambridge University Press, 2000.

Wiesner, Merry E. *Women and Gender in Early Modern Europe.* Cambridge: Cambridge University Press, 1993.

Wiesner, Merry E. *Working Women in Renaissance Germany.* New Brunswick, NJ: Rutgers University Press, 1986.

Willard, Charity C. *Christine de Pizan: Her Life and Works.* New York: Persea Books, 1984.

Williamson, Margaret. *Sappho's Immortal Daughters.* Cambridge, MA: Harvard University Press, 1995.

Williamson, Marilyn. *Raising Their Voices: British Women Writers, 1650–1750.* Detroit, MI: Wayne State University Press, 1990.

Wilson, Adrian. *The Making of Man-Midwifery: Childbirth in England, 1660–1770.* Berkeley: University of California Press, 1995.

Winn, Colette H. "De sage (-) femme à sage (-) fille: Louise Boursier, Instruction a ma Fille (1626)." In *L'éducation des filles sous l'Ancien Regime. Numéro spécial en homage à Linda Timmermans.* Edited by Colette H. Winn. *Papers on French Seventeenth-Century Literature,* 24, no. 46 (1997): 61–83.

Winn, Colette H. "Les *Discours* de Marie Le Gendre et l'Académie du Palais." In *La Femme lettrée à la Renaissance.* Edited by Michael Bastiaensen, 165–175. Brussels: Université Libre de Bruxelles, Institut Interuniversitaire Renaissance et Humanisme, 1997.

Winn, Colette H. "Marie Le Gendre et l'échec du stoïcisme." In *Women's Writing in the French Renaissance.* Proceedings of the Fifth Cambridge French Renaissance Colloquium, 7–9 July 1997. Edited by Philip Ford and Gillian Jondorf, 207–220. Cambridge: Cambridge French Colloquia, 1999.

Winn, Colette H., and François Rouget. "Introduction." *Album de poesies (Manuscrit francais 25455 de la BNF).* Paris: Honoré Champion, 2004.

Winn, Colette, ed. *The Dialogue in Early Modern France, 1547–1630: Art and Argument.* Washington DC: Catholic University of America Press, 1993.

Wood, Diane S. *Hélisenne de Crenne: At the Crossroads of Renaissance Humanism and Feminism.* Ruther-ford, NJ: Farleigh Dickinson University Press, 2000.

Wood, Jeryldene M. *Women, Art, and Spirituality: The Poor Clares of Early Modern Italy.* Cambridge: Cambridge University Press, 1996.

Woodbridge, Linda. *Women and the English Renaissance: Literature and the Nature of Womankind, 1540–1620.* Champaign: University of Illinois Press, 1984.

Woodrough, Elizabeth, ed. *Women in European Theatre.* Oxford: Intellect Books, 1995.

Wormald, Jenny. *Mary Queen of Scots: Politics, Passion and a Kingdom Lost.* New York: Tauris Park, 2001.

Wunder, Heide. *He Is the Sun, She Is the Moon: Women in Early Modern Germany.* Translated by Thomas Dunlap. Cambridge, MA: Harvard University Press, 1998.

Yandell, Cathy. *Carpe Corpus: Time and Gender in Early Modern France.* Newark, DE: University of Delaware Press, 2000.

Yavneh, Naomi. "The Spiritual Eroticism of Leone's Hermaphrodite." In *Playing with Gender: A Renaissance Pursuit.* Edited by Jean Brink, Maryanne C. Horowitz, and Allison Coudert, 85–98. Champaign and Chicago: University of Illinois Press, 1991.

Zahl, Paul F. M. *Five Women of the English Reformation.* Grand Rapids, MI: William B. Eerdmans, 2001.

Zancan, Marina. "Gaspara Stampa: Rime." In *Letteratura Italiana: Le Opere.* Vol. 2. Edited by Aldo Asor Rosa, 407–436. Milan: Einaudi, 1992.

Zancan, Marina. "Lettere di Caterina da Siena." In *Letteratura italiana. Le Opere: Dalle Origini al Cinquecento.* Edited by A. Asor Rosa, 1: 593–633. Turin: Einaudi, 1992.

Zanette, Emilio. *Suor Arcangela Tarabotti monaca del Seicento veneziano.* Venice-Rome: Istituto per la Collaborazione Culturale, 1960.

Zannini, Gian Ludovico Masetti. *Stampatori e librai a Roma nella seconda meta' del Cinquecento.* Rome: 1980.

Zarri, Gabriella. "Gender, Religious Institutions and Social Discipline: The Reform of the Regulars." In *Gender and Society in Renaissance Italy.* Edited by J. C. Brown and R. C. Davis. London and New York: Longman, 1998.

Zarri, Gabriella. *Il monachesimo femminile in Italia dall'alto medioevo al secolo XVII a confronto con l'oggi.* Atti del VI Convegno del "Centro di Studi Farfensi," Santa Vittoria in Matenano, 21–24 September 1995, SanPietro in Cariano (Verona): Il Segnodei Gabrielli editori, 1997.

Zarri, Gabriella. *Per lettera: La scrittura epistolare femminile tra archivio e tipografia, secoli XV–XVII.* Rome: Viella, 1999.

Zarri, Gabriella. "The Third Status." In *Time, Space, and Women's Lives in Early Modern Europe.* Edited by Anne Jacobson Schutte, Thomas Kuehn, and Silvana Seidel Menchi, 181–199. Kirksville, MO: Truman State University Press, 2001.

Zarri, Gabriella, ed. *Donna, disciplina creanza cristiana.* Rome: Edizioni di Storia e Letteratura, 1996.

Zarrilli, Carla. "Forteguerri, Laudomia." Vol. 49: 153–155. Rome: Instituto dell'Enciclopedia Italiana, 1997.

Zerbi Fanna, M. "Lucrina Fetti pittrice." *Civiltà mantovana* 23–24 (1989): 35–53.

Zerner, Henri. "Diane de Poitiers, maîtresse de son image." In *Actes du colloque Le mythe de Diane en France au XVIe siècle, Albineana* 14 (2002): 335–343.

Ziegler, Georgianna. " 'More Than Feminine Boldness': The Gift Books of Esther Inglis." In *Women, Writing, and the Reproduction of Culture.* Pages 19–37. Syracuse, NY: Syracuse University Press, 2000.

Zorzi, Alvise. *Cortigiana veneziana: Veronica Franco e i suoi poeti, 1546–1591.* Milan: Camunia, 1986.

Index

Marinella, Lucrezia, 98, 140–141, 150, **234–237,** 309, 323, 334, 353
Marlowe, Christopher, 129, 218
Marot, Clément, 159, 229, 269, 317, 322
Marquets, Anne de, **237–239,** 373
Marriage, **239–243**
  control of sexuality, 251–252
  divorce, 240
  love and, 240
  patrilineage, 241
  Protestant Reformation and, 240
  protofeminist critiques and commentaries, 75–76, 134, 141, 142
  social class and, 240–241
  unmarried women, 242, 285
  See also Dowry system
Martin, Dorcas, 370, 372
Martyrs, 320
  Anne Askew, 34–35, 290, 315
  Calvinists, 315
  Elizabeth Barton, 38
  Margaret Clitherow, 84
  See also Religious persecution
Mary I, Queen of England, 7, **243–245,** 298, 315
  Anne of Cleves and, 22
  Jane Grey and, 176
Mary of Guise, **234**
Mary Stuart (Queen of Scots), 7, 128, 218, **245–249,** 299, 323
  Bess of Hardwick and, 49
  Mary of Guise and, 234
Mary Tudor, **249,** 370, 371, 372
Marzi, Frasia, 152
Masculinity, **249–252**
Masques:
  Amazons and, 7, 110
  Anna of Denmark and, 18, 19, 218, 359, 398
  Anne Killigrew and, 193
  Elizabeth Cary and, 64
  Henrietta Maria and, 182
  Mary Stuart and, 218
  Mary Wroth and, 218, 398
  patronage and, 217, 359–360
  transvestism, 375
Matraini, Chiara, 152, 206, 215, **253–254**
Medici, Cosimo I de. *See* Cosimo I de Medici
Medicine and health, **255–262**
  alchemy, 4–6
  child and infant mortality, 75

childbirth and reproductive knowledge, 260–261
classical knowledge, 257
contraception and birth control, **91**
cosmetics, 223–224
domestic knowledge and practice, 255–256
Greek learning and, 124
hospital and nursing careers, 259–260, 392
laywomen and pharmacology practice, 264–268
legal status of female practitioners, 256–258
medical guilds, 257
medical texts, 266
nurses and healers, 224
old age, 285–286
plague, 68, 69, 75, 79, 81, 111, 161, 176, 346
professionalization and women, 256, 394
recipes, 95–96, 255–256
religious healers, 258
syphilis, 91, 103, 104, 132
textbooks, 57–58
witchcraft accusations, 258–259
See also Childbirth and reproduction; Midwives; Nurses and healers; Pregnancy and obstetrics
Melville, Elizabeth, 370, 371
Memoirists, 181, 204, 231–233, 272–274
Menstruation, 1
Merchant correspondence, 213, 214
Merici, Angela, 93
Meun, Jean de, 140
Meurdrac, Marie, 6
Michelangelo, 15, 89, 164
Midwives:
  incompetency myth, 262
  licensing and regulation, 261, 263
  Louise Bourgeois, **57–58**
  male midwifery, **262–264**
  textbook for, 57–58
  witchcraft allegations, 258–259
Mildmay, Grace, 95–96, 266
Milton, 136
Minut, Charlotte de, 212
The Mirror of the Sinful Soul (Marguerite of Navarre), 229, 230, 289
Mirtilla, 10, 11–12, 63, 361
Misogynistic writings, 310
  Amazons in, 7
  Aristotle, 236
  Boccaccio's *Corbaccio,* 236